Austrian Review of International and European Law

Austrian Review of International and European Law

VOLUME 20

The titles published in this series are listed at *brill.com/aril*

Austrian Review of International and European Law

VOLUME 20 (2015)

Edited by

Stephan Wittich
Jane A. Hofbauer
Gerhard Loibl

BRILL
NIJHOFF

LEIDEN | BOSTON

Suggested citation: 20 ARIEL (2015)

Typeset by Scarlett Ortner

ISSN 1385-1306
E-ISSN 1573-6512
ISBN 978-90-04-37507-9 (hardback)

Copyright 2018 by Koninklijke Brill NV, Leiden, The Netherlands.
Koninklijke Brill NV incorporates the imprints Brill, Brill Hes & De Graaf, Brill Nijhoff, Brill Rodopi, Brill Sense and Hotei Publishing.
All rights reserved. No part of this publication may be reproduced, translated, stored in a retrieval system, or transmitted in any form or by any means, electronic, mechanical, photocopying, recording or otherwise, without prior written permission from the publisher.
Authorization to photocopy items for internal or personal use is granted by Koninklijke Brill NV provided that the appropriate fees are paid directly to The Copyright Clearance Center, 222 Rosewood Drive, Suite 910, Danvers, MA 01923, USA. Fees are subject to change.

This book is printed on acid-free paper and produced in a sustainable manner.

Austrian Review of International and European Law

Editors

Stephan Wittich
Department of International Law, University of Vienna

Jane A. Hofbauer
Section for International Law and International Human Rights Law, Bundeswehr University Munich

Gerhard Loibl
Vienna School of International Studies

Managing Editor

Philipp Andreas Janig
Section for International Law and International Human Rights Law, Bundeswehr University Munich

Editorial Board

Wolfgang Benedek
Peter Hilpold
August Reinisch
Kirsten Schmalenbach
Sigmar Stadlmeier
Karl Zemanek

Gerhard Hafner
Manfred Nowak
Helmut Tichy
Christoph Schreuer
Friedl Weiss

Advisory Board

Jean d'Aspremont
James Crawford
Pierre-Marie Dupuy
Malgosia Fitzmaurice
Hubert Isak
Jan Klabbers
André Nollkaemper
Anne Peters
Christian Tams
Andreas Zimmermann

Ilias Bantekas
Thomas Desch
Martti Koskenniemi
Andrea Gattini
Yann Kerbrat
Ursula Kriebaum
Alain Pellet
Bruno Simma
Christian Tomuschat

Manuscripts, editorial communications and book reviews as well as books for review are welcome and may be sent to:

Austrian Review of International and European Law
c/o Department of International Law
University of Vienna
Juridicum
Schottenbastei 10-16
A-1010 Vienna
Austria
ariel.int-law@univie.ac.at
http://intlaw.univie.ac.at/index.php?id=ariel

Please note that it is the policy of the *Austrian* Review to only consider exclusive submissions for publication!

Editorial

This is the 20th volume of the Austrian Review, a project that started in 1996 as a two issue 'semi-quarterly' journal, that unfolded as a 'real' quarterly with four issues per year in 1997 and that finally assumed the yearbook format in 1999. With regard to the structure and substance of the Review things have been pretty much the same since then; we only undertook a modest refurbishment of its appearance as of volume 17 (2012) that we think has provided the Review with a more modern and appealing look.

While the Austrian Review is a periodical open to all kinds of submissions in the field of international and European law irrespective of the authorship and whether solicited or not, we still try to do justice to the idea that it is a 'national' yearbook, albeit not so much for 'idealistic' purposes than for pragmatic reasons. This can be seen particularly in the annual digest of Austrian practice making available to the interested public decisions of Austrian courts, as well as parliamentary, diplomatic and other documents dealing with questions of international law, that we compile, edit, translate and publish annually in the Review. This is, frankly speaking, an awful lot of work and, on behalf of the board of editors, I would like to sincerely thank all those who have contributed to this digest in the past and to those who are still on board. We also continuously encourage younger Austrian scholars and practitioners to use the Review as a 'door-opener' for their academic career. It is with a modest sense of satisfaction that we observe an increasing number of younger academics who discover the value of the Review as a forum for their scholarly contributions worthy of being published.

20 years of existence signifies that the transition from teenage years via adolescence to adulthood is once and for all over; and it is of course a wonderful occasion to celebrate this 'runder Geburtstag' comprising two decades. For that purpose we thought it might be a good idea to publish several articles discussing from different angles a topic that combines questions of theory with problems of practice. Prof. Karl Zemanek was kind enough to provide the kick-off article on 'court generated state practice' to which a number of authors added their own thoughts.

The approaches to the overall topic vary significantly, and while some provide direct 'reactions' to Prof. Zemanek's initial ideas (Georg Nolte and Santiago Torres Bernárdez), others come up with broader observations on the relationship between court practice, treaty interpretation, and custom

(Markus P Beham, Malgosia Fitzmaurice and Panos Merkouris, and Serena Forlati). Christina Binder and Ralph Janik, in their contributions, address considerations of legitimacy of court generated state practice, whereas still other authors focus more generally on the aspect of subsequent practice against the background of specific examples (Ilias Bantakes and Jan Klabbers) or on the position of a particular state on the practice, as it were, of subsequent practice (Gerhard Hafner). All in all, we think that this is a very fine collection of analytical articles on a topic that is beset with uncertainties in both theory and practice.

This birthday volume is rounded out by an article on a stock-taking of EU development cooperation by Peter Hilpold who adduces a vision how that cooperation should – or may – unfold in the future. As usual, the Austrian digest as well as book reviews and notes conclude the present volume.

After 20 years of continuing efforts, we are a little proud of having established the Austrian Review as a recognized annual periodical in the field of international and European law. There are numerous 'parents' of this modest success, ranging from the 'founding fathers' in 1996, the individual authors, to our dependable and loyal publisher as well as our more than reliable editorial team (notably Jane Alice Hofbauer, Philipp Janig, and Scarlett Ortner). It is with great pleasure that Jane Alice Hofbauer who has worked as managing editor over the last years will assume the position of a co-editor. This is but a token of gratitude for all the work she has invested in the Review. At the same time, Phililpp Janig will take over her task as managing editor and continue to provide his invaluable support to the Review.

A distinct word of gratefulness is due to the Austrian Federal Ministry for Europe, Integration and Foreign Affairs that has repeatedly supported the Review by financial subsidies that cover some of the expenditures necessarily incurred in the process of publication. We sincerely thank you all!

We hope the readers will enjoy this anniversary volume and wish the Review a flourishing future. Ad multos annos!

Stephan Wittich
on behalf of the board of editors

Contents

Editorial vii

Agora: The Opening

Karl Zemanek
Court Generated State Practice? 3

Critique and Defense

Georg Nolte
Court Generated State Practice? A Response to Karl Zemanek 17

Santiago Torres Bernárdez
Court Generated State Practice? (Karl Zemanek) – A Commentary 25

Broader Approaches to Court Generated State Practice

Markus P Beham
Could State Practice Ever *Not* Play a Role in the Formation of
Custom? The Ghosting of Tacit Agreements in International Law 35

Malgosia Fitzmaurice & Panos Merkouris
Re-Shaping Treaties While Balancing Interests of Stability and
Change: Critical Issues in the Amendment/Modification/Revision
of Treaties 41

Serena Forlati
On 'Court Generated State Practice': The Interpretation of Treaties
as Dialogue between International Courts and States 99

On the Legitimacy of Court Generated State Practice

Christina Binder
A Legitimacy Perspective on Court Generated State Practice 113

Ralph Janik
How Many Divisions Does the European Court of Human
Rights Have? Compliance and Legitimacy in Times of Crisis 125

On the Practice of Subsequent Practice

Ilias Bantekas
Uniformity in Model Laws as Subsequent Practice under Article 31
of Vienna Convention on the Law of Treaties 147

Jan Klabbers
Subsequent Agreement Outside/In: The Kigali Principles
on Protection of Civilians 165

Gerhard Hafner
Modification of Treaties by Subsequent Practice – Some
Comments on the Austrian Position 175

Recent Developments

Peter Hilpold
EU Development Cooperation: A Stock-Taking and a Vision
for the Future 189

Austrian Practice in International Law 2015/ Österreichische Praxis zum Internationalen Recht 2015

Structure 261

Jane Alice Hofbauer, Philipp Janig,
Michael J Moffatt and *Stephan Wittich*
Part I: Austrian Judicial Decisions Involving Questions of International
Law/Österreichische Judikatur zum Internationalen Recht 277

Markus P Beham and *Gerhard Hafner*
Part II: Austrian Diplomatic and Parliamentary Practice in
International Law/Österreichische Diplomatische und
Parlamentarische Praxis zum Internationalen Recht 365

Book Reviews

Jens David Ohlin, The Assault on International Law
(Ralph Janik) 449

Susan Pedersen, The Guardians: The League of Nations and the
Crisis of Empire (Ralph Janik) 450

Michael Potacs, Rechtstheorie (Markus P Beham) 452

Book Notes

Matthias Niedobitek (ed.), Europarecht – Grundlagen der Union
and Matthias Niedobitek (ed.), Europarecht – Politiken der Union
(Markus P Beham) 455

Agora:

The Opening

Court Generated State Practice?

Karl Zemanek[*]

The Vienna Convention on the Law of Treaties (VCLT) of 1969 provides in para 1 of its Article 31, which regulates the interpretation of treaties:

> There shall be taken into account, together with the context
> [...]
> (b) any subsequent practice in the application of the treaty which establishes the agreement of the parties regarding its interpretation;

Underlying this provision is the obvious assumption that the conduct of the parties in applying the provisions of a treaty was indicative of their understanding of them and thus may help to clarify their meaning when it cannot be definitely determined by the process indicated in para 1 of Article 31. Whether the constant application of a treaty provision in a manner that differs from what an interpretation of the provision with the means of Article 31(1) VCLT would amount to an amendment of the treaty, is a controversial question. The ILC draft for the Vienna Conference proposed a relevant article[1] which, however, was not adopted.[2] The ILC recently resumed the consideration of the subject and its *Draft Conclusions on subsequent agreements and*

---

[*] Emeritus Professor of International Law, University of Vienna; Emeritus Member of the Institut de droit international.

[1] The proposed Article 38 read: 'A treaty may be modified by subsequent practice in the application of the treaty establishing the agreement of the parties to modify its provisions', see ILC, 'Report of the International Law Commission on the Work of its 18th Session' (1966) UN Doc A/CN.4/191, 236.

[2] United Nations Conference on the Law of Treaties, '1st Session – 38th Meeting of the Committee of the Whole (COW)' (25 April 1968) UN Doc A/CONF.39/C.1/SR.38, 210 (deletion of the proposed Article 38 was adopted by 53 votes to 15, with 26 abstentions).

subsequent practice in relation to the interpretation of treaties[3] propose the following Conclusion 7:

> (3) It is presumed that the parties to a treaty, by […] a practice in the application of the treaty, intend to interpret the treaty, not to amend or modify it. The possibility of amending or modifying a treaty by subsequent practice of the parties has not been generally recognized. The present draft conclusion is without prejudice to the rules on the amendment of treaties […] under customary international law.[4]

Apart from merely establishing a presumption that could eventually be rebutted, the words 'amending or modifying a treaty' obstruct the solution of the problem. The treaty is not amended, since that could only be done by the process indicated in Article 40 VCLT. It is the performance of a specific duty or the exercise of a specific right arising under the treaty which is modified by the common practice of the parties, giving the provision which establishes the right or duty a meaning that would not be obtained were the provision interpreted in accordance with Article 31(1) VCLT. This does not formally amend the treaty; the wording of the provision remains the same. Hence the parties could revert at any time to a common practice in conformity with the ordinary meaning of the provision, though the first instances of such a practice would appear unlawful until they become general, a phase inherent in the change of custom (as exemplified by the reduction of state immunity to acts of public power).

In that optic, it is evident that such a modification could occur if the conduct of the parties is consistent and driven by *opinio iuris*; the specific right and/or obligation resulting from the treaty would then, as long as the required conditions persist, be changed by custom. Hafner[5] comes to the same conclusion, albeit by a different reasoning, when he states:

> Practice, however, cannot modify the treaty but rather the rights and obligations resulting therefrom, provided that the practice has gained a legal quality as customary international law.

---

[3] ILC, 'Report on the International Law Commission on the Work of its 66th Session' (2014) UN Doc A/69/10, 166.

[4] *Ibid.*, at 169 (emphasis added).

[5] Gerhard Hafner, 'Subsequent Agreements and Practice: Between Interpretation, Informal Modification, and Amendments' in Georg Nolte (ed), *Treaties and Subsequent Practice* (2013) 105, 115-116.

Yet he also points to the domestic constitutional problems which that practice may create when ratification of the original treaty had required parliamentary consent. As executive practice it is, on the other hand, a tempting option for governments to avoid, domestically and/or internationally, a possibly cumbersome procedure.

Most writers who question the possibility of modifying rights and/or obligations under a treaty by subsequent practice refer, however, to the rejection by the Vienna Conference of the relevant article proposed by the ILC as being indicative of the existing *opinio iuris,* and thus to what they consider a decisive denial of the possibility. Yet Simma[6] has rightly pointed out that the rejection was mostly due to the fact that the VCLT was intended to apply only to treaties in written form,[7] and a process belonging to customary law may have appeared out of place in that framework to the minds of the delegates to the Conference. And there exist, indeed, instances which let one doubt whether the statement that treaty modification by subsequent practice 'has not been generally recognized' corresponds to reality.

One example is Article 27(3) of the UN Charter which provides that decisions of the Security Council on non-procedural matters 'shall be made by an affirmative vote of nine members including the concurring votes of the permanent members'. In spite of the ordinary meaning of the words 'affirmative' and 'concurring', practice has turned them into meaning 'not objecting',[8] although the preparatory work suggests the contrary intention of the (future) five permanent members. The practice started with the Soviet Union abstaining in 1946 on the Spanish question, though it stressed that this was not to be considered a precedent. When the United Kingdom abstained in 1949 on the admission of Israel to the United Nations, it declared that this should not prevent the Security Council from taking a decision, a formula which was repeated for many years afterwards whenever a permanent member would abstain on a non-procedural decision. The nascent practice was apparently provoked by the permanent members' growing awareness that being compelled to a yes or no position unduly limited their room for political manoeuvre. The International Court of Justice found in its Advisory

---

[6] Alfred Verdross and Bruno Simma, *Universelles Völkerrecht* (3rd edn 1984) para 793.

[7] See Art 1 read in conjunction with Art 2(1)(a) Vienna Convention on the Law of Treaties, 23 May 1969, 1155 UNTS 331.

[8] For a detailed consideration see Bruno Simma and Stefan Brunner, 'Article 27' in Bruno Simma (ed), *The Charter of the United Nations: A Commentary* (1995) 430.

Opinion on *Namibia* that '[t]his procedure [...] has been generally accepted by Members of the United Nations and evidences a general practice of that Organization'.[9] One must therefore conclude that, while the text of the UN Charter has not formally been amended, the established practice on Article 27(3) differs to the extent that it has transformed the voting right of a permanent member into a true 'veto', which means that it must be exercised to prevent a decision. Should one consider a practice established within the UN as 'not generally recognized'?

In fact, the International Court of Justice, in two Advisory Opinions (that is, *Reparation for Injuries Suffered in the Service of the United Nations*[10] and *Certain Expenses of the United Nations*[11]), had developed the functional interpretation of the UN Charter and therewith sanctioned the innovative practice of the member states in the organization. Now 'established practice' is part of the 'rules of the organization'.[12]

Another example are across-the-board reservations. Article 2(1)(d) VCLT defines a reservation as a statement which excludes or modifies 'the legal effect of certain provisions of the treaty'. The ordinary meaning of 'certain provisions' would suggest that a reservation must identify the provision or provisions of the treaty to which it is made. Hence a statement which makes the implementation and/or application of the treaty generally dependent on its compatibility with domestic constitutional law or with religious law (Sharia), without specifying the provisions of the treaty which the statement affects (across-the-board reservation), would not be a reservation but a simple statement of intent without legal effect.

Yet the ILC *Draft Guidelines to Practice on Reservation to Treaties*[13] prove the opposite. The meticulously researched state practice cited in the commentaries to Guideline (GL) 1[14] and to GL 3.1.5.2[15] shows conclusively

---

[9] *Legal Consequences for States of the Continued Presence of South Africa in Namibia (South West Africa) notwithstanding Security Council Resolution 276 (1970)* [1971] ICJ 16, 22, paras 21-22 (Advisory Opinion of 21 June).

[10] *Reparation for Injuries Suffered in the Service of the United Nations* [1949] ICJ 174 (Advisory Opinion of 11 April).

[11] *Certain Expenses of the United Nations (Article 17, Paragraph 2, of the Charter)* [1962] ICJ 151 (Advisory Opinion of 20 July).

[12] See the definition in Art 2(1)(j) Vienna Convention on the Law of Treaties between States and International Organizations or between International Organizations, 21 March 1986 (not yet in force), UN Doc A/CONF.129/15.

[13] ILC, 'Reservations to treaties' (19 May 2011) UN Doc A/CN.4/L.779.

[14] *Ibid.*, paras 15-16, 21-22.

[15] *Ibid.*, paras 4, 7-8.

that, without exception, across-the-board reservations have been accepted by other states as reservations. While objections to such reservations have been raised on the ground that, because of their unspecified generality, their compatibility could not be assessed, or that they were incompatible with the object and purpose of the respective treaty, no instance is known in which their nature as reservation was disputed. This obviously is the case because, if they were to be measured against the object and purpose of the treaty, they had to be taken as legally valid acts relating to the treaty, hence as reservations, in the first place. The Guidelines draw a cautious conclusion. After repeating the definition of a reservation of Article 2(1)(d) VCLT in para 1 of GL 1.1, para 2 of the GL adds that this definition 'is to be interpreted' as including across-the-board reservations, thus referring to state practice as a means of interpretation under Article 31(3)(b) VCLT as well as a source of the modification. In sum that means that the right of states to make a statement with the effect of a reservation under the VCLT has been modified by the general practice of states. Denying that possibility now, after decades of constant general state practice, would amount to a *venire contra factum proprium* if it were limited to one or a few states, justifiable only if it was the beginning of a new general practice.

The obvious conclusion to be drawn is that, if all or a greater number of parties have practical problems with the application of a particular treaty provision because the drafters had not foreseen the circumstances causing them, states tend to adjust the obligation arising under the provision by subsequent practice. This form of modification is thus not alien to international law.

*

However, the problem assumes another dimension when a treaty establishes a supervisory body that engages in the former's interpretation. Simma has pointed out a possible dilemma in the following terms:

> Another issue arises in regard to the reactions of states parties to a treaty to views or activities of supervisory bodies established by these treaties. For instance, could we say that a lack of opposition by states parties to the International Covenant on Civil and Political Rights to a view of the Human Rights Committee considering the interpretation and application of the Covenant could lead to some sort of acquiescence *vis-à-vis* that view and, in that sense, would constitute state practice, consisting of not doing

anything? Could a state be bound by just keeping quiet *vis-à-vis* more or less daring interpretations of the law by these treaty bodies?[16]

The Human Rights Committee indeed offers a good example for examination. According to Article 40(4) of the International Covenant on Civil and Political Rights (CCPR) it may issue general comments when it considers them appropriate and, over the years, has adopted a number of General Comments, nearly all of them concerning the interpretation of substantive provisions of the CCPR. In the domain of general international law, the best known is perhaps its 'General Comment on issues relating to reservations made on ratification or accession to the Covenant or the Optional Protocols, or in relation to declarations under article 41 of the Covenant'.[17] General Comments are not binding on the parties, but that explains their effect inadequately. They state the Committee's understanding of the CCPR and, eventually, of pertinent rules of general international law and thus determine the Committee's attitude towards the conduct of the treaty parties in these matters. They may have an indirect influence on the conduct of these parties and Article 40(5) CCPR entitles them consequently to submit observations on such commentaries. Whether that right was exercised in respect of General Comment No. 24 could not be ascertained because the respective website[18] does not show relevant entries. That makes the significance of Simma's remarks clear. Supposing that no observations had been submitted by the parties, does the principle of *qui tacet consentire videtur* apply? Would silence amount to acquiescence?

Silence plays a certain role in the formation of customary international law as it does in aggregating the instances of subsequent practice of the parties in applying a treaty. Not all potential actors provide the relevant conduct at the same time and those who have not acted yet, but remained silent in the face of the conduct of others, are presumed to consider that conduct lawful unless and until they speak out or act differently when the occasion arises. But that model cannot be transferred one-to-one to the views of treaty bodies. A duty to object requires that the act requiring reaction affects the legal rights of a state, and non-binding views do not affect them *legally*, though they

---

[16] Bruno Simma, 'Miscellaneous Thoughts on Subsequent Agreements and Practices' in Georg Nolte (ed), *Treaties and Subsequent Practice* (2013) 46, 47-48.

[17] Human Rights Committee, 'CCPR General Comment No. 24: Issues Relating to Reservations Made upon Ratification or Accession to the Covenant or the Optional Protocols thereto, or in Relation to Declarations under Article 41 of the Covenant' (4 November 1994) UN Doc CCPR/C/21/Rev.1/Add.6.

[18] See <http://tbinternet.ohchr.org/_layo> accessed 20 July 2017.

may do so in many other ways. Silence is therefore not indicative in this instance. Evidence of acceptance has to be sought in the subsequent conduct of states. And that is the crucial point: do states act in conformity with General Comment No 24? This is not the place for an exhaustive examination of the relevant practice, wherefore some random examples must suffice.[19] Yet they show that, in spite of the General Comment's opposition to across-the-board reservations, the practice continued after its adoption. When they acceded to the CCPR, Botswana, the Maldives, Pakistan and Turkey reserved the precedence of domestic constitutional provisions over treaty obligations, and Bahrain, Mauretania, Pakistan did the same for Sharia law. On the other hand, the frequency of objections to such reservations has increased. The reservation by Pakistan, for instance, was objected to by Austria, Belgium, Canada, the Czech Republic and Denmark, among others. The findings are thus mixed: some states did not heed the opinion expressed in the General Comment, while other states were perhaps motivated or encouraged by the Comment to object to defective reservations. But that would qualify rather as application of the relevant provisions of the VCLT than as distinct 'subsequent practice' of the parties to the CCPR. In any case, the supposed silence of the parties to the CCPR on General Comment No 24 was not followed by a consistent conforming practice, which makes it difficult to assess how states judge its operational validity, though the existing practice does not suggest that states feel obliged to act in conformity with the General Comment. Acceptance may be more uniform when a General Comment concerns a substantive provision of the CCPR[20] and induces parties to the Covenant to conduct which results in a situation emulating that of the following section, even without the instrumentality of an eventual judgment compelling a hesitant state to a conforming subsequent practice. Judge Simma's question may thus be answered as follows: when faced with the non-binding view of a treaty body, the addressee's silence does neither signify acquiescence nor is it evidence of state practice. Only the actual conforming conduct of states could transform the view by 'subsequent practice' into a legally binding obligation.

*

---

[19] These are taken from the UN Audiovisual Library of International Law, <www.un.org/law/avl> accessed 20 July 2017.

[20] See, *e.g.*, Human Rights Committee, 'CCPR General Comment No. 6: Article 6 (Right to Life)' (30 April 1982) UN Doc HRI\GEN\1\Rev.1, 6; Human Rights Committee, 'General Comment No. 34 – Article 19: Freedom of opinion and expression' (12 September 2011) UN Doc CCPR/C/GC/34; also see *supra* note 15.

The invoked scenario of judicially generated state practice comes into view when one examines the question in the context of treaty-based regimes which have a judicial supervisory organ that renders binding decisions in case of the eventual violation of a protected right of individuals, and thus on the interpretation of that right, like the European Court of Human Rights (ECtHR). It is then the court which decides whether the practice of the parties in applying the right has evolved since the treaty's inception and whether that practice puts a new and different complexion on the protected right than its understanding resulting from the textual interpretation applying the means of Article 31(1) VCLT would suggest.

Since the rights protected by a human rights treaty are implemented in the domestic sphere of states, their eventual violation or evolution is caused by the latter's legislative or administrative practice. State practice relating to this part of international law does not, or does only incidentally, develop in the interaction of states. It consists of what each contracting party practices in its own legal domain and only the sum of those individual conducts constitutes the 'subsequent practice of the parties' in the sense of Article 31(3)(b) VCLT.

The ECtHR frequently refers to that practice to keep its interpretation of the rights protected by the European Convention of Human Rights (ECHR) in line with the contracting parties' evolving conception of them.[21] In those instances the Court reviews the practice across the Council of Europe member states for a consensus with respect to the interpretation of a right. Leading cases are *Soering*[22] and *Öcalan*.[23]

However, the evolutive concept which determines the interpretative strategy of the ECtHR and finds expression in its understanding of the ECHR as the 'constitutional instrument of European public order (*ordre public*)'[24] and as 'a living instrument which must be interpreted in the light of present

---

[21] The respective practice of the ECtHR is documented and analysed in detail in Georg Nolte's Second Report to the ILC Study Group on Treaties Over Time, see Georg Nolte, 'Jurisprudence Under Special Regimes Relating to Subsequent Agreements and Subsequent Practice' in Georg Nolte (ed), *Treaties and Subsequent Practice* (2013) 210, 244-268; and by George Letsas, 'Strasbourg's Interpretive Ethic: Lessons for the International Lawyer' (2010) 21 EJIL 509.

[22] *Soering v The United Kingdom*, ECtHR, Application No 14038/88, Judgment of 7 July 1989, para 103.

[23] *Öcalan v Turkey*, ECtHR, Application No 46221/99, Judgment of 12 May 2005, para 163.

[24] *Loizidou v Turkey* (Preliminary Objections), ECtHR, Application 15318/89, Judgment of 23 March 1995, para 73.

day circumstances',[25] as well as its construction of the rights protected by the ECHR as 'having an autonomous meaning in the context of the Convention and not on the basis of their meaning in domestic law'[26] have led the Court further. In some cases it was satisfied by identifying a qualified majority of states which by their practice reflected an authoritative standard. Thus, in *Demir and Baykara* it referred to 'the vast majority of European States'[27] and in *A v The United Kingdom* to 'most, if not all, signatory States to the Convention'[28] to underpin its interpretation. This still reflects a conventional understanding of 'state practice', which is commonly only evidenced by the actions of some but not all states concerned, so long as those which have not actively contributed to it can be presumed not to oppose it.

Occasionally, however, the Court sets a certain standard despite the fact that a European consensus cannot be identified. In *Goodwin*,[29] for instance, it attached 'less importance to the lack of evidence of a common European approach to the resolution of the legal and practical problems posed' and relied instead on the 'clear and uncontested evidence of a continuing international trend in favour'. In another case it found that human trafficking 'cannot be considered compatible with a democratic society and the values expounded in the Convention'.[30] A further sign of the Court's tendency to construe the rights protected by the ECHR in a manner conforming to assumed international (or European) legal currents is its reliance on international legal instruments bearing on the case under consideration even when the state whose conduct is examined is not a party to them. Thus it held in *Demir and Baykara*:

> In this context, it is not necessary for the respondent State to have ratified the entire collection of instruments that are applicable in respect of the precise subject matter of the case concerned. It will be sufficient for the Court that the relevant international instruments denote a continuous evolution in the

---

[25] *Tyrer v The United Kingdom*, ECtHR, Application No 5856/72, Judgment of 25 April 1978, para 31.

[26] *Engel and Others v The Netherlands*, ECtHR, Application No 5100/71, 5101/71, 5102/71, 5354/72 and 5370/72, Judgment of 8 June 1976, para 81.

[27] *Demir and Baykara v Turkey*, ECtHR, Application No 34503/97, Judgment of 12 November 2008, para 52.

[28] *A v The United Kingdom*, ECtHR, Application No 35373/97, Judgment of 17 December 2002, para 80.

[29] *Christine Goodwin v The United Kingdom*, ECtHR, Application No 28957/95, Judgment of 11 July 2002, para 85.

[30] *Rantsev v Cyprus and Russia*, ECtHR, Application No 25965/04, Judgment of 7 January 2010, para 282.

norms and principles applied in international law or in the domestic law of the majority of the member States of the Council of Europe and show, in a precise manner, that there is common ground in modern societies [...].[31]

However, inapplicable international instruments, or trends manifest in some states' domestic legislation or social policy, or even mere doctrines, are not elements of 'state practice' in the sense of Article 31(3)(b) VCLT. They may harden into it in time if they translate into constant and general conduct, but do not yet fulfil that condition.

So how should one classify the creativity of the ECtHR's interpretative practice in terms of international law? Roberts has offered the following considerations which *mutatis mutandis* provide an answer to that question:

> In theory, states and states alone make international law while decisions of international courts and tribunals are merely subsidiary means of determining international law rather than sources of international law *per se*. In practice, when states delegate power to international courts and tribunals to resolve disputes under treaties and/or to interpret and apply those treaties, they impliedly delegate some law-making functions to those judicial bodies. Those judicial decisions are then routinely cited as evidence of what the law is, even when these decisions clearly develop rather than merely apply the law.[32]

What is relevant in the present context is the fact that under the regime established by the ECHR states have contracted away their authority to interpret the Convention and hence to determine their obligations under the Convention. That gives the ECtHR leeway to develop these obligations in accordance with the conception of the underlying values which it assumes to exist at the moment of deciding an appropriate case. That will, in reality, lead to a modification of the obligation under the Convention, a process which was analyzed in the first section of this paper, here however effected in a very special manner.

The Court recognizes that possibility, although it makes the mistake mentioned in the first section, of confusing the modification of an obligation resulting from the Convention with an amendment of the latter. Already in *Soering* it found 'that an established practice within the member States could

---

[31] *Demir and Baykara v Turkey*, ECtHR, Application No 34503/97, Judgment of 12 November 2008, para 86.

[32] Anthea Roberts, 'Subsequent Agreements and Practice: The Battle over Interpretive Power' in Georg Nolte (ed), *Treaties and Subsequent Practice* (2013) 95.

give rise to an amendment of the Convention'.[33] In *Öcalan* it went beyond the abstract possibility and argued:

> It may be questioned whether it is necessary to await ratification of Protocol No. 6 by the three remaining States before concluding that the death penalty exception in Article 2 § 1 has been significantly modified. Against such a consistent background, it can be said that capital punishment in peacetime has become to be regarded as an unacceptable […] form of punishment that is no longer permissible under Article 2.[34]

In *Al-Saadoon and Mufdhi* it came finally to the conclusion:

> It can be seen, therefore, that the Grand Chamber in Öcalan did not exclude that Article 2 had already been amended so as to remove the exception permitting the death penalty. Moreover, as noted above, the position has evolved since then. All but two of the Member States have now signed Protocol No. 13 and all but three of the States which have signed have ratified it. These figures, together with consistent State practice in observing the moratorium on capital punishment, are strongly indicative that Article 2 has been amended so as to prohibit the death penalty in all circumstances.[35]

In these cases the Court dealt with a rather classical instance of the modification of obligations resulting from a treaty through subsequent practice or agreement. Yet that is only part of the picture. Judgments of the Court have an ensuing, generalizing effect. The evolutionary interpretation of the provisions of the ECHR which gives a new meaning to obligations arising under it, may – and usually will – cause a change in the conduct of the parties. In turn this process, when consolidated into constant subsequent practice, will definitely modify these obligations. The process differs from the effect of General Comments by the Human Rights Committee examined in the second section of this paper because a new reading of an obligation under the ECHR gained by evolutionary interpretation practically compels parties to adapt their legislation or administrative practice accordingly, or risk individual complaints when continuing a practice that is at variance with the understanding of the obligation by the Court. It is a self-induced process

---

[33] *Soering v The United Kingdom*, ECtHR, Application No 14038/88, Judgment of 7 July 1989, para 103.

[34] *Öcalan v Turkey*, ECtHR, Application No 46221/99, Judgment of 12 May 2005, para 163.

[35] *Al-Saadoon and Mufdhi v The United Kingdom*, ECtHR, Application No 61498/08, Judgment of 2 March 2010, para 120.

because a significant number of adaptations enable the Court to claim them as evidence of the new understanding of the respective provision of the ECHR and hence as state practice, thereby transforming what was initially a specific interpretation into a modified obligation.

It is thus not the Court's judgment which amounts to 'subsequent practice', but the adoption by the parties of the specific interpretation by the Court of a protected right as correct rendering of the obligation created by the respective treaty provision and the following adaptation of the corresponding domestic law which leads to that 'subsequent practice in the application of the treaty which establishes the agreement of the parties regarding its interpretation'. Whether one qualifies that as 'court induced' or 'court ordered' state practice is a matter of subtlety, depending on how compelling one considers the risk of eventual individual complaints.

*

One can draw a general conclusion. The foregoing examination shows that the words 'court generated state practice' in the title of this essay overstate the effect. 'State practice' remains 'state' practice even when it is initiated by a court or by a supervisory organ. Excepting the occasional Advisory Opinion of the International Court of Justice stimulating the law of international organizations, state practice initiated by a supervisory body or a court seems to be particular to special regimes or sub-systems which have such a permanent body. The leverage of their pronouncements depends on the construction of the regime or sub-system. Whether the evolutive interpretation of a bilateral treaty by the ICJ, giving it a contemporary meaning,[36] later gave rise to new state practice beyond the performance of the judgment, is not documented.

---

[36] See, *e.g.*, *Aegean Sea Continental Shelf Case (Greece v Turkey)* (Jurisdiction) [1978] ICJ 3, 33, para 77 (Judgment of 19 December); *Dispute Regarding Navigational and Related Rights (Costa Rica v Nicaragua)* [2009] ICJ 213, 242-243, paras 64-67 (Judgment of 13 July).

Critique and Defense

Court Generated State Practice?
A Response to Karl Zemanek

Georg Nolte*

The editors of the *Austrian Review of International and European Law* have asked me to briefly contribute a short comment on Karl Zemanek's illuminating piece 'Court Generated State Practice?'. I limit myself to pointing to certain aspects of the work of the International Law Commission.

*

According to Karl Zemanek, it is 'the obvious assumption' of Article 31(3)(b) of the Vienna Convention of the Law of Treaties

> that the conduct of the parties in applying the provisions of a treaty was indicative of their understanding of them and may thus help to clarify their meaning when it cannot be definitely determined by the process prescribed by para 1 of Article 31.[1]

In its recent work on the topic 'Subsequent agreements and subsequent practice in relation to the interpretation of treaties',[2] the International Law Commission addressed the question of the relationship between paras 1 and 3 of Article 31. It came to the conclusion, on the basis of the Commission's 1966 commentary to the Draft Articles on the Law of Treaties, that subsequent practice under Article 31(3)(b) is a primary means on interpretation which 'shall' be taken into account 'together with' all the other means of interpretation contained in Article 31 in a unitary process of interpretation.[3]

---

* Professor of Law, Humboldt University; Member of the International Law Commission; Membre associé de l'Institut de Droit International.

[1] Karl Zemanek, in this volume, at 3.

[2] ILC, 'Report of the International Law Commission on the Work of the 65th Session' (2013) UN Doc A/68/10, 9; ILC, 'Report of the International Law Commission on the Work of the 66th Session' (2014) UN Doc A/69/10, 166; ILC, 'Report of the International Law Commission on the Work of the 67th Session' (2015) UN Doc A/70/10, 84.

[3] See ILC (2013), *supra* note 2, at 11, Draft Conclusion 1(5).

Accordingly, the commentary by the Commission to Draft Conclusion 1 on the topic states:

> (7) Article 31(1) is the point of departure for any treaty interpretation according to the general rule contained in article 31 as a whole. This is intended to contribute to ensuring the balance in the process of interpretation between an assessment of the terms of the treaty in their context and in the light of its object and purpose, on the one hand, and the considerations regarding subsequent agreements and subsequent practice in the following draft conclusions. *The reiteration of article 31(1) as a separate paragraph is not, however, meant to suggest that this paragraph, and the means of interpretation mentioned therein, possess a primacy in substance within the context of article 31 itself. All means of interpretation in article 31 are part of a single integrated rule.* [emphasis added]
>
> (8) Paragraph 3 reproduces the language of articles 31(3)(a) and (b) of the Vienna Convention, in order to situate subsequent agreements and subsequent practice, as the main focus of the topic, within the general legal framework of treaty interpretation. Accordingly, the chapeau of article 31(3) 'there shall be taken into account, together with the context' is maintained in order to emphasize that the assessment of the means of interpretation mentioned in paragraph 3 (a) and (b) of article 31 are an integral part of the general rule of interpretation set forth in article 31.
>
> (12) The Commission considered it important to complete draft conclusion 1 by emphasizing in paragraph 5 that, notwithstanding the structure of draft conclusion 1, moving from the general to the more specific, the process of interpretation is a 'single combined operation', which requires that 'appropriate emphasis' is placed on various means of interpretation. The expression 'single combined operation' is drawn from the Commission's commentary to the 1966 draft articles on the Law of Treaties. There the Commission also stated that it intended 'to emphasize that the process of interpretation is a unity'.

Thus, according to the Commission, there is no primacy, in the process of interpretation, of the means of interpretation which are mentioned in para 1 of Article 31. This signifies that para 3 of Article 31 does *not* only come into play when the meaning of the treaty 'cannot be definitely determined by the process indicated in para 1 of Article 31'.[4] One may or may

---

[4] Karl Zemanek, in this volume, at 3.

not agree with this proposition, but it is based on substantial classical and modern authority.

*

This point of departure has certain implications for the question whether a treaty can be modified (or amended) by the subsequent practice of the parties in its application. On this basis, a 'constant application of a treaty provision in a manner that differs from what an interpretation of the provision with the means of Article 31(1)' does not necessarily 'amount to an amendment of the treaty'.[5]

It is, of course, correct that a different subsequent practice does not amend the treaty in the sense of Article 40 VCLT.[6] Article 40, after all, prescribes a formal procedure. If, however, the term 'amendment' is understood from the point of view of its effect (which is the change of a legal obligation arising under a treaty) then the use of this term by the Commission does make sense, in particular in view of such occasional usage by different institutions and authors.[7] Indeed, the commentary on Draft Conclusion 7(3) alerts the reader that the Commission is aware of the relevant provisions of the Vienna Convention, but also of certain difficulties of delimitation, when it notes:

> It is often difficult to draw a distinction between agreements of the parties under a specific treaty provision which attributes binding force to subsequent agreements, simple subsequent agreements under article 31, paragraph 3 (a) which are not binding as such, and, finally, agreements on the amendment or modification of a treaty under articles 39–41.[8]

*

Karl Zemanek assumes that the current work of the Commission on *Subsequent agreements and subsequent practice in relation to the interpretation of treaties* also concerns customary international law. This, however, is not the case. It is true that the Commission, in its work in the 1960s on the Draft Articles on the Law of Treaties, originally considered the possible effect of

---

[5] *Ibid.*

[6] *Ibid.*

[7] When the European Court of Human Rights uses the term amendment in this context it is necessary to refer to it in a Draft Conclusion in order to dispel any possible misunderstanding, see *Soering v United Kingdom*, ECtHR, Application No 14038/88, Judgment of 7 July 1989, para 103.

[8] ILC (2014), *supra* note 2, at 186, para 21.

subsequent practice in the application of the treaty and that of customary law on a treaty together. The Draft Articles on the Law of Treaties, in their state after the First Reading in 1964, contained an Article 68 which addressed both possibilities and which read:[9]

Draft Article 68
Modification of a treaty by a subsequent treaty, by subsequent practice or by customary international law

The operation of a treaty may also be modified –

By a subsequent treaty between the parties relating to the same subject matter to the extent that their provisions are incompatible;

By subsequent practice of the parties in the application of the treaty establishing their agreement to an alteration or extension of its provisions; or

By the subsequent emergence of a new rule of customary law relating to matters dealt with in the treaty and binding upon all the parties.

However, in his Sixth Report on the Law of Treaties of 1966,[10] reflecting the comments made by governments after the First Reading,[11] the Special Rapporteur, Sir Humphrey Waldock, expressed the following view:

14. In any event, the Special Rapporteur feels that article 68, as at present constructed, is out of place in the section on 'modification' of treaties. Articles 65-67 concern the alteration of the operation of treaties by acts of the parties done in relation to the treaty. Those articles may therefore properly be regarded as relating to the modification of treaties. The same is true of sub-paragraph (b) of the present article, since it concerns the subsequent practice of the parties in the application of the treaty. But sub-paragraphs (a) and (c) concern the impact on a treaty of acts done outside and not in relation to it.

---

[9] ILC, 'Report of the International Law Commission on the Work of its 16th Session' (1964) UN Doc A/CN.4/173, 198.

[10] ILC, 'Sixth Report on the Law of Treaties, by Sir Humphrey Waldock' (1966) UN Doc A/CN.4/186 and Add. 1, 2/Rev. 1, 3-7.

[11] ILC, 'Comments by Governments on Parts I, II and III of the Draft Articles on the Law of Treaties Drawn up by the Commission at its Fourteenth, Fifteenth and Sixteenth Session' (1966) Yearbook of the ILC 1966 (Vol II) UN Doc A/CN.4/SER.A/1966/Add.1, 287.

15. In the light of the foregoing observations the Special Rapporteur thinks that the Commission should reconsider the whole article. ... A possible solution, he feels, may be: (1) to remove sub-paragraph (a) and regard it as covered by article 63 [which later became article 30]; (2) to omit sub-paragraph (c) and re-examine how the question of the inter-temporal law should be dealt with in Article 69, para. 1; and (3) to retain only sub-paragraph (b) in the present article.[12]

The Commission, following the proposal of the Special Rapporteur, did not further pursue the possible effect of customary law, or customary practice, on a treaty.

*

The formulation in the present Draft Conclusion 7(3) according to which 'the possibility of amending or modifying a treaty by subsequent practice of the parties has not been generally recognized'[13] is not a categorical statement and it does not reject such a possibility, as Karl Zemanek seems to assume. It rather represents an effort to reconcile the position of those who, like Zemanek, point to certain instances in which this possibility appears to have been recognized with respect to particular provisions – *e.g.* Article 27(3) UN Charter, or Article 2(1)(d) VCLT –, and the position of those who explain such cases as being instances in which the respective provision has received a particularly wide interpretation, or simply as being exceptional. This is why the Commission, in para (1) of Draft Conclusion 7 introduced its consideration of the question of the possibility of modifying a treaty by subsequent practice by stating:

> Subsequent agreements and subsequent practice under article 31, paragraph 3, contribute, in their interaction with other means of interpretation, to the clarification of the meaning of a treaty. This may result in narrowing, widening, or otherwise determining the range of possible interpretations,....[14]

This Draft Conclusion confirms, once again, that the Commission does not consider that the ordinary meaning of the terms of the treaty necessarily plays a determinative role for the question whether a particular subsequent practice remains within the range of possible interpretations of a treaty, or whether it represents a modification, or a claim to modify a treaty. On the other hand, the

---

[12] ILC (Waldock), *supra* note 10, at 91, paras 14 and 15.
[13] ILC (2014), *supra* note 2, at 169.
[14] *Ibid.*

Commission did not want to go so far as to recognize that the jurisprudence of the European Court of Human Rights, according to which the subsequent practice of the parties can be a most relevant factor in its determination that a provision of the Convention was modified, confirmed or reflected a general rule under the law of treaties. In particular, the Commission was not prepared to recognize that this jurisprudence confirmed a general rule under the law of treaties according to which a modifying effect can be produced by practice which does not establish the agreement of *all* parties to a treaty.

A different approach is certainly arguable. In the course of the work on this topic I originally envisaged a somewhat broader recognition by the Commission of the possibility of modifying a treaty by subsequent practice of the parties,[15] and in particular that the Commission would recognize that the jurisprudence of the European Court of Human Rights has some broader significance under the general law of treaties.[16] In the further course of the work, and as a result of debates in the Commission, however, I concluded that a more restrictive formulation should be proposed.[17] Hence in the formulation 'has not been generally recognized'. The word 'generally' indirectly refers to those cases which Karl Zemanek addresses and which are perhaps not so exceptional. By choosing this formulation, the Commission has certainly arrived at a compromise. This compromise is, however, based on the agreement among the members of the Commission that any modification by the subsequent practice of the parties in the application of the treaty, if it is possible at all, does not take place easily and would require either clear and

---

[15] See Introductory Report for the ILC Study Group on Treaties over Time, 'Jurisprudence of the International Court of Justice and Arbitral Tribunals of Ad Hoc Jurisdiction Relating to Subsequent Agreements and Subsequent Practice' in Georg Nolte (ed), *Treaties and Subsequent Practice* (2013) 200-208; Second Report for the ILC Study Group on Treaties over Time, 'Jurisprudence under Special Regimes Relating to Subsequent Agreements and Subsequent Practice' in Georg Nolte (ed), *Treaties and Subsequent Practice* (2013) 305.

[16] Second Report for the ILC Study Group on Treaties over Time, *supra* note 15, at 305 (Conclusion 17).

[17] Third Report for the ILC Study Group on Treaties over Time, 'Subsequent Agreements and Subsequent Practice of States Outside of Judicial or Quasi-Judicial Proceedings' in Georg Nolte (ed), *Treaties and Subsequent Practice* (2013) 353-356; ILC, 'Second Report on Subsequent Agreements and Subsequent Practice in Relation to the Interpretation of Treaties, by Georg Nolte' (26 March 2014) UN Doc A/CN.4/671, 49-69.

convincing evidence, or some additional and specific element which would not result from the general law of treaties.

*

One additional element which could explain the exceptional nature of a modifying effect may be, as Karl Zemanek suggests, a specific judicial power which results from the treaty. I personally have doubts, however, whether it is advisable to recognize a more or less specific 'law-making' power of courts, as Zemanek and others suggest. This would mean to upgrade the informal persuasive authority of courts by giving such informal authority a formal status as a means of interpretation, or even as a power to modify a treaty. In my view, this position conflates factual effects and legal significance. It raises questions of conceptual clarity and systemic legitimacy. I would rather leave it at the courts 'recognizing' state practice by their judgments, within the broad range that Articles 31 and 32 of the VCLT provide. This does not exclude that states may then take these judgments into account in their further practice. In this sense courts can certainly 'generate' state practice which, however, will again need to be properly recognized be the courts. But it would go beyond the scope of this small contribution to elaborate more fully on these questions.

Be this as it may, Karl Zemanek has revisited a fundamental question of the current international legal order and he proposes a challenging response. I am grateful for the opportunity to contribute a comment.

Court Generated State Practice?
(*Karl Zemanek*) – A Commentary

Santiago Torres Bernárdez[*]

Being requested to write a comment on the above essay of Professor Karl Zemanek to be published in an Agora in the Jubilee issue of ARIEL, I will begin acknowledging that I deem it an honour to assume the task as well as a pleasure because it has allowed me to become acquainted with a further very fine contribution of Professor Karl Zemanek on the elucidation of some wisely selected specific issues of public international law in need of clarification.

In the present case, the selected issue poses the question of whether 'subsequent practice' of the state parties to a treaty is susceptible legally of being generated by an international court or supervisory body entrusted with certain functions by the treaty concerned. In other words, whether there it is in order or correct to admit that the said 'subsequent state practice' is or could be in such a context the practice in fact of the court or a supervisory body, namely of a third with respect to the parties to the treaty.

*

In the first section of the essay, Professor Zemanek recalls that in the 'law of treaties' the role and issues posed by the 'subsequent practice' may relate to the 'interpretation' or to the 'amendment (modification)' of treaties. The subsequent practice in the interpretation of treaties has been codified by the provision set forth in paragraph 3(b) of Article 31 of the VCLT whose text is quoted at the head of the essay. This provision has become therefore, with the full support of the states and doctrine, one of the constituent interpretative elements of the 'general rule of interpretation' of treaties embodied in said Article 31. As stated by Professor Zemanek, underlying this provision of the VCLT is 'the obvious assumption that the conduct of the parties in applying the provisions of a treaty was indicative of their understanding of them'.[1]

---

[*] Member of the Institut de Droit International and International Arbitrator. Former Registrar and Judge ad hoc in the International Court of Justice (ICJ) and former Director in the Codification Division of the United Nations Office of Legal Affairs.

[1] Karl Zemanek, in this volume, at 3.

In contrast, the role and effects of 'subsequent practice' is more controversial or problematic with respect to the amendment (modification) of treaties. As indicated in the essay, the relevant article of the ILC Draft Articles on the Law of Treaties, namely Article 38, was not adopted by the Vienna Conference. In fact, it was the only full casualty of the ILC Draft Articles (by a vote in the Committee of the Whole of 53 votes to 15, with 26 abstentions, Austria being one out of the 15 states which voted in favour of maintaining the Article). No alternative provision to the rejected ILC Draft Article being submitted, the 1969 VCLT has no provision on the amendment (modification) of treaties by 'subsequent practice' of the state parties thereto.

In this respect, Conclusion 7 of the recent 2014 ILC 'Draft Conclusions on subsequent agreements and subsequent practice in relation to the interpretation of treaties' seems to have frozen the described outcome of the Vienna Conference (1968-1969) by, on one hand, establishing the presumption that the parties to a treaty by a practice in its application intend to interpret the treaty, not to amend or modify it, and, on the other hand, by declaring that the possibility of amending or modifying a treaty by subsequent practice has not been generally recognized.

It is evident that Professor Zemanek is unhappy with above development adopting a critical position on that ILC conclusion. This critical position manifests itself in three ways: (i) by qualifying the above ILC presumption as refutable because it could eventually be rebutted; (ii) by considering that a different subsequent common practice would modify the performance by the parties of specific rights or duties arising under the treaty rather than amend the treaty via instrument and that it is, consequently, erroneous to use wording implying the contrary when the text of the provision remains the same and the parties could revert to the former common practice at any time, thereby bringing the different practice or custom to an end; and in particular (iii) by refuting the proposition that the eventual amending (modifying) effect of specific duties or rights arising under the treaty by a different subsequent common practice of the parties 'has not been generally recognized', concluding in that respect in the following terms:

> The obvious conclusion (of the practice reviewed in the essay) is that, when all or a greater number of parties have practical problems with the application of a particular treaty provision because the drafters had not foreseen the circumstances causing them, states tend to adjust the obligation arising under the provision by subsequent practice. This form of modification is thus not alien to international law.[2]

---

[2] Karl Zemanek, in this volume, at 3.

I am fully in agreement with the first and second proposition of Professor Zemanek. As to the third one, I can go along as well if formulated in the cautious terms of the quoted passage because the modification of the ordinary meaning of terms of particular treaty rights and obligations by 'subsequent practice' of the parties, as stated by Professor Zemanek, is certainly 'not alien to international law'. There are selective examples confirming this in quite important fields of international relations as referred to in the essay. But – the issue at the time of the Vienna Conference as well as today – is rather, in my opinion, a different one, namely whether or not there is in the matter a general practice accepted as law across-the-board susceptible of becoming the subject of a codified written rule of general application. The ILC made an attempt with its Article 38 proposal but on the basis of very feeble evidence (a mere passage of a contemporaneous 1963 Award in the arbitration between France and the United States regarding the interpretation of a bilateral air transport agreement) and failed. It seems that the general approach on the matter has not evolved much since then.

The VCLT therefore does not regulate the modification of specific treaty rights or obligations by 'subsequent practice' of the parties and, consequently, as stated in the Preamble of the Convention, the question continues to be governed by the relevant rules of customary international law exclusively. Furthermore, as with respect to interpretation, a 'subsequent practice' suitable eventually of modifying specific treaty rights or obligations must be a practice establishing the *agreement* of the parties to the treaty regarding the modification of those rights or obligations. Thus, when such an agreement is present the silence of the VCLT cannot be an obstacle to the application of those particular rights or obligations as modified by the different agreed subsequent practice, so long as one remains outside of the *ius cogens* realm. All in all, the present situation appears more akin to *pacta sunt servanda* than an eventual codified rule questioned or reserved by a number of states.

*

In the second section of his essay, Professor Zemanek deals first with the issue of the legal evaluation of the reactions of state parties to a treaty when faced with non-binding views of supervisory bodies established by those treaties (*i.e.* the Human Rights Committee's comments on the interpretation of provisions of the CCPR). The position of Professor Zemanek in the matter is given in the form of an answer to the question raised by Judge Simma whether the lack of opposition expressed by state parties to a view of the supervisory body could lead to some sort of acquiescence *vis-à-vis* that view and in that sense would qualify as state practice. In other words, supposing that no reaction or observations had been submitted by the state parties, does *qui taceret consentire videtur* apply and does the supervisory body's view become 'subsequent practice' of the state parties without further ado for law of treaties purposes?

Professor Zemanek's answer is roundly negative. As he explains, in public international law

> the duty to object requires that the act necessitating the reaction affects the legal rights of a state, and non-binding views not affect them *legally*, though they may do so in many other ways. Evidence of acceptance has to be sought in the subsequent conduct of the states.[3]

And further:

> When faced with the non-binding view of a treaty body, the addressee's silence does neither signify acquiescence nor is it evidence of state practice. Only the actual conforming conduct of states could transform the view (of the body) by 'subsequent practice' into a legal binding obligation.[4]

I cannot be more in agreement with those propositions which are well illustrated in the essay by the example of the diversity of reactions of states to the Human Rights Committee's opposition to across-the-board reservations to CCPR in General Comment No. 24.

Thereafter, the second section moves to the scenario of 'court generated state practice' evoked in the title of the essay. It is indeed a different scenario because, as explained by Professor Zemanek, now the supervisory body is a court rendering binding decisions on alleged violation of a given protected right and, consequently, on the interpretation of that right. The body which decides whether or not the practice of the parties in applying the right at issue has evolved since the inception of the application of the treaty to the point of differing from the understanding resulting from an interpretation in accordance with Article 31 of the VCLT is in the present scenario a judicial body and the decision manifests itself in a court's judgment.

Professor Zemanek approaches this aspect by reference to the *modus operandi* of the European Court of Human Rights (ECtHR) under the particular regime established by the European Convention of Human Rights and Fundamental Freedoms (ECHR), a field of international law in which the internationally protected rights are implemented in the domestic legal order

---

[3] *Ibid.*, at 8-9.
[4] *Ibid.*

of the state parties to the Convention. In such a context, the 'subsequent practice of the parties' in the sense of Article 31(3)(b) of the VCLT consists, as explained by Professor Zemanek, in the sum of the individual conducts in the matter of each European state party in its own legal domain. At this point, Professor Zemanek distinguishes rightly, on the basis of ECtHR case law, between decisions of the Court which accord with the conventional understanding of the 'state practice' of Article 31 of the VCLT and Court's decisions of another kind.

For example, when looking for a consensus concerning the interpretation of a given protected right in the domestic legal order of the member states of the Council of Europe, the ECtHR is generally satisfied with the concurrent practice of 'most, if not all, signatory states of the Convention', or 'a qualified majority of the parties' or 'the vast majority of European states' to justify the Court's interpretation of the protected right concerned. This certainly, as underlined by Professor Zemanek, accords with the conventional understanding of 'subsequent practice' of the state parties to the treaty of Article 31 which does not required the active contribution of 'all' state parties concerned, being sufficient that those which have not actively contributed to it can be presumed not to oppose the new practice.[5]

However, there are also occasions in which decisions of the ECtHR set certain interpretative standards of protected rights despite the fact that a European consensus cannot be identified, as well as situations in which the Court tends to overcome the lack of uncontested evidence by invoking values expounded by the Convention or of a democratic society, or by presuming an European or international legal current, or by doctrinal considerations or by relaying on international legal instruments even when the state whose conduct is at issue is not a party to them. Then, as rightly pointed out by Professor Zemanek, none of those elements partake the conventional understanding of 'subsequent practice' of the state parties of Article 31(3)(b) of the VCLT.

In all those decisions, the *creativity* (the term is used by Professor Zemanek) of the ECtHR's interpretation is evident because they develop rather than apply the law. But, at the same time they are decisions in line with the evolutionary concept of the protected human rights underlying the Convention and the contracting states' understanding of the Convention as a 'living instrument' and a 'constitutional instrument of European public order'. These principles manifest themselves in the Preamble of the Convention (*i.e.* the reference to pursue 'the maintenance and *further realisation* of Human Rights

---

[5] See ILC commentary to Article 27, paragraph (16), of its Draft Articles on the Law of Treaties

and Fundamental Freedoms'[6]) and in the text of some of its provisions, as well as in the practice of adding articles to the ECHR through the adoption of successive Protocols. As to the provisions, it should be noted that Article 46 limits the binding force of the final judgments of the ECtHR by *ratione personae* criteria (the parties) only, excluding the *ratione materiae* additional limitation (in respect of the particular case) of Article 59 of the Statute of the ICJ and Article 296 of the 1982 Convention on the Law of the Sea.

For Professor Zemanek, following Roberts' views, the ECtHR's decisions that develop rather than apply the law cannot be explained or justified in terms of the 'subsequent practice' of Article 31 of the VCLT, but by

> the fact that under the regime established by the ECHR states have contracted away their authority to interpret the Convention and hence to determine their obligations under the Convention. That gives the ECtHR leeway to develop these obligations, relying on the conception of the underlying values it assumes to prevail at the moment of deciding an appropriated case.[7]

In any case, an initiative of the ECtHR may lead ultimately to a modification of the obligation under the European Convention at issue. As explained by Professor Zemanek, when the evolutionary interpretation of the obligation adopted by the Court concerning the obligation creates a new meaning it usually leads to a change in the conduct of the state parties which, in turn, when consolidated into a constant 'subsequent practice' of them, modifies the conventional obligation concerned. The process would differ however from the effect of the General Comments of the UN Human Rights Committee because a new reading of an obligation under the ECHR gained by evolutionary interpretation of the Court practically would compel states to adapt their legislation or administrative practice accordingly.

We share this proposition of Professor Zemanek, as well as the further one that it is not the ECtHR's judgment as such which amounts to 'subsequent practice' in the sense of Article 31 VCLT but the following definite adoption by the state parties of the specific ECtHR's interpretation as the correct reading of the treaty provision setting forth the right subject of the interpretation. Nevertheless, it is undeniable that at the origin of this new 'subsequent practice' lays an initiative of the Court which induces the state parties to adopt

---

[6] Convention for the Protection of Human Rights and Fundamental Freedoms, 4 November 1950, 213 UNTS 222 (emphasis added).

[7] Karl Zemanek, in this volume, at 12.

the new practice, in a more or less compelling manner depending on the risks for them of the eventual filing of individual applications for non-compliance.

*

I am in full agreement with Professor Zemanek's general conclusion of his essay that, for the purpose of Article 31 of the VCLT, 'subsequent practice' remains 'state subsequent practice' even when it is initiated and/or induced by a court or by another supervisory organ. The answer therefore to the query posed in the very title of his essay is negative. There is not a 'court *generated* state practice' as such, but there are examples of genuine 'state practice' *originally initiated or induced* by decisions of international courts or supervisory organs. However, so long as they have not been consolidated into a *genuine state practice*, those decisions will not fall under the 'subsequent practice in the application of the treaty' referred to in Article 31(3)(b) of the VCLT because to be so the practice concerned has to establish, as explicitly stated in the provision, 'the agreement of the parties (to the treaty) regarding its interpretation'.

I would like also to underline that one of the main merits of the commented essay lays in the fact that its tenor and conclusions protect the global international legal order of potentially distorting inroads resulting from unjustified extrapolations of elements or features of a given international special regime or sub-system into the realm of the codified general rules of international law on interpretation of treaties. So-called 'evolutionary interpretations' are nowadays frequently alleged to conceal attempts to justify free interpretations or to avoid the application of the rules on interpretation of treaties set forth in Articles 31, 32 and to 33 of the VCLT. It is therefore in order to recall that those rules were codified bearing in mind that: 'the interpretation of treaties in good faith *and according to the law* is essential if the *pacta sunt servanda* rule is to have any real meaning'.[8]

Professor Zemanek's essay is not unfriendly at all to existing or future conventional special regimes or sub-systems encompassing an international court or supervisory body entrusted with competences concerning the interpretation of the treaty-base concerned, but certainly aims at avoiding confusion of apples with oranges. It distinguishes clearly, on the one hand, the exercise of a given international court or supervisory body of its own competences from the crystallization of a genuine 'subsequent practice' of the state parties to the treaty in the sense of Article 31(3)(b) of the VCLT and, on

---

[8] ILC Commentary to Articles 27 and 28, paragraph (5), of its Draft Articles on the Law of Treaties (emphasis added).

the other hand, the latter 'subsequent practice' from the former initiative or undertaking adopted by the court or body within the particular conventional regime or sub-system in question pursuant to the competences vested upon them by the state parties to the treaty.

The above clarifications close right with the system of the interpretation of treaties codified by the VCLT because (i) all the rules on *interpretation* codified are *general rules* and (ii) none these general rules are of *ius cogens* character. Consequently, the state parties to conventional special regimes or sub-systems may set forth particular modalities or mechanisms for the interpretation of the treaty as, for example, providing for a given participation of a court or supervisory body in the process *of* interpretation and application of the treaty (as in the studied cases of the ECtHR and the UN Human Rights Committee).

But, what is legally beyond the reach of those special regimes or sub-systems is to amend or change the nature of the interpretative elements constituting the general rules on interpretation of treaties codified by the VCLT, the subsequent practice in the application of the treaty by the state parties thereto of Article 31 of the Convention included.

In sum, Professor Zemanek's essay provides the reader with a learned and opportune clarification of an important topic of the law of treaties having a doctrinal as well as a practical value for international jurists.

Broader Approaches to Court Generated State Practice

Could State Practice Ever *Not* Play a Role in the Formation of Custom? The Ghosting of Tacit Agreements in International Law

*Markus P Beham**

The two 'kick-off' texts accompanying Karl Zemanek's Round Table at the Section of International Law and International Relations of the University of Vienna in May 2016 and published in this anniversary volume of the Austrian Review whirl up more than one bagful of doctrinal dust. Within the constraints of the present agora, one particular issue stands out to the present author: The terminological – and conceptual – conundrum in the relationship between 'subsequent agreements and subsequent practice' and customary international law. In particular, it will be argued that a strictly analytical, positivist approach to both treaties and custom as distinct sources of international law may provide a solution by replacing the notion of amendment or modification through customary international law with the idea of subsequent tacit agreements (not excluding, however, the possibility of parallel formation of custom).

Conclusion 7 of the *Draft Conclusions on subsequent agreements and subsequent practice in relation to the interpretation of treaties* by the International Law Commission (ILC) differentiates between 'application', 'interpretation', 'amendment', and 'modification' of a treaty, holding that '[t]he possibility of amending or modifying a treaty by subsequent practice of the parties has not been generally recognized'. Notwithstanding the question of 'the rules on the amendment of treaties [...] under customary international law', Georg Nolte writes that the current work of the ILC on subsequent agreements and subsequent practice in relation to the interpretation of treaties does not concern customary international law.[1] Drawing upon the *travaux préparatoires* of the Vienna Convention on the Law of Treaties (VCLT), he concludes that the ILC 'did not further pursue the possible effect of customary

---

* Lecturer at the Section for International Law and International Relations of the University of Vienna and Associate at Freshfields Bruckhaus Deringer LLP.
[1] See Georg Nolte, in this volume, at 19.

law, or customary practice, on a treaty'.[2] Karl Zemanek points out with Bruno Simma that this was due to the fact that 'the VCLT was intended to apply only to treaties in written form'.[3]

This statement leads to the heart of the problem of defining and distinguishing both the respective source, with which one is dealing and the connected (unilateral) acts. Can 'subsequent agreements and subsequent practice' *not* have an effect upon customary international law? Should any of the cited developments such as that regarding Article 27(3) of the Charter of the United Nations be deemed 'customary international law'? Indeed, Cassese spoke of a 'customary modification' and called the voting procedure a 'customary process'.[4] It has even been argued that

> far from supplanting customary law, and reducing its field of operation to a minimum, the codifying of great tracts of international law will, on account of the practical and political difficulties of amending multilateral treaties, whether codifying or otherwise, give over the development of international law almost entirely into the hands of custom, operating upon and beyond the codifying treaties.[5]

Such informal 'modifications' of the Charter of the United Nations have also been referred to as 'dynamic interpretations' or as a '*de facto* modification of the Charter'.[6] The International Court of Justice (ICJ), however, in its *Namibia* Advisory Opinion simply framed it as an act of interpretation of the Charter.[7] This also seems to be the approach of the third paragraph of Conclusion 7 of the *Draft Conclusions on subsequent agreements and subsequent practice*

---

[2] *Ibid.*, at 21.

[3] See Karl Zemanek, in this volume, at 5.

[4] Antonio Cassese, *International Law* (2nd edn, 2005) 166.

[5] Hugh WA Thirlway, *International Customary Law and Codification: An Examination of the Continuing Role of Custom in the Present Period of Codification of International Law* (1972) 146.

[6] See Nico J Schrijver, 'The Future of the Charter of the United Nations' (2006) 10 Max Planck Yearbook of United Nations Law 1, 13. *Cf.* also Oscar Schachter, *International Law in Theory and Practice* (1991) 118-119.

[7] As Akehurst points out, some refer to it as an 'amendment', whereas the *Namibia* Advisory Opinion refers to it as an 'interpretation'. See Michael Akehurst, 'The Hierarchy of the Sources of International Law' (1974-1975) 47 BYIL 273, 278.

in relation to the interpretation of treaties.[8] It seems possible here to frame the same development in different lights.

This fact alone is *per se* not disconcerting from the perspective of legal theory. But how far does 'interpretation' – for every act of application is always also an interpretation – go, before it should become an 'amendment' or a 'customary modification'? And is not an act of interpretation in itself enough to trigger the formation of a rule of customary international law? The 2014 Report of the ILC itself holds that 'the dividing line between the interpretation and the amendment or modification of a treaty is in practice sometimes "difficult, if not impossible, to fix"'.[9] Already in the comments to the Draft Articles on the Law of Treaties, the ILC held that 'though the line may sometimes be blurred between interpretation and amendment of a treaty through subsequent practice, legally the processes are distinct'.[10] As a rule of thumb, an amendment or modification might always be assumed, once the boundaries of the ordinary meaning are breached. At the same time, any subsequent practice with regard to a treaty always also constitutes a form of informal interpretative declaration. However, none of these acts with relation to a treaty should be blurred with the formation of custom.

Much of the discourse on treaties and custom – not just within the present context[11] – seem to omit oral agreements (should one not choose to take

---

[8] 'It is presumed that the parties to a treaty, by an agreement subsequently arrived at or a practice in the application of the treaty, intend to interpret the treaty, not to amend or to modify it.'

[9] ILC, 'Report of the International Law Commission on the Work of its 66th Session' (2014) UN Doc A/69/10, Commentary to Conclusion 7, 188, para 24.

[10] Draft Articles on the Law of Treaties with Commentaries, YILC 1966-II, Commentary to Article 38, para 1.

[11] Bilateral customary international law is often viewed as consensual in the sense of an agreement. See, *inter alia*, Anthony A D'Amato, *The Concept of Custom in International Law* (1971) 234 and 250; Alain Pellet, 'Article 38' in Karin Oellers-Frahm, Christian J Tams, Christian Tomuschat, and Andreas Zimmermann (eds), *The Statute of the International Court of Justice. A Commentary* (2nd edn, 2012) 731, 831, para 246; Malcolm N Shaw, *International Law* (7th edn, 2014) 66. However, the nature of the dispute of the *Rights of Passage* case shows that the underlying issue was more reminiscent of a servitude in domestic law. Also, the persistent objector theory assumes a consensualist view of customary international law. *Cf.* Gennady M Danilenko, *Law-Making in the International Community* (1993) 42. Still, it has become part of '[m]ainstream accounts of the principles governing the formation and application of rules of customary international law' (Ted L Stein, 'The Approach of the Different Drummer: The Principle of the Persistent Objector in International Law' (1985) 26(2) Harvard International Law Journal 457, 457).

a voluntarist approach to the formation of customary international law[12]). Apart from the issue of Article 103 of the Charter of the United Nations, why should it not be possible to simply frame what is called 'practice' here as a tacit agreement between the respective states? In fact, the ILC did take this view into account:

> Indeed, the Commission recognized that a treaty may sometimes be modified even by an oral agreement or by a tacit agreement evidenced by the conduct of the parties in the application of the treaty. Accordingly, in stating that the rules of part II regarding the conclusion and entry into force of treaties apply to amending agreements, the Commission did not mean to imply that the modification of a treaty by an oral or tacit agreement is inadmissible. On the contrary, it noted that the legal force of an oral agreement modifying a treaty would be preserved by the provision in article 3, sub-paragraph (b), and it made express provision in article 38 for the modification of a treaty by the subsequent practice of the parties in its application.[13]

The ICJ specifically recognised this approach in the *Dispute regarding Navigational and Related Rights*, stating that

> the subsequent practice of the parties, within the meaning of Article 31(3) (b) of the Vienna Convention, can result in a departure from the original intent on the basis of a tacit agreement between the parties.[14]

The term 'subsequent practice' invites the connotation of 'state practice' and, in turn, of customary international law. However, it would be more satisfying in terms of a systematic approach to simply solve conflicts between treaties and customary international law in terms of the simple conflict of norms *formulae* of *lex posterior* and *lex specialis*. Whereas any 'subsequent agreements and subsequent practice' could – just as any agreement – result

---

[12] For a brief overview of consensualist doctrine in the first half of the 20th century including Anzilotti, Cavaglierie, Triepel, and Strupp, see Louis Le Fur, 'La Coutume et les Principes Généraux du Droit Comme Sources du Droit International Public' in Charles Appleton (ed), *Recueil d'Études sur les Sources du Droit en l'Honneur de François Gény. Tome III. Les Sources des Diverses Branches du Droit* (1934) 362, 362-363. For the Soviet take on voluntarism see Grigory I Tunkin, *Theory of International Law* (2003) 133.

[13] Draft Articles on the Law of Treaties with Commentaries, YILC 1966-II, Commentary to Article 35, para 4.

[14] *Dispute regarding Navigational and Related Rights* (*Costa Rica v Nicaragua*) [2009] ICJ 213, 242, para 64 (Judgment of 13 July).

in a '*Doppelgänger* ou un reflet de miroir coutumier',[15] this would not *per se* amend or modify the underlying treaty.[16] As opposed to having to imagine a treaty with a sort of 'customary parasite', there would simply arise a conflict of norms in case of conflicting content.

Drawing upon the idea of tacit agreements, just as in private law,[17] states would, through their 'subsequent practice' modify a treaty by what is in essence a new agreement. Thus, the first act of a state with regard to a particular provision would constitute an offer, the subsequent reaction of the other party (parties) an acceptance (or not). Mostly, this chain will consist of a unilateral act followed by acquiescence. Of course, domestic law concerns may arise in such an environment,[18] but these are the same concerns shared by states failing to implement obligations of an unmodified ratified treaty.

In the case of courts – or treaty bodies, for that matter – endowed with the power to interpret treaty provisions, it can only be opportune to speak of state practice following 'the adoption by the parties of the specific interpretation by the Court of a protected right as correct', as Zemanek writes.[19] As Alain Pellet holds with regard to General Assembly resolutions, the correct approach 'in assessing their legal value' is not to focus on 'what *they* say, but what *the States* have had to say about them'.[20]

However, what about state appointed judges or members such as those of the ILC? While these are, of course, supposed to act as independent judges or experts, this fact could only be established by a thorough (biographical) analysis of each such member. The indication that the particular individual

---

[15] Georges Abi-Saab, 'Les Sources du Droit International: Essai de Déconstruction' in Manuel Rama-Montaldo (ed), *El Derecho Internacional en un Mundo en Transformacion. Liber Amicorum en Homenaje al Professor Eduardo Jiménez de Aréchaga / Le Droit International Dans un Monde en Mutation. Liber Amicorum en Hommage au Professeur Eduardo Jiménez de Aréchaga / International Law in an Evolving World. Liber Amicorum in Tribute to Eduardo Jiménez de Aréchaga* (1994) 29, 45.

[16] Contrary, Austrian Statement at the 69th Session of the 6th Committee on the Report of the International Law Commission on the Work of its 66th Session, 29 October 2014, New York, see Markus P Beham and Gerhard Hafner, 'Austrian Diplomatic and Parliamentary Practice in International Law/ Österreichische Diplomatische und Parlamentarische Praxis zum Internationalen Recht' (2014) 19 Austrian Review of International and European Law 305, 322-324.

[17] *Cf.*, *e.g.*, Article 29 United Nations Convention on Contracts for the International Sale of Goods, 11 April 1980, 1489 UNTS 3.

[18] *Cf.* ILC (2014), *supra* note 9, Commentary to Conclusion 7, 191, para 34.

[19] Karl Zemanek, in this volume, at 14.

[20] Pellet, *supra* note 11, at 825, para 231.

is, in fact, setting state practice might be clearer in cases, in which the nomination was part of a specific agenda of the state. One might also think of the appointment of *ad hoc* judges in this context, although a detailed study might prove the exact opposite. The paradox is similar to that of arguments brought by state appointed counsel in proceedings. In how far should strategic steps taken in an arbitration proceeding be considered the practice of a particular state?

These observations hold true with respect to an analysis of the formation of customary international law. Taking the view that subsequent practice with regard to treaties constitutes a new tacit agreement over the subject matter or simply on the application of the respective treaty provision, courts or treaty bodies would be restricted to application and interpretation alone, unless these organs are endowed with the power to conclude agreements, which would revert the question, whether these acts constitute state practice, to an attribution to the respective states.

Re-Shaping Treaties While Balancing Interests of Stability and Change: Critical Issues in the Amendment/Modification/Revision of Treaties

Malgosia Fitzmaurice & Panos Merkouris[*]

I. Introduction

The present article aims to examine trends in amendment/modification/ revision (A/M/R) practices in international law, both pre- and post-VCLT, and how these reflect the constant tug-of-war between the competing interests of stability of international relations and the necessity to change in order to avoid stagnation. However, any study on trends, whether viewed as reflecting either linear or circular concepts, requires a study of the drafting history of any existing generally applicable set of rules on A/M/R. The International Law Commission (ILC) was well aware of the maze of complexities surrounding any discussion on A/M/R provisions and procedures. An exhaustive analysis of the relevant debates during the ILC meetings goes beyond the scope of the present article. The authors have instead decided to focus on the most controversial issues relating to A/M/R and examine these both from a doctrinal and an empirical angle. For this reason, in Section II the most critical aspects of the drafting history of the relevant articles of the Vienna Convention on the Law of Treaties (VCLT)[1] will be examined in order to draw some initial conclusions as to the trends at that time regarding A/M/R. In Section III, interesting forms of A/M/R will be examined, which either emerged post-VCLT, or existed pre-VCLT (such as the tacit acceptance procedure) but have shown a remarkable surge in application in the last few decades. Finally,

---

[*] Malgosia Fitzmaurice is Professor of Public International Law, Queen Mary, University of London (m.fitzmaurice@qmul.ac.uk); Panos Merkouris is Assistant Professor of Public International Law, University of Groningen (p.merkouris@ rug.nl). The authors would like to thank Mr. Vincent Beyer, Ms. Meaghan Beyer, Ms. Lauren Elrick and Ms. Iris Kwakkel for their invaluable assistance in collating and categorizing amendment, modification and revision provisions from the IEA Database Project.

[1] Vienna Convention on the Law of Treaties, 23 May 1969, 1155 UNTS 331.

in Section IV the A/M/R clauses of treaties will be statistically examined to reveal whether any conclusions arrived at the previous sections can be confirmed or whether any additional trends can be identified.

It goes without saying that when dealing with such a broad topic certain concessions, by necessity, have to be made. In Sections III and IV, the focus has been mainly on multilateral environmental agreements (MEAs). This is not because A/M/R practice in other fields of international law is devoid of interest, far from it.[2] However, for the purposes of this article it was considered better to adopt a 'narrow and deep' approach rather than a 'broad and shallow' one. MEAs were selected as the ideal focal point for several reasons; firstly, because an examination of the A/M/R of all treaties would be impossible within the confines of this article. Second, because MEAs due to their technical nature and their particular object and purpose seem to best reflect the constant battle between stability and change and finally, because there is a great number of MEAs from which useful statistical data can be drawn.

II. The Drafting History of Article 39-41 VCLT

A. Characteristics and Definitions of Rules Relating to A/M/R

1. Need for A/M/R Articles in the VCLT

The *Institut de Droit international* in 1960, while examining the modification of multilateral treaties, came to the conclusion that it was desirable to insert into such treaties amendment provisions in order to allow them to adapt to changing circumstances and enhance their relevance in a constantly shifting

---

[2] For various presentations of and commentaries to the drafting history of the VCLT see Olivier Corten and Pierre Klein (eds), *The Vienna Convention on the Law of Treaties: A Commentary* (2011); Oliver Dörr and Kirsten Schmalenbach (eds), *The Vienna Convention on the Law of Treaties: A Commentary* (2012); Mark E Villiger, *Commentary on the 1969 Vienna Convention on the Law of Treaties* (2009). For the purposes of this article the authors have chosen to focus on and refer directly to the primary documents of the drafting history of the VCLT, *i.e.* the discussions at the ILC and the Vienna Conference on the Law of Treaties (rather than to the respective Commentaries), in order to offer an analysis tailored specifically to the topic at hand and also highlight certain key issues that have so far eluded analysis.

legal landscape. Despite this, the members of the *Institut* were rather reluctant to adopt or suggest the existence of any specific rules regarding A/M/R.[3]

In the ILC there were some doubts as to the possibility of distilling a ubiquitously applicable set of rules from the wide gamut of A/M/R procedures used in treaty practice[4] and some arguments set against such an inclusion in the VCLT,[5] with one member even characterizing the work of the ILC as '*bourgeois*'.[6] The main point of those opposing the adoption of such rules was that despite the desirability of such rules, those issues were rooted in politics and diplomacy,[7] satisfactorily covered by other provisions on the law of treaties, or that any rules adopted would be prone to vagueness and abuse.[8]

Despite these objections, the ILC – as evidenced by the existence of Articles 39-41 VCLT – saw the issue in a different light. Although the A/M/R of a treaty 'was a matter of diplomacy and politics, it nonetheless also had legal aspects and the ILC was more than competent to concern itself with those',[9] and those rules should be 'raised to the rank of positive rules of international law.'[10] There were a number of reasons that proved the necessity of the ILC undertaking such a task. First, the approach that A/M/R was firmly rooted in the sphere of politics and diplomacy had led to recourse to the *rebus sic standibus* and the *inter se* principles to allow for the A/M/R of a treaty. Regrettably, the function of those principles in the context of A/M/R was manifestly sub-optimal.[11] Second, A/M/R rules would be the ideal balancing point between the competing interests of stability and change. They would safeguard the stability of treaties while at the same time

---

[3] Institut de Droit international, 'Modification et terminaison des traités collectifs' (1961/I) 49 Annuaire de l'Institut de Droit international 229-291.

[4] ILC, 'Summary record of the 747th meeting' (1964) UN Doc A/CN.4/SR.747, para 19 (Waldock); on the multifaceted nature of amendment/modification and its connection with other VCLT provisions see ILC, 'Third Report on the law of treaties, by Sir Humphrey Waldock' (1964) UN Doc A/CN.4/167 and Add.1-3, 47, paras 1-2.

[5] ILC (747th meeting), *supra* note 4, at paras 6 (Amado), 26 (Waldock).

[6] *Ibid.*, at para 6 (Amado).

[7] See for instance, Lord Arnold D McNair, *Law of Treaties* (1961) 534.

[8] ILC (747th meeting), *supra* note 4, at para 11 (Tsuruoka).

[9] ILC, 'Summary record of the 744th meeting' (1964) UN Doc A/CN.4/SR.744, para 9 (Lachs).

[10] *Ibid.*, at para 61 (Bartos); also in favour ILC, 'Summary record of the 745th meeting' (1964) UN Doc A/CN.4/SR.745, paras 4 (Yasseen) and 56 (Tunkin).

[11] ILC (Third report Waldock), *supra* note 4, at 48, para 4.

ensure that peaceful change could occur in order to avoid stagnation.[12] Finally, A/M/R rules would be useful for a multitude of other reasons including the proliferation of treaties and the importance of those rules for international organizations.[13] In this context, Article 39 VCLT (then Draft Article 67) as considered rather useful to retain[14] as it was the only provision of that cluster relating to amendment and modification that applied to both bilateral and multilateral agreements.[15] Thus, such an all-encompassing scope of application would best serve one of the purposes for the adoption of A/M/R rules, *i.e.* to function as guidelines that would streamline the process of A/M/R of treaties.

Similarly nobody disputed the fact that *inter se* agreements were an essential technique, and a necessary safety valve, for the adjustment of treaties to the dynamic needs of international society. If such a technique

---

[12] ILC (744th meeting), *supra* note 9, at paras 13-15 (Castrén); ILC (745th meeting), *supra* note 10, at para 49 (El-Erian); ILC, 'Summary record of the 746th meeting' (1964) UN Doc A/CN.4/SR.746, para 2 (Pal).

[13] ILC, 'Report of the International Law Commission on the work of its Eighteenth Session' (4 May-19 July 1966) UN Doc A/6309/Rev.1, 231-232, para 1.

[14] ILC (745th meeting), *supra* note 10, at paras 34 (Briggs), 54-55 (El-Erian).

[15] ILC, 'Summary record of the 859th meeting' (1966) UN Doc A/CN.4/SR.859, para 29 (Briggs). This has to be contrasted with Article 40 of the VCLT, which is entitled 'Amendment of multilateral treaties'. This was intentional, in order to highlight the difference *ratione materiae* between Articles 39 and 40. Article 40 VCLT applies only to multilateral treaties since as mentioned any rule designed to apply only to amendment of bilateral treaties would be devoid of any true purpose as it was tantamount to a question of negotiation and agreement; ILC (A/6309/Rev.1), *supra* note 13, at 233, para 5.

In a similar vein, although, it was generally recognized that *inter se* agreements were essentially new instruments and different from amendments (ILC (746th meeting), *supra* note 12, at paras 7 (Lachs), 22 (Ruda), 32 (Jiménez de Aréchaga)), a point that kept creeping up was that from an effects-perspective, amendment and modification may appear very similar, if not identical; ILC (747th meeting), *supra* note 4, at paras 23-24 (Waldock); ILC, 'Summary record of the 754th meeting' (1964) UN Doc A/CN.4/SR.54, paras 4 (Briggs), 22 (Lachs); United Nations Conference on the Law of Treaties, '1st Session – 37th meeting of the Committee of the Whole (COW)' (1968) UN Doc A/CONF.39/11, at paras 39 and 50-52. In order to highlight the difference between amendment and *inter se* agreement, and to bolster the differences in requirements and effects the Drafting Committee inserted what would become Article 40(2) VCLT so that the state parties would clarify *ab initio* their intention and it would be clear whether Article 40 or 41 VCLT was applicable; ILC (754th Meeting), in this note, paras 8-9 (Waldock), 24 and 74 (Briggs), 28 (de Luna), 30 (Ago), 82 (Castrén); ILC, 'Summary record of the 764th meeting' (1964) UN Doc A/CN.4/SR.764, paras 76 (Castrén), 85 (Bartos), 88 (Yasseen), 94 (Lachs), 103-104 (de Luna). This was clearly established and inserted in the provision during the 764th meeting, paras 29-33.

had not existed, there would have been stagnation in many treaty relation. The *inter se* procedure had been the means resorted to for that necessary evolution.[16] One of the earliest examples of a treaty providing explicitly for *inter se* agreements was Article 19 of the 1883 International Convention for the Protection of Industrial Property.[17]

The importance of *inter se* agreements was not lost on the ILC. Although originally the ILC envisaged one provision for both amendment and modification, the discussion surrounding *inter se* agreements ballooned so quickly that it became blatantly obvious that they deserved an Article of their, not to mention the fact that if such an Article was not adopted then Articles 39 and 40 VCLT 'would become meaningless.'[18]

The above analysis should not give the wrong impression that the A/M/R choices reflected in the VCLT rules were intended as the primary and preferred method of A/M/R. On the contrary, the diversity of the state practice on A/M/R guided the ILC to the conscious choice not to 'frame a comprehensive code of rules regarding the amendment of treaties .... [but to] include a formulation of the basic rules concerning the process of amendment'[19]. Articles 39-41 VCLT reflect the choice of the drafters that primacy should be given to the treaty text, in accordance with the *pacta sunt servanda* principle[20] and that the rules on A/M/R would of a 'residual character.'[21]

---

[16] ILC (746th meeting), *supra* note 12, at para 35 (Jiménez de Aréchaga); see also ILC, 'Second Report on the Law of Treaties, by Mr. H. Lauterpacht' (1954) UN Doc A/CN.4/87 and Corr.1, 136; ILC, 'Third Report on the Law of Treaties, by Mr. G.G. Fitzmaurice' (1958) UN Doc A/CN.4/115 and Corr.1, 43, para 89; ILC (Third report Waldock), *supra* note 4, at 49.

[17] For recent examples of *inter se* agreements see Seyed Ali Sadat-Akhavi, *Methods of Resolving Conflicts between Treaties* (2003) 114-119; Study Group of the ILC, 'Report on Fragmentation of International Law: Difficulties Arising from the Diversification and Expansion of International Law, finalized by Martti Koskenniemi' (2006) UN Doc A/CN.4/L.682, paras 297 *et seq*.

[18] ILC (746th meeting), *supra* note 12, at para 57 (Waldock).

[19] *Ibid*.

[20] ILC (Third report Waldock), *supra* note 4, at 47, para 2.

[21] *Ibid*., at 50, paras 10-11; ILC (A/6309/Rev.l), *supra* note 13, at 231-232, para 2, 233, para 7; ILC (744th meeting), *supra* note 9, at para 62 (Bartos); ILC (746th meeting), *supra* note 12, at paras 33 (Jiménez de Aréchaga), 54-55 (Tunkin).

2. Definitional Issues of A/M/R

Making a conscious choice on the 'residual character' of the VCLT A/M/R rules was not the end of the ILC's troubles on the issue. Another major hurdle that the ILC had to surmount in order to adopt a set of rules relating to A/M/R was a definitional one. Two definitional issues can be discerned. First, state practice indicated that states tended to use the terms 'amendment', 'revision' and 'modification' rather loosely or even interchangeably.[22]

The ILC basically faced two possible courses of action; either to try and decipher from the practice of the League of Nations the terminology or to adopt a set of terms and define them in an explanatory note or in the commentary.[23] Considering that most ILC members felt that there was only a difference of degree between 'amendment' and 'revision'[24] and that the distinction being so artificial should be dropped,[25] the ILC went for the second option, using only the terms 'amendment' and 'modification' and clarifying that

> [it] considered it sufficient in the present articles to speak of 'amendment' as being a term which covers both the amendment of particular provisions and a general review of the whole treaty. As to the term 'revision', the Commission recognized that it is frequently found in State practice and that it is also used in some treaties. Nevertheless, having regard to the nuances that became attached to the phrase 'revision of treaties' in the period preceding the Second World War, the Commission preferred the term 'amendment'. This term is here used to denote *a formal* amendment of a treaty intended to alter its provisions with respect to all the parties. The more general term 'modification' is used in [Article 41 VCLT] in connexion with an *inter se* agreement concluded between certain of the parties only, and intended to vary provisions of the treaty between themselves alone, and also in connexion with a variation of the provisions of a treaty resulting from the practice of the parties in applying it [which was included in Draft Article 38, but was eventually left out of the text of the VLCT].[26]

---

[22] United Nations, *Final Clauses of Multilateral Treaties: Handbook* (2003) 96.

[23] ILC (744th meeting), *supra* note 9, at para 33 (de Luna).

[24] *Ibid.*, at para 17 (Castrén); ILC (746th meeting), *supra* note 12, at para 49 (Yasseen).

[25] ILC (Third report Waldock), *supra* note 4, at 48, para 6; ILC (744th meeting), *supra* note 9, at paras 20 (Liang), 33 (de Luna); ILC (746th meeting), *supra* note 12, at paras 10 (Rosenne), 31 (Jiménez de Aréchaga).

[26] ILC (A/6309/Rev.l), *supra* note 13, at 232, para 3.

Several decades later the UN Handbook, *Final Clauses of Multilateral Treaties*, offered its two cents on the issue without, however, deviating from the VCLT's drafting choices. According to the Handbook, 'modification normally refers to alterations of certain provisions of a treaty only among certain parties to that treaty'.[27] The term 'revision' is not used in the VCLT, however, it does appear in several treaties and it usually refers 'to a general alteration affecting the treaty as a whole, as opposed to an amendment that partially alters some of the treaty provisions.'[28]

The second definitional issue was the normative essence of the ability of states to propose an amendment? Was it a 'right'[29] or a 'faculty'?[30] The matter became more convoluted because the choice of the term would affect corresponding obligations.[31] The ILC eventually took the Gordian knot approach. Since it was extremely debatable, it cut out from the text of Article 39 any qualifying term, be that 'right' or 'faculty'. It followed Tunkin's suggestion to use the terms 'a treaty *may* be amended', since such a non-committal expression would help the ILC avoid all the major theoretical problems.[32]

B. Critical Issues relating to the Process of A/M/R in the VCLT

Having made choices as to the nature and definition of A/M/R, the ILC then had to turn to the actual content of the relevant cluster of provisions. An exhaustive analysis of the relevant debates is outside the scope of this article. Of importance are, however, two issues. The first one, on the specific rights and obligations of states attached to activating an A/M/R procedure and the second one, which is also connected to our analysis in Section IV, concerning the debate on requiring adherence to the unanimity rule in one way or another.

1. Rights and Obligations of States during A/M/R Procedures

One of the main reasons for the adoption of Articles 39 and 40 was that in earlier times, treaties were amended or revised by certain parties without

---

[27] United Nations, *supra* note 22, at 107.
[28] *Ibid.*, at 96.
[29] ILC (744th meeting), *supra* note 9, at paras 30 (Verdross), 81 (Amato), 78 (Bartos).
[30] *Ibid.*, at paras 24 (Ago), 28 (Rosenne); Pal does not seem to take a position on the matter using both terms, however, it has to be noted that he used the term 'faculty' with greater frequency, *ibid.*, at para 68 (Pal).
[31] *Ibid.*, at paras 74-76 (Ago); para 78 (Bartos), paras 82-83 (Ruda); ILC (745th meeting), *supra* note 10, paras 13-15 (Paredes).
[32] ILC (744th meeting), *supra* note 9, at para 85 (Tunkin).

the consultation of other parties. One of the most notorious examples of the pitfalls of the A/M/R system is the Concert of Europe, in which the major powers would conclude new treaties on same subject-matters, without securing the consent of all the parties to the previous treaty. This, of course, gave rise to situations of conflicting obligations and treaties.[33]

By the 1960s some writers had concluded that state parties do not have a 'right' to participate in discussions relating to amendment, since this was more of a 'practical rather than legal'[34] matter and that if such a rule existed, even if it prevented conflicting obligations, it 'would also be a formidable factor of stagnation.'[35] However, the vast majority of the ILC members were of a different view. According to them, state parties not only had a right to be notified of any proposal for amendment,[36] but also a right to participate in the negotiations,[37] which flowed logically from the principle of good faith[38] and struck the ideal balance between the competing interests.[39]

A side issue with respect to Article 40(2) was its limits *ratione personae*. Should the right to be notified and involved in the negotiations also extend to non-parties? The issue was hotly contested within the ILC,[40] with concerns being expressed that although there could be instances where this was desirable,[41] there was great danger that over-expanding the circle of participants in these discussions would lead to stagnation of international law. After a lot of deliberation and a final amendment proposed by the Netherlands during the Vienna Conference,[42] which struck the golden mean, Article 40(2)

---

[33] ILC (Third report Waldock), *supra* note 4, at 48, para 4.

[34] Edwin C Hoyt, *The Unanimity Rule in the Revision of Treaties: A Re-Examination* (1959) 250.

[35] Jean Leca, *Les techniques de révision des conventions internationales* (1961) 204 (authors' translation).

[36] ILC (745th meeting), *supra* note 10, at paras 35 (Briggs), 43 (Yasseen), 52 (El-Erian), 68 (de Luna), 25 (Castrén).

[37] ILC (746th meeting), *supra* note 12, at para 42 (Reuter); ILC (A/6309/Rev.1), *supra* note 13, at 233, paras 8-9.

[38] ILC (Third report Waldock), *supra* note 4, at para 14.

[39] ILC (A/6309/Rev.1), *supra* note 13, at 233-234, para 10.

[40] ILC (745th meeting), *supra* note 10, at paras 32 (Waldock), 35 (Briggs), 43 (Yasseen), 69 (de Luna).

[41] ILC, 'Summary record of the 875th meeting' (1966) UN Doc A/CN.4/SR.875, para 44 (Briggs).

[42] Netherlands, 'Amendment Proposal to Article 40' UN Doc A/CONF.39/C.1/L.232.

VCLT was adopted, giving a limited number of non-state parties certain rights regarding notification and participation in the discussions of an amendment.

Conversely, the issue that arose from the rights of the state parties receiving notification of an amendment proposal was whether those states also had obligations. The ILC was of the opinion that the receiving states had an obligation of 'good faith' to give due consideration of the proposal.[43] However, putting this concept into black letter law proved extremely difficult as it could be abused by leaving the door open to arbitrary denunciations of treaties on the pretended ground that the other party had not given 'due consideration'. For this reason it was omitted from the final text of the VCLT.[44]

2. Unanimity Rule

Although it was accepted that the 'jurist recognizes no immutable instruments'[45] and that A/M/R was necessary *inter alia* 'in order to minimize the danger of normative conflict'[46], the optimal method in order to ensure such changes to treaties was uncertain. During the ILC meetings the question that the members had to tackle was whether the unanimity rule merited being included in the VCLT A/M/R provisions.

The inclusion of the unanimity rule was argued both in favour[47] and against,[48] with an interesting proposal by Rosenne suggesting that it could be restricted to treaties with a limited number of parties (the problem, however, being that this was an ill-defined category).[49] We shall return in Section IV to this proposal, as its importance will emerge more clearly there, when we examine patterns emerging from the practice relating to the A/M/R provisions included in MEAs. In the end, however, and despite Rosenne's proposal, the ILC concluded that the rapid growth in the number of international treaties

---

[43] ILC (A/6309/Rev.1), *supra* note 13, at 233, para 6; ILC (Third report Waldock), *supra* note 4, at 50, para 12; ILC (744th meeting), *supra* note 9, at para 51 (Briggs); ILC (745th meeting), *supra* note 10, at para 54 (El-Erian); with one ILC member, however, considering that any reference to 'good faith' would be an 'empty admonition', *ibid.*, at para 17 (Paredes). However, this 'good faith' obligation did not entail an obligation to negotiate, *ibid.*, at paras 42 (Yasseen), 68 (de Luna).

[44] ILC (A/6309/Rev.1), *supra* note 13, at 233, para 6.

[45] Charles Rousseau, *Principes généraux du droit international public: Tome 1* (1944) 616.

[46] ILC (745th meeting), *supra* note 10, at para 64 (de Luna).

[47] ILC (747th meeting), *supra* note 4, at para 12 (Tsuruoka).

[48] ILC (746th meeting), *supra* note 12, at para 8 (Rosenne).

[49] *Ibid.*, at para 15 (Rosenne).

had rendered the unanimity rule impractical.[50] In Article 39 VCLT, the terms agreed upon were 'between the parties' and not 'between all the parties' in order to highlight the difference between amendment and termination and the shift from the unanimity rule.[51]

The unanimity rule was also discussed in connection to Article 41 VCLT. A/M/R is a multi-faceted concept that has several cross-overs with other areas of the law of treaties. One such connection that was hinted at, in connection to promoting the unanimity rule, was with termination.[52] However, Waldock and de Luna clarified that modification should be distinguished from termination as they had different results as to the obligations of the parties.

Another way in which the unanimity rule in connection to Article 41 was proposed was by means of an analogy with the system on reservations. During the Vienna Conference, Australia[53] and France[54] submitted amendments that echoed Fitzmaurice's typology of obligations[55] and Article 20(2) VCLT. They were based on the premise that '*inter se* agreements [were] primarily possible in the case of those multilateral treaties which operated in fact on a bilateral basis'.[56] Consequently, in the case of a restricted multilateral treaty the unanimity principle would be activated and any *inter se* agreement would require the acceptance by all state parties.

Several states opposed such an approach as it did not reflect practice and it would put too disproportionate a restraint on the ability to conclude *inter se* agreements, not to mention prejudge the content of Article 20(2) VCLT, which at that time had yet to be approved.[57] For that reason, no mention of such a limit to *inter se* agreements found its way in Article 41 VCLT. Whether the aforementioned objections to the Australian and French amendment proposals

---

[50] ILC (A/6309/Rev.l), *supra* note 13, at 231-232, para 1.

[51] ILC, 'Summary record of the 753rd meeting' (1964) UN Doc A/CN.4/SR.753, paras 39-41 and 46 (Waldock).

[52] ILC (744th meeting), *supra* note 9, at para 85 (Tunkin); ILC (745th meeting), *supra* note 10, at para 67 (de Luna).

[53] Australia, 'Amendment Proposal to Article 41' UN Doc A/CONF.39/C.1/L.237.

[54] France, 'Amendment Proposal to Article 41' UN Doc A/CONF.39/C.1/L.46.

[55] Reciprocal and non-reciprocal. The former subdivided into bilateral and bilateralisable, whereas the latter into interdependent and integral, ILC (Third report Fitzmaurice), *supra* note 16, at 41-45, paras 77-94.

[56] ILC, 'Summary record of the 860th meeting' (1966) UN Doc A/CN.4/SR.860, paras 66 (Tunkin), 62 (de Luna).

[57] United Nations, *supra* note 57, at paras 47-48; United Nations Conference on the Law of Treaties, '2nd Session – 86th meeting of the Committee of the Whole (COW)' (1969) UN Doc A/CONF.39/11/Add.1, paras 5-11.

were well-founded or not is a point to which we shall return in Section IV, when we examine state practice relating to A/M/R provisions in MEAs.

In summation, both during the ILC and the Vienna Conference on the Law of Treaties –despite some interesting proposals to the contrary – the solution opted for by the ILC was that the unanimity rules should take more of a residual role with respect to A/M/R.[58]

III. Critical Trends & Issues in A/M/R of Treaties

A. Introduction

The first part of the present article referred to the traditional ways of the amendment of a treaty, as enshrined in the 1969 VCLT, and the debate concerning the drafting of Articles 39-41 by the ILC. As it was explained, not only were the rules incorporated in the VCLT meant to be of a 'residual nature' but a number of issues came up, that were either left out of the final text or the wording adopted was intentionally open-ended in order to allow for state practice to find its own way through a process of trial and error.

For instance, there are differences in the classification between such concepts of the law of treaties, as amendment, modification and revision (the last one not having been included in the 1969 VCLT). This obscure and far from clear-cut classification is, however, not the only issue, either definitional or substantive, that has arisen in theory and in the practice of states. Consequently, and for the purpose of ensuring the completeness of this article, the most critical ones will be brought to the attention of the reader and analyzed.[59] These are:

- the tacit amendment procedure;[60]
- the subsequent practice of Conferences of the Parties/Meetings of the Parties (COPs/MOPs) in MEAs[61]; and

---

[58] ILC (753rd meeting), *supra* note 51, at paras 39-41 (Waldock), 58 (de Luna).

[59] See in depth on this, Irina Buga, 'Subsequent Practice and Treaty Modification' in Michael J Bowman and Dino Kritsiotis (eds), *Conceptual and Contextual Perspectives on the Modern Law of Treaties* (forthcoming 2018 - on file with the authors); Athina Chanaki, *L'adaptation des traités dans les temps* (2013).

[60] Also referred to as tacit acceptance procedure and 'opting-out' procedure.

[61] A phenomenon noted and analyzed by Professor Nolte during his work on *Treaties over Time* in the ILC. See in detail Georg Nolte (ed), *Treaties and Subsequent Practice* (2013), in particular 337-338.

- the difference between interpretation and A/M/R of a treaty.[62]

The first two have been selected as they are approaches to treaty A/M/R that have mainly developed through state practice and deviate from classical approaches to A/M/R, such as the requirement that a certain number or percentage of the member states adopt the amendment and the need for explicit provision of consent to be bound. Furthermore, whereas the former had already emerged pre-VCLT it has evolved and risen in prominence post-VCLT. The latter is a post-VCLT creature that has emerged through the decisions of COPs/MOPs of MEAs.

However, A/M/R is defined not only by the elements of which it consists, *i.e.* by the various A/M/R procedures, but also by the manner in which it is distinguished from other actions in the 'life-cycle' of the treaty. This brings us to the third issue, which although not an A/M/R procedure *per se* is equally important as it purports to identify the demarcation line between A/M/R and interpretation. Although this problem was briefly touched upon during the VCLT *travaux préparatoires*,[63] it has gradually, and also due to the ILC's work on the importance of subsequent agreements/practice in treaty interpretation, been receiving a long overdue attention.

B. Tacit Acceptance Procedure

In general, Hathaway, Saurabh Sanghvi and Solow distinguish between:

- The so-called consensus amendments. These are amendments to a treaty that require the unanimous consent of all parties represented in the international body, the function of which is amending of a treaty. These agreements require that all states represented in the regulatory body of a treaty agree to any future policy that the body adopts (*e.g.* Open Skies Agreement). This Treaty requires consensus which is defined as 'the absence of any objection by a state party to the taking of a decision or making a recommendation, before it can act.'
- The so-called opt out amendments. These are based on the premise that the regulatory body of a treaty proposes an amendment to a treaty. If the amendment is approved than the state parties to a

---

[62] See analysis *infra* in Section III.D.
[63] In more detail see *infra* Section III.D.

Re-Shaping Treaties: Issues in the Amendment/Modification/Revision 53

treaty have a determined period of time within which they can reject them. If a certain number of state parties do not agree with an amendment (a 'blocking minority'), the amendment may not be adopted altogether. Otherwise, it will be adopted, but effective only in respect to the parties that did not object to it.[64] The examples of this system are treaties concluded within the IMO regime (see below Sections III.B.1.-III.B.4.).

- Finally, a third category distinguished by Hathaway, Saurabh Sanghvi and Solow are the so-called binding amendments. This category includes, *e.g.*, the World Trade Organization ('WTO') and the Montreal Protocol. The WTO can amend its agreements through a Ministerial Conference. The WTO encourages the use of consensus at these Conferences. It can, however, make changes if there exists a supermajority that overrules the objections of any one of the state parties. With respect to the Montreal Protocol, its COPs can adopt changes to certain annexes by a two-thirds majority vote, even over the objection of the remaining parties.

This Section will be devoted to the tacit procedure in the meaning of the second category as the most common and significant in practice. The third category will be dealt with in Section III.C.

1. Tacit Acceptance Procedure in International Treaties

The procedure of tacit acceptance ('opting-out procedure') has been known for a long time in relation to organizations such as the International Labour Organization (ILO), the World Health Organization (WHO), the International Telecommunications Union (ITU), the World Meteorological Organization (WMO), the International Civil Aviation Organization (ICAO), the International Maritime Organization (IMO) and the International Whaling Commission (IWC). This procedure is not uncommon in relation to organs established by environmental treaties such the Consultative Meeting of the Contracting Parties established by the 1972 Convention on the Prevention of Marine Pollution by Dumping of Wastes and other Matter (London Convention),[65] but is best known as applied by the IMO in the treaties concluded

---

[64] Oona A Hathaway, Haley N Saurabh Sanghvi and Sara Solow, 'Tacit Amendments', 10-16, <https://law.yale.edu/system/files/documents/pdf/cglc/TacitAmendments.pdf> accessed 29 June 2017.

[65] Convention on the Prevention of Marine Pollution by Dumping of Wastes and Other Matter, 29 December 1972, 1046 UNTS 120.

under its auspices. Within the framework of the IMO, the International Convention for the Prevention of Pollution from Ships (MARPOL)[66] and the International Convention for the Safety of Life at Sea (SOLAS)[67] were the first instruments to introduce these procedures.

This procedure, however, is not exclusive to these organizations and is also widely used in other international institutions such as many international fisheries commissions such as the North-East Atlantic Fishery Commission (NEAFC),[68] the Northwest Atlantic Fisheries Organization (NAFO),[69] the Convention on International Trade in Endangered Species of Wild Fauna and Flora (CITES)[70] and the International Whaling Commission.[71]

The system of 'opting-out' is a mechanism which was a precursor of the expanding phenomenon of the so-called autonomous institutional arrangements (AIAs), as described by Churchill and Ulfstein, and the increasing legislative powers of COPs/MOPs, including amendments to treaties.[72]

The procedures, which characterize the legal acts of an organization set up under a treaty by way of involving the 'tacit acceptance' system, are: firstly, the acts are adopted by a majority vote, and, secondly, that member states can lodge an objection and, thus, avoid being bound by the act. The essential characteristic is based on the premise that a member state is automatically bound by the act of the organization unless it takes specific action to avoid being so bound (*i.e.* by way of 'opting-out').[73] Thus, this system encompasses in equal measure the legal problems of consent to be bound by a treaty and

---

[66] International Convention for the Prevention of Pollution from Ships, 2 November 1973, 1340 UNTS 184.

[67] International Convention for the Safety of Life at Sea, 1 November 1974, 1184 UNTS 278.

[68] North-East Atlantic Fishery Convention, 18 November 1980, 285 UNTS 129.

[69] International Convention for the Northwest Atlantic Fisheries, 8 February 1949, 157 UNTS 158.

[70] Convention on International Trade in Endangered Species of Wild Fauna and Flora, 3 March 1973, 993 UNTS 243.

[71] International Convention for the Regulation of Whaling, 2 December 1946, 161 UNTS 72.

[72] Robin R Churchill and Geir Ulfstein, 'Autonomous Institutional Arrangements in Multilateral Environmental Agreements: A Little-Noticed Phenomenon in International Law' (2000) 94 AJIL 623. This issue will be analyzed in more detail *infra*, in Section III.C.

[73] On the subject see in particular Krzysztof Skubiszewski, 'A New Source of the Law of Nations Resolutions of International Organisations' in Paul Guggenheim and Maurice Battelli (eds), *Recueil d'études de droit international en hommage à Paul Guggenheim* (1968) 508-520.

the law-making or at least rule-making acts of an international organization, which may result in a treaty being amended.

2. Legality and *Telos* of the Tacit Acceptance Procedure

The power of the organization to *prima facie* curb the obligation for expression of consent by the member states is rooted in the constituent treaty of the international organization. Consequently, one might refer to a 'derivative treaty obligation'[74], *i.e.* although the organization creates law that is directly binding on states, its *pouvoir de légiférer* is ultimately founded in the treaty establishing the organization. In this manner the principles of *pacta sunt servanda, pacta tertiis nec nocent nec prosunt* and of state sovereignty remain intact. This is further reinforced by the structure of the 'opting-out procedure', which allows a member state to object to the proposed amendment and thus not be bound.

The *telos* of the 'tacit acceptance procedure' is to combine the principle of state sovereignty (the right of a member state to lodge an objection) whilst at the same time, by making it politically unattractive to lodge an objection, to encourage the creation of a uniform system for all the states, which are party to the convention in question. Opinions differ as to whether the act of an international organization operating under the tacit acceptance (opting-out) system has an independent law-making character, or constitutes, in effect, an agreement analogous to an agreed amendment to the treaty between the States concerned.[75] On the one hand, the view has been expressed by some authors that such acts, having been taken by a majority vote of the organization concerned, and becoming binding on the member states without their explicit agreement (as was traditionally always required for the formation of an international treaty), do have a law-making character independent of the will of the member states.[76]

---

[74] Paul C Szasz, 'International Norm-Making' in Edith Brown Weiss (ed), *Environmental Change and International Law: New Challenges and Dimensions* (1992) 65.

[75] Roberto Ago, 'Die Internationalen Organisationen und Ihre Funktionen im inneren Tätigkeitsgebiet der Staaten' in Hans Wehberg, Walter Schätzel and Hans-Jürgen Schlochauer (eds), *Rechtsfragen der internationalen Organisation: Festschrift für Hans Wehberg zu seinem 70 Geburtstag* (1956) 20-38; Hans Blix, *Treaty Making Power* (1960) 293-296.

[76] Krzysztof Skubiszewski, *Uchwaly Prawotworcze Organizacji Miendzynarodowych. Przeglad Zagadnien I Analiza Wstepna (Law-Making Resolutions of International Organisations. Survey of Problems and the Preliminary Analysis)* (1965) 69.

On the other hand, the view has equally been expressed that the 'tacit acceptance' procedure is no more than a system developed for the purpose of accelerating and simplifying the process of concluding a kind of international treaty; or of amending or modifying an existing treaty.[77] The procedure of tacit acceptance combines the principle of consent to be bound and at the same time encourages the creation of uniform rules applicable to all state parties to the treaty. [78]

3. *Raison d'Être* of the Tacit Acceptance Procedure: The IMO Example

In relation to the amendment of the treaties within the realm of the IMO tacit acceptance was only one of the means to do so. In order to better understand the purpose of the establishment and the role of tacit acceptance as a method of amending treaties, the classical procedure of amendment of certain treaties concluded under the IMO auspices will be first described.[79]

The early IMO conventions were characterized by a complex and cumbersome procedure relating to amendments, which only came into force after a certain percentage of contracting states, usually two-thirds, had ratified them. This meant that at times more ratifications were required to amend a convention than were originally required for its entry into force, in particular in relation to conventions with multiple state parties. Such a classical amendment procedure was a source of difficulties. As Lost-Sieminska explains, such an example were the amendments to the SOLAS Convention which entered into force twelve months after the date on which the amendments were ratified by two-thirds of the contracting governments, including two-thirds of the governments represented on the Maritime Safety Committee (MSC). In the early days of the SOLAS Convention, such a provision did not pose undue problems since at the time of the adoption of the Convention amendments required ratification by only fifteen countries for their entry into force, seven of which had fleets consisting of at least one million gross tons of merchant shipping. However, the late 1960s witnessed the expansion of the number of state parties to SOLAS, which had reached 80 and the tonnage was

---

[77] Grigory I Tunkin (transl. by William E Butler), *Theory of International Law* (1974) 106. The same view is expressed by Chanaki, *supra* note 59, at 183.

[78] Chanaki, *supra* note 59, at 183.

[79] Dorota Lost-Sieminska, 'The International Maritime Organisation' in Michael J Bowman and Dino Kritsiotis (eds), *Conceptual and Contextual Perspectives on the Modern Law of Treaties* (forthcoming 2018 - on file with the authors).

continuously rising due to the emergence of new countries which developed their shipping industry. Such an expansion of the number of state parties had an impact on the total number required to amend the Convention, leading to instances where the acceptance of amendments took a longer time than that of the ratification of the Convention itself.

The rapid advancement of technology in the shipping industry resulted in amending the SOLAS Convention six times after it entered into force in 1965. In 1974, a new Convention was adopted in order to incorporate all these amendments as well as other minor changes. This new Convention has been subsequently amended on numerous occasions.[80]

Complex requirements concerning amendments to the IMO conventions resulted in long delays in bringing them into force. The tacit acceptance procedure was introduced to remedy this state of affairs. Following the examples of the ICAO, the WHO and the other above-listed organizations, the IMO conventions applied the tacit acceptance procedure to the amendment of provisions of a technical nature, included in the annexes and appendices of treaties. The classical amendment procedure has been retained for non-technical articles, 'which have limited practical importance.[81] In more detail, the IMO states:

> Tact acceptance is now incorporated into most of the IMO's technical Conventions.
>
> It facilitates quick and simple modification of the Conventions to keep pace with the rapidly –evolving technology in shipping world. Without tacit acceptance, it would have proved impossible to keep Conventions up to date and IMO's role as the international forum for technical issues involving shipping would have been placed in jeopardy.[82]

As expected, the tacit acceptance procedure has greatly sped up the amendment process. Amendments generally enter into force within 18 to 24 months. On the contrary, the classical amendment procedure of the 1960 SOLAS Convention did not result in any of the amendments adopted between 1966 and 1973 in entering into force due to insufficient number of ratifications.[83] Due to its effectiveness, the tacit acceptance procedure has been applied in the

---

[80] *Ibid.*

[81] *Ibid.*

[82] IMO, 'Introduction', <http://www.imo.org/en/About/Conventions/Pages/Home.aspx> visited on 1 May 2016.

[83] Lost-Sieminska, *supra* note 79.

majority of the IMO's technical conventions and also has been incorporated in other instruments such as on liability for oil pollution damage.

The advantages of tacit acceptance are numerous, in particular due to its quick, simple and efficient modification of conventions to conform to the development of technology in shipping industry. A very important element of this procedure is, as it was observed, that it provides certainty as to the date upon which an amendment becomes effective, rather than leaving this to the timing of individual acceptances. Lost-Sieminska notes that

> in reality, the classical amendment procedure meant that amendments would never have entered into force and, as a consequence, every State would have adopted its own national rules for shipping safety and environmental protection, inevitably leading to chaos.[84]

Most of the amendments of technical annexes of the SOLAS Convention are 'deemed to have been accepted at the end of two years from the date on which it is communicated to Contracting Governments' unless the amendment is objected to by more than one third of the contracting governments, or contracting governments owning not less than 50% of the world's gross merchant tonnage. The MSC may vary this period by up to one year.

The MARPOL provides for an amendment to be deemed to have been accepted at the end of a period determined by the appropriate body at the time of its adoption, which period shall not be less than ten months. The entry into force of such amendments can be blocked in a similar fashion as with the SOLAS Convention, *i.e.* if they are objected to by not less than one third of the state parties or by parties owning not less than 50% of the world's gross merchant tonnage.[85] The whole procedure of adoption of amendments under the SOLAS Convention and MARPOL is very complex, due to the binary solution regarding the consideration of amendments: amendment after the consideration by the Organization (*i.e.* IMO committees consider the proposed amendment) and amendment by the COP, in which case only the parties consider the amendments.[86]

In the IMO practice, all decisions, including the adoption of amendments, are taken by consensus. In case of a lack of consensus, both SOLAS and MARPOL provide that a two-thirds majority of the parties adopts amend-

---

[84] *Ibid.*
[85] *Ibid.*
[86] *Ibid.*

ments.[87] It appears that, at least within the framework of the IMO sponsored treaties, tacit acceptance is a simplified and effective method of speeding up entry into force of amendments, however, the undisputed efficiency of this method appears to be hindered by the unclear and complex relationship between the role of the Marine Environment Protection Committee (MEPC) and the parties, and the role of the MEPC and the parties versus the Assembly in the adoption of amendments.[88] The troubled relationship between the state parties to MARPOL and the MEPC as the body responsible for this Convention is an example of the procedural difficulties regarding the decision on amendments. There are currently 171 states eligible for membership of the committee: 170 members of the Organization and one state that is a non-member of the Organization but is a Party to MARPOL. Of those states only 75 are parties to the 1997 Protocol.[89] Such a structure illustrates very well the difficulty regarding the situation in which the majority of the MEPC will have a different view than the two-thirds of the parties.[90]

Notwithstanding the internal problems concerning the adoption of the amendments to the IMO conventions, the use of the system of tacit acceptance appears to be applied recently even more extensively than before. Such an example is the Guidelines for Ships Operating in Arctic Ice-Covered Waters that were adopted by the MSC and MEPC in 2002, *i.e.* the so-called Polar Code. The method of transposing it into 'hard' binding law was subject to much discussion. Finally, it was decided that it be will adopted through dissecting the Code into various parts and attaching these in the form of annexes to the existing Conventions, such as the SOLAS and the MARPOL, adopting them through the tacit acceptance procedure.[91]

To give an example outside the IMO framework, in order to demonstrate that the tacit acceptance procedure is not merely a specialized tool unique to the workings of the IMO, the CITES may be turned to. The CITES COP has adopted criteria for the consideration by its Parties regarding proposals concerning amending Appendices I (species of wild fauna and flora threatened with extinction) and II (species of wild fauna and flora which may become extinct unless a strict regulation of their trade has been enacted) of the

---

[87] In the SOLAS a two-thirds of the contracting governments and in the MARPOL a two-thirds majority of the parties, *ibid*.

[88] See in depth on this aspect, *ibid*.

[89] MARPOL Annex VI.

[90] Lost-Sieminska, *supra* note 79.

[91] *Ibid*.

CITES.[92] The updating of these lists is carried out under a tacit acceptance procedure.[93] Interestingly enough the possibility of 'opting-out' for the state parties is called a 'reservation' in CITES.[94]

4. Characterization of the Tacit Acceptance Procedure

In the view of the authors of the present article, the legal character of the tacit acceptance ('opting-out') procedure has more recently been defined as a simplified amendment to a treaty, rather than an expression of a unilateral act of an organization. The most notable feature of this procedure is its efficiency in the adoption of amendments. However, one of the characteristics of this method of amendment of a treaty is that it is used in relation to amendments of the provisions, which are of a technical nature; not in a relation to provisions that set out the main rights and obligations of state parties to the treaty.

As a final thought, it is interesting to note that the awkwardness of characterizing the tacit acceptance procedure that we face at the international level is reflected in equal measure at the domestic level. Demonstrative of this is the fact that in certain states, such as Poland, the procedure of tacit acceptance, at least within the IMO, is treated as an amendment to a treaty, not a *sensu stricto* act of an international organization, and thus is subject to the same procedure of internal approval (parliamentary and other) *as a formal amendment to a treaty.*[95] However, in other states, such as Croatia and Nigeria, the tacit acceptance procedure is *automatically transposed into the national legal order.*

---

[92] CITES, Resolution Conf 9.24 (Rev. CoP13), <https://cites.org/eng/res/all/09/E09-24R13.pdf> accessed 29 June 2017.

[93] Art XV(1) and (2) Convention on International Trade in Endangered Species of Wild Fauna and Flora, 3 March 1973, 993 UNTS 243.

[94] Art XV(3) Convention on International Trade in Endangered Species of Wild Fauna and Flora, 3 March 1973, 993 UNTS 243.

[95] Information obtained through Dorota Lost-Sieminska, the Head of the Legal Section of the IMO and Iva Parlov (expert maritime lawyer in Croatia). In Poland, originally the changes to the IMO Conventions adopted within the Maritime Environment Protection Committee were subject to the ratification by the Parliament *en bloc* according to Article 14 of the Law on International Treaties (Official Journal No 39, item 443, 2002 with amendments). Recent practice is simplified through the act Council of Minsters (the same Statute). However, if changes are significant, the procedure of ratification will be employed.

C. COPs/MOPs in MEAs and Amendment/Modification Thereof

1. Legal Characterization of COPs/MOPs

As was mentioned above, the tacit acceptance procedure was the precursor of the so-called 'autonomous institutional arrangements',[96] although the latter must be distinguished from the former as it partakes of different characteristics.[97] This connection, yet differentiation, between the tacit amendment procedure and AIAs has dictated the structure of our analysis. Consequently, having concluded our research into the tacit acceptance procedure we will now proceed to examine the recent phenomenon concerning the extensive powers of organs of MEAs, in particular COPs/MOPs, the legal character of which has been variously termed as 'AIAs', 'managerial treaty making',[98] or simply as a diplomatic conference.[99] Notwithstanding that this subject-matter has attracted a sizeable body of literature, there is still little understanding as to the legal character of COPs/MOPs and the effects of their decisions on treaty regimes.[100] Nolte in his seminal work, *Treaties and Subsequent Practice*, stated that they are situated somewhere in between a diplomatic conference and an international organization.[101] They constitute useful *fora* for state parties to evolve treaty regimes and cooperate. They are treaty bodies in the sense that they are created on the basis of treaties; they are not

---

[96] Churchill and Ulfstein, *supra* note 72, at 623-659.

[97] Hathaway, Saurabh Sanghvi and Solow, *supra* note 64.

[98] José E Alvarez, *International Organisations as Law-Makers* (2006) 316.

[99] Alan E Boyle, 'Saving the World? Implementation and Enforcement of International Environmental Law through International Institutions' (1991) 3 Journal of Environmental Law 225.

[100] For example: Churchill and Ulfstein, *supra* note 72; Jutta Brunnée, 'COPing with Consent: Law-making Under Multilateral Environmental Agreements' (2002) 15 LJIL 1; Jutta Brunnée, 'Reweaving the Fabric of International Law? Patterns of Consent in the Environmental Framework Agreements' in Rüdiger Wolfrum and Volker Röben (eds), *Developments of International Law in Treaty-Making* (2005) 101; René Lefeber, 'Creative Legal Engineering' (2000) 13 LJIL 1; Malgosia Fitzmaurice, 'Consent to be Bound-Anything New under the Sun?' (2005) 74 Nordic Journal of International Law 483.

[101] Nolte, *supra* note 61, at 365.

to be equated, however, with bodies which comprise independent experts or bodies with a limited membership.[102]

> ...COPs are more or less periodical settings which are open to all parties of a treaty.
>
> As such, they can be seen as the continuing common venue of the parties of a treaty where authoritative interpretations in terms of the VCLT can take place. COPs represent a vehicle for the continuing and evolving expression of the will of the parties, allowing for the concretization and adaptation of treaty provisions over time. [103]

COPs/MOPs adopt various legal acts, which may be classified as 'internal' and 'external'. The first category of acts relates to the structure and performance of COPs/MOPs themselves.[104] The second category of acts concern decisions affecting substantive obligations of the state parties. However, although this in theory seems like a pretty straightforward distinction, practice demonstrates that it is far from a clear-cut one.[105]

2. Link between COP/MOP Decisions and Subsequent Practice Relating to A/M/R

a. COP/MOP Decisions as a Means of Concretization of Treaty Rules

Nolte has identified and distinguished several different functions of COPs/MOPs relating to subsequent practice concerning the specification of treaty provisions and the amendment procedure in the MEAs. Firstly, it may be said that subsequent agreements and subsequent practice in cases of COPs/MOPs can contribute to the specification of the meaning of treaty rules, thus leading to a modification of the text of the treaty.[106] It is argued that this technique may be extremely apposite to a framework treaty, as it permits state parties

---

[102] *Ibid.*

[103] *Ibid.*

[104] Such as adoption of rules of procedure, finances, establishment of subsidiary bodies.

[105] Nolte, *supra* note 61, at 367. He gives several examples of such situations, such as the evolution of a financial mechanism as a part of the institutional architecture developed over time by the COP to the UNFCCC and the CMP to the Kyoto Protocol.

[106] *Ibid.*, at 336.

through decisions of COPs/MOPs to provide greater precision to very general and at times vague provisions of the original framework treaty.

b. COP/MOP Decisions as a Non-Treaty Based Means of A/M/R

Another group identified by Nolte is state practice that suggests that state parties to the treaty aim to modify the treaty through subsequent agreement or subsequent practice without using an available amendment procedure.[107]. The most prominent example of such practice in the MEAs is a decision of the MOP of the 1985 Montreal Protocol of Substances that Deplete the Ozone Layer (Montreal Protocol),[108] on the basis of which several amendments to this Protocol were adopted. The procedure for the amendment of the Montreal Protocol is provided for in Article 9(5) of the 1985 Vienna Convention on for the Protection of Ozone Layer (Vienna Convention).[109] However, the second MOP of the Montreal Protocol in 1990 adopted Decision II/2 on several amendments to the Protocol, which were set out together with their entry into force in Annex II to the MOP's Final Report. Article 2 of the Annex stated the following:

> The Amendment will enter into force on January 1 1992, provided that at least twenty instruments of ratification, acceptance of approval of the Amendment have been deposited by States or regional economic integration organization that are Parties to the Montreal Protocol on Substance that Deplete the Ozone Layer. In the event that this condition has not been

---

[107] Such examples may be found in MEAs dealing with the law of sea, see Nolte, *supra* note 61, at 353-355.

[108] Montreal Protocol on Substances that Deplete Ozone Layer, 16 September 1987, 1522 UNTS 293.

[109] Art 9(5) reads as follows: 'Ratification, approval or acceptance of amendments shall be notified to the Depositary in writing. Amendments adopted in accordance with paragraphs 3 or 4 above shall enter into force between parties having accepted them on the ninetieth day after the receipt by the Depositary of notification of their ratification, approval or acceptance by at least three-fourths of the Parties to this Convention or by at least two-thirds of the parties to the protocol concerned, except as may otherwise be provided in such protocol. Thereafter the amendments shall enter into force for any other Party on the ninetieth day after that Party deposits its instrument of ratification, approval or acceptance of the amendments.' Vienna Convention for the Protection of Ozone Layer, 22 March1985, 1513 UNTS 324.

fulfilled by that date, the Amendment shall enter into force on the ninetieth day following the date on which it has been fulfilled.[110]

Nolte explains that this MOP decision is a subsequent agreement by the state parties which, it can be said, goes well beyond the scope of interpretation by providing a modification of the amendment procedure set in the Vienna Convention.[111]

c.   COP/MOP Decisions as a Parallel Means of A/M/R

Finally, there is also the possibility that subsequent practice runs in parallel with a formal amendment procedure. Such cases could arise when the parties to the treaty agree on the A/M/R of one of its provisions or on the establishment of a regime aiming at fulfilling the treaty, where the state parties then begin to comply with their agreement before they have completed a formal amendment procedure which was initiated in parallel.[112] The Kyoto Protocol's Article 18 may be given as an example, which states as follows:

> The Conference of the Parties serving as the meeting of the Parties to this Protocol shall, at its first session, approve appropriate and effective procedures and mechanisms to determine and to address cases of non-compliance with the provisions of this Protocol, including through the development of an indicative list of consequences, taking in to account the cause, type, degree and frequency of non-compliance. Any procedures and mechanisms under this Article entailing binding consequences shall be adopted by means of an amendment to this Protocol.

The parties to the Kyoto Protocol adopted Decision 27/CMP.1, creating the mechanism for compliance, *i.e.* the Compliance Committee comprising of two branches, the facilitative and the enforcement one.[113] The latter of these branches has a wide gamut of functions which can include the suspension

---

[110] Montreal Protocol MOP, Report of the 2nd Meeting of the Parties to the Montreal Protocol, (UNEP/Ozl.Pro.2/3 Decision II /2), cited in Nolte, *supra* note 61, at 355.

[111] Nolte, *supra* note 61, at 355.

[112] *Ibid.* Nolte poses the question of whether if the formal amendment is not completed, the subsequent practice can, nonetheless, be assumed as expressing the treaty obligation.

[113] Kyoto Protocol CMP, Report of the Conference of the Parties serving as the Meeting of the Parties to the Kyoto Protocol on its First Session, FCCC/KP/CMP/2005/8/Add.3, 92-103, cited in Nolte, *supra* note 61, at 355.

of a party from the flexibility mechanisms, which constitute a core of the functioning of the Kyoto Protocol. The state parties have the option of appealing the decisions of the enforcement branch before the CMP, which may be described as quasi-judicial functions of the CMP. Therefore, it may be stated that such a mechanism establishes binding consequences for the state parties. The Kyoto Protocol, however, was never amended in accordance with the provisions set out in the treaty text,[114] and all further developments of the compliance mechanism were effectuated through the decisions of the CMP.

The Basel Convention on Transboundary Movement of Hazardous Wastes (Basel Convention)[115] is another example of such an activity of the COP. In this case, the COP adopted by consensus a decision banning the export of hazardous wastes from OECD member states to non-OECD member states.[116] Such a decision, without a formal amendment of a Convention, resulted in protests from many state parties to the Convention. In 1995, an official amendment was adopted by inserting a new preambular paragraph 7 *bis* and a new Article 44 to the Convention. This amendment has not yet entered into force.

D. The Juxtaposition of A/M/R with Interpretation

1. The Interconnectivity of A/M/R with Other Aspects of the 'Life-Cycle' of Treaties

During the preparatory work of the ILC the similarities of both the characteristics of and the solutions relating to A/M/R with other aspects of the 'life-cycle' of a treaty kept coming up. There were three main areas where that interconnectivity was prominent: reservations (Article 20 VCLT), successive same subject-matter treaties (Article 30 VCLT), and interpretation (Article 31 VCLT).

---

[114] Panos Merkouris, 'The UNFCCC and the Kyoto Protocol: The Challenges of Trying to Clean One's Own Nest' in Malgosia Fitzmaurice and Attila Tanzi (eds), *Encyclopedia of International Environmental Law: Multilateral Environmental Agreements* (forthcoming 2017 – on file with the authors).

[115] Nolte, *supra* note 61, at 356; Basel Convention on Transboundary Movement of Hazardous Wastes and Their Disposal, 22 March 1989, 1673 UNTS 57.

[116] Basel Convention COP, Report of the Second Meeting of the Conference of the Parties to the Basel Convention, UNEP/CHW.230 Decision II/12, 20, cited in Nolte, *supra* note 61, at 356.

In more detail, when discussing the retention of the unanimity rule, Rosenne in the ILC meetings,[117] and Australia[118] and France[119] during the Vienna Conference suggested that the approach should be similar to that of reservations and in particular Article 20(2) VCLT. They were based on the premise that unanimity should be the norm in the case of treaties with a limited number of parties ('restricted multilateral treaties').[120]

With respect to normative conflict and successive treaties, the link emerged as the result of a draft Article which eventually was left in its entirety on the cutting floor of the VCLT *travaux préparatoires*. In the discussions surrounding the form that the amending instrument should have, the possibility of instruments and methods other than 'in written form' was acknowledged. This led to Draft Article 68, which identified three venues through which a treaty could be modified: i) through subsequent agreement (Draft Article 68(a)); ii) through subsequent practice (Draft Article 68(b)); and iii) through the emergence of a new customary rule (Draft Article 68(c)).[121] The ILC decided to dispense with 68(a) as it was considered superfluous since the same topic was addressed by Article 30 VCLT.[122]

2. A/M/R and Interpretation

However, the connection was more prominent with respect to interpretation. This can be seen even in the terminology to describe A/M/R. For instance, as was already mentioned in Section II, when attempting to determine the difference between 'amendment' and 'modification', de Luna suggested the trichotomy amendment *secundum/infra legem*, *praeter legem* and *contra*

---

[117] ILC (746th meeting), *supra* note 12, at para 15 (Rosenne).

[118] Australia, *supra* note 53.

[119] France, *supra* note 54.

[120] This solution did not find its way into the final text of the VCLT as several states opposed it as not reflecting state practice. See United Nations Conference on the Law of Treaties (37th COW), *supra* note 15, at paras 47-48; United Nations, *supra* note 58, at paras 5-11.

[121] For an extensive analysis of the drafting history of Draft Article 68(c) see Nancy Kontou, *The Termination of Treaties in Light of New Customary International Law* (1994).

[122] ILC (A/6309/Rev.1), *supra* note 13, at 236, para 2; ILC, 'Summary record of the 866th meeting' (1966) UN Doc A/CN.4/SR.866, paras 2 (Castrén), 6 (Jiménez de Aréchaga), 11 (Ago), 12 (Rosenne), 15 (Tunkin), 21 (de Luna), 25 (Briggs), 35 (Yasseen).

legem.[123] This echoes the theories that interpretation can also be *infra legem*, *praeter legem* and *contra legem*.[124]

But leaving similarities in terminology or effects aside, the difficulty of clearly identifying the line where interpretation turns into A/M/R was evident in the discussion surrounding the aforementioned Draft Article 68, and later on Draft Article 38. Draft Article 68(c), which provided for amendment by subsequent custom, had a fate similar to 68(a). It was also put on the chopping block for a variety of reasons: it was better left to be considered under the Draft Article on intertemporal law;[125] 'the question formed part of the general topic of the relation between customary norms and treaty norms which is too complex for it to be safe to deal only with one aspect of it in [one] article';[126] and it was irrelevant as the solution in any given situation would be provided by identifying the intention of the parties.[127] The argument relating to intertemporal law is quite interesting, because that Article was also left out of the VCLT. The reasoning was that the first leg of the doctrine of intertemporal law (determining the existence of a rule) was provided for by Article 30 of the VCLT, while the second leg (determining the continued manifestation of a rule) would be covered by Article 31 of the VCLT. However, references to intertemporal law eventually were left out from Article 31 because the issue was too complex.[128] In the end, Drat Article 68(c) was omitted for being complex and superfluous as it would be dealt with under the Draft Article on intertemporal law. The latter, in turn, was left out for the exact same reasons, as part of it would be incorporated in Article 30 VCLT, and finally any reference to intertemporal law was once

---

[123] ILC (764th meeting), *supra* note 15, at para 104 (de Luna).

[124] Anastasios Gourgourinis, *Equity and Equitable Principles in the World Trade Organization: Addressing Conflicts and Overlaps between the WTO and Other Regimes* (2015).

[125] ILC, Summary record of the 766th meeting' (1964) UN Doc A/CN.4/SR.766, para 121 (Waldock). Ironically enough, this Article was also, in the end, discarded. For an analysis of the drafting history of Draft Article 56 see Panos Merkouris, *Article 31(3)(c) VCLT and the Principle of Systemic Integration: Normative Shadows in Plato's Cave* (2015) Chapter 2.

[126] ILC (A/6309/Rev.1), *supra* note 13, at 236, para 2; ILC (866th meeting), *supra* note 122, at paras 10 (Jiménez de Aréchaga), 11 (Ago), 12 (Rosenne), 20 (Tunkin), 24 (de Luna), 25 (Briggs), 41-42 and 67 (Waldock), 58 (Rosenne).

[127] ILC (A/6309/Rev.1), *supra* note 13, at 236, para 2; ILC (866th meeting), *supra* note 122, at para 50 (Ago).

[128] For a detailed analysis of the history of Draft Article 58, see Merkouris, *supra* note 125, Chapter 2.

again omitted from Article 30 because of its complexity. The issue kept being passed along like a hot potato, from one Article to the next and in the end got lost somewhere in the transition from one Draft Article to the next. Interestingly, the *Institut de Droit international* faced similar difficulties more recently, in 1995, when discussing a Resolution on 'Problems Arising from a Succession of Codification Conventions on a Particular Subject'. Following the example of the ILC, it avoided making any pronouncements on the issue of modification by subsequent custom.[129] The reason being that it was too complex of an issue to be dealt with 'as an ancillary point at the end of a Conclusion [in the Resolution].'[130]

However, unlike paragraphs (a) and (c) of Draft Article 68, paragraph (b) which provided for modification by subsequent practice managed to survive the trial by fire of the ILC discussions and go through to the Vienna Conference on the Law of Treaties.

Despite its survival, a major concern was that 'the line may sometimes be blurred between interpretation and amendment of a treaty through subsequent practice.'[131] However, several members of the ILC felt that the two processes were distinct and should be treated in the VCLT as such.[132] The ILC acknowledged that when dealing with bilateral treaties it may be difficult to distinguish whether subsequent practice is evidence of a new agreement modifying the original treaty or an authentic interpretation of the treaty. The examples used were *Temple of Preah Vihear* (where practice was considered an authentic interpretation) and the *Air Transport Services Agreement* (where the treaty was considered modified by practice).[133]

---

[129] Institut de Droit international, 'Problems Arising from a Succession of Codification Conventions on a Particular Subject' (1995/I) 66 Annuaire de l'Institut de Droit international 248.

[130] Comments by Higgins, in *ibid.*, at 207.

[131] ILC, 'Report of the International Law Commission Covering the Work of its Sixteenth Session' (1964) UN Doc A/5809, 198, para 2; ILC (766th meeting), *supra* note 125, at para 122 (Waldock); ILC, 'Summary record of the 767th meeting' (1964) UN Doc A/CN.4/SR.767, paras 37 (Verdross), 39 (Waldock), 41 (Pal), 43 (Ago), 44-45 (Yasseen), 46-50 (Tunkin).

[132] ILC (767th meeting), *supra* note 131, at 198, para 2; ILC (866th meeting), *supra* note 122, at paras 4 (Castrén), 7-8 (Jiménez de Aréchaga), 11 (Ago), 26 (Briggs), 36 (Yasseen). Against: ILC (767th meeting), *supra* note 131, at paras 35 (Verdross), 36 (de Luna); ILC (A/6309/Rev.l), *supra* note 13, at 300 (Israel).

[133] ILC (767th meeting), *supra* note 131, at 198, para 2; ILC, 'Sixth Report on the Law of Treaties, Sir Humphrey Waldock' (1964) UN Doc A/CN.4/186 and Add. 1-7, 87-91, paras 1-15 and in particular para 8; ILC (A/6309/Rev.l), *supra* note 13, at 236, para 1.

a.   Parties & (Non)-Essential Provisions

But in multilateral treaties things are different. And at this point another critical point with respect to the function of Draft Article 68(b) emerged. Subsequent practice for interpretation must establish the agreement of all the parties. Modification, on the other hand, especially in cases of treaties creating bilateral or bilateralizable obligations was not clear whether it required the participation of all the parties, or just certain of the parties.[134] As Waldock summarised it:

> [c]learly, on the plane of interpretation, *the treaty has only one correct interpretation*. But in practice it may have applications between particular parties which diverge from the interpretation and application of it by the general body of the parties. It hardly seems possible to classify such cases under the head of 'interpretation by subsequent practice' without seeming to throw overboard the essential concept of the integrity of the text of a multilateral treaty.[135]

The discussion within the ILC did not help clarify the issue, with members arguing both the expansive and restrictive interpretation of the term 'parties' with equal fervor.[136] The group against the expansive interpretation of the term 'parties' submitted that this was taken the analogy with *inter se* agreements a bit too far. Since in the case of subsequent practice, the safeguards of Article 41 (notification of parties) did not exist.[137] Additionally, it was difficult to establish whether the actual agreement between the parties had actually come into existence between certain of the parties.[138]

The ILC in its Commentary tried to smooth over the debate by adopting the middle ground. It claimed that

> [i]n formulating the rule in this way the Commission intended to indicate that the subsequent practice, even if every party might not itself have ac-

---

[134]   ILC (Sixth report Waldock), *supra* note 133, at 90, para 9.

[135]   *Ibid.* [emphasis added].

[136]   ILC, 'Summary record of the 876th meeting' (1966) UN Doc A/CN.4/SR.876, paras 19-64; ILC, 'Summary record of the 883rd meeting' (1966) UN Doc A/CN.4/SR.883, paras 76-80.

[137]   ILC (866th meeting), *supra* note 122, at paras 19 (Tunkin), 23 (de Luna), 27 (Briggs), 31 (Tsuruoka), 38 (Yasseen), 45 (El-Erian).

[138]   *Ibid.*, at para 57 (Tunkin).

tively participated in the practice, must be such as to establish the agreement of the parties as a whole to the modification in question.[139]

Finally, we need to mention an interesting point that Tunkin raised; whether a distinction should be drawn between essential and minor provisions. The latter being open to modification by subsequent practice, but not the former. He was, however, the first to admit that he merely wished to raise the issue but had no ready answer to offer.[140] Waldock agreed with Tunkin, but he felt it as such an extremely delicate issue that 'as a draughtsman ... [he] would shrink from the task of having to cover the points in the text of sub-paragraph *(b)*.'[141] The ILC, equally, selected not to delve deeper into the topic.

b.   Rejection of Draft Article 38

Having survived the discussions in the ILC, one would expect that Draft Article 38 (which, in essence was Draft Article 68(b)) would to a greater or lesser degree also survive the test of the Vienna Conference. That was a far cry from what actually happened. Draft Article 38 was rejected by an overwhelming majority. Several states took the floor and expressed serious misgivings about the wisdom of including that Article in the VCLT.[142] The main reasons for the rejection of this Article can be summarised in the following points:

- it was expedient to deal in the VCLT with such complex issues as the relationship between customary law and treaty law;[143]
- the Article was superfluous as it duplicated Article 31(3)(b) and other VCLT provisions;[144]

---

[139] ILC (A/6309/Rev.1), *supra* note 13, at 236, para 2.

[140] ILC (866th meeting), *supra* note 122, at para 18 (Tunkin).

[141] *Ibid.*, at para 64 (Waldock).

[142] The only states that spoke in favour of Draft Article 38 were Israel, Italy, Austria, Cambodia, Switzerland, and Argentina.

[143] United Nations Conference on the Law of Treaties (37th COW), *supra* note 15, at paras 57 (Finland), 58 (Japan).

[144] *Ibid.*, at paras 57 (Finland), 58 (Japan), 59 (Venezuela), 62 (Vietnam), 67-68 (Spain); United Nations Conference on the Law of Treaties, '1st Session – 38th meeting of the Committee of the Whole (COW)' (1968) UN Doc A/CONF.39/11, paras 2 (Russia), 28 (Turkey), 48 (Israel).

- it raised grave concerns of conflict with the states' respective constitutional law;[145]
- it conflicted or weakened *pacta sunt servanda*;[146]
- it was open to abuse;[147]
- it would disrupt international relations since 'if States were given the impression that any flexible attitude towards the application of a treaty was tantamount to agreement to modify the treaty, they would tend in future to become much more circumspect and rigid in their attitudes';[148]
- it was unclear whether it applied to only to non-essential provisions,[149] and also what was meant by 'practice' and 'parties';[150] and finally
- it was contrary to law and democracy.[151]

In a last ditch attempt to save Draft Article 38 Expert Consultant Waldock tried to address the concerns raised by the states[152] but to no avail. The amendment deleting Draft Article 38 was adopted by 53 votes to 15, with 26 abstentions.

---

[145] United Nations Conference on the Law of Treaties (37th COW), *supra* note 15, at paras 58 (Japan), 63 (France), 68 (Spain); United Nations Conference on the Law of Treaties (38th COW), *supra* note 144, at paras 4 (Russia), 17 (Poland), 27 (Turkey), 36 (Uruguay), 40-41 (Cuba), 43 (Philippines).

[146] United Nations Conference on the Law of Treaties (37th COW), *supra* note 15, at paras 60 (Venezuela), 63 (France), 70 (Spain), 75 (Chile); United Nations Conference on the Law of Treaties (38th COW), *supra* note 144, at paras 3 (Russia), 6 (USA), 30-32 (Guinea), 38 (Tanzania), 40 (Cuba), 42 (Portugal), 47 (Netherlands), 53 (Czechoslovakia).

[147] United Nations (*Conference on the Law of Treaties*), *supra* note 15, at para 61 (Vietnam).

[148] *Ibid.*, at para 63 (France).

[149] *Ibid.*, at para 69 (Spain).

[150] *Ibid.*, at paras 71-74 (Spain), 76-77 (Canada); United Nations Conference on the Law of Treaties (38th COW), *supra* note 144, paras 13-16 (Poland), 18 (China), 34-35 (Uruguay), 44-46 (Netherlands), 52 (Czechoslovakia).

[151] United Nations Conference on the Law of Treaties (38th COW), *supra* note 144, at para 21 (Colombia).

[152] *Ibid.*, at paras 55-57.

3. The Difference between A/M/R and Interpretation

Although the above analysis demonstrates the difficulties in distinguishing between A/M/R and interpretation, which among other reasons led to the eventual discarding of Draft Articles 68 and 38, this is not an impossible task. There are certain key differences, which although not a *passe-partout*, can offer guidance in traversing the mercurial waters of the overlap between A/M/R and interpretation. There are two areas that need to be addressed; the difference between A/M/R and evolutive interpretation, and the difference between A/M/R and interpretation by subsequent agreements/practice.

a. The Difference between A/M/R and Evolutive Interpretation

The critical difference between A/M/R and evolutive interpretation is one of limits. Gardiner rightly underscores the fact that

> [t]he indication that evolutive interpretation must be based on the concepts already in the treaty suggests that this has more limited potential for extending meanings than does concordant practice of the parties. Since the parties, are, acting collectively through their concordant practice, sovereign to make further treaty provisions, they can take interpretation further than can a person or body charged with the role of independent interpretation.[153]

Whereas A/M/R can go beyond the text, *i.e. contra legem*, evolutive interpretation cannot. This is also the view expressed by certain judges in *Feldbrugge v the Netherlands* when they opined that:

> [a]n evolutive interpretation allows variable and changing concepts already contained in the Convention to be construed in the light of modern-day conditions ... but it does not allow entirely new concepts or spheres of application to be introduced in the Convention: that is a legislative function that belongs to the Member States of the Council of Europe[154]

And by the Human Rights Committee in *Atasoy and Sarkut v Turkey* where it held that evolutive interpretation 'cannot go beyond the letter and spirit of the treaty or what the State parties initially and explicitly so intended.'[155]

---

[153] Richard K Gardiner, *Treaty Interpretation* (2nd edn 2015) 275.

[154] *Feldbrugge v the Netherlands*, ECtHR, Application No 8562/79, Judgment of 29 May 1986, paras 23-24.

[155] *Atasoy and Sarkut v Turkey*, Human Rights Committee, Communications Nos 1853 and 1854/2008, Views of 29 March 2012.

Re-Shaping Treaties: Issues in the Amendment/Modification/Revision 73

Judge Bedjaoui in his Separate Opinion in the *Gabčíkovo-Nagymaros Project* case, was also attune to the fact that evolutive interpretation should not be unconstrained but should abide by certain limits, or 'precautions' as he called them:

> Taken literally and in isolation, there is no telling where this statement may lead. The following precautions must be taken:
>
> - an 'evolutionary interpretation' can only apply in the observation of the general rule of interpretation laid down in Article 31 of the Vienna Convention on the Law of Treaties;
>
> - the 'definition' of a concept must not be confused with the 'law' applicable to that concept;
>
> - the 'interpretation' of a treaty must not be confused with its 'revision'.[156]

Of course there are a number of other limits/'precautions' to evolutive interpretation,[157] including that evolutive interpretation should not end up becoming a 'revision' of the treaty, *i.e.* an A/M/R.[158] However, since this is the exact point of our analysis to consider it as one of the fundamental limits of evolutive interpretation here would be somewhat self-referential and of no practical usefulness. However, thankfully there are other limits/'precautions' that can prove more helpful for the purposes of our inquiry. In the context of distinguishing between A/M/R and evolutive interpretation the three most critical limits/'precautions' are: the intention of the parties, the object and purpose of the treaty and the text of the treaty.[159] Whereas A/M/R may go beyond these limits and alter the contours of each and every one of them, evolutive interpretation cannot.

---

[156] *Gabčíkovo-Nagymaros Project* (*Hungary v Slovakia*) [1997] ICJ 7, 120, para 5 (Judgment of 25 September, Separate Opinion of Judge Bedjaoui).

[157] Such as *ius cogens* norms, non-retroactivity, judicial activism. For a complete list and detailed analysis see Panos Merkouris, '(Inter)temporal Considerations in the Interpretative Process of the VCLT: Do Treaties Endure, Perdure or Exdure?' (2014) 45 Netherlands Yearbook of International Law 121, 150-151; Merkouris, *supra* note 125, Chapter 2.

[158] *Gabčíkovo-Nagymaros Project*, Separate Opinion of Judge Bedjaoui, *supra* note 156; *Kasikili/Sedudu Island* (*Botswana v Namibia* [1999] ICJ 1045, 1113, para 2 (Judgment of 13 December, Declaration of Judge Higgins).

[159] Merkouris, *supra* note 125, Chapter 2; Merkouris, *supra* note 157, at 150-151 and cases cited therein.

b. The Difference between A/M/R and Interpretation by Subsequent Agreements/Practice

On the other hand, the distinction between A/M/R and interpretation under 31(3)(a) & (b) is slightly more problematic as they both employ reference to subsequent agreements or practice. So what is the critical difference between them? Here it will prove useful to distinguish between modification and amendment.

Modification, in the VCLT sense, *i.e.* that of an *inter se* agreement, does not raise any issues. The reason is simple.

> '[M]odification' in the Convention's sense could never be achieved purely by practice as envisaged in article 31(3)(b) because that provision is predication [sic] on agreement of *all* the parties, while modification is by the Vienna Convention's usage (article 41 in particular) operative for only *some* of the parties.[160]

Consequently, no issue of conflation will arise between modification and interpretation by reference to subsequent agreements/practice.

Things become more complicated as to what concerns amendment. As Waldock insightfully noted:

> Subsequent practice when it is consistent and embraces all the parties would appear to be decisive of the meaning to be attached to the treaty, at any rate when it indicate that the parties consider the interpretation to be binding upon them. In these cases, subsequent practice as an element of treaty interpretation and as an element in the formation of a tacit agreement overlap and the meaning derived from the practice becomes an authentic interpretation established by agreement. Furthermore, if the interpretation adopted by the parties diverges, as sometimes happens, from the natural and ordinary meaning of the terms, there may be a blurring of the line between *interpretation* and the *amendment* of a treaty by subsequent practice.[161]

Two questions need to be addressed. Firstly, whether the distinction between interpretation and A/M/R in this context is of any practical importance, and second whether amendment by subsequent practice is customary international law or is it more of a concept *in statu nascendi* and thus, at least for the moment, the debate on its difference from interpretation is merely an academic exercise.

---

[160] Gardiner, *supra* note 153, at 267 at note 169 (emphasis in the original).

[161] ILC (Third report Waldock), *supra* note 4, at para 25.

With respect to the former, Gardiner drives the point home by presenting both sides of the argument. The opinion, that searching for the difference between amendment and interpretation is like waiting for Godot, is based on the following two premises. The first is an effects-based one. Irrespective of whether one applies a treaty as a result of an *interpretation* reflecting the agreement of the parties or an *amendment* reflecting the agreement of the parties, the result is exactly the same. The qualification does nothing to change the application of the treaty.[162] Second,

> if one accepts that every application of a treaty is preceded, no matter for how fleeting a moment, by an act of interpretation, any subsequent practice or subsequent agreement to an amendment constituted by practice would each form a valid component of an interpretation.[163]

However, Gardiner continues, such an aphoristic equation between interpretation and amendment fails to take into account 'the importance of treaty relations, procedural difficulties, and [the effect of] decisions of courts and tribunals.'[164] With respect to treaty relations, for instance, a procedure may be presumed to have been followed for amendments that give not only parties but also potential parties the opportunity to participate. As to what concerns procedural difficulties, these may arise in scenarios similar to *Pope & Talbot*, where one organ was vested with the power of interpreting a treaty, whereas another has the power to determine a dispute and characterize whether the act of the first body was indeed an interpretation or an act *ultra vires*.[165] This is also relevant as to the effect of international courts and tribunals, that not only have to legally characterize certain acts, but also their judgments may echo through time, although judgments of international courts and tribunals are in principle only binding on the parties to the proceedings, they 'have an effect comparable to precedent.'[166]

With respect to the second question, the answer is not quite clear. The preparatory work of Draft Article 68 and 38 analyzed above in Section III.D. seems to indicate that states accepted the amendment by subsequent practice as customary international law (although this was by no means a general consensus). The reason that most states objected to its inclusion to the VCLT was its complexity. International jurisprudence seems also to accept

---

[162] Gardiner, *supra* note 153, at 275.

[163] *Ibid*.

[164] *Ibid*.

[165] *Ibid.*, at 275, referring to *Pope & Talbot*.

[166] *Ibid*.

this possibility, although most relevant *dicta* are quite open-ended. Case law seems to be swinging like a pendulum from outright rejection to unequivocal acceptance. Sometimes 'interpretation' is used when 'amendment' is probably (or possibly) meant and *vice versa*; other times the relevant court does not explicitly say whether it considers a particular subsequent practice as interpretative or amending in nature.[167]

In such a doctrinal and jurisprudential quicksand, the ILC approach, as reflected in Conclusion 7, seems to be – if not the correct one –, definitely the most utilitarian one.

Conclusion 7

Possible effects of subsequent agreements and subsequent practice in interpretation

1. Subsequent agreements and subsequent practice under article 31, paragraph 3, contribute, in their interaction with other means of interpretation, to the clarification of the meaning of a treaty. This may result in narrowing, widening, or otherwise determining the range of possible interpretations, including any scope for the exercise of discretion which the treaty accords to the parties.

2. Subsequent practice under article 32 can also contribute to the clarification of the meaning of a treaty.

3. *It is presumed that the parties to a treaty, by an agreement subsequently arrived at or a practice in the application of the treaty, intend to interpret the treaty, not to amend or to modify it.* The possibility of amending or modifying a treaty by subsequent practice of the parties has not been generally recognized. The present draft conclusion is without prejudice to the rules on the amendment or modification of treaties under the Vienna Convention on the Law of Treaties and under customary international law.[168]

This Conclusion creates a presumption in favour of interpretation, similar to the presumption against conflict that we see in situations of normative conflict.[169] In this manner, in most cases the scenario of having to qualify

---

[167] In more detail, see ILC, 'Second Report on Subsequent Agreements and Subsequent Practice in Relation to Interpretation of Treaties, by Georg Nolte' (2014) UN Doc A/CN.4/671, at 50-60 and cases cited therein.

[168] ILC, 'Report of the International Law Commission on the Work of its 68th Session' (2016) UN Doc A/71/10, Chapter VI, 121. See also commentary on the third paragraph, *ibid.*, at 173-180.

[169] Joost Pauwelyn, *Conflict of Norms in Public International Law: How WTO Law Relates to Other Rules of International Law* (2003).

a subsequent practice as either amending or interpreting the treaty will be avoided, ensuring the consistency and integrity of the text.

IV. A/M/R Provisions in MEAs

A. (Non-)Inclusion of A/M/R Provisions in MEAs

Having examined in the previous sections the drafting history of Articles 39-41 VCLT as well as areas and trends in amendment and modification which raise highly theoretical and practical issues relating to the law of treaties, and before we conclude this article, it was felt that it might be useful to examine which direction contemporary treaty-law making is going with respect to A/M/R and whether practice confirms certain of our preliminary findings.

A complete examination of the entire *corpus* of treaties, for pragmatic considerations, would fall outside the scope of this article. It would perhaps be better suited for a new UN Handbook on Final Clauses. For this reason, the authors had by necessity to be selective. The treaties which were examined were, firstly, multilateral treaties since – as was already established in Section II – amendment and modification of bilateral treaties does not really make sense as this would be equivalent to the process of negotiation.[170] Secondly, those treaties were ones that could be characterized as environmental ones. The reason being that MEAs offer a large pool from which valid data can be derived as to the existence or not of trends in A/M/R clauses. Of course, whether a treaty should be considered as environmental or not would rest on the chosen definition. For this reason, the authors have selected to use the definition and the database of the International Environmental Agreement (IEA) Database Project of the University of Oregon.[171] An additional reason for focusing on MEAs was that they are a prime example of how this tug-of-war between stability and change is reflected in treaties. On the one hand, there is need for stability in the protection of the environment, on the other hand, the science and the methods connected to both endangerment and protection of the environment are evolving at break-neck speed, and MEAs need to adapt and evolve themselves in order to avoid becoming irrelevant and obsolete.

---

[170] See *supra* note 15.

[171] According to the IEA database, its working definition is '[IEA is] an intergovernmental document intended as legally binding with a primary stated purpose of preventing or managing human impacts on natural resources.' The database and the definition can be found at: <http://iea.uoregon.edu/node/6> accessed 29 June 2017.

In the tables created and produced below the following premises have been followed:

- If a MEA provides for different A/M/R procedures for different articles, both of these procedures have been accounted for.
- If a MEA provides for unanimity/consensus and in the case that unanimity/consensus cannot be secured allows for a different procedure, then this has been considered as counting both under unanimity/consensus (as this is the initial preference of the drafters of the MEA) and under the alternative procedure, unless otherwise explicitly stated.
- Amendments have not been included in the tallying of the treaties, as the original treaty (and its amendment procedure) usually remains relatively unscathed. It was felt that several consecutive amendments of a particular treaty may skew statistically the results. The only cases where an amendment has been taken into account for statistical purposes has been when the amendment amends the amending procedure or introduces a new one where none existed.
- It was stated that the VCLT articles on amendment and modification are of a residual nature. But how residual are they in actual practice? In how many MEAs did the parties consider that the VCLT rules (or prior to those, customary international law) was a sufficient safeguard of the interests of the parties? Table 1 juxtaposes the MEAs which have an A/M/R clause and those that do not:[172]

---

[172] In some instances, especially when dealing with Protocols, the instrument may not specify an exact process of A/M/R but may either directly refer back to the A/M/R provisions of the Convention with which the Protocol is connected (see for instance Art 14 of the Black Sea Biodiversity and Landscape Conservation Protocol: 'Article 14 - Adoption of any amendments to the articles and amendments to the annexes of the Protocol shall be made according to the procedures established by the Articles XX and XXI of the Convention'; 2002 Black Sea Biodiversity and Landscape Conservation Protocol to the Convention on the Protection of the Black Sea Against Pollution, <http://www.blacksea-commission.org/_convention-protocols-biodiversity.asp> accessed 29 June 2017), or may have an article establishing the relationship/connection of the Protocol to the Convention for a number of issues, including but not explicitly mentioning A/M/R (see for instance Art 32 of the Cartagena Protocol which provides: 'Article 32: Relationship with the Convention - Except as otherwise provided in this Protocol, the provisions of the Convention relating to its protocols shall apply to this Protocol.'; Cartagena Protocol on Biosafety to the Convention On

Re-Shaping Treaties: Issues in the Amendment/Modification/Revision   79

	No Provision	Existence of Provision	Total
1800-1899	12	2	14
1900-1919	1	1	2
1920-1939	9	6	15
1940-1959	31	14	45
1960-1969	31	35	66
1970-1979	32	60	92
1980-1984	10	30	40
1985-1989	10	35	45
1990-1994	36	77	113
1995-1999	19	61	80
2000-2004	7	70	77
2005-2009	4	32	36
2010-2016	0	28	28
Total	202	451	653

Table 1: Existence or non-existence of A/M/R clauses in MEAs

The following Chart visually captures the ratio of the (non-)existence of A/M/R clauses in MEAs by time-period:

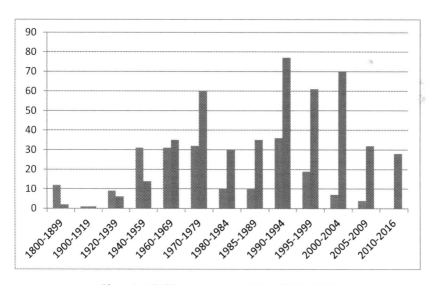

Chart 1: A/M/R provisions in MEAs (1800-2016)

The final tally of 202 MEAs not containing any provision, compared to 455 MEAs containing one or more provisions, translates respectively to 30,93%

Biological Diversity, 29 January 2000, 2226 UNTS 208). In the latter case, these Protocols have also been considered as having an A/M/R provision.

and 69,07% of all MEAs. This percentage differentiation may not seem that much, but one needs to bear in mind that the above tables and charts contain information taken from a time period starting from the 19th century. The information contained in them is put in the proper perspective if we examine how the ratio between A/M/R non-containing and containing MEAs, has changed at different periods in time. For this reason, we have grouped the MEAs into four chronological periods: i) 1800-1899, *i.e.* one century; ii) 1900-1969, *i.e.* until the adoption of the VCLT at which time all states would be to a greater or lesser degree aware of the information and the discussions within the ILC and the Vienna Conference on the Law of Treaties; iii) 1970-1999, *i.e.* until the end of the century; and iv) 2000-2016. The last two categories were split up, despite them being much shorter from a temporal point of view, since the number of treaties contained therein is high compared to the first two groups. The ratio that is thus revealed is depicted below:

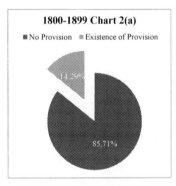
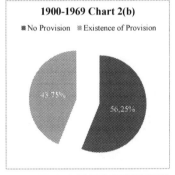
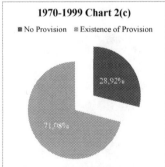
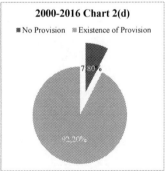

Chart 2: Ratio of A/M/R-containing MEAs to A/M/R-non-containing MEAs

The above Chart demonstrates clearly that states are increasingly inclined to regulate between themselves the manner in which a MEA will be amended or modified. From being a clear minority (14,29%) in the 19th century, A/M/R-containing MEAs rose to 43,75% by the time the VCLT was adopted, and that trend continued, with MEAs containing references to A/M/R becoming the majority by the end of the 20th century. In the period 1970-1999 the ratio between A/M/R-containing MEAs versus the non-containing ones was 71,08% versus 28,92%. This shift towards specificity as to what concerned A/M/R of MEAs has continued in the 21st century as well, as easily reflected in the percentages between these two groups of MEAs, *i.e.* 92,2% compared to 7,8% of MEAs that make no reference to A/M/R. Clearly, despite the existence of the VCLT rules on amendment and modification states seem to feel much more comfortable providing for their own amendment/modificaiton procedures than relying on the VCLT's residual rules.

This gradual progression in favour of incorporation of A/M/R provisions in MEAs becomes even more pronounced if one takes into account two additional factors. Firstly, the lack of inclusion of A/M/R can be explained by the fact that a number of the examined treaties were of a limited duration. Consequently, there was no need for providing for an A/M/R provision. Second, a lot of the documents that do not contain A/M/R provisions are protocols[173] to existing treaties, and they neither provide for a separate A/M/R procedure, nor do they refer back to the original treaty. If one focuses only on the original MEAs and not the protocols thereto,[174] the afore-identified trend of including an A/M/R provision in a MEA becomes even more evident. In more detail, the percentages of Chart 2 become: i) for the period 1800-1899: 83,33% *vs* 16,67%, in favour of non-existence of an A/M/R provision; ii) for the period 1900-1969: 50,88% *vs* 49,12%, in favour of non-existence of an A/M/R provision; iii) for the period 1970-1999: 20,54% *vs* 79,46%, in favour of inclusion of an A/M/R provision; and iv) for the period 2000-2015: a staggering 6,47% *vs* 93,53%, again in favour of inclusion of an A/M/R provision. For reasons of consistency, however, for the remainder of the analysis we will continue to use the data provided for in Table 1, which takes into account all treaties, irrespective of whether they are protocols or not.[175]

---

[173] There are various adjectives used, *e.g.*, additional, supplementary, or amending protocols.

[174] Unless the protocol has provided for a specific A/M/R procedure.

[175] Also because not all protocols fall in this category since there are quite a few that provide for their own process of A/M/R or clearly refer back to the Convention to which they are connected and which provides for such a procedure.

Table 2 breaks down Table 1, into the exact kind of provision that the MEAs contain.

	A	M	R	A+M	A+R	M+R	A+M+R	No Provision	Total
1800-1899		2						12	14
1900-1919		1						1	2
1920-1939	2	2	2					9	15
1940-1959	10		3	1				31	45
1960-1969	19		8	1	6		1	31	66
1970-1979	34	2	7	1	16			32	92
1980-1984	27		1		2			10	40
1985-1989	29	1	2		3			10	45
1990-1994	63	2	4	3	5			36	113
1995-1999	53	1	3	1	3			19	80
2000-2004	61	1		4	4			7	77
2005-2009	24	1	1	1	5			4	36
2010-2016	26				1		1		28
Total	348	13	31	12	45		2	202	653

Table 2: Specific nature of A/M/R clause (or lack thereof) in MEAs

It has to be pointed out that in the above table the provisions have been categorized on the basis of the terms used in the MEA. It is true that – as described in Section II – there was an extensive debate as to the normative content to be attached to each of the terms. It was recognized that practice so far (until the 1960s) was somewhat inconsistent or vague, with states using amendment, modification and revision sometimes interchangeably. To make matters even worse, the situation has not abated since. In fact, the term 'revision' or 'review' continues to pop up in MEAs, whereas modification is sometimes used in a manner where from the context one can reach the conclusion that it may also refer to amendments and not merely *inter se* agreements. This is not always the case, and there has been a shift in the terminology used post-VCLT, but for reasons of simplicity the above table follows the terminology as defined by the ILC in its commentary to the draft articles on the law of treaties.

B. Adoption and Entry Into Force of Proposed A/M/Rs of MEAs

What remains now is to break down the above A/M/R provisions into further specific categories in order to identify whether particular patterns emerge. However, that is not as simple as it may seem at first sight. There are two important stages in the process leading to the A/M/R of a multilateral treaty. First, we have the 'adoption stage', *i.e.* when an amendment proposal is submitted how it is adopted by the state parties. In the stage of adoption the various categories examined (*e.g.* the required majority) is either unconditional or on the basis of certain conditions.[176] For reasons of simplicity, we have decided to focus on the various majorities both as separate categories, and *en bloc*, but not to further sub-divide these into majorities with conditions and without.

Furthermore, even when an amendment has been adopted, that does not necessarily mean that *eo ipso* the amendment enters into force (and also for which parties it enters into force). For that reason, the tables on adoption are supplemented by tables regarding the entry into force of the adopted amendments. Specifically, for the entry into force tables the analytical lens has been that of for which parties the amendment enters into force, *i.e.* for the ratifying/accepting states or for all states. In the latter case, what has also been examined is whether states that do not wish to be bound by the amendment have an option to 'opt-out' or not.

1. Adoption

Having made the above clarifications regarding the investigative approach taken, let us now break down the A/M/R clauses into the specific adoption procedure they provide for:

	Consensus	Unanimity	Common (Mutual) Accord/Agreement	Simple Majority	Qualified Majority	Other	Not specified[177]	Total
1800-1899			1				1	2
1900-1919			1					1
1920-1939	1	1		1			2	5
1940-1959		1			8	2	4	15
1960-1969		9	1	1	16	1	11	39
1970-1979	1	7			24	3	31	66
1980-1984	3	11			9	3	6	32
1985-1989	9	6			17		8	40
1990-1994	20	18	3	2	29	6	15	93
1995-1999	16	14	10	3	19	6	5	73
2000-2004	22	9	11	3	28	2	10	85
2005-2009	10	7	1		11	1	4	34
2010-2016	13	6	3	1	8		3	34
Total	95	89	31	11	169	24	100	519

Table 3: A/M/R clauses: 'adoption stage

---

[176] See for instance: Arts. 31 and 10(3) of the Agreement Creating The Eastern Pacific Tuna Fishing Organization, which requires for the amendment of certain provisions not only a 2/3rd majority of state parties present, but also 'half plus one of Latin American Eastern Pacific Coastal States', 1989 Agreement Creating The Eastern Pacific Tuna Fishing Organization, <http://iea.uoregon.edu/treaty-text/1989-easternpacifictunaorganizationentxt> accessed 29 June 2017.

[177] The fact that there are a number of treaties, which although containing a provision on A/M/R do not specify the voting procedure for adoption seems prima facie a bit bizarre. A closer look, however, at the relevant provisions shows that a substantial percentage of these provisions relate to Review Conferences, consequently there is no need for the treaty to provide for a voting procedure in such a conference, as

And if we look further into the variations of majority voting:

	Consensus	Unanimity	Common (Mutual) Accord/Agreement	Simple Majority	Qualified Majority: 2/3	Qualified Majority: 3/4	Qualified Majority: Other	Other	Not Specified	Total
1800-1899			1						1	2
1900-1919			1							1
1920-1939	1	1		1					2	5
1940-1959		1			8			2	4	15
1960-1969	9		1	1	13	1	2	1	11	39
1970-1979	1	7			14	8		3	31	66
1980-1984	3	11			6	3		3	6	32
1985-1989	9	6			9	8			8	40
1990-1994	20	18	3	2	17	11	1	6	15	93
1995-1999	16	14	10	3	13	6		6	5	73
2000-2004	22	9	11	3	14	13	1	2	10	85
2005-2009	10	7	1		8	1	2	1	4	34
2010-2016	13	6	3	1	6	2			3	34
Total	95	89	31	11	108	53	8	24	100	519

Table 4: A/M/R clauses: 'adoption stage' – Expanded version

The figures of the above tables have been calculated on the basis of what adoption procedures are mentioned in each MEA. Multiple identical procedures in the same MEA have been counted only once. For instance, sometimes the procedure for the adoption of amendments to the Convention is the same as those of an Annex or an Appendix.[178] If, however, we account for these procedures in our calculations, the above Tables 3 and 4 should be amended in the following manner:

	Consensus	Unanimity	Common (Mutual) Accord/Agreement	Simple Majority	Qualified Majority	Other	Not specified	Total
1800-1899			1				1	2
1900-1919			1					1
1920-1939	1	1		1			2	5
1940-1959		1			8	2	4	15
1960-1969	10		1	1	17	1	11	41
1970-1979	1	8			34	3	31	77
1980-1984	4	11			12	3	6	36
1985-1989	17	7			28		8	60
1990-1994	28	21	3	2	42	7	16	119
1995-1999	25	16	10	5	30	7	5	98
2000-2004	33	10	11	3	45	2	10	114
2005-2009	12	7	1		14	1	4	39
2010-2016	18	9	3	1	14		3	48
Total	139	101	31	13	244	26	101	655

Table 5: A/M/R clauses: 'adoption stage' – Multiple identical procedures accounted for

---

it is no different than any other conference held to negotiate a new treaty. In any event, the parties to the Review Conference can always agree on the particular voting procedure. Furthermore, another big portion is taken up by treaties that provide merely for the number of States that is required in order for a proposal to be considered for discussion and adoption, but not for the adoption itself.

[178] Note, however, that MEAs, which distinguish between existing and new obligations for the purposes of entry into force (see for instance Art XVI of the Agreement for the Establishment of a Commission for Controlling the Desert Locust in the Western Region, 22 November 2000, 2179 UNTS 221) have only been counted once as the relevant provisions do not differentiate between these two categories of obligations as to what pertains to adoption.

Re-Shaping Treaties: Issues in the Amendment/Modification/Revision   85

	Qualified Majority: 2/3	Qualified Majority: 3/4	Qualified Majority: Other	Other	Not Specified	Total
1800-1899					1	2
1900-1919						1
1920-1939					2	5
1940-1959	8			2	4	15
1960-1969	14	1	2	1	11	41
1970-1979	20	12	2	3	31	77
1980-1984	7	5		3	6	36
1985-1989	15	13			8	60
1990-1994	26	15	1	7	16	119
1995-1999	19	11		7	5	98
2000-2004	26	18	1	2	10	114
2005-2009	11	1	2	1	4	39
2010-2016	10	4			3	48
Total	156	80	8	26	101	655

Table 6: A/M/R clauses: 'adoption stage' – Multiple identical procedures accounted for – Expanded version

Another striking insight from Tables 3-6 is that the requirement for unanimity (both *stricto sensu* and *lato sensu*)[179] although not resorted to as frequently as other procedures taken in aggregate, is far from a thing of the past. If we compare the A/M/R clauses in MEAs that require consensus, with those that require unanimity *lato sensu* and with those that provide for another procedure,[180] we arrive at Table 7:

	Consensus	Unanimity *lato sensu*	Other Method	Total
1800-1899		1		1
1900-1919		1		1
1920-1939	1	1	1	3
1940-1959		1	10	11
1960-1969		10	18	28
1970-1979	1	7	27	35
1980-1984	3	11	12	26
1985-1989	9	6	17	32
1990-1994	20	21	37	78
1995-1999	16	24	28	68
2000-2004	22	20	33	75
2005-2009	10	8	12	30
2010-2016	13	9	9	31
Total	95	120	204	419

Table 7: Consensus, unanimity lato sensu and other methods in MEA A/M/R clauses

---

[179] We use this term to refer to A/M/R clauses that employ the term 'unanimity' or other terms, which in all likelihood could be equated with unanimity, such as 'common accord', 'common agreement' 'mutual agreement' etc.

[180] Treaties which although referring to A/M/R do not specify a particular procedure for adoption are omitted.

If we again account for multiple identical procedures, we arrive at Table 8:

	Consensus	Unanimity *lato sensu*	Other Method	Total
1800-1899		1		1
1900-1919		1		1
1920-1939	1	1	1	3
1940-1959		1	10	11
1960-1969		11	19	30
1970-1979	1	8	37	46
1980-1984	4	11	15	30
1985-1989	17	7	28	52
1990-1994	28	24	51	103
1995-1999	25	26	42	93
2000-2004	33	21	50	104
2005-2009	12	8	15	35
2010-2016	18	12	15	45
Total	139	132	283	554

Table 8: Consensus, unanimity lato sensu and other methods in A/M/R clauses of MEAs – Multiple identical procedures accounted for

This data would seem to indicate that both unanimity and consensus are alive and well in modern age.

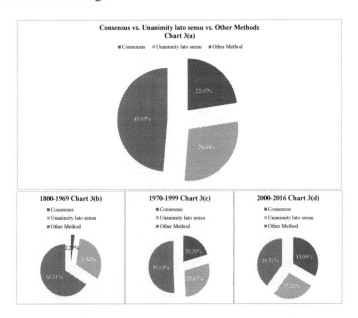

Chart 3: Consensus, unanimity lato sensu and other methods in A/M/R clauses

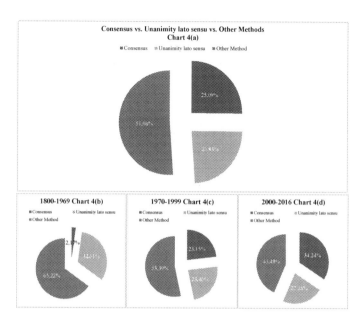

Chart 4: Consensus, unanimity lato sensu and other methods in A/M/R clauses – Multiple identical procedures accounted for

However, although this may be true, the impression that is given by Tables 7 and 8 and Charts 3 & 4 (a)-(d) is a slightly 'magic picture.' There are two reasons for this. Firstly, as mentioned in the beginning of Section IV, if a MEA provides both for consensus and alternatively, if the parties fail to reach a consensus, for an entirely different procedure, then this has been counted in both the rows for consensus and for that other procedure. However, at the end of the day what would matter would be the second procedure. If we take this into account then the scales tip a little more in favour of the other procedures compared to consensus and unanimity. In more detail, such kind of 'alternative constructions' can be found in: i) one treaty in the period 1980-1984; ii) four in the period 1985-1989; ii) ten in the period 1990-1994; iii) seven in the period 1995-1999; iv) nine in the period 2000-2004; v) one in the period 2005-2009 and vi) five in the period 2010-2016. If multiple identical procedures are factored in, these numbers are updated to: i) one procedure in the period 1980-1984; ii) nine in the period 1985-1989; ii) fourteen in the period 1990-1994; iii) eleven in the period 1995-1999; iv) fifteen in the period 2000-2004; v) one in the period 2005-2009 and vi) eight in the period 2010-2016. This would then translate to a reduced influence of consensus and a more pronounced presence of qualified majorities in the A/M/R provisions of MEAs. More specifically:

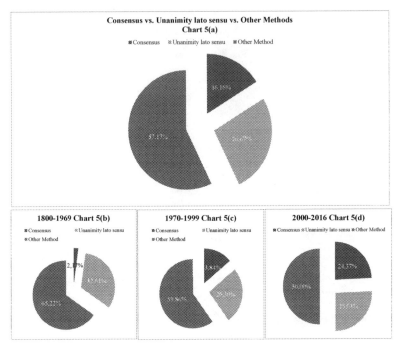

Chart 5: Consensus, unanimity lato sensu and other methods in A/M/R clauses – The influence of 'alternative' contructions & multiple identical procedures

An additional interesting point is that this 'alternative construction' of A/M/R provisions, whereby consensus is the objective striven for but if it is not attained then amendments and modifications can be introduced by various majorities, is a rather recent phenomenon at least with respect to MEAs. Instances of such A/M/R provisions seem to be completely missing in the 19th and early 20th century. The practice becomes more prominent only after 1985,[181] which would seem to be an indication that parties to MEAs seem to want to avoid the normative fragmentation of MEAs (thus striving for consensus), but acknowledge the difficulties associated with achieving consensus especially in MEAs of wide participation. Thus they balance this with a second-tier voting procedure that is activated once consensus is not

---

[181] See previous paragraph.

achieved and that allows amendments to be adopted as long as a predetermined majority has been achieved.[182]

However, the 'alternative construction' of A/M/R clauses in MEAs is not the entire story. The second reason, and perhaps the most important one, why the data of Tables 7 and 8 and Charts 3 & 4 (a)-(d) should be taken with a grain of salt, is that in a large number of cases where unanimity is required MEAs with a small number of parties are concerned, *e.g.*, MEAs governing a river, a river basin, a lake, a region of land or sea etc. This point is very critical because it echoes the discussions in the ILC relating to the connection between A/M/R and reservations, as well as the French amendment on 'restricted multilateral treaties' and the Australian one proposed during the Vienna Conference.[183] The reasons for the propensity of A/M/R clauses requiring unanimity in these kind of MEAs is very similar to the reasons that led to the adoption of Article 20(2) VCLT which provides that:

> [w]hen it appears from the limited number of the negotiating States and the object and purpose of a treaty that the application of the treaty in its entirety between all the parties is an essential condition of the consent of each one to be bound by the treaty, a reservation requires acceptance by all the parties.

The same logic would seem to be behind the preference of States when entering such MEAs to opt for the unanimity rule.

2. Entry Into Force

Having examined the clauses of MEAs relating to the 'adoption stage' of an A/M/R proposal, we will now move to the 'entry into force stage'. As mentioned above, the research focus is on who is bound by the proposal when it enters into force and when it can be binding on states that have not explicitly ratified/accepted it, how forceful and unavoidable that binding effect is for them.

---

[182] As a final point of interest regarding the 'alternative construction' of A/M/R clauses is the 2005 Treaty on the Conservation and Sustainable Development of the Forest Ecosystems of Central Africa. <http://extwprlegs1.fao.org/docs/pdf/mul71928.pdf> accessed 29 June 2017. This MEA, instead of following the classical formula of 'consensus or qualified majority', has opted for a different approach. According to Article 28, amendments to this treaty are to be adopted 'unanimously or by consensus'.

[183] See Section II.B.2.

The analysis of the relevant provisions has yielded a plethora of interesting results. These have influenced the identification of the various categories of A/M/R clauses as to their 'entry into force' effects. Three are the main groups identified: i) the amendment becomes binding only for the ratifying/accepting state parties; ii) the amendment becomes binding on all state parties, even those which have not ratified/explicitly accepted the amendment; and iii) the entry into force requirements and procedure is not specified in the treaty text.[184]

Of importance are the first two categories. The first can be further divided into two sub-categories: i) the amendment becomes binding for each ratifying/accepting state party; and ii) the amendment becomes binding for each ratifying/accepting state party but first certain conditions need to be met. These would usually be in the form of a certain number of state parties having first to deposit instruments of ratification/acceptance/approval before the amendment can enter into force.[185]

The second category can also be divided in multiple sub-categories. At this point we would like to remind the reader of the three-pronged categorization made by Hathaway, Saurabh Sanghvi and Solow, who distinguished between 'consensus' amendments, 'opting-out' amendments and 'binding' amendments.[186] The last two are apposite in the context of our analysis, as they also revolve around the inevitability or not of a state being bound by an adopted amendment proposal to which it may have objections. Digging deeper into the relevant A/M/R clauses it becomes gradually evident that not only is the permissibility of an objection a critical aspect but also the effects that such an objection may have both to the objecting state and/or the other state parties. More specifically, and following from our previous analysis this category will be named for reasons of simplicity 'tacit acceptance *lato sensu*' so as to include both 'opting-out' amendments and 'binding' amendments, but so as to also allow for additional *sui generis* sub-categories that also share the common element of states being bound tacitly.

The four sub-categories identified are the following: i) amendments that are binding on all state parties and no objection is permitted[187] ii) amendments that are binding on all state parties and objection is permitted but it amounts

---

[184] Or will be determined at a different stage by another body, see for instance Art 31 of the 1989 Agreement Creating the Eastern Pacific Tuna Fishing Organization (*supra* note 176).

[185] See for instance Art X of the Agreement on the Conservation of Gorillas and their Habitats, 26 October 2007, 2545 UNTS 55.

[186] See analysis in Section III.B.

[187] See, *e.g.*, Art 19(3) of the African Nuclear Weapons Free Zone Treaty, 11 April 1996, 35 ILM 698.

to denouncement of or withdrawal from the treaty;[188] iii) amendments that are binding on all state parties and objections are permitted. This is the classical 'opting-out' procedure;[189] and iv) amendments that are binding on all state parties, and objections are permitted. However, in the case of this sub-category, even one objection by one state party stops the amendment from entering into force for all state parties.[190] These four sub-categories reflect the force of the objection by a state party. The first sub-group is one of 'inexistence of objection'. There is no provision providing for the option of an objection to the amendment.[191] The second one is a 'weak' form of objection; either the state remains silent and tacitly accepts the binding effect of the amendment, or it objects but then is forced to withdraw from or denounce the treaty.[192] The third one is the 'regular' form of objection, where the objection prevents the amendment from entering into force for the objecting states.[193] The final sub-group is where the objection of one state produces the maximum effect.

---

[188] See, *e.g.*, Art 17 of the Agreement on The Network Of Aquaculture Centres in Asia and the Pacific, 8 January 1988, 1560 UNTS 201; Art 15 of the Protocol to Amend the International Convention on Civil Liability for Oil Pollution Damage, 27 November 1992, 1956 UNTS 255; Art 37 of the Convention on the Contract for the Carriage of Goods by Inland Waterway, 2001, available at: <http://iea.uoregon.edu/treaty-text/2000-contractcarriagegoodsinlandwaterwayentxt> accessed 29 June 2017; Art 17 of the Agreement on the Institutionalisation of the Bay of Bengal Programme as an Inter-governmental Organisation, 2003, available at: <http://iea.uoregon.edu/treaty-text/2003-bayofbengalintergovernmentalorganizationentxt> accessed 29 June 2017.

[189] See, *e.g.*, Art 30 of the Convention on Civil Liability for Damage Resulting From Activities Dangerous to the Environment, 21 June 1993, 32 ILM 1228; Art X of the Agreement on the Conservation of African-Eurasian Migratory Waterbirds, 16 June 1995, 2365 UNTS 203; Art 21(5) of the Protocol to the United Nations Framework Convention on Climate Change (Kyoto Protocol), 11 December 1997, 2303 UNTS 162.

190 Art XXI(3) of the Convention on Future Multilateral Cooperation in the Northwest Atlantic Fisheries, 24 October 1978, 1135 UNTS 370; Art 35(3) of the Convention on the Conservation and Management of the High Seas Fishery Resources in the South Pacific Ocean, 2009 available at: <https://www.sprfmo.int/assets/Basic-Documents/Convention-and-Final-Act/2272946-v1-SPRFMO-Convention.pdf> accessed 29 June 2017.

[191] This procedure can be called TA/NO ('Tacit Acceptance – No Objection'). This and the following abbreviations will be used on the relevant Tables and the main text.

[192] This procedure can be called TA/WO ('Tacit Acceptance – Weak Objection').

[193] This procedure can be called TA/RO ('Tacit Acceptance – Regular Objection').

It bars the amendment from entering into force for any state party. This would be the 'strong' form of objection.[194]

With these considerations in mind, the analysis of the relevant A/M/R clauses leads us to the following Tables:

	Ratifying/Accepting States		Tacit Acceptance *lato sensu*					
	Ratifying/Accepting States-Parties	Ratifying/Accepting States-Parties with Conditions	Tacit Acceptance / No Objection (TA/NO)	Tacit Acceptance/ Weak Objection (TA/WO)	Tacit Acceptance / Regular Objection (TA/RO)	Tacit Acceptance / Strong Objection (TA/SO)	Not Specified	Total
1800-1899							2	2
1900-1919							1	1
1920-1939	2	1					2	5
1940-1959	4	5	5		1		4	19
1960-1969	10	12	10	1	2		10	45
1970-1979	7	26	8		15	1	26	83
1980-1984	1	24	3		2	1	2	33
1985-1989	1	25	3	1	10		6	46
1990-1994	6	47	16	3	12	1	11	96
1995-1999	7	34	10	1	14	1	15	82
2000-2004	6	48	8	4	10	1	9	86
2005-2009	2	18	3		2	2	8	35
2010-2016	2	22	1		5	1	3	35
Total	48	262	67	11	73	8	99	568

Table 9: A/M/R clauses: 'entry into force stage

And if we factor in multiple identical procedures we have the following:

	Ratifying/Accepting States		Tacit Acceptance *lato sensu*					
	Ratifying/Accepting States-Parties	Ratifying/Accepting States-Parties with Conditions	Tacit Acceptance / No Objection (TA/NO)	Tacit Acceptance/ Weak Objection (TA/WO)	Tacit Acceptance / Regular Objection (TA/RO)	Tacit Acceptance / Strong Objection (TA/SO)	Not Specified	Total
1800-1899							2	2
1900-1919							1	1
1920-1939	2	1					2	5
1940-1959	4	5	5		2		4	20
1960-1969	11	15	11	1	3		10	51
1970-1979	7	26	8		18	1	26	86
1980-1984	2	25	3		2	1	2	35
1985-1989	1	27	3	1	10		6	48
1990-1994	6	56	21	3	15	1	11	113
1995-1999	7	40	13	1	16	2	15	94
2000-2004	6	58	8	4	15	1	9	101
2005-2009	2	21	3		3	2	8	39
2010-2016	2	26	2	1	5	1	3	40
Total	50	300	77	11	89	9	99	635

Table 10: A/M/R clauses: 'entry into force stage' – multiple identical procedures accounted for

From the above, it is clear that although the tacit acceptance procedures are not as prominent as the classical methods of consent to be bound, they are far from immaterial.

---

[194] This procedure can be called TA/SO ('Tacit Acceptance – Strong Objection').

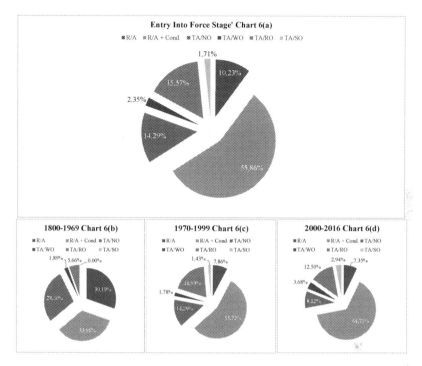

Chart 6: 'entry into force stage'

A distinction that needs to be made is between TA/WO procedures and procedures where all state parties need to ratify/accept an amendment and those that fail to do so cease to be parties to the treaty in question. An example of such a procedure can be found in Article 38(5) of the 1983 International Tropical Timber Agreement which provides that '[a]ny member which has not notified its acceptance of an amendment by the date on which such amendment enters into force shall cease to be a party to this Agreement as from that date'.[195] Although, this could *prima facie* appear very similar to the TA/WO procedure there are a number of crucial differences. In TA/WO, if the state party does nothing it is bound by the amendment. In the case of the Tropical Timber Agreement, however, if the party remains inactive it ceases to be a party to the Agreement. In TA/WO this effects manifests itself only if the state party objects to the amendment, an option that is not offered in the Tropical Timber Agreement. Finally, in TA/WO we are dealing with a true case of tacit acceptance; even though not all states have adopted or accepted

---

[195] International Tropical Timber Agreement, 18 November 1983, 1393 UNTS 120.

the amendment, after the expiry of a specific time-period they are all bound (unless a state chooses to withdraw from the treaty). In the Tropical Timber Agreement case, however, we are not actually dealing with tacit acceptance. Indeed, the amendment enters into force when a number (not all) state parties have accepted it. However, the amendment *does not become binding* on all other state parties *tacitly*. Article 38 requires that all states explicitly accept the amendment. If they do not, then they are considered as having withdrawn from the Agreement. Consequently, in this case we are not dealing with a genuine situation of tacit acceptance, and that is the reason why this provision and other similar ones have been considered as falling under the sub-group of 'ratifying/accepting states with conditions'.

The treaties and provisions providing for any form of 'tacit acceptance' may seem quite numerous considering the fact that 'tacit acceptance' is a departure from the classical forms of consent to be bound. However, if one looks closer at the specific provisions, out of these very few actually provide for 'tacit acceptance' amendment either as the sole method of amendment, or at least of substantive and critical provisions of the Convention/Protocol proper. This should not come as a surprise. This method of amendment, as has also been reaffirmed by our research, is usually reserved either for amendments to provisions that do not entail new obligations for the state parties[196] or for amendments of Annexes and Appendices, *i.e.* for amendments of documents that are technical in nature and require regular and extremely fast updating. However, exactly because of the nature of the amended provisions and documents of these two groups, it is logical that one would not expect to find multiple instances of tacit acceptance A/M/R provisions of the treaty proper. Despite this, the importance of the existing tacit acceptance A/M/R provisions in the existing MEAs should not be understimated, as they breathe life and ensure the viability of some of the most important and successful global treaties.[197]

C. Amendment of Amendment Procedures

A wide gamut of additional interesting correlations emerges from the study of the A/M/R provisions in MEAs. However, an exhaustive presentation of all

---

[196] Which in turn would be more inclined to accept them even tacitly; see for instance Art X of the Agreement for the Establishment of a General Fisheries Council for the Mediterranean, 24 September 1949, 126 UNTS 237; Art XVI of the Agreement for the Establishment of a Commission for Controlling the Desert Locust in the Western Region, 22 November 2000, 2179 UNTS 221.

[197] See Section III.B.

these permutations is beyond the scope of this article and the intention of the authors. However, before concluding, we will indulge ourselves with a final observation and a nod to 'self-referential' systems and paradoxes. These have been analyzed in mathematics, philosophy and law.[198] In the present context, the amendments that amend amending procedures are of importance. These are not so common, yet they are invaluable in determining the approach of the state parties with respect to A/M/R. Four examples are offered below:

- The Convention on the Prevention of Marine Pollution by Dumping of Wastes and Other Matter[199] and its 1978 amendment.[200] Although the 1978 amendment, strictly speaking amended the amendment procedure of the original treaty, in actuality the changes introduced were clarificatory rather than substantive ones. The amendment simply clarified that the Meeting of the Contracting Parties could decide on amendments not only of the Convention, but also of the Annex.

- More interesting is the Convention on Conservation of Nature in the South Pacific[201] and its 2000 amendment.[202] The original treaty had no provision on amendment. One such was introduced with the 2000 amendment whereby amendments would be adopted by a ¾ majority.

---

[198] See Roy Sorensen, *A Brief History of the Paradox: Philosophy and the Labyrinths of the Mind* (2005); Herbert LA Hart, *Essays in Jurisprudence and Philosophy* (1983); Gunther Teubner, '"And God Laughed ...": Indeterminacy, Self-Reference and Paradox In Law' (2001) 12 German Law Journal 376; Laurence Goldstein, 'Four Alleged Paradoxes in Legal Reasoning' (1979) 38(2) Cambridge Law Journal 373; John M Rogers and Robert E Molzon, 'Some Lessons about the Law from Self-Referential Problems in Mathematics' (1991-1992) 90 Michigan Law Review 992.

[199] Convention on the Prevention of Marine Pollution by Dumping of Wastes and Other Matter, 13 November 1972, 1046 UNTS 120.

[200] <http://iea.uoregon.edu/pages/view_treaty.php?t=1978-Amendment-1972-MarinePollutionDumpingWastesOtherMatter.EN.txt&par=view_treaty_html> accessed 29 June 2017.

[201] Convention on Conservation of Nature in the South Pacific, 12 July 1976, 976 IEL 45.

[202] <http://iea.uoregon.edu/pages/view_treaty.php?t=2000-Amendments-1976-NatureSouthPacific.EN.txt&par=view_treaty_html> accessed 29 June 2017.

- The Constitution of the European Commission for the Control of Foot and Mouth Disease[203] is another interesting example. Article XIV provided for adoption of amendments with a 2/3 majority and no state would be bound without expressing its consent. Things changed dramatically with the 1962 amendment.[204] Firstly, it distinguished between amendments involving and amendments not involving additional obligations for the state parties. For the latter, this involved immediate effect for all state parties upon the decision of the Council. For the former, a tacit acceptance procedure with a 2-year grace period was introduced. Consequently, the treaty went from a 2/3 majority, to tacit acceptance procedure in the 'blink of an amendment.'

- The final example concerns the International Convention for the Prevention of Pollution of the Sea by Oil[205] and its 1962 amendment.[206] Although in both the original and the amended treaty the procedure established is the tacit acceptance one, the amendment increases the level of integration and the role of international organs in the amendment procedure. For instance, the Assembly of the Organization and, more importantly, the Maritime Safety Committee are basic actors in the amendment procedure, whereas in the original treaty the Bureau was the only one involved and even then mostly in a 'communication facilitator' role.

Not only, are these four examples widely diverse, but also very few to extract any solid conclusions with respect to the amendment of amendment procedures. However, one point sticks out. With the exception of the first example,[207] in all the cases the new procedure promoted either closer co-operation or speedier amendment procedures (or both). In none of them did

---

[203] Constitution of the European Commission for the Control of Foot and Mouth Disease, 11 December 1953, 191 UNTS 285.

[204] <http://iea.uoregon.edu/pages/view_treaty.php?t=1962-Amendments-1953-EuropeanCommissionFootMouthDisease.EN.txt&par=view_treaty_html> accessed 29 June 2017.

[205] International Convention for the Prevention of Pollution of the Sea by Oil, 12 May 1954, 327 UNTS 3.

[206] <http://iea.uoregon.edu/pages/view_treaty.php?t=1962-Amendment-1954-Oil-Pollution.EN.txt&par=view_treaty_html> accessed 29 June 2017.

[207] Which, if we are to be completely accurate, is an amendment of the amendment procedure only in name.

we witness a step back, a return to earlier more slowly paced methods of amendment. Whether this is indeed a common characteristic of the direction that these amendments always take the original treaty is something that would require further research in treaty practice from other fields of law.

V. Conclusion

The present article's aim was to examine the current trends in the A/M/R of treaties. In order to do so and heading the aphorism that 'whoever forgets his past is doomed to repeat it', the authors started by going through the preparatory work both of the 'first order' (the Vienna Conference) and of the 'second' one (ILC meetings, drafts and reports). We were introduced to a veritable cornucopia of ideas and issues that either found their way in the text of the VCLT, or were unceremoniously discarded; that sparked fiery debates or were quickly condemned to *lethe*; and that were either resolved or considered too complex or dividing to benefit from inclusion in the VCLT. However, a common theme in all the discussions was the need to balance the competing interests of on the one hand the stability of international relations, and on the other hand the need for change. The former was required in order for states to have a feeling of security that would be a catalyst to further international cooperation. The latter was essential in order to avoid stagnation.

This tug-of-war between stability and change was also reflected in Section III, where current and more 'informal' methods of A/M/R were examined. The characteristics of the tacit acceptance procedure were scrutinized, which allows for much faster amendment procedures binding on all, but its application is sometimes restricted on the basis of the nature of the amendments proposed. COP/MOP decisions and their binding effect were also put under the microscope. Although this new method suggests that 'autonomous institutional arrangements' is a phenomenon that may promote new methods of A/M/R, this, however, should not be equated with a complete negation of stability in favour of moving forward. This explains the existence of various theories attempting to describe AIAs within the old-fashioned, formal contours of the established methods of consent to be bound; finally, the re-emergence of the discussion of modification by subsequent practice (and its connection to interpretation), almost half a century after the ILC discussions shows the cyclicality of some of the arguments and that although matters are far from clear, maybe the balancing point of the competing interests as to this particular method of modification may have shifted just a bit. Finally, in

Section IV we examined a number of A/M/R clauses in MEAs to arrive at a number of interesting results (*e.g.* amendments of amending procedures, the preference for unanimity in 'interdependent'-like MEAs, preference for *ad hoc* A/M/R provisions rather than the 'residual' ones of the VCLT, varying degrees of force of the objection in 'tacit acceptance procedures') only to see behind them again the eternal dance between stability and change; the common thread uniting not only the ideas of this article, but the theory and practice relating to A/M/R and, even more, the progress of international law.

On 'Court Generated State Practice': The Interpretation of Treaties as Dialogue between International Courts and States

Serena Forlati[*]

I. International Courts and the Interpretation of Treaties

International case law is of particular relevance for the purposes of the interpretation of international legal rules, including international treaties, to the point that international courts and tribunals are sometimes qualified as exercising a 'law making' function.[1] This qualification is usually not accepted by international courts themselves, as it would amount to overstepping the mandate which they were granted by the states that established them.[2] The International Court of Justice (ICJ) Advisory Opinion on the *Legality of the Threat or Use of Nuclear Weapons* is particularly clear in stating that 'the Court cannot legislate ... it states the existing law and does not legislate. This is so even if, in stating and applying the law, the Court necessarily has to

---

[*] Associate Professor of International Law, University of Ferrara.

[1] See only Bruno Simma, 'Foreword' and Armin von Bogdandy and Ingo Venzke, 'Beyond Dispute: International Judicial Institutions as Lawmakers' in Armin von Bogdandy and Ingo Venzke (eds), *International Judicial Lawmaking: On Public Authority and Democratic Legitimation in Global Governance* (2012), respectively v and 3.

[2] The reference to 'states' is made for the sake of simplicity, as also other international legal entities (notably, international governmental organisations) can contribute to the setting up of international judicial systems and may have a role in developing subsequent practice similar to the one of states – as set forth also by Article 31(3)(b) of the Vienna Convention on the Law of Treaties between States and International Organizations or between International Organizations, 21 March 1986 (not yet in force). Their role is, in this respect, radically different from the one of individuals, investors or NGOs, who may be subject to the jurisdiction of specific international tribunals but play no role in their establishment. However, specifically with reference to Article 31(3)(b) the peculiar position of international organizations' practice is usually discussed in different terms, which rather concern the effects of their own practice for the purposes of interpretation of their constituent instrument (see para I).

specify its scope and sometimes note its general trend'.[3] At the same time, the task of contributing to the elucidation and development of international law is more or less explicitly entrusted to at least some international courts: it is prominent for the ICJ but concerns also other permanent courts and institutional arbitration.[4]

However, the boundaries between evolutive interpretation of treaties and modification of the obligations enshrined therein are at times difficult to draw; it is thus not easy to understand how the role of international courts and tribunals interpreting of international treaties fits into the framework of the rules on interpretation set forth by the VCLT. Some authors consider that, while the parties to a treaty share the competence to interpret it, the interpretation by an international tribunal may amount to an 'authentic interpretation' of the treaty;[5] other scholars point to the existence, in this regard, of a 'shared interpretive competence' of the parties and international courts,[6] and pronouncements of international tribunals are at times treated as 'subsequent practice' on the same basis as states' behaviours for the purposes of interpretation,[7] whereas this contention is expressly rejected in

---

[3] *Legality of the Threat or Use of Nuclear Weapons* [1996] ICJ 226, 237, para 18 (Advisory Opinion of 8 July).

[4] See also for further references Serena Forlati and Paula Wojcikiewicz Almeida, 'Is Non-Compliance with Judgments a Failure of International Adjudication? A Case Study on the International Court of Justice' in Hélène Ruiz Fabri and Lorenzo Gradoni (eds), *Debacles. Illusions and Failures in the History of International Adjudication* (forthcoming).

[5] Serge Sur, *L'interprétation en droit international public* (1974) 123: 'La compétence concurrente d'interprétation entraine donc des prétentions juridiques opposes mais égales, qui ne sont ni l'une ni l'autre une interprétation authentique ou quasi-authentique du droit. Sous certaines conditions, et notamment le consentement tacite ou non des autres Etats, ou l'intervention d'un organe juridictionnel, une telle interprétation pourra être reconnue comme interprétation authentique'. This approach echoes the idea that international courts are 'common organs' of the disputing parties, that is difficult to accept today (see further below, section III).

[6] Anthea Roberts, 'Subsequent Agreements and Practice: The Battle over Interpretive Power' in Georg Nolte (ed), *Treaties and Subsequent Practice* (2013) 95, at 101.

[7] See *Macoun v Commissioner of Taxation*, High Court of Australia (2015) 90 AUR 93, 120151 HCA 44, paras 79ff (referring to an ILOAT judgment): and Joined Cases C464/13 and C465/13, *Europaeische Schule Muenchen v Oberto and O'Leary*, ECLI:EU:C:2015:163, para 65, as regards the case law of the Complaints Board of European Schools (see also para 72 on the qualification of the board as a 'court or tribunal'). These cases are discussed in the responses

other contexts.[8] While the Draft Conclusions adopted so far in first reading by the International Law Commission distinguish carefully between practice relevant for the purposes of Article 31(3)(b) VCLT and other forms of practice, which may nonetheless be relevant for the purposes of treaty interpretation, they do not elaborate on the role of international judicial bodies in this specific perspective.

Professor Zemanek's insightful discussion of the role of international courts in generating practice relevant under Article 31(3)(b) of the Vienna Convention on the Law of Treaties (VCLT) rightly points to this issue and raises a number of questions pertaining to the interaction between adjudicative bodies and practice of the parties in the interpretation of treaty-based obligations. My comments will draw from one of his concluding remarks, dealing specifically with the evolutionary interpretation of the European Convention on Human Rights (ECHR) by the European Court of Human Rights (ECtHR) and the potential of this case law to induce a generally accepted interpretation (or even modification) of the Convention. Professor Zemanek argues, in this respect, that 'it is ... not the Court's judgment that amounts to "subsequent practice", but the adoption by the parties of the specific interpretation by the Court of a protected right as correct'. I share this view and intend to offer, firstly, some additional remarks as to why, although the acts of international institutions and their organs may be of direct relevance for the purposes of Article 31(3)(b) VCLT, the findings of international courts do not come into play in this respect. I will draw from the generally accepted assumption that Article 31(3)(b) reflects customary international law and is, therefore, relevant also for states that are not parties to the Convention.[9] Secondly, I

---

respectively by Australia and by Spain to the Request for information contained in Chapter III of the Report of the Sixty-Seventh session of the International Law Commission (2015), <www.un.org>, accessed 20 July 2017.

[8] See notably WTO, *Japan: Alcoholic Beverages*, discussed *infra* note 40.

[9] The stance according to which 'it is well established that Articles 31 to 33 of the Convention reflect rules of customary international law' has been often upheld by the ICJ (see recently *Question of the Delimitation of the Continental Shelf Between Nicaragua and Colombia beyond 200 Nautical Miles from the Nicaraguan Coast (Nicaragua v Colombia)* (Preliminary Objections) [2016] ICJ para 33 (Judgment of 17 March). *Cf.* Draft Conclusion 2 [1](1), 'Subsequent agreements and subsequent practice in relation to the interpretation of treaties. Text of the draft conclusions provisionally adopted by the International Law Commission on first reading', in ILC, 'Report of the International Law Commission on the Work of its Sixty-Eighth Session' also for further references (2 May-10 June and 4 July-12 August 2016) UN Doc A/71/10, 120.

will discuss the situation arising when the interpretation of a treaty by an international court is *not* endorsed by the states subject to its jurisdiction.

II. 'Subsequent Practice' Under Article 31(3)(b) Vienna Convention and the Practice of International Organizations

It is often noted that subsequent practice relevant to the interpretation of a treaty may take a variety of different forms,[10] including silence,[11] and may be developed also by entities other than the parties themselves. Linderfalk observes, for instance, that '"practice" does not necessarily emanate only from the parties themselves, or the non-state organ, possibly an international organization – with which the application might have been entrusted'.[12]

Yet, not all these interpretation exercises are relevant for the purposes of Article 31(3)(b) VCLT. This provision stipulates that the interpretation of treaties should take into account '[a]ny subsequent practice in the application of the treaty which establishes the agreement of the parties regarding its interpretation'.[13] As also the drafting history confirms,[14] it is precisely *the agreement of the parties* that gives this form of subsequent practice its 'specific function and value for the interactive process of interpretation under the general rule of interpretation of article 31'[15] – a function that is

---

[10] Giovanni Distefano, 'La pratique subséquente des Etats parties à un traité' (1994) 40 Annuaire français de droit international 41, 42.

[11] See *Border and Transborder Armed Actions* (*Nicaragua v Honduras*) (Jurisdiction) [1988] ICJ 69, 87, para 36 (Judgment of 2 December).

[12] Ulf Linderfalk, *On the Interpretation of Treaties* (2007) 166. See also Laurence Boisson de Chazournes, 'Subsequent Practice, Practices and "Family-Resemblance": Towards Embedding Subsequent Practice in its Operative Milieau' in Georg Nolte (ed), *Treaties and Subsequent Practice* (2013) 46, 53 *et seq*.

[13] Emphasis added. See on this provision Jean-Marc Sorel and Valérie Boré Eveno, 'Article 31, Convention of 1969' in Olivier Corten and Pierre Klein (eds), *The Vienna Conventions on the Law of Treaties* (2011) 804.

[14] The choice as to the wording of the text currently in force emphasizes this requirement in terms that are stronger than those Sir Humphrey Waldock had proposed ('understanding', rather than 'agreement'): see Distefano, *supra* note 10, at note 21.

[15] ILC, 'Second Report on Subsequent Agreements and Subsequent Practice in Relation to the Interpretation of Treaties, by Georg Nolte' (26 March 2014) UN Doc A/CN.4/671, para 49.

of particular cogency for the purposes of treaty interpretation.[16] Thus, it is difficult to disagree with the contention that, '[t]o be relevant, practice must be attributable to the parties to the treaty'.[17] This principle is embodied in ILC Draft Conclusion 5(1).[18]

Notably, international organizations develop a significant practice in interpreting their own constitutive instruments although they are not parties to them. This practice could easily be considered for the purposes of Article 31(3)(b) whenever the interested organization is not endowed with international legal personality, acting rather as a 'common organ' of the states that have established it.[19] The situation is however more complex as regards the practice of organizations which do have international legal personality. While the treatment of the issue especially by the International Court of Justice has been the object of extensive analysis,[20] it may be worth to briefly recall the stances it adopted in this regard in its Advisory Opinions on *IMCO Maritime Safety Committee, the Legality of the Use of Nuclear Weapons and on the Wall in Palestine*.

The *Maritime Safety Committee* Opinion includes no specific elaboration as to why the practice of the IMCO Assembly could throw 'some light on the Court's consideration of the question'[21] submitted to it, that but it has been suggested that this practice should be read 'implicitly' as practice 'of states party to the treaty setting up the organization'.[22]

In the second case, the ICJ did take into specific account the autonomy and independent nature of international organizations, stressing that

> the constituent instruments of international organizations are also treaties of a particular type; their object is to create new subjects of law endowed with a certain autonomy, to which the parties entrust the task of realizing common goals. Such treaties can raise specific problems of interpretation

[16] This is stressed by Bruno Simma, 'Miscellaneous Thoughts on Subsequent Agreements and Practice' in Georg Nolte (ed), *Treaties and Subsequent Practice* (2013) 46.

[17] Richard K Gardiner, *Treaty Interpretation* (2011) 235.

[18] ILC, *supra* note 9.

[19] This has a parallel in the treatment of decisions by 'Conferences of the parties', on which see Draft Article 11[10] of the ILC Draft.

[20] See notably ILC, *supra* note 9, Commentary to Draft Article 12[11] also for further references.

[21] *Constitution of the Maritime Safety Committee of the Inter-Governmental Maritime Consultative Organization* [1960] ICJ 150, 167-168 (Advisory Opinion of 8 June 1960).

[22] Gardiner, *supra* note 17, at 232.

owing, *inter alia*, to their character which is conventional and at the same time institutional; the very nature of the organization created, the objectives which have been assigned to it by its founders, the imperatives associated with the effective performance of its functions, as well as its own practice, are all elements which may deserve special attention when the time comes to interpret these constituent treaties.[23]

At the same time, the Advisory Opinion ruled out the relevance of the resolution requesting the Advisory Opinion for the purposes of establishing an agreement between the WHO members as to the competence of the organization to put forward the request. This stance relies, *inter alia*, on the attitude taken by states at the moment of voting – as specific reference was made to the fact that the adoption of the resolution had met with opposition.[24]

This same element was also underlined in the *Wall* Advisory Opinion, where the ICJ upheld an evolutive interpretation of Article 12 UN Charter on the basis of the '*accepted* practice of the General Assembly';[25] moreover, allegations of procedural irregularities in the adoption of the resolution were rejected as in similar instances the validity of the adopted resolutions were 'never disputed'.[26] It would thus seem that the key element for the purposes of Article 31(3)(b) VCLT were not the General Assembly resolutions as such, but rather the ('negative' or 'positive') reaction of the organizations' members to such resolutions, including the attitude they took in the voting process.

While this reading of the ICJ case law is not unanimously accepted,[27] the contention can be made that resolutions of political organs of international organizations (notably of the UN General Assembly) if adopted unanimously or with no significant dissent, are in substance subsequent agreements directly

---

[23] *Legality of the Use by a State of Nuclear Weapons in Armed Conflict* [1996] ICJ 66, 75, para 19 (Advisory Opinion of 8 July).

[24] *Ibid.*, at para 27. Reference is made to the fact that 'Resolution WHA46.40 ... adopted, not without opposition, ... could not be taken to express or to amount on its own to a practice establishing an agreement between the members of the Organization to interpret its Constitution as empowering it to address the question of the legality of the use of nuclear weapons'. See further Gardiner, *supra* note 17, at 248.

[25] *Legal Consequences of the Construction of a Wall in the Occupied Palestinian Territory* [2004] ICJ 136, 150, para 28 (Advisory Opinion of 9 July).

[26] *Ibid.*, at 152, para 33.

[27] See for a different reading of ICJ case law Luigi Crema, 'Subsequent Agreements and Subsequent Practice Within and Outside the Vienna Convention' in Georg Nolte (ed), *Treaties and Subsequent Practice* (2013) 15.

relevant to the interpretation of treaties[28] (although admittedly a careful factual appreciation is required in this regard). This possibility is acknowledged also by Conclusion 12[11] of the ILC Draft,[29] but could certainly not apply as regards the practice of international courts and tribunals in the interpretation of treaties.

III. 'Subsequent Practice' Under Article 31(3)(b) Vienna Convention and Pronouncements of International Courts and Tribunals

International courts and tribunals are also part of the realm of international institutions. Notably, the ICJ shares the international legal personality of the United Nations and other international tribunals, such as the International Criminal Court, are autonomous international organizations.[30] The idea that even non-institutional arbitral tribunals may be endowed with international legal personality, which met with significant opposition in the past,[31] can more easily be accepted today.[32] That the outcome of international judicial activities cannot, therefore, be directly attributed to the states which have established the relevant court or tribunal is confirmed also by the case law of the ECtHR. Albeit in contexts that did not have a direct bearing on issues

---

[28] See Anthony Aust, *Modern Treaty Law and Practice* (3rd edn, 2013) 213; Benedetto Conforti, *La funzione dell'accordo nel sistema delle Nazioni Unite* (1968); James Crawford, 'A Consensualist Interpretation of Article 31(3) of the Vienna Convention on the Law of Treaties' in Georg Nolte (ed), *Treaties and Subsequent Practice* (2013) 29, 31; Gardiner, *supra* note 17, as quoted above, and corresponding text).

[29] See also ILC, *supra* note 9, Commentary to Draft Article 12[11], especially paras 12 *et seq*.

[30] Under Arts 1 and 4(1) ICC Statute the Court is a 'permanent institution' which 'shall have international legal personality'.

[31] See only the discussion of Gaëtano Morelli, 'La théorie générale du procés international' (1937-III) 61 Recueil des cours 257, 275.

[32] Carlo Santulli, *Droit du contentieux international* (2005) 86-87.

of treaty interpretation, cases such as *Boivin*,[33] *Galić*[34] or *Beygo*[35] are to the effect that international judicial pronouncements should be treated, in this respect, on the same basis as the acts of political bodies of international organizations endowed with international legal personality.

At the same time, such pronouncements could not be considered as expressing *the agreement* of the parties. This would be precluded, on the one hand, by the formal argument relating to international legal personality discussed above. On the other hand, even if one accepts the 'substantialist' qualification of the acts of political organs as 'agreements', this reasoning could not apply to the delegation of interpretive authority by states to international courts. Indeed, independence is perceived as an essential feature of jurisdiction, not only at the domestic but also at the international level;[36] this applies not only to permanent tribunals but also in non-institutional arbitration, as the recent example of the *Croatia/Slovenia* arbitration shows. In that instance, the arbitral tribunal stressed in its Partial Award that the right to an independent judge is essential to procedural fairness;[37] perhaps more importantly for the purposes of this discussion, the developments of the case are a perfect illustration of the fact that even party-appointed arbitrators should exercise

---

[33] *Boivin v 34 Member States of the Council of Europe*, ECtHR, Application No 73250/01, Decision of 9 September 2008. This stance is under the proviso that state parties to the ECHR may be responsible for violations of protected rights through acts of international organizations endowed with international legal personality in cases of manifest infringement of such rights.

[34] *Galić v The Netherlands*, ECtHR, Application No 22617/07), Decision of 9 June 2009, para 39, on activities of the United Nations and specifically of the ICTY.

[35] The European Court of Human Rights also confirme, that acts of international organizations endowed with international legal personality cannot be attributed to their member states (at least when there is no allegation of manifest infringement of protected rights): see, *e.g.*, *Boivin*, supra note 33, as regards the activities of both Eurocontrol and the ILOAT Tribunal; *Beygo v 46 Member States of the Council of Europe*, ECtHR, Application No 36099/06), Decision of 16 June 2009, as regards the Council of Europe Administrative Tribunal.

[36] *Effects of Awards of Compensation Made by the UN Administrative Tribunal* [1954] ICJ 47, 53 (Advisory Opinion of 13 July), qualifying the Tribunal 'not as an advisory organ or a mere subordinate committee of the General Assembly, but as an *independent* and truly judicial body pronouncing final judgments without appeal within the limited field of its functions' (emphasis added).

[37] *In the Matter of an Arbitration under the Arbitration Agreement between the Government of the Republic of Croatia and the Government of the Republic of Slovenia, Signed on 4 November 2009*, PCA, Partial Award of 30 June 2016, para 227 (available at <www.pca-cpa.org> together with the final award, issued on 29 June 2017).

their function independently from any instructions/wishes of the state that appoints them.[38] This only confirms that the authoritativeness of international judgments and their impact beyond the boundaries of the specific dispute that they decide upon is not linked to Article 31(3)(b) VCLT.

This conclusion does not detract in any way from the acknowledgment that international judicial institutions have a special place within the 'epistemic community'[39] called upon to interpret and apply international treaties. The WTO Appellate Body has made this point clearly as regards the status of adopted panel reports within the WTO system when holding:

> Adopted panel reports are an important part of the GATT *acquis*. They are often considered by subsequent panels. They create legitimate expectations among WTO Members, and, therefore, should be taken into account where they are relevant to any dispute. However, they are not binding, except with respect to resolving the particular dispute between the parties to that dispute… For these reasons, we do not agree with the Panel's conclusion in paragraph 6.10 of the Panel Report that 'panel reports adopted by the GATT CONTRACTING PARTIES and the WTO Dispute Settlement Body constitute subsequent practice in a specific case' as the phrase 'subsequent practice' is used in Article 31 of the *Vienna Convention*.[40]

This conclusion does not concern only the WTO dispute settlement system[41] (that is akin to a judicial system notwithstanding its peculiarities), but applies much more broadly, and is indeed a feature of international adjudication even when the binding force of pronouncements does not depend on formal approval by a political body. The ability of international jurisdictions to act as agents of development within specific treaty regimes (and of international

---

[38] On these developments see Arman Sarvarian and Rudy Baker, 'Arbitration between Croatia and Slovenia: Leaks, Wiretaps, Scandal' *EJILTalk!* (28 July and 7 August 2015); Philippe Sands, 'Developments in Geopolitics – The End(s) of Judicialization?' *EJILTalk!* (15 October 2015).

[39] See Andrea Bianchi, 'Law, Time and Change: The Self-Regulatory Function of Subsequent Practice' in Georg Nolte (ed), *Treaties and Subsequent Practice* (2013) 133, 138.

[40] WTO, *Japan: Alcoholic Beverages II – Report of the Appellate Body* (4 October 1996) WT/DS8/AB/R, WT/DS10/AB/R and WT/DS11/AB/R, 4 October 1996.

[41] That this is the Appellate Body's view is made clear by the remark made *ibid.*, at fn 30, to the effect that 'the Statute of the International Court of Justice has an explicit provision, Article 59, to the same effect. This has not inhibited the development by that Court (and its predecessor) of a body of case law in which considerable reliance on the value of previous decisions is readily discernible'.

law in general) depends on different factors, in a combination that varies in different jurisdictions and can also shift over time. Among those, the permanent nature of a judicial system, with the ensuing possibility to build a coherent case law, is particularly important, as Professor Zemanek also points out with reference to the ECHR. A persuasive reasoning reached in a procedurally fair way can also bear an influence in this regard, as it enhances the legitimacy of adjudication. Another central aspect, however, is precisely that international courts and tribunals make an independent and impartial assessment of the law. While Professor Sur qualifies judicial interpretation as 'authentic' interpretation,[42] independence marks the 'added value' of adjudication in the international legal order, where it may otherwise be difficult to overcome the 'dialogue of the deaf' between parties holding conflicting views on issues of treaty interpretation. This element explains why also *ad hoc* arbitral tribunals, which are not part of a permanent institutional framework, can play a role that is similar to the one of permanent courts. Incidentally, moreover, independence is also a feature of expert bodies whose members sit in their individual capacity, rather than as representatives of states,[43] and is the main basis for the authoritativeness of their pronouncements on matters of treaty interpretation. Whereas notably the lack of binding effects of expert bodies' pronouncements may well justify a distinct treatment, as in Professor Nolte's *Fourth Report on Subsequent Agreements and Subsequent Practice in Relation to the Interpretation of Treaties*[44] and in the Draft Conclusions provisionally adopted by the Drafting Committee,[45] it is noteworthy that also the systemic impact of judicial interpretation of treaties (beyond the limits set by the principle of *res judicata*) is not based on the formally binding nature of judicial decisions. Pronouncements of international tribunals, as well as those of expert bodies, are not as such the 'authentic' interpretation of a treaty in the sense of Article 31(3)(b) VCLT: only acceptance by the parties to the interpreted treaty, be it in the form of acquiescence, can express their agreement as to interpretation adopted by international courts and tribunals.

---

[42] Sur, *supra* note 5 and corresponding text.

[43] Christian Tomuschat, *Human Rights between Idealism and Realism* (3rd edn, 2016) 219-220.

[44] ILC, 'Fourth Report on Subsequent Agreements and Subsequent Practice in Relation to the Interpretation of Treaties, by Georg Nolte' (6 March 2016) UN Doc A/CN.4/694.

[45] Draft conclusion 13[12] dealing with pronouncements of expert treaty bodies does not apparently apply to courts (see however paragraph 2).

IV. The Interaction between International Courts and States and the (Evolutive) Interpretation of Treaties

It may be worth stressing that what matters here is not so much the possibility of more or less open refusal by states to abide by judgments and awards directly addressed to them. This is a well-known phenomenon also in present day international law, which should however be distinguished from the reactions of states not formally bound by *res judicata*: only the latter would be properly relevant as 'court generated state practice'. Positive reactions, amounting to acceptance of specific judicial interpretation of treaties, may take a variety of different forms, such as official declarations,[46] adaptation of domestic legislation,[47] express endorsement in amendments to the treaties,[48] or simply the fact that the relevant interpretation is not as such challenged in subsequent cases. This is the most frequent outcome, especially when subsequent cases pend before the same jurisdiction, and is often due to expediency an open challenge to a given (evolutive) interpretation of a treaty before the Court which has adopted it is not likely to be successful, whereas defences based on distinguishing may have more chances in this respect. One telling example relates to the *Sejdovic* case, where Italy tried to challenge the policy of indicating measures of general nature in pilot judgments, that the ECtHR had recently inaugurated in *Broniowski v Poland*,[49] without, however, any effect on the new policy, which continues to date. Moreover, also political considerations often lead to acquiesce to unfavourable developments in the

---

[46] See, *e.g.*, on the *Philippines/China* award on the South China Sea dispute, the Declaration by the United States (which however have not ratified UNCLOS), as quoted by David J Firestein, 'The US-China Perception Gap in the South China Sea' *The Diplomat* (19 August 2016), and the more nuanced declaration issued by the High Representative on behalf of the EU on the Award rendered in the Arbitration between the Republic of the Philippines and the People's Republic of China (Press release No 442/16 of 15 July 2016 <www.consilium.europa.eu>).

[47] See for some examples Council of Europe Parliamentary Assembly, 'Impact of the European Convention on Human Rights in States Parties: Selected Examples', overview prepared by the Legal Affairs and Human Rights Department, AS/Jur/Inf (2016)04, 8 January 2016.

[48] This was the case, for instance, as regards the judicial review over acts the European Parliament and the standing of that same institution to submit complaints to the Court of Justice under what is now Article 263 TFEU. Subsequent treaty practice may however also point to dissatisfaction with specific interpretive trends.

[49] *Broniowski v Poland*, ECtHR, Application No 56581/00, Judgment of 1 March 2006, paras 115ff.

case law of permanent jurisdictions as the possible alternative, namely leaving the relevant jurisdictional system, is not a desired outcome.

Yet, states do rely also on other options out of dissatisfaction with specific interpretive trends, including various forms of individual and collective 'backlash' against international jurisdictions that bring to the forefront the parties' role as 'masters' of the relevant treaties.[50] Less dramatic reactions usually occur within treaty frameworks featuring strong jurisdictional systems, such as the one of the European Union and of the ECHR; in those contexts disagreement is often addressed in the form of 'judicial dialogue' between domestic and international jurisdictions. However this dialogue does not necessarily lead to positive results: for instance, the Italian Constitutional Court has a tradition of 'openness' towards international law as interpreted by international courts, but some recent stances reflect strong criticism with the interpretation of treaties (and custom) by international judgments.[51] Italy may well be isolated as regards the substance of some of these stances, but also a radical decision such as the Brexit has been linked to uneasiness with the pervasive role of the CJEU in the framework of the European Union.

It is not possible here to address such issues in detail; however, the examples discussed above seem to confirm that the complex interaction between the parties to international agreements and international tribunals called upon to interpret such agreements can be seen as a dialogue, not only between international and domestic judicial but also, more generally, between international courts and states. While this idea is certainly not new,[52] the notion of 'court generated state practice' helps identifying more precisely the terms of this dialogue.

---

[50] See only Karen Alter, James T Gathii and Laurence Helfer, 'Backlash against International Courts in West, East and Southern Africa: Causes and Consequences' (2016) 27 EJIL 293.

[51] Besides the well-known Judgment No 238/2014 on the *Jurisdictional Immunities* case, reference can be made to Judgment No 49/2015 which openly challenges the interpretation of Article 7 ECHR by the Strasbourg Court in *Varvara v Italy*, indicating that Italian courts are bound to follow only settled case law of the ECtHR.

[52] See Anthea Roberts, 'Power and Persuasion in Investment Treaty Interpretation: The Dual Role of States' (2010) 104 AJIL 179, 193-194.

On the Legitimacy of Court
Generated State Practice

A Legitimacy Perspective on Court Generated State Practice

Christina Binder[*]

I. Introduction

Karl Zemanek's article refers to the jurisprudence of the European Court of Human Rights (ECtHR) as a prime example for 'court generated state practice', namely when the dynamic interpretation of the ECtHR exceeds the wording of the European Convention on Human Rights (ECHR). In doing so, Karl Zemanek adopts a classic law of treaties' perspective: To what extent is the ECtHR's dynamic interpretation of the Convention based on the rules of treaty interpretation (Articles 31 *et seq.* of the Vienna Convention on the Law of Treaties (VCLT)) and may thus be understood as based on 'subsequent practice in the application of the treaty' in the meaning of Article 31(3)(b) VCLT? What are possible justifications for 'interpretations' which reach further than the VCLT's rules of treaty interpretation since they exceed the wording of the ECHR without firm basis in the practice of the treaty parties?[1] And, respectively, what is the value of any practice which is induced (or generated) by the ECtHR's interpretation, *i.e.* of 'court generated state practice'?

---

[*] Christina Binder is Professor of International Law and International Human Rights Law at the University of the Federal Armed Forces in Munich and Lecturer at the Department of European, International and Comparative Law at the University of Vienna. She was visiting fellow at the Lauterpacht Center for International Law in Cambridge (2007-2008), at the Max Planck Institute for Comparative Public Law and International Law in Heidelberg (2008-2010) and at McGill University in Montréal (summer 2015). She is member of the ILA Committees on the Implementation of the Rights of Indigenous Peoples and on Feminism in International Law. Christina is member of the Executive Boards of the European Society of International Law (ESIL) and of the European University Center for Human Rights and Democratisation (EIUC). She can be reached under c.binder@unibw.de.

[1] Legally speaking, the ECHR circumscribes the scope of states parties' obligations in human rights terms. It also defines the competences of the ECtHR as regards the application and interpretation of the Convention (Art 32 ECHR).

According to Karl Zemanek, the very acceptance of the ECtHR's jurisdiction by the contracting parties to a certain extent provides the basis for the Court's dynamic interpretation:

> What is relevant in the present context is the fact that under the regime established by the ECHR states have contracted away their authority to interpret the Convention and hence to determine their obligations under the Convention. That gives the ECtHR leeway to develop these obligations in accordance with the conception of the underlying values which it assumes to exist at the moment of deciding an appropriate case. That will, in reality, lead to a modification of the obligation under the Convention...[2]

The ECtHR's authority is thus derived, as explained by Karl Zemanek, from the ECHR's parties' consent to the Court's jurisdiction through the ratification of the ECHR.

Still, this consent is not unlimited. Especially the resistance by certain states shows the thin grounds on which the ECtHR's authority is built, particularly where it leaves the 'firm grounds' of the Convention. For example, the United Kingdom strongly objected to the ECtHR's evolutionary interpretation in the prisoner voting cases.[3] It even threatened to leave the ECHR system and to withdraw from the Convention.[4] The Russian Constitutional Court puts limits

---

[2] Karl Zemanek, in this volume, at 12.

[3] See *Hirst v The United Kingdom (No. 2)*, ECtHR, Application No 74025/01, Judgment of 6 October 2005; *Greens and M.T. v The United Kingdom*, ECtHR, Application No 60041/08 and 600054/08, Judgment of 23 November 2010; *Firth and Others v The United Kingdom*, ECtHR, Application No 47784/09 et al, Judgment of 12 August 2014; *McHugh and Others v The United Kingdom*, ECtHR, Application No 51987/08 and 1,014 others, Judgment of 10 February 2015; *Millbank and Others v The United Kingdom*, ECtHR, Application No 44473/14 et al, Judgment of 30 June 2016.

[4] Anushka Asthana and Rowena Mason, 'UK must leave European Convention on Human Rights, says Theresa May' *The Guardian* (25 April 2016) <https://www.theguardian.com/politics/2016/apr/25/uk-must-leave-european-convention-on-human-rights-theresa-may-eu-referendum> accessed 20 July 2017; A. Wagner, 'Theresa May Plans UK Withdrawal From European Convention on Human Rights – Report', 28 December 2016, available at https://rightsinfo.org/theresa-may-plans-uk-withdrawal-human-rights-convention-reports/ accessed 20 July 2017; The ECHR, in principle, allows for withdrawal in accordance with Art 58 ECHR:

> 1. A High Contracting Party may denounce the present Convention only after the expiry of five years from the date on which it became a party to it and after six months' notice contained in a notification addressed to the Secretary General of the Council of Europe, who shall inform the other

to the execution of the ECtHR's judgments[5] when rejecting the latter's case law, as, for example, in *Anchugov & Gladkov v Russia*.[6] Both the United Kingdom and Russia therefore challenged the authority of the ECtHR and questioned the Court's – in their view – overly broad interpretation of the ECHR as an intrusion into their national sovereignty. Such contestation risks to undermine the very basis of the ECHR's system. It illustrates that states may even reverse their acceptance of the ECtHR's jurisdiction as an *ultima ratio* consequence.

High Contracting Parties. 2. Such a denunciation shall not have the effect of releasing the High Contracting Party concerned from its obligations under this Convention in respect of any act which, being capable of constituting a violation of such obligations, may have been performed by it before the date at which the denunciation became effective. 3. Any High Contracting Party which shall cease to be a member of the Council of Europe shall cease to be a Party to this Convention under the same conditions. 4. The Convention may be denounced in accordance with the provisions of the preceding paragraphs in respect of any territory to which it has been declared to extend under the terms of Article 56.

No state has so far left the ECHR. Conversely, in the region of the Americas, Trinidad/Tobago and Venezuela withdrew from the ACHR. For details on both Trinidad and Tobago´s and Venezuela´s withdrawal see 'Venezuela Denounces American Convention on Human Rights as IACHR Faces Reform' International Justice Resource Center, 19 September 2012 <http://www.ijrcenter.org/2012/09/19/venezuela-denounces-american-convention-on-human-rights-as-iachr-faces-reform/> accessed 20 July 2017.

[5] See Russian Constitutional Court, 19 April 2016, concerning *Anchugov and Gladkov*, <http://www.ksrf.ru/ru/News/Pages/ViewItem.aspx?ParamId=3281> accessed 20 July 2017. Marina Aksenova, 'Anchugov and Gladkov is not Enforceable: The Russian Constitutional Court Opines in its First ECtHR Implementation Case' *Opinio Juris* (25 April 2016) <http://opiniojuris.org/2016/04/25/anchugov-and-gladkov-is-not-enforceable-the-russian-constitutional-court-opines-in-its-first-ecthr-implementation-case/> accessed 20 July 2017. Early 2017, the Russian Constitutional Court also refused the execution of the just satisfaction ordered in *OAO Neftyanaya Kompaniya Yukos v Russia*, ECtHR, Application No 14902/04, Judgment (just satisfaction) of 31 July 2014 (RCC 19 January 2017), for details see Maxim Timofeyev, 'Money Makes the Court go Round: The Russian Constitutional Court's Yukos Judgment' *Verfassungsblog* (26 January 2017) <http://verfassungsblog.de/money-makes-the-court-go-round-the-russian-constitutional-courts-yukos-judgment/> accessed 20 July 2017.

[6] *Anchugov and Gladkov v Russia*, ECtHR, Application No 11157/04 and 15162/05, Judgment of 4 July 2013; On the political commentary regarding ECHR criticism in Russia see Andriy Osavoliyk, 'Russia's Ignoring of European Court of Human Rights Decisions' *Open Dialogue* (5 February 2016) <http://en.odfoundation.eu/a/7280,russia-s-ignoring-of-european-court-of-human-rights-decisions> accessed 20 July 2017.

The ECtHR thus has to be careful not to undermine the basis of states' consent by an all too dynamic interpretation of the ECHR. This stands in clear tension to its very role as guardian of the ECHR: The Court has to adapt the Convention, which was adopted more than 65 years ago, to today's realities, evolving social needs and expanded human rights standards by means of a dynamic interpretation. The ECtHR thus is in a true dilemma and faces the delicate task to keep the ECHR as a 'living instrument'[7] without putting at risk states parties' acceptances of its jurisdiction.

The tension is clearest when the grounding of the ECtHR's case law in the wording of the ECHR seems doubtful. In cases, thus, where the Court's authority cannot be derived merely from its source, *i.e.* states' consent to the ECHR. Hence, which means exist to further respondent states' acceptance of the ECtHR's judgments?

II. A Legitimacy Perspective of the ECtHR's Case Law

Given the doubtful *legality* of the ECtHR's dynamic jurisprudence, it appears promising to examine the ECtHR's case law by adopting a more legitimacy-oriented view. Such perspective seems warranted since it helps to establish the exercise of the Court's authority more broadly than to only derive it from states' consent as expressed through their ratification of the Convention.

A. Generalities on Legitimacy

To examine an international monitoring institution's operation from the perspective of its legitimacy is a rather new approach. In traditional international law, there was no real need for it. Since international monitoring institutions generally remained within their mandate and acted within the scope of the competences conferred to them in the treaty which established them, the principles of state consent and legality were considered largely sufficient bases for the exercise of their authority. Especially the principle of legality connected the latter to the original state consent. This has changed with the increased activity of international monitoring institutions.[8] The ECtHR is a

---

[7] *Tyrer v UK*, ECtHR, Application No 5856/72, Judgment of 25 April 1978, para 31: 'The Court must also recall that the Convention is a living instrument which, as the Commission rightly stressed, must be interpreted in the light of present-day conditions.'

[8] See Daniel Bodansky, 'The Legitimacy of International Governance: A Coming Challenge for International Environmental Law' (1999) 93 AJIL 596, 610; Rüdiger

telling example: the Court's dynamic/evolutive interpretation of the ECHR, as was shown, departs from the 'secure' basis of state consent quite frequently.

Recalling the definition of legitimacy as 'quality that leads people (or states) to accept authority – independent of coercion, self-interest or rational persuasion – because of a general sense that the authority is justified'[9], legitimacy not only is a general justification and requirement for the exercise of authority. The strength of a norm perceived as legitimate lies also in the fact that it pulls, in Thomas Franck's terms, those to whom it is addressed towards consensual compliance.[10] Scholars have suggested different models and elements that may induce legitimacy in the exercise of a particular authority.[11] They distinguished broadly between source, procedure and result-oriented approaches, or a combination thereof. Put differently, authority can be legitimated by its origin or source (traditionally state consent); it can also be considered as legitimate because it involves procedures which are adequate and fair; or because of its success in producing desired outcomes.[12] Functional aspects – including the expertise of the respective institution – may also be taken into account. These perspectives will be drawn upon in the following to shed new light on the ECtHR's dynamic case law.

B. Procedural Legitimacy

When critically assessing the ECtHR's dynamic jurisprudence, the procedural legitimacy of the Court weighs strongly. The ECtHR derives this legitimacy from its composition as well as from the procedures guiding the deliberation process (decision-making). The Court's composition, in this respect, benefits from the high authority and experience of its judges who enjoy the guarantees

---

Wolfrum, 'Legitimacy of International Law and the Exercise of Administrative Functions: The Example of the International Seabed Authority the International Maritime Organization (IMO) and International Fisheries Organizations' (2008) 9 German Law Journal 2041, 2044.

[9] Daniel Bodansky, 'Legitimacy' in Ellen Hey, Jutta Brunnée and Daniel Bodansky (eds), *Oxford Handbook of International Environmental Law* (2007) 704, 707.

[10] Thomas Franck, *The Power of Legitimacy Among Nations* (1990).

[11] See, *e.g.*, Wolfrum, *supra* note 8, at 2040; Bodansky, *supra* note 8, at 611 *et seq.*

[12] In addition to the abovementioned scholars, see also Jost Delbrück, 'Exercising Public Authority beyond the State: Transnational Democracy and/or Alternative Legitimation Strategies?' (2003) 10 Indiana Journal of Global Legal Studies 29, 42.

of impartiality, independence and legal expertise.[13] The involvement of the Council of Europe's (CoE's) Parliamentary Assembly in the (s)election of judges also provides for some democratic legitimacy.[14] Turning to the procedures involved to reach a judgment, especially the techniques aiming at a decision's normative correctness seem of relevance when assessing the ECtHR's dynamic interpretation of the ECHR.[15]

Respectively, the ECtHR finds legitimacy in its general fair trial requirements.[16] Also, as a rule, a judge of the nationality of the respondent state sits on the case.[17] Since this generally furthers the (Grand) Chamber's understanding

---

[13] Arts 21, 23(1) ECHR. The judges' independence was further strengthened with the entry into force of Protocol No 14 in June 2010 which extended the terms of office to nine years and abolished the possibility of re-election.

[14] There are two phases to the election process. Firstly, a national selection procedure, where each state party compiles a list of three qualified candidates, and secondly, the election process by the Parliamentary Assembly.

[15] A different dimension are factually comprehensive decisions. These are however of reduced relevance here. See for further reference Christina Binder, 'Anything New Since the End of the Cold War? or International Law Goes Domestic: International Electoral Standards and Their Legitimacy' (2011) 27 Anuario Español de Derecho Internacional 437.

[16] Such as public hearings, Art 40 ECHR; see also the welcome possibility to allow for third party intervention in accordance with Art 36 ECHR.

[17] Art 26 ECHR: Single-judge formation, Committees, Chambers and Grand Chamber

1. To consider cases brought before it, the Court shall sit in a single-judge formation, in committees of three judges, in Chambers of seven judges and in a Grand Chamber of seventeen judges. The Court's Chambers shall set up committees for a fixed period of time.

2. At the request of the plenary Court, the Committee of Ministers may, by a unanimous decision and for a fixed period, reduce to five the number of judges of the Chambers.

3. When sitting as a single judge, a judge shall not examine any application against the High Contracting Party in respect of which that judge has been elected.

4. There shall sit as an *ex officio* member of the Chamber and the Grand Chamber the judge elected in respect of the High Contracting Party concerned. If there is none or if that judge is unable to sit, a person chosen by the President of the Court from a list submitted in advance by that Party shall sit in the capacity of judge.

5. The Grand Chamber shall also include the President of the Court, the Vice-Presidents, the Presidents of the Chambers and other judges chosen in accordance with the rules of the Court. When a case is referred to the Grand

of the national background and the domestic legislative framework of a case, it contributes to a judgment's legitimacy. Likewise, the possible referral of cases which raise serious legal questions of general interest to the Grand Chamber contributes to the Court's legitimacy, given the inclusive composition of the Chand Chamber's 17 sitting judges. Numerous cases are Grand Chamber judgments.[18] Especially where the judgment is reached without any strong dissenting opinions attached, this furthers the legitimacy of the judgments passed by the ECtHR.

Furthermore, the ECtHR developed a promising technique to expand the scope of the ECHR. The ECtHR generally bases its dynamic interpretation of the Convention's provisions on a comparison between the ECHR's parties' legislative frameworks to discern whether a (higher) common European standard has formed. Especially where this draws on a true European consensus, such as in *Öcalan*[19] or *Soering*,[20] this appears as an adequate development of Convention standards and may be understood as subsequent practice by states parties in the meaning of Article 31(3)(b) VCLT.[21]

Critical for the ECtHR's procedural legitimacy, is, of course, how many states have adopted according legislation and how widespread and consistent state practice supporting the ECtHR's dynamic interpretation of the ECHR is. General rules of public international law provide guidance. They require a

---

Chamber under Article 43, no judge from the Chamber which rendered the judgment shall sit in the Grand Chamber, with the exception of the President of the Chamber and the judge who sat in respect of the High Contracting Party concerned.

[18] Of the approximately 20000 judgments issued by the ECtHR by April 2017, 426 stem from the Grand Chamber. See <http://hudoc.echr.coe.int/eng#{%22langua geisocode%22:[%22ENG%22],%22documentcollectionid2%22:[%22GRAND CHAMBER%22]}> accessed 20 July 2017.

[19] *Öcalan v Turkey*, ECtHR, Application No 46221/99, Judgment of 12 May 2005, para 162f.

[20] *Soering v The United Kingdom*, ECtHR, Application No 14038/88, Judgment of 7 July 1989, para 102.

[21] As Karl Zemanek rightly maintains, in case of vertical obligations such as those incorporated in human rights treaties, relevant state practice in the meaning of Article 31(3)(b) VCLT/development of customary international law is not established by state interaction but rather by internal legislation which grants the according rights. (Karl Zemanek, in this volume, at 8-10) This, of course, under the assumption that states acted with the according *opinio iuris*; *i.e.* that they adopted legislation in pursuit of a presumed legal obligation. Given the binding jurisdiction of the ECtHR and states' risk to be held accountable in case of non-compliance, this can, however, safely be assumed.

widespread uniform practice especially of those states which are particularly affected.[22] It is thus not necessary that *all* states have adopted the respective legislation. If at least a considerable or overwhelming majority of states has done so, in line with the general rules of international law, the other states may be assumed to tacitly consent to the higher standard unless they openly object.[23] For example, in *Demir and Baykara v Turkey* the ECtHR relied on a 'vast majority of European states', and in *A v UK* the ECtHR referred to 'most, if not all signatory states to the Convention.'[24]

However, in other cases, the ECtHR's interpretation does not seem to be based on the conforming legislation of the majority of state parties. For example, in *Hirst v UK*[25] and *Frodl v Austria*[26] the ECtHR found that the *ex lege* deprivation of the prisoners' voting rights in the United Kingdom and Austria constituted a breach of the right to free elections (Article 3 of Protocol No 1), notwithstanding the fact that the pertinent legislation of the state parties to Protocol No 1 was not uniform since only a minority of states had no restrictions on prisoners' voting rights.[27] The ECtHR's dynamic interpretation of treaty standards regarding the right to free elections was thus not based on a 'subsequent practice' in accordance with Article 31(3)(b) VCLT and not firmly grounded in state consent. In fact, the ECtHR has also

---

[22] See as to the requirements for the formation of customary international law the International Court of Justice (ICJ) in the *North Sea Continental Shelf* case: *North Sea Continental Shelf (Federal Republic of Germany v Denmark; Federal Republic of Germany v Netherlands)* [1969] ICJ 4, 43, para 74 (Judgment of 20 February): 'State practice, including that of States whose interests are specially affected, should have been both extensive and virtually uniform in the sense of the provision invoked.'

[23] Karl Zemanek, in this volume, at 11 'Conventional understanding of state practice which is commonly only evidenced by the action of some but not all states concerned, so long as those which have not actively contributed to it can be presumed not to oppose it.'

[24] See Zemanek, in this volume, at 11.

[25] *Hirst, supra* note 3.

[26] *Frodl v Austria*, ECtHR, Application No 20201/04, Judgment of 8 April 2010. See also subsequent cases, *Greens MT, supra* note 3; *Scoppola v Italy*, ECtHR, Application No 126/05, Judgment of 22 May 2012; *Anchugov, supra* note 6.

[27] See Joint Dissenting Opinion of the Judges Wildhaber, Costa, Lorenzen, Kovler and Lebens to *Hirst v UK*, para 6. For example, in *Hirst*, the ECtHR aimed at identifying 'common European standards'. Problematically, the Court disregarded though that only 18 out of 45 contracting states had no restrictions on prisoners' voting rights. (See Joint Dissenting Opinion of the Judges Wildhaber, Costa, Lorenzen, Kovler and Lebens to *Hirst, supra* note 3, at paras 33ff).

relied on other methods/justifications to explain its dynamic interpretation, such as, *e.g.,* more general and value-oriented considerations (see, *e.g.,* in *Goodwin v UK* or *Rantsev v Cyprus and Russia*).[28] Even if the latter is of a more doubtful validity, it seems safe to assume that the Court's generally coherent methodology on which it bases its dynamic interpretation of Convention standards overall favours its legitimacy.[29]

C. Substantive/Outcome-Based Legitimacy

The legitimacy of the ECtHR's case law is also supported by substantive/result-oriented approaches. The latter are concerned, most bluntly speaking, with an institution's output; its appearance of doing 'a good job in governing', which also relates to its effectiveness. Drawing on Treves' discussion of the

---

[28] Karl Zemanek, in this volume at, 11: *Goodwin v The United Kingdom*, ECtHR, Application No 28957/95, Judgment of 11 July 2002: The ECtHR attached 'less importance to the lack of evidence of a common European approach to the resolution of the legal and practical problems posed' and relied on the 'clear and uncontested evidence of a constituting international trend in favour'; *Rantsev v Cyprus and Russia*, ECtHR, Application No 25965/04, Judgment of 7 July 2010: The ECtHR stated that human trafficking 'cannot be considered compatible with a democratic society and the values expounded in the Convention.'; See also *Demir and Baykara v Turkey*, ECtHR, Application No 34503/97, Judgment of 12 November 2008: '85. The Court, in defining the meaning of terms and notions in the text of the Convention, can and must take into account elements of international law other than the Convention, the interpretation of such elements by competent organs, and the practice of European States reflecting their common values. The consensus emerging from specialised international instruments and from the practice of Contracting States may constitute a relevant consideration for the Court when it interprets the provisions of the Convention in specific cases.' Generally on this issue see also George Letsas, 'The ECHR as a Living Instrument – Its Meaning and Legitimacy' in Andreas Føllesdal, Birgit Peters and Geir Ulfstein (eds), *Constituting Europe: The European Court of Human Rights in a National, European and Global Context* (2010) 106.

[29] The ECtHR thus has, in principle strong procedural safeguards and methodological techniques to reach normatively correct decisions. Conversely, the Court's fact finding capacities are more limited. The Court usually appreciates facts as established by national courts on the basis of written applications by the parties and, because it lacks resources, only most exceptionally engages in fact finding or on-site visits itself. It is simply beyond the capacities of an international judicial institution to obtain a comprehensive picture of a domestic election, notwithstanding the welcome liberal practice of the ECtHR concerning the admissibility of *amicus curiae*, which provide additional insights into a country's situation. This may at times hamper the Court's capacity to resort to a comprehensive consideration of facts especially in more complex situations.

legitimacy of judicial decisions, this will particularly address the inherent characteristics of a judgment (*i.e.* consistent application of relevant law and quality of legal reasoning) and the relation between a judgment and its execution (in more general terms to what extent the outcome is accepted by the respective community).

With regard to the ECtHR, there are a number of indications which support its claim to possess substantive/outcome-based legitimacy. As a rule, the Court draws extensively on its previous case law in the reasoning. Such references are welcome since they have the practical effect of system building by informal precedent,[30] further the consistency of the Court's judgments and stabilize the normative expectations of the states parties to the ECHR.[31] The ECtHR's technique of interpretation when comparing different states' legal orders to inquire whether a new European standard on a matter has emerged (documented in the Court's considerations) mentioned above, furthers transparency. It thus contributes to the outcome-based legitimacy of the ECtHR's judgments.

Moreover, as regards the relation between a judgment and its execution, states' compliance is of major importance. One may distinguish between the Council of Europe's means to further execution and the actual compliance by respondent states. As regards the former, a relevant starting point is the binding nature of the ECtHR's judgments; a state is obliged to comply with them in accordance with Article 46 ECHR. There exists also an organ which is (*inter alia*) tasked to monitor the execution of judgments; being the Committee of Ministers. The publication of individual states' compliance records on the Council of Europe's website and the Committee of Minister's supervisory powers which were increased with the entry into force of Protocol No 14 – the Committee may now re-refer cases of non-compliance back to the ECtHR – pressure states to abide by judgments.[32] The Council of Europe's institutional framework thus provides a minimum of outcome-based legitimacy to the ECtHR's dynamic interpretation by pushing states to comply with the Court's judgments.

---

[30] The Court is not formally bound by its previous decisions. For further reference on precedent and system building see Marc Jacob, 'Lawmaking Through International Adjudication' (2011) 12 German Law Journal 1005.

[31] See for further reference, Armin von Bogdandy and Ingo Venzke, 'Beyond Dispute: International Judicial Institutions as Lawmakers' in Armin von Bogdandy and Ingo Venzke (eds), *International Judicial Lawmaking – On Public Authority and Democratic Legitimation in Global Governance* (2012) 3.

[32] Note, however, that so far, no case has been brought before the ECtHR based on this mechanism.

In practice, states' compliance with the judgments of the ECtHR is mixed. Most states abide by the Court's judgments or at least indicate their willingness to do so. In some cases, however, there have been delays in execution.[33] Other countries fail to provide the relevant information on the status of execution to the Committee of Ministers.[34] Notwithstanding these instances of failed or delayed compliance, the ECtHR's substantive/outcome-based legitimacy is cautiously positive.

C. Legitimacy and 'Court Generated State Practice': An Evaluation

Procedural and substantive legitimacy dimensions contribute to the authority of the ECtHR's judgements and therewith support the acceptance of the Court's dynamic interpretation of Convention standards. However, as was shown, there is still room for improvement. Thus, and especially when engaging in dynamic (far-reaching) interpretations of the ECHR therewith abandoning the 'safe ground' of state consent, the ECtHR should strive to even further develop these procedural and substantive legitimacy dimensions. This, for example, by consistently arguing its cases or by further developing the motivation of its arguments. The therewith enhanced legal security and according stabilisation of normative expectations should increase respondent states' acceptance of the ECtHR's judgments even in cases of far reaching interpretations. The development of 'court generated practice' should be stimulated accordingly.

This is particularly welcome since such subsequent conforming practice expands the ECtHR's case law and establishes higher human rights standards for all treaty parties. As affirmed by Karl Zemanek, 'court generated state practice' may subsequently modify state parties' obligations under the

---

[33] See, *e.g.*, the Report by the Rapporteur Mr Klass de Vries to the Committee on Legal Affairs and Human Rights (PACE, AS/Jur/2015) 17). The Annual Report of the CoE Committee of Ministers compiles precise statistics on the execution of judgments every year, noting some cause for concern as regards the length of execution. Thus, *e.g.*, in 2016 only 65% of the judgments ordering just satisfaction were paid within the deadlines (compared to 71% in 2015). See 10th Annual Report of the Committee of Ministers, 'Supervision of the Execution of Judgments and Decisions of the European Court of Human Rights 2016', 10 <https://rm.coe.int/CoERMPublicCommonSearchServices/DisplayDCTMContent?documentId=0900001680706a3d> accessed 12 July 2017.

[34] *Ibid.*

ECHR.[35] *Inter partes* obligations from a particular case are turned into *erga omnes* obligations. 'Court generated state practice' thus heals the deficiencies of the ECtHR's (originally) overly dynamic interpretations of Convention standards where the ECtHR has left the safe grounds of (original) state consent. Ideally, 'court generated state practice' therewith has the potential to 'close the circle' also from a legitimacy perspective. It reunites all three dimensions of legitimacy, *i.e.* source-based, procedural and substantive/result-oriented ones. Likewise for these reasons, the Court should strive to further subsequent state practice insofar possible.

---

[35] Zemanek, in this volume, at 11-12.

How Many Divisions Does the European Court of Human Rights Have?
Compliance and Legitimacy in Times of Crisis

Ralph Janik[*]

I. Introduction

Professor Zemanek's elaborations on what he identifies as 'Court Generated State Practice' raises a somewhat underexplored doctrinal issue: The 'creativity of the ECtHR's interpretative practice', in particular when it comes to setting standards absent the lack of a European consensus, and the resulting to modifications of obligations under the European Convention on Human Rights (ECHR). To a certain extent, the European Court of Human Rights (ECtHR) is effectively turning the interrelationship between state practice and the court as an interpretative organ on its head: As ECHR member states will adapt to findings of the ECtHR, they will ultimately modify its obligations:

> [...] a self-induced process because a significant number of adaptions enables the Court to claim them as evidence of the new understanding of the respective provision of the ECHR and hence as state practice, thereby transforming what was initially a specific interpretation into a modified obligation.[1]

These notions also require a careful consideration of the limits of the ECtHR and its jurisprudence. Like all international courts, it often needs to strike the balance between potential non-compliance with its judgments and granting states too much leeway. Be it Islamic clothing, the non-refoulement principle, or the state of emergency: The ECtHR cannot escape hovering between the necessity to uphold certain minimum human rights guarantees and the

---

[*] Researcher and Lecturer, Department for European, International and Comparative Law, Section for International Law and International Relations, University of Vienna.

[1] Karl Zemanek, in this volume, at 13-14.

'margin of appreciation' doctrine as a means to calibrate different, at times conflicting societal interests.

This long-standing tension has increasingly come to the fore amid recent global developments and the challenges posed to the European continent. Compliance with its judgments and court generated state practice in particular requires legitimacy of the ECtHR in the eyes of the respective state. It is thus necessary to examine what role the ECtHR can and should play in times of crisis.

II. The Fragility of Human Rights Law

The year 2016 was not a good year for Europe and the European Union. The increasing influx of asylum seekers has been accompanied by the rise of populist movements as well as an intensification of the debate on the role of Islam in Europe. Many have furthermore attributed the wave of terrorism not only to the fight against the 'Islamic State' but also to Europe's lax security standards and the impossibility of detecting potential or actual terrorists before entering European soil. Lastly, one also needs to mention the aftermath of the attempted *coup d'état* in Turkey and the successful referendum on granting president Erdogan additional powers.

All of these events and developments have had a tremendous impact on hitherto unquestioned and commonly accepted basic principles of international human rights law.

Some governments have openly debated whether it is about time to change the basic definition of a refugee in the 1951 Geneva Convention.[2] The question whether Article 18 of the Charter of fundamental rights of the European Union enshrines a 'right to asylum' or at least a 'right to seek asylum' (similar to the generally accepted understanding of Article 14

---

[2] Jon Stone, 'Theresa May wants to change the international definition of "refugee"' *Independent* (London, 6 October 2015) <www.independent.co.uk/news/uk/politics/theresa-may-wants-to-change-the-international-definition-of-refugee-a6681976.html> accessed 20 July 2017; Ole Mikkelsen, 'Denmark wants Geneva Convention debate if Europe cannot curb refugee influx' *Reuters* (Copenhagen, 28 December 2015) <www.reuters.com/article/us-europe-migrants-denmark-idUSKBN0UB10020151228> accessed 20 July 2017; Australia has openly questioned the definition contained in the 1951 Refugee Convention for long, see Adrienne Millbank, 'The Problem with the 1951 Refugee Convention' (2000) Research Paper No. 5 2000-01 <www.aph.gov.au/About_Parliament/Parliamentary_Departments/Parliamentary_Library/pubs/rp/rp0001/01RP05> accessed 20 July 2017.

Universal Declaration of Human Rights or the 2016 New York Declaration for Refugees and Migrants[3]) needs to be resolved more urgently than ever. The principle of non-refoulement is increasingly under duress as states are debating over the necessary threshold of risk for the returnee to be treated in violation of Article 3 ECHR.[4] The EU-Turkey-refugee deal, then, was criticised as a violation of the prohibition of collective expulsion and, in some cases at least, the principle of non-refoulement.[5]

What is novel about the current refugee crisis is that many perceived it as an *external* threat to the well-being, security, and welfare systems of the European states, first and foremost of those bearing the brunt. After all, the last fundamental threat to Europe's existence originating *outside* its borders was the 1683 Battle of Vienna. Throughout its modern history, Europe was threatened from within, be it for religious reasons, disputes between the respective monarchies, or the rise of nationalism in the 19th until the mid-20th century. It has only ceased to be a continent of war in the last decades, turning, as it was emphasized upon the award of the Nobel peace prize to the European Union, into a continent of peace. Taking into account its entire life-span, at least ever since the Peace of Westphalia as the starting point of its modern history, this seems like an historic aberration. Peace is not to be taken for granted.

The refugee crisis is also novel in the sense that it is currently not clear for how long it will last. It does not derive from a single and somewhat isolated event but a myriad of factors.

For one, the war in Syria, one of the driving forces of the refugee crisis, has been raging ever since 2012[6] (while the domestic tensions broke out already in late February 2011), with no end in sight. As the history of warfare has

---

[3] UNGA Res 71/1, New York Declaration for Refugees and Migrants (19 September 2016) UN Doc A/RES/71/1, para 27.

[4] In addition to criticism on deportations to Afghanistan, the New Year's Eve sexual assaults in German have triggered an emotional debate in Germany on the human rights situation to North African countries such as Morocco, Tunisia, or Algeria.

[5] Mauro Gatti, 'The EU-Turkey Statement: A Treaty That Violates Democracy (Part 1 of 2)' (*EJIL:Talk!*, 18 April 2016) <www.ejiltalk.org/the-eu-turkey-statement-a-treaty-that-violates-democracy-part-1-of-2/> accessed 20 July 2017; Amnesty International, 'A Blueprint for Despair: Human Rights Impact of the EU-Turkey Deal' (2017) <www.amnesty.eu/content/assets/Reports/EU-Turkey_Deal_Briefing_Formatted_Final_P4840-3.pdf> accessed 20 July 2017.

[6] ICRC, 'Syria: ICRC urges full respect for international humanitarian law' *ICRC News Release 12/161* (4 August 2012) <www.icrc.org/eng/resources/documents/news-release/2012/syria-news-2012-07-31.htm> accessed 20 July 2017.

shown, conflicts like these, *i.e.* proxy wars showing a high level of foreign involvement, may last even for decades. Even if the conflict eventually comes to its end, it is not clear how many refugees will be ready to return. After years abroad, people often end up being caught between alienation from their homeland and a low level of integration in their new country of residence. In addition, many only return if there exists sufficient hope that things are about to improve. In other words: What is needed is trust into the (new) state apparatus. Ethnically and religiously divided countries populated by large numbers of young men without sufficient future perspectives like Syria, Afghanistan, or many African states are particularly prone to fail when it comes to ensuring long-term stability and peace. The prospects for nation building are dim, success stories are hard to find. US strategic planning under president Obama and most likely even more so under Donald Trump (who announced that the US should no longer engage in 'rebuilding other countries'[7]), is still affected by the occupation of Iraq. The future of Syria heavily depends on Iran, Russia, and al-Assad (and, to a lesser extent, Turkey).[8]

The refugee crisis has furthermore added another facet to the general debate of the role of Islam in Europe. While the ECHR recognizes secularism and a restrictive separation of the church from the state, the freedom of religion cannot be constrained at will. On the other hand, the so-called veil ban has shown its reluctance to interfere with governmental policies in highly sensitive areas.

Another significant challenge to the ECHR has come from Turkey. After the unsuccessful coup attempt, the government of Recep Tayyip Erdoğan began cracking down not only on the actually involved soldiers but a wide range of individuals and groups possibly posing a threat to its rule, among them academics, journalists and/or individuals suspected to be associated with or sympathetic to Erdogan's former companion Fetullah Gülen or other opposition parties and groups. At the time of writing, it still remains to be seen whether Erdogan will implement his announcement to impose the death penalty on 'traitors', *i.e.* those involved in the coup.

---

[7] The full transcript of this speech is available at Ryan Teague Beckwith, 'Read Donald Trump's 'America First' Foreign Policy Speech' *Time* (New York City, 27 April 2016) <http://time.com/4309786/read-donald-trumps-america-first-foreign-policy-speech/> accessed 20 July 2017.

[8] Liz Sly and Suzan Haldamous, 'At Russia-led talks, Syrian rebels and government meet for the first time' *Washington Post* (Astana, 23 January 2017) <www.washingtonpost.com/world/at-russia-led-talks-syrian-rebels-and-government-meet-for-the-first-time/2017/01/23/e6373d5e-df65-11e6-8902-610fe486791c_story.html> accessed 20 July 2017.

The ECtHR faces a fundamental dilemma in all of these areas. On the one hand, states have in general shown their willingness to adhere to its judgments even in sensitive areas. On the other hand, while the ECtHR may successfully 'order' a specific type of behaviour, at times even against the will of the respective states, these standards are increasingly threatened by events outside of its control. History in general and when it comes to human rights protection in particular is not a linear development toward progress. Sometimes we take one step forward and two steps back. We shall thus briefly return to the very fundament of international law and the impact of the emergence of the individual as one of its subjects.

III. The Legitimacy of Human Rights

From today's perspective, classic international law, for better or worse, was a comparatively simple affair. States were more or less the sole subjects of international law,[9] while individuals, to use Akehurst's vivid comparison, enjoyed a status similar to that of animals in domestic law.[10] Or, as Oppenheim put it, they were not subjects but *objects*: Although possessing rights 'in conformity with or according to International Law', he emphasized 'that these rights would not exist had the single States not created them by their Municipal Law'. One also needs to remember that these rights predominantly applied to foreign individuals and not *vis-à-vis* the nationals of the respective state.[11] While cases of cruelty of a state against its own population could eventually even lead to forceful (outside) interventions on their behalf, Oppenheim nevertheless made it clear that such 'so-called rights of mankind' were not guaranteed by international law.[12]

This basic conception of the relationship between the state and the individual already changed after the First World War[13] and later due to the adoption

---

[9] *Cf.* Antonio Cassese, 'States: Rise and Decline of the Primary Subjects of the International Community' in Bardo Fassbender and Anne Peters (eds), *The Oxford Handbook of the History of International Law* (2012) 49.

[10] Peter Malanczuk, *Akehurst's Modern Introduction to International Law* (7th rev edn 1997) 91.

[11] Lassa Oppenheim, *International Law: A Treatise, Volume I: Peace* (2nd edn 1912) 363-364.

[12] *Ibid.*, at 369.

[13] See, *e.g.*, the Declaration of the International Rights of Man adopted by the *Institut de Droit International* at its New York session of 12 October 1929, for

of the UN Charter, which, by its multiple references to human rights, 'established the human person as a second focal point', thereby – knowingly or not – 'profoundly changing the parameters of traditional international law.'[14]

After all, human rights obligations are not predominantly owed to other states but towards individuals residing in the territory of the respective state or otherwise under its control.[15] Human rights law thus escapes the traditional notion of international law as a system of reciprocal rights and duties.

Respect for international human rights law thus still hinges upon its *legitimacy* in the eyes of the respective government. The modern state as enunciated already by Thomas Hobbes rests on the fundamental idea of institutionalizing and monopolizing power on behalf of its constituent individuals. It is not an end in itself, but serves the purpose of protecting individuals from violence committed among themselves and, *a fortiori*, must not itself become a perpetrator. Seemingly novel concepts such as the Responsibility to Protect are not entirely new re-definitions of sovereignty but based on conceptualizations which can be traced back to the very origin of modern statehood and international (human) rights law.[16]

In cases of human rights violations, a state and its rulers can be influenced, pressured, and subjected to sanctions or even to forcible interventions. Any means to effectuate law can only serve as *ultima ratio*. Yet, in order to function, the law itself still needs to be accepted by its addressees.

IV. The ECtHR and Court Generated State Practice

Europe is generally seen as a human rights role model where one finds the most-nuanced and well-developed human rights regime. To quote Luzius Wildhaber, the ECtHR and its hitherto unprecedented complaints procedure

---

an English version see George A Finch, 'The International Rights of Man' (1941) 35 AJIL 662.

[14] Karl Zemanek, 'New Trends in the Enforcement of erga omnes Obligations' (2000) 4 Max Planck Yearbook of United Nations Law 1, 3.

[15] *Cf.* the widely-discussed ECtHR's decisions in *Banković and Others v Belgium and Others*, ECtHR, Application 52207/99, Decision of 12 December 2001; or *Al-Jedda v The United Kingdom*, ECtHR, Application No 27021/08, Judgment of 7 July 2011.

[16] See, for a broader discussion of the historic origins in philosophical and political theory, Irene Etzersdorfer and Ralph Janik, *Staat, Krieg und Schutzverantwortung* (2015).

can be seen as 'the most spectacular illustration' of how the notion of sovereignty and the role of have evolved during the 20th century.[17]

One must nevertheless not forget its shortcomings and main challenges. In particular during times of crisis and political upheavals, the danger of lacking effectivity is always looming. Politicians may be keen on making political gains by portraying the ECtHR and its judges as agents of alien interferences into domestic affairs. Execution has remained the ECHR's and ECtHR's Achilles heel. Judgments are not self-executing and enforcement does not lie within the ECtHR, but a political organ (the Committee of Ministers) and its non-adversarial process 'based essentially on peer pressure and effective enforcement of judgments, but also on a commonality of political interest and often a self-interested tolerance of the practical problems associated with execution.'[18] States and their common will still have the final say. Whenever the thin line between law and politics is blurred, the potential detrimental impact on the ECHR's effectiveness is all too evident:

> There is perhaps also a tendency in such politically sensitive cases to deal with them as political questions and not, as they should be seen, as legal or rule of law questions relating to the execution of a binding court judgment. This is the natural gravitation of a political body and may also be inevitable given the intractable nature of the underlying political problems reflected in some cases. Unfortunately, apart from raising questions concerning compliance with Article 46, it reveals the limits of the concept of collective enforcement under the Convention in disputes concerning allegations of widespread violations, damages the reputation of the Committee, and undermines the integrity of the Convention system as a whole.[19]

The ECtHR's credibility can also suffer in cases concerning systemic violations resulting from a lack of adequate financial and other capacities in a state and thus affecting large numbers of individuals, such as detainees living under conditions which have been found detrimental to the prohibition of torture, inhumane or degrading treatment or punishment. The original decision triggering countless follow-up cases logged on the same basis would thus probably not solve the problem but instead lead to lengthy proceedings and further complicate execution. If the root cause of the problem remains

---

[17] Luzius Wildhaber, 'The European Court of Human Rights: The Past, The Present, The Future' (2007) 22 American University Law Review 521, 522.

[18] David Harris et al, *Harris, O'Boyle & Warbrick Law of the European Convention on Human Rights* (3rd edn 2014) 180.

[19] Ibid., at 199.

untackled, for lack of will, resources, or structural difficulties, the ECtHR renders judgments with no apparent effect.[20]

Hence, there remains an inevitably tension between human rights as they *should* be—human rights as a, to use the emphatic description of Jürgen Habermas, *Realistic Utopia*, since they 'anchor the ideal of a just society in the institutions of constitutional states themselves'[21] – and what they actually *can* be in light of the political and factual circumstances. This tension lies at the very heart of what professor Zemanek eminently identified as 'Court Generated State Practice'. As a supervisory body, the ECtHR enjoys

> leeway to develop [the ECHR's and its protocols'] obligations in accordance with the conception of underlying values which it assumes to exist at the moment of deciding an appropriate case. That will, in reality, lead to a modification of the obligation under the Convention.[22]

The ECtHR, in its jurisprudence, thus goes beyond the mere application of the law as accepted by the member states but becomes a *Change Agent* similar to domestic courts (such as the US Supreme Court and lower-level courts[23]): If states and their courts accept its interpretations, the resulting change in conduct essentially modifies the respective obligations. This process shows both the limits and the powers of the ECtHR.

On the one hand, it needs to be aware of the fact that attempting to facilitate the development of human rights law is contingent upon the susceptibilities of the member states. Reforms take time, while they can often be brought about only incrementally and in non-sensitive areas. States like Turkey[24] or Russia[25] have been particularly reluctant to implement and adhere to ECtHR judgments visibly demonstrating the limits of the ECtHR's actual impact.

---

[20] Luzius Wildhaber, 'The place of the European Court of Human Rights in the European Constitutional landscape' (2002) <www.confeuconstco.org/reports/rep-xii/Report%20ECHR-EN.pdf> accessed 20 July 2017, at 6-7.

[21] See Jürgen Habermas, 'The Concept of Human Dignity and the Realistic Utopia of Human Rights' (2010) 41 Metaphilosophy 464, 476.

[22] Karl Zemanek, in this volume, at 12.

[23] Jeffrey Sutton, 'Courts as Change Agents: Do we want more—or less?' (2014) 127 Harvard Law Review 1419.

[24] See Başak Çalı, 'Turkey's relationship with the European Court of Human Rights shows that human rights courts play a vital role, but one that can often be vastly improved' (*LSE Blog*, 14 March 2012) <http://blogs.lse.ac.uk/europpblog/2012/03/14/turkey-echr/> accessed 20 July 2017.

[25] See, *e.g.*, Iryna Marchuk, 'Flexing Muscles (Yet Again): The Russian Constitutional Court's Defiance of the Authority of the ECtHR in the Yukos Case' (*EJIL:Talk!*,

On the other hand, the process of generating state practice can occasionally be relatively independent from actual state practice, at least at the beginning. In so doing, the ECtHR has often functioned as a catalyst for domestic reforms of all sorts.[26] Beyond governmental activities, a survey of domestic courts in France, Germany, and the United Kingdom indeed confirms that they

> are at considerable pains to avoid friction with the European Court […] they have in fact come to embrace the role of faithful trustees of the rights of the European Convention.[27]

One pertinent and, in light of recent developments particularly pressing example (aside from those identified in professor Zemanek's paper) for this oscillation between the ECtHR's contribution to enact positive change while simultaneously having to exercise self-restraint is the prohibition of refoulement of rejected asylum seekers in general and those posing a security threat to the respective states in particular.

V. The Refugee Crisis

A. Refugee Law

Refugee law does *prima facie* not fall within the scope of the ECHR. The European Convention on Human Rights and its protocols do not include any provisions expressly dealing with refugee law. Article 2(1) of the Additional Protocol No 4 only stipulates that '[e]veryone shall be free to leave any country, including his own' without mentioning a right to seek or even be granted asylum.

In general, sovereignty entails the freedom to decide on the entry and stay of foreign individuals including heads of state, diplomats, or members of

---

13 February 2017) <www.ejiltalk.org/flexing-muscles-yet-again-the-russian-constitutional-courts-defiance-of-the-authority-of-the-ecthr-in-the-yukos-case/> accessed 20 July 2017.

[26] See Dia Anagnostou (ed), *The European Court of Human Rights: Implementing Strasbourg's Judgments on Domestic Policy* (2013).

[27] Eirik Bjorge, *Domestic Application of the ECHR: Courts as Faithful Trustees* (2015) 4. See, on the high level of acceptance of ECtHR judgments by Austrian courts, *e.g.* Walter Berka, *Verfassungsrecht* (2016) 457 and the general overviews of Austrian state practice in this and the preceding volumes of the *Austrian Review of International and European Law*.

government.[28] As the ECtHR has made it clear, states enjoy the right '[...] as a matter of well-established international law and subject to their treaty obligations, to control the entry, residence and expulsion of aliens.'[29]

This right, however, is not absolute as it needs to be balanced against the necessity to uphold fundamental humanitarian principles. Customary international law imposes a general prohibition of arbitrary and unreasonable expulsions.[30] Refugee law and general human rights law have further reduced this broad level of discretion: While there is no generally accepted right to asylum in international law,[31] the non-refoulement principle obliges state to abstain from deporting, expelling, or extraditing refugees and other individuals to countries where they face a high risk of torture or inhumane treatment. There can thus be an obligation to accept the continuous residence of refugees and even their admission at the border under certain circumstances.[32]

States have nevertheless remained keen on protecting their vital security interests.[33] Article 33(2) of the 1951 Refugee Convention thus exempts refugees endangering the respective country or its community from claiming the benefit of this provision.[34] Due to its potential impact on those affected, a high

---

[28] Robert Jennings and Arthur Watts, *Oppenheim's International Law, Volume 1: Peace* (9th edn 1992) 940 *et seq.*, 1034 *et seq*. See also Case C-364/10 *Hungary v Slovak Republic* [2012] ECLI:EU:C:2012:630, para 51; see also German Constitutional Court (BVerfG), Decision of the 2nd Chamber of the 2nd Senate of 8 March 2017, 2 BvR 483/17.

[29] *Moustaquim v Belgium*, ECtHR, Application No 12313/86, Judgment of 18 February 1991, para 43.

[30] Robert Jennings and Arthur Watts, *Oppenheim's International Law, Volume 1: Peace* (9th edn 1992) 940.

[31] Guy S Goodwin-Gill and Jance McAdam, *The Refugee in International Law* (2007) 358; see also Roman Boed, 'The State of the Right of Asylum in International Law' (1994) 5 Duke Journal of Comparative and International Law 1; *cf.*, however, María-Teresa Gil-Bazo, 'Asylum as a General Principle of International Law' (2015) 27 International Journal of Refugee Law 3, who argues that asylum constitutes a legally binding general principle establishing a right to be granted asylum. See also William Thomas Worster, 'The Contemporary International Law Status of the Right to Receive Asylum' (2014) 26 International Journal of Refugee Law 477.

[32] Goodwin-Gill and McAdam, *supra* note 31, at 208.

[33] See the precursors to Article 33(3) of the 1951 Refugee Convention as described in Andreas Zimmermann and Philipp Wennholz, 'Article 33, para. 2' in Andreas Zimmermann (ed), *The 1951 Convention Relating to the Status of Refugees and its 1967 Protocol: A Commentary* (2011) 1396.

[34] Article 33(2) Convention Relating to the Status of Refugees, 22 April 1954, 189 UNTS 137.

threshold and standard of proof nevertheless needs to be met, *i.e.* 'conviction by a final judgment of a particularly serious crime'[35] such as 'homicide, rape, child molesting, wounding, arson, drugs trafficking, and armed robbery.'[36] Still, once this standard was met state practice has confirmed the principal interest of states to give overriding priority to their security needs.

B. Non-Refoulement and the ECtHR

Already in its 1961 decision on the admissibility in *X against Federal Republic of Germany* the European Commission held that

> the deportation of a foreigner to a particular country might in exceptional circumstances give rise to the question whether there had been 'inhuman treatment' within the meaning of Article 3 of the Convention.[37]

As the Court emphasized in *X against Austria and Yugoslavia*, this finding equally applied to extradition cases.[38]

After several insulated cases in the following years,[39] the ECtHR became more actively involved in asylum-related matters during the early 1990s and thus at a time when the difficulties of deporting rejected asylum seekers were already apparent.[40] The jurisprudential basis remains the *Soering* decision and its finding that Article 3 'enshrines one of the fundamental values of the democratic societies making up the Council of Europe' and that there was an 'inherent obligation not to extradite'[41] to the US since the claimant could have faced the death penalty.

---

[35] James C Hathaway, *The Rights of Refugees under International Law* (2005) 344, 350.

[36] *Ibid.*, at 349.

[37] *X against The Federal Republic of Germany*, ECtHR, Application No 1465/62, Decision of 6 October 1962 (1962) 5 Yearbook of the European Convention on Human Rights 256, 260.

[38] *X against Austria and Yugoslavia*, ECtHR, Application No 2143/64, Decision of 30 June 1964 (1964) 7 Yearbook of the European Convention on Human Rights 314, 328-329.

[39] See the cases mentioned and discussed by Terje Einarsen, 'The European Convention on Human Rights and the Notion of an Implied Right to de facto Asylum' (1990) 2(3) International Journal of Refugee Law 361, 365-366.

[40] See Kay Hailbronner, 'The Right to Asylum and the Future of Asylum Procedures in the European Community' (1990) 2 International Journal of Refugee Law 341.

[41] *Soering v The United Kingdom*, ECtHR, Application No 14038/88, Judgment of 7 July 1989, para 88.

Starting with *Cruz Varas* from 20 March 1991, the ECtHR explicitly extended this rationale to the expulsion of asylum seekers.[42] In *Hirsi*,[43] the ECtHR went as far as applying these obligations to state conduct on the High Seas since the affected individuals were under the control of the (Italian) authorities.

The ECtHR's reading of the *absoluteness* of prohibition of torture, inhumane or degrading treatment or punishment also *deliberately* goes beyond the non-refoulement principle established in the 1951 Refugee Convention[44] which explicitly allows for the expulsion of individuals posing a threat to national security even if there is a risk of persecution.[45] As the ECtHR emphasized in *Chahal*, there is no 'room for balancing the risk of ill-treatment against the reasons for expulsion in determining whether a State's responsibility under Article 3 [...] is engaged.'[46]

The Court furthermore refrained from further distinguishing between the various forms of ill-treatment.[47] The prohibition to deport is thus not only applicable in connection with torture but also inhumane or even mere degrading treatment. For example, in *Ahmed* the ECtHR concluded that deporting someone to a country where 'he faces a serious risk of being subjected there to torture *or* inhuman *or* degrading treatment' would constitute a violation of Article 3 regardless of convictions or the general magnitude of the threat

---

[42] *Cruz Varas and Others v Sweden*, ECtHR, Application No 15576/89, Judgment of 20 March 1991, para 70 (note, however, that the ECtHR did not find a violation of Article 3 due to the changed political environment in Chile after the transition towards democracy, see *ibid.*, para 82). See also *Vilvarajah and Others v The United Kingdom*, ECtHR, Application No 13163/87, 13164/87, 13165/87, 13447/87, 13448/87, Judgment of 30 October 1991, paras 103-104.

[43] *Hirsi Jamaa and others v Italy*, ECtHR, Application No 27765/09, 23 February 2012.

[44] See *Ahmed v Austria*, ECtHR, Application No 25964/94, Judgment of 17 December 1996, para 41.

[45] Article 33 Convention Relating to the Status of Refugees, 22 April 1954, 189 UNTS 137.

[46] *Chahal v the United Kingdom*, ECtHR, Application No 22414/93, 15 November 1996, para 81.

[47] See Commission on Human Rights, 'Civil and Political Rights, Including the Questions of Torture and Detention: Torture and Other Cruel, Inhuman or Degrading Treatment, Report on the Special Rapporteur on the Question of Torture, Manfred Nowak' (23 December 2005) UN Doc E/CN.4/2006/6, paras 34-41.

stemming from asylum seeker:[48] '[T]he activities of the individual in question, however undesirable or dangerous, cannot be a material consideration.'[49]

The ECHR, as applied by the European Commission and later the ECtHR, thus severely restricts the above-mentioned sovereign right to control the entry and stay within a State's territory. As the Commission held already in *X against Austria and Yugoslavia*:

> [...] although extradition and the right of asylum are not, as such, among the matters governed by the Convention [...] the Contracting States have nevertheless accepted to restrict the free exercise of their powers under general international law, including the power to control and exit of aliens, to the extent and within the limits of the obligations which they have assumed under the Convention.[50]

Member states to the ECHR are thus effectively prevented from rejecting migrants or refugees at their borders if there are sufficient grounds to believe that they may be subjected to torture, inhumane, or even mere degrading treatment. The ECtHR's jurisprudence on Article 3, along with Articles 8 and 13 ECHR, has effectively established a factual right to asylum through the backdoor.[51]

The ECtHR's jurisprudence on expulsion is also remarkable since the above-mentioned older cases were not based on state practice but a coherent and resolute understanding of Article 3. The *Soering*-rationale furthermore resulted from a *bona fide* interpretation of the CCPR, the American Convention on Human Rights, and in particular the Convention Against Torture (and its Article 3). As the Court routinely emphasizes, the prohibition of ill-treatment and not merely of torture does not allow for any circumvention on the basis for security-related reasons regardless of state interests. The community takes a step back behind the individual even although governments indeed try to justify expulsions of individuals posing a risk to the community: A clear-cut example of court-ordered state practice?

In any case, the ECtHR's rigorous understanding of the absoluteness of Article 3 has led to increasing criticism in recent years when it comes to the question of how to deal with Islamist radicals, terrorist-suspects, criminals,

---

[48] *Ahmed v Austria*, *supra* note 44, para 46 (emphasis added).

[49] *Ibid.*, para 41.

[50] *X against Austria and Yugoslavia*, *supra* note 38, at 328.

[51] That *Soering* would amount to a de facto right to asylum was already argued in 1990 and thus before the pertinent decisions discussed above were rendered, see Einarsen, *supra* note 39.

and refugees in general (*i.e.* regardless of any convictions). In the United Kingdom, one of the countries most affected by this jurisprudence and interim measures halting deportations, prominent voices have openly been calling for a re-assessment of its ECHR membership.[52]

It remains to be seen how the ECtHR will deal with the increase of deportations to instable, oppressive, or even war-torn countries. At the centre of the debate stands the safety in Afghanistan. After the EU signed an agreement with the Afghan government, in particular Germany, Austria, or Sweden increased the numbers of deportations.[53] It remains to be seen how the ECtHR will deal with these cases. The heart of the dispute is the threshold as to what exactly constitutes a 'serious risk' of being subjected to ill-treatment. If the ECtHR indeed rules against such deportations, this could result in increasing internal pressure to question or even defy the ECHR within those states most severely affected by the refugee crisis. While a withdrawal of one or even several states does not seem likely at this point, more and more calls to ignore its decisions by simply abstaining from execution could ultimately turn into a significant challenge to the ECHR as a whole and the ECtHR's legitimacy in particular.

VI. The Margin of Appreciation Doctrine

The ECtHR's resoluteness in deportation cases also stands in stark contrast to its general approach in sensitive areas. As epitomized by the margin of appreciation doctrine, the ECtHR is careful to avoid an overextension of its powers: After all, the various justifications and explanations for the ECtHR's reluctance to impose (too) far-reaching restrictions in sensitive matters – the legitimate regulatory role of democratic governments, the political nature

---

[52] Martin Beckford, 'European Court of Human Rights blocks more deportations from UK than any other country' *The Telegraph* (London, 1 May 2012) <www.telegraph.co.uk/news/uknews/law-and-order/9239417/European-Court-of-Human-Rights-blocks-more-deportations-from-UK-than-any-other-country.html> accessed 20 July 2017.

[53] Tommy Wilkes, 'Afghans deported from Europe arrive home, to war and unemployment' *Reuters* (Kabul, 31 March 2017) <www.reuters.com/article/us-afghanistan-refugees-idUSKBN1721VJ> accessed 20 July 2017; see also Maeve McClenaghan, 'Refugee crisis: Afghanistan ruled safe enough to deport asylum-seekers from UK' *Independent* (London, 3 March 2016) <www.independent.co.uk/news/uk/home-news/refugee-crisis-afghanistan-ruled-safe-enough-to-deport-asylum-seekers-from-uk-a6910246.html> accessed 20 July 2017.

of many disputes, the subsidiarity principle, its relationship with domestic courts of all instances and the resulting institutional comity, or the differing moral values and sentiments in the various ECHR member states[54] – arguably ultimately all stem from the ECtHR's concern over compliance. The Court, just like any other international body,[55] fears non-compliance, thus imposing self-restraint so as to save its jurisprudential weight for areas where it matters the most and where no ample room for deliberations can be left open. If the Court also showed less restraint with respect to provisions explicitly containing a restrictive clause, its legitimacy could be severely threatened.

A. Muslim Headwear

The veil ban and other types of regulating Muslim headwear discussed or implemented in a number of European countries is a case in point. Governments in states like Austria, Germany, France, Belgium, Sweden, or the Netherlands are confronted with an increasingly nervous electorate due to the growing size of Muslim minorities and even the prospect of Islamization. These fears and pressures to take action are further exacerbated by more extremist and populist opposition groups and parties waiting in the wings. Moderate parties are thus desperate to impose clearly visible measures and avoid the impression of helplessness or idly standing by: In this sense, they have often reverted to *Symbolpolitik*, *i.e.* taking measures merely to show that 'something is being done' in light of the seeming impossibility to address pressing issues at their core – after all, a sufficiently promising formula to ensure the integration of newly-arriving or already-present Muslim communities is still lacking and will perhaps never be found. Europe is trying to escape the downward spiral of increasing mutual alienation between Non-Muslims and Muslims.

---

[54] *Cf.* Steven Greer, *The Margin of Appreciation: Interpretation and Discretion under the European Convention on Human Rights* (2000); Dominic McGoldrick, 'A Defence of the Margin of Appreciation and an Argument for its Application by the Human Rights Committee' (2016) 65 International and Comparative Law Quarterly 21.

[55] As the issue of non-adherence to Security Council 1267 smart sanctions regime due to its failure to meet generally required due process standards has shown, even the Security Council is not immune from concerns over the lawfulness and thus the legitimacy of its decisions, see the second annual report of the Special Rapporteur Ben Emmerson, see 'Promotion and Protection of Human Rights and Fundamental Freedoms While Countering Terrorism: Note by the Secretary General' (26 September 2012) UN Doc A/67/396, para 20: 'Experience has shown that the absence of an independent judicial review mechanism at the United Nations level has seriously undermined the effectiveness and the perceived legitimacy of the regime.'

Religious symbols like the burqa, the niqab, or the simple headscarf have thereby become central components of the debate on the relationship between the construed notions of 'us' and 'them', *i.e.* Europe and Islam and the general debate over somewhat simplifying questions such as whether 'Islam is part of Europe' and attempts to formulate a 'moderate', quasi-enlightened, softened version compatible with European values at its core.

While the veil ban and other types of regulating Islamic female headwear involve a number of human rights, first and foremost the right to religious freedom and the prohibition of discrimination,[56] the ECtHR seems to have been well aware of its limited impact and role in this area.

In *Dahlab*, it weighed 'the right of a teacher to manifest her religion [by wearing a headscarf] against the need to protect pupils by preserving religious harmony' and held that

> having regard, above all, to the tender age of the children for whom the applicant was responsible as a representative of the State, the Geneva authorities did not exceed their margin of appreciation.[57]

The ECtHR adopted a similar reasoning when holding that the prohibition to wear a headscarf on the premises Turkish medical school was compatible with Article 9 in *Sahin*:

> In delimiting the extent of the margin of appreciation in the present case, the Court must have regard to what is at stake, namely the need to protect the rights and freedoms of others, to preserve public order and to secure civil peace and true religious pluralism, which is vital to the survival of a democratic society.[58]

For some time it seemed that the ECtHR would not deem broad prohibitions to wear a certain religious dress in public (and thus not only when exercising certain functions or inside of certain places) as compatible with Article 9: After the applicants in *Ahmet Arslan and Others v Turkey* were fined for wearing the characteristic clothing of their group, *i.e.* a turban, salvar (knee-length pants) and a tunic in the streets of Ankara, the ECtHR limited

---

[56] Sally Pei, 'Unveiling Inequality: Burqa Bans and Nondiscrimination Jurisprudence at the European Court of Human Rights' (2013) 122 The Yale Law Journal 1089.

[57] *Dahlab v Switzerland*, ECtHR, Application No 42393/98, Judgment of 15 February 2001.

[58] *Case of Leyla Şahin v Turkey*, ECtHR, Application No 44774/98, Judgment of 10 November 2005, para 110.

the margin of appreciation since the applicants were common people not working on behalf of a state or exercising any official competences.[59]

While one could have expected that the ECtHR would stick to this approach in connection with the prohibition to wear a full-face veil (while formally neutral, this measure effectively addressed the niqab) in public, it reverted to a wide margin of appreciation in *S.A.S. v France*. Taking into account the French government's argumentation concerning public safety and guaranteeing 'the conditions of living together' as a 'choice of society', the Court concluded that it had

> a duty to exercise a degree of restraint in its review of Convention compliance, since such review will lead it to assess a balance that has been struck by means of a democratic process within the society in question.[60]

In other words: The wide margin of appreciation granted to France in light of its emphasis on the need to protect social interaction and the need to be able to grasp facial expressions led the Court to acknowledge the limits of its jurisprudential powers.

One can only wonder what would have happened had the ECtHR ruled against the niqab ban. It may well be the case that the court was reluctant to risk its legitimacy in such a sensitive area by explicitly noting its acceptance of the French government's line of argumentation. Finding a violation of the ECHR would have triggered further criticism from populist or even moderate political forces within the respective state. Once again, the court seemed eager to preserve its powers for clear-cut cases and provisions.

B. The State of Emergency

The ECtHR's approach to declarations of a state of emergency is an even clearer example of the necessity to exercise self-restraint whenever vital issues are at stake. Numerous writers have noted the limits of the observance of international law if a state 'deems its highest political interests to be in jeopardy' or even amid fears concerning its survival.[61]

---

[59] *Ahmet Arslan and Others v Turkey*, ECtHR, Application No 41135/98, Judgment of 23 February 2010.

[60] *Case of S.A.S. v France*, ECtHR, Application No 43835/11, Judgment of 1 July 2014, para 154. See also *Belcacemi and Oussar v Belgium*, ECtHR, Application No 37798/13, Judgment of 11 July 2017, and *Dakir v. Belgium*, ECtHR, Application No 4619/12, Judgment of 11 July 2017.

[61] See, *e.g.*, Lassa Oppenheim, *The Future of International Law* (1921) 58.

Starting with *Lawless*, the court has always accepted the determination of the respective government concerning the existence of a state of emergency.[62] In this regard, one must not forget that a state of emergency may not be necessarily invoked to safeguard the life of a nation as a whole but merely that of the respective government.

An extended state of emergency may turn the relationship between norm and exception upside down. Thus, General Comment No 29 on Article 4 of the International Covenant on Civil and Political Rights holds that re-establishing 'a state of normalcy where full respect for the Covenant can again be secured' needs to be the 'predominant objective' of the state and that such measures had to be 'of an exceptional and temporary nature.'[63] At the same time, the very nature of terrorist threats and their non-foreseeability has led the ECtHR to allow extended periods of a state of emergency.[64] In *A and Others v UK* it also accepted the possibility of a pre-emptive state of emergency: 'Since the purpose of Article 15 is to permit States to take derogating measures to protect their populations from future risks.'[65]

Understandable as this line of reasoning may be, given the need to counter terrorist threats and in light of the natural limits of the ECtHR's influence in such vital areas, its self-restraint when it comes to a government's assessment of a state of emergency comes at the high price of proneness to abuse. Non-representative, oppressive, or what may be called illiberal democratic

---

[62] In *the Greek case*, however, the Commission rejected the state of emergency declared by the military junta after its overthrow because 'a displacement of the lawful Government by force of arms by the Communists and their allies' was not imminent and there was no 'threat, imminent in that it would be realised before or soon after the May elections, of such political instability and disorder that the organised life of the community could not be carried on', see *The Greek Case*, European Commission of Human Rights, Application No 3321/67, 3322/67, 3323/67, 3344/67, Report of the Sub-Commission, Volume I, Part 1, <http://hudoc.echr.coe.int/app/conversion/pdf/?library=ECHR&id=001-73020&filename=001-73020.pdf> accessed 20 July 2017, paras 119, 124.

[63] Human Rights Committee, 'CCPR General Comment No. 29: Article 4: Derogations during a State of Emergency', (24 August 2001) UN Doc CCPR/C/21/Rev.1/Add.11, para 2; the ECtHR has quoted this passage in *A and Others v The United Kingdom*, ECtHR, Application No 3455/05, Judgment of 19 February 2009, para 110.

[64] *Gary Marshall v United Kingdom*, ECtHR, Application No 41571/98, Decision of 10 July 2001.

[65] *A and Others v The United Kingdom*, supra note 62, para 177.

governments[66] may invoke Article 15 to solidify and fortify their power. The less a government is based on the acceptance of the general population, the more it will need to rely on brute force and the restriction of general freedoms.[67] Even governments legitimated by a majority or at least a substantial percentage of votes may nevertheless still impose harsh measures in order to crackdown the opposition.

The question remains as to what the impact of a potential rejection of a state's invocation of the state of emergency may be. For one, such a determination would send a powerful signal not only to the government but also to all other members to the ECHR. In this sense, the margin of appreciation should arguably be as narrow as possible. If the purpose the ECHR 'is to preclude the exercise of arbitrary power', one can only agree with the conclusion of Oren Gross and Fionnuala Ní Aoláin that

> [i]n times of national emergency, when the danger of arbitrary power being used is very much a real one and the specter of authoritarianism looms large, it falls to the supranational Court to exercise special protection of the rights protected under the European Convention. Rather than being content with playing a supporting, subsidiary role to that played by the states parties themselves in protecting human rights, the Court must assume a primary responsibility for such protection. In order to fulfil its responsibility the Court must reject latitudinarian constructions of the margin of appreciation doctrine.[68]

VII. Conclusion

The ECtHR enjoys sufficient legitimacy to set generally binding accepted standards and ultimately modify the obligations contained in the ECHR – often way beyond their original intent and scope. Recent developments nevertheless darken the outlook for this success story. Be it the refugee

---

[66] See Fareed Zakaria, 'The Rise of Illiberal Democracy' *Foreign Affairs* (November/December 1997) <www.foreignaffairs.com/articles/1997-11-01/rise-illiberal-democracy> accessed 20 July 2017.

[67] *Cf.* Hannah Arendt, *On Violence* (1970).

[68] Oren Gross and Fionnuala Ní Aoláin, 'From Discretion to Scrutiny: Revisiting the Application of the Margin of Appreciation Doctrine in the Context of Article 15 of the European Convention on Human Rights' (2001) 23(3) Human Rights Quarterly 625, 649.

crisis, the integration of and interaction with Muslim minorities along with the rise of populist movements, or the upheavals in Turkey: The ECtHR oscillates between the threat of becoming irrelevant and acting as a change agent (what some term judicial activism). In so doing, it has exercised considerable restraint in highly sensitive matters such as the regulation of Muslim headwear or invocations of the state of emergency.

At the same time, the ECtHR has flexed its jurisprudential muscles by adopting a rigorous interpretation of Article 3 ECHR in connection with expulsion or deportation cases by extending the non-refoulement principle not only if there is a serious risk of torture but also of inhumane or even mere degrading treatment. It has thereby effectively introduced a de-facto right to asylum going beyond the definition of a refugee contained in the 1951 Geneva Convention and severely restricted the freedom of states to control the entry to and stay of foreigners.

It remains to be seen whether this high standard will hold. From today's perspective, it seems as if Europe and the ECtHR are about to face their most severe challenges in recent history. One can only hope that we are about to look back on such sorrows with a grin soon enough.

On the Practice of Subsequent Practice

Uniformity in Model Laws as Subsequent Practice under Article 31 of Vienna Convention on the Law of Treaties

Ilias Bantekas[*]

I. Introduction

The life and quality of a treaty is by no means a foregone conclusion. In the past, where treaties were few and apart, member states either strove to fortify them or took every possible action to destroy them. This is no longer the case, as treaties, particularly of a multilateral character, affect far more actors than the foreign offices that participate in their drafting, signature and ratification. There is nowadays a plethora of direct and indirect stakeholders that have an interest in the functioning of a treaty. Specialized NGOs, victim groups, those affected by the measures adopted in a treaty, corporations, academics and other actors may enter into conduct that ultimately greases the wheels of state practice. This may include public interest litigation, scholarly writings, petitions to national parliaments, public protests and many others. Hence, a state may eventually be forced to amend its original stance *vis-à-vis* certain strands of the treaty in question. In equal measure, sustained transnational judicial dialogue, as well as a pronouncement of an international tribunal, may alter the course of state practice in one way or another.[1]

Increasingly, states resort to forms of international agreement other than treaties.[2] This includes memoranda of understanding (MoU), model laws and

---

[*] Professor of Law, Brunel and Northwestern (HBKU) Universities and independent arbitrator.

[1] See Ronald J Krotoszynski, '"I'd like to Teach the World to Sing (In Perfect Harmony)": International Judicial Dialogue and the Muses – Reflections on the Perils and the Promise of International Judicial Dialogue' (2006) 104 Michigan Law Review 1321; Philip M Moremen, 'National Court Decisions as State Practice: A Transnational Judicial Dialogue?' (2006) 32 North Carolina Journal of International Law and Commercial Regulation 259.

[2] See Ramses A Wessel, 'Informal International Law-Making as a New Form of World Legislation?' (2011) 8 International Organizations Law Review 253.

private agreements and these may encompass only states as parties, as well as states alongside non-state entities, such as inter-governmental organizations and private actors, such as investors. Hence, a particular subject matter may not be covered by a treaty this does not in any way mean that its inter-state regulation is no less significant or that states do not take the 'obligations' contained in the instrument under consideration seriously. In practice, model laws require the same degree of involvement as ordinary treaties and UNCITRAL or the OECD retain extensive *travaux preparatoires*, concluded over many rounds and years of debates. This clearly shows that states participating in the deliberation of model laws view them no less seriously than treaties. As this article goes on to demonstrate, the concept of 'uniformity' is the cornerstone underlying model laws and by and large conforms, *mutatis mutandis* to the concept of 'subsequent practice' as enshrined in Article 31(1)(b) of the Vienna Convention on the Law of Treaties. To the degree, therefore, that a model law is domesticated, whether through incorporation or transformation, in several legal orders and all such orders contribute to a sustained transnational judicial dialogue, which is itself predicated and reinforced by transnational arbitral tribunals, this corresponds to a subsequent practice that renders the model law uniform across all states. Such uniformity is hard to detect in respect of most multilateral treaties, for several reasons. Although it is beyond the scope of this article, it is worth noting that the vast majority of multilateral treaties generate little domestic case law, a limited amount of jurisprudence from international courts and tribunals and hence the emergence of a sustained transnational or international judicial dialogue is difficult. Model laws on the other hand provide exactly the opposite type of state practice, but they are not ordinarily the subject matter before treaty or UNSC-based international courts and tribunals, although some of the provisions of the Model Law have been the subject matter, by analogy, of the CISG Advisory Council (a quasi-judicial international mechanism), which is examined at the end of this article. However, in this article international arbitral tribunals and domestic courts dealing with international issues are treated as producing the same outcomes as an international court or tribunal.

Article 2A of the UNCITRAL Model Law on International Commercial Arbitration (Model Law) provides that:

(1) In the interpretation of this Law, regard is to be had to its international origin and to the need to promote uniformity in its application and the observance of good faith.

(2) Questions concerning matters governed by this Law which are not expressly settled in it are to be settled in conformity with the general principles on which this Law is based.[3]

Article 2A concerns the interpretation of the Model Law by domestic courts and executive bodies. Given that the Model Law is not a treaty it is not straightforward that treaty-based interpretation rules are directly applicable. At the same time, given its purpose and international outlook, any construction premised solely on domestic law would defeat its *raison d'etre* (*i.e.* uniformity), despite the fact that the aim of UNCITRAL is for states to adopt the Model Law as part of their domestic law. While it is clear that Article 2A has been modeled after Article 7 of the International Convention on Sale of Goods (CISG),[4] the fact that the latter is a treaty and its focus is solely on international sales militates against an absolute reliance on that provision and its pertinent commentaries in order to construe Article 2A, although some degree of analogy is no doubt inevitable. The assumption of this author is that the Model Law produces legal effects that are similar to treaties; this extends beyond Model Law states. This conclusion is justified by the fact that if one or more Model Law states fulfill the 'obligations' emanating therefrom, the very adoption of the Model Law by other states gives rise to a legitimate expectation[5] (and reciprocity) that the same 'obligations' will be honored by them also. The absence of any form of persistent objection[6]

---

[3] Art 2A UNCITRAL Model Law on International Commercial Arbitration 1985, with amendments as adopted in 2006 (2008) <www.uncitral.org/pdf/english/texts/arbitration/ml-arb/07-86998_Ebook.pdf> accessed 21 July 2017.

[4] This later inspired Art 3 UNCITRAL Model Law on Electronic Commerce 1996 (1999) <www.uncitral.org/pdf/english/texts/electcom/05-89450_Ebook.pdf> accessed 21 July 2017; Art 8 UNCITRAL Model Law on Cross-Border Insolvency 1997 (2014) <www.uncitral.org/pdf/english/texts/insolven/1997-Model-Law-Insol-2013-Guide-Enactment-e.pdf> accessed 21 July 2017; Art 4 UNCITRAL Model Law on Electronic Signatures 2001 (2002) <www.uncitral.org/pdf/english/texts/electcom/ml-elecsig-e.pdf> accessed 21 July 2017; Art 2 UNCITRAL Model Law on International Commercial Conciliation 2002 (2004) <www.uncitral.org/pdf/english/texts/arbitration/ml-conc/03-90953_Ebook.pdf> accessed 21 July 2017.

[5] This may be defined as 'damage or prejudice incurred by reliance on conduct or statements made by competent authorities'. This restrictive estoppel is consistent with general practice and academic writings. See Thomas Cottier and Jörg P Müller, 'Estoppel' in Rüdiger Wolfrum (ed), *Max Planck Encyclopedia of Public International Law*, vol III (2012) 671, para 3.

[6] Jonathan I Charney, 'The Persistent Objector Rule and the Development of Customary International Law' (1986) 56 British Yearbook of International Law 1.

entails acquiescence in respect of these 'obligations' and raises legitimate promissory estoppel claims by the compliant state(s).[7]

Paragraph 1 of Article 2A introduces three overarching principles upon which any construction of the Model Law should be predicated or that in any event should be taken into consideration. These principles are: (a) the Model Law's international origin; (b) the promotion of uniformity and; (c) good faith. Although these may to a lesser or larger degree constitute substantive principles, here they are meant solely as aids of construction or interpretative tools. Paragraph 2 is a gap-filling (residual) provision which allows courts and tribunals to apply other general principles but fails to provide further information. Whatever their content their residual character necessitates that they are consistent with the three principles set out in paragraph 1 of Article 2A.

The article will proceed to analyze Article 2A through the methodology of a commentary so as to provide the reader with a more holistic view of the subject matter of this article and its connection with the theme of the special issue.

II. Travaux Préparatoires and Background

Article 2A was first adopted in 2006 and as already noted was inspired and modelled after Article 7 CISG in an attempt to promote and enhance the uniformity of the Model Law.[8] Despite its importance, one finds very little discussion in the 2006 *travaux*,[9] and hence the assumption must have been that the principles enunciated in Article 2A were either self-evident or that they were already settled (to a larger or lesser degree) on the basis of judicial and arbitral pronouncements in the context of Article 7 CISG; or that they

---

[7] *Case Concerning the Temple of Preah Vihear* (*Cambodia v Thailand*) (Merits) [1962] ICJ 101, 143-144 (Judgment of 26 May, Dissenting Opinion of Sir Percy Spencer).

[8] The promotion of uniformity was high on the agenda, see UNGA, 'Draft Resolution, Revised Articles of the Model Law on International Commercial Arbitration of the United Nations Commission on International Trade Law, and the Recommendation Regarding the Interpretation of Article II, Paragraph 2, and Article VII, Paragraph 1, of the Convention on the Recognition and Enforcement of Foreign Arbitral Awards, done at New York, 10 June 1958' (25 October 2006) UN Doc A/C.6/61/L.8, para 1.

[9] UNGA, 'Report of the United Nations Commission on International Trade Law on the work of its thirty-ninth session' (2006) UN Doc A/61/17, paras 174-175.

were discernible in general international law. This conclusion is justified by the fact that unification was already on the agenda since the first draft of the Model Law in the mid-1980s[10] and hence was not an innovation of the 2006 revision. Indeed, one of the key arguments behind the launch of the Model Law in 1985 was the desire to revise the 1958 New York Convention on the Recognition and Enforcement of Foreign Arbitral Awards, but such a task seemed formidable and the prospect of a model law was much more attractive.[11] The idea of addressing discrepancies among jurisdictions in the application and interpretation of the New York Convention resurfaced in the 2006 discussions leading to the revision of pertinent provisions of the Model Law. Although discussed in the context of other provisions, the issue of uniformity was raised in relation to the written form of the arbitration agreement in Article II(2) of the New York Convention with a view to inserting corresponding references in the Model Law.[12] This led to the adoption of a wholly revised provision (Article 7) on the written form of the arbitration agreement and a new paragraph 2 in respect of Article 35.

III. Paragraph 1

Paragraph 1 concerns the interpretation of the Model Law by judges and executive bodies. It embodies three important concepts, namely: (a) aids of interpretation; (b) the notion of uniformity in the application of the Model Law, as opposed to mere uniformity in its incorporation or transformation

---

[10] UNGA Res 40/72 (11 December 1985) UN Doc A/RES/40/72. See also Aron Broches, 'The 1985 UNCITRAL Model Law on International Commercial Arbitration: An Exercise in International Legislation' (1987) 18 Netherlands Yearbook of International Law 3.

[11] UNGA, 'Report of the Secretary-General: Study on the Application and Interpretation of the Convention on the Recognition and Enforcement of Foreign Arbitral Awards (New York, 1958)' (20 April 1979) UN Doc A/CN.9/168.

[12] See UNCITRAL, 'Settlement of Commercial Disputes, Preparation of Uniform Provisions on Written Form of Arbitration Agreements, Article II(2) of the Convention on the Recognition and Enforcement of Foreign Arbitral Awards (New York, 1958), Note by the Secretariat' (14 December 2005) UN Doc A/CN.9/WG.II/WP.139; UNCITRAL, 'Settlement of Commercial Disputes, Preparation of Uniform Provisions on Written Form of Arbitration Agreements, Proposal by the Mexican Delegation' (20 April 2005) UN Doc A/CN.9/WG.II/WP.137; UNCITRAL, 'Settlement of Commercial Disputes, Preparation of a Model Legislative Provision on Written Form for the Arbitration Agreement, Note by the Secretariat' (19 July 2005) UN Doc A/CN.9/WG.II/WP.136.

in the domestic sphere[13] and; (c) the observance of good faith by all those applying the Model Law. As will be demonstrated, all of these concepts are inextricably linked and one cannot be understood or construed without reference to all the others.

A. 'Interpretation of this Law'

Paragraph 1 of Article 2A is addressed to all those entities or persons that are called upon to apply the Model Law in the domestic sphere. This includes judges as well as administrative entities, in addition to quasi-judicial bodies such as ombudspersons.[14] Given that the Model Law is not a treaty – and hence does not require incorporation or transformation into domestic law – nor is there an expectation that states adapt it verbatim into their legal systems, reference to 'this Law' means the statute that corresponds to the adaptation of the Model Law into the domestic sphere. However, as we shall see in a subsequent section, the internationalist approach to the Model Law ultimately demands that its fundamental principles override any conflicting domestic provisions.

Even so, it is not clear from the wording of Article 2A whether the various principles enunciated therein constitute rules, aids (tools) or objectives of interpretation. This is an important observation because if they are classified as rules (or canons) of interpretation, in the sense of Articles 31-33 VCLT, local courts must construe the domestic arbitration statute first and foremost on the basis of the pertinent rules/principles. If on the other hand, they are viewed as mere aids or tools, the courts may rely upon them, but their decision will not suffer from any irregularity should they choose to ignore them in favor of other rules of construction imposed or made available under domestic law. The Explanatory Note of the UNCITRAL Secretariat to the 2006 version of the Model Law stipulates that Article 2A is meant, among

---

[13] The examination of incorporation or transformation is not pertinent in the context of the Model Law because its adoption does not raise the constitutional issues associated with the reception of treaties into the domestic sphere, see Christoph H Schreuer, 'The Interpretation of Treaties by Domestic Courts' (1971) 45 British Yearbook of International Law 255; Pierre-Marie Dupuy, 'International Law and Domestic (Municipal) Law' in Rüdiger Wolfrum (ed), *Max Planck Encyclopedia of Public International Law*, vol V (2012) 836.

[14] Art 2A is addressed to arbitrators only to the degree that they are called upon to interpret the Model Law or where it constitutes the governing law of the parties' agreement.

others 'to facilitate interpretation',[15] thus clearly suggesting that the principles constitute aids or tools, as opposed to rules of interpretation. This result is also confirmed by those domestic statutes that are predicated on the Model Law, such as Sections 8(1) and (2) of the 2010 Irish Arbitration Act, which refer to the *travaux* of the Model Law as a possible aid to its interpretation. By extension, given the international origin of the Model Law, the customary principles of interpretation in Articles 31 and 32 VCLT, otherwise reserved for treaties, constitute useful aids of interpretation, namely the teleological (object and purpose) and supplementary (*travaux*) approaches.[16]

It is useful to spell out those principles enunciated in Article 2A of the Model Law which serve as aids of interpretation. These are: (a) the international origin of the Model Law; (b) the promotion of uniformity and; (c) the observance of good faith. These principles serve a dual role. On the one hand they are interpretative tools whereas on the other they clearly also constitute objectives or goals to which Model Law nations should strive.

It should be emphasized that because the Model Law is not a treaty, Article 2A does not impose an autonomous interpretation. Treaties are self-contained systems,[17] save where they specifically refer to external means and sources of interpretation – or where their subject matter is restricted by customary law or *jus cogens*. The legal nature of the Model Law, however, entails that in construing questions arising from its application recourse may be had to sources and principles that are external to it, such as treaties, general principles, *lex mercatoria* and domestic law.[18]

Finally, one should assess the significance of the practice of Model Law states by which they choose not to incorporate Article 2A in their arbitral

---

[15] UNCITRAL Model Law on International Commercial Arbitration 1985, with amendments as adopted in 2006 (2008) <http://www.uncitral.org/pdf/english/texts/arbitration/ml-arb/07-86998_Ebook.pdf> accessed 21 July 2017, at 24, para 4.

[16] According to Bachand this is justified by the fact that the Model Law is a transnational instrument requiring an 'internationalist interpretative approach'. Frédéric Bachand, 'Judicial Internationalism and the Interpretation of the Model Law: Reflections on Some Aspects of Article 2A' in Frédéric Bachand and Fabien Gélinas (eds), *The UNCITRAL Model Law After 25 Years: Global Perspectives on International Commercial Arbitration* (2013) 235, 249.

[17] As is the case with Art 7 United Nations Convention on Contracts for the International Sale of Goods (CIGS), 11 April 1980, 1489 UNTS 3.

[18] See Martin Gebauer, 'Uniform Law, General Principles and Autonomous Interpretation' (2000) 5 Uniform Law Review 683.

statutes, as opposed to those that do.[19] By the end of 2015, only sixteen Model Law states had incorporated Article 2A in their arbitral laws (as well as several states in the USA and Australia). Even so, the absence of incorporation should not be viewed as determinative of a state's rejection of the aids and principles contained in Article 2A. For one thing, many states may not find it expedient to amend their arbitral statutes in the aftermath of the 2006 revision of the Model Law. Secondly, the practice of the courts of industrialized nations, whether Model Law adherents or not, demonstrates a strong inclination towards internationalization and uniformity. It is assumed, therefore, that unless a state expressly rejects the principles and aids contained in Article 2A these are presumed to apply in its application and interpretation of the Model Law.

B. Promotion of Uniformity

The promotion of uniformity is both an aid to interpretation of the Model Law as well as an underlying principle. Indeed, the role and function of uniformity is to enhance certainty, but Article 2A does not put forward a clear methodology by which to achieve such uniformity. Uniformity has been defined as the 'varying degree of similar effects on a legal phenomenon across boundaries of different jurisdictions resulting from the application of deliberate efforts to create specific shared rules in some form'.[20] Before we go on to examine the various forms and varieties of uniformity, it is appropriate to ascertain the sources from which it may emanate: (a) model or uniform laws; (b) principles declared by NGOs, such as the UNIDROIT Principles of International Commercial Contracts;[21] (c) standard contract terms, such

---

[19] As is the case, for example, with Sec 9 Hong Kong Arbitration Ordinance (HKAO); Art 2 Slovenian Arbitration Law.

[20] Camilla Baasch Andersen, 'Defining Uniformity in Law' (2007) 12 Uniform Law Review 5.

[21] See Michael J Bonell, 'Unification of Law by Non-Legislative Means: The UNIDROIT Draft Principles for International Commercial Contracts' (1992) 40 American Journal of Comparative Law 617; Robert Ashby Pate, 'The Future of Harmonization: Soft Law Instruments and the Principled Advance of International Lawmaking' (2010) 13 Touro International Law Review 142. The UNIDROIT Principles have been identified by several domestic courts and arbitral tribunals, in CISG-related disputes, to constitute general principles under Art 7(2) CISG, see UNCITRAL, 'Digest of Case Law on the United Nations Convention on Contracts for the International Sale of Goods' (2012) <www.uncitral.org/pdf/english/clout/CISG-digest-2012-e.pdf> accessed 21 July 2017, at 46.

as those adopted by FIDIC in relation to construction and; (d) multilateral treaties, such as CISG and the New York Convention.[22]

Before we explore the type of uniformity that is envisaged, or is otherwise more appropriate, in respect of the Model Law, it is useful to set out the types of uniformity that are generally available. At the apex one finds *textual* or *absolute* uniformity, the aim of which is to 'transplant' the instrument in question verbatim in the legal system of the participating or member states.[23] This type of uniformity is exceptional and difficult to implement in practice. It is demanded in respect of EU Regulations and is envisaged (but by no means demanded) in the case of most treaties (bilateral and multilateral), save where member states are offered the possibility of extensive reservations – which cannot, however, violate the instrument's object and purpose.[24] Whereas in the EU context textual uniformity is viable because of the large cultural, economic and legal convergence,[25] it is doomed to failure in situations where such convergence is absent among a group of states, even if ultimately they

---

[22] The situation with treaties is somewhat different because parties are obliged to adapt the treaty into their domestic law without significant changes. Even if reservations are allowed these must not be in conflict with the treaty's object and purpose, see Art 19 Vienna Convention on the Law of Treaties, 23 May 1969, 1155 UNTS 331. This is not tantamount to textual uniformity because, unless otherwise stated, states are allowed to implement treaties into their domestic law in accordance with existing legal rules and principles.

[23] An extensive literature regarding the textual interpretation of CISG under Art 7 therefore exists, see Larry A DiMatteo, *International Sales Law: A Global Challenge* (2016) 66ff; Peter Schlechtriem and Ingeborg Schwenzer (eds), *Commentary on the UN Convention on the International Sale of Goods (CISG)* (2nd edn 2005).

[24] See Harry M Flechtner, 'The Several Texts of the CISG in a Decentralized System: Observations on Translations, Reservations and Other Challenges to the Uniformity Principle in Article 7(1)' (1998) 17 Journal of Law and Commerce 187.

[25] Even so, in the field of criminal law, the principle of 'mutual recognition' was not based on textual uniformity. Para 8 of the Vienna Action Plan rejected the notion of procedural criminal law harmonisation and unification ideology by proclaiming that the aim of the member states was not to create 'a common territory where uniform detection and investigation procedures would be applicable to all law enforcement agencies in Europe in the handling of security matters', see Action Plan of the Council and the Commission on how best to implement the provisions of the Treaty of Amsterdam on an area of freedom, security and justice - Text adopted by the Justice and Home Affairs Council of 3 December 1998 [1999] OJ C19/1. This was achieved through *approximation*, which foresaw as a starting point the gradual adoption of common definitions for a set of core

'transplant' the text of the agreement verbatim in their domestic laws.[26] Textual uniformity was never envisaged or pursued in respect of the Model Law as this would not only have dissuaded many states from adopting it, but would have been practically impossible in practice as it would have required a wholesale amendment of fundamental areas of law, such as contract and civil procedure. Such strict uniformity is not desirable in the context of the Model Law.

Below textual uniformity one encounters *applied* uniformity. The intention here is not to achieve word-by-word textual correspondence across jurisdictions, but rather to develop a uniform understanding and a uniform interpretation of the text/rules in question.[27] In this manner, there is no requirement that texts actually meet or correspond linguistically. Applied uniformity is indeed the hallmark of Article 7(1) CISG.[28] In the process of achieving applied uniformity there is typically a harmonization of values and norms – this also arises as an outcome from a sustained process of applied uniformity.

Another type of uniformity is so-called *functional* uniformity or *functional similarity*. Here, the objective is to create similar rules across jurisdictions, even in the absence of a general cross-border framework of applied uniformity in order to achieve a functional similarity of substantive or procedural trade rules, which ultimately leads to harmonization. Functional uniformity is therefore a short-cut hybrid between applied and textual uniformity.[29]

---

offences bearing a transnational nature, see Anne Weyembergh, 'Approximation of Criminal Laws, the Constitutional Treaty and the Hague Programme' (2005) 42 Common Market Law Review 1567.

[26] See Alan Watson, *Legal Transplants: An Approach to Comparative Law* (2nd edn 1993).

[27] Schlechtriem and Schwenzer, *supra* note 23, at 6.

[28] There exists an extensive jurisprudence on Art 7(1) CISG and despite the fact that its wording is very close to that of Art 2A of the Model Law – and in fact the latter was inspired by the former – we shall avoid replicating or applying this body of law in order to analyse Art 2A of the Model Law. This approach is justified for several reasons. Firstly, CISG is a treaty (subject to many reservations), whereas the Model Law is not. Secondly, the CISG concerns substantive rules where the focus of the Model Law is largely on rules of civil procedure. This, of course, is not impediment to applying CISG case law *mutatis mutandis* to Art 2A of the Model Law, see UNCITRAL, 'Digest of Case Law on CISG', *supra* note 21, 42ff.

[29] Several commentators refer to it also as 'harmonisation', see Andersen, *supra* note 20, at 28.

Article 2A(1) of the Model Law expressly refers to applied ('application') uniformity, although in some cases functional similarity may have to be introduced until applied uniformity has been fully and universally achieved. By way of illustration, legal systems that do not provide for an equivalent of interim measure requests by arbitral tribunals cannot be expected to develop a pertinent culture overnight and hence the availability of interim measures must be introduced as a first step.

Having established the preferred test/method for uniformity, one must next adopt an appropriate methodology. However, this process cannot be undertaken (only) unilaterally, but in conjunction with other Model Law states. Article 2A offers no assistance in this respect. Given that the Model Law is predicated on respect for the diversity of legal cultures and legal principles (*e.g.* as to the definition of contract or agreement, the choice of public policy rules, or in respect of contractual gap-filling by the courts among others) functional uniformity is required in respect of fundamental principles underlying the operation of international commercial arbitration. An indicative example is the removal of the *Diwan* (an executive body which among others passed judgment on the validity of the arbitration clause) from the arbitral process in the 2012 Saudi Arbitration Law.[30] Thereafter, applied uniformity requires the adoption of a particular culture that is not necessarily dependent on reciprocity – in fact reciprocity may be viewed as alien to applied uniformity.[31] Rather, the courts and executive must assume an internationalist view point that is consistent with the prevailing practice in the courts of other jurisdictions as well as the practice of arbitral tribunals themselves. Although this may be seen as an arduous task, relevant trends and practices are nowadays easily accessible through databases such as CLOUT, the UNCITRAL Digest of Case Law or the Yearbook of International Commercial Arbitration and in any event, academic writings are abundant on legal aspects of the Model Law.

C. 'International Origin'

The 'international origin' of the Model Law is inextricably linked to the promotion of its uniform application. This is justified on account of several

---

[30] For an analysis of the role of the *Diwan* prior to the 2012 Law, see Abdulrahman Baamir and Illias Bantekas, 'Saudi Law as Lex Arbitri: Evaluation of Saudi Arbitration Law and Judicial Practice' (2009) 25 Arbitration International 239.

[31] No doubt, the promotion of uniformity 'forces' other states towards reciprocity, in which case reciprocity constitutes a fruit or a desired outcome.

reasons. Firstly, the combination of the Model Law's international origin and the need for applied uniformity culminates in the adoption of an *internationalist* approach, which, as already explained, constitutes a method of interpretation. Secondly, the international origin of the Model Law emanates from several processes, namely: (a) UNCITRAL conferences with the participation of government experts and the formulation of official *travaux*; (b) general principles of arbitration law;[32] (c) customary international law and; (d) relevant multilateral treaties, such as the New York Convention, ICSID, CISG and others. The idea, therefore, is that the Model Law reiterates existing principles and does not introduce new rules. As a result, in their application of the Model Law, local courts and executive bodies must construe their adapted arbitral statute in accordance with the source of the rule under consideration (*i.e.* treaty, custom, other).

The internationalist approach is consistent with the objective of applied uniformity. However, if Article 2A required courts to consider only the Model Law's international origin but not the pursuit of uniformity, an assessment of the pertinent sources would not necessitate recourse to an internationalist outlook (*i.e.* to the decisions of domestic courts, practice of states, arbitral tribunals and arbitral institutions). Practice suggests that the courts of industrialized or arbitration-friendly nations take into consideration the international origin of the Model Law (or other similar instruments)[33] on the basis of an internationalist approach whereby significant reference is made to foreign judgments on the basis that they are reflective of customary international law or general principles.[34]

---

[32] In the sense of Art 38(1)(c) Statute of the International Court of Justice, 26 June 1945, 33 UNTS 993.

[33] As is the case with *Fothergill v Monarch Airlines* [1981] AC 251, at 282, 290.

[34] See pertinent case law in this respect from Hong-Kong, Australia and Singapore in Stewart D Lewis, 'Testing the Harmonisation and Uniformity of the UNCITRAL Model Law on International Commercial Arbitration' (PhD Thesis, University of Leicester 2015) 133ff. Lewis demonstrates that the courts of these three nations make significant citations to the judgments of foreign courts and although a significant degree of applied uniformity is ultimately achieved, few adoptions of the *ratio descidendi* of these foreign judgments is taken on board.

D. 'Observance of good faith'

Good faith is used in domestic[35] and international law as both a substantive[36] and a procedural[37] principle, as well as method of treaty interpretation. In the context of Article 2A(1) it is meant as an aid of interpretation given what we have already said in previous sections and on account of the other two principles identified therein. Beyond treaty interpretation to which we shall return shortly, it is interesting to note that the ICJ and other international arbitral tribunals have taken good faith to constitute a cardinal principle, at the very least, in the creation and implementation of legal obligations[38] as well as in the context of bilateral or multilateral negotiations.[39] The customary nature of good faith and its underlying function in both substantive and procedural international law has been viewed by commentators as sharing a high degree of proximity with justice and equity, which is further concretized in specific

---

[35] Especially in the field of contract law, see Art 1134 French Civil Code; Art 242 German Civil Code (*BGB*); Art 5(3) Swiss Confederation Constitution; Art 1-201(20) United States Uniform Commercial Code.

[36] Art 2(2) Charter of the United Nations, 24 October 1945, 1 UNTS 16; Art 86 Rome Statute of the International Criminal Court, 17 July 1998, 2187 UNTS 90; Arts 24(4),(5) Agreement on Trade-Related Aspects of Intellectual Property Rights, 15 April 1994, 1869 UNTS 299; Art 300 United Nations Convention on the Law of the Sea, 10 December 1982, 1833 UNTS 396.

[37] Arts 3(10), 4(3) WTO Understanding on Rules and Procedures Governing the Settlement of Disputes <www.wto.org/english/docs_e/legal_e/28-dsu.pdf> accessed 21 July 2017; Art 23 ICSID Rules of Procedure for Conciliation Proceedings <https://icsid.worldbank.org/en/Documents/resources/2006%20CRR_English-final.pdf> accessed 21 July 2017, at 81; Art 11 Permanent Court of Arbitration Optional Conciliation Rules <https://pca-cpa.org/wp-content/uploads/sites/175/2016/01/Permanent-Court-of-Arbitration-Optional-Conciliation-Rules.pdf> accessed 21 July 2017. In the *Israeli Wall* Advisory Opinion and *Ariel Incident of 10 August 1999* the ICJ relied on Art 2(2) UN Charter in order to substantiate a procedural duty to settle disputes in good faith, see *Legal Consequences from the Construction of a Wall in the Occupied Palestinian Territory* [2004] ICJ 136, 174, para 94 (Advisory Opinion of 9 July); *Aerial Incident of 10 August 1999* (*Pakistan v India*) (Jurisdiction) [2000] ICJ 12, 33, para 53 (Judgment of 21 June).

[38] *Nuclear Tests Case* (*Australia v France*) (Merits) [1974] ICJ 253, 268, para 46 (Judgment of 20 December).

[39] *Delimitation of the Maritime Boundary in the Gulf of Maine Area* (*Canada v USA*) (Judgment) [1984] ICJ 246, 292, para 87 (Judgment of 12 October).

applicable rules, such as 'acquiescence, estoppel or duties of information or disclosure'.[40]

The aforementioned observations are important in our examination of good faith as a principle of construction, chiefly because Article 2A is addressed to states (*i.e.* judges and executive organs).[41] Moreover, the obligation to pursue uniformity in conjunction with the international origin of the Model Law suggest that the enforcer of the Model Law should exercise good faith in all cases before him, in his discharge of the duties assumed by the state. Although the Model Law is not binding as such, the fact that one or more Model Law states have discharged their 'obligations' thereunder gives rise to a legitimate expectation that other Model Law states also fulfill their obligations. In this manner, good faith is not merely a moral duty but a legal one, the violation of which can in theory incur state responsibility. In any event, where one or more states fulfill their 'obligations' under the Model Law, others are deemed to acquiesce in respect of similar performance, in addition to any reciprocity.

As a result of these considerations, it is pertinent to resort to the VCLT in order to clarify the content of good faith in Article 2A(1). Article 26 VCLT expresses the *pacta sunt servanda* principle, namely that agreements must be performed in good faith. Good faith is not only an element of *pacta sunt servanda*, but its very foundation. In the case of the Model Law, as has already been explained, its binding nature arises from the legitimate expectations of compliant states that all others will act likewise. From a strict textual interpretation perspective, Article 31(1) VCLT stipulates that agreements shall be interpreted in good faith in accordance with their context and the agreement's object and purpose. Of particular interest in this connection is Article 31(3)(b) and (c) VLCT, which apply *mutatis mutandis* to the Model Law. Subparagraph (b) points out that along with context, account shall be taken of 'any subsequent practice in the application of the treaty which establishes the agreement of the parties regarding its interpretation'. The judicial practice of states with respect to the Model Law and the New York Convention is extensive and certainly constitutes 'subsequent practice', thereafter giving rise to reciprocity, legitimate expectations and acquiescence. Subparagraph (c) notes that account shall also be taken of 'any relevant rules of international law applicable in the relations between the parties'. This not only encompasses customary law and other treaties such as the VCLT and

---

[40] Markus Kotzur, 'Good Faith (Bona Fide)' in Rüdiger Wolfrum (ed), *Max Planck Encyclopedia of Public International Law*, vol IV (2012) 508, para 23.

[41] *Ibid.*, para 20.

the New York Convention but also rules accepted by states but which have been established by private practice, essentially *lex mercatoria*.[42] A widely accepted industry-based rule, whether procedural or substantive, is as much a rule of international law as a provision in an inter-state agreement.

IV. Paragraph 2

Paragraph 2 was meant as a gap-filling or residual provision within the context of the interpretative function of paragraph 1 of Article 2A. Although its main quality is flexibility, the absence of any indication as to what is meant or encompassed under the term 'general principles on which this Law is based' creates considerable ambiguity and lack of certainty for litigators. It also provides judges and the executive with an unnecessary degree of discretion.

A. 'General Principles on Which This Law is Based'

Paragraph 2 is a residual or gap-filling clause. As a consequence, the term 'general principles' does not include the three principles (international origin, uniformity and good faith) found in paragraph 1. The second question is whether the term encompasses general principles of international or domestic laws. The key to answering this question is the first part of the sentence of paragraph 2 and particularly 'matters governed by this Law'. Matters governed by the Model Law cover a broad range of fields. Some are quintessentially of a public international law nature, such as immunities from enforcement, while others pertain to domestic law, as is the case with the permissibility of oral agreements; yet others are mixed, with party autonomy having been established by multilateral treaties (*e.g.* New York Convention) and general principles of domestic (contract) laws. Hence, although there are several principles underlying the entirety of the Model Law (*e.g.* party autonomy, right to fair trial), there are others that are specific to some or all of its articles. Their existence is a matter of proof and depending on their origin (general principle, custom, treaty), the parties must rely on the appropriate methodology for demonstrating the existence of each principle claimed.

What is clear, however, is that the term 'general principles' does not encompass principles derived or existing solely in one legal system, or a minority of legal systems, especially where the rule/principle found there

---

[42] See Illias Bantekas, 'The Private Dimension of the International Customary Nature of Commercial Arbitration' (2008) 25 Journal of International Arbitration 449.

is antithetical to the practice of the majority of states. This is justified by the fact that the Model Law is 'based' on internationally agreed rules as it is the product of an inter-governmental process that is not divorced from other multilateral developments, such as the New York Convention and case law that is supportive of international commercial arbitration. Moreover, as a residual provision, paragraph 2 cannot be construed in isolation or in conflict with paragraph 1 of Article 2A; rather, it must be consistent with it. This means that any residual general principles identified by the parties or the courts under paragraph 2 must take into consideration the international origin of the Model Law, promote uniformity and observe good faith.[43]

At the time of writing there were no known cases whereby a general principle under paragraph 2 of Article 2A had been identified by a court or tribunal.[44] On the contrary, the case law on Article 7(2) CISG is extensive, but significant caution must be exercised before accepting any analogies. Firstly, the content of Article 7(2) CISG is broader, stipulating that in the absence of general principles recourse is to be made to rules of private international law. Secondly, the scope and subject matter of CISG is largely different to that of the Model Law and a principle common to the CISG and the Model Law in name may not be so in substance. The CISG Digest lists the following general principles as identified by national courts and arbitral tribunals in accordance with Article 7(2) CISG: party autonomy; good faith; estoppel; place of payment of monetary obligations; currency of payment; burden of proof; full compensation; informality; dispatch of communications; mitigation of damages; binding usages; set-off; right to withhold performance and the principle of simultaneous exchange of performances; right to interest; costs of one's own obligations; changed circumstances and right to renegotiate; *favor contractus*.[45] It is beyond the scope of this short article to identify which of these may be adapted for the purposes of Article 2A(2) of the Model Law, but if the context and purpose is similar there is no impediment why a court or tribunal cannot apply any one of these in a residual manner *mutatis*

---

[43] An example of a general principle identified by the ICJ, and which is relevant to arbitral proceedings, concerns the right of parties in review proceedings to have an opportunity to submit oral statements, see *Application for Review of Judgment No 158 of the UN Administrative Tribunal* [1973] ICJ 166, para 36 (Advisory Opinion of 12 July).

[44] The UNCITRAL does not attempt to identify any general principle under Art 2A(2), see UNCITRAL, '2012 Digest of Case Law on the Model Law on International Commercial Arbitration' (2012) <www.uncitral.org/pdf/english/clout/MAL-digest-2012-e.pdf> accessed 21 July 2017, at 15.

[45] UNCITRAL, 'Digest of Case Law on CISG 2012', *supra* note 21, 42ff.

mutandis.[46] In any event, it should be pointed out that the CISG is construed by the CISG Advisory Council, which although not a treaty-based judicial mechanism, enjoys significant authority among CISG member states in the same manner as the UN Human Rights Committee.[47] Its opinions provide a source not only of guidance but of an authoritative interpretation of the CISG and are not lightly dismissed by CISG member states.

V. Conclusion

The Model Law and institutions such as CISG provide a novel way of understanding and implementing international co-operation and are both perhaps unknown to general international lawyers. Uniformity, rather than formal agreement is perhaps also the way forward in areas traditionally occupied by treaty law, given that the intended outcome is the active engagement of states without the pressure that comes from a treaty (both before and after ratification). The emergence of an extensive body of case law emanating from arbitral tribunals and courts and emanating from the application of the Model Law demonstrates that states are more apt to honestly enforce an instrument which they have allowed to mature in their domestic legal order, as opposed to something they had to incorporate wholesale without having the time and space to think about its practicalities, as is usually the case with treaties transformed by acts of parliament.

Although international lawyers do not generally perceive commercial or trade practice, particularly if instigated by private actors, as an extension of state practice, in the case at hand the transnational effects of uniformity have culminated, or have the potential to culminate in subsequent practice that reinforces the instrument in question.

---

[46] The UNCITRAL Model Law on International Commercial Conciliation with Guide to Enactment and Use 2002 (2004) <https://www.uncitral.org/pdf/english/texts/arbitration/ml-conc/03-90953_Ebook.pdf> accessed 21 July 2017, at 27, para 41, identifies four general principles.

[47] See <www.cisgac.com/> accessed 21 July 2017.

Subsequent Agreement Outside/In: The Kigali Principles on Protection of Civilians

Jan Klabbers[*]

I. Introduction

In the life of a treaty, it is a vital question how subsequent practice or agreement between the parties to that treaty helps to shape or re-shape the treaty concerned. This applies not merely to 'regular' treaties, but also to those that are constitutive of international organizations.[1] Perhaps the best example of the last two decades is the case of NATO, whose organizational treaty, the North Atlantic treaty, was changed beyond recognition by the common accord of its parties. The modalities of the change were highly intriguing: NATO's constitution was never formally amended but was, instead, revised by means of innocuous sounding documents such as 'strategy documents': adopting a new defense strategy was considered to be within the purview of the NATO Treaty, even if such a new defense strategy went beyond what observers might think of as the limits of NATO. Thus, if NATO originally was thought of as purely defensive, operative only – if at all – in case one member state would come under attack by an outside state, the new and revamped NATO operates mostly outside the territory of its member states, and does so without acting in self-defense (in any recognized sense of that term); instead, it engages mostly in what are best seen as policing tasks, yet those tasks were conspicuously absent from the treaty as concluded in 1949. In short, NATO's treaty has been revised, somewhat underneath the radar screen, by the subsequent agreement and practice of its member states – about as informal a revision as it can get.[2]

---

[*] Academy Professor (Martti Ahtisaari Chair), University of Helsinki; Visiting Research Professor, Erasmus School of Law, Rotterdam.

[1] The classic study of change of organizational constitutions remains Ralph Zacklin, *The Amendment of the Constitutive Instruments of the United Nations and Specialized Agencies* (first published 1968, 2005).

[2] For a useful overview, see Stefan Bölingen, *Die Transformation der NATO im Spiegel der Vertragsentwicklung: Zwischen sicherheitspolitischen Herausforderungen und völkerrechtlicher Legitimität* (2007).

With international organizations there is an additional element to be factored in, and that is the practice of the organs which, on some conception of the organization at least, can also be seen as the subsequent practice of member states assembled in that particular organ.[3] The classic example is the changed understanding of the word 'concurring' in article 27, paragraph 3, of the United Nations Charter, addressing decision-making by the Security Council.[4] Ever since the Soviet Union's early boycott of the Council entailed that a decision had to be taken in the absence of one of the five permanent members, the term 'concurring' has come to mean not strictly 'approving', but rather 'not disapproving'. While the dictionary meaning of 'concurring' suggests the need of an affirmative vote, the way the word has constantly been interpreted in UN circles is different, suggesting merely the absence of a negative vote. This has been the practice of the Council since the early 1950s, and was given the stamp of approval by the International Court of Justice in 1971, after South Africa had raised the argument that decisions thus reached by the Council lacked validity. The Court, in response, held that the practice was the consistent practice of the Council, and was considered as generally accepted. The Court underlined that the practice had persisted over a period of many years, had been consistent and uniform, had been accepted by the UN's member states, and 'evidences a general practice of that Organization.'[5]

A question that has thus far given rise to little principled debate is what to do with subsequent practice or agreement adopted by some of an organization's member states, in conditions where the practice or agreement is purposefully adopted outside the organization's framework but clearly meant to influence the work of the organization.[6] It is to this seemingly esoteric practice that the remainder of this contribution will be devoted, largely in the form of a discussion of the so-called Kigali Principles, adopted by a

---

[3] Those who think organizations are but vehicles for their member states might be inclined to such a view; those who feel the organization has a distinct legal identity might be less inclined to take such a view – for them, the practice of an organ is organizational practice, distinct from member state practice. See further on these two approaches Jan Klabbers, *An Introduction to International Organizations Law* (3rd edn 2015).

[4] Charter of the United Nations, 26 June 1945, 1 UNTS XVI.

[5] See *Legal Consequences for States of the Continued Presence of South Africa in Namibia (South West Africa) Notwithstanding Security Council Resolution 276 (1970)* [1977] ICJ 16, 22, para 22 (Advisory Opinion of 21 June).

[6] A related phenomenon is the treaty conflict created so as to change the underlying general regime. For a fine recent study, see Surabhi Ranganathan, *Strategically Created Treaty Conflicts and the Politics of International Law* (2014).

handful in states in 2015 and addressing the protection of civilians by and in peacekeeping missions.

II. Influence from Outside?

The formalist (or even not so formalist) international lawyer, when confronted with a bid by member states of an organization to influence the organization but without respecting the prescribed organizational procedures, may be curt in her response: if and where formal procedures for revision exist, these ought to be used – the rule of law, however defined, demands nothing less.[7] Surely, when a constitutionally prescribed procedure exists, it ought to be utilized, lest the development of the law collapses into the exercise of naked political power. And judicial support for this proposition is offered by the (then) ECJ, in the *Second Defrenne* case: where amendment procedures exist, it is not acceptable to aim to revise a treaty by ignoring those prescribed procedures, as doing so affects the procedural safeguards designed to protect various stakeholders.[8]

The formalist (or not so formalist) lawyer would be right, but practice shows more variety: it happens with some regularity that departure from established procedure is considered acceptable, even before the same ECJ.[9] And on some level, this is to be expected: the non-formalist (or even not so non-formalist) lawyer will recognize that law mostly sets out to accurately reflect power configurations, and if existing law stands in the way of doing so, then it just needs to be bypassed. The rule of law may be a good thing, but is rather, in the language that has come to prevail, Utopian; it needs to be (and inevitably will be) balanced by means of something more Apologetic.[10]

There are, on closer scrutiny, quite a few examples of practices that emerge outside organizations between some or all of their members, but with the

---

[7] Article 41 VCLT by and large supports the same point: a modification of an organization's constitution by some members *inter se* is bound to affect the rights and obligations of the other member states, and therewith not encouraged, see Vienna Convention on the Law of Treaties, 23 May 1969, 1155 UNTS 331.

[8] Case C-43/75 *Defrenne v Sabena* [1976] ECR 455, para 58.

[9] See Joined Cases C-181/91 and C-248/91 *European Parliament v Council and Commission* [1993] ECR I-3685 (admittedly, this did not quite involve a revision of the any of the EU Treaties, but a departure from the regular budgetary procedure).

[10] See Martti Koskenniemi, *From Apology to Utopia: The Structure of International Legal Argument* (1989).

aim of somehow affecting whatever it is the organization does. The EU, for instance, for all its legal safeguards, has proved to be fertile ground.[11] The emergence of the European Council is an example from relatively early years, created as a vehicle for the Heads of State and Government to discuss the broad outlines of European politics and policies, but outside the institutional framework provided by the EEC Treaty, as it then was. Much the same applies (and from much the same time period) to the gradual emergence of a European foreign policy, originally in the extra-curricular form of European Political Cooperation. And something similar, but not involving all member states, happened in the mid-1980s with the conclusion of the Schengen Agreement between, at first, a handful of EU member states.

Examples can also be found outside the EU context, although it is also fair to say that since the EU is the most 'constitutionalized' among international organizations, it is in particular here that in formal mechanisms become visible. With other organizations, the line between 'formal and 'informal' is not nearly as sharply drawn; formal and informal amendments may shade into each other, making it more difficult to distinguish them analytically. Still, one can think of examples, some successful, some less so. Above, NATO was already mentioned, as was the re-interpretation of Article 27(3) UN Charter. One rather visible attempt to change the UN from the outside was the introduction, some fifteen years ago, of the notion of Responsibility to Protect, which has spawned many writings and even has a journal specifically devoted to it, though without being considered a particularly successful example of changing the world. The Responsibility to Protect (often affectionately referred to as R2P) was launched by the International Commission on Intervention and State Sovereignty (ICISS), a non-governmental platform set up for the occasion on instigation and with support of some UN member states, in order to influence the way the UN responds to humanitarian crises. Admittedly, one may argue that it was not set up to influence only the UN (it is addressed, in principle, to states and to all organizations with a task in maintaining the peace), but equally clearly its main target was the UN.

R2P has yet to start to work properly: it may have spawned many writings, but has resulted in little concrete action, and one could be forgiven for thinking that, as an attempt to influence global politics in any direct manner, it has

---

[11] Indeed, in the EU it is even acknowledged that member states be given the chance to deepen the cooperation between some of them inter se, under the heading of 'géométrie variable'. The seminal study is Filip Tuytschaever, *Differentiation in European Union Law* (1999).

by and large failed.[12] R2P was followed, if that is the correct way of putting it, in 2015 by the promulgation of the so-called Kigali Principles: a highly intriguing initiative of a few states, including the Netherlands and Rwanda,[13] to get states to pledge support for protecting civilians in times of crisis.[14] It is obvious from the contents of the principles that these are meant to give more concrete 'hands and feet' to international peacekeeping operations, and to make it possible for the commanding officers of those missions to circumvent the bureaucratic decision-making processes of international organizations.

III. Retour à Rwanda

The Kigali Principles are, in a sense, a belated response to everything that went wrong in the Rwandan genocide of 1994, where the UN stood by and did a whole lot of nothing while some 800,000 people were being slaughtered.[15] The five initiating states organized an event in Kigali, in 2015, hosted by Rwanda and with the participation of the 30 largest troop contributing states and ten largest donor states to peacekeeping. Partly this was no doubt inspired by regular problems experienced in the field (Rwanda knows a bit about failed protection of civilians), partly perhaps also in a bid for election to the Security Council: the Netherlands was eagerly campaigning at the time, and eventually ended up sharing a seat with Italy. The result of their

---

[12] While not inaccurate, this would be too simple: the influence of R2P may not reside in direct action, but in indirectly changing perceptions of what are and what are not acceptable exercises of international authority. And here R2P may have had a tremendous impact, in making sovereignty conditional on approval by the international community. The point is eloquently made in Anne Orford, *International Authority and the Responsibility to Protect* (2011).

[13] The origin of the Kigali Principles is not uncontested: different sources mention different states involved in the initial stages. All are agreed though that Rwanda and the Netherlands were involved.

[14] The text and some accompanying materials can be found at International Conference on the Protection of Civilians, 'The Kigali Principles on the Protection of Civilians' (2015) <http://civilianprotection.rw/wp-content/uploads/2015/09/REPORT_PoC_conference_Long-version.pdf> accessed 24 March 2017.

[15] See generally, *e.g.*, Michael Barnett, *Eyewitness to a Genocide: The United Nations and Rwanda* (2002). For further discussion focusing on the legal concept of omission, see Jan Klabbers, 'Sins of Omission: The Responsibility of International Organizations for Inaction' (2016) Jean Monnet Center Working Paper 2/2016 <www.jeanmonnetprogram.org/wp-content/uploads/JMWP-02-Klabbers.pdf> accessed 24 March 2017.

work is the adoption of the Kigali Principles, a set of pledges that other states have subsequently been asked to endorse, and to date 39 states (including the original five) have done so.

The relevance of the Kigali Principles resides partly in their substance. Thus, remarkably, one of the Principles gives the commander of peacekeeping troops the authority to act in case he or she deems it necessary for the protection of civilians (pledge # 7). Another aims to have compulsory consultation of troop contributing countries in decision-making by the Security Council (# 16), and yet another of the pledges promises that the endorsing states shall take sanctions against their own military if these fail to protect civilians where protection had been due (# 13).

But interesting as the substance is, more remarkable are form and process. Not only is it intriguing that the Kigali Principles come in the form of pledges[16] rather than obligations formulated in the regular way, but in particular the chosen process is fascinating: aiming to influence UN decision-making, but doing so outside the regular UN mechanisms. This could have been, after all, yet another General Assembly resolution, perhaps even a Security Council resolution of uncertain provenance or a Presidential Statement perhaps. Instead, all of this was avoided.

IV. The Politics (and Law) of Procedure

As noted, the Kigali Principles were adopted on the initiative of a small number of states, outside the regular UN mechanisms. This raises two immediate questions: why abandon the UN machinery? And how does this affect the legal status of the Kigali Principles, in particular in relation to the UN?

One of the reasons to operate outside the UN machinery was no doubt pragmatic. Peacekeeping is often closely associated with the UN, but nonetheless, peacekeeping also takes place by other international organizations, such as the African Union. Hence, it could be suggested that a focus on the UN alone would be too narrow. On the other hand, some of the 18 pledges contained in the Principles are clearly addressed solely at the Security Council: it is the Council which is asked to consult with troop contributing states (# 16), and it is the Council that needs to ensure that mandates are

---

[16] These are rare in international law, and the idea of a pledge is rarely used in order to discuss international legal instruments. An isolated exception is Lea Brilmayer, 'From "Contract" to "Pledge": The Structure of International Human Rights Agreements' (2006) 77 British Yearbook of International Law 163.

matched with resources (# 17). It is the UN that is asked to provide clarity on the rules of engagement of missions (# 9); the UN with whom capacity gaps should be discussed (# 5) and whose standby arrangements may need to be reviewed (# 11) while the UN Secretariat is expected to play a useful role in relation to logistics (# 18). Hence, there is a clear indication that at least partly, the aim is to influence operations and working methods of the UN and in particular the Security Council.[17]

There may also have been something of 'UN fatigue' at play: the UN adopts so many reports and resolutions, that few stand out and are noticed. Political initiatives may – and often do – get lost in the labyrinthine paper factory that is the UN. Indeed and rather intriguingly given the non-utilization of UN machinery, the Kigali Principles were explicitly presented as the follow-up to a High Level UN Report, and several high-ranking UN officials (including one assistant-secretary general) were present and speaking in Kigali. Moreover, the UN machinery has been used to mobilize member states, with 'endorsement sessions' having been organized at headquarters in New York, asking member states to step forward and formally announce their endorsement. At present, 39 have done so, including France, the United Kingdom and the United States, but not China or Russia. Hence, there is something of a procedural link, albeit a tenuous one, with the UN, despite the attempt to circumvent the UN.

Now the UN does not have a particularly good track record when it comes to incorporating revision in the formal way. The Charter is immensely difficult to amend (with a veto for the five permanent members of the Council), and accordingly, has only been amended a few times on relatively minor points.[18] Attempts by the General Assembly to influence actual initiatives of the Security Council can be highly effective (it effectively frustrated the work of the ICTY in its early years by its reluctance to make funds available[19]), but the General Assembly is less fit to provide hands and feet to UN legal concepts. A classic example is the Definition of Aggression, a laudable attempt to further define the notion of aggression (mentioned but left undefined in article 39 UN

---

[17] By contrast, there is only one specific reference to a different entity: pledge # 11 mentions the African Union, but even then mostly as a possible regional partner for the UN.

[18] For brief but useful discussion, see Nico Schrijver, 'UN Reform: A Once-in-a-Generation Opportunity?' (2005) 2 International Organizations Law Review 271.

[19] See generally Jan Klabbers, 'Checks and Balances in the Law of International Organizations' in Mortimer NS Sellers (ed), *Autonomy in the Law* (2007) 141.

Charter) that went belly-up in the face of global discord.[20] The fear must have been that trying to change peace-keeping through the Assembly would result in a quagmire of rather sticky, syrupy politics, at best possibly leading to a weak and watered-down compromise to make sure China or Russia would not completely block it. Hence, the initiators must have thought that it was better to move outside the UN frame.

Whether it works is, of course, a different matter. The Security Council is under no legal obligation to consult troop contributing states, and the Kigali Principles do not, and cannot, create such a legal obligation. As a legal matter, it would seem obvious that an agreement between 39 states (out of the 193 member states of the UN) is not capable of influencing the activities of an organization nominally owned and controlled by all 193 together.[21]

Then again, this would (again) be too simple. What the Kigali Principles aim to achieve is to start a discussion on peacekeeping and the protection of civilians, and to place some pressure on the Security Council in particular to change its ways. It is here also that the curious nature of the formulations (in the form of 'pledges') comes in: the individual states concerned – all 39 of them – can be seen to have made several promises which, even though the Kigali Principles are marketed as legally non-binding, nonetheless can have a strong normative effect. Obviously, many of the pledges are hedged with caveats (states shall strive 'within our capabilities' and such like formulations), but some might nonetheless be legally enforceable. Thus, there is a quite hard pledge to 'take disciplinary action against our own personnel if and when they fail to take action to protect civilians […]' (pledge # 13). Surely, this is the sort of provision that, under some circumstances, can give rise to litigation, at least when no disciplinary action is forthcoming. Activists may also consider threatening the endorsing states with legal action, perhaps before a domestic court, once they are on the Council and are seen to vote in a way going against their pledges, or if such a state proposes to include in a Security Council resolution a caveat or restriction that might prevent civilians from being protected (pledge # 4).[22]

---

[20] The classic discussion is Julius Stone, 'Hopes and Loopholes in the 1974 Definition of Aggression' (1977) 71 American Journal of International Law 224.

[21] The general theory of international organizations law insists that the member states together determine what it is the organization can and cannot do, see Jan Klabbers, 'The EJIL Foreword: The Transformation of International Organizations Law' (2015) 26 European Journal of International Law 9.

[22] Here it is useful to remember that the ICJ held Greece to account after it failed, within NATO, to sponsor the application for membership of the Former Yugoslav Republic of Macedonia, despite having bilaterally promised FYROM to do so, see

By and large, the Kigali Principles will not immediately rewrite the law on peacekeeping, and will not immediately succeed in bringing the protection of civilians center stage. And perhaps that is a good thing too: the Kigali Principles would place considerable power in the hands of contingent commanders, for instance (pledge # 7), going against the classic division of labour (however *idealtypisch* perhaps[23]) according to which the political decisions are to made by politicians and executed by the military, rather than also made by the military.

V. By Way of Conclusion

It happens every now and then that the member states of international organizations realize that the most effective way to influence the organization may be to circumvent it – the Kigali Principles seem to be an attempt to do precisely that. The legal effects and status of such attempts will come to derive not just from constitutional considerations, but also from the general political response of the member states. If taken up by the organization and the other member states, these principles will sooner or later come to be seen as part of the UN and its legal order. If by and large ignored, then they will end up becoming one further example of just how difficult it is to set the UN in motion, all good intentions notwithstanding. The law here, including the law on subsequent practice and agreement, can do little more than channel those political responses (acceptance or rejection) to initiatives coming from outside the regular machinery. But the law can neither fully prohibit nor endorse such initiatives: both would be suicidal.

Application of the Interim Accord of 13 September 1995 (*The Former Yugoslav Republic of Macedonia v Greece*) [2011] ICJ 644 (Judgment of 5 December).

[23] For useful discussion, see Antonia Chayes, *Borderless Wars: Civil Military Disorder and Legal Uncertainty* (2015).

Modification of Treaties by Subsequent Practice – Some Comments on the Austrian Position

Gerhard Hafner[*]

I. Introduction

The question as to whether treaties may be amended by subsequent practice had kept the ILC very busy in the course of its elaboration of the Draft Articles on the Law of Treaties. Professor Zemanek implicitly addresses this problem in his article on 'Court-Generated State Practice', in which he concludes that it is not the court or supervisory organ that creates state practice, but rather the reaction of states to a decision of such a body. In that way, a court or supervisory organ can only initiate or catalyze the creation of state practice.[1] This view is also confirmed by the relative legal effect of court decisions since, as confirmed by Article 59 of the Statute of the International Court of Justice, they are binding only upon the parties to the dispute, with certain variations concerning intervening states. Accordingly, states not parties to a dispute are not bound by a decision resulting from it. Such states maintain their discretionary power to conform to the decision or not. It will always remain up to them to act in conformity with the relevant decision, notwithstanding the risk of a later negative judgment should a state's own acts later be judged as not in conformity with the first judicial decision. Accordingly, courts can possibly determine the interpretation only of those treaties to which all parties to the dispute are bound, mostly only bilateral, but hardly multilateral treaties.

The conclusion offered in Zemanek's contribution seems to assume that the subsequent practice of states is able to modify a treaty. However, Zemanek frames this result in a distinct way by arguing that it is not the treaty that

---

[*] Prof. ret. of international law, Vienna University.
[1] See Karl Zemanek, in this volume, at 14.

is modified by subsequent practice, but the obligation(s) resulting from the treaty.[2]

II. Austria's Position Regarding Draft Article 38 of the Text of the ILC on the Law of Treaties

In this regard, his view differs from that of the ILC itself, which coined this problem as 'modification of treaties by subsequent practice'. This formulation was the title of draft article 38 of the Draft Articles on the Law of Treaties as submitted by the ILC to the General Assembly.[3] This draft article read as follows:

> Article 38. *Modification of treaties by subsequent practice*
> A treaty may be modified by subsequent practice in the application of the treaty establishing the agreement of the parties to modify its provisions.

At the Conference on the Law of Treaties held in Vienna during 1968-1969, various amendments regarding this draft provision were proposed by Finland,[4] Japan,[5] Venezuela,[6] the Republic of Vietnam[7] and France[8] in the Committee of the Whole. The amendments tabled by Finland, Japan, Venezuela and the Republic of Vietnam were identical and proposed a deletion of this provision, whereas France proposed to add an introductory sentence to the existing text. Finally, a roll-call decision on the first four proposals was taken which resulted in 53 votes in favour of, and only 15 against the deletion, with 26 abstentions. Accordingly, this article was dropped and not recommended to the Conference.[9]

---

[2] *Ibid.*

[3] See United Nations Conference of the Law of Treaties, First and second session, Official Records, Document of the Conference (1971) UN Doc A/CONF.39/11/Add.2, at 55.

[4] UN Doc A/CONF.39/C.1/L.143.

[5] UN Doc A/CONF.39/C.1/L.200.

[6] UN Doc A/CONF.39/C.1/L.206.

[7] UN Doc A/CONF.39/C.1/L.220.

[8] UN Doc A/CONF.39/C.1/L.241: This text proposed, as an introductory phrase of this provision, an insertion of the text: 'Provided its provisions or the conditions of its conclusion are no bar [...]'.

[9] UN Doc A/CONF.39/11/Add.2, at 158.

The Western European states were divided with regard to this vote: Whereas states like the United Kingdom, the Federal Republic of Germany, Greece or Liechtenstein supported the deletion, others like Switzerland or Denmark opposed it. Austria likewise supported the draft article and voted against the deletion.[10] The Austrian delegate recognized the existence of the rule stated in article 38 as a principle of international law. According to this delegate, this provision dealt with the problem facing all legislators and authors of treaties as soon as negotiations had been completed; he referred to several examples of multilateral treaties between Austria and other states which had been modified by subsequent practice. In his view, this article was not contrary to the principle of *pacta sunt servanda* and Austria would vote in favour of retaining the article in its present form or as modified by the French amendment.[11]

III. The Austrian Views in the Context of the Topic 'Subsequent Agreements and Subsequent Practice in Relation to the Interpretation of Treaties' of the International Law Commission

A. Austria's Written Reply to the Request of the International Law Commission

When the ILC discussed the topic of subsequent agreements and subsequent practice in relation to the interpretation of treaties (originally called 'Treaties over Time'), it again encountered the problem reflected in draft article 38. The Austrian reply[12] to the request of the ILC to submit comments regarding treaties and subsequent practice referred to a statement made by the Austrian delegate to the 6th Committee of the General Assembly in 2010: This statement first referred to the accession of Austria to the European Union in 1995, when many provisions of EU law contradicted provisions of treaties either with third states or with other EU member states. As far as subsequent practice (except that established by subsequent treaties) was concerned, another example provided in this statement was the Paris Agreement between Italy and

---

[10] *Ibid.*

[11] UN Doc A/CONF.39/11, at 212.

[12] Text on file with the author.

Austria of 1946 (also known as the Gruber–De Gasperi Agreement)[13] which has been the subject of extensive subsequent agreements and practice. This agreement has been implemented in several steps over a period of nearly 50 years. Negotiations for its implementation led to the so-called 'South Tyrol Package' in 1969, which contained all the measures to be taken for the benefit of the German-speaking ethnic group in South Tyrol, including a guarantee of substantial autonomy. A 'calendar of operations' set forth a time-table for the implementation of the measures outlined in the 'Package' for both Austria and Italy and subsequently for the settlement of the dispute between the parties. According to Austria's view as expressed in its reply to the ILC, these measures constituted subsequent practice establishing the agreement of the parties regarding the interpretation of the Paris Agreement as reflected in Article 31 paragraph 3(b) of the Vienna Convention on the Law of Treaties.

The reply further referred to the Austrian State Treaty of 15 May 1955[14] that has been the subject of subsequent practice in form of the obsolescence of the provisions regarding the military and air clauses as contained in Articles 12 to 16 and Article 22 paragraph 13. In light of the fundamentally changed political realities in Europe since 1990, Austria regarded these provisions as no longer applicable. After consultations with the other signatories of the Treaty, Austria declared these provisions obsolete in 1990. The other signatories of the Treaty accepted this declaration either explicitly or implicitly.[15]

A further case quoted in this reply was the Agreement between Austria and Germany concerning mutual assistance in cases of disasters and other serious incidents,[16] signed on 23 December 1988. In accordance with the political situation at the time, this agreement still contained the so-called Berlin clause which extended the agreement's application to the region of Berlin (West-Berlin). However, by the time of ratification German reunification had

---

[13] Paris Agreement of 5 September 1946; English text as annex to Article 10 of the Treaty of Peace with Italy, 10 February 1947, 49 UNTS 3, No. 747; <https://history.state.gov/historicaldocuments/frus1946v04/d297>.

[14] Federal Law Gazette No 152/1955.

[15] Different view is presented in particular by Marcelo Kohen. According to him, '[i] t was in fact the agreement of the parties (Article 54(b) of the 1969 Convention) which formed the basis of the termination of Articles 12 to 16 of the Austrian State Treaty.', see Marcelo G Kohen, 'Desuetude and Obsolescence of Treaties' in Enzo Cannizzaro (ed), The Law of Treaties Beyond the Vienna Convention (2011) 350, 358. However, this view does not explain the legal effect for those State Parties that were neither informed nor asked for their consent.

[16] Abkommen zwischen der Republik Österreich und der Bundesrepublik Deutschland über die Gegenseitige Hilfeleistung bei Katastrophen oder Schweren Unglücksfällen, Federal Law Gazette No 489/1992.

already occurred. Therefore, in the Austrian Federal Law Gazette a note was added to the Berlin clause stating that it was to be regarded as obsolete.[17]

The reply also referred to the Austro-Swiss Treaty of Commerce of 1926 that, upon common conclusion by Austria and Switzerland, was declared as inapplicable[18] due to Austria's accession to the European Union as well as the European common commercial policy that no longer left room for bilateral agreements. 'As a consequence, the Treaty of Commerce was declared terminated due to obsolescence in 2000 due to mutual non-application'. In Austria's view, this step had only a declaratory effect.

As to the jurisprudence of the Austrian Constitutional Court, the reply quoted the decision of March 1973 according to which the Treaty of Commerce concluded between Germany and Austria in 1930 had been invalidated by desuetude, and where the Court explicitly referred to this concept of international law.[19] The Court found that the conduct of both parties demonstrated that they no longer considered the treaty applicable: Austrian authorities had not applied equal national treatment to German citizens purchasing real property as provided for by the treaty. Germany had not published the treaty in its official treaty list and had never protested against its non-application by Austria. Moreover, according to the law of the then European Economic Community, the Council of the EEC would have had to give its consent to the continued application of the Treaty of Commerce, which Germany never sought. All these factors indicated that this treaty had fallen into desuetude. Likewise, certain other treaties concluded before World War II between Austria and its northern and eastern neighbours later fell into desuetude since, in practice, the Iron Curtain rendered them inapplicable.

---

[17] *Ibid.*

[18] See also Federal Law Gazette III No 68/2001. A different view is offered by Kohen: 'Indeed, the Treaty ceased to be in force with the Austrian Anschluss by Germany in 1938. After the Second World War, the Western Allied Authorities asked the Austrian government to notify them which treaties concluded with the German Reich should be proposed for re-application in the relations between it and the Federal Republic of Germany. The Austrian list did not include the 1930 Commercial Treaty, nor did the German Federal government approach Austria with the view to its possible reapplication. Hence, the idea of desuetude is completely alien as a ground for the termination of the 1930 Commercial Treaty.', Kohen, *supra* note 15, 357 [footnote omitted]. However, the author does not explain why the 'Anschluss' terminated the treaty. In Austria's view, Austria continued to exist, albeit as a *nudum ius*, since the 'Anschluss' has been seen as an illegal occupation.

[19] Austrian Constitutional Court, Judgment of 13 March 1973 (VfGH Slg. Nr. 7014/1973, at 197 *et seq*).

B. Austria's Oral Comments in the 6th Committee of the General Assembly of the United Nations

The issue of the effects of subsequent agreements and practice became more relevant when the ILC proposed draft conclusion 7 that is mainly discussed by Professor Zemanek in his contribution. It reads as follows:

Conclusion 7

Possible effects of subsequent agreements and subsequent practice in interpretation

1. Subsequent agreements and subsequent practice under article 31, paragraph 3, contribute, in their interaction with other means of interpretation, to the clarification of the meaning of a treaty. This may result in narrowing, widening, or otherwise determining the range of possible interpretations, including any scope for the exercise of discretion which the treaty accords to the parties.

2. Subsequent practice under article 32 can also contribute to the clarification of the meaning of a treaty.

3. It is presumed that the parties to a treaty, by an agreement subsequently arrived at or a practice in the application of the treaty, intend to interpret the treaty, not to amend or to modify it. The possibility of amending or modifying a treaty by subsequent practice of the parties has not been generally recognized. The present draft conclusion is without prejudice to the rules on the amendment or modification of treaties under the 1969 Vienna Convention and under customary international law.

The Austrian view was expressed in the various comments upon the reports of the ILC in the 6th Committee of the General Assembly.

In 2010, Austria presented the above list of cases that were subsequently made subject of a written reply to the ILC.[20]

In 2011, the Austrian delegate concurred with most of the preliminary conclusions elaborated so far, but proposed to distinguish between different

---

[20] Melanie Fink, Gerhard Hafner and Gregor Novak, 'Austrian Diplomatic and Parliamentary Practice in International Law/Österreichische Diplomatische und Parlamentarische Praxis zum Internationalen Recht' (2010) 15 ARIEL 339, 351. In this note, Austria referred also to the termination of certain agreements on the basis of Article 59 VCLT: 'When Estonia acceded to the European Union in 2003, the Agreement on mutual external commercial relations of 1993 between this State and Austria was declared terminated pursuant to Article 59 para. 1 lit a of the Vienna Convention on the Law of treaties of 1969' (Federal Law Gazette

types of treaties according to their substance and, consequently, their object and purpose. Human rights treaties were frequently interpreted by a different method compared to other treaties. It should also be examined up to which extent treaties containing synallagmatic obligations were interpreted differently from treaties containing *erga omnes* obligations. This distinction was reflected also in the qualification of the evolutionary approach as a special kind of interpretation by subsequent practice since, in this case, it was not the practice of the state parties regarding the relevant treaty that was relevant for the interpretation, but the general development and evolution of the political environment. However, neither the issue of the variety of treaties nor that of the evolutionary approach were further developed in the later statements.[21]

In 2012, the Austrian delegate addressed the issue of modification versus interpretation and confirmed a preference of resorting to interpretation over formal modification, because it allowed States to avoid national approval procedures for treaty modification. This statement also recalled that a proposal according to which treaties could be modified by subsequent practice was defeated at the Vienna Conference on the Law of Treaties.[22]

A year later and after the renaming of the topic as 'Subsequent agreements and subsequent practice in relation to the interpretation of treaties', Austria quoted the case *Methanex Corporation v United States of America* in which the NAFTA Free Trade Commission's interpretation of NAFTA provisions

---

   III No 84/2001). The same ground of termination was applied to several other agreements such as
- the Agreement of 1992 on mutual external commercial and trade relations between Austria and Latvia (Federal Law Gazette No 71/1996) when Latvia joined the European Union (Federal Law Gazette III No 42/2004),
- the Agreement of 1992 on mutual external commercial relations between Austria and Slovenia (Federal Law Gazette No 40/1993) due to the accession of Slovenia to the European Union in 2003, (Federal Law Gazette III No 99/2004)
- the Agreement of 1979 on cooperation in the field of veterinary between Austria and the CSSR and
- the Agreement of 1982 concerning postal and telecommunication service between these two States due to the accession of the Czech Republic to the European Union.

[21] Melanie Fink Gerhard Hafner and Gregor Novak, 'Austrian Diplomatic and Parliamentary Practice in International Law/Österreichische Diplomatische und Parlamentarische Praxis zum Internationalen Recht' (2011) 16 ARIEL 427, 440.

[22] Markus P Beham, Gerhard Hafner, 'Austrian Diplomatic and Parliamentary Practice in International Law/Österreichische Diplomatische und Parlamentarische Praxis zum Internationalen Recht' (2012) 17 ARIEL 395, 410.

were deemed a 'subsequent agreement'[23]. Accordingly, interpretative declarations by treaty bodies were regarded as 'subsequent agreements' in the sense of Article 31 paragraph 3(a) of the VCLT.

As regards the role of subsequent practice in the interpretation of a treaty, the statement emphasized that the subsequent practice of only one or of less than all parties to a treaty could only serve as a supplementary means of interpretation under the restrictive conditions of Article 32 of the VCLT.[24]

In 2014, the Austrian delegate supported the draft conclusion 7(3) by stating that the parties to a treaty were presumed not to amend or modify a treaty by subsequent agreement or practice, but rather to interpret treaty provisions. This presumption was seen as reflecting the application of treaty obligations in good faith and the principle of *pacta sunt servanda*. Nevertheless, in Austria's view, the statement contained in the second sentence of draft conclusion 7(3) that 'the possibility of amending or modifying a treaty by subsequent practice of the parties has not been generally recognized' raised some questions. If this second sentence was connected to the proposed definition of 'subsequent practice' in draft conclusion 4 (2), which was only regarded as 'an authentic means of interpretation', it would not extend to amendments or modifications. However, Austria did not generally exclude the possibility of a modification by a subsequent practice:

> Notwithstanding the fact that during the 1969 Vienna Codification Conference on the Law of Treaties former draft article 38 on the modification of treaties by subsequent practice was not adopted, it seems clear that a 'subsequent practice' establishing an agreement to modify a treaty should be regarded as a treaty modification and not merely as an interpretation exercise.[25]

However, the further text of this statement qualified this conclusion insofar as it made this conclusion dependent on the clear intention of the parties, on the one hand, and referred to the modification of rights and obligations under the treaty through a rule of customary international law, on the other:

---

[23] *Methanex Corporation v United States of America*, Final Award on Jurisdiction and Merits, 3 August 2005, II B, paras. 20, 21.

[24] Markus P Beham and Gerhard Hafner, 'Austrian Diplomatic and Parliamentary Practice in International Law/Österreichische Diplomatische und Parlamentarische Praxis zum Internationalen Recht' (2013) 18 ARIEL 313, 331.

[25] Markus P Beham and Gerhard Hafner, 'Austrian Diplomatic and Parliamentary Practice in International Law/Österreichische Diplomatische und Parlamentarische Praxis zum Internationalen Recht' (2014) 19 ARIEL 305, 323.

Also where no such intention of the parties can be established, general international law does not exclude that states parties to a treaty may create customary international law through their subsequent practice, if accompanied by opinio iuris, and thereby modify the rights and obligations contained in the treaty. This consequence is even reinforced by the fact that international law does not know any hierarchy between the sources of international law. Thus, the change of international law based on custom by treaty rules and vice versa is a generally accepted phenomenon which the formulation of the second sentence of draft conclusion 7 paragraph 3 should not be understood to exclude.[26]

IV. The Assessment of This Position

These Austrian declarations and statements started from the recognition of the possibility of the modification of treaties by subsequent practice, but became more nuanced in the course of the further discussion of the topic in the ILC. The statements excluded this possibility unless the modification was accompanied by an *opinio iuris* resulting in the creation of a norm of customary international law. These statements several times referred to the Paris Agreement of 1946 between Austria and Italy: the operation calendar and the 'Package' as well as the South Tyrol Statute of Autonomy of 1972 was referred to as constituting subsequent practice in relation of the Paris Agreement. Since this practice resulted in an interpretation of the Paris Agreement, the jurisdiction of the International Court of Justice with regard to South Tyrol would directly relate to the Paris Agreement instead of obligations and rights different from those of this agreement.[27] Although the statement in 2014 did not exclude the possibility of a modification by subsequent practice, it nevertheless required for this purpose the existence of an *opinio iuris* converting this practice into a rule of customary international law.

Austria's treaty practice only partially coincides with the view expressed in the 6th Committee: The official view regarding the various measures such as the 'Package' or the 'calendar of operations' are claimed to constitute subsequent practice to the Paris Agreement of 1946.[28] In the case of the

---

[26] *Ibid.*

[27] Gerhard Hafner, 'Einige Anmerkungen zur Zuständigkeit des Internationalen Gerichtshofs im Fall Südtirol' (to appear).

[28] Bundesministerium für auswärtige Angelegenheiten (ed), *Jahrbuch der österreichischen Außenpolitik. Außenpolitischer Bericht 1992* (1992) 192.

Treaty of Commerce concluded between Germany and Austria of 1930, the Constitutional Court referred to desuetude as a legal ground for treaty's termination. Accordingly, the termination, or obsolescence, of the treaty required the creation of a contradicting rule of customary international law insofar as the previous non-application of the treaty was accompanied by a corresponding *opinio iuris*. In 1985, the same Court delivered a decision using similar reasoning regarding the non-application of the Treaty between Austria-Hungary and Italy of 11 February 1906 concerning fees applicable to the acquisition of real estate by citizen of the other state party when it decided that this treaty was terminated by way of desuetude. The Court explained desuetude as follows: 'But desuetude, as a reason of termination does not only mean a simple non-application of existing norms, but rather the formation of derogating customary law contrary to positive treaty law.'[29]

In contrast thereto, the ground for termination of treaties based on obsolescence that Austria invigorated on the occasion of the termination of certain provisions of the State Treaty of 1955 does not rely on practice, but rather on the changed situation that do not justify the expectation of a further application of the treaty in the eyes of the parties: Accordingly, the non-application of the Berlin clause in the Agreement between Austria and Germany concerning mutual assistance in cases of disasters and other serious incidents of 1988 was explained by reference to the fundamentally changed political situation[30] as was likewise the case with the non-application of certain provisions of the Austrian State Treaty of 15 May 1955.[31]

However, obsolescence was also referred to in cases where a certain practice existed in the form of persistent mutual non-application: this situation occurred in the case of the Austro-Swiss Treaty of Commerce of 1926,[32] or the Agreement of Commerce of 1928 including the Protocol of Signature[33] between Austria and France.[34] However, in all these cases, Austria emphasized the common conclusion of the state parties regarding the applicability of

---

[29] Peter Fischer and Gerhard Hafner, 'Aktuelle österreichische Praxis zum Völkerrecht' (1986) 36 Österreichische Zeitschrift für öffentliches Recht und Völkerrecht 365, 384.

[30] Federal Law Gazette No 489/1992.

[31] See also Felix Ermacora, 'Die Obsoleterklärung von Bestimmungen des österreichischen Staatsvertrages 1955' (1991) 42(3) Austrian Journal of Public and International Law 319, 323.

[32] Federal Law Gazette III No 68/2001.

[33] Federal Law Gazette No 208/1928.

[34] Federal Law Gazette III No 37/2004.

obsolescence. Accordingly, this approach could be interpreted in different ways.

On the one hand, the applicability of obsolescence has been confirmed by both State Parties with a declaratory effect. In this situation, it could be argued that Austria interprets obsolescence in different ways; the common denominator would only be the termination of a treaty when the observance could no longer be expected in the eyes of the parties either due to the persistent practice or to the changed political circumstances. Such an approach undoubtedly blurs the distinction between obsolescence and desuetude, tends in the direction of an expectation-reliance approach, but remains close to the principle of good faith[35] referred to in Article 31 VCLT.[36] In particular, if the common conclusions are regarded as a manifestation of an *opinio iuris* and were combined with the persistent mutual practice, this ground for termination would be identical with the desuetude. Accordingly, Austria, in these cases, could have relied on desuetude as was the case with the Treaty of Commerce of 1930 concluded between Germany and Austria However, although in the cases of obsolescence of bilateral treaties, Austria stressed the common conclusions of the state parties, they were said to be only of declaratory effect so that the real ground of termination was the persistent mutual practice alone.

On the other hand, the common conclusion of the state parties referred by Austria can be seen as producing a subsequent agreement in the sense of Article 31 paragraph 3(a) ('any subsequent agreement between the parties regarding the interpretation of the treaty or the application of its provisions') with the effect of the termination of the treaty.

Accordingly, this practice belittles the strictness of the view that the modification of treaties by subsequent practice requires the existence of an *opinio iuris*, unless the common conclusions are regarded as a reflection of an *opinio iuris*. Otherwise, the instrument of obsolescence in its second version, which relies on a persistent mutual practice alone, seems to amount to a manifestation of the possibility of the modification of a treaty by subsequent practice. It differs from this mode of modification only insofar as it is restricted to the inapplicability of individual provisions or of a treaty and does not extend to a positive modification of the substance of rights and obligations resulting from a treaty.

---

[35] See, *e.g.*, Case T-115/94 *Opel Austria GmbH v Council of the European Union* [1997] ECR II43 quoted by Steven Reinhold, 'Good Faith in International Law' (2013) 2 UCL Journal of Law and Jurisprudence 40, 60.

[36] *Ibid.*, at 40, 60.

Recent Developments

EU Development Cooperation:
A Stock-Taking and a Vision for the Future

Peter Hilpold[*]

I. Introduction

The dynamic evolution of EU law finds one of its foremost expressions in the area of development cooperation. Here, the most ambitious goals and disinterested ideals intersect with pronounced economic and political interests both of the EU as a whole as well as of the single member states. Therefore, difficult compromises have to be made. The provisions on development cooperation now explicitly form part of the norms on 'External Action' (Part V of the TFEU). This policy is, however, not only directed to the outside but it has considerable internal repercussions.

The meaning of development cooperation is subject to continuous change. As will be shown in the following, the EU has been re-orienting itself in this field continuously anew and an important refocusing is under way right now. Over the last decades, there has been, first of all, considerable uncertainty as to what development aid should mean in economic terms. The EU has not been the only international actor being confronted with this question. This has rather been a challenge for any subject active in this field: for states, the competent UN institutions and for non-governmental organizations. For the last half a century an enormous development has taken place in this field. The respective approaches have moved from a rather primitive stage based on simple resource transfers to highly sophisticated concepts attempting to implement forms of all-encompassing, sustainable and lasting development. As a consequence, in its endeavours to operationalize the concept of development cooperation and to conceive a set of tools to effectively implement this policy the Union has not been alone. In fact, the respective ideas and notions

---

[*] Peter Hilpold is Professor of International Law, European Law and Public Comparative Law at the University of Innsbruck. This contribution is based on commentaries on the Articles 208-211 TFEU published by this author in Smith & Herzog, Law of the European Union which are here updated and further developed.

have been further developed in an intense dialogue with other international institutions and in the ambit of international bodies. The Union has been nothing more than an active discussant in this process, albeit a very important one. The field where the contributions by the Union were ground-breaking was that of political conditionality. As will be shown, in this area the Union led the way and introduced a policy that was copied on a world-wide scale. In the beginning, heavy criticism was levelled against this policy and the EU was accused of intervening in other states' domestic affairs and of imposing its own values on others. In the meantime, however, criticism of this kind has become rare and it has become broadly recognized that such a policy can give a decisive contribution for the diffusion of values broadly shared on the universal level. The fear that the EU would thereby pursue egoistic goals has proved to be unfounded. This policy has perhaps been egoistic in that sense that the EU and its member states had recognized that the propagation and the defence of these core values on a universal level was in the immediate internal interest of the EU and its member states. Such self-interest in the realization of broadly shared values is, however, tolerated.

On a whole it can be said that the EU development policy is becoming ever more part of a holistic universal design to which the Union is giving an important contribution but which is to be seen, at the same time, as a universal project. In the following it will be shown how the EU development policy has evolved from a limited endeavour with a strong egoistic foundation to an instrument designed to actively influence world politics in order to bring about a more peaceful, solidary and rights-based international society.

II. The Beginnings

Formally, the development policy has been part of EC law only since the entering into force of the Treaty of Maastricht. On a factual basis, however, this policy has been evolving over a very long period and the Treaty of Maastricht only rendered official what had become *acquis communautaire* long time before.

The first basis for this later policy can already be found in the EEC Treaty of 1957.[1] It included provisions on association of the overseas countries

---

[1] For an excellent overview of the historical roots of the EU development policy see Dieter Frisch, 'Entwicklungszusammenarbeit, Vorbemerkung zu den Artikeln 130u bis 130y' in Hans von der Groeben, Jochen Thiesing and Claus-Dieter Ehlermann (eds), *Kommentar zum EU-/EG-Vertrag*, vol. 3 (1999) 2014. See also

and territories in Article 198ss [ex-182ss, ex-131ss], introduced upon the insistence of France (assisted by other colonial powers such as Belgium, Italy and the Netherlands), who wanted to maintain its special relationship with its colonies also in the newly founded EEC, that prepared the ground for such later developments.[2] This special relationship was mostly about financial aid and privileged trade – two cornerstones of development policy as it was understood in the 50s and the 60s of the last century.

More rapidly than originally thought, the colonial empires kept by some EC member states crumbled and the former special relationship with their dependent territories had to be substituted by a different institute. In fact, the gaining of independence did not solve the development problem but sometimes even accentuated it, as it had not been anticipated or assisted by a sound nation-building process. In any case, the newly independent states kept entertaining most of their economic relations primarily with their former colonial masters and the preservation of these relations – albeit possibly in a more equal form – remained vital for the development process to succeed. On the side of the former colonial powers there was, on the other hand, a strong interest to maintain these spheres of influence that should guarantee, amongst others, preferred access to raw materials.

As is well known, the association regime was enlarged step-by-step paralleling to a large extent the accession process to the EC. In particular, it was the accession of the United Kingdom to the EC that radically changed the face of this institute with dozens of former British colonies now seeking to be integrated into the association regime. While with the Yaoundé I Agreement (from 1965 to 1970)[3] and the Yaoundé II Agreement (from 1970 to 1975) mainly developing countries from the francophone world were associated to the EC, already in 1969 a specific agreement, the so-called 'Arusha Agreement' was concluded with Kenya, Tanzania and Uganda, thereby associating three former British colonies to the EC.

At the beginning of the 1970s the time was ripe for a first thorough rethinking of international development policy. Not only had the subjective situation for the EC changed with the accession of the United Kingdom, Denmark und Ireland in 1973, but totally new challenges also arose outside the EC with developing countries grouping together and speaking with one voice. This

---

Lorand Bartels, 'The Trade and Development Policy of the European Union' in Marise Cremona (ed), *Developments in EU External Relations Law* (2008) 128.

[2] On this subject see Peter Hilpold, 'Commentaries to the Articles 198ss TFEU' in Heinz Mayer (ed), *EUV und AEUV, Kommentar* (2010).

[3] The agreement was concluded in Yaoundé, the capital of Cameroon.

was the time when the foundations for an International Law of Development were laid and there was a widely felt perception that this branch of law would finally revolutionize traditional international law.[4] Although these hopes (or, respectively, woes) proved to be wrong and since long this area of law has all but fallen in oblivion,[5] at the time of its first forming – which proceeded with an enormous dynamic – it still exerted an enormous attractiveness and had a visible impact on law-making, both on an international level as well as on the level of the Community. With regard to the former, first of all the activities of the United Nations Conference on Trade and Development (UNCTAD) have to be mentioned. It is within this international institution, created in 1964 as a discussion forum for developing countries (the 'GATT of the poor'), that the demands for a more equal and a more participative international order were advanced in ever more pronounced form. On occasion of the UNCTAD II Conference in New Delhi in 1968 agreement was found on a General Preference System which had to be transposed afterwards in other international normative systems and finally also in national and Community law.[6] In the 1970s, a radical redistribution of international wealth was demanded and large catalogues of demands, drafted in a normative language, were issued and adopted by the UN General Assembly, partly with the opposition of the developed world. The best examples in kind were the Declaration on the Establishment of a New International Economic Order[7] and the Charter of

---

[4] See, in this regard, Subrata R Chowdury *et al*, *The Right to Development in International Law* (1992); Milan Bulajic, *Principles of International Development Law: Progressive Development of the Principles of International Law Relating to the New International Economic Order* (1993); Christian Tomuschat, 'New International Economic Order' in Rudolf Bernhardt (ed), *Encyclopedia of Public International Law*, vol. III (1997) 578.

[5] See, *e.g.*, Peter Slinn, 'The International Law of Development: A Millennium Subject or a Relic of the Twentieth Century?' in Wolfgang Benedek *et al* (eds), *Development and Developing International and European Law* (1999) 299; and Thomas W Waelde, 'A Requiem for the "New International Economic Order" – The Rise and Fall of Paradigms in International Economic Law and a Post-Mortem with Timeless Significance' in Gerhard Hafner *et al* (eds), *Liber Amicorum Professor Ignaz Seidl-Hohenveldern in Honour of his 80th Birthday* (1998) 771.

[6] On this subject see Peter Hilpold, 'Das neue Allgemeine Präferenzschema der EU' [1/1996] Europarecht 98.

[7] UNGA Res 3201 (S-VI), Declaration on the Establishment of a New International Economic Order (1 May 1974) UN Doc A/9559.

Economic Rights and Duties of States.[8] It is against this international background that the main activities of the EC in the field of development policy have to be seen.[9] As unilateral measures the EEC in 1971 set into force its own General Preference System.[10]

III. The Lomé Agreements

Over time, the Lomé Agreement of 1975[11] with 46 African, Caribbean and Pacific (ACP) countries as the treaty-based cooperation framework designed to replace the Yaoundé and the Arusha regime and to overcome the many deficiencies of these agreements, became far more important. The Yaoundé and the Arusha treaties were widely criticized not only for their selective nature but more fundamentally because the association concept was perceived by many developing countries as a neo-colonialist plot[12] and as harmful to their interests in the worst case or as ineffectual in the best. Much criticism also came from several member states as they objected to the strong francophone bias of this system having consequences also on the economic level as the commercial advantages from this cooperation were mainly reaped by firms in French speaking member states.[13]

As a whole, there was a broad consensus that the development promotion aspects had to be stronger emphasized. This was true, even though an explicit competence by the EEC was still lacking in this field. As the time was not yet ripe for a reform of the treaties in this sense, a bottom-up or soft law approach[14] was adopted according to which the Commission prepared a

---

[8] UNGA Res 3281 (XXIX), Charter of Economic Rights and Duties of States (12 December 1974) UN Doc A/9631. While the former document was adopted by consensus the latter one met with harsh resistance by important industrialized countries.

[9] See Anna K Dickson, 'The Demise of the Lomé Protocols: Revising European Development Policy' (2000) 5 European Foreign Affairs Review 197.

[10] See Hilpold, *supra* note 6.

[11] ACP-EEC Convention of Lomé [1976] OJ L25/2.

[12] Frisch, *supra* note 1, at paras 3, 14.

[13] Frisch, *supra* note 1, at para 4.

[14] Peter Hilpold, 'Konditionalität in den Beziehungen zwischen der EU und den AKP-Staaten: Menschenrechte, Demokratie, Rechtsstaatlichkeit und verantwortungsvolle Regierungsführung' [2002/2] Zeitschrift für europarechtliche Studien 239, at 241.

'Memorandum concerning a Community development cooperation policy'[15] followed by a 'First programme of action'[16]. The Commission asked not only for a deepening of the development policy and a widening of its scope but also for the adoption of a comprehensive approach that would touch all areas of Community activities and for a better coordination of the relevant activities by the Community and the member states. Considering the fact that at that time no hard law basis for such a policy was given, this was a bold move that should soon bring concrete results. In fact, compared to the previous situation, the Lomé Agreement of 1975 created a totally new framework. As it seemed to fulfil large part of the demands advanced by the developing countries it was widely hailed as an innovative instrument which should be best suited to meet the challenges for the development policy of the future. The following elements were of particular relevance:[17]

- It contained a renouncement on reciprocity in international trade relations in line with demands brought forward by developing countries within the GATT;
- In line with the prevailing political and economic thinking in the field of development economics of that time, the economic relations between industrialized and developing countries should be stabilized and protected against short-term market fluctuations of a speculative nature. As the goods mainly traded by developing countries (agricultural products and raw materials) are characterized by extreme price elasticity, earnings of these countries are subject to enormous fluctuations with, in some cases, disastrous consequences for the budgetary situation. On the other side, also the industrialized countries are interested in principle in stable raw material markets and prices. As it turned out, however, the attempt to manipulate the market in this field was doomed to fail; and
- Finally, the Lomé Agreement provided for privileged market access for agricultural products. It was probably this aspect of the Agreement that had – in the long run – the most significant impact

---

[15] European Commission, 'Memorandum Concerning a Community Development Cooperation Policy' (27 July 1971) (1971) 4 EC Bull. suppl. 5.

[16] European Commission, 'First Programme of Action' (2 February 1972) (1972) 5 EC Bull. suppl. 2.

[17] See Andreas Zimmermann, 'Commentary to Article 177 TEC' in Hans von der Groeben and Claus-Dieter Ehlermann (eds), *Kommentar zum Vertrag über die Europäische Union*, vol. 3 (2003) 1470, para 5.

on trade relations between the EEC and the ACP countries. As will be seen later on, the success of these provisions has been in the end, however, also the reason for intense criticism against the Lomé framework as a whole, as thereby discrimination was introduced among developing countries (between those making part of the EEC-ACP framework and those staying outside). Ultimately, this criticism was of decisive importance for the complete overhaul of the whole cooperation framework.
- The export earnings of the developing countries, especially with agricultural products, should be stabilized according to the so-called 'STABEX system'.[18]

The Lomé Agreement was renewed every five years. On each of these occasions, this Agreement was partly reformulated and the development aims were refocused. The single steps of this process were the following:

- Lomé I (1975-1980);
- Lomé II (1980-1985);
- Lomé III (1986-1990); and
- Lomé IV (1990-2000).

In 1995, a mid-term review process was undertaken which brought about substantial revisions of the text. The revised Lomé IV Agreement is also known as 'Lomé IV-bis Agreement'.

On 2 August 2000, the partnership agreement between the EC and the ACP countries entered into force. This agreement shall last 20 years. While Lomé I was concluded with 46 ACP countries, this number rose to 50 with Lomé II, to 64 with Lomé III and to 66 with Lomé IV. The subsequent agreement of Cotonou tied 77 ACP states to the EC. In the meantime, this number has risen to 79. According to Article 94 of the Cotonou Agreement, any independent state whose structural characteristics and economic and social situation are comparable to those of the ACP states may become party of this agreement.

The various agreements from Lomé I to Cotonou mirror profound changes in development politics over a period of 25 years (1975 to 2000). In the economic sphere, the leading elements were more and more softened and in

---

[18] A system of export earnings stabilization set up by the European Community in accordance with the African, Caribbean, and Pacific (ACP) states. Under the system, the EC helps developing countries withstand fluctuations in the price of their agricultural products by paying compensation for lost export earnings.

part even disappeared. Preferential market access, basically for agricultural products in the EC, was the keystone of cooperation. The preferential regime brought this order into conflict with GATT/WTO law and the long lasting 'Banana conflict' is the best known expression of such a contention.[19] Interestingly enough, it is now more and more doubted whether this preferential regime was – in the end – really beneficial to the ACP states, as they do not seem to have gained a lasting development advantage over other developing countries outside the regime.[20] Openly distractive and damaging policies such as the dumping of the EC's excess food production on the developing countries' markets, carried out regularly in the name of food aid, were, however, abandoned.

Formally, the opening of the market took place under the non-reciprocal conditions. In practice, however, trade concessions by the EC had to be traded in by concessions in other fields (especially human rights, good governance as well as social and environmental standards)[21] by the ACP countries. On

[19] The Banana conflict was finally solved by two agreements (Geneva Agreement on Trade in Bananas between the European Union and Brazil, Colombia, Costa Rica, Ecuador, Guatemala, Honduras, Mexico, Nicaragua, Panama, Peru and Venezuela of 31 May 2010 and the Agreement on Trade in Bananas between the European Union and the United States of America of 8 June 2010). See Council Decision 2011/194/EU of 7 March 2011, OJ L88/66.

Thereby the transition from a quota system for banana imports in the EU (which strongly privileged bananas from ACP countries) to a tariff-only systems was agreed. The WTO-inconsistent import restrictions applied before by the EU had to be abolished. On the evolution of this dispute see Peter Hilpold, *Die EU im GATT/WTO-System* (3rd edn 2009) 355 *et seq.* On the final agreement see Eckart Guth, 'The End of the Bananas Saga' (2012) 46 Journal of World Trade 1.

[20] See, *e.g.*, 'Green Paper on Relations between the European Union and the ACP Countries on the Eve of the 21st Century: Challenges and Options for a New Partnership', COM (96) 570; Christopher Stevens, 'The EU-ACP relationship after Lomé' in Pitou van Dijck and Gerrit Faber (eds), *The External Economic Dimension of the European Union* (2000) 223, at 228 *et seq.*; Joseph A McMahon, 'Negotiating in a Time of Turbulent Transition: The Future of Lomé' (1999) 36 Common Market Law Review 599; Dickson, *supra* note 9. Recently, in a thorough analysis of the principle of non-discrimination, it has been argued that exceptions to this principle are often not only detrimental to the international trading system as a whole but also to the interests of the countries that should be the very beneficiaries of these exceptions. See also the so-called 'Sutherland-Report, The Future of the WTO' (2004) 19–27.

[21] The issue of such standards became particularly prominent on a general level, with the introduction of the new Generalised System of Preferences for the 10-year period starting with 1995. These standards had the function to condition the behaviour of the developing countries both in a negative and in a positive

a whole, the cooperation between the EC and the ACP countries over time became more and more variegated. From the beginning, the Lomé agreements were officially not characterized as association agreements any longer but as partnership agreements to avoid any implication of inferiority for any of the parties. Although technically they were clearly association agreements along the way from Lomé I to Cotonou, the idea of a partnership between the EC and the former colonies of its member states was further approached under different aspects. Each agreement addressed the issues considered by the ACP countries to be pivotal for effective development. Thus, for example, in the Lomé II Agreement the issue of investment was added; in Lomé III new titles followed, among others, on transport and communication and on cultural and social cooperation.[22] Particularly innovative were, however, the provisions in the Lomé IV Agreement; they addressed the problem of debt reduction, the environmental issue and the human rights problem.

Debt reduction is still an important issue in the relations between industrialized and developing countries. The most important question arising in this context is whether this instrument is useful at all in the end.[23] The international finance crisis has presented this problem in a new light and with new emphasis. In any case, it can never apply on a general scale but only selectively, under extreme circumstances and for the least-developed countries because any other policy would lead to moral hazard in borrowing and endanger the functionality of the financial markets.[24]

Also the environmental issue has gained importance ever since. With the environment more and more being perceived to be a common good of all nations and the affirming of the conviction that only through a global approach the most urgent environmental problems can be solved, developing countries become important interlocutors in this international discussion. This

---

way in the sense that deviations from internationally agreed standards could be punished by a withdrawal of concessions while particular achievements in these fields could be awarded with extra bonuses. See Paul Waer and Bart Driessen, 'The New European Union Generalised System of Preferences' (1995) 29 Journal of World Trade 97; Hilpold, *supra* note 6.

[22] Karin Arts, *Integrating Human Rights into Development Cooperation: The Case of the Lomé Convention* (2000) 128 *et seq.*

[23] For a differentiating approach, see Raghuram Rajan, 'Debt Relief and Growth', [2005] Finance & Development 56-57. Even the recent debt relief plan by the G8 for Africa has met with harsh criticism, see George Monbiot, 'A Truckload of Nonsense' *The Guardian* (14 June 2005).

[24] Kenneth S Rogoff, 'Moral Hazard in IMF Loans – How Big a Concern?' [2002] Finance & Development 56-57.

is especially true as central environmental resources are located in developing countries. Besides being of global relevance these resources constitute also an important asset in the process of development planning, both in a short-term and in a long-term perspective (thereby leading to partly conflicting goals). In the last years innovative instruments have been devised to make these goods tradable, thereby letting developing countries gain property rights on at least part of the international welfare created by environment conservationist policies.[25]

The most radical changes Lomé IV brought about regarded, however, the field of human rights. The human rights issue was addressed already in the Lomé III Agreement, although in a prudent and timid way.[26] Article 4 of the Agreement made an indirect reference to human rights by emphasizing the necessity of respecting people's dignity. Only in Annex I human rights were explicitly mentioned, even though the connection of human rights with development was somewhat contorted and confusing.[27]

In contrast, with Article 5 of the Lomé IV Agreement the human rights issue was at the center of the discussion. The achievement of high human rights standards was no longer a secondary element of the development process but became an autonomous goal and a constitutive element of development itself.

Article 5 of the Lomé IV Agreement read as follows:

> 1. Cooperation shall be directed towards development centred on man, the main protagonist and beneficiary of development, which thus entails respect for and promotion of all human rights. Cooperation operations shall thus be conceived in accordance with this positive approach, where respect for human rights is recognised as a basic factor of real development and where cooperation is conceived as a contribution to the promotion of these rights.
>
> In this context development policy and cooperation shall be closely linked to respect for and enjoyment of fundamental human rights and to the

---

[25] In particular, the so-called 'debt for equity swaps' have to be mentioned here. On the basis of such instruments developing country debt is cancelled if the debtor country agrees to implement an environmental protection or conservation project. Parties to such an agreement can be governments but also NGOs and private banks can operate as intermediaries. This instrument has been successfully tested in several countries (for example, in Bolivia, Costa Rica, Ecuador, the Philippines and Madagascar) but has potential for still broader application.

[26] See Peter Hilpold, 'EU Development Cooperation at a Crossroads: The Cotonou Agreement of 23 June 2000 and the Principle of Good Governance' (2000) 7 European Foreign Affairs Review 53, at 59.

[27] Ibid.

recognition and application of democratic principles, the consolidation of the rule of law and good governance. The role and potential of initiatives taken by individuals and groups shall be recognized in order to achieve in practice real participation of the population in the development process in accordance with Article 13.

In this context good governance shall be a particular aim of cooperation operations.

Respect for human rights, democratic principles and the rule of law, which underpins relations between the ACP States and the Community and all provisions of the Convention, and governs the domestic and international policies of the Contracting Parties, shall constitute an essential element of this convention.

2. The contracting parties therefore reiterate their deep attachment to human dignity and human rights, which are legitimate aspirations of individuals and peoples. The rights in question are all human rights, the various categories thereof being indivisible and inter-related, each having its own legitimacy: non-discriminatory treatment; fundamental human rights; civil and political rights; economic, social and cultural rights.

Every individual shall have the right, in his own country or in a host country, to respect for his dignity and to protection by the law.

ACP-EC cooperation shall help abolish the obstacles preventing individuals and peoples from actually enjoying to the full their economic, social, political and cultural rights and this must be achieved through development which is essential to their dignity, their well-being and their self-fulfilment.

The Contracting Parties hereby reaffirm their existing obligations and commitment in international law to strive to eliminate all forms of discrimination based on ethnic group, origin, race, nationality, colour, sex, language, religion or any other situation. This commitment applies more particularly to any situation in the ACP States or in the Community that may adversely affect the pursuit of the objectives of the Convention. The Member States (and/or, where appropriate, the Community itself) and the ACP States will continue to ensure, through the legal or administrative measures which they have or will have adopted, that migrant workers, students and other foreign nationals legally within their territory are not subjected to discrimination on the basis of racial, religious, cultural or social differences, notably in respect of housing, education, health care, other social services and employment.

3. At the request of the ACP States, financial resources may be allocated, in accordance with the rules governing development finance cooperation,

> to the promotion of human rights in the ACP States and to measures aimed at democratisation, a strengthening of the rule of law and good governance. Practical steps, whether public or private, to promote human rights and democracy, especially in the legal domain, may be carried out with organisations having internationally recognised expertise in this sphere.
>
> In addition, with a view to supporting institutional and administrative reform, the resources provided for in the Financial Protocol for this purpose can be used to complement the measures taken by the ACP States concerned, within the framework of its indicative programme, in particular at the preparatory and start-up stage of the relevant projects and programmes.

The respect for human rights was characterized as a 'basic factor of real development' and this meant that from this point on, efforts to promote human rights obedience should be a necessary element of any development initiative.

On 21 July 1986, the Community's Foreign Ministers meeting in the Council on human rights, democracy and development declared that respecting, promoting, and guaranteeing human rights was a key factor in international relations and a cornerstone of European cooperation as well as of relations between the Community and its member states and other countries. These ideas were further developed in a Communication to the Council adopted by the Commission on 13 March 1991[28] where general lines of conduct concerning the relationship between development cooperation policies, respect for and promotion of human rights, and support for democratic processes in developing countries were conceived. These concepts were again taken up in a Declaration on Human Rights adopted by the Luxembourg European Council of 29 June 1991[29] and by a resolution of the Council of 28 November 1991 on human rights, democracy, and development.[30] Human rights were linked to democracy and development and qualified as an explicit aim of EC development policy. The Council took a clear position towards a positive approach in favouring the respect of human rights. While sanctions should

---

[28] (1991) 3 EC Bull. 69.

[29] (1991) 6 EC Bull. I, at 45.

[30] (1991) 11 EC Bull. point 2.3.1. See Der-Chin Horng, 'The Human Rights Clause in the European Union's External Trade and Development Agreements' (2003) 9 European Law Journal 677, at 682; and Mercedes Candela Soriano, 'L'Union Européenne et la Protection des Droits de l'Homme dans la Coopération au Développement: Le Role de la Conditionalité Politique' (2002) 13 Revue trimestrielle des droits de l'homme 875, at 880.

not be ruled out as a measure of last resort, a clear preference was given to political dialogue.[31]

Beginning with the early 90s, the EC has inserted human rights clauses in all its agreements with third countries (and not only with developing countries). With the Treaty of Nice a corresponding clause was introduced for agreements with third countries not constituting developing countries (Article 181a para 1, subpara 2, now Article 212 para 1, referring to the 'principles and objectives of EU external action').

The human rights clauses consist mainly of two elements: the 'essential element clause' and the 'additional clause' or 'non-execution' clause. The first clause goes as follows:

> Respect for democratic principles and fundamental human rights [established by the Universal Declaration of Human Rights] inspires the internal and international policies of the Parties and constitutes an essential element of this agreement.[32]

The 'additional clause' was usually a mere suspension clause. It was used in the first agreements with Estonia, Latvia, Lithuania[33] and Slovenia[34] and was called the 'Baltic clause'. These clauses did not operate in a totally satisfactory way as they provided only for the most extreme cases that should lead to the immediate suspension of the agreement without consultation with the other treaty partner.[35]

The 'Bulgarian clause' which is now usually applied provides on the other hand for a far more flexible and diplomatic mechanism which pays also more respect to the sovereignty of the treaty parties. Should the parties fail to meet their treaty obligations a consultation procedure is started and

---

[31] Vaughne Miller, 'The Human Rights Clause in the EU's External Agreements', House of Commons Library Research Paper 04/33, 16 April 2004.

[32] Elena Fierro, 'Legal Basis and Scope of the Human Rights Clauses in EC Bilateral Agreements: Any Room for Positive Interpretation?' (2001) 7 European Law Journal 41, citing page 273-13 (Rel. 4) of the Cooperation agreement between the European Community and the Lao People's Democratic Republic, OJ 1997 L 334/15.

[33] Agreement between the European Economic Community and the Republic of Estonia on Trade and Commercial and Economic Co-Operation, OJ 1992 L 403/2 (Latvia 403/11, Lithuania 403/20).

[34] Cooperation Agreement between the European Economic Community and the Republic of Slovenia, OJ 1993 L 189/2.

[35] Der-Chin Horng, *supra* note 30.

afterwards appropriate measures can be taken. Special care is taken for the need of urgency measures. On a whole, a clear *favor contractus* is perceptible in this clause. The 'Bulgarian clause' declares as follows:

> If either Party considers that the other Party has failed to fulfil an obligation under this Agreement, it may take the appropriate measures. Before so doing, except in cases of special urgency, it shall supply the Joint Committee with all relevant information required for a thorough examination of the situation with a view to seeking a solution between the Parties. In the selection of measures, priority must be given to those which least disturb the agreement. These measures shall be notified immediately to the Joint Committee if the other Party so requests.

With regard to the specific way these human rights clauses operated, a decision was taken to adopt primarily a 'positive' approach according to which priority should be given to incentives for greater adherence to internationally agreed standards and for closer cooperation in this field.[36] Initially, however, it was not clear how this approach should be implemented. Furthermore, the question remained open what should be the consequence of a violation of these principles. Only with the Lomé IV-bis Agreement this situation has changed and human rights conditionality became fully applicable. The relevant provision, subpara 3 of Article 5(1) of the Agreement, reads as follows:

> Respect for human rights, democratic principles and the rule of law, which underpins relations between the ACP States and the Community and all provisions of the Convention, and governs the domestic and international policies of the Contracting Parties, shall constitute an essential element of the Convention.

This provision was to be read together with Article 366a(2) and (3) of Lomé IV-bis Agreement, the so-called 'non-compliance clause':

> If one Party considers that another Party has failed to fulfil an obligation in respect of one of the essential elements referred to in Article 5, it shall invite the Party concerned, unless there is special urgency, to hold consultations with a view to assessing the situation in detail and, if necessary, remedying it.

---

[36] On the advantages of 'positive' measures over sanctions see Bruno Simma, Jo B Aschenbrenner and Constance Schulte, 'Human Rights Considerations in the Development Cooperation Activities of the EC' in Philip Alston, Mara R Bustelo and James Heenan (eds), *The EU and Human Rights* (1999) 571, at 578 with further references.

For the purposes of such consultations, and with a view to finding a solution:

- the Community side shall be represented by its Presidency, assisted by the previous and next member states to hold the Presidency, together with the Commission;
- the ACP side shall be represented by the ACP state holding the Co-Presidency, assisted by the previous and next ACP states to hold the Co-Presidency. Two additional members of the ACP Council of Ministers chosen by the party concerned shall also take part in the consultations.

The consultations shall begin no later than 15 days after the invitation and as a rule last no longer than 30 days.

At the end of the period referred to in the third subpara of para 2 if in spite of all efforts no solution has been found, or immediately in the case of urgency or refusal of consultation, the party which invoked the failure to fulfil an obligation may take appropriate steps, including, where necessary, the partial or full suspension of application of this Convention to the party concerned. It is understood that suspension would be a measure of last resort.

The party concerned shall receive prior notification of any such measure which shall be revoked as soon as the reasons for taking it have disappeared. There can be no doubt that this whole system was primarily based on principles of negative conditionality. The violation of essential elements of this agreement should allow for the application of sanctions according to the procedure described above. The intent proclaimed in the past to move closer to positive conditionality was only partly set into practice. Furthermore, it was not clear in which way the various 'essential elements' mentioned in subpara 3 of Article 5(1) were interrelated. The need was felt for a clear framework on the basis of which priorities could be set in order to employ scarce resources in the most effective way. In fact, once it became clear in which way the single essential elements determined each other it should also be possible to identify the areas where – depending on specific characteristics of each individual situation – concrete action was most needed.

IV. The Agreement of Cotonou of 23 September 2000

A. The Relevance of the Principle of 'Good Governance'

One could get the impression that in the Agreement of Cotonou of 23 September 2000 the relevant framework was identified in the principle of 'good governance'. This concept, which was first used in the 1989 World Bank Report,[37] should provide a workable concept to effectively apply conditionality in international development cooperation. It is, however, not yet really clear what specific role this principle shall play in the context of the EC-ACP relationship in the future. This results from a brief overview of the relevant provisions, Articles 9 and 96 of Cotonou Agreement. Article 9 para 2 subpara 4 reads as follows:

> Respect for human rights, democratic principles and the rule of law, which underpin the ACP-EU Partnership, shall underpin the domestic and international policies of the Parties and constitute the essential elements of this Agreement.

The consequences of a violation of essential elements are set out in Article 96 of the Agreement:

> *Essential elements: consultation procedure and appropriate measures as regards human rights, democratic principles and the rule of law.*
>
> 1. Within the meaning of this Article, the term „Party" refers to the Community and the Member States of the European Union, of the one part, and each ACP State, of the other part.
>
> 1a. Both Parties agree to exhaust all possible options for dialogue under Article 8, except in cases of special urgency, prior to commencement of the consultations referred to in paragraph 2(a) of this Article.
>
> a) If despite the political dialogue conducted regularly between the Parties, a Party considers that the other Party has failed to fulfil an obligation stemming from respect for human rights, democratic principles and the rule of law referred to in paragraph 2 of Article 9, it shall, except in cases of special urgency, supply the other Party and the Council of Ministers with the relevant information required for a thorough examination of the situation with a view to seeking a solution acceptable to the Parties. To this end, it

---

[37] See Simma, Aschenbrenner and Schulte, *supra* note 36.

shall invite the other Party to hold consultations that focus on the measures taken or to be taken by the party concerned to remedy the situation.

The consultations shall be conducted at the level and in the form considered most appropriate for finding a solution.

The consultations shall begin no later than 15 days after the invitation and shall continue for a period established by mutual agreement, depending on the nature and gravity of the violation. In any case, the consultations shall last no longer than 60 days.

If the consultations do not lead to a solution acceptable to both Parties, if consultation is refused, or in cases of special urgency, appropriate measures may be taken. These measures shall be revoked as soon as the reasons for taking them have disappeared.

b) The term „cases of special urgency" shall refer to exceptional cases of particularly serious and flagrant violation of one of the essential elements referred to in paragraph 2 of Article 9, that require an immediate reaction.

The Party resorting to the special urgency procedure shall inform the other Party and the Council of Ministers separately of the fact unless it does not have to do so.

c) The 'appropriate measures' referred to in this Article are measures taken in accordance with international law, and proportional to the violation. In the selection of these measures, priority must be given to those which least disrupt the application of this agreement.

...

With regard to the principle of good governance, Article 9 para 3 of the Cotonou Agreement contains the following provision:

In the context of a political and institutional environment that upholds human rights, democratic principles and the rule of law, good governance is the transparent and accountable management of human, natural, economic and financial resources for the purposes of equitable and sustainable development. It entails clear decision-making procedures at the level of public authorities, transparent and accountable institutions, the primacy of law in the management and distribution of resources and capacity building for elaborating and implementing measures aiming in particular at preventing and combating corruption.

From the wording of this provision the impression may be gained that the principle of good governance is the overarching concept that should lend itself to give structure to the whole conditionality debate.

As already set out,[38] the concept of good governance is, however, still a rather vague one and the integration of this notion in the Cotonou Agreement may be seen as an experiment to 'harden' it. For the moment, however, there is an apparent conflict between the binding nature of the Cotonou Agreement and the lack of precision of the concept of good governance. As it is not considered as an 'essential element' in the Articles 9 and 96 of the Agreement the consultation process and the sanction mechanism set out in Article 96 do not find application. According to Article 97, only in case of corruption a consultation procedure and appropriate measures may find application.[39] For the rest the provisions on 'good governance' remain a *lex imperfecta*. It is obvious that this situation is the result of a compromise. To create at this stage a fully implementable concept of 'good governance' would probably have been too hard an infringement with the prevailing view of state sovereignty. Nevertheless, the concept of 'good governance' is here to stay. Whether this principle will live up to the expectations associated with it is not yet clear. It can however be said without doubt that the prominent place given to this principle is expression of the intent by the European Community to thoroughly reconsider important elements of its development policy. It is no coincidence that it should have been the Agreement of Cotonou where the principle of good governance – and together with it also respect for human rights and democracy – obtained such a strong position. First of all, it was the changed international environment that allowed for the imposition of values during the negotiation process which only slightly more than a decade earlier would have been considered to be mainly the expression of western ideological values. Secondly, it was also the first time that the new provisions on development cooperation introduced by the Maastricht Treaty manifested their full impact.[40] As the EC/EU and its member states are committing themselves ever stronger in the field of development cooperation also the call for more effectiveness

---

[38] Hilpold, *supra* note 26, at 68.

[39] Hilpold, *supra* note 14, at 252.

[40] Although being in force already at the time when the Lomé IV-bis Agreement was concluded, the philosophy behind these provisions had trickled down fully only at a later moment.

of these measures grows. Good governance is considered to be a key to the effectiveness of development assistance.[41]

Of course, the Agreement of Cotonou brought about not only a new philosophy on the role of human rights and governance but also – and probably even more visibly – a new perception on what this model of cooperation should achieve on the economic level and what instruments should be applied to reach this end.

As a result of the negotiations on a revision of the Cotonou Agreement concluded on 23 February 2005, the provisions on the political dialogue were further strengthened. This dialogue was intended to be of a more systematic nature in the future. It shall prevent situations requiring recourse to the consultation procedures envisaged in Articles 96 and 97. For this purpose more details on the political dialogue have been set out in a new Annex VII to the Cotonou Agreement.

B. The Cotonou Agreement as the Pivotal Document for EU Development Cooperation with ACP Countries

The Cotonou Agreement has undergone a second revision in 2010. As will also be shown below both the revision of 2005 and that of 2010 were directed at rendering this agreement more efficient and at strengthening the political component. In 2010, regard was taken of new challenges for the state community as a whole and for the parties involved in the EU-ACP development cooperation process in particular. Thus, specific provisions on climate change, food security, regional integration, state fragility and aid effectiveness were inserted.

On a whole, it can be said that this Agreement came about when a fundamental re-focusing of EU development cooperation was under way according to which it was tried to abandon the concentration on the ACP area in favour of those developing countries most in need. The Cotonou Agreement was, at the same time, expression of an attempt to uphold, as far as possible, the original focus. This difficult balancing act is still ongoing.

The overall political and economic context in which the EC-ACP relationship was designed to operate had changed dramatically. From a political viewpoint, the end of the East-West conflict had immediate repercussions on the Third World. The development discussion was freed from ideological

---

[41] European Commission, 'Governance and development. Communication from the Commission to the Council, the European Parliament and the European Economic and Social Committee' COM (2003) 615 final, at 4.

burdens of the past and developing countries came to be seen as a group of nations deserving equal attention. This change of perspective was partly reflected also in the law of the European Union where the insertion of Articles 177-181 in the EC Treaty in 1991 can be regarded as a decisive step towards the creation of a truly general development policy.[42]

With regard to the economic context, the entry into force of the Uruguay Agreement has brought about a gradual erosion of preferences the ACP countries had previously enjoyed as tariff and non-tariff barriers were further lowered on a general plane.[43] In the negotiating process the great challenge was, therefore, on the one hand, to overcome the elements of conflict with WTO law and, on the other, to offer new perspectives of development to this group of nations.

The development challenge now has to be tackled at the backdrop of an international environment that has profoundly changed in respect to the situation when this policy was first officially introduced by the Treaty of Maastricht. One of the greatest perils for further development – and actually for the preservation of the development stage already achieved – are fragile and failing states. The 2010 revision of the Cotonou Agreement has dedicated particular attention to this new threat.[44] Furthermore, by this revision agreement, the following threats have been newly addressed: organized crime, piracy and trafficking of, notably, people, drugs and weapons. Moreover, as stated in Article 11 para 1: 'The impacts of global challenges like international financial market shocks, climate change and pandemics also need to be taken into account.'[45]

C. Economic Cooperation Within the Cotonou Framework

The most immediate impulse to abandon the Lomé regime came from GATT/WTO law.[46] In the early 90s of the last century serious doubts were voiced

---

[42] See, in this sense, McMahon, *supra* note 20.

[43] *Ibid.*

[44] Art 11, para 1 of the revised Cotonou Agreement, 25 June 2005. On this challenge see also Peter Hilpold, '*Jus Post Bellum* and the Responsibility to Rebuild – Identifying the Contours of an Ever More Importance Aspect of R2P' (2015) 6 Journal of International Humanitarian Legal Studies 284. See also among SDGs of 2015 Goal 16.

[45] Art 11, para 1, subpara 2 of the revised Cotonou Agreement, 25 June 2005.

[46] Jürgen Huber, 'The Past, Present and Future ACP-EC Trade Regime and the WTO' (2000) 11 EJIL 427.

whether the association of the ACP countries to the EC was compatible with GATT law as the non-reciprocal trade preferences were alleged to be in violation of the most-favoured-nation (MFN) principle. Although Part IV of GATT allowed for non-reciprocal trade preferences for developing countries these were to apply on a generalized and not on a selective basis. On 9 December 1994 temporary relief was provided by the contracting parties through a waiver which was to last until the expiry of the Lomé IV-bis Agreement scheduled for 29 February 2000. In view of the fact that waivers did not have the objective to grant permanent exemptions from GATT/WTO rules and considering also that with the entry into force of the new WTO law on 1 January 1995 waivers had come under closer scrutiny, a successor regime had to be found that was compatible with WTO law. As this implied the withdrawal of far-reaching concessions negotiations with ACP countries proved to be tough. Soon it became clear that no radical change after the expiry of the Lomé IV-bis Agreement would be possible. Care had rather to be taken for the introduction of a provisional regime that would also provide further time for the negotiation of the definite successor regulation. In the end, this aim was actually achieved and the necessary consent by the WTO obtained. From 2000 to the end of 2007 the non-reciprocal trade preferences were kept in force. The waiver necessary for this derogation from WTO law was granted on 14 November 2001.[47] Transition from a non-reciprocal to a reciprocal system proved, however, not to be as smooth as originally thought. In many senses, this process is still ongoing.

The Lomé Agreements were not suited to bring about the economic progress within the ACP countries the parties had initially aimed at. It appeared that economic and social progress in the ACP group was slow or even non-existent.[48] A further spread of poverty was noticed. The main reason

---

[47] World Trade Organization, 'European Communities – The ACP-EC Partnership Agreement, Decision of 14 November 2001', WT/MIN(01)/15, <https://www.wto.org/english/thewto_e/minist_e/min01_e/mindecl_acp_ec_agre_e.htm> accessed 12 July 2017. See also Federico Lenzerini, 'Le relazioni tra Organizzazione Mondiale del Commercio e Comunità Europea nel settore della Cooperazione allo Sviluppo' in Francesco Francioni *et al* (eds), *Organizzazione Mondiale del Commercio e diritto della Comunità Europea nella prospettiva della risoluzione delle controversie* (2005) 189.

[48] Olufemi Babarinde and Gerrit Faber, 'From Lomé to Cotonou: ACP-EU Partnership in Transition' in Olufemi Babarinde and Gerrit Faber (eds), *The European Union and the Developing Countries – The Cotonou Agreement* (2005) 1, at 5 *et seq*. See also Nsongurua J Udombana, 'Back to Basics: The ACP-EU Cotonou Trade Agreement and Challenges for the African Union' (2004) 40 Texas International Law Journal 59 and Heribert Weiland, 'Globalisierung auf Raten. Zum

for this situation could be found in the fact that the initiatives set within this framework were not capable of giving an incentive for the creation of a strong private sector which should become the decisive force of self-sustaining development.[49]

In a certain sense, the philosophy behind this cooperation regime was one of a traditional international law viewpoint. Interlocutors of the EC and its member states were primarily governments and it was by no means guaranteed that the aid provided would trickle down to reach broader masses. In view of the amounts of resources at play the serious question had to be posed whether they were well spent. In a Commission green paper of 1996[50] it was pointed out that

> beyond political stability, which is a fundamental precondition for growth, and initial endowments, sound policies play a major role in influencing exports and growth. Macroeconomic stability, realistic and stable exchange rates, good institutions and good governance, and efficient resource allocation policies, in particular stable and credible import and taxation regimes, as well as reduced trade protection ... are significant determinants of competitiveness and hence export performance.[51]

The concession of unilateral preferences by the EU to the ACP countries has proved to be irreconcilable with WTO law, which was one of the main reasons for the total overhaul of the EC-ACP cooperation regime. The Cotonou Agreement purports to 'foster the smooth and gradual integration of the ACP States into the world economy'[52] and aims at 'full conformity with the provisions of the WTO'.[53]

---

neuen Cotonou-Abkommen zwischen der EU und den AKP-Staaten' in Heinrich Oberreuter, Armin A Steinkamm and Hanns-Frank Seller (eds), *Weltpolitik im 21. Jahrhundert, Festschrift Jürgen Schwarze* (2004) 418.

[49] Udombana, *supra* note 48, at 66 *et seq.* and Weiland, *supra* note 48, at 423 *et seq*.

[50] European Commission, 'Green Paper on Relations between the European Union and the ACP countries on the Eve of the 21st Century – Challenges and Options for a New Partnership', COM (96) 570 final of 20 November 1996.

[51] *Ibid.*, at para 17. The Green Paper stated further: 'The Union must redesign its aid policy towards the ACP countries from the scratch [...] the colonial and post-colonial era is over.'

[52] Art 34, para 1 ACP-EU Partnership Agreement, 23 June 2000 (Cotonou Agreement).

[53] Art 34, para 4 Cotonou Agreement.

The so-called Economic Partnership Agreements (EPAs), which are essentially Free Trade Areas concluded by the EU with groups of ACP countries, shall be at the center of economic cooperation. As GATT/WTO law is rather demanding in this regard,[54] a transitional period had to be allowed for the necessary adaptations to be made.

The transitional period lasted until 31 December 2007 during which the non-reciprocal trade preferences applied under the Fourth ACP-EC Convention were to be maintained. As mentioned, due to a waiver,[55] the WTO conformity of this transitional measure was guaranteed. The details of this regime were regulated in Annex V to the Cotonou Agreement (deleted by the 2010 reform).

Originally, a clear time-frame was given according to which the transition from non-reciprocal trade to reciprocal trade should be completed. This goal proved to be unachievable and over the years the parties became aware of the complexities of this process. The 2010 revision of the Cotonou agreement ushered in a complete revision of Article 36 of the agreement. This provision now goes as follows:

Article 36
Modalities

1. In view of the objectives and principles set out above, the Parties agree to take all the necessary measures to ensure the conclusion of new WTO-compatible Economic Partnership Agreements, removing progressively barriers to trade between them and enhancing cooperation in all areas relevant to trade.

2. The Economic Partnership Agreements, as development instruments, aim to foster smooth and gradual integration of the ACP States into the world economy, especially by making full use of the potential of regional integration and South-South trade.

3. The Parties agree that these new trading arrangements shall be introduced gradually.

---

[54] See Peter Hilpold, 'Regional Integration According to Article XXIV GATT – Between Law and Politics' (2003) 7 Max Planck Yearbook of United Nations Law (2003) 219.

[55] WTO, *supra* note 47. This waiver was granted during the Doha WTO Ministerial 2001 and expired on 31 December 2007.

A specific time-frame, formerly mentioned in Article 37 of the Cotonou Agreement, is now missing.

It is not yet clear whether EPAs will successfully take the place of the existing preference regime. In principle, these agreements could have a very far-reaching coverage comprising goods, services, direct foreign investment, technical assistance and harmonization of regulation.[56]

The newly drafted para 2 of Article 35 of the Cotonou Agreement gives proof to the new understanding of the intricacies of development acquired in the meantime by the EU:

> Economic and trade cooperation shall build on regional integration initiatives of ACP States.
>
> Cooperation in support of regional cooperation and integration as defined in Title I and economic and trade cooperation shall be mutually reinforcing. Economic and trade cooperation shall address, in particular, supply and demand side constraints, notably interconnectivity of infrastructure, economic diversification and trade development measures as a means of enhancing ACP States' competitiveness. Appropriate weight shall therefore be given to the corresponding measures in the ACP States' and regions' development strategies, which the Community shall support, in particular through the provision of aid for trade.

Ideally, there should be, therefore, a sequence in the sense that first groups of ACP countries integrate among each other and afterwards they conclude a FTA with the EU. As regional integration among developing countries has been – on average – not very successful it is doubtful whether this is a workable approach.[57] It is argued in literature that integration between the ACP countries and between the EU and the relevant ACP groups should proceed simultaneously.[58]

The newly drafted Article 37A addresses the problem of preference-erosion for ACP states as a consequence of further multilateral and bilateral trade liberalization. The solution offered to overcome this problem is a rather timid one: The parties shall endeavour to overcome the negative impact of

---

[56] Gerrit Faber, 'Economic Partnership Agreements and Regional Integration among ACP Countries' in Olufemi Babarinde and Gerrit Faber (eds), *The European Union and the Developing Countries* (2005) 85, at 87.

[57] *Ibid.*, at 92 *et seq.*

[58] *Ibid.*, at 96 *et seq.*

this development, for as long as it is feasible. Thereby, the parties admit that preference erosion is a fact that is unavoidable in the long run.

In the past, within the Cotonou agreement, also in the context of economic integration specific regard has been taken of the so-called Least Developed Countries (LDC). As a consequence of the 2010 reform, this category no longer enjoys specific consideration within this field. Still, some specific provisions on LDCs can be found in the Articles 84ss. of the Cotonou Agreement. According to Article 84 LDCs shall be accorded special treatment 'in order to enable them to overcome the serious economic and social difficulties hindering their development so as to step up their respective rates of development.'

It was hoped that the essence of 'special treatment' should be clarified in the ambit of the Doha Round. Up to this moment, these hopes have been disappointed as the Doha Round negotiations have stalled. These countries continue, however, to profit from specific preferences in the ambit of the EU's Generalised Scheme of Preferences (GSP).

The European Union has granted free access to essentially all products from 49 LDCs as of 1 January 2015.[59] The intention was to apply the GSP to fewer beneficiaries while rendering it at the same time more effective. To this end the GSP scheme was divided into three arrangements.[60]

- There is, first of all, a general arrangement to be granted to all those developing countries which share a common developing need and are in a similar stage of development. These countries are granted duty arrangements for about 66% of all EU tariff lines. Not all developing countries are, however, eligible for these benefits. In fact, countries which are classified by the World Bank as high-income or upper-middle income countries were retained not

---

[59] This step was taken with the so-called 'Everything But Arms Regulation' (introduced by Council Regulation (EC) 416/2001 amending Regulation (EC) No 2820/98 applying a multiannual scheme of generalised tariff preferences for the period 1 July 1999 to 31 December 2001 so as to extend duty-free access without any quantitative restrictions to products originating in the least developed countries, OJ L060/43). On the basis of Regulation (EU) 978/2012 (applying a scheme of generalised tariff preferences and repealing Council Regulation (EC) No 732/2008, OJ L303/1) containing the EU GSP presently in force no duties and quantitative restrictions find application on imports of products from LDCs. As of 1 January 2015 the GSP+ regime applies to 13 countries.

[60] See for this classification and the relating explanations the preambular provisions in Regulation 978/2012, *supra* note 59.

to be in need of such grants as they have successfully completed their transition to competitive market economies. Furthermore, the concession of privileges to such countries would increase the competitive pressure to lower-income countries.[61] Furthermore, for the sake of consistency, also those countries that benefitted from a different preferential market access arrangement with the Union were excluded from the general GSP scheme.[62] As a consequence, at the moment the group benefitting from the general regime comprises 34 countries and territories.

- Furthermore, there is a Special Incentive Arrangement for Sustainable Development and Good Governance, or 'GSP+' initiative. This initiative applies to developing countries if[63]

    • they are considered to be vulnerable due to a lack of diversification and insufficient integration within the international trading system;

    • they have ratified all the conventions listed in Annex VIII of Reg. 978/2012 and provided the monitoring process to these convention did not reveal any serious failure in the implementation of these conventions and no reservation has been formulated to any of these conventions that would have been prohibited by the relevant instrument or be incompatible with its object and purpose.[64]

---

[61] *Ibid.*, at para 9 of the preambular provisions.

[62] *Ibid.*

[63] *Ibid.*, at Art 9.

[64] This appears to be a very ingenious way to further enhance human rights compliance in third countries. As it has been shown, the European Union has conducted a human rights promotion policy towards third countries for quite a long time. The EU concentrated, however, primarily on the assumption of these obligations while barely taking regard of the implementation process. On this basis many countries created the semblance of a human rights friendly policy while in reality their human rights record remained poor. Now form alone is no longer sufficient: substance counts.

On the basis of the GSP+-initiative the same 66% tariff lines that benefit from the general GSP scheme are completely exempted from duties.[65]

- The third initiative concerns 'Special Arrangements for the Least-Developed Countries' ('Everything But Arms' – EBA).[66] Countries that have been identified by the UN as a 'least-developed country' are eligible for full duty-free, quota-free access for all products except arms and ammunition.[67] Currently, there are 49 beneficiaries of this regime.[68]

While ACP countries have always been the main targets of EC development cooperation, over the years a network of cooperation agreements has been built up also with countries of other regions.[69] In this context the cooperation agreements with several countries and territories of the Mediterranean region[70] (Algeria, Egypt, Jordan, Lebanon, Morocco, Tunisia, West Bank and Gaza

---

[65] Presently there are 13 beneficiaries of this scheme: Armenia, Bolivia, Cape Verde, Costa Rica, Ecuador, El Salvador, Georgia, Guatemala, Mongolia, Pakistan, Panama, Paraguay and Peru.

[66] Regulation 978/2012, *supra* note 59, at Art 17ff.

[67] European Commission, 'The EU's Generalised Scheme of Preferences (GSP)' (October 2014) <http://trade.ec.europa.eu/doclib/docs/2014/november/tradoc_152865.pdf> accessed 12 July 2017, at 3.

[68] Regulation 978/2012, *supra* note 59, at Annex IV.

[69] See, for details, Thomas Oppermann, *Europarecht* (1999) para 1746 *et seq*.

[70] See, in this context, the MEDA programme based on MEDA Regulation 1488/96, OJ L 189/1, as amended by Regulation 2698/2000, OJ L 311/1. MEDA II is more program-oriented and strategic than its predecessor. It is meant to be a preparatory initiative for the creation of a Euro-Mediterranean free-trade area to be set up by 2010. See Euromed Special Feature No 21 of 3 May 2001. See also the Barcelona Declaration adopted at the Euro-Mediterranean Conference 27–28 November 1995 where the foundations for the Barcelona Process, a new regional relationship, was laid; for a recent overview of this relationship, see Peter Schlotter, 'Die Europäische Union als außenpolitischer Akteur? – Zur Kohärenz der EU-Mittelmeerpolitik und zur Rolle der Kommission' (2005) 4/05 Integration 316.

Strip), with Israel,[71] with the Latin American region and with Asian countries[72] as well as with South Africa[73] have to be mentioned.

A general, all-encompassing policy of development is, however, only in the making at the most.[74]

---

[71] See, in particular, the Euro-Mediterranean Agreement establishing an association between the European Communities and their Member States, on the one part, and the State of Israel, on the other part, concluded on 20 November 1995 and which entered into force on 1 June 2000, OJ L 147/3. It was amended by a Protocol signed on 30 March 2004 to extend the application of this agreement as of 1 May 2004 to the 10 new EU member states. In 2007 it was superseded by the European Neighbourhood and Partnership Instrument (ENPI). See <http://www.medea.be/en/themes/euro-mediterranean-cooperation/meda-programme/> accessed on 16 August 2017.

[72] See Council Regulation (EEC) 443/92, OJ L52. A policy of financial and technical cooperation with the Asian and the Latin American (ALA) developing countries outside the ACP-EEC relationship has been pursued since 1976. Later it was supplemented by economic cooperation programs. In this context ever-increasing importance was attributed to the promotion of human rights, to the support for the process of democratization, good governance, environmental protection, trade liberalization and the strengthening of the cultural dimension, by means of an increasing dialogue on political, economic and social issues conducted in the mutual interest; see Regulation 443/92, Article 1. With regard to Asia, in particular, the general strategy that guides all EC actions in this region – including development assistance – is contained in the 2001 Commission Communication 'Europe and Asia: A Strategic Framework for Enhanced Partnership'. See, in this context, the EC Commission's Strategy Paper and Indicative Programme for multi-country programs in Asia, 2005-2006.

[73] Although this country has adhered to the Cotonou Agreement, the provisions of the EU-South Africa Trade, Development and Cooperation Agreement (TDCA) take precedence over the Cotonou Agreement. In particular, the provisions of the Cotonou Agreement on development finance cooperation and those on economic and trade cooperation will not apply, see Protocol No. 3 to the Cotonou Agreement. The TDCA provisionally came into force in January 2000. While for the EU extensive trade liberalisation obligations for industrial goods (and lesser ones in the field of agricultural products) apply, the situation for South Africa is the opposite. The TDCA contains also a variety of provisions on economic development cooperation.

[74] This is not to say that specific endeavours by the Commission would be lacking. See, for example, the thorough study contained in the Communication from the Commission to the Council and the European Parliament, 'The European Community's Development Policy', COM(2000) 212 final. In recent years, the Union tries to connect the development issue with other fundamental challenges such as environmental protection, climate change, security, fight against terrorism and state-building. The 'European Consensus on Development', the 'Agenda for Change' (2012) and the Communication 'A Decent Life for All: From Vision

On a whole, the EU had to thoroughly redefine its development policy as the old privileges for the former colonies of single member states could no longer be maintained. This process is still going on as it is not yet clear how to reconcile the reciprocity requirement imposed by Article XXIV GATT and the need to grant special and differential treatment, an element to which also the Cotonou Agreement refers to. It is uncontestable that already the existing legal regime provides instruments and ways for successful development cooperation. In fact, the conclusion of free trade agreements will allow for the creation of preferential regimes that should boost trade and development.[75] Furthermore, it will be possible also in the future to privilege ACP countries in the field of unilateral measures. Privileges of this kind are actually in place and find broad appreciation. In general, however, WTO law imposes strict limits for deviations from reciprocity and it is hard to imagine how the volume of preferences once in force within the Lomé system could be re-established within the Cotonou framework. Of course, the Lomé regime has proven to be rather ineffectual and the new development cooperation system should make a difference also in this sense. How this should be achieved still has to be sorted out. As evidenced by the developments on the international level of the last two decades, the search for a genuine and effective international development policy has become a paramount concern for the international community.[76] Economic development is also closely interconnected with

---

to Collective Action' (2014) provide a refreshing new look at the development issue.

[75] This is at least the traditional view of the role of free trade areas (as well as customs unions). See in this regard the literature starting with Jacob Viner, *The Customs Union Issues* (1950) up to the report by the WTO, *Regionalism and the World Trading System* (1995). A different attitude is, however, perceptible in a later report by the WTO, see WTO, 'Regional Trade Integration under Transformation' (2002), <http://www.wto.org/english/tratop_e/region_e/sem_april02_e.htm> accessed 12 July 2017. Lately, the criticism by the WTO towards regionalism seems to abound; see, in particular, the so-called 'Sutherland-Report', WTO, 'The Future of the WTO – Addressing Institutional Challenges in the New Millennium', at 19. See, in general on this issue, Hilpold, *supra* note 54. See also Peter Hilpold, 'Regionale Integrationsabkommen im GATT/WTO-System' (2015) 62 Wirtschaftspolitische Blätter 227, and the literature cited therein.

[76] See in this context the United Nations Millennium Declaration adopted by all UN member states in 2000 (UNGA Res 55/2 (LV), United Nations Millennium Declaration (18 September 2000) UN Doc A/RES/55/2). See also the so-called 'Sachs-Report', UN Millennium Project, 'Investing in Development: A Practical Plan to Achieve the Millennium Development Goals' (2005) <http://www.unmillenniumproject.org> accessed 12 July 2017. For a general analysis of this discussion, see Peter Hilpold, 'Reforming the United Nations: New Proposals in

several other pivotal concerns of the international community of the present days such as the fight against terrorism, against new infectious diseases and the effective implementation of the prohibition of the use of force.[77] For the future it is, therefore, very probable that the shape of the European Union's development policy will be much more influenced by the international discussion on this subject than it has been the case in the past. At the same time the prominent role played by the European Union in the field of international cooperation assures that the EU can also give a decisive contribution to the formation of these new international standards.

On a whole, it can be said that the EU development policy has undergone – especially in the last decade – a far-reaching reformulation whereby its scope of application has been amply broadened. Historic ties now count less and the effective needs of the single countries are now far more important. An ever-increasing importance is attributed to the evaluation of the effectiveness of this policy.[78]

D. Institutional Aspects of the Cotonou Agreement

There is a dispute in literature whether the Cotonou Agreement is to be seen as a continuation of the Lomé system or whether it constitutes rather a total departure from it. There are surely elements of both. The guiding idea remained the same: to provide an instrument that should enhance the development of the ACP but the elements by which this should be achieved changed considerably as will be shown subsequently.

Already the formal structure of the Cotonou Agreement diverges clearly from that of the Lomé IV-bis Agreement. While the latter comprised 369 articles the former is limited to exactly 100 articles. The bulk of the provisions that regulate the actual working on the new relationship between the EC and the ACP countries was relegated to the annexes. On a whole, it represents a stocktaking of a long experience on development cooperation and an attempt to redress the major deficiencies that have shown up in this context. The

---

a Long-Lasting Endeavour' (2005) LII Netherlands International Law Review (2005) 389.

[77] See, in particular, the Report presented by the High-level Panel of Eminent Persons to the UNSG Kofi Annan of 1 December 2004, entitled 'A More Secure World: Our Shared Responsibility', UN Doc A/59/565. A new 'Responsibility to Protect' is evolving and in this context the European Union has to play a prominent role. See Peter Hilpold (ed), *The Responsibility to Protect* (2015).

[78] See also the European Commission Report on the public consultation on the future of EU development policy of June 2005.

primary goal to reduce poverty shall be achieved through five instruments of which the Cotonou agreement is mainly composed of:

- strengthened political dimension;
- broader integration of private actors and of the civil society as a whole;
- cooperation approach addressing more clearly poverty reduction;
- conclusion of new economic and trade partnerships; and
- more focused financial cooperation.

Article 2 of the Agreement declares fundamental principles, underpinning the ACP-EC cooperation:

- equality of partners and ownership of the development strategies;
- participation of all sections of society, including the private sector and civil society organizations;
- dialogue; and
- differentiation and regionalism: the needs, the performance and the long-term development strategy of each cooperation partner shall be taken into consideration. Special attention shall be given to the needs of the least-developed countries, of landlocked and island countries. The 2nd revision agreement of 2010 has emphasized that particular emphasis shall be put on regional integration, including at continental level.

The Cotonou Agreement is concluded for a period of 20 years.[79] At first sight, this constitutes an important modification with respect to the past. On the other hand, the important financial protocols are defined only for five-year periods. Thus, only the general framework is characterized by long-term stability. The flexibility of the financial provisions makes sure that periodical adaptations of the policies pursued are possible. As will be shown later on, a cornerstone of this new relationship, the Economic Partnership Agreements, still have to be defined in detail and will become operative only in the years to come.

As already mentioned, the Cotonou Agreement has already undergone two revisions according to Article 95, which foresees such adaptations in five year intervals. By the revision of 2005 it was attempted to bring the Cotonou Agreement more in line with the general orientations of the EC development

---

[79] Art 95 Cotonou Agreement.

policy and to streamline it with regard to actual political needs. Furthermore, it was also tried to relate the cornerstone of the EC development policy more closely to the activities set on the UN level. To this end, the preamble of the Cotonou Agreement contains a special reference to the UN Millennium Development Goals (MDGs) adopted by the UNGA in 2000.[80]

In 2010, this approach was continued. New priorities were set (fight against organized crime, piracy and trafficking of, notably people, drugs and weapons, need to tackle challenges like international financial market shocks, climate change[81] and pandemics[82]; necessity to address situations of fragility; Article 11 of the Cotonou Agreement). The difficulty to meet the ambitious timetable for the conclusion of EPAs was recognized and therefore more flexibility was granted in this regard. Furthermore, some institutional reforms were undertaken.

The institutional provisions are to be found in Articles 14–17 of the Cotonou Agreement. According to Article 14, the institutions of this agreement are the Council of Ministers, the Committee of Ambassadors and the Joint Parliamentary Assembly.

The Council of Ministers is the most powerful, political organ.[83] It comprises, on the one hand, the members of the Council of the European Union and members of the Commission of the European Union, and, on the other hand, a member of the government of each ACP state. The office of the President of the Council of Ministers is held alternatively by a member of the Council of the European Union and a member of the government of an ACP state. As a rule, the Council meets once a year and whenever it seems necessary. The decisions are taken by consensus.[84]

The Committee of Ambassadors comprises, on the one hand, the permanent representative of each EU member state and a representative of the Commission and, on the other, the head of mission of each ACP state to the European Union. This Committee primarily assists the Council of Ministers

---

[80] As will be explained below, these MDGs were superseded in 2015 by the Sustainable Development Goals (SDGs) which, on the one hand, build on the MDGs but, on the other hand, are more comprehensive and far-reaching.

[81] See the provision in Art 32A on 'climate change'.

[82] See also the extensive provision in Art 31A on HIV/AIDS.

[83] Andreas Zimmermann, 'Commentary to Article 179 TEC' in Hans von der Groeben and Jürgen Schwarze (eds), *EU-/EG-Vertrag-Kommentar* (2003) para 38.

[84] Art 14 Cotonou Agreement.

in the fulfilment of its tasks and, in this context, fulfils a monitoring function with regard to the implementation of the agreement.[85]

The Joint Parliamentary Assembly[86] assumes – to a certain extent – a representative role.[87] It is composed of an equal number of EU and ACP representatives. The members of the Joint Parliamentary Assembly are members of the European Parliament and members of parliament or other representatives nominated by the respective parliament. Exceptionally there is also the possibility that an ACP state may nominate its representatives for the Assembly if there is no parliament.[88] The Joint Parliamentary Assembly is a merely consultative body which meets twice a year, alternatively in the European Union and in an ACP state.

By the 2010 reform a new institution was added: the 'Meeting of Heads of State or Government' (Article 14A). This new institution assures both closer interaction between the Cotonou institutions and the participating governments as well as an immediate presence of the governments within the Cotonou setting.

E. Political Dialogue

One of the major innovations of the Cotonou Agreement is about the inclusion of substantially extended provisions on the basis of political dialogue. The parties have already accumulated some experience in the past but the results were not always satisfying. Now Article 2 of the Agreement considers a political dialogue not only as a fundamental principle but also attributes it a 'pivotal role'. This is not merely an emphatic enunciation. The EU as well as the ACP countries have evidenced the importance attributed to political dialogue during the first revision conference to the Cotonou Agreement between May 2004 and February 2005. In the ambit of the conference the political dimension was strengthened and political dialogue more amplified. According to Article 8 of the Cotonou Agreement the 'Parties shall regularly engage in a comprehensive, balanced and deep political dialogue leading to commitments on both sides'. On the basis of the First Revision Agreement (in force since 1 July 2008), political dialogue is attributed now a much more formal role within the Cotonou framework. Such a dialogue is mandatory

---

[85] Art 16 Cotonou Agreement.

[86] Art 17 Cotonou Agreement.

[87] Zimmermann, *supra* note 83, at para 40.

[88] In this case, however, these representatives need the prior approval of the Joint Parliamentary Assembly.

before recourse is taken to the consultation procedure according to Article 96 of the Agreement.[89] In Annex VII 'Political dialogue as regards human rights, democratic principles and the rule of law', introduced by the First Revision Agreement, detailed advice is given on how to structure this dialogue. Much care is taken to guarantee that the dialogue takes place according to internationally recognized standards and norms and with reference to jointly agreed agendas, priorities and benchmarks. This reform was hailed as an important step forward in order to make sure that the application of these provisions is felt to be a less subjective issue and, as a consequence, to render their implementation less confrontational. It has also been agreed that the political dialogue shall be systematic and formal.[90] As it involves each country, a further contribution is given in order to render this instrument acceptable on a broad basis.

With regard to material reforms, particular emphasis was laid on the fight against terrorism,[91] non-proliferation[92] and the introduction of an obligation to support the International Criminal Court.[93]

On a whole, it can be said that these provisions on political dialogue opened up truly new avenues in North-South cooperation that could assume an exemplary role on a global scale. Thereby the basis was created for a more effective and meaningful dialogue than it was the case in the past, even if in the literature it has been argued that the EC has been partly too keen to push through their own position in this field.[94] In 2010 it was tried to remediate somewhat to this deficit by emphasizing the fact that political conditionality applies in a reciprocal way and it is therefore not dictated by the EU to its partners.[95]

---

[89] Only the following consultations under Article 96 can go ahead without preceding intensified political dialogue: (1) if there is special urgency or (2) when there is a persistent lack of compliance with commitments taken by one of the Parties during an earlier dialogue, (3) or by a failure to engage in a dialogue in good faith.

[90] Annex VII Cotonou Agreement.

[91] Art 11a Cotonou Agreement.

[92] Art 11b Cotonou Agreement.

[93] Art 11 para 6 Cotonou Agreement. See also Sandra Bartelt, 'Commentary to Article 209' in Ulrich Becker *et al* (eds), EU-Kommentar (2012) 1965, para 24.

[94] See Karin Arts, 'Political Dialogue in a "New" Framework' in Olufemi Babarinde and Gerrit Faber (eds), *The European Union and the Developing Countries* (2005) 155, at 173.

[95] Art 9, para 4, subpara 4 Cotonou Agreement.

With this latest reform it was generally tried to further fine-tune the goals and objectives of political dialogue within the Cotonou Agreement. Particular emphasis is now put on fight against all forms of discrimination. The subject of 'climate change' has been newly added.

F. Financial Cooperation

Financial cooperation, a 'euphemism for aid'[96], as it was called, is regulated in Articles 62 to 78 as well as in two annexes to the Cotonou Agreement. The relevant financial resources do not make part of the EU budget but are derived from the European Development Fund (EDF) which is supported directly by member states' payments.[97] The revision agreements continued to maintain the existing situation. At the moment, for the period 2014-2020, the 11th European Development Fund with a total allocation of 30.5 billion is in force. In the past, repeatedly the integration of the EDF in the EU budget was requested. There would be good arguments for such a move, in particular the creation of more transparency, but on the other hand it was opined that preserving a special fund for ACP countries would not only allow for more flexibility but also strengthen the EU development budget as a whole.[98] Of course, also the old political, cultural and economic allegiances with these countries play a role when the decision was taken to postpone a radical reshuffling of the whole financing system to the period after 2020. The bulk of the means from EDF goes to Africa. In line with the 'Agenda for Change' (2011) the EU wanted to allocate resources to projects with the greatest impact.[99] As a rule, three priority sectors per country should be chosen (for fragile states four). Primary recipients are Ethiopia (745 million), Tanzania (626 million), the Democratic Republic of Congo (620 million) and Niger (596 million).[100]

---

[96] See Udombana, *supra* note 48, at 83.

[97] Andreas Hecker, 'Commentary to Article 179 TEC' in Carl Lenz and Klaus-Dieter Borchardt (eds), *EU- und EG-Vertrag* (2003) 1785, para 11.

[98] See Kilnes *et al*, 'More or Less? A Financial Analysis of the Proposed 11th European Development Fund' (2012) European Centre for Development Policy Management, Brief Note No 29, 2.

[99] See Brussel Office Weblog, <http://brussels.cta.int/index.php?option=com_k2&view=item&id=9097:edf-2014-2020-following-the-money> accessed 12 July 2017.

[100] Amounts in Euro. For these data see the source in the previous footnote.

G.   An Assessment and an Outlook

With regard to its relations with the ACP countries the EU is, at the moment, in the process of a difficult re-adjustment of its position and its policy. The previous policy of non-reciprocity and selective privileges for this group of countries has been subject of heavy criticism and is no longer sustainable in its original form. It has also become clear that aid of this kind has no lasting effects and can even be detrimental if it flows mainly to the established corrupt and autocratic elites. Nonetheless, the need for further aid is still given. There can be no doubt that the primary focus of EU development cooperation initiatives remains on Africa. However, new approaches and instruments are needed and the Agreement of Cotonou can be seen as an attempt to reconceive development cooperation. This agreement is, however, at the same time expression for the need of a re-orientation as it sticks to traditional visions of development aid. It can therefore be qualified as an instrument of transition and, at the same time, as a field of experimentation. Many elements that make out present EU development cooperation had been conceived and subjected to a first try within the EU-ACP relationship, and with the Agreement of Cotonou this tradition is continued. At the same time, however, EU development cooperation has taken a broader perspective and its further evolution takes place in an intense dialogue with a series of competent international institutions. Furthermore, it has to be considered that the internal political climate of the EU has profoundly changed. The sensibility for those goals and perspectives that stand at the center of political conditionality and for a fairer distribution of international wealth has greatly augmented. It is, therefore, very likely that the further development of the EU-ACP relationship will be strongly influenced by these developments. As shown, the last reforms to the Agreement of Cotonou already reflect these processes and it is most likely that the further reforms to this agreement will go along the same way.

V. Going from Amsterdam to Nice to Lisbon

A. The Treaty of Amsterdam, the Treaty of Nice and the Proposed 'Constitution for Europe'

Neither the Treaty of Amsterdam nor the Treaty of Nice brought about greater changes for the provisions on development cooperation.[101] The essence of these rules has remained largely untouched. The former Treaty strengthened the position of the European Parliament by applying the co-decision procedure according to Article 251 TEC to development cooperation. The latter treaty introduced Article 181a into Community law (now Article 212 TFEU). This provision created the normative basis for economic, financial and technical cooperation with third countries that are not developing countries. Thereby, instruments created in the field of development cooperation can now find application also beyond this area without necessity to overstretch the concept of development country. It can be argued that this new conceptual clarity will be in the interest also of the developing countries as this allows for a more effective targeting of the relevant measures. Really important changes in the field of development cooperation were contained in the Treaty establishing a Constitution for Europe[102] especially with regard to the extension of the scope of this policy as with regard to the instruments available for its implementation.[103] As is well known, this Treaty never entered into force but important parts of this Treaty, and among them also the provisions on development cooperation, came to life within the Treaty of Lisbon.

B. The Treaty of Lisbon

The provisions formerly contained in the Articles 177-181 TEC are now to be found in the Articles 208-211 TFEU. This re-location of the relevant provisions had substantial implications. They now form an integral part of Title III on 'Cooperation with Third Countries and Humanitarian Aid'

---

[101] For the structure of EU development cooperation in 2003 see Ursula Werther-Pietsch, 'Die Entwicklungszusammenarbeit der Europäischen Union' in Bea de Abreu Fialho Gomes *et al* (eds*), Die Praxis der Entwicklungszusammenarbeit* (2003) 129.

[102] Treaty Establishing a Constitution for Europe, 16 December 2004, OJ C 310.

[103] Andreas Zimmermann, 'Gemeinschaftliche Entwicklungspolitik im Vertrag über eine Verfassung für Europa' in Rainer Hofmann and Andreas Zimmermann (eds), *Eine Verfassung für Europa* (2005) 167.

(Articles 208-213 TFEU) which makes part of title V on 'External Action'. Article 208 refers to the 'principles and objectives of the Union's External Action'. Many of the principles and objectives formerly contained in Article 177 TEC (now Article 208 TFEU) could therefore be deleted from the text of this provision as they now are part of the overarching framework which has been enriched with further principles and objectives and which offers a far more coherent overall setting in a European Union now considerably more 'politicized' than before and attributing far larger importance to the democratic component embodied by the European Parliament.

While in the past Community action in the field of development cooperation was governed by the principle of subsidiarity, now the Union competence is of a parallel nature and therefore Union and member states act on an equal footing.[104] This is also made clear by Article 4 para 4 TFEU which provides as follows:

> In the areas of development cooperation and humanitarian aid, the Union shall have competence to carry out activities and conduct a common policy; however, the exercise of that competence shall not result in Member States being prevented from exercising theirs.

Now the ordinary legislation rules apply and thereby the European Parliament has a greater say in this field. Its role has become equal to that of the Council.[105]

A further important structural change regards the location of the principle of coherence. While up to the Treaty of Lisbon a specific article was dedicated to this principle (Article 178 TEC), now it has been integrated into Article 208 para 1, 2nd sentence with a somewhat strengthened wording. As will be seen below, the new wording now requires that Union 'take[s] account of the objectives of development cooperation in the policies that it implements which are likely to affect developing countries' (while in the past it sufficed that the Union 'contributed' to them.

The EU continues to be represented externally by the European Commission, notwithstanding the introduction of a High Representative for Foreign

---

[104] See Article 4 para 4 TFEU, according to which '[i]n the areas of development cooperation and humanitarian aid, the Union shall have competence to carry out activities and conduct a common policy; however, the exercise of that competence shall not result in Member States being prevented from exercising theirs.'. See Wolfgang Benedek, 'Commentary to Article 208' in Eberhard Grabitz, Meinhard Hilf and Martin Nettesheim (eds.), *EUV/AEUV* (2016) para 18.

[105] *Ibid.*, at para 19.

Affairs and Security Policy[106] and this holds true also for the development policy which is purely external in nature. Nonetheless, development policy activities have to be coordinated with those of the High Representative. The High Representative coordinates a series of aid instruments and in this he/she has to cooperate with the newly created European Diplomatic Service (EDS). A new Directorate-General for International Cooperation and Development (DE DEVCO) has been created that is responsible for formulating European international cooperation and development policy and delivering aid. It resulted from a merger of the EuropeAid Cooperation Office (AIDCO) and the Directorate General for Development and Relations with ACP States and was first entitled as 'DG Development and Cooperation – EuropeAid (as of 1 January 2011) and got its actual name as of 1 January 2015.

VI. The Competence Situation After Lisbon and the Five C's

As already mentioned, the position of the development policy has been enhanced by the Treaty of Lisbon. In the past, the text in Article 177 TEC spoke of this policy being 'complementary'. There was broad agreement that this did not mean that the EC's development policy should be of a subordinate nature. On the contrary, it was maintained that both policies were standing on the same footing[107] and as a consequence they had to be coordinated. What complementarity really means results, first of all, from statistical data. These data are evidencing that the means provided by the EU member states on their own by far exceed those coming directly from the EU.[108]

Complementarity may also refer to the relationship between the donor and the recipient. In this context, according to the 'European Consensus on Development', '[t]he best way to ensure complementarity is to respond to partner countries' priorities, at the country and regional level.'[109]

---

[106] According to the Treaty of Amsterdam which introduced this post, its title was 'High Representative for Common Foreign and Security Policy'.

[107] See extensively on this issue and with unequivocal clarity the opinion by GA Antonio La Pergola in Case C-268/94, *Portuguese Republic v Council of the European Union*, [1994] ECR I-6177, para 14 *et seq*.

[108] See G Vernier, 'Commentary to Article 177 TEC' in Philippe Léger, *Commentaire article par article des traités UE et CE* (2000) para 9.

[109] European Commission, 'The European Consensus on Development' (2006) 20, para 30.

Article 209 para 1 contains a general competence provision in the field of development cooperation. This provision is, of course, not the only one, which touches upon competence issues within development cooperation[110] but it is surely the most important one. As the CJEU has stated on several occasions, a measure (or an agreement) has to be characterized according to its 'essential object' (and not on the basis of its formal designation) and the legal basis for its adoption has to be chosen accordingly.[111] Reference to more than one legal bases is allowed only if an 'essential object' of a measure, its 'main focus', cannot be determined and if the relevant procedures are not mutually incompatible.[112]

Recently, the CJEU has restated its jurisprudence in a case concerning (also) the issue of development cooperation:[113]

> According to settled case-law, the choice of the legal basis for a European Union measure, including the measure adopted for the purpose of concluding an international agreement, must rest on objective factors amenable to judicial review, which include the aim and content of that measure. If examination of a European Union measure reveals that it pursues a twofold purpose or that it has a twofold component and if one of those is identifiable as the main or predominant purpose or component, whereas the other is merely incidental, the measure must be founded on a single legal basis, namely, that required by the main or predominant purpose or component. By way of exception, if it is established that the measure pursues several objectives which are inseparably linked without one being secondary and indirect in relation to the other, the measure must be founded on the various corresponding legal bases. However, no dual legal basis is possible where the procedures required by each legal basis are incompatible with each other (see, inter alia, Case C130/10 Parliament v Council EU:C:2012:472, Paragraphs 42 to 45 and the case-law cited).
>
> In this instance, it must be determined whether, among the provisions of the Framework Agreement, those relating to readmission of nationals of the contracting parties, to transport and to the environment also fall within

---

[110] See, in particular, Arts 207, 217 TFEU.

[111] Case C-268/94, *Portuguese Republic v Council of the European Union*, [1996] ECR I-6177, para 39. See in general Case C-300/89, *Commission of the European Communities v Council of the European Communities*, [1991] ECR I-02867, para 22, the leading case as to this question.

[112] See Rudolf Streinz and Tobias Kruis, 'Commentary to Article 209 TFEU' in Rudolf Streinz (ed), *EUV/AEUV, Kommentar* (2012) 1999, para 1.

[113] Case C-377/12, *European Commission v Council*, [2014] ECLI:EU:2014:1903.

development cooperation policy or whether they go beyond the framework of that policy and therefore require the contested decision to be founded on additional legal bases.

According to Article 208(1) TFEU, European Union policy in the field of development cooperation is to be conducted within the framework of the principles and objectives – as resulting from Article 21 TEU – of the European Union's external action. The primary objective of that policy is the reduction and, in the long term, the eradication of poverty and the European Union must take account of the objectives of development cooperation in the policies that it implements which are likely to affect developing countries. For implementation of that policy, Article 209 TFEU, upon which, inter alia, the contested decision is founded, provides in particular, in Paragraph 2, that the European Union may conclude with third countries and competent international organisations any agreement helping to achieve the objectives referred to in Article 21 TEU and Article 208 TFEU.[114]

In the past, Article 179 contained the formulation that this competence provision applied 'without prejudice' to other competence provisions within the Treaty. By the deletion of this provision the pivotal role of Article 209 as a competence basis for the implementation of the development cooperation policy was further emphasized. This modification of the norm text appears to be justified also by the fact that its purview was considerably extended as a consequence of the integration of the provision on the conclusion of agreements with third countries and pertinent international organizations.

In general, the following rule can be applied: the provisions on trade policy (Article 207) prevail over those on development policy[115] while measures with regard to food and humanitarian aid, the fight against drugs and measures in the sanitary area are – if taken with regard to developing countries – to be based on Article 209.[116]

---

[114] *Ibid.*, at paras 34ff.

[115] On this basis the General Preference System could be continued taking reference solely to Article 133. See Andreas Zimmermann and Bernd Martenczuk, 'Commentary to Article 179 TEC' in Jürgen Schwarze (ed.), *EU-Kommentar* (2000) 1704, para 3.

[116] Natascha Solar, 'Commentary to Article 179 TEC' in Heinz Mayer (ed), *Kommentar zu EU- und EG-Vertrag* (2000) para 6.

Complementarity represents one of the five C's which characterize the EU development policy as a whole.[117] The further elements are:

- coherence (Article 208 para 1, 2nd subpara, 2nd sentence TFEU): The aims set out in Article 208 have to be taken into regard in the implementation process of other policies if they touch upon development policies. According to the 'European Consensus on Development', '[t]he EU shall take account of the objectives of development cooperation in all policies that it implements which are likely to affect developing countries'.[118] Awareness for the need to grant policy coherence dates to the farther past but the financial crisis had made greater coherence unpostponable. In 2009 the Commission issued a communication on 'Policy Coherence for Development' (PCD) requiring focusing on a few priority issues (like combating climate change or making migration work for development) and harnessing non-ODA financial flows for development.[119] Still, however, the concept of coherence remains somewhat ambiguous.[120]

- coordination (Article 210 para 1 TFEU): Measures in the field of development policy by the European Union have to be planned and carried out together with those of the Member States. Coordination is a necessary corollary of complementarity: To reach their utmost effectivity parallel (complementary) competences by the EU and their member states have to be coordinated. According to the

---

[117] See in this regard Wolfgang Benedek, 'Prologue to Articles 177–181 TEC', in Eberhard Grabitz and Meinhard Hilf, *Das Recht der Europäischen Union* (2003) paragraph 18; Benedek, *supra* note 104, at para 22. Other authors mention three C's (coherence, complementarity, coordination) with a somewhat larger reach. See, for example, Rudolf Streinz and Tobias Kruis, 'Commentary to Article 208 TFEU' in Rudolf Streinz (ed), *EUV/AEUV, Kommentar* (2012) 1989, para 14.

[118] European Commission, 'The European Consensus on Development' (2006) 22, para 35.

[119] European Commission, 'Policy Coherence for Development – Establishing the Policy Framework for a Whole-of-the-Union Approach' (15 September 2009) COM(2009) 458 final.

[120] Christophe Hillion, 'Tous pour un, un pour Tous! – Coherence in the External Relations of the European Union' in Marise Cremona (ed), *Developments in EU External Relations Law* (2008) 10.

'Agenda for change' of 2011[121] '[f]ragmentation and proliferation of aid is still widespread and even increasing'.[122] The Commission proposes 'joint multi-annual programming documents' resulting in a 'single joint programming document'.[123]

- cooperation: This element is closely related to the previous one although they are not fully equivalent. In fact, cooperation emphasized the element of solidarity more than coordination.
- consistency: This last requirement has gained greater attention only recently. Development cooperation should be entered into with countries in effective need of such measures and not made dependent from other conditions.

These five C's can also be seen as auxiliary instruments and concepts in order to give more effect to the EU development policy as a whole and, ultimately, to create the much proclaimed 'added value' in this field.[124] In fact, in an area where success or failure of a policy depends so much on the ability to fine-tune the relevant measures the persistence of parallel competences both by the EU and its member states constitutes, at first sight, a drawback. There can be no doubt that an important reason for this enduring parallelism is to be found in a rivalry between the EU and its member states determined by political considerations. As this policy is associated with the disbursement of large sums it provides potentially considerable political clout. Therefore, this parallelism has to be accepted as a fact also for the future and it constitutes a great challenge for the years to come not only to avoid possible frictions between those actors but to find ways and means for a cooperative approach that justifies the maintenance of this peculiar competence situation also on objective grounds.[125]

---

[121] European Commission, 'Increasing the Impact of EU Development Policy: An Agenda for Change' (13 October 2011) COM(2011) 637 final.

[122] *Ibid.*, at 10.

[123] *Ibid.*, at 11. See also Benedek, *supra* note 104, at para 60.

[124] See, *e.g.*, Vernier, *supra* note 108, at 1398, para 9.

[125] See in this context European Commission, 'The European Community's Development Policy' (26 April 2000) COM(2000) 212 final, at 13: 'It is for the EC to promote coordination and ensure complementarity between the Community and Member States in the broader international framework. One of the most critical aspects of coordination within the EU is to enhance the ability of the EU to present common positions in international bodies, thus realizing the potential for increased European influence... . Building on past experience of coordination,

The five C's also point to the aim of aid effectiveness that has moved center-stage in the last years. Already at the European Council in Barcelona in March 2002 a specific commitment has been assumed to enhance trade effectiveness. This aspect has been further emphasized at the second High Level Forum on Aid Effectiveness of Paris in March 2005 where international donors and aid recipients formulated monitorable commitments with regard to ownership, harmonization, alignment, results and mutual accountability.[126] The need to ensure aid effectiveness was further confirmed at the 4th High Level Forum on Aid Effectiveness in Busan 2011[127], the Nairobi High Level Forum in 2016[128] and in the "New European Consensus on Development" of 7 June 2017[129].

In a certain sense, the five C's anticipated an approach towards development that became center-stage on the international level by the adoption of the Sustainable Development Goals (SDGs) in 2015, as will be shown below.[130] As will also be shown below, this further evidences the fact that in the conception of development instruments and approaches there is close interaction between the international and the European level.

---

the European Union has to move ahead and to establish a division of labour to achieve commonly established goals.'

[126] EU Report on Millennium Development Goals 2000-2004 of 12 April 2005. With regard to the important issue of ownership, see Peter S Heller, 'Making Aid Work' (2005) 42(3) Finance & Development 9.

[127] OECD, 'The Busan Partnership for Effective Development Co-Operation', <http://www.oecd.org/development/effectiveness/busanpartnership.htm> accessed on 16 August 2017.

[128] Global Partnership for Effective Development Co-Operation, 'Second High-Level Meeting (2016)', <http://effectivecooperation.org/events/2016-high-level-meeting/> accessed on 16 August 2017.

[129] European Commission, 'European Consensus on Development', <https://ec.europa.eu/europeaid/policies/european-development-policy/european-consensus-development_en> accessed on 16 August 2017. See paras 113ff of this document.

[130] It will also be shown that, to a certain extent, the philosophy standing behind the SDGs can be found already in the Millennium Development Goals (MDGs) of 2000.

VII. Development Policy Goals After Lisbon

A. The Paramount Importance of the Fight Against Poverty

The development policy of the EU primarily pursues the objective of poverty reduction and, in the long term, the eradication of poverty.[131] Contrary to the pre-Lisbon situation, no further specific goals of development policy are mentioned in Article 208. However, para 1 of Article 208 states that 'Union policy in the field of development cooperation shall be conducted within the framework of the principles and objectives of the Union's external action.'

Accordingly, the EU seeks to promote the following values (also) in the field of development cooperation as they are stated in Article 21 para 1 TEU:

- democracy;
- the rule of law;
- the universality and indivisibility of human rights and fundamental freedoms;
- respect for human dignity;
- the principles of equality and solidarity; and
- respect for the principles of the United Nations Charter and international law.

This new norm that puts the fight against poverty at the center provides a leaner norm structure that emphasizes the most eminent goal disregarding the broader context. The panoply of goals to be pursued by development policy has therefore not been reduced but amplified and strengthened.

These goals of development cooperation introduced with the Treaty of Maastricht have to be read together with the 2030 Agenda for Sustainable Development adopted by the UN General Assembly on 25 September 2015[132] which continued the development of the MDGs which had been adopted by the UN General Assembly in 2000.[133]

---

[131] Art 208 para 1 subpara 1, 1st sentence TFEU.

[132] UNGA Res 70/1, Transforming our world: the 2030 Agenda for Sustainable Development (21 October 2015), UN Doc A/RES/70/1.

[133] UNGA Res 55/2 (LV), United Nations Millennium Declaration (18 September 2000) UN Doc A/RES/55/2.
The MDGs were the following:

The MDGs had constituted an important step forward in international developments politics as they provided a coherent and highly inspirational point of reference for re-conceiving the attitude of the industrialized world towards the development issue. At the same time, however, they were partly over-reaching and illusionary, and partly incomplete. Furthermore, the financial crisis starting in 2008 made a dent in the capabilities by the developed world to engage in larger unilateral resource transfers.

As a consequence, it became clear that the deadline of 2015 could not be maintained and intense efforts were undertaken to devise new orientation, a post-2015 agenda, even though the general framework set by the Millennium Declaration should be upheld. An important contribution was given by the Rio+20 Conference on Sustainable Development in 2012 where consensus was found among the UN member states to draw up a new agenda for the 2015-2030 period.[134] It was agreed to formulate 17 sustainable development goals to be put forward for adoption by head of states at a UN summit in New York in September 2015. The establishment of new 'Global Partnership for Poverty Eradication and Sustainable Development after 2015' as an overarching framework with universally applicable goals, shared responsibility, the involvement of civil society, the private sector and academia and the creation

---

1. Eradicate extreme poverty and hunger. Lessen by a half the number of people in extreme poverty, and the number of people who suffer from hunger by 2015;

2. Achieve universal primary education. Ensure by 2015 that all children will be able to complete a full course of primary schooling;

3. Promote gender equality and empower women. Eliminate gender disparity in primary and secondary education by 2005, and in all levels of education by 2015;

4. Reduce child mortality. Reduce by two-thirds the under-five mortality rate by 2015;

5. Improve maternal health. Reduce by three-quarters the maternal mortality rate by 2015;

6. Combat HIV/AIDS, malaria, and other diseases. Lessen by a halt the spread of HIV/AIDS, malaria, and other major diseases, and begin to reverse the spread by 2015;

7. Ensure environmental sustainability. Lessen by a half the proportion of people without sustainable access to safe drinking water by 2015; and

8. Develop a global partnership for development. Further develop an open, rule-based, predictable, non-discriminatory trading and financial system.

[134] See Pamela S Chasek *et al.*, 'Getting to 2030: Negotiating the Post-2015 Sustainable Development Agenda' (2016) 25 Review of European Community and International Environmental Law 5.

of an effective monitoring[135] was envisaged. This partnership had to be based on human rights, good governance, the rule of law, support for democratic institutions, inclusiveness, non-discrimination, and gender equality. At the launching conference of the 2030 Agenda for Sustainable Development in 2015, the UNGA had to admit that progress had been uneven, particularly in Africa, least-developed countries, landlocked developing countries and small island developing states.[136] As it was stated, 'the eight MDGs failed to consider the root causes of poverty or gender inequality, many of the underlying environmental issues or the holistice nature of development'.[137] The 2030 Agenda did, however, not abandon the MDGs. Rather, the new Agenda builds on the MDGs and develops them further in order to better reach the most vulnerable.[138] It goes beyond traditional goals such as poverty eradication and improvement of health, education, food security and nutrition and instead sets broader societal objectives that include the economy as a whole as well as broader social issues and the environment.[139] The new approach is based on sustainable development and human rights.[140] Perhaps most importantly, it includes the goal to 'promote peaceful and inclusive societies for sustainable development, provide access to justice for all and build effective, accountable and inclusive institutions at all level' (Goal 16). In a broader sense, Goal 16 refers to the issue of 'good governance' which

---

[135] With regard to monitoring the quality of EU aid internationally agreed targets shall be used such as those contained in the Paris Declaration (2005) and in the Accra Agenda for Action (2008) and revised by the Busan high-level forum, which created the Partnership for Effective Development Cooperation (2011). See European Commission, 'International Cooperation and Development' (2014) 7, <https://europa.eu/european-union/topics/development-cooperation_en> accessed 18 July 2017.

[136] UNGA Res 70/1, Transforming our world: the 2030 Agenda for Sustainable Development (21 October 2015), UN Doc A/RES/70/1, para 16.

[137] See Chasek *et al.*, *supra* note 134, at 7.

[138] UNGA Res 70/1, Transforming our world: the 2030 Agenda for Sustainable Development (21 October 2015), UN Doc A/RES/70/1, para 16.

[139] *Ibid.*, at para 17.

[140] See 'The New European Consensus on Development – "Our world, our dignity, our future"', Joint Statement by the Council and the Representatives of the Governments of the Member States Meeting within the Council, the European Parliament and the European Commission, 7 June 2017, https://ec.europa.eu/europeaid/new-european-consensus-development-our-world-our-dignity-our-future_en, accessed on 16 August 2017.

is surely crucial for lasting development and overcoming inequalities also within given national societies.[141]

The 2030 Agenda for Sustainable Development consists of the following 17 goals:

Goal 1. End poverty in all its forms everywhere;

Goal 2. End hunger, achieve food security and improved nutrition and promote sustainable agriculture;

Goal 3. Ensure healthy lives and promote well-being for all at all ages;

Goal 4. Ensure inclusive and equitable quality education and promote lifelong learning opportunities for all;

Goal 5. Achieve gender equality and empower all women and girls;

Goal 6. Ensure availability and sustainable management of water and sanitation for all;

Goal 7 Ensure access to affordable, reliable, sustainable and modern energy for all;

Goal 8. Promote sustained, inclusive and sustainable economic growth, full and productive employment and decent work for all;

Goal 9. Build resilient infrastructure, promote inclusive and sustainable industrialization and foster innovation;

Goal 10. Reduce inequality within and among countries;

Goal 11. Make cities and human settlements inclusive, safe, resilient and sustainable;

Goal 12. Ensure sustainable consumption and production patterns;

Goal 13. Take urgent action to combat climate change and its impacts;

Goal 14. Conserve and sustainably use the oceans, seas and marine resources for sustainable development;

Goal 15. Protect, restore and promote sustainable use of terrestrial ecosystems, sustainably manage forests, combat desertification, and halt and reverse land degradation and halt biodiversity loss;

Goal 16. Promote peaceful and inclusive societies for sustainable development, provide access to justice for all and build effective, accountable and inclusive institutions at all levels;

---

[141] Hilpold, *supra* note 26. This aspect is of particular relevance in post-conflict situations. See on this issue Hilpold, *supra* note 44.

Goal 17. Strengthen the means of implementation and revitalize the Global Partnership for Sustainable Development.

The fight against poverty has been attributed paramount importance also in the past. Hence, both in the MDGs as in the SDGs this goal is ranked first in the hierarchy. Many of the further goals can be seen as a specification of the first one. The SDGs (and previously the MDGs) elaborated by the UN best exemplify how interrelated the various goals are and how the fight against poverty may be key to overcome the development challenge.

Although there is no unanimous consensus in the ongoing worldwide development policy discussion, *i.e.* whether the SDGs constitute an exclusive, overarching set of goals, there is an emerging consensus that poverty eradication should remain the goal of any new development policy strategy. The 2030 Agenda further develops the attempt, already present in the MDGs, to achieve this objective by the setting of concrete and simple targets.[142]

In any case, it can be argued that the MDGs profoundly influenced the European development policy and eventually also the drafting of Article 208. A similar and even more enhanced influence which departs from international law and moves towards EU law emanates from the SDGs.[143]

It is highly probable that the adoption of the post-2015 agenda will also have important implications for further activities under the UN Framework Convention on Climate Change.[144] In fact, the Paris Agreement of 2015, an agreement negotiated within the Framework Convention, emphasizes

---

[142] See in this regard European Commission, *supra* note 78, at 14. See also Philip Alston, 'Ships Passing in the Night: The Current State of the Human Rights and Development Debate Seen through the Lens of the Millennium Development Goals' (2005) 27 Human Rights Quarterly 755 and, more recently, European Commission, 'Fighting Hunger together with the European Union' (2015), <https://ec.europa.eu/europeaid/fighting-hunger-together-european-union_en> accessed on 16 August 2017.

[143] From a more nuanced perspective it can also be argued that this influence is reciprocal. In fact, the SDGs, with their emphasis on human rights and good governance, correspond even more closely to the very characteristics of EU law than it has been the case with the MDGs.

[144] See European Commission, 'A Global Partnership for Poverty Eradication and Sustainable Development after 2015' COM(2015), at 44; German Federal Government, 'Post-2015 Agenda for Sustainable Development – Key Positions of the German Government' (February 2014), <https://sustainabledevelopment.un.org/content/documents/8778germany.pdf> accessed 18 July 2017, and Global Policy Forum, 'Post-2015 Sustainability Agenda', <https://www.globalpolicy.org/social-and-economic-policy/the-millenium-development-goals/post-2015-development-agenda.html> accessed 18 July 2017.

the achievement of the SD.[145] Already in 2007, the EU started the Global Climate Change Alliance (GCCA) aiming at fostering effective dialogue and cooperation on climate change with landlocked developing countries and small island developing states. In 2014, a new, enhanced initiative with more generous funding, the Global Climate Change Alliance+ (GCCA) was started. According to this program, climate change must be an integral consideration in national development plans, policies and budgets, vulnerable countries shall be helped to prepare for climate-related hazards and furthermore understanding shall be increased about the specific consequences of climate change in the short, medium and long term.[146]

From the very beginning, the EU gave much relevance to the measurement of actual progress towards the MDGs.[147] From the official UN list of 48 MDG indicators, several key indicators have been sorted out, on the basis of which the performance of countries and regions, which receive development assistance, are assessed. These are the following:

1. Proportion of the population having daily income below $1 a day;
2. Prevalence of child malnutrition (underweight children) under-five years of age;
3. Net enrolment ratio in primary education;
4. Children under-five years of age mortality rate;
5. Proportion of one-year old children immunized against measles;
6. Proportion of births attended by skilled health personnel;
7. HIV prevalence among 15-24 years old pregnant women; and
8. Proportion of the population with sustainable access to an improved water source.

Whether a situation of poverty is given can therefore not be measured only in financial or economic terms. Poverty is rather a complex phenomenon

---

[145] See paras 6.4-6.7 of the Agreement. On this agreement see Sabine Rauch, *Das Pariser Klimaschutzabkommen – Grundlagen und Perspektiven* (2017).

[146] See Global Climate Change Alliance, <http://www.gcca.eu/print/about-the-gcca/what-is-the-gcca> accessed 16 August 2017.

[147] European Commission, 'EU Report on Millennium Development Goals 2000-2004. EU Contribution to the Review of the MDGs at the UN 2005 High Level Event' SEC(2005) 456, at 8.

and so are the strategies to fight it. In fact, the UN defined poverty in the following terms:

> Fundamentally, poverty is a denial of choices and opportunities, a violation of human dignity. It means lack of basic capacity to participate effectively in society. It means not having enough to feed and clothe a family, not having a school or clinic to go to, not having the land on which to grow one's food or a job to earn one.[148]

This broad vision of the goals of development cooperation, comprising not only the fight against poverty in a stricter sense, has been confirmed by the CJEU in C-377/12, the first judgment on development cooperation in the post-Lisbon context.[149] In this judgment the Court confirmed that 'European Union policy in the field of development cooperation is not limited to measures directly aimed at the eradication of poverty, but also pursues the objectives referred to in Article 21(2) TEU [...]'.[150] It further reminds that '[a]s the Advocate General notes in points 40 and 41 of his Opinion and as is apparent in particular from Paragraphs 5 and 7 of the European Consensus, the main objective of development cooperation is the eradication of poverty in the context of sustainable development, including pursuit of the Millennium Development Goals'.[151]

On a whole, the MDGs and to some extent also already the SDGs have strongly influenced the understanding and the continuing re-conception of EU development politics. The traditional development goals, centred on the figth against poverty, remain important targets but it cannot be denied that the discussion has evolved further. As already spelled out and as will be re-iterated in the conclusions, the post-2015 agenda has brought about a partial re-orientation towards a holistic concept of development that understands industrialized and developing countries as partners of a common project and that puts particular emphasis on a rights-based approach that should be implemented in a national legal environment based on good governance and the rule of law.

---

[148] Economic and Social Council, 'Statement of Commitment for Action to Eradicate Poverty Adopted by Administrative Committee on Coordination' ECOSOC/5759, 20 May 1998, para 3.

[149] Case C-377/12, *European Commission v Council*, [2014] ECLI:EU:2014:1903; The 'leading case' before was Case C-268/94, *Portuguese Republic v Council of the European Union*, [1996] ECR I-6177, para 39.

[150] *Ibid.*, at para 37.

[151] *Ibid.*, at para 42.

B. Further Principles and Objectives of Development Cooperation

In the following the further principles and objectives of development cooperation, as they result by reference of Article 208 TFEU to Article 21 TEU, shall be specified.

1. Safeguarding the Union's Values, Fundamental Interests, Security, Independence and Integrity

This is an 'egoistic' objective that is common to all countries pursuing a development policy. In plain language, it is made clear that development cooperation is useful and beneficial for the 'assisting' or 'donor' country or entity as much as it is for the recipient. As a corollary of this statement it results that this policy has to be tailored accordingly. This is also made clear by the European Security Strategy (ESS) of 12 December 2003 where the EU confirmed *inter alia* that development cooperation can be a powerful tool for enhancing international security and thereby also the security of the EU and its member states.[152]

2. 'Consolidate and Support Democracy, the Rule of Law, Human Rights and the Principles of International Law'

This objective was already present in the previous Article 177 TEC with a somewhat different wording ('development and consolidation of democracy, the rule of law, of human rights and fundamental freedoms').

In the past, this author has stated the following with regard to this objective in its previous formulation:

> From the system of the Treaty and the wording of the relevant provision it becomes clear that the development and the consolidation of democracy, the rule of law, of human rights and fundamental freedoms are not independent goals enjoying the same relevance as those enlisted in Paragraph 1 of Article 177. They are rather of an auxiliary nature and furthermore

---

[152] 'Trade and development policies can be powerful tools for promoting reform. As the world's largest provider of official assistance and its largest trading entity, the European Union and its Member States are well placed to pursue these goals.' European Council, 'European Security Strategy – A Secure Europe in a Better World' (2003) 10.

they are worded very cautiously.[153] The limited role attributed to these principles is a direct consequence of the competence situation of the EC in this field which is of a restricted dimension.[154] Nonetheless, there can be no doubt that these elements are continuously gaining more importance as the insight in the complexities of the development process grows and there is a broad awareness that a lasting development progress cannot be achieved if development incentives do not take place in a somewhat consolidated and participatory political and legal environment.[155]

The slight changes in the wording of this goal refer to major changes in substance occurred in the meantime. In fact, no longer reference is made to the 'development' of democracy, the rule of law and human rights but rather to their 'consolidation'. Thereby, it is made clear that the European Union has gone a long way in this process and much has been achieved. The EU is proud about these achievements. It would be inappropriate to speak about 'development' (of such rules) as they already exist and the EU has given a decisive contribution for their elaboration. Now the time has come to consolidate them and to support them on the international plane.

This policy is clearly directed towards the cooperating partners even though it has considerable repercussion for the Union and its member states. Again it becomes evident that the principles and objectives of development cooperation explain their effects both externally and internally. The values and goals indicated in this indent define much of the EU's identity, in particular the way it wants to be seen on the international level. One drawback could be seen in the fact that these values and goals are not defined in EU legal instruments but, on the other hand, there are sufficient international instruments and documents available[156] that can be referred to in order to obtain at least the essential elements of such a definition: For the principle of democracy see, e.g., the 1990 Copenhagen Conference on the Human Dimension of the CSCE or the Charter of Paris for New Europe of 1990, with regard to the rule of law, the CJEU has developed a broad jurisprudence, human dignity is recognized on a world-wide scale as a pre-requisite for any form of human

---

[153] Hilpold, *supra* note 26; Andreas Zimmermann and Bernd Martenczuk, 'Commentary to Article 177 ECT' in Jürgen Schwarze (ed), *EU-Kommentar* (2000) 1700, para 24.

[154] Hilpold, *supra* note 26, at 65.

[155] Hilpold, *supra* note 26. See also Benedek, *supra* note 117, at para 25.

[156] For a detailed analysis see Stefan Oeter, 'Article 21' in Hermann-Josef Blanke and Stelio Mangiameli (eds), *The Treaty on European Union (TEU)* (2013) 833, at 844ff.

rights protection, solidarity is becoming a principle governing vast areas of international relations[157] and respect for the principles of the United Nations and international law has become a 'mantra' for the EU with continuous pledges by EU politicians and officials to uphold and further develop these principles on the universal level.[158] However, as has been convincingly argued in literature[159], there is not one common vision of international law but there

---

[157] See Peter Hilpold, 'Solidarität als Prinzip des Staatengemeinschaftsrechts' (2013) 51 Archiv des Völkerrechts 239; Ronald SJ MacDonald, 'Solidarity in the Practice and Discourse of Public International Law' (1996) 8 Pace International Law Review 259; Karel Wellens, 'Solidarity as a Constitutional Principle: Its Expanding Role and Inherent Limitations' in Ronald SJ Macdonald and Douglas M Johnston (eds), *Towards World Constitutionalism* (2005) 775; Rüdiger Wolfrum, 'Solidarity amongst States: An Emerging Structural Principle of International Law' (2009) 49 Indian Journal of International Law 8; Peter Hilpold, 'Solidarität als Rechtsprinzip – völkerrechtliche, europarechtliche und staatsrechtliche Betrachtungen' (2007) 55 Jahrbuch des öffentlichen Rechts 195; and Rüdiger Wolfrum and Chie Kojima (eds) *Solidarity: A Structural Principle of International Law* (2010). For the relevance of the solidarity principle within the European Monetary Union see Hermann-Josef Blanke and Stefan Pilz, *Die Fiskalunion* (2014); and Peter Hilpold, 'Eine neue europäische Finanzarchitektur – Der Umbau der Wirtschafts- und Währungsunion als Reaktion auf die Finanzkrise' in Peter Hilpold and Walter Steinmair (eds), *Neue europäische Finanzarchitektur – Die Reform der WWU* (2013) 3.

[158] Reality often shows, however, a different picture with the EU tending to go for its own. The most remarkable case in kind is surely the *Kadi* case where both GA Poiares Maduro as well as the CJEU emphasized the EU's commitment to the international legal order while at the same time they attributed priority to the immediate EU interests and goals. See the Opinion by GA Poiares Maduro in Case C-402/05 P, para 24: '*[...] although the Court takes great care to respect the obligations that are incumbent on the Community by virtue of international law, it seeks, first and foremost, to preserve the constitutional framework created by the Treaty.*' The CJEU, in Joined Cases C-402/05 P and C-415/05 P of 3 September 2008, para 291, first paid lip service to respect international law while afterwards emphasizing the predominance of the 'very foundations of the Community legal order' (para 304). See on this case Peter Hilpold, 'EU Law and UN Law in Conflict: The Kadi Case' (2009) 13 Max Plank UNYB 141; Peter Hilpold, 'UN Sanctions Before the ECJ: the Kadi Case' in August Reinisch (ed), *Challenging Acts of International Organizations Before National Courts* (2010) 18; Peter Hilpold, 'Kadi die Dritte – EU-Recht und UN-Recht weiter auf Kollisionskurs' [22/2010] Eurpäische Zeitschrift für Wirtschaftsrecht 844; and Peter Hilpold, 'Im Spannungsverhältnis zwischen UN-Recht und EU-Recht – die unendliche Kadi-Saga' (2011) 22 Europäisches Wirtschafts- und Steuerrecht 45.

[159] See Frank Hoffmeister, 'The Contribution of EU Practice to International Law' in Marise Cremona (ed), *Development in EU External Relations Law* (2008) 37.

are several.[160] The German model refers primarily to UN law containing the core values of international law, while the French seeks to pursue national interests through international law and the British interpret international law from a common law perspective, according to which the international legal order is a developing set of norms but not necessarily a complete one.[161] Nonetheless, there are important fields – and they continuously grow in size – where these visions converge. One of these fields is surely that of conditionality. As has been shown above, human rights conditionality finds its roots already in the Lomé III Agreement of 1984 but only with the Lomé IV-bis Agreement of 1995 conditionality reached the status of a fully defined and actionable legal principle.

As respect for human rights, democratic principles and the rule of law have been qualified in this context as essential elements, the whole nature of the Lomé Agreement has changed. In fact, these elements were given such a weight that their violation could discharge the cooperation partner from its obligations and bring financial flows and privileged trade to a halt.

Although the qualification as 'essential elements' would have rendered Article 60 of the Vienna Convention on the Law of Treaties (Vienna Convention) applicable, a specific and precise mechanism was created upon which parties had to rely in case of an infringement of these principles. This procedure regulated in Article 366a of the Lomé Agreement remained, however, somewhat ambiguous as it hinted at an unresolved conflict between partnership and cooperation. In fact, on the basis of the partnership idea the application of sanctions required the holding of prior consultations. On the other hand, these consultations did not necessarily influence the final decision on the sanctions to apply nor did it impede the taking of sanctions in cases of special urgency. Thus, the cooperative process was confined to a first (possible) fact-finding and fact-assessing procedure. The final decisions were to be taken – and carried out – unilaterally. Despite official declarations to the contrary, the human rights policy of the EU was still largely based on the 'negative' approach which corresponded to the unilateral elements in the structure of the provisions described above. The results of this new instrument were not fully satisfactory as a lasting success of the single initiatives in the field of human rights could not be guaranteed. It was noticed that the relationship between democracy and the rule of law on the one hand and the

---

[160] *Ibid.*, at 125, referring to Ricardo Gosalbo-Bono, 'Some Reflections on the CFSP Legal Order' (2006) 43 Common Market Law Review 337, at 380-384.

[161] *Ibid.*

protection of human rights, on the other hand, had to be further clarified. Still unclear was the relation of these principles with the concept of development.

The drafters of the successor regime to the Lomé Agreement, the Cotonou Agreement, had the precise intent to improve this situation. In this agreement, paramount importance was attributed to the principle of good governance, which should become the overarching concept on the basis of which the elements mentioned above should be structured and brought in a harmonious order. An important clarification has been undertaken by the EU Commission in a Communication to the Council and the European Parliament of 1998 – at a time when discussions about a successor regime to Lomé IV-bis Agreement had already started. In this document, good governance is defined as the management of public affairs in a transparent, accountable, participative and equitable manner showing due regard for human rights and the rule of law:

> It encompasses every aspect of the State's dealing with civil society, its role in establishing a climate conducive to economic and social development and its responsibility for the equitable division of resources.[162]

The Cotonou Agreement in Article 9 para 3 contains a similar definition of good governance:

> In the context of a political and institutional environment that upholds human rights, democratic principles and the rule of law, good governance is transparent and accountable management of human, natural, economic and financial resources for the purposes of equitable and sustainable development. It entails clear decision-making procedures at the level of public authorities, transparent and accountable institutions, the primacy of law in the management and distribution of resources and capacity building for elaborating and implementing measures aiming in particular at preventing and combating corruption.

The Commission Communication of 1998 adds the further elements:

> Equity and the primacy of law in the management and allocation of resources call for an independent and accessible judicial system that guarantees all citizens basic access to resources by recognising their right to act against inequalities. In the specific context of governance, this involves establishing a legal and regulatory framework that encourages private enterprise and investment.

---

[162] European Commission, 'Communication from the Commission to the Council and the European Parliament' COM(1998) 146 final.

The institutional capacity to manage a country's resources effectively in the interests of economic and social development implies an ability to draft, implement and supervise policies addressing the needs of the people. The government and civil society must be able to implement an equitable development model and guarantee the judicious use of all resources in the public interest. Building public and private institutional capacities is vital because it directly determines economic and social development, and especially the effectiveness of development cooperation.

Transparency, which entails being accountable and organising effective procedures and systems for monitoring the management and allocation of resources, implies that resource management is open to scrutiny and subject to controls. It is both a key factor in establishing trust between the various agents of development and a guarantee of institutional integrity.

Development without the public participation in the decision-making processes concerning the management and allocation of resources is inconceivable. Participation calls for the various agents of development to exchange views on major decisions relating to the management and allocation of resources and development programming. This dimension also concerns the scope to be given to private initiative, enterprise and civil society in development.

In the Communication on Governance and Development of 20 October 2003, the Commission has given further elucidation on this concept.[163] On this occasion the Commission has stressed that the concept of governance provides a terminology that is more pragmatic than democracy, human rights, etc. For the Commission this is a meaningful and practical concept relating to the very basic aspects of the functioning of any society and political and social systems.[164] It described good governance as a basic measure of stability, quality and performance of a society.[165]

As demonstrated above, it is evident that much discussion is needed to give further content and consistency to the principle of good governance but nonetheless the European Community felt prepared to attribute to this concept such an important role in the Agreement of Cotonou (though is constitutes still 'only' a 'fundamental element' and not an 'essential element' of the agreement).

---

[163] European Commission, *supra* note 41.
[164] *Ibid.*, at 3.
[165] *Ibid.*

EU human rights conditionality is not limited to its special relationship with ACP states. Human rights clauses have rather become an essential element of all cooperation agreements with third countries, independently from their development status.[166] The EU Annual Report on Human Rights of 2005 states:

> The EU views human rights clauses in agreements with third countries as an incentive for the promotion of human rights. The Commission issued in May 1995 a Communication on the inclusion of respect for democratic principles and human rights in agreements between the Community and third countries which includes a list of targeted measures that may be taken in response to serious human rights violations or serious interruptions of democratic process. Such measures, ranging from the alteration of the contents of cooperation programmes to the suspension of elements of the agreement, are regularly applied. However, the principal role of the clause is to provide the EU with a basis for positive engagement on human rights and democracy issues with third countries.[167]

As the concepts involved are still in large parts undetermined and furthermore subject to a rapid evolution the EU has considerable leeway for their concretization.[168] This activity has ultimately important consequences also for the formation of an international consensus on these concepts on a global scale.

At the moment, the most evolved 'hard' provisions on conditionality are probably to be found in the Cotonou Agreement. The 2005 revision to this agreement has emphasized the importance of dialogue prior to the application of sanctions[169] and in 2010 it was emphasized that '[t]he principles underlying the essential and fundamental elements as defined in this Article shall apply equally to the ACP States on the one hand, and to the European Union and its member States, on the other hand'.[170] Therefore, in principle, conditionality is an instrument applicable also against the EU and its member states.

---

[166] See Peter Hilpold, 'Human Rights Clauses in EU-Association Agreements' in Stefan Griller and Birgit Weidel (eds), *External Economic Relations and Foreign Policy in the European Union* (2002) 359.

[167] European Council, 'EU Annual Report on Human Rights 2005' (2005) 32.

[168] See Zimmermann/Martenczuk, *supra* note 153, at 1691, para 26.

[169] See Lorand Bartels, 'The Trade and Development Policy of the European Union' in Marise Cremona (ed), *Developments in EU External Relations Law* (2008) 128, at 153.

[170] Art 9, para 4 subpara 4 Cotonou Agreement.

On a whole, it can be said that the EU has given important contributions for the definition and the further development of these concepts, although, in the end, their meaning can be identified only by common international consent. In fact, it would not be wise for the EU to unilaterally define concepts of this kind that by their very nature are destined for universal use and need also international contributions for their definition in order to obtain the broadest-possible acceptance.

There can be no doubt that the promotion of democracy, good governance and the rule of law is a goal sincerely felt by the EU. This is not only proven by an extensive practice in this field but also by a specific reference to this task in the ESS:

> Contributing to better governance through assistance programmes, conditionality and targeted trade measures remains an important feature in our policy that we should further reinforce. A world seen as offering justice and opportunity for everyone will be more secure for the European Union and its citizens.[171]

The ongoing attempts to re-formulate the EU development policy is informed by the attempt to attribute even more importance to human rights, democracy, and good governance. Thus, the EU Annual Report on Human Rights and Democracy in the World[172] announces a strictly rights-based approach:

> The Agenda for Change, the EU Strategic Framework on Human Rights and Democracy and the Communication towards a Post-2015 Development Framework were calling for a move to a Rights Based Approach (RBA). The negotiation on the DCI has introduced a RBA as a key objective of the Regulation for the period 2014-2020.
>
> To this purpose, the EU has been mandated to develop a toolbox for working towards a rights-based approach, encompassing all human rights, to development cooperation.[173]

---

[171] Zimmermann/Martenczuk, *supra* note 153, at 1691, para 26.

[172] European Council, 'EU Annual Report on Human Rights and Democracy in the World in 2013' (2014), 11107/14.

[173] *Ibid.*, at 45.

3. Sustainable Economic, Social and Environmental Development of the Developing Countries

This goal is to be found in Article 21 para 2 lit (d): ('foster the sustainable economic, social and environmental development of developing countries, with the primary aim of eradicating poverty').

A similar provision was to be found in the pre-Lisbon text of Article 177 TEC ('[t]he sustainable economic and social development of the developing countries, and more particularly the most disadvantaged among them'). The modifications have, therefore, been rather slight: Article 21 para 2 lit (d), which is now guiding external action as a whole, concentrates on the eradication of poverty, a goal which has now become of overarching importance. At the same time we have, however, to take into regard that 'poverty' has to be defined broadly so that in substance little has changed.

The concept of 'sustainable development' is intimately related to the broad field of environmental protection and with the Treaty of Lisbon explicit reference is now made to environment in the context of development cooperation. It has been shown in literature that this concept has been known in its very essence for quite a long time, both in national law and in international law.[174] It became prominent, however, only after it had been included in the Brundtland Report of 1987 where it was defined as 'a development which fulfils the present needs without risking that future generations cannot fulfil their own needs'.[175] Since the so-called 'Earth Summit', the World Summit on Sustainable Development, convened in Rio de Janeiro in 1992, the principle of sustainability has been at the focal point of any discussion on the further development of international economic law.[176] The concept of sustainability in the field of environmental protection touches in several ways upon the development issue:

- Environmental protection requires international action and the cooperation of the developing countries is essential in this context;

---

[174] Rudolf Dolzer, 'Wirtschaft und Kultur im Völkerrecht' in Wolfgang Vitzthum (ed), *Völkerrecht* (2004) 478, para 35, referring – with regard to international law – to the preamble provision in GATT.

[175] UNGA, 'Report of the World Commission on Environment and Development' (4 August 1987) UN Doc A/42/427.

[176] See also the results of the World Summit on Sustainable Development in Johannesburg, 26 August – 4 September 2002.

- As the development process is following generally a similar path according to which the developing countries aim first at the building-up of highly polluting industries before feeling able to concentrate on cleaner high-tech industries or services, to narrow the development gap earlier can contribute to a considerable reduction of the world-wide pollution;
- A lag in the development process is regularly associated with high population growth which puts additional strain on the future environmental sustainability of the biosphere; and
- Probably in no area the impact of development on the protection of the environment becomes more evident than in that of climate protection. The United Nations Framework Convention on Climate Change of 1992 together with the Kyoto Protocol of 1997 and the Paris Agreement of 2015 can be seen not only as an instrument for environmental protection of unprecedented reach but also as an important step towards a new global economic order protecting particularly the interests of the developing countries.[177]

It is, however, not only the environment that this provision points at. The reference to a sustainable economic and social development makes this goal absolutely unique in the international development policy as it sets conditions that should guarantee lasting effects of such a policy and which should furthermore ensure that this policy does not become too narrowly interpreted.

Sustainability in the mere economic field requires, first of all, adequate planning of all initiatives and a thorough assessment of the consequences. In this context it can become evident, for example, that food aid provided outside a specific, urgent need can do more harm than good and is, therefore, detrimental to sustainable economic development.[178]

Sustainability is furthermore required also in the social field. This requirement poses, probably, one of the most eminent challenges to the planning process of the European development policy, if due regard is paid to it. In fact, this requirement makes clear that it is not only the welfare of a developing country in absolute terms that counts, but at least as much the distribution

---

[177] As is well-known, lately, the migration problem has become a major challenge for the European Union. Again, there is a strong nexus between climate change, migration and development policy that the EU intends to address. See the 'New European Consensus on Development', *supra* note 140, at 20.

[178] Christian Pitschas, 'Commentary to Article 177 TEC' in Rudolf Streinz (ed), *EUV/EGV-Kommentar* (2003) 1765, para 16 with further references.

of it. The European development policy has, therefore, to make sure that the respective initiatives do not have a disruptive effect on social cohesion but also – positively – that social cohesion is furthered by these measures.

It is clear that all these concerns are even more accentuated for the most disadvantaged countries as it can be argued that the higher the degree of development is, the lesser will be the impact of EU development initiatives on the social and the economic fabric of a developing country, both in the positive and in the negative sense.

Already the 'European Consensus on Development' of 2006[179] highlighted the importance of environmental sustainability for any form of development policy.[180] This aspect has now become of paramount importance as has been evidenced by the 'Agenda for Change' of 2012. Therein, the EU development policy was identified as a key instrument for achieving 'the transition to a green economy, including resource efficiency, and also contribute to food and nutrition security, environmental protection and climate change mitigation and adaptation'.[181] Furthermore, strong coordination between the EU's climate and development policies was qualified as 'vital'.[182]

Programs in the field of 'climate change and environment' are suitable for financing within the Financing instrument for development cooperation for the period 2014-2020.[183] By the 2010 revision of the Cotonou Agreement Article 32a was introduced in this agreement which refers to 'climate change'. Finally, building on the commitments made at the 2012 United Nations Conference on Sustainable Development (Rio+20) goals and objectives in the field of environmental protection rank high in the post-2015 agenda. By the introduction of the SDGs in 2015 sustainability has become a pivotal element of development.

---

[179] European Commission, 'The European Consensus on Development' (2006).

[180] *Ibid.*, at 46, para 105.

[181] Council Conclusions, 'Increasing the Impact of EU Development Policy: An Agenda for Change' (14 May 2012), para 8.

[182] *Ibid.*, at para 12.

[183] Regulation (EU) 233/2014 of 11 March 2014 establishing a financing instrument for development cooperation for the period 2014-2020 [2014] OJ L77/44.

4. Encourage the Integration of All Countries into the World Economy, Including Through the Progressive Abolition of Restrictions on International Trade

Also this objective was already contained in Article 177 TEC, albeit with a slightly different wording ('smooth and gradual integration into the World Economy').

In this indent, formal expression is given to a principle that has characterized the EU development policy from its very beginnings and which corresponds also to the prevailing view always held by Western market-oriented countries in general. It is assumed that the political economy model at the basis of the success of the dominant economies and which requires the recourse to free trade in the external economic relations, could and should be adopted also by developing countries as the experience of the last two centuries has evidenced that there is no superior model available.[184] It has, however, also been generally recognized that the liberalization process can only be a gradual one as an immediate, unconditional market opening would make the building-up of a home-grown industry impossible.[185] As this exception, if improperly applied, could lead to particularly deleterious forms of protectionism, a difficult balancing is required where the final goal, the full integration of these economies in the world trading system, should never be lost from sight.

The proposition set out in this indent corresponds also fully to the approach adopted in this field by the WTO. While GATT law was somewhat ambiguous on this issue during the Uruguay Round a straightforward decision was taken to aim at a full integration of the developing countries. Only for the least developed countries larger exceptions should be granted.[186]

It is doubtable whether this approach was a fortunate one. Within the Doha Round, started in 2001, solutions are looked for that should better cater for

---

[184] See generally on this issue, Michael J Trebilcock and Robert Howse, *The Regulation of International Trade* (2005).

[185] The infant industry argument stands behind this position, see *ibid.*, at 8.

[186] See Michael Finger and L Alan Winters, 'What Can the WTO Do for Developing Countries?' in Kym Anderson and Bernard Hoekman (eds), *The Global Trading System* (2002) 71; Peter van den Bossche, *The Law and Policy of the World Trade Organisation* (2005) 694; see also Wil D Verwey, 'The Preferential Status of Developing Countries in International Trade Law after the Uruguay Round' in Erik MG Denters and Nico Schrijver (eds), *Reflections on International Law from the Low Countries* (1998) 48.

the needs of developing countries.[187] The previous formulation (in Article 177 TEC) referred to 'graduation' and it can be assumed that with the 'progressive abolition of restrictions on international trade' the same concept is meant. 'Graduation' is an established principle in international economic law. First of all, the graduation principle is one of the most characteristic elements of the GSP which, being based on the Enabling Clause of 1979,[188] allows for the granting of unilateral preferences that can be differentiated according to a broad set of criteria.

As shown above, the EC's GSP was challenged by India before the WTO Dispute Settlement Body under the allegation that this system constituted a violation of the GATT most favoured nation principle.[189] The WTO panel ruled in favour of India in 2003 finding that the Special Arrangements to Combat Drug Production and Trafficking provided in Council Regulation (EC) 2501/2001 was inconsistent with Article I:1 GATT.[190] The Appellate Body, however, has taken a position more favourable to the EC. In substance it argued that the enabling clause did not refer to the developing countries as a group and that different treatment of developing countries with different development, financial and trade needs was allowed. Also drug-trafficking could be an expression of a development problem. As the EC failed, however, to demonstrate that the preferences granted under the Drug Arrangements would be conceded to all developing countries that evidence a similar drug

---

[187] See Michael J Trebilcock, *International Trade La*w (2015) 197: 'The future scope of special and differential treatment for developing countries has become a major fault line between developing and developed countries in the current Doha Round of multilateral trade negotiations, and in part explains the dramatic proliferation of PTAs in recent years.'

[188] GATT, 'Differential and More Favourable Treatment Reciprocity and Fuller Participation of Developing Countries' (Decision of 28 November 1979 (L/4903)), < https://www.wto.org/english/docs_e/legal_e/tokyo_enabling_e.pdf> accessed 12 July 2017.

[189] See also Matthew S Dunne *et al*, 'International Trade' (2005) 39 The International Lawyer 209, at 218.

[190] In particular, the GATT panel found that the phrase 'developing countries' in para 2(a) of the enabling clause refers to all developing countries. No differences in preferences except those contemplated by the UNCTAD negotiators would be allowed. See Gene M Grossmann and Alan O Sykes, 'A Preference for Development: The Law and Economics of GSP' (2005) 4 World Trade Review 41, at 50.

problem, the EC GSP was again qualified as being of a discriminatory nature.[191]

Graduation stands in close connection with the principle of more favorable and beneficial treatment (MFBT). Both are logically interconnected as a privileged treatment is justified only if and inasmuch specific needs are given. The principle of graduation provides for a dynamic element in the application of MFBT. Advancements in the degree of development shall lead to a reduction of the granted privileges. On the other hand, as soon as this treatment is no longer necessary it has to cease to exist.

According to the formulation of this goal previously in force, integration into the world economy has to take place in a 'smooth' way. Smoothness of integration should result, first of all, directly from graduality but at the same time it points at something more, namely the fact that the integration process should not lead to discontinuities in the development process or even to internal disruption. Indirectly, it refers also to the social aspect of development. The integration of developing countries in the world economic system with all the connected changes (restructuring of single economic branches, lay-off of workers, etc.) should not lead to unbearable social costs. The requirement of smoothness requires, therefore, the right balancing of all elements. It can lead to a slowdown or to an acceleration of the integration process, depending on the specific situation.

It can be argued that the element of 'smoothness' now makes part of the element of progressiveness.

---

[191] Grossmann/Sykes, *supra* note 190, at 52. See also Claudio Di Turi, 'Il sistema di preferenze generalizzate della Comunità Europea dopo la controversia con l'India sul regime speciale in tema di droga' (2005) LXXXVIII Rivista di diritto internazionale 721; James Harrison, 'Incentives for Development: The EC's Generalised System of Preferences, India's WTO Challenge and Reform' (2005) 42 Common Market Law Review 1663. For the new GSP scheme, see the Communication from the Commission to the Council, the European Parliament and the European Economic and Social Committee of 7 July 2004 entitled 'Developing Countries, International Trade and Sustainable Development: The Function of the Community's Generalised System of Preferences (GSP) for the Ten-Year Period from 2006 to 2015', setting out the guidelines for the application of the GSP scheme for the period 2006 to 2015; and Council Regulation (EC) 980/2005, OJ 2005 L169/1 implementing those guidelines for the period until 31 December 2008.

5. Compliance with International Commitments

The Union and the member states have to comply with the commitments and to take account of the objectives they have approved in the context of the United Nations and other competent international organizations.

At first sight, this obligation seems to be only of a declaratory nature. Such a sight would make, however, the whole provision redundant or reduce it to a statement of a mere political character. First of all, this provision ties the Union and the member states together when it comes to make sure that international obligations of these entities have to be respected. Although both entities keep their respective legal obligations distinct[192] they have to display loyal cooperation according to Article 4 para 3 TFEU. This provision is furthermore explicable by the fact that in this field competences are most often shared between the Union and the member states.[193]

Second, and even more importantly, this provision opens the EU development policies in its orientation broadly towards general international trends. As it can be assumed that the EU and/or its member states are participating in a considerable part in the major multilateral international instruments of relevance in the field of development, it is hereby made sure that EU development law will always be friendly towards international law. Furthermore, this provision provides the EU development law with an important dynamic component. While development law and policy outside the EU undergoes fast changes, the Union counterpart cannot remain static and insensitive to new needs and trends.

The expressions 'context' and 'competent' have to be interpreted broadly. Commitments made and objectives approved within international organizations have to be obeyed even if the EU or its member states have not been members in the formal sense.[194] 'Competent' does not mean that the respective organizations need to be exclusively or even predominantly active in the field of development policy. A primary competence in this area has, however, to be given.

---

[192] See also Natascha Solar, 'Commentary to Article 177 TEC' in Heinz Mayer (ed), *Kommentar zu EU- und EG-Vertrag* (2005) para 25; Zimmermann, *supra* note 17, at 1470, para 74; Kirsten Schmalenbach, 'Commentary to Article 177 TEC' in Christian Calliess and Matthias Ruffert (eds), *Kommentar des Vertrages über die Europäische Union und des Vertrages zur Gründung der Europäischen Gemeinschaft – EUV/EGV* (2002) para 19.

[193] See Benedek, *supra* note 117, at para 43.

[194] See in this sense Zimmermann, *supra* note 17, at 1470, para 74.

The EU, together with its members, is a great spender of development aid but still much needs to be done. According to the EU the world has the technology and resources to eradicate extreme poverty in our lifetime and put the world on a sustainable path to ensure a decent life for all by 2030.[195]

6. Assisting Populations, Countries and Regions Confronting Natural or Man-Made Disasters

Experience shows that developing countries are particularly vulnerable for natural or man-made disasters. Their infrastructure is often not resilient enough to confront such challenges. When disaster hits, resources are needed that are often not available in developing countries. Furthermore, it is to say that many developing countries are situated in regions particularly exposed to such disruptions (earthquakes, flooding, storms and so on). The EU has recognized that disaster risk reduction (DRR) has a high cost-benefit ratio in the context of development cooperation.[196]

Disaster relief is therefore one of the priorities of developing cooperation and suitable for financial assistance.[197]

VIII. Financing

With regard to financing, the European Investment Bank (EIB)[198] is of considerable importance which has been active in the field of development cooperation since 1963 granting loans at reduced interest rates and conditions for the financing of projects in developing countries.[199]

---

[195] See European Commission, 'A Decent Life for All: From Vision to Collective Action' COM(2014) 335 final, 2.

[196] See the European Commission, 'EU Strategy for Disaster Risk Reduction in Developing Countries' COM(2009) 84 final, 2.

[197] See, *e.g.*, Regulation (EU) 233/2014 of 11 March 2014 establishing a financing instrument for development cooperation for the period 2014-2020 [2014] OJ L77/44 which under 'A. Common Areas of Cooperation under Geographic Programmes', 'III. Other areas of significance for development', refers to 'Resilience and disaster risk reduction'. See also Andreas Zimmermann, 'Commentary to Article 208' in Hans von der Groeben, Jürgen Schwarze and Armin Hatje (eds), *Europäisches Unionsrecht* (2015) 374, para 79.

[198] Art 209 para 3 TFEU.

[199] See Streinz/Kruis, *supra* note 112, at 2008, para 32.

Beyond that, specific financing instruments have been introduced. Some are dedicated exclusively to development projects, others partly. On 2 December 2013 the Council adopted the regulation on the Multiannual Financial Framework mentioning the External Action Financing instruments.[200] This Framework refers to six instruments with the following amount agreed for spending over the six years period (2014-2020):

Instrument for Pre-accession Assistance (IPA):	€ 11,699 million
European Neighbourhood Instrument (ENI):	€ 15,433 million
Development Cooperation Instrument (DCI):	€ 19,662 million
Partnership Instrument (PI):	€ 955 million
Instrument contributing to Stability and Peace (IfSP):	€ 2,339 million
European Instrument for Democracy & Human Rights(EIDHR)	€ 1,333 million

In the field of development cooperation, the Development Cooperation Instrument (DCI) is the most important one. For the period 2014-2010 this instrument has been established by Regulation No. 233/2014 of 11 March 2014. Under this instrument the EU may finance:

- geographic programs aimed at supporting development cooperation with developing countries that are included in the list of recipients of Official Development Assistance (ODA) established by the OECD/DAC, except for countries eligible for other funds;
- thematic programs to address development-related global public goods and challenges and support civil society organizations and local authorities in partner countries;
- a Pan-African program to support the strategic partnership between Africa and the Union.[201]

Geographic programs stand at the center of the DCI. They may be of a regional or a bilateral character and they shall encompass cooperation in appropriate areas of activity. Thematic programs shall add value to, and be complementary

---

[200] European Commission, 'The Multiannual Financial Framework: The External Action Financing Instruments (MEMO/13/1134)' (11 December 2013).

[201] Art 1 Regulation (EU) 233/2014 of 11 March 2014 establishing a financing instrument for development cooperation for the period 2014-2020 [2014] OJ L77/44.

to and coherent with, actions funded under geographic programs.[202] Subjects are environment and climate change, sustainable energy, human development, including decent work, social justice and culture, food and nutrition security and sustainable agriculture, and migration and asylum. For both geographic programs and thematic programs strategic papers shall be elaborated.

The Pan-African program is of a complementary nature. According to Article 9 of Reg. 233/2014, the objective of Union assistance under this program shall be to support the strategic partnership between Africa and the Union, and subsequent modifications and additions thereto, to cover activities of a trans-regional, continental or global nature in and within Africa.

Outside the EU budget remains the European Development Fund (EDF) created by an intergovernmental agreement of June 2013.[203] The 11th EDF (2014-2020), which applies provisionally pending ratification, covers cooperation with ACP countries and Overseas Countries and Territories (OCTs).[204] It is sustained that keeping the EDF outside the EU budget will allow for a more flexible use of this instrument and for a more efficient, long-term planning. Furthermore, this could also be a means to protect the overall level of the development aid budget which, in times of financial restraint, is also subject to closer scrutiny.[205]

IX. Conclusions: Towards a True Partnership based on the respect of human rights, democracy, the rule of law and gender equality

EU development cooperation has a history of more than half a century. In this period, this policy has undergone profound changes whereby its main traits have been completely modified. There can be no doubt that initially, the EEC and its member states started from a paternalistic and in a certain sense also egoistic attitude. By the way, in this attitude the EEC and its member states were not alone. It was a rather common relationship between 'donor' countries and recipients. Now, this situation has changed. The respective

---

[202] Art 6 Regulation (EU) 233/2014 of 11 March 2014 establishing a financing instrument for development cooperation for the period 2014-2020 [2014] OJ L77/44.

[203] European Commission, *supra* note 200.

[204] *Ibid.*

[205] See also above Section VI.F. Financial Cooperation.

process has taken place slowly, often even nearly imperceptibly, but over the years the changes were substantial. The focus is now on a truly egalitarian partnership. For many reasons the original approach could not be maintained further. First of all, industrialized and developing countries do not form closed groupings that would not be subject to change over time. On the contrary, it could be noticed that over a longer period some developing countries can become politically and economically strong while so-called industrialized countries may go the opposite direction. The factual pre-conditions for a strong hierarchical relationship between these two groups are simply not given. Furthermore, such a relationship would run counter to a basic principle of modern international law, the principle of sovereign equality of all states.[206]

It took some time for the state community to fully internalize this philosophy[207] but states have gone great lengths in this regard in the last decades. The EU has been an active sponsor of this process, may be also because the continuous enlargement process has increased the difference of economic and political strength between the single member states, thereby prompting weaker countries to emphasize their sovereign equality.

This process has been fostered, however, not only by political susceptibilities. This search for a more equal partnership has grown out also by economic considerations and by new insights into the nature of global commons and global challenges.

In fact, it has been noticed that asymmetrical integration with limited market opening on both sides was often associated with next to no growth and economic development. On the contrary, such trade relations were conducive to the preservation of traditional trading structures that were typical for the colonial and the immediate post-colonial situation. It is hoped that reciprocal trade integration as it is regulated in Article XXIV GATT will change this and spur both competition and development. As has been shown, it is not intended to fully apply the rules on regional integration. It shall be taken notice of the factual difference between industrialized countries and developing countries. Is the concept of 'Economic Partnership Agreements' more than a buzzword? It is true that is has largely to be filled with details and content

---

[206] See Art 2 para 1 of the UN Charter. At the San Francisco Conference this term was deliberately adopted as a 'new term'. See Bardo Fassbender, 'Commentary to Article 2 Paragraph 1' in Bruno Simma *et al* (eds), *The Charter of the United Nations* (2012) 153, para 47.

[207] See now in particular UNGA Res 2625 (XXV), Declaration on Principles of International Law concerning Friendly Relations and Co-operation among States in accordance with the Charter of the United Nations (24 October 1970) UN Doc A/8028.

but nonetheless the intention can be noticed to give it a workable meaning. The reference to 'partnership' brings to bear that this relationship shall be egalitarian and it shall be tried to overcome in this context all elements of hierarchy. The first consequences of this approach can be seen in the field of conditionality policy, a set of rules widely criticized in the past for being the expression of unilateralism and for a mindset qualifying the EU member states as countries with an impeccable human rights and rule of law record and for implicitly submitting that their trading parting should be the natural addressees for lecturing and guidance by the first world. The EU has tried to dispel this criticism first by making the insertion of conditionality rules in trade and cooperation agreements mandatory with whomever they are concluded[208] and afterwards by accepting that these principles apply also against the EU. This has been spelled out very clearly by the 2010 reform of the Cotonou Agreement adding the following subpara 4 to Article 9 para 4:

> The principles underlying the essential and fundamental elements as defined in this Article shall apply equally to the ACP States on the one hand, and to the European Union and its Member States, on the other hand.

The switch to partnership is, however, not only to be seen as a re-qualification of the specific relationship between the EU and the developing world (and, in particular, with countries of the ACP area). This partnership shall rather reach out to a far broader set of goals and involve countries far beyond the traditional relationship between industrialized and developing countries. In its most recent documents the EU points out that industrialized and developing countries should attempt to pursue goals common to the whole state community.

In its Communication of 2 June 2014 fittingly entitled 'A Decent Life for All: From Vision to Collective Action'[209], the Commission emphasized, on the one hand, the paramount importance of 'eradicating poverty and achieving sustainable development'[210] but on the other it underscored that this challenge is to be addressed in a globalized and inter-linked world. Consensus is looked for 'for a new transformative post-2015 agenda'. The Commission points out

---

[208] See European Commission, 'Communication on the Inclusion of Respect for Democratic Principles and Human Rights in all Agreements between the Community and Third Countries' COM(95) and EU Council Conclusions of 29 May 1995 ((1995) 5 EU Bull. point 1.2.3).

[209] European Commission, 'A Decent Life for All: From Vision to Collective Action' COM(2014) 335 final.

[210] *Ibid.*, at 2.

that '[t]his includes tackling issues of global concern that were not sufficiently covered in the MDGs such as inclusive and sustainable growth, inequalities, sustainable consumption and production, migration and mobility, decent work, digital inclusion, health and social protection, sustainable management of natural resources, climate change, disaster resilience and risk management, and knowledge and innovation.'[211]

With regard to financing, in the post-2015 development policy, in the implementation process of the 2030 agenda, more emphasis will have to be given to private financing, to raise domestic tax revenues and to create a supportive investment climate.[212]

We see that the idea of developing cooperation has gone a long way from its early times when it was mainly understood as requiring a resource transfer from industrialized countries to developing ones – and preferably to those with which before longstanding colonial ties had existed. Development has become a multidimensional issue that no longer knows two opposed groups, an upstairs and a downstairs, patronizing donors and grateful, submissive receivers. Development has become a common project where the parties involved may have partly diverging tasks but widely identical goals. It has become a dialogue based on the respect of human rights, democracy, the rule of law and gender equality.[213] As has been shown, the term of 'partnership' has been used for quite some time in the EU development cooperation context but only recently it seems to be taken seriously. If the policy is continued along this line, EU development cooperation is really set for a great leap forward and may become lasting and sustainable in the sense of the new SDGs.

---

[211] *Ibid.*, at 3.

[212] See European Report on Development, 'Combining Finance and Policies to Implement a Transformative Post-2015 Development Agenda' (2015) 26ff. See also the 'New European Consensus on Development' of 2017, *supra* note 140, at 48f: 'Enhancing domestic resource mobilization is key to all governments´ efforts to achieve inclusive growth, poverty eradication and sustainable development'.

[213] See the 'New European Consensus on Development' of 2017, *supra* note 140, at 7.

Austrian Practice in
International Law 2015/

Österreichische Praxis zum
Internationalen Recht 2015

Edited by
Gerhard Hafner and *Stephan Wittich*

Structure 261

Jane Alice Hofbauer, Philipp Janig, Michael J. Moffatt and *Stephan Wittich*

Part I: Austrian Judicial Decisions Involving Questions of International
Law/Österreichische Judikatur zum Internationalen Recht 277

Markus P. Beham and *Gerhard Hafner*

Part II: Austrian Diplomatic and Parliamentary Practice in International Law/
Österreichische Diplomatische und Parlamentarische Praxis zum
Internationalen Recht 365

Structure

AA. International law in general/Völkerrecht – allgemein

I. Nature, basis, purpose/Natur, Grundlage, Funktionen
   1. In general/Allgemeines
   2. *Ius cogens*
   3. Soft law
II. History/Geschichte

BB. Sources of international law/Völkerrechtsquellen

I. Treaties/Verträge
II. Custom/Völkergewohnheitsrecht
III. General principles of law/Allgemeine Rechtsgrundsätze
IV. Judicial decisions/Gerichtsentscheidungen
V. Opinions of writers/Lehrmeinungen
VI. Equity/Billigkeit
VII. Unilateral acts, including acts and decisions of international organisations and conferences/Einseitige Akte, einschließlich der Akte und Beschlüsse von internationalen Organisationen und Konferenzen
VIII. Comity/Courtoisie (*comitas gentium*)
IX. Codification and progressive development/Kodifikation und progressive Weiterentwicklung

CC. The law of treaties/Recht der Verträge

I. Conclusion and entry into force of treaties/Abschluß und Inkrafttreten völkerrechtlicher Verträge
   1. Conclusion/Abschluß
   2. Reservations and declarations/Vorbehalte und Erklärungen
   3. Provisional application and entry into force/Vorläufige Anwendung und Inkrafttreten
II. Observance, application and interpretation of treaties/ Einhaltung, Anwendung und Auslegung von Verträgen
   1. Observance of treaties/Einhaltung von Verträgen
   2. Application of treaties/Anwendung von Verträgen

3. Interpretation of treaties/Auslegung von Verträgen
4. Treaties and third states/(Verträge und) Drittstaaten

III. Amendment and modification of treaties/Änderung und Modifikation von Verträgen
IV. Invalidity, termination and suspension of operation of treaties/Ungültigkeit, Beendigung und Suspendierung von Verträgen

1. General rules/Allgemeine Bestimmungen
2. Invalidity/Ungültigkeit
3. Termination and suspension of operation including denunciation and withdrawal/Beendigung und Suspendierung von Verträgen, einschließlich der Kündigung von Verträgen und des Rücktritts vom Vertrag
4. Procedure/Verfahren
5. Consequences of invalidity, termination or suspension of operation/Folgen der Ungültigkeit, Beendigung oder Suspendierung von Verträgen

V. Depositaries, notifications, corrections and registration/ Depositär, Notifikationen, Berichtigungen und Registrierung
VI. Consensual arrangements, other than in treaty-form/ Willensübereinkünfte in anderer Form

DD. Relationship between international law and internal law/Völkerrecht und innerstaatliches Recht

I. In general/Allgemeines
II. Application and implementation of international law in internal law/Innerstaatliche Anwendung und Durchführung des Völkerrechts
III. Remedies under internal law for violations of international law/Innerstaatliche Rechtsmittel bei Völkerrechtsverletzungen

EE. Subjects of International law/Völkerrechtssubjekte

I. States/Staaten

1. Status and powers/Status und Befugnisse

   a. Personality/Rechtspersönlichkeit
   b. Sovereignty and independence/Souveränität und Unabhängigkeit
   c. Non-intervention/Interventionsverbot
   d. Domestic jurisdiction/Vorbehaltener Wirkungsbereich
   e. Equality of states/Gleichheit
   f. State immunity/Staatenimmunität

g. Other powers, including treaty-making powers/Andere Befugnisse, einschließlich der Vertragsabschlußbefugnis

2. Recognition/Anerkennung

   a. Recognition of states/Anerkennung von Staaten
   b. Recognition of governments/Anerkennung von Regierungen
   c. Types of recognition/Arten der Anerkennung

      aa. *de facto\de jure*
      bb. conditional\unconditional/bedingt\unbedingt

   d. Acts of recognition/Anerkennungsakte
      aa. implied\express/stillschweigend\ausdrücklich
      bb. collective\unilateral/kollektiv\einseitig

   e. Effects of recognition/Wirkungen der Anerkennung
   f. Non-recognition and its effects/Nicht-Anerkennung und deren Wirkungen
   g. Withdrawal of recognition/Rücknahme der Anerkennung

3. Types of states/Arten von Staaten

   a. Unitary states, federal states and confederations/
      Einheitsstaaten, Bundesstaaten und Staatenbünde
   b. Personal unions, real unions/Personalunionen, Realunionen
   c. States under protection/Protektorate

4. Formation, continuity, succession and extinction of states/Entstehung von Staaten, Kontinuität, Staatennachfolge und Untergang von Staaten

   a. Conditions for statehood/Elemente der Staatlichkeit
   b. Formation/Bildung von Staaten
   c. Identity, continuity/Identität, Kontinuität
   d. Extinctions/Untergang von Staaten

      aa. Cases of state succession/Fälle der Staatennachfolge

         i. Union, with or without demise of former state/Zusammenschluß unter Auslöschung oder Fortbestand eines bisherigen Staates
         ii. Separation/Abspaltung
         iii. Newly independent states

      bb. Effects of state succession/Rechtliche Folgen der Staatennachfolge

         i. Territory and other areas under national jurisdiction/Staatsgebiet und andere der Jurisdiktion unterstehende Gebiete
         ii. Nationality/Staatsangehörigkeit
         iii. Succession in respect of treaties/Staatennachfolge in Verträge
         iv. Archives/Archive
         v. Debts/Schulden

vi. Property/Staatsvermögen
vii. Responsibility/Staatenverantwortlichkeit
viii. Other rights and obligations/Sonstige Rechte und Pflichten

5. Self-determination/Selbstbestimmung

II. International organisations/Internationale Organisationen

1. In general/Allgemeines

   a. Status and Powers/Status und Befugnisse

      aa. Personality/Rechtspersönlichkeit
      bb. Powers, including treaty-making power/Befugnisse einschließlich der Vertragsabschlußbefugnis
      cc. Privileges and immunities of the organisation/Privilegien und Immunitäten der Organisation

   b. Participation of states in international organisations and in their activities/Mitgliedschaft in internationalen Organisationen, Teilnahme an ihren Aktivitäten

      aa. Admission/Zulassung
      bb. Suspension, withdrawal, expulsion/Suspension der Mitgliedschaft, Austritt, Ausschluß
      cc. Obligations of membership/Verpflichtungen aus der Mitgliedschaft
      dd. Representation of states, including privileges and immunities/Vertretung der Staaten, einschließlich ihrer Privilegien und Immunitäten

   c. Legal effect of acts of international organisations/Rechtswirkung von Akten internationaler Organisationen
   d. Personnel of international organisations, including their privileges and immunities/Bedienstete internationaler Organisationen, einschließlich ihrer Privilegien und Immunitäten
   e. Responsibility of international organisations (see MM.)/Verantwortlichkeit internationaler Organisationen (siehe MM.)
   f. Succession of international organisations/Nachfolge internationaler Organisationen

2. Particular types/Arten internationaler Organisationen

   a. Universal organisations/Universelle Organisationen
   b. Regional organisations/Regionalorganisationen
   c. Organisations constituting integrated (*e.g.*, economic) communities/ Internationale Gemeinschaften (z.B. wirtschaftlicher Natur)
   d. Other types of organisations/Andere Arten von Organisationen

III. Other subjects of international law and entities and groups/Andere Völkerrechtssubjekte, Einheiten und Gruppen

    1. Insurgents/Insurgenten
    2. Belligerents/Kriegsführende
    3. The Holy See/Der Heilige Stuhl
    4. Mandated and trust territories/Treuhand- und Mandatsgebiete
    5. Dependent territories/Abhängige Gebiete
    6. Special regimes/Besondere Regime
    7. Others (indigenous people, minorities, national liberation movements, *etc.*)/Sonstige (indigene Völker, Minderheiten, Nationale Befreiungsbewegungen)

FF. The position of the individual (including the corporation) in international law/Die Stellung der Einzelperson (einschließlich der juristischen Person) im Völkerrecht

    I. Nationality/Staatsangehörigkeit
    II. Diplomatic and consular protection (see MM.)/Diplomatischer und konsularischer Schutz (siehe MM.)
    III. Aliens or non-nationals/Fremde
    IV. Members of minorities/Angehörige von Minderheiten
    V. Stateless persons/Staatenlose
    VI. Refugees/Flüchtlinge
    VII. Immigration and emigration, extradition, expulsion, asylum/ Einwanderung und Auswanderung, Auslieferung, Ausweisung, Asyl

        1. Immigration and emigration/Einwanderung, Auswanderung
        2. Extradition/Auslieferung
        3. Expulsion/Ausweisung
        4. Asylum/Asyl

    VIII. Human rights and fundamental freedoms/Menschenrechte und Grundfreiheiten
    IX. Expropriation/Enteignung
    X. Crimes under international law/Völkerrechtliche Verbrechen
    XI. Criminal responsibility of the individual (see MM.)/Strafrechtliche Verantwortlichkeit des Einzelmenschen (siehe MM.)

GG. Organs of the state and their legal status/Die Staatsorgane und ihr rechtlicher Status

    I. Head of state/Das Staatsoberhaupt
    II. Minister/Minister
    III. Other organs of the state/Andere Staatsorgane
    IV. Diplomatic missions and their members/Diplomatische Vertretungen und ihre Mitglieder
    V. Consulates and their members/Konsulate und ihre Mitglieder
    VI. Special missions/Spezialmissionen
    VII. Trade delegations, information centres, *etc.*/Handelsvertretungen, Informationseinrichtungen *etc.*
    VIII. Armed forces/Streitkräfte
    IX. Protecting powers/Schutzmächte

HH. Jurisdiction of the state/Jurisdiktion (Hoheitsgewalt)

    I. Basis of jurisdiction/Grundlage der Jurisdiktion

        1. Territorial principle/Territorialitätsprinzip
        2. Personal principle/Personalitätsprinzip
        3. Protective principle/Schutzprinzip
        4. Universality principle/Universalitätsprinzip
        5. Other principles/Andere Grundlagen

    II. Types of jurisdiction/Arten der Jurisdiktion

        1. Jurisdiction to prescribe/Legislative Jurisdiktion
        2. Jurisdiction to adjudicate/Urteilsjurisdiktion
        3. Jurisdiction to enforce/Durchsetzungsjurisdiktion

    III. Extra-territorial exercise of jurisdiction/Extraterritoriale Ausübung von Hoheitsgewalt

        1. General/Im allgemeinen
        2 Consular jurisdiction/Konsularjurisdiktion
        3. Jurisdiction over military personnel abroad/Jurisdiktion über im Ausland stationiertes Militärpersonal
        4. Others (artificial islands, *terra nullius, etc.*)/Sonstiges (künstliche Inseln, *terra nullius* etc.)

    IV. Limitations upon jurisdiction (servitudes, leases, *etc.*)/ Einschränkungen der Hoheitsgewalt (Servituten, ähnliche Gebrauchsrechte)
    V. Concurrent jurisdiction/Konkurrierende Jurisdiktion

II. State territory/Das Staatsgebiet

  I. Territory/Das Gebiet

     1. Elements of territory/Gebietsteile

        a. Land, internal waters, rivers, lakes and land-locked seas (see also JJ. and KK.) Land, Binnengewässer, Flüsse, Seen und Binnenmeere (siehe auch JJ. Und KK.)
        b. Sub-soil/Unterirdisches Gebiet
        c. Territorial sea (see KK.)/Küstenmeer (siehe KK.)
        d. Airspace (see LL.)/Luftraum (siehe LL.)

     2. Good neighborliness/Gute Nachbarschaft

  II. Boundaries and frontiers/Grenzen

     1. Delimitation/Delimitation
     2. Demarcation/Demarkation
     3. Stability/Stabilität

  III. Acquisition and transfer of territory/Gebietserwerb und Gebietsübertragung

     1. Acquisition/Gebietserwerb
     2. Transfer/Gebietsübertragung

JJ. International watercourses/Internationale Gewässer

  I. Rivers and Lakes/Flüsse und Seen

     1. Definiton/Definition
     2. Navigation/Schiffahrt
     3. Irrigation/Bewässerung
     4. Uses for other purposes/Sonstige Nutzungen
     5. Protection of the environment/Umweltschutz
     6. Institutional aspects/Institutionelle Aspekte

  II. Subterranean waters/Grundwasser
  III. Canals/Kanäle

KK. Seas/Meere

  I. Internal waters, including ports and bays/Innere Gewässer, Hafenanlagen, Buchten
  II. The territorial sea/Das Küstenmeer
  III. Straits/Meerengen
  IV. Archipelagic waters/Archipelagische Gewässer
  V. Contiguous zone/Anschlußzone

VI. Exclusive economic zone, exclusive fisheries zone/Ausschließliche Wirtschaftszone, ausschließliche Fischereizone
VII. Continental shelf/Festlandsockel
VIII. High seas/Die Hohe See

    1. Freedom of the sea/Grundsatz der Meeresfreiheit
    2. Hot pursuit/Nachteile
    3. Visit and search/Durchsuchung
    4. Piracy/Piraterie
    5. Conservation of living resources/Bewahrung der lebenden Ressourcen

IX. Islands, rocks and low-tide elevations/Inseln, Felsen, trocken-fallende Erhebungen
X. Enclosed and semi-enclosed seas/Eingeschlossene und halbeingeschlossene Meere
XI. International sea-bed area/Internationaler Meeresboden
XII. Land locked and geographically-disadvantaged states/Binnenstaaten und geographisch benachteiligte Staaten
XIII. Protection of the maritime environment/Schutz der Meeresumwelt
XIV. Maritime scientific research/Wissenschaftliche Meeresforschung
XV. Cables and pipelines/Kabel, Rohrleitungen
XVI. Artificial islands, installations and structures/Künstliche Inseln, Anlagen und Bauwerke
XVII. Tunnels/Tunnels
XVIII. Vessels/Schiffe

    1. Legal regime/Recht der Schiffahrt

        a. Warships/Kriegsschiffe
        b. Public vessels other than warships/Andere Staatsschiffe
        c. Merchant ships/Handelsschiffe

    2. Nationality/Nationalität von Schiffen
    3. Jurisdiction over vessels/Jurisdiktion über Schiffe

        a. Flagstate/Flaggenstaat
        b. Coastal state/Küstenstaat
        c. Port state/Hafenstaat
        d. Other exercise of jurisdiction/Sonstige Ausübung der Jurisdiktion

LL. Air Space, outer space and Antarctica/Luftraum, Weltraum, Antarktis

I. Air Space/Luftraum
   1. Legal status/Rechtsstellung
   2. Uses/Nutzungen
   3. Legal regime of aircraft/Rechtlicher Status des Luftfahrzeuges

II. Outer space/Weltraum
   1. Legal status/Rechtsstellung
   2. Uses/Nutzungen
   3. Legal regime of spacecraft/Rechtlicher Status des Weltraumobjektes

III. Antarctica/Die Antarktis
   1. Legal status/Rechtsstellung
   2. Uses/Nutzungen

MM. International responsibility/Völkerrechtliche Verantwortlichkeit

I. General conception/Konzept der völkerrechtlichen Verantwortlichkeit

II. General issues of responsibility/Allgemeines zur völkerrechtlichen Verantwortlichkeit

   1. The elements of responsibility (*e.g.*, unlawfulness of the act, attribution to the state)/Die Elemente der Staatenverantwortlichkeit (z.B. unerlaubter Akt, Zurechenbarkeit)
   2. Circumstances excluding responsibility (self-defence, necessity, reprisals)/Ausschluß der Verantwortlichkeit (Selbstverteidigung, Notstand, Repressalien)
   3. Procedure/Verfahren

      a. Diplomatic protection/Diplomatischer Schutz

         aa. Nationality of claims
         bb. Exhaustion of local remedies/Ausschöpfung der innerstaatlichen Rechtsmittel

      b. Consular protection/Konsularischer Schutz
      c. Peaceful settlement (see NN.)/Friedliche Streitbeilegung (siehe NN.)

   4. Consequences of responsibility (restitutio in integrum, damages satisfaction, guarantees)/Folgen der völkerrechtlichen Verantwortlichkeit (*restitutio in integrum*, Schadenersatz, Genugtuung, Sicherheitsleistungen)

III. Responsible entities/Träger der Verantwortlichkeit

1. States/Staaten
2. International organisations/Internationale Organisationen
3. Entities other than states and international organisations/Andere Einheiten
4. Individuals and groups of individuals, including corporations/
   Individuen und Gruppen einschließlich juristischer Personen

NN. Pacific settlement of disputes/Friedliche Streitbelegung

I. The concept of an international dispute/
   Vorliegen eines internationalen Streites
II. Means of settlement/Methoden zur Streitbelegung

1. Negotiations and consultations/Verhandlungen und Konsultationen
2. Good offices/Die Guten Dienste
3. Enquiry and fact-finding/Untersuchung
4. Mediation/Vermittlung
5. Conciliation/Vergleich
6. Arbitration/Schiedsgerichtsbarkeit

   a. Arbitral tribunals and commissions/Schiedsgerichte und -kommissionen
   b. Permanent Court of Arbitration/Ständiger Schiedshof

7. Judicial settlement/Gerichtliche Streitbelegung

   a. International Court of Justice/Der Internationale Gerichtshof
   b. Courts or tribunals, other than the ICJ/Sonstige Gerichte und Gerichtshöfe

8. Settlement within international organisations/Streitbeilegung
   innerhalb der internationalen Organisationen

   a. United Nations/Vereinte Nationen
   b. Organisations other than the United Nations/Andere Organisationen

9. Other means of settlement/Sonstige Methoden der Streitbelegung

OO. Coercive measures short of the use of force/Zwangsmaßnahmen unter der Schwelle der Gewaltanwendung

I. Unilateral acts/Einseitige Akte

1. Retorsion/Retorsion
2. Countermeasures/Gegenmaßnahmen
3. Pacific blockade/Friedliche Blockade
4. Intervention (see also EE.)/Intervention (siehe auch EE.)
5. Other unilateral acts/Andere einseitige Akte

II. Collective measures/Kollektivmaßnahmen
   1. United Nations/Vereinte Nationen
   2. Collective measures outside the United Nations/
      Kollektivmaßnahmen außerhalb der Vereinten Nationen

PP. Use of force/Gewaltanwendung

   I. Prohibition of use of force/Gewaltverbot
   II. Legitimate use of force/Rechtmäßiger Gewaltgebrauch
      1. Self-defense/Selbstverteidigung
      2. Collective measures/Kollektivmaßnahmen
         a. United Nations/Vereinte Nationen
         b. Outside the United Nations/Außerhalb der Vereinten Nationen
      3. Others/Sonstiges
   III. Disarmament and arms control/Abrüstung und Rüstungskontrolle

QQ. The law of armed conflict and international humanitarian law/Recht des bewaffneten Konfliktes und internationales humanitäres Recht

   I. International armed conflict/Der internationale bewaffnete Konflikt
      1. Definition/Definition
      2. The laws of international armed conflict/Das Recht
         des internationalen bewaffneten Konflikts
         a. Sources/Rechtsquellen
         b. The commencement of international armed conflict and its effects (*e.g.*, diplomatic and consular relations, treaties, private property, nationality, trading with the enemy, *locus standi personae in judicio*)/Der Beginn des internationalen bewaffneten Konfliktes und seine Rechtsfolgen (z.B. diplomatische und konsularische Beziehungen, Verträge, Privateigentum, Staatsangehörigkeit, Feindhandel, *locus standi personae in judicio*)
         c. Land warfare/Landkrieg
         d. Sea warfare/Seekrieg
         e. Air warfare/Luftkrieg
         f. Distinction between combatants and non-combatants/Kombattanten – Nicht-Kombattanten
         g. International humanitarian law (droit humanitaire international)/Internationales humanitäres Recht
         h. Belligerent occupation/Kriegerische Besetzung
         i. Conventional, nuclear, bacteriological and chemical weapons/ Konventionelle, nukleare, bakteriologische und chemische Waffen

j. Treaty relations between combatants (cartels, armistices *etc*.)/Vertragliche Beziehungen zwischen den Kombattanten (Absprachen, Waffenstillstände)

k. Termination of international armed conflict, treaties of peace/Beendigung des internationalen bewaffneten Konfliktes, Friedensverträge

    3. Reparations/Reparationen

II. Non-international armed conflict/Nicht-internationaler bewaffneter Konflikt

RR. Neutrality, non-belligerency/Neutralität, Nicht-Kriegführung

I. The laws of neutrality/Neutralitätsrecht

    1. Land warfare/Landkrieg
    2. Sea warfare/Seekrieg
    3. Air warfare/Luftkrieg

II. Permanent neutrality/Dauernde Neutralität

III. Neutrality in the light of the Charter of the United Nations/ Neutralität im Licht der Satzung der Vereinten Nationen

IV. Policy of neutrality and non-alignment/Neutralitätspolitik, Bündnisfreiheit

V. Non-belligerency/Nicht-Kriegführung

SS. Legal aspects of international relations and cooperation in particular matters/Rechtliche Aspekte der internationalen Beziehungen und Zusammenarbeit in bestimmten Bereichen

I. General economic and financial matters/Wirtschaftliche und Finanzwirtschaftliche Angelegenheiten

    1. Trade/Handel
    2. Loans/Kredite
    3. Investments/Investitionen
    4. Taxes/Steuern
    5. Monetary matters/Monetäre Angelegenheiten
    6. Development/Entwicklung

II. Transport and communications/Transport, Kommunikation

III. Environment/Umwelt

IV. Natural Resources/Natürliche Ressourcen

V. Technology/Technologie

VI. Social and health matters/Soziale und gesundheitliche Angelegenheiten

VII. Cultural matters/Kulturelle Angelegenheiten

VIII. Legal matters (*e.g.*, judicial assistance and crime control *etc.*)/Rechtliche Angelegenheiten (z.B. Rechtshilfe und Verbrechensbekämpfung *etc.*)

IX. Military and security matters/Militärische Angelegenheiten, Sicherheitsangelegenheiten

PART I
Austrian Judicial Decisions Involving Questions of International Law/
Österreichische Judikatur zum Internationalen Recht

Jane Alice Hofbauer[*], *Philipp Janig*[**], *Michael J. Moffatt*[***] *and Stephan Wittich*[****]

Index of Judgments and Decisions[*****]

BB. Sources of international law/Völkerrechtsquellen

   BB.I. – *See CC.II.3., HH.II.2.*

CC. The law of treaties/Recht der Verträge

   CC.II.3. – *See also HH.II.2.*

   Provincial Administrative Court (Lower Austria), Decision LVwG-AV-172/001-2015 of 24 August 2015 – treaty interpretation – Treaty of Friendship and Establishment between the Republic of Austria and the Empire of Iran from 9 September 1959 – domestic interpretation rules (historical).. 280

DD. Relationship between international law and internal law/Völkerrecht und innerstaatliches Recht

   DD.II. – *See CC.II.3.*

---

[*] Researcher and lecturer, Section for International Law and International Human Rights Law, Bundeswehr University Munich, and editor.

[**] Researcher and lecturer, Section for International Law and International Human Rights Law, Bundeswehr University Munich.

[***] Researcher and lecturer, Section for International Law and International Relations, University of Vienna.

[****] Professor, Section for International Law and International Relations, University of Vienna, and editor.

[*****] The digest covers the period from 1 January 2015 to 31 December 2015.

FF. The position of the individual (including the corporation) in international law/Die Stellung der Einzelperson (einschließlich der juristischen Person) im Völkerrecht

FF.III. – *See FF.VII.4.*

FF.VII.2.-1 – Supreme Court, Decision 13Os27/15t (13Os30/15h) of 15 April 2015 – extradition for criminal prosecution – European Convention on Human Rights – Art 3 and 6 ECHR – extraterritorial effects of the ECHR – diplomatic assurances – penal system of the Russian Federation 287

FF.VII.2.-2 – Supreme Court, Decision, 14Os60/15b (14Os73/15i) of 4 August 2015 – extradition for execution of a criminal sentence – diplomatic assurances – European Convention on Human Rights – Art 3 and 6 ECHR – Russian Federation 300

FF.VII.4. – Constitutional Court, Decision U528/2013 of 7 October 2015 – violation of the prohibition of discrimination among aliens as regards the rejection of an asylum application – omission of conducting the necessary investigations regarding the persecution of an Iraqi member of the armed forces/interpreter – political opinion.. 315

FF.VIII. – *See also* FF.VII.2.-1, FF.VII.2.-2, FF.VII.4.

Supreme Administrative Court, Judgment Ro 2014/09/0053 of 20 May 2015 – freedom of expression – European Convention on Human Rights – Art 10 ECHR – Art 17 ECHR – Art 9 Austrian State Treaty – prohibition of National Socialism – doubt expressed by a university professor regarding the Holocaust – Art 6 ECHR – applicability of fair trial rights to disciplinary proceedings – impartiality of judges 327

HH. Jurisdiction of the state/Jurisdiktion (Hoheitsgewalt)

HH.II.2. – Supreme Court, Decision 8Ob28/15y of 24 March 2015 – bilateral enforcement agreement between Austria and Turkey – (partial) recognition (by analogy) of foreign court decisions – *ordre public* – right to be heard – contestation of legitimacy – nullification of paternity *res judicata* – jurisdiction to adjudicate... 349

HH.II.3. – *See* HH.II.2.

SS. Legal aspects of international relations and cooperation in particular matters/Rechtliche Aspekte der internationalen Beziehungen und Zusammenarbeit in bestimmten Bereichen

SS.I.3. – *See* CC.II.3.

BB. Sources of international law/Völkerrechtsquellen

I. Treaties/Verträge

See CC.II.3., HH.II.2.

CC. The law of treaties/Recht der Verträge

II. Observance, application and interpretation of treaties/ Einhaltung, Anwendung und Auslegung von Verträgen

3. Interpretation of treaties/Auslegung von Verträgen

See also HH.II.2.

CC.II.3.

Provincial Administrative Court (Lower Austria), Decision LVwG-AV-172/001-2015 of 24 August 2015

Landesverwaltungsgericht (Niederösterreich), Entscheidung LVwG-AV-172/001-2015 vom 24. August 2015

Keywords

Treaty interpretation – Treaty of Friendship and Establishment between the Republic of Austria and the Empire of Iran from 9 September 1959 – domestic interpretation rules (historical)

Vertragsinterpretation – Freundschafts- und Niederlassungsvertrages zwischen der Republik Österreich und dem Kaiserreich Iran vom 09. September 1959 – innerstaatliche Auslegung (historische)

Facts and procedural history (summary)

The complainant received a decree from the governmental authorities of Lower Austria, giving her a negative confirmation regarding her purchase of real estate. The decree was based on §15 no 1 of the Land Transfer Law of Lower Austria in connection with Articles 5, 8 and 14 of the Treaty of Friendship and Establishment between the Republic of Austria and the Empire of Iran from 9 September 1959 (Federal Law Gazette No 45/1966) [Treaty of Friendship and Establishment].

The decree's reasoning was primarily based on the argument that the Treaty of Friendship and Establishment only foresaw the equal treatment of self-emplyoyed persons and not of persons who were not self-employed. While Ms *** was an Iranian national, she had not provided any evidence regarding her self-employment. Hence, the Treaty of Friendship and Establishment was not applicable in the present case.

Ms ***, stating that she was from a wealthy family, and thus did not rely on any type of income – appealed against this decision. She argued that §6 of the Austrian Civil Code provided that the interpretation of legal provisions – and thus also international treaties – primarily must consider the distinct meaning of the terms together with their context. No other content should be implied than can be deduced from the wording. Article 14 of the Treaty of Friendship and Establishment unambigiously showed that Article 8 was not applicable to those persons, who were non-self-employed. According to her line of arguments, it was evident that the purpose of the provision that it only applied to self-emplyed persons. The heading 'interpretation' in the Austrian Civil Code preceded provisions on interpretation in the proper sense (§6), the loophole-filling interpretation (§7) and the so-called authentic interpretation (§8) of laws. These provisions had a wider-ranging importance in the Austrian legal system as the rules of interpretation were only codified in this statute.

The Provincial Administrative Court (Lower Austria) held (excerpts)

[…]

Ms *** is an Iranian national and neither employed nor self-employed and lives from her father's fortune. […]

The following provisions are relevant:

§15 No 1 of the Land Transfer Law of Lower Austria stipulates that the provisions of this act regarding the legal acquisition of title by foreign persons are not applicable to nationals which are placed on an equal footing with Austrian nationals by virtue of international and European law.

Article 5, 8 and 14 of the Treaty of Friendship and Establishment […] read as follows:

Article 5:

In accordance with the legislation of the Contracting Parties, the nationals of one of the High Contracting Parties enjoy treatment no less favorable than the treatment accorded to investors of any third state as regards the right to exercise any form of self-employment freely on the territory of the other Party.

Where one of the High Contracting Parties reserves the exercise of a type of self-employment to nationals, the other Contracting Party may also exclude nationals of the former from the exercise of such employment.

Article 14:

It is understood that the provisions of this treaty, according to which the nationals and the corporate entities listed in Article 6 enjoy treatment no less favourable than is accorded to nationals or corporate entities of any other state, are not applicable to:

a) preferential treatment which one of the High Contracting Parties has granted or will grant to a third state due to any multilateral agreement,

b) nationals of the other High Contracting Party, which are engaged in non-self-employment.

Number 226 of the supplements to the stenographic protocol of the national council IX. legislative period shows the following regarding the government bill on Treaty of Friendship and Establishment in the report of the Foreign Affairs Committee:

> 'The present treaty contains general provisions of a declaratory nature and provisions on the establishment of physical and juristic persons, provisons on the protection of property of the nationals of both parties, provisions on the applicable law in family matters, provisions on overall estate planning, on the mutual assistance in civil and commercial matters and on the exemption from military and civil service in the state of residence. [...]
>
> The nationals of both parties enjoy treatment no less favorable than the treatment accorded to investors of any third state on the territory of the other state when undertaking any form of self-employment [...].'

It is undisputed that the complainant is an Iranian national and is not engaged in any type of non-self-employment in Austria.

However, the Treaty of Friendship and Establishment is only applicable to nationals of the other High Contracting Party who are exercising some form of self-employment. This is evident from the report of the Foreign Affairs Committee regarding the government bill on the Treaty of Friendship and Establishment which – in contrast to the legal opinion of the complainant – is relevant for the interpretation [of said treaty]. This particularly as its elaborations regarding the international treaty are a more specific interpretation thereof than according to the general rules of interpretation contained in the Austrian Civil Code. According to this report, the equal treatment only extends to self-employed persons. The complainant, however, does not even claim to be self-employed.

Quite the opposite, the complainant explains that – from an economic perspective – she is solely supported by her father [...].

In order to fulfil the terms of the treaty, i.e. 'not non-self-employment', the 'economic' status of the complainant as a 'person of private means' does not constitute a sufficient category of a negative confirmation for the purpose of the treaty as any (economic) dependency – as is given in the case of non-self-employment – excludes this.

E contrario, the self-employment which is required by law and mentioned in the report of the Foreign Affairs Committee is certainly not given in the present context of the complainant.

Hence, the preferential treatment foreseen in the Treaty of Friendship regarding the acquisition of property is not applicable as regard the complainant.

[…]

German Original

Entscheidungsgründe:

Mit Bescheid der NÖ Landesregierung vom ***, Zl. ***, wurde der Antrag von Frau ***, vertreten durch ***, Rechtsanwalt, auf Erlassung einer Negativbestätigung, betreffend den Erwerb von 106/642 Anteilen an der Liegenschaft EZ ***, Grundbuch ***, Grundstück Nr. ***, entsprechend dem Kaufvertrag vom ***, abgewiesen.

Gestützt ist diese Entscheidung auf § 15 Z 1 NÖ Grundverkehrsgesetz 2007, LGBl. 6800-5, idF LGBl. Nr. 8/2015 iVm Art. 5, 8 und 14 des Freundschafts- und Niederlassungsvertrages zwischen der Republik Österreich und dem Kaiserreich Iran vom 09. September 1959, BGBl. 45/1966.

Begründet wird diese Entscheidung im Wesentlichen damit, dass aus dem Freundschafts- und Niederlassungsvertrag zwischen der Republik Österreich und dem Kaiserreich Iran hervorgehe, dass sich die Gleichstellung auf selbständige Erwerbstätige beziehe. Unter Berücksichtigung des Art. 5 seien Art. 8 und 14 so zu verstehen, dass nur selbständig Erwerbstätige gleichgestellt seien. Frau *** sei zwar iranische Staatsbürgerin, habe jedoch keinen Nachweis einer selbständigen Tätigkeit erbracht. Infolgedessen sei der zwischen der Republik Österreich und dem Kaiserreich Iran geschlossene Freundschafts- und Niederlassungsvertrag auf den vorliegenden Sachverhalt nicht anwendbar.

Gegen diese Entscheidung richtet sich die fristgerecht erhobene Beschwerde vom ***, in der beantragt wurde, den angefochtenen Bescheid dahingehend abzuändern, als der Antrag auf Erlassung einer Negativbestätigung bewilligt werde. Begründend wurde zusammengefasst ausgeführt, dass § 6 ABGB normiere, dass bei der Auslegung gesetzlicher Vorschriften und daher auch bei Staatsverträgen vorrangig der eigentümlichen Bedeutung der Worte in ihrem Zusammenhang Bedeutung zukomme. Es dürfe kein anderer Inhalt unterstellt werden als aus der Bedeutung der Worte hervorgehe. Aus Art. 14 des Freundschaftsvertrages zwischen der Republik Österreich und dem Kaiserreich Iran gehe eindeutig hervor, dass Art. 8 auf jene Personen nicht anwendbar sei, die eine unselbständige Erwerbstätigkeit ausüben würden. Es gehe daher ganz klar aus dem Wortsinn diese Bestimmung hervor, dass Art. 8 auf jene Personen anwendbar sei, die keine unselbständige Erwerbstätigkeit ausüben. Unter der Überschrift „Auslegung" seien im ABGB vorbildliche Bestimmungen über die Auslegung im eigentlichen Sinn (§ 6), die lückenfüllende Ergänzung (§ 7) und die sogenannte authentische Interpretation (§ 8) von Gesetzen normiert, die mangels sonstiger in der österreichischen Rechtsordnung positivierter Rechtsanwendungsregeln von allgemeiner, über den Bereich des bürgerlichen Rechts weit hinausgehender Bedeutung seien. Die Auslegung habe mit der Erforschung des Wortsinnes der Norm zu beginnen. Da ein Gesetz grundsätzlich aus sich selbst auszulegen sei und mit seinem Wortlaut seiner Systematik und seinem Zusammenhang mit anderen Normen über der Meinung der Redaktoren stehe, seien andere Erkenntnisquellen über die Absicht des Gesetzgebers erst heranzuziehen, wenn die Ausdrucksweise zu zweifeln Anlass biete. Gerade bei Staatsverträgen sei zu beachten, dass dem Wortsinn die größte Bedeutung zukomme, da es nicht auf die Interpretation eines einzelnen der Vertragsteile ankomme, wie ein Vertrag auszulegen sei.

Im vorliegenden Fall sei daher klar und eindeutig geregelt, dass alle Personen, die nicht unselbständig erwerbstätig seien, die Begünstigungen des Art. 8 des Staatsvertrages erfahren würden. Ein Bericht irgendeines außenpolitischen Ausschusses über die Regierungsvorlage sei aufgrund des eindeutigen Wortlautes unbeachtlich. Die Beschwerdeführerin stamme aus einer begüterten Familie und müsse daher weder selbständig noch unselbständig tätig sein, um ihren Lebensunterhalt zu verdienen. So sei auch die gegenständliche Liegenschaft ohne Kreditaufnahme bezahlt worden. Die Beschwerdeführerin sei daher als Privatier anzusehen und falle daher unter die Begünstigungen des Art. 8.

Bereits aus dem Akteninhalt ergibt sich folgender unbestrittener entscheidungsrelevanter Sachverhalt:

Mit Schriftsatz der nunmehrigen Beschwerdeführerin vom *** wurde die Erlassung einer Negativbestätigung, wonach eine Genehmigungspflicht des Kaufvertrages bei Rechtserwerb durch ausländische Personen nicht erforderlich ist, für den Kaufvertrag, abgeschlossen zwischen *** als Verkäufer und *** als Käufer beantragt.

Frau *** ist iranische Staatsbürgerin und weder unselbständig noch selbständig erwerbstätig und lebt vom Vermögen ihres Vaters.

Ausdrücklich wurde im Antrag vorgebracht, dass Frau *** nicht unselbständig in Österreich tätig ist. Der Kaufvertrag, abgeschlossen am ***, betreffend das Grundstück Nr. *** hinsichtlich 106/642 Anteilen in der KG ***, EZ ***, wurde diesem Antrag ebenso beigelegt, wie eine Kopie des Reisepasses.

Dieser Sachverhalt stützt sich im Wesentlichen auf das Vorbringen der Beschwerdeführerin.

Rechtlich gelangen folgende Bestimmungen zur Anwendung:

Gemäß § 15 Z 1 NÖ Grundverkehrsgesetz gelten die Bestimmungen dieses Gesetzes über den Rechtserwerb durch ausländische Personen nicht für Staatsangehörige aufgrund des Völker- oder Gemeinschaftsrechtes österreichischen Staatsangehörigen gleichgestellt.

Artikel 5, 8 und 14 des Freundschafts- und Niederlassungsvertrages zwischen der Republik Österreich und dem Kaiserreich Iran vom 09. September 1959, BGBl. Nr. 45/1966 lauten wie folgt:

Art. 5:

Im Einklang mit der Gesetzgebung der Vertragschließenden Parteien genießen die Angehörigen einer Hohen Vertragschließenden Partei bezüglich des Rechtes der Ausübung einer selbständigen Erwerbstätigkeit auf dem Gebiet der anderen Partei die gleiche Behandlung, die den Angehörigen der meistbegünstigten Nation zuteil wird.

Insoweit eine der Hohen Vertragschließenden Parteien die Ausübung einer selbständigen Erwerbstätigkeit Inländern vorbehält, kann auch die andere Vertragsschließende Partei die Angehörigen der ersteren von der Ausübung dieser Erwerbstätigkeit ausschließen.

Art. 8:

Die Angehörigen einer der Hohen Vertragschließenden Parteien haben das Recht, im Rahmen der auf dem Gebiete der anderen Partei in Kraft stehenden Gesetze und sonstigen Vorschriften daselbst jede Art von Rechten sowie von beweglichem oder unbeweglichem Eigentum zu erwerben, zu besitzen und zu veräußern. Sie werden in dieser Hinsicht unter der Voraussetzung der Gegenseitigkeit wie die Angehörigen der meistbegünstigten Nation behandelt.

Art. 14:

Es besteht Einverständnis darüber, daß die Bestimmungen des vorliegenden Vertrages, denen zufolge die Angehörigen und die in Artikel 6 bezeichneten Gesellschaften einer der Hohen Vertragschließenden Parteien auf dem Gebiet der anderen Partei die gleiche Behandlung wie die Angehörigen oder Gesellschaften der meistbegünstigten Nation erfahren, nicht anwendbar sind:

a) auf Begünstigungen, die eine der Hohen Vertragschließenden Parteien dritten Staaten auf Grund einer multilateralen Vereinbarung gewährt oder in Zukunft gewähren sollte,

b) auf Angehörige der anderen Hohen Vertragschließenden Partei, die eine unselbständige Erwerbstätigkeit ausüben.

Aus 226 der Beilagen zu den stenographischen Protokollen des Nationalrates IX. GP. ist aus dem Bericht des Außenpolitischen Ausschusses über die Regierungsvorlage (217 der Beilagen): Freundschafts- und Niederlassungsvertrag zwischen der Republik Österreich und dem Kaiserreich Iran Folgendes zu entnehmen:

„Das vorliegende Vertragswerk enthält neben allgemeinen Bestimmungen lediglich deklaratorischen Charakter unter anderem Niederlassungsbestimmungen für physische und juristische Personen, Bestimmungen über den Schutz des Eigentums der beiderseitigen Staatsangehörigen, Bestimmungen über das in Familiensachen anzuwendende Recht, Vorschriften über die Nachlaßregelung, über die Rechtshilfe

in Zivil- und Handelssachen und über die Befreiung von militärischem und zivilem Dienst im Aufenthaltsstaat. [...]
Die beiderseitigen Staatsangehörigen genießen auf dem Gebiet des anderen Staates bei Ausübung einer selbständigen Erwerbstätigkeit die gleiche Behandlung, die den Angehörigen der meistbegünstigten Nation zuteil wird, wobei bei Vorbehalt einzelner selbständiger Erwerbstätigkeiten für Inländer die materielle Gegenseitigkeit angewandt wird. [...]"

Unstrittig steht fest, dass die Antragstellerin iranische Staatsbürgerin ist und keiner unselbständigen Erwerbstätigkeit in Österreich nachgeht.

Der Freundschafts- und Niederlassungsvertrag zwischen der Republik Österreich und dem Kaiserreich Iran ist jedoch nur auf Angehörige der anderen Hohen Vertragschließenden Partei, die eine selbständige Erwerbstätigkeit ausüben, anwendbar. Dies ergibt sich aus dem Bericht des Außenpolitischen Ausschusses über die Regierungsvorlage zum Freundschafts- und Niederlassungsvertrag, der entgegen der Rechtsmeinung der Beschwerdeführerin sehr wohl zur Auslegung heranzuziehen ist, zumal durch die darin enthaltenen Ausführungen zum vorliegenden völkerrechtlichen Vertragswerk eine speziellere Interpretation desselben erfolgt als durch die allgemeinen Auslegungsregelungen des ABGBs . Laut diesem Bericht bezieht sich eine Gleichstellung lediglich auf selbständige Erwerbstätige. Eine selbständige Erwerbstätigkeit wird von der Beschwerdeführerin nicht einmal behauptet.

Ganz im Gegenteil führt die Beschwerdeführerin aus, in wirtschaftlicher Hinsicht ausschließlich von ihrem Vater unterstützt zu werden, sodass jedwede Annahme einer selbständigen Erwerbstätigkeit schon von vornherein aus diesem Grund ausscheidet.

Für die nach dem Wortlaut des Vertrages geforderte „nicht unselbständige Erwerbstätigkeit" stellt der „wirtschaftliche" Status der Beschwerdeführerin als „Privatier" keine nach dem Sinn des Vertragswerkes für eine Negativbestätigung ausreichende Kategorie dar, da eine (wirtschaftliche) Abhängigkeit, wie dies eben bei unselbständig Erwerbstätigen gegeben ist, dies ausschließt.

Die vom Gesetz im Umkehrschluss und im Zusammenhang mit dem Bericht des Außenpolitischen Ausschusses geforderte selbständige Erwerbstätigkeit liegt bei der Antragstellerin und nunmehrigen Beschwerdeführerin jedenfalls nicht vor.

Aus diesem Grund ist auch die im Freundschaftsvertrag vorgesehene Begünstigung - hinsichtlich des Eigentumserwerbes – auf die Beschwerdeführerin nicht anwendbar.

Eine öffentliche mündliche Verhandlung konnte gemäß § 24 Abs. 4 VwGVG entfallen.

Zur Zulässigkeit der ordentlichen Revision:

Die ordentliche Revision war im gegenständlichen Fall allerdings zuzulassen, da eine Judikatur zur Auslegung der Bestimmung des § 15 NÖ Grundverkehrsgesetz iVm Völkerrechtlichen Verträgen, wie insbesondere dem Freundschafts- und Niederlassungsvertrag zwischen der Republik Österreich und dem Kaiserreich Iran, fehlt.

DD. Relationship between international law and internal law/ Völkerrecht und innerstaatliches Recht

II. Application and implementation of international law in internal law/Innerstaatliche Anwendung und Durchführung des Völkerrechts

See CC.II.3.

FF. The position of the individual (including the corporation) in international law/Die Stellung der Einzelperson (einschließlich der juristischen Person) im Völkerrecht

III. Aliens or non-nationals/Fremde

See FF.VII.4.

VII. Immigration and emigration, extradition, expulsion, asylum/ Einwanderung und Auswanderung, Auslieferung, Ausweisung, Asyl

2. Extradition/Auslieferung

FF.VII.2.-1

Supreme Court, Decision 13Os27/15t (13Os30/15h) of 15 April 2015

Oberster Gerichtshof, Entscheidung 13Os27/15t (13Os30/15h) vom 15. April 2015

Keywords

Extradition for criminal prosecution – human rights – European Convention on Human Rights – Art 3 and 6 ECHR – extraterritorial effects of the ECHR – diplomatic assurances – penal system of the Russian Federation

Auslieferung zur Strafverfolgung – Menschenrechte – Europäische Menschenrechtskonvention – Art 3 und 6 EMRK – Extraterritorial Effekte der EMRK – Diplomatische Zusicherungen – Strafvollzug in der Russischen Föderation

Facts and procedural history (summary)

On 24 March 2014, the Prosecutor General's Office of the Russian Federation requested the extradition of Dr Anatoly R***** for criminal prosecution. The Regional Criminal Court of Vienna declared the extradition permissible, as no death penalty would be imposed on the person concerned and no other obstacles precluding extradition were present. The affected individual appealed that decision. The Higher Regional Court affirmed the permissibility of the extradition, dependent on several conditions as outlined in a letter of assurances of the Prosecutor General's Office of the Russian Federation, namely that

1) the conditions of detention are not inhumane or degrading within the meaning of Art 3 ECHR;

2) the physical and mental integrity of the extradited person is to be preserved and their medical care, if required, to be ensured;

3) Dr Anatoly R***** has at any time the right to contact the diplomatic mission of Austria, which is entitled to visit the aforementioned at any time and unannounced, in the absence of any surveillance measures;

4) the Austrian diplomatic mission is informed of the place of detention of Dr Anatoly R***** and the Austrian diplomatic mission is immediately informed of a possible relocation of the person concerned to another prison;

5) Dr Anatoly R***** has the right to communicate with his defence lawyer unrestricted and unsupervised;

6) the relatives of the extradited person have the right to visit him in prison (BS 1 f).

Moreover, the Higher Regional Court required, as conditions for the permissibility of the extradition, the requesting state to observe certain procedural guarantees as outlined in its decision. Based on these factors, the Higher Regional Court considered that the risk of the individual concerned being subjected to treatment in violation of Art 3 ECHR was so small that it appeared merely theoretical. As a result, it declared the extradition permissible.

The General Procurator's Office lodged a nullity appeal to preserve the integrity of the law against that decision. Likewise, the person concerned lodged an application for re-hearing of criminal proceedings.

The Supreme Court held

In the extradition matter AZ 311 HR 50/14g of the Regional Criminal Court of Vienna, the decision of the Higher Regional Court of Vienna, as appellate court, from 20 January 2015, AZ 22 Bs 248/14b (ON 82) violates Sections 33 (1) and

(3) Extradition and Mutual Assistance Act (*ARHG*) in conjunction with Art 3 and 6 ECHR.

The decision is lifted and the Higher Regional Court of Vienna is instructed to reach a new decision.

With regard to his application for re-hearing of criminal proceedings (*Erneuerungsantrag*) directed against that decision, Dr Anatoly R***** is referred to this decision.

Insofar as the application for renewal is directed against the decision of the Federal Minister of Justice taken in the extradition matter, it is dismissed, likewise the application for suspensive effect.

Reasons:

With the decision of 10 July 2014, GZ 311 HR 50/14g-55, the judge of the Regional Criminal Court of Vienna declared the extradition of Dr Anatoly R*****, requested by note of the Russian Federation of 24 March 2014, Nr 81/3-757-09, for criminal prosecution due to the suspicions described in the request and documents (ON 30), to be permitted under the condition that the death penalty is not imposed on the person concerned. According to the reasoning of the court of first instance, the assurances of the Russian Federation in the present case, according to which the death penalty will not be imposed on Dr Anatoly R***** as Art 59 (1) Point 1 of the Criminal Code of the Russian Federation excludes that possibility, are sufficient (BS 6 f) and also no other obstacles precluding extradition are present (BS 17).

The appeal of the affected individual (ON 57) directed against that decision was rejected by the Higher Regional Court by way of decision from 20 January 2015, AZ 22 Bs 248/14b, as the extradition, with reference to the letter of assurances from 15 December 2014 made by the Prosecutor General's Office of the Russian Federation, was made dependent on the following conditions, namely that

1) the conditions of detention are not inhumane or degrading within the meaning of Art 3 ECHR;

2) the physical and mental integrity of the extradited person is to be preserved and their medical care, if required, to be ensured;

3) Dr Anatoly R***** has at any time the right to contact the diplomatic mission of Austria, which is entitled to visit the aforementioned at any time and unannounced, in the absence of any surveillance measures;

4) the Austrian diplomatic mission is informed of the place of detention of Dr Anatoly R***** and the Austrian diplomatic mission is immediately informed of a possible relocation of the person concerned to another prison;

5) Dr Anatoly R***** has the right to communicate with his defence lawyer unrestricted and unsupervised;

6) the relatives of the extradited person have the right to visit him in prison (BS 1 f).

The existence of obstacles excluding extradition that might derive from Art 3 and 6 ECHR has been rejected by the Higher Regional Court with extensive reasoning (BS 9 to 12). In doing so, the statements of the Austrian embassy (BS 10), the assurances of the Russian authorities considered binding under international law and reliable (S 2 in ON 30; BS 12 f), as well as the "in principle alarming state of the Russian penal system" were taken into account (BS 12 f).

Irrespective of these considerations the appellate court felt compelled, due to the aforementioned statement of the Austrian embassy and a judgment of the European Court of Human Rights (ECtHR 10 December 2012, 42525/07 und 60800/08, *Ananyev et al/Russia*), in which repeatedly violations of Art 3 ECHR by the country of destination in connection with its penal system were found, to oblige the requesting state, through the Federal Ministry of Justice, to observe procedural guarantees outlined in the decision as condition of an extradition. It further added that their observance has already been abundantly assured by the Prosecutor General's Office of the Russian Federation. In weighing the given circumstances, the risk of an inhumane treatment of the appellant had been reduced to such a low degree that it appears merely theoretical (BS 14). In this context the appellate court also referred to the possibility of monitoring the compliance with the pertinent guarantees through the Federal Ministry for Europe, Integration and Foreign Affairs and explained that in case of a non-compliance with the guarantees – which was not to be expected in the present case – also the reopening of the proceedings along with a return (*Zurückstellung*) of the extradited person would be possible. In that case, the reliability of Russian assurances pro futuro would be put in question to such an extent that future transfers would even had to be deemed impermissible (BS 14).

The Federal Minister of Justice has authorised the extradition of Dr Anatoly R***** for criminal prosecution in reference to the assurances given by the Russian Federation on 27 June 2014 and 15 December 2014 and taking into consideration the principle of speciality (*Spezialitätsgrundsatz*) (ON 86).

In the decree from 5 February 2015, GZ BMJ 4060431/0002-IV 4/2015, the Federal Ministry of Justice held the legal opinion that the extradition could not be declared permissible on the condition of compliance with the conditions (ON 86).

The application for re-hearing of criminal proceedings of Dr Anatoly R*****, combined with an application for suspensive effect and invoking a violation of Art 2, 3 and 6 ECHR, is directed against the decision of the Higher Regional Court as well as the authorization of the extradition by the Minister of Justice (Sec 363a (1) Code of Criminal Procedure (*StPO*)).

The nullity appeal for observance of the law lodged by the General Procurator's Office is directed against the decision of the Higher Regional Court of Vienna of 20 January 2015, AZ 22 Bs 248/14b (ON 82).

Decision

On the nullity appeal to preserve the integrity of the law:

As the General Procurator's Office correctly points out, the decision of the Higher Regional Court of Vienna is not in conformity with the law.

Pursuant to Sec 33 (3) Extradition and Mutual Assistance Act (*ARHG*), the court has to comprehensively examine the permissibility of the extradition in light of requirements for and obstacles to extradition. In doing so, it has to take into consideration international agreements, as well as the subjective rights of the person concerned under statutory law and the federal constitution. Although Sec 1 Extradition and Mutual Assistance Act (*ARHG*) provides for priority of international agreements over the Extradition and Mutual Assistance Act (*ARHG*), the obstacles to extradition arising from the ECHR and its additional protocols must be observed in any event, insofar as they are oppose to an extradition according to the jurisprudence of the ECtHR (see explanatory remarks to government bill 294 BlgNR 22. GP 33; *Martetschläger* in WK² ARHG § 1 MN 3; *Göth-Flemmich* in WK² ARHG Vor §§ 10-25 MN 6, § 33 MN 8).

The Federal Minister of Justice may deny an extradition on the basis of political considerations ("interests of the Republic of Austria") or of reasons of international law (Sec 34 (1) first and second sentence Extradition and Mutual Assistance Act (*ARHG*), explanatory remarks to government bill 294 BlgNR 22. GP 33), he is bound to a final and enforceable decision of the court declaring the extradition impermissible (Sec 34 (1) last sentence Extradition and Mutual Assistance Act (*ARHG*)).

For the state of residence, an extradition may constitute a violation of Art 3 ECHR, if there are serious reasons to believe that the affected individual could be at actual risk of being subjected to treatment contrary to Art 3 ECHR in the requesting state (see ECtHR 7 July 1989, 14038/88, *Soering/United Kingdom*, EuGRZ 1989, 314; RIS-Justiz RS0123229; RS0123201; *Göth-Flemmich* in WK² ARHG § 19 MN 7 with further references). The mere possibility of infringements, which may occur in every state under the rule of law, does not lead to the illegality of the extradition (RIS Justiz RS0118200).

The affected individual has to conclusively prove the considerable likelihood of a current and serious (grave) danger (RIS-Justiz RS0123229). Such proof is unnecessary only if the requesting state exhibits a constant practice of massive and systematic violations of human rights.

The conditions of detention may constitute inhuman or degrading treatment, even if they are not designed to humiliate and debase a detainee. They violate Art 3 ECHR if they cause considerable mental and physical suffering, diminish human dignity or arouse feelings of humiliation and debasement. Such assessment requires consideration of all circumstances, including overcrowding, inadequate heating or ventilation, excessive heat, sanitary conditions, sleeping conditions, nutrition, recreation and contact with the outside world, as well as a cumulative effect as the case may be (RIS-Justiz RS0123229 [T4]; ECtHR 15 July 2002, 47095/99, *Kalashnikov/Russia*; *Meyer-Ladewig*, EMRK[3] Art 3 MN 29).

In case of an extradition to a state party of the Convention, as the Russian Federation in this case, the responsibility of the requested state is limited, if the affected individual may obtain legal protection in the requesting state against violations of the Convention. A co-responsibility of the extraditing state only exists if there is a risk of torture or other severe and irreparable maltreatment and effective legal protection – also through the ECtHR – may not be obtained in due time (13 Os 139/12h with further references).

Although the extradition proceedings themselves do not fall in the scope of Art 6 ECHR, its procedural guarantees may (exceptionally) be relevant for the decision on the permissibility of the extradition, where the affected individual demonstrates that there is a risk of suffering a flagrant denial of fair trial ("a flagrant denial of justice") in the requesting state (see ECtHR 7 July 1989, 14038/88, *Soering/United Kingdom*, EuGRZ 1989, 314; RIS Justiz RS0123200; *Meyer-Ladewig*, EMRK[3] Art 6 MN 167; further references in *Göth-Flemmich* in WK² ARHG § 19 MN 14).

Against this background, the initial approach of the appellate court to focus, in the context of Art 3 and 6 ECHR, on evidence provided by the affected individual does not give rise to concern.

The court has to declare the extradition permissible, if, after its examination, it considers that all legal requirements for extradition have been met and no obstacles to extradition are present. However, should doubts persist as to the existence of an obstacle precluding extradition, the court has to attempt to dispel such doubts prior to a decision on the permissibility of extradition. If that is unsuccessful, it has to declare the extradition to be impermissible (see *Göth-Flemmich* in WK² ARHG Vor §§ 10-25 MN 7; *Murschetz*, Auslieferung und Europäischer Haftbefehl 189, 295f).

The decision of the Higher Regional Court from 20 January 2015, AZ 22 Bs 248/14b, does not conform to these examination criteria.

In the present case, the Higher Regional Court considered the risk of a 'treatment of the appellant in violation of human rights' (apparently in reference to Art 3 ECHR) as being sufficiently reduced by (mere) virtue of obliging the requesting state to observe certain procedural guarantees (outlined in the decision) 'as condition in case of extradition' (BS 1 f and 14).

However, a declaration on the permissibility of the extradition requires that an examination determines the non-existence of obstacles precluding extradition. Conditioning the declaration on the permissibility of the extradition on the requirement that the Russian Federation will, in the future, comply with the

Convention in relation to the affected individual contradicts Sec 33 (1) and (3) Extradition and Mutual Assistance Act (*ARHG*) in conjunction with Art 3 and 6 ECHR.

Incidentally, diplomatic assurances may only be relied upon, if they are suited to eliminate the risk of the affected individual and are deemed both binding and reliable by the Court (see *Göth-Flemmich* in WK² ARHG Vor §§ 10-25 MN 7).

For the purpose of guaranteeing adequate protection against torture and abuse of extradited persons, diplomatic assurances will be rendered generally insufficient where objective sources report the usage or toleration of practices contrary to the principles of the Convention (ECtHR 20 May 2010, 21055/09, *Khaydarov/Russia*; see also *Göth-Flemmich* in WK² ARHG Vor §§ 10-25 MN 8). In such cases, the overall human rights situation in the receiving State excludes the possibility of accepting any assurances from the outset (see ECtHR 17 January 2012, 8139/09, *Othman [Abu Qatada]/United Kingdom*).

The consideration of the Higher Regional Court, whereby, in case of a non-observance of the conditions, the reliability of assurances of the requesting state would be called into question to such a degree that future extraditions had to be declared impermissible does not remove the potential risk of Dr Anatoly R***** being subjected to treatment contrary to Art 3 ECHR in the receiving state.

The remarks on the erroneous link of the declaration of permissibility of the extradition to conditions also apply, as should be noted, to the part of the decision of the court of first instance not objected to by the Higher Regional Court, insofar as it declares the extradition of Dr Anatoly R***** to be permissible under the condition that no death penalty will be imposed. According to Art 11 European Convention on Extradition of 13 December 1957 (Federal Law Gazette No 320/1969), which finds application in relation to the Russian Federation, and the reservation of Austria thereto (see also Sec 20 (1) Extradition and Mutual Assistance Act (*ARHG*)), the extradition may be denied, should the requesting state not give assurances the court (*Göth-Flemmich* in WK² ARHG §33 MN 9) considers adequate that the death penalty will not be imposed. The assurances of the Russian Federation underlying the declaration of permissibility was correctly considered to be sufficient by the court of first instance, as there are already legal bars on an imposition of the death penalty in the requesting state, namely Art 59 (2) No 1 of the Criminal Code of the Russian Federation. The attaching of conditions to the decision does not account for the assessment of the assurances as being sufficient.

As negative effects of the pertinent violation of the law on the affected individual may not precluded, the Supreme Court saw itself called upon to endow its determination with the specific effects detailed in the decision below (Sec 292 last sentence Code of Criminal Procedure (*StPO*)).

Should the appellate court again base itself on diplomatic assurances of the Prosecutor General's Office of the Russian Federation in connection with the alarming state of the Russian penal system in the new proceedings, it will have to take into account that such assurances may only serve to eliminate a risk if the pertinent authority has the possibility to bind the state, for instance if it falls within its authority to order any enforcement in a specific manner, conforming with the requirements of the ECHR (see on the admissibility of diplomatic assurances as an adequate instrument of protection the criteria developed by the ECtHR in the proceedings *Othman [Abu Qatada]/United Kingdom*, as described by Schneider, EuGRZ 2014, 174).

With regard to his application for re-hearing of criminal proceedings directed against the decision of the Higher Regional Court, Dr Anatoly R***** was to be referred to the decision on the nullity appeal to preserve the integrity of the law (RIS-Justiz RS0126458).

German Original

Spruch

In der Auslieferungssache AZ 311 HR 50/14g des Landesgerichts für Strafsachen Wien verletzt der Beschluss des Oberlandesgerichts Wien als Beschwerdegericht vom 20. Jänner 2015, AZ 22 Bs 248/14b (ON 82), § 33 Abs 1 und 3 ARHG iVm Art 3 und 6 MRK.

Dieser Beschluss wird aufgehoben und dem Oberlandesgericht Wien eine neue Entscheidung aufgetragen.

Mit seinem gegen jenen Beschluss gerichteten Erneuerungsantrag wird Dr. Anatoly R***** auf diese Entscheidung verwiesen.

Soweit sich der Erneuerungsantrag gegen die in der Auslieferungssache ergangene Entscheidung des Bundesministers für Justiz wendet, wird er zurückgewiesen, desgleichen der Antrag auf Zuerkennung aufschiebender Wirkung.

Text

Gründe:

Mit Beschluss vom 10. Juli 2014, GZ 311 HR 50/14g-55, erklärte der Einzelrichter des Landesgerichts für Strafsachen Wien die mit Note der Russischen Föderation vom 24. März 2014, Nr 81/3-757-09, begehrte Auslieferung des Dr. Anatoly R***** zur Strafverfolgung wegen der im Ersuchen samt Unterlagen beschriebenen Verdachtslage (ON 30) unter der Bedingung für zulässig, dass über den Betroffenen nicht die Todesstrafe verhängt wird. Der erstgerichtlichen Begründung zufolge seien die vorliegende Zusicherung der Russischen Föderation, wonach über Dr. Anatoly R***** keine Todesstrafe verhängt wird, aufgrund von Art 59 Abs 2 Punkt 1 des Strafgesetzbuches der Russischen Föderation, der dies ausschließe, ausreichend (BS 6 f) und auch keine sonstigen Auslieferungshindernisse gegeben (BS 17).

Der dagegen gerichteten Beschwerde der betroffenen Person (ON 57) gab das Oberlandesgericht mit Beschluss vom 20. Jänner 2015, AZ 22 Bs 248/14b, mit der Maßgabe nicht Folge, dass unter Bezugnahme auf die von der Generalstaatsanwaltschaft der Russischen Föderation abgegebene Garantieerklärung vom 15. Dezember 2014 die Auslieferung von folgenden Bedingungen abhängig gemacht wird, nämlich dass

1) die Haftbedingungen nicht unmenschlich oder erniedrigend im Sinn von Art 3 MRK sind;

2) die physische und psychische Integrität der ausgelieferten Person und ihre allenfalls erforderliche medizinische Versorgung gewahrt sein muss;

3) Dr. Anatoly R***** jederzeit das Recht hat, sich an die diplomatische Vertretung Österreichs zu wenden und diese berechtigt ist, den Genannten jederzeit und unangemeldet ohne jegliche Überwachungsmaßnahmen zu besuchen;

4) der österreichischen diplomatischen Vertretung der Ort der Inhaftierung des Dr. Anatoly R***** bekannt gegeben und die österreichische Vertretung über eine allfällige Verlegung des Betroffenen in ein anderes Gefängnis unverzüglich informiert wird;

5) Dr. Anatoly R***** das Recht hat, mit seinem Verteidiger uneingeschränkt und unbewacht zu verkehren;

6) die Angehörigen des Ausgelieferten das Recht haben, ihn im Gefängnis zu besuchen (BS 1 f).

Der Nachweis des Vorliegens von Auslieferungshindernissen, die sich aus Art 3 und 6 MRK ergeben könnten, wurde vom Oberlandesgericht mit ausführlicher Begründung verneint (BS 9 bis 12). Dabei fanden die Stellungnahmen der österreichischen Botschaft (BS 10), die als völkerrechtlich verbindlich und verlässlich angesehene Zusicherung russischer Behörden (S 2 in ON 30; BS 12 f) und auch der „grundsätzlich besorgniserregende Zustand des russischen Strafvollzugs" Berücksichtigung (BS 12 f).

Ungeachtet dieser Erwägungen sah sich das Beschwerdegericht aber auch aufgrund der bereits erwähnten Stellungnahme der österreichischen Botschaft und einer Entscheidung des Europäischen Gerichtshofs für Menschenrechte EGMR 10. 12. 2012, 42525/07 und 60800/08, *Ananyev* ua/Russland), worin wiederholt Verletzungen des Art 3 MRK durch den Zielstaat im Bereich des Strafvollzugs festgestellt wurden, veranlasst, den ersuchenden Staat im Weg des Bundesministeriums für Justiz zur Einhaltung der aus dem Spruch ersichtlichen Verfahrensgarantien als Bedingung für den Fall der Auslieferung zu verpflichten. Dabei fügte es hinzu, dass deren Einhaltung von der Generalstaatsanwaltschaft der Russischen Föderation bereits im Übermaß zugesichert worden sei. In

Würdigung der gegebenen Umstände lasse sich das Risiko einer menschenrechtswidrigen Behandlung des Beschwerdeführers auf ein so geringes Maß herabsetzen, dass es nur noch theoretisch erscheine (BS 14). In diesem Zusammenhang verwies das Rechtsmittelgericht auch auf die Möglichkeit der Kontrolle der Einhaltung der abgegebenen Garantien durch das Bundesministerium für Europa, Intergration und Äußeres und führte aus, dass bei einem - fallbezogen nicht zu erwartenden - Nichteinhalten der Garantie auch die Wiederaufnahme des Verfahrens samt Zurückstellung des Ausgelieferten in Betracht käme. In diesem Fall wäre die Verlässlichkeit russischer Zusicherungen pro futuro derart in Frage gestellt, dass künftige Überstellungen sogar als unzulässig eingestuft werden müssten (BS 14).

Vom Bundesminister für Justiz wurde die Auslieferung des Dr. Anatoly R***** zur Strafverfolgung unter Bezugnahme auf die von der Russischen Föderation am 27. Juni 2014 und 15. Dezember 2014 abgegebenen Zusicherungen unter Beachtung des Spezialitätsgrundsatzes bewilligt (ON 86).

Im Erlass vom 5. Februar 2015, GZ BMJ4060431/0002-IV 4/2015, vertrat das Bundesministerium für Justiz die Rechtsauffassung, dass die Auslieferung nicht unter der Maßgabe der Einhaltung von Bedingungen für zulässig erklärt werden könne (ON 86).

Gegen den Beschluss des Oberlandesgerichts, aber auch gegen die Bewilligung der Auslieferung durch den Bundesminister für Justiz richtet sich der mit einem Antrag auf Zuerkennung aufschiebender Wirkung verbundene, eine Verletzung von Art 2, 3 und 6 MRK reklamierende Erneuerungsantrag des Dr. Anatoly R***** (§ 363a Abs 1 StPO).

Die von der Generalprokuratur erhobene Nichtigkeitsbeschwerde zur Wahrung des Gesetzes wendet sich gegen den Beschluss des Oberlandesgerichts Wien vom 20. Jänner 2015, AZ 22 Bs 248/14b (ON 82).

Rechtliche Beurteilung

Zur Nichtigkeitsbeschwerde zur Wahrung des Gesetzes:

Wie die Generalprokuratur zutreffend aufzeigt, steht der Beschluss des Oberlandesgerichts Wien mit dem Gesetz nicht im Einklang.

Gemäß § 33 Abs 3 ARHG hat das Gericht die Zulässigkeit der Auslieferung in rechtlicher Hinsicht umfassend in Bezug auf Auslieferungsvoraussetzungen und -hindernisse zu prüfen. Dabei hat es auf zwischenstaatliche Vereinbarungen ebenso Bedacht zu nehmen wie auf die der betroffenen Person nach Gesetz und Bundesverfassung zukommenden subjektiven Rechte. Auch wenn § 1 ARHG den Vorrang zwischenstaatlicher Vereinbarungen vor dem ARHG normiert, sind jedenfalls die sich aus der MRK und ihren Zusatzprotokollen ergebenden Auslieferungshindernisse zu beachten, sofern sie nach der Rechtsprechung des EGMR einer Auslieferung entgegenstehen (vgl EBRV 294 BlgNR 22. GP 33;

Martetschläger in WK² ARHG § 1 Rz 3; *GöthFlemmich* in WK² ARHG Vor §§ 10-25 Rz 6, § 33 Rz 8).

Der Bundesminister für Justiz kann eine Auslieferung aus politischen Erwägungen („Interessen der Republik Österreich") oder aus völkerrechtlichen Gründen ablehnen (§ 34 Abs 1 erster und zweiter Satz ARHG, EBRV 294 BlgNR 22. GP 33), an eine die Auslieferung rechtskräftig für unzulässig erklärende Entscheidung des Gerichts ist er gebunden (§ 34 Abs 1 letzter Satz ARHG).

Eine Auslieferung kann für den Aufenthaltsstaat eine Verletzung von Art 3 MRK bedeuten, wenn stichhaltige Gründe für die Annahme bestehen, dass die betroffene Person der tatsächlichen Gefahr einer Art 3 MRK widersprechenden Behandlung im Empfangsstaat ausgesetzt sein könnte (vgl EGMR 7. 7. 1989, 14038/88, *Soering/Vereinigtes Königreich*, EuGRZ 1989, 314; RIS-Justiz RS0123229; RS0123201; *GöthFlemmich* in WK² ARHG § 19 Rz 7 mwN). Die bloße Möglichkeit von Übergriffen, die in jedem Rechtsstaat vorkommen können, macht die Auslieferung nicht unzulässig (RISJustiz RS0118200).

Die betroffene Person hat die erhebliche Wahrscheinlichkeit einer aktuellen, ernsthaften (gewichtigen) Gefahr schlüssig nachzuweisen (RIS-Justiz RS0123229). Ein solcher Nachweis ist nur dann verzichtbar, wenn der ersuchende Staat eine ständige Praxis umfassender und systematischer Menschenrechtsverletzungen aufweist.

Haftbedingungen können eine unmenschliche oder erniedrigende Behandlung darstellen, auch wenn sie nicht darauf abzielen, den Gefangenen zu demütigen oder zu erniedrigen. Sie verletzen Art 3 MRK, wenn sie erhebliches psychisches oder physisches Leid verursachen, die Menschenwürde beeinträchtigen oder Gefühle von Demütigung und Erniedrigung erwecken. Zu berücksichtigen sind dabei alle Umstände, so zB Überbelegung, mangelhafte Heizung oder Lüftung, übergroße Hitze, sanitäre Verhältnisse, Schlafmöglichkeit, Ernährung, Erholung und Außenkontakte sowie gegebenenfalls ihr kumulativer Effekt (RIS-Justiz RS0123229 [T4]; EGMR 15. 7. 2002, 47095/99, *Kalashnikov/Russland*; *Meyer-Ladewig*, EMRK³ Art 3 Rz 29).

Bei einer Auslieferung an einen Konventionsstaat wie hier an die Russische Föderation ist die Verantwortlichkeit des ersuchten Staats eingeschränkt, wenn die betroffene Person im Zielstaat Rechtsschutz gegen Konventionsverletzungen erlangen kann. Eine Mitverantwortung des ausliefernden Staates besteht nur dann, wenn Folter oder sonstige schwere und irreparable Misshandlungen drohen und effektiver Rechtsschutz - auch durch den EGMR nicht rechtzeitig zu erreichen ist (13 Os 139/12h mwN).

Zwar fällt das Auslieferungsverfahren selbst nicht in den Anwendungsbereich des Art 6 MRK, doch können dessen Verfahrensgarantien für die Entscheidung über die Zulässigkeit der Auslieferung dann (ausnahmsweise) Relevanz erlangen, wenn die betroffene Person nachweist, dass ihr im ersuchenden Staat eine offenkundige Verweigerung eines fairen Verfahrens („a flagrant denial of justice") droht (vgl EGMR 7. 7. 1989, 14038/88, *Soering/Vereinigtes Königreich*, EuGRZ 1989, 314; RISJustiz RS0123200; *Meyer-Ladewig*, EMRK[3] Art 6 Rz 167; weitere Nachweise bei *Göth-Flemmich* in WK[2] ARHG § 19 Rz 14).

Vor diesem Hintergrund begegnet der ursprüngliche Ansatz des Beschwerdegerichts, unter dem Aspekt der Art 3 und 6 MRK auf einen Nachweis durch die betroffene Person abzustellen, keinen Bedenken.

Geht das Gericht nach seiner Prüfung vom Vorliegen aller rechtlichen Voraussetzungen für die Auslieferung und vom Fehlen von Auslieferungshindernissen aus, hat es die Auslieferung für zulässig zu erklären. Bestehen hingegen noch Zweifel am Vorliegen eines Auslieferungshindernisses, muss das Gericht versuchen, sie *vor* der Entscheidung über die Zulässigkeit der Auslieferung auszuräumen. Gelingt dies nicht, hat es die Auslieferung für unzulässig zu erklären (vgl *Göth-Flemmich* in WK[2] ARHG Vor §§ 10-25 Rz 7; *Murschetz*, Auslieferung und Europäischer Haftbefehl 189, 295 f).

Diesen Prüfkriterien entspricht der Beschluss des Oberlandesgerichts vom 20. Jänner 2015, AZ 22 Bs 248/14b, nicht.

Das Oberlandesgericht hat vorliegend das Risiko „einer menschenrechtswidrigen Behandlung des Beschwerdeführers" (erkennbar im Sinn des Art 3 MRK) als (nur) dadurch ausreichend herabgesetzt erachtet, dass es den ersuchenden Staat zur Einhaltung bestimmter (im Spruch ersichtlicher) Verfahrensgarantien „als Bedingung für den Fall der Auslieferung" verpflichtete (BS 1 f und 14).

Eine Erklärung der Zulässigkeit der Auslieferung setzt aber als Ergebnis der Prüfung das Nichtvorliegen von Auslieferungshindernissen voraus. Den Ausspruch über die Zulässigkeit der Auslieferung an die Bedingung zu knüpfen, dass sich die Russische Föderation in Bezug auf die betroffene Person in Zukunft konventionskonform verhält, widerspricht § 33 Abs 1 und 3 ARHG iVm Art 3 und 6 MRK.

Auf eine diplomatische Zusicherung darf übrigens nur dann vertraut werden, wenn sie geeignet ist, die Gefahr für die betroffene Person zu beseitigen, sie muss aus Sicht des Gerichts verbindlich und verlässlich sein (vgl *GöthFlemmich* in WK[2] ARHG Vor §§ 1025 Rz 7).

Wenn objektive Quellen von der Anwendung oder Tolerierung von Praktiken berichten, die den Prinzipien der Konvention entgegenstehen, sind diplomatische Zusicherungen generell nicht ausreichend, um adäquaten Schutz vor Folter oder Misshandlung der ausgelieferten Person zu gewährleisten (EGMR 20. 5. 2010, 21055/09, *Khaydarov/Russland*; vgl auch *Göth-Flemmich* in WK[2] ARHG Vor §§ 1025 Rz 8). In diesen Fällen schließt es die allgemeine Menschenrechtslage im Empfangsstaat bereits von vornherein aus, irgendeine Zusicherung zu akzeptieren. Sonst wird die allgemeine Lage in einem Land selten dazu führen, dass einer Zusicherung gar kein Gewicht zugemessen werden kann (vgl EGMR 17. 1. 2012, 8139/09, *Othman [Abu Qatada]/Vereinigtes Königreich*).

Mit der Erwägung des Oberlandesgerichts, im Fall der Nichteinhaltung der Bedingungen wäre die Verlässlichkeit von Zusicherungen des ersuchenden Staats in Auslieferungsverfahren derart in Frage gestellt, dass künftig Auslieferungen als unzulässig eingestuft werden müssten, wird eine Dr. Anatoly R***** allenfalls betreffende Gefahr einer Art 3 MRK widersprechenden Behandlung im Empfangsstaat nicht ausgeräumt.

Die Ausführungen zur verfehlten Verknüpfung des Ausspruchs der Zulässigkeit der Auslieferung mit Bedingungen gelten, wie angemerkt sei, auch für den vom Oberlandesgericht unbeanstandet gelassenen Spruch des Erstgerichts, soweit er die Auslieferung des Dr. Anatoly R***** unter der Bedingung der Nichtverhängung der Todesstrafe für zulässig erklärt. Nach Art 11 des im Verhältnis zur Russischen Föderation zur Anwendung gelangenden Europäischen Auslieferungsübereinkommens vom 13. Dezember 1957 (BGBl 320/1969) und des dazu erklärten Vorbehalts Österreichs (vgl auch § 20 Abs 1 ARHG) kann die Auslieferung abgelehnt werden, sofern nicht der ersuchende Staat eine vom Gericht (*Göth-Flemmich* in WK² ARHG § 33 Rz 9) als ausreichend erachtete Zusicherung gibt, dass die Todesstrafe nicht ausgesprochen wird. Die der Zulässigerklärung zugrunde gelegte Zusicherung der Russischen Föderation wurde vom Erstgericht in der Begründung zu Recht als ausreichend erachtet, weil dem Ausspruch der Todesstrafe im ersuchenden Staat bereits rechtliche Hindernisse, und zwar Art 59 Abs 2 Punkt 1 des Strafgesetzbuches der Russischen Föderation, entgegenstehen. Die Beifügung der Bedingung im Spruch trägt der Einschätzung der Zusicherung als ausreichend aber nicht Rechnung.

Da eine Benachteiligung der betroffenen Person durch die aufgezeigte Gesetzesverletzung nicht ausgeschlossen werden kann, sah sich der Oberste Gerichtshof veranlasst, ihre Feststellung auf die im Spruch ersichtliche Weise mit konkreter Wirkung zu verbinden (§ 292 letzter Satz StPO).

Falls das Beschwerdegericht im Zusammenhang mit besorgniserregenden Zuständen im Bereich des Strafvollzugs auch im neuen Verfahren auf eine diplomatische Zusicherung durch die Generalstaatsanwaltschaft der Russischen Föderation abstellt, wird zu beachten sein, dass eine solche Zusicherung nur dann der Beseitigung einer Gefahr dienen kann, wenn die genannte Behörde die Möglichkeit hat, den Staat zu binden, wenn es etwa in ihre Kompetenz fällt, den Vollzug in einer konkreten, den Vorschriften der MRK entsprechenden Strafvollzugsanstalt anzuordnen (vgl zur Zulässigkeit einer diplomatischen Zusage als ausreichendes Schutzinstrument die Verfahren *Othman* [*Abu Qatada*]/*Vereinigtes Königreich* dazu herausgearbeiteten Beurteilungskriterien des EGMR, dargestellt von *Schneider*, EuGRZ 2014, 174).

Mit seinem gegen die Entscheidung des Oberlandesgerichts gerichteten Erneuerungsantrag war Dr. Anatoly R***** auf die Erledigung der Nichtigkeitsbeschwerde zur Wahrung des Gesetzes zu verweisen (RIS-Justiz RS0126458).

Soweit der Antragsteller auch die in der Auslieferungssache ergangene Entscheidung des Bundesministers für Justiz, also keine strafgerichtliche Entscheidung oder Verfügung kritisiert, verfehlt er den gesetzlichen Bezugspunkt (§ 363a Abs 1 StPO).

Mit Blick auf die Kompetenznorm des § 362 Abs 5 StPO hat der Oberste Gerichtshof zwar mit Beschluss vom 9. März 2015, 13 Os 27/15t-8, die Befugnis in Anspruch genommen, den Vollzug der mit Erneuerungsantrag bekämpften Entscheidung des Oberlandesgerichts zu hemmen. Ein diesbezügliches Antragsrecht kommt der betroffenen Person aber nicht zu (RIS-Justiz RS0125705).

In diesem Umfang waren die Anträge des Dr. Anatoly R***** daher als unzulässig zurückzuweisen.

Mit Blick auf die Frage allfälligen Auflebens der in § 29 Abs 6 erster Satz ARHG normierten Höchstfrist der Auslieferungshaft von einem Jahr ist festzuhalten, dass die Zulässigkeit der Auslieferung nach dem eindeutigen Wortlaut des § 29 ARHG keine Voraussetzung für die Auslieferungshaft bildet (RIS-Justiz RS0120452). Weder durch die Aufhebung des Beschlusses auf Zulässigerklärung der Auslieferung durch den Obersten Gerichtshof noch durch die vom Bundesministerium für Justiz für diesen Fall bereits in Aussicht genommene Aufhebung der Bewilligung durch den Bundesminister für Justiz leben die in § 29 Abs 5 und Abs 6 ARHG normierten Fristen wieder auf (vgl für den Bereich der Untersuchungshaft RIS-Justiz RS0098035; *Kirchbacher/Rami*, WKStPO § 178 Rz 7; § 29 Abs 1 zweiter Satz ARHG).

Die Auslieferungshaft bleibt aber weiterhin durch den Verhältnismäßigkeitsgrundsatz (§ 29 Abs 1 ARHG iVm § 173 Abs 1 StPO) begrenzt. Auch das besondere Beschleunigungsgebot in Haftsachen (§§ 9 Abs 2, 177 Abs 1 StPO) ist unverändert zu beachten. Sollte die Auslieferung rechtskräftig für unzulässig erklärt werden, ist die Auslieferungshaft aufzuheben.

FF.VII.2.-2

Supreme Court, Decision, 14Os60/15b (14Os73/15i) of 4 August 2015

Oberster Gerichtshof, Beschluss, 14Os60/15b (14Os73/15i) vom 4. August 2015

Keywords

Extradition for execution of a criminal sentence – diplomatic assurances – European Convention on Human Rights – Art 3 and 6 ECHR – Russian Federation

Auslieferung zur Strafvollstreckung – Diplomatische Zusicherungen – Europäische Menschenrechtskonvention – Art 3 und 6 EMRK – Russische Föderation

Facts and procedural history (summary)

On 27 October 2010, the Regional Court of Leningrad (St. Petersburg) located in the city of Kaliningrad, sentenced Timur I***** to six years in a 'strict corrective labour colony' for the crimes of prepared and attempted circulation of narcotics on a particularly large scale.

By decision of 21 December 2012, the competent judge of the Vienna Regional Criminal Court, declared extradition for the execution of a custodial sentence as requested by the Prosecutor General's Office of the Russian Federation on 21 June 2012, (not in-) admissible. The decision was affirmed on appeal by the Higher Regional Court of Vienna on 16 April 2013. In response to an application for re-hearing of criminal proceedings filed by the person concerned and a subsequent nullity appeal to preserve the integrity of the law filed by the Procurator General's Office, both aforementioned decisions were set aside by the Supreme Court due to breaches of Article 3 (1) Second Additional Protocol to the European Convention on Extradition and Article 6 (1) European Convention on Human Rights [ECHR] and the matter was remitted to the Vienna Regional Criminal Court. The Supreme Court had considered the (initial) assurance offered by the Prosecutor General's Office of the Russian Federation inadequate in light of the second sentence of Article 3 (1) Second Additional Protocol to the European Convention on Extradition, while the competent courts had declared extradition (not in-) admissible solely on such basis and thus had not even verified the conformity of proceedings held in absentia with the requirements of the ECHR.

After a new decision by the Vienna Regional Criminal Court of 23 April 2014, once more declaring extradition admissible, that decision too was set aside and the case again remitted to the court of first instance, this time, however, for procedural reasons and by the Higher Regional Court of Vienna.

With its decision of 5 September 2014, the Vienna Regional Criminal Court declared extradition (not in-) admissible for a third time. It viewed new assurances offered by the Prosecutor General's Office of the Russian Federation on 29 August 2012, as sufficient to satisfy the requirements of the European Convention on Extradition and also considered the requisite lack-of-further-obstacles-to-extradition-test met. The subsequent appeal of the person concerned dated 20 January 2015 was not granted by the Higher Regional Court of Vienna. It referred to the new assurances received and also extradition now being rendered conditional upon four requirements, namely that the applicant would

1) Not be subjected to torture, cruel, inhuman or degrading treatment or punishment (Article 3 ECHR) and permitted to consult with his attorney in private for an unlimited period of time;

2) Be held in a correctional facility commensurate with the requirements of the ECHR and the European Prison Rules of 11 January 2006, disposing of adequate medical facilities and ensuring the possibility of family visits;

3) Be able to receive visits from officials of the Austrian Embassy in the Russian Federation at any time and without supervision, requiring immediate notification of the place of incarceration and any relocation;

4) Have the possibility of turning to Austrian diplomatic representations in the Russian Federation at any time.

Although the court of appeal had assessed that the proceedings conducted in absentia were insufficient to meet the requirements of Article 6 (1) ECHR, it noted that the enhanced assurances received were satisfactory in light of the European Convention on Extradition and, subsequent to a a statement of the Austrian Embassy in Moscow dated 17 October 2014, proof of obstacles to extradition in terms of Articles 3 and 6 ECHR lacking. Despite these considerations and in light of both the aforementioned statement of the Austrian Embassy in Moscow and a decision of the European Court of Human Rights [ECtHR] (10 December 2012, 42525/07 and 60800/08, *Ananyev and others/Russia*), which had identified repeated breaches of Article 3 ECHR within the Russian penal system, the court of appeal saw itself prompted to request that the Federal Ministry of Justice render any extradition contingent upon observance of the (procedural) guarantees detailed in the relevant dictum. The fact that the Prosecutor General's Office of the Russian Federation had already agreed to such observance by letter of 11 December 2014, led the Court to surmise that the risk of Article 3 ECHR being breached had been minimized to the point of constituting a merely theoretical risk. Furthermore, the Austrian Federal Ministry for Europe, Integration and Foreign Affairs would be able to supervise the observance of assurances provided and, in the event of non-compliance, proceedings could be reopened, possibily resulting in the return of the extradited person. If such a scenario where to materialize, the reliability of future Russian assurances in extradition proceedings would be questionable to the point of rendering prospective transfers inadmissible.

By reference to the assurances of the Russian Federation - particularly those provided by letter of 11 December 2014, – and, as envisaged by the decision of the Higher Regional Court of Vienna, on 28 January 2015, the Federal Minister of Justice approved the extradition of Timur I***** for the purpose of his prosecution, while nevertheless expressing the legal opinion that extradition could not be declared admissible based on the observance of conditionalities.

After Timur I***** was detained by order of 24 March 2015 and the date of surrender to Russian authorities was set for 17 April 2015 by letter of 7 April 2015, upon application of the [Austrian] prosecution, extradition was preliminarily deferred by decision of the Vienna Regional Criminal Court dated 16 April 2015 and reference to an analogous decision taken by the Supreme Court in a similar case one day prior, resulting in the revocation of the surrender date and release of Timur I*****.

The application for the re-hearing of criminal proceedings submitted by the person concerned is directed against the decisions of the Vienna Regional Criminal Court dated 5 September 2014 and the Higher Regional Court of Vienna dated 20 January 2015, alleging breaches of ECHR Articles 3, 6 and '8 or 9 as the case may be'.

The Supreme Court held (excerpts)

[...]

On the 'nullity appeal to preserve the integrity of the law':

As accurately demonstrated by the Procurator General's Office, the decision of the Higher Regional Court of Vienna is inconsistent with the law:

Pursuant to Section 33 (3) Extradition and Mutual Assistance Act [Auslieferungs- und Rechtshilfegesetz, ARHG], the Court is tasked with examining the admissibility of extradition, by performing a legally comprehensive analysis of requirements for and obstacles to extradition. In doing so, it must equally heed both intergovernmental agreements and the subjective rights of the affected individual as accorded by the Federal Constitution. Notwithstanding the priority of intergovernmental agreements over the ARHG pursuant to Section 1 ARHG, obstacles to extradition as envisaged by the ECHR and its additional protocols, must be observed in any event, insofar as opposed to extradition pursuant to ECtHR jurisprudence (see explanatory remarks to government bill 294 BlgNR 22. GP 33; *Martetschläger* in WK2 ARHG § 1 MN 3; *Göth-Flemmich* in WK2 ARHG Vor §§ 10-25 MN 6, § 33 MN 8).

The Federal Minister of Justice may refuse extradition based on political considerations ('interests of the Republic of Austria'), or on grounds of public international law (first and second sentences of Section 34 (1) ARHG, explanatory remarks to government bill 294 BlgNR 22. GP 33) and is bound to any final and enforceable decision of the [competent] court determining the inadmissibility of an extradition (last sentence of Section 34 (1) ARHG).

For the State of residence, an extradition may constitute a breach of Article 3 ECHR where there are serious reasons to believe that the affected individual might actually be subjected, in the receiving State, to treatment contrary to that required by Article 3 ECHR (see ECtHR 7 July 1989, 14038/38, *Soering/ United Kingdom*, EuGRZ 1989, 314; RIS-Justiz RS0123229, RS0123201; *Göth-Flemmich* in WK² ARHG § 19 MN 7 with further references). The mere possibility of an assault, which may occur in any State governed by the rule of law, does not render extradition inadmissible (RIS-Justiz RS0118200).

The affected individual must conclusively prove the considerable likelihood of a current and serious (grave) danger (RIS-Justiz RS0123229). Such proof may only be waived, where the requesting State exhibits a constant practice of comprehensive and systematic Human Rights abuses.

Detention conditions may constitute inhuman or degrading treatment, even if they are not designed to humiliate and debase a detainee. They breach Article 3 ECHR, where they cause considerable mental and physical suffering, diminish human dignity or arouse feelings of humiliation and debasement. Such assessment requires consideration of all circumstances, including overcrowding, inadequate heating or ventilation, excessive heat, sanitary conditions, sleeping conditions, nutrition, recreation and contact with the outside world, as well as a cumulative effect as the case may be (RIS-Justiz RS0123229 [T4]; ECtHR 15 July 2002, 47095/99, *Kalashnikov/Russia*; Meyer-Ladewig, EMRK³ Art 3 MN 29).

In the context of extradition to an ECHR Member State, responsibility of the extraditing State is limited, if the person concerned can attain sufficient and timely legal protection against breaches of the Convention in the receiving State (*Göth-Flemmich* in WK² ARHG § 19 MN 10 with further references). Any such assumption is, however, refuted (see Section 4 (3) Asylum Act 2005 [Asylgesetz 2005, AsylG 2005]), where the opposite has been conclusively proven (based on the aforementioned criteria) by the person concerned, or a specific endangerment of such person due to existing systemic deficiencies in terms of fundamental rights protection within the receiving State – regardless of its legal obligations (particularly pursuant to the ECHR) - must be assumed by the Court based on objective sources (ECtHR judgments of 21 January 2011 [GC], 30696/09, *M.S.S./Belgium and Greece* [particularly MN 326, 328, 330 f, 342 f, 352 ff and 362 ff] and of 4 January 2014 [GC], 29217/12, *Tarakhel/Switzerland* [particularly MN 101 ff]; *Grabenwarter/Pabel*, EMRK⁵ § 20 MN 44).

Although extradition proceedings do not fall within the ambit of Article 6 ECHR, the procedural safeguards of that Article can (by way of exception) apply to the decision on the permissibility of the extradition, where the person concerned can prove that they would risk suffering a flagrant denial of justice in the requesting State (see ECtHR 7 July, 1989, 14038/88, *Soering/United Kingdom*, EuGRZ 1989, 314; RIS-Justiz RS0123200; Meyer-Ladewig, EMRK³ Art 6 MN 167; *Göth-Flemmich* in WK² ARHG § 19 MN 14 with further references).

Against this backdrop, the original approach taken by appellate court, which turned on proof provided by the person concerned as regards Articles 3 and 6 ECHR, does not give rise to concern.

The Court is obliged to declare extradition admissible, if, after its examination, the Court surmises that all legal prerequisites for an extradition have been met and obstacles to extradition are lacking. If, however, doubts persist as to whether or not an obstacle to extradition may remain, the Court is obliged to attempt to dispel such doubts before a decision on the admissibility of extradition may be taken. If unsuccessful in its endeavor, the Court must declare extradition inadmissible (see *Göth-Flemmich* in WK² ARHG Vor §§ 10-25 MN 7; *Murschetz*, Auslieferung und Europäischer Haftbefehl 189, 295 f).

The decision of the Higher Regional Court of 20 January 2015, AZ 22 Bs 296/14m, does not reflect these examination criteria.

In the case at hand, the court of appeal considered the 'risk of an Article 3 ECHR breach' sufficiently reduced, by (mere) virtue of obliging the requesting State to heed certain procedural safeguards (enumerated in the pertinent dictum) as a precondition 'in the event of extradition' (BS 1 f and 7).

Any declaration rendering extradition admissible is, however, contingent upon prior determination of a lack of obstacles thereto. Tying the declaration of admissible extradition to the condition that the Russian Federation will, in the future, comply with the Convention as regards the person concerned, contradicts Section 33 (1) and (3) ARHG in conjunction with Articles 3 and 6 ECHR.

Incidentally, diplomatic assurances may only be relied upon, if they are suited to eliminate the endangerment of the person concerned and deemed both binding and reliable by the Court (see *Göth-Flemmich* in WK² ARHG Vor §§ 10-25 MN 7).

For the purpose of guaranteeing adequate protection against torture and abuse of extradited persons, diplomatic assurances will be rendered generally insufficient where objective sources report the application or toleration of practices contrary to the principles of the Convention (ECHR 20 May 2010, 21055/09, *Khaydarov/Russia*; see also *Göth-Flemmich* in WK² ARHG Vor §§ 10-25 MN 8). In such cases, the overall human rights situation in the receiving State excludes the possibility of accepting any assurance from the outset (see ECHR 17 January 2012, 8139/09, *Othman [Abu Qatada]/United Kingdom*).

The consideration of the Higher Regional Court, whereby 'the reliability of future Russian assurances' in extradition proceedings would be questionable to the point of 'rendering prospective transfers inadmissible' if the conditions were not met, does not remove the potential danger of Timur I***** being subjected to treatment contrary to that required by Article 3 ECHR (see AZ 13 Os 27/15t, 30/15f).

Given that the possibility of the person concerned suffering negative effects as a result of the described violation of the law cannot be excluded, the Supreme Court saw itself called upon to endow its determination with the specific effects detailed in the dictum below (last sentence of Section 292, Code of Criminal Procedure [Strafprozessordnung, StPO].

On the application for re-hearing of criminal proceedings

The subsidiary legal remedy of an application for re-hearing of criminal proceedings not founded on a judgment of the ECtHR – such as the present - is, mutatis mutandis, subject to the same admissibility requirements applicable before the ECtHR pursuant to Articles 34 and 35 ECHR (RIS-Justiz RS0122737; 14 Os 103/14z; 14 Os 28/15z).

As a result, applications for re-hearing of criminal proceedings are inadmissible against decisions which are appealable by the applicant (see: 13 Os 47/11b, 54/11g) and the objective application must be dismissed insofar as it is (substantively) directed against the decision of the Vienna Regional Criminal Court of 5 September 2014, GZ 353 HR 244/14w-128.

As regards the submissions of the applicant directed against the decision of the Higher Regional Court and pertaining to a breach of Article 3 ECHR, he may be referred to the settlement of those submissions by the nullity appeal to preserve the integrity of the law successfully brought by the Procurator General's Office, given that the nullity appeal coincides with the application for re-hearing of criminal proceedings insofar as it pertains to *that* alleged fundamental rights breach and a commensurate remedy has been provided by the declaration of such breach combined with the specific effects of the order issued pursuant to the last sentence of Section 292 StPO (RIS-Justiz RS0126458).

Insofar as the application – equally pertaining to the decision of the appellate court – alleges further breaches of ECHR Articles 6 and 'Articles 8 or 9 as the case may be', it proves to be partly inadmissible (as demonstrated above) pursuant to Article 35 ECHR and partly unfounded:

Based on the determination that the trial in the Russian Federation which was conducted against the person concerned in absentia did not meet the requirements of Article 6 ECHR, the Higher Regional Court *examined* the supplementary and enhanced assurances of the receiving State authorities (whereby, in summary, pursuant to the Russian code of criminal procedure, convictions in absentia must [in any event] be set aside 'for procedural reasons' and pertinent case files forwarded to the Court for the purpose of a retrial, which must then conduct a regular trial heeding rights of defence, if the person concerned asserts their disagreement with the judgment, and, either personally on the occasion of their arrest or appearance before judicial bodies, or through a defense attorney, files an appropriate application, while such procedure would also be guaranteed in the case at hand - if Timur I***** where to make such assertions and file such applications; ON 50, ON 93 and ON 101) at length and these – partly by virtue of (admissible; see RIS-Justiz RS0124017 [particularly T2, T3, T4]) reference to the decision of the appellate court dated 21 May 2014, AZ 22 Bs 140/14w (ON 111) -, endowed with comprehensive reasoning, were considered sufficient pursuant to both the second sentence of Article 3 (1) of the Second Additional Protocol to the European Convention on Extradition and Section 19a (2) ARHG (BS 5 f; see *Murschetz*, Auslieferung und Europäischer Haftbefehl, 205; see also [the objectively inapplicable] Section 11 (1) (4) Federal law on judicial cooperation in criminal matters with the Member States of the European Union [Bundesgesetz über die judizielle Zusammenarbeit in Strafsachen mit den Mitgliedstaaten der Europäischen Union, EU-JZG] as well as the Supreme Court decision handed down in the context of those proceedings of 28 January 2014, AZ 14 Os 149/13p, 179/13z, 180/13x).

Insofar as the applicant advances the (unfounded) allegation that his 'privacy' and 'religious practice' would 'in any event ... be inadmissibly restricted' due to his 'religion and ethnicity (Muslim/Tajik)' in the event of his incarceration, amounting to a breach of ECHR 'Article 8 or 9 as the case may be', the pertinent application fails due to a lack of exhaustion of remedies, given that no such arguments were submitted in the appeal against the decision of the Vienna Regional Criminal Court of 5 September 2014, GZ 353 HR 244/14w-128 (see RIS-Justiz RS0122737 [T13]).

Moreover, this submission does not demonstrate a – merely nominally mentioned – breach of fundamental rights in a clear and specific fashion (once more RIS-Justiz RS0122737 [T17], RS0128393).

As a result, pursuant to Section 363c (2) StPO (partially by analogy; see 17 Os 11/12i, EvBl 2013/41, 273), the application for re-hearing of criminal proceedings was not granted.

German Original

Spruch

(I) In der Auslieferungssache AZ 353 HR 244/14w des Landesgerichts für Strafsachen Wien verletzt der Beschluss des Oberlandesgerichts Wien als Beschwerdegericht vom 20. Jänner 2015, AZ 22 Bs 296/14m, § 33 Abs 1 und Abs 3 ARHG iVm Art 3 und 6 Abs 1 MRK.

Dieser Beschluss wird aufgehoben und dem Oberlandesgericht Wien eine neue Entscheidung aufgetragen.

(II) In diesem Umfang wird Timur I***** mit seinem Antrag auf Erneuerung des Verfahrens gemäß § 363a StPO auf diese Entscheidung verwiesen.

(III) Im Übrigen wird dem Antrag nicht Folge gegeben.

Text

Gründe:

Timur I***** (alias Timur C***** [T*****, vgl ON 27 und ON 29 im Akt AZ 353 HR 244/14w des Landesgerichts für Strafsachen Wien]) war mit Urteil des Rayonsgerichts Leningrad (St. Petersburg) der Stadt Kalininrad vom 27. Oktober 2010 wegen der am 27. November und 16. Dezember 2009 begangenen Straftaten nach Art 30 Abs 3 iVm Art 228.1 Abs 2 lit b („Versuch des ungesetzlichen InVerkehrBringens von Betäubungsmitteln in besonders großem

Ausmaß, der aus nicht von der Person abhängigen Umständen nicht zu Ende geführt wurde") sowie Art 30 Abs 1 iVm Art 228.1 Abs 3 lit d („Vorbereitung des ungesetzlichen In-Verkehr-Bringens von Betäubungsmitteln in besonders großem Ausmaß, die aus nicht von der Person abhängigen Umständen nicht zu Ende geführt wurde") des Strafgesetzbuchs der Russischen Föderation in Abwesenheit schuldig erkannt und zu einer Freiheitsstrafe von sechs Jahren „in einer Besserungskolonie mit strengem Regime" verurteilt worden (ON 26 S 5 und 11 ff).

Mit Beschluss vom 21. Dezember 2012, GZ 313 HR 59/11s-56, erklärte der Einzelrichter des Landesgerichts für Strafsachen Wien die von der Russischen Föderation mit Note der Generalstaatsanwaltschaft der Russischen Föderation vom 21. Juni 2012, Nr 81/3-289-11 (ON 26), begehrte Auslieferung des Timur I***** zur Vollstreckung dieser Freiheitsstrafe für (nicht un-)zulässig.

Das Oberlandesgericht Wien gab der dagegen erhobenen Beschwerde der betroffenen Person mit Beschluss vom 16. April 2013, AZ 22 Bs 39/13s, nicht Folge (ON 63).

Mit Erkenntnis vom 28. Jänner 2014, AZ 14 Os 149/13p, 179/13z, 180/13x, sprach der Oberste Gerichtshof aufgrund einer aus Anlass eines Antrags der betroffenen Person auf Erneuerung des Auslieferungsverfahrens nach § 363a StPO von der Generalprokuratur dagegen erhobenen Nichtigkeitsbeschwerde zur Wahrung des Gesetzes aus, dass die beiden vorgenannten Beschlüsse Art 3 Abs 1 des Zweiten Zusatzprotokolls zum Europäischen Auslieferungsübereinkommen sowie Art 6 Abs 1 MRK verletzen, hob diese Beschlüsse auf und verwies die Sache an das Landesgericht für Strafsachen Wien, weil er die (damals) zugrunde gelegte Zusicherung der Generalstaatsanwaltschaft der Russischen Föderation nicht als ausreichend im Sinn des Art 3 Abs 1 zweiter Satz des Zweiten Zusatzprotokolls zum Europäischen Auslieferungsüberein-kommen erachtete, die Gerichte die Auslieferung jedoch alleine auf dieser Basis für (nicht un-)zulässig erklärt und deshalb die Konventionskonformität des in Russland geführten Abwesenheitsverfahrens überhaupt nicht geprüft hatten.

Die betroffene Person wurde mit ihrem Erneuerungsantrag unter einem auf diese Entscheidung verwiesen (ON 75).

Den Beschluss des Einzelrichters des Landesgerichts für Strafsachen Wien vom 23. April 2014, mit dem die begehrte Auslieferung des Timur I***** wieder für (nicht un-)zulässig erklärt worden war (ON 108), hob das Oberlandesgericht Wien als Beschwerdegericht in Stattgebung einer dagegen erhobenen Beschwerde der betroffenen Person (ON 110) aus formalen Gründen erneut auf und verwies die Auslieferungssache zu neuer Verhandlung und Entscheidung an das Erstgericht zurück (ON 115).

Mit Beschluss vom 5. September 2014, GZ 353 HR 244/14w-128, erklärte der Einzelrichter des Landesgerichts für Strafsachen Wien die von der Russischen Föderation mit Note der Generalstaatsanwaltschaft der Russischen Föderation vom 21. Juni 2012, Nr 81/328911 (ON 26), begehrte Auslieferung des Timur I***** zur Vollstreckung der mit dem eingangs erwähnten Urteil über ihn verhängten sechsjährigen Freiheitsstrafe ein drittes Mal für (nicht un)zulässig. In der Begründung führte das Erstgericht aus, dass die ursprüngliche durch die Zusicherung vom 7. April 2014 (ON 102) ergänzte Erklärung der Generalstaatsanwaltschaft der Russischen Föderation vom 29. August 2012 (ON 50 S 7) eine ausreichende Zusicherung einer Neudurchführung des Verfahrens im Sinn des Art 3 Abs 1 zweiter Satz des Zweiten Zusatzprotokolls zum Europäischen Auslieferungsübereinkommen darstelle (BS 5) und auch keine sonstigen Auslieferungshindernisse vorlägen (BS 9).

Der dagegen gerichteten Beschwerde der betroffenen Person (ON 129) gab das Oberlandesgericht mit Beschluss vom 20. Jänner 2015, AZ 22 Bs 296/14m, „mit der Maßgabe nicht Folge, dass unter Bezugnahme auf die von der Generalstaatsanwaltschaft der Russischen Föderation abgegebene Garantieerklärung vom 11. Dezember 2014 die Auslieferung von folgenden Bedingungen abhängig gemacht wird, nämlich dass der Betroffene

1) im ersuchenden Staat keinen Foltern, grausamen, unmenschlichen, die Menschenwürde erniedrigenden Behandlungs- und Bestrafungsmaßnahmen unterzogen wird (Art 3 MRK), sowie unter vier Augen unbewacht und ohne zeitliche Beschränkung Besuch von seinem Verteidiger empfangen kann;

2) in einer Haftanstalt angehalten wird, die den Vorschriften der Menschenrechskonvention (MRK) und den Europäischen Strafvollzugsgrundsätzen vom 11. Jänner 2006 gerecht wird und in der eine angemessene medizinische Versorgung sowie der Besuch von Angehörigen sichergestellt ist;

3) von Amtspersonen der Österreichischen Botschaft in der Russischen Föderation jederzeit ohne Überwachung besucht werden kann, wozu erstere über den Ort der Inhaftierung und von allfälligen Verlegungen unverzüglich zu informieren sind;

4) sich jederzeit an Mitglieder der österreichischen diplomatischen Vertretung in der Russischen Föderation wenden kann".

Das Beschwerdegericht ging zunächst von der Konventionswidrigkeit des in Russland geführten Abwesenheitsverfahrens (Verstoß gegen Art 6 Abs 1 MRK) aus (BS 5 f), erachtete jedoch wie das Erstgericht die Zusicherung der Behörden des Zielstaats als ausreichend im Sinn des Art 3 Abs 1 zweiter Satz des Zweiten Zusatzprotokolls zum Europäischen Auslieferungs-übereinkommen sowie des § 19a Abs 2 ARHG (BS 5 f). Der Nachweis des Vorliegens von Auslieferungshindernissen, die sich aus Art 3 und 6 MRK ergeben könnten, wurde vom Oberlandesgericht unter Berücksichtigung einer Stellungnahme der österreichischen Botschaft in Moskau vom 17. Oktober 2014 (ON 131) verneint (BS 6 f).

Ungeachtet dieser Erwägungen sah sich das Beschwerdegericht aber auch aufgrund der bereits erwähnten Stellungnahme der österreichischen Botschaft und einer Entscheidung des Europäischen Gerichtshofs für Menschenrechte (EGMR 10. 12. 2012, 42525/07 und 60800/08, *Ananyev* ua/Russland), worin wiederholte Verletzungen des Art 3 MRK durch den Zielstaat im Bereich des Strafvollzugs festgestellt wurden, veranlasst, den ersuchenden Staat im Weg des Bundesministeriums für Justiz zur Einhaltung der aus dem Spruch ersichtlichen (Verfahrens-)Garantien als Bedingung für den Fall der Auslieferung zu verpflichten. Dabei fügte es hinzu, dass eine solche von der Generalstaatsanwaltschaft der Russischen Föderation bereits in einem Schreiben vom 11. Dezember 2014 zugesichert worden sei, wodurch sich die Risken einer Verletzung des Art 3 MRK so weit minimieren ließen, dass sie nur noch theoretisch erschienen. In diesem Zusammenhang verwies das Rechtsmittelgericht auch auf die Möglichkeit der Kontrolle der Einhaltung der abgegebenen Garantien durch das Bundesministerium für Europa, Integration und Äußeres und führte aus, dass bei Nichteinhalten der Garantie auch die Wiederaufnahme des Verfahrens samt Zurückstellung des Ausgelieferten in Betracht käme. In diesem Fall wäre die Verlässlichkeit russischer Zusicherungen pro futuro derart in Frage gestellt, dass künftige Überstellungen sogar als unzulässig eingestuft werden müssten (BS 7 f).

Vom Bundesminister für Justiz wurde die Auslieferung des Timur I***** zur Strafverfolgung im Umfang dieses Beschlusses des Oberlandesgerichts Wien unter Bezugnahme auf die von der Russischen Föderation insbesondere mit Schreiben vom 11. Dezember 2014, Nr 81/328911 (ON 133) abgegebenen Zusicherungen bewilligt.

Bereits in diesem Erlass vom 28. Jänner 2015, GZ BMJ-4046440/0002-IV 4/2015, vertrat das Bundes-ministerium für Justiz die Rechtsauffassung, dass die Auslieferung nicht unter der Maßgabe der Einhaltung von Bedingungen für zulässig erklärt werden könne (ON 139).

Ein mit Auslieferungsbrief vom 7. April 2015 auf den 17. April 2015 festgesetzter Termin zur Übergabe der betroffenen Person an die russischen Behörden (ON 159) wurde aus Anlass eines Antrags der Staatsanwaltschaft auf vorläufigen Aufschub der Durchführung der Auslieferung mit Beschluss des Landesgerichts für Strafsachen Wien vom 16. April 2015 unter Bezugnahme auf die einen gleichgelagerten Sachverhalt betreffende - Entscheidung des Obersten Gerichtshofs vom 15. April 2015, AZ 13 Os 27/15t, 30/15f) widerrufen (ON 161) und Timur I***** am 16. April 2015 aus der mit Beschluss desselben Gerichts vom 24. März 2015 (ON 152) über ihn verhängten Überstellungshaft nach § 36 Abs 1 ARHG entlassen (ON 162).

Gegen die Beschlüsse des Landesgerichts für Strafsachen Wien vom 5. September 2014, GZ 353 HR 244/14w-128, und des Oberlandesgerichts Wien vom 20. Jänner 2015, AZ 22 Bs 296/14m (ON 138), richtet sich der eine Verletzung von Art 3, Art 6 und „Art 8 bzw Art 9" MRK reklamierende Antrag der betroffenen Person auf Erneuerung des Verfahrens nach § 363a StPO.

Rechtliche Beurteilung

Die von der Generalprokuratur erhobene Nichtigkeitsbeschwerde zur Wahrung des Gesetzes wendet sich gegen die letztgenannte Entscheidung des Beschwerdegerichts.

Zur Nichtigkeitsbeschwerde zur Wahrung des Gesetzes:

Wie die Generalprokuratur zutreffend aufzeigt steht der Beschluss des Oberlandesgerichts Wien mit dem Gesetz nicht im Einklang:

Gemäß § 33 Abs 3 ARHG hat das Gericht die Zulässigkeit der Auslieferung in rechtlicher Hinsicht umfassend in Bezug auf Auslieferungsvoraussetzungen und -hindernisse zu prüfen. Dabei hat es auf zwischenstaatliche Vereinbarungen ebenso Bedacht zu nehmen wie auf die der betroffenen Person nach Gesetz und Bundesverfassung zukommenden subjektiven Rechte. Auch wenn § 1 ARHG den Vorrang zwischenstaatlicher Vereinbarungen vor dem ARHG normiert, sind jedenfalls die sich aus der MRK und ihren Zusatzprotokollen ergebenden Auslieferungshindernisse zu beachten, sofern sie nach der Rechtsprechung des Europäischen Gerichtshofs für Menschenrechte (EGMR) einer Auslieferung entgegenstehen (vgl EBRV 294 BlgNR 22. GP 33; *Martetschläger* in WK² ARHG § 1 Rz 3; *Göth-Flemmich* in WK² ARHG Vor §§ 1025 Rz 6, § 33 Rz 8).

Der Bundesminister für Justiz kann eine Auslieferung aus politischen Erwägungen („Interessen der Republik Österreich") oder aus völkerrechtlichen Gründen ablehnen (§ 34 Abs 1 erster und zweiter Satz ARHG, EBRV 294 BlgNR 22. GP 33), an eine die Auslieferung rechtskräftig für unzulässig erklärende Entscheidung des Gerichts ist er gebunden (§ 34 Abs 1 letzter Satz ARHG).

Eine Auslieferung kann für den Aufenthaltsstaat eine Verletzung von Art 3 MRK bedeuten, wenn stichhaltige Gründe für die Annahme bestehen, dass die betroffene Person der tatsächlichen Gefahr einer Art 3 MRK widersprechenden Behandlung im Empfangsstaat ausgesetzt sein könnte (vgl EGMR 7. 7. 1989, 14038/88, *Soering/Vereinigtes Königreich*, EuGRZ 1989, 314; RIS-Justiz RS0123229, RS0123201; *GöthFlemmich* in WK² ARHG § 19 Rz 7 mwN). Die bloße Möglichkeit von Übergriffen, die in jedem Rechtsstaat vorkommen können, macht die Auslieferung nicht unzulässig (RIS-Justiz RS0118200).

Die betroffene Person hat die erhebliche Wahrscheinlichkeit einer aktuellen, ernsthaften (gewichtigen) Gefahr schlüssig nachzuweisen (RIS-Justiz RS0123229). Ein solcher Nachweis ist nur dann verzichtbar, wenn der ersuchende Staat eine ständige Praxis umfassender und systematischer Menschenrechtsverletzungen aufweist.

Haftbedingungen können eine unmenschliche oder erniedrigende Behandlung darstellen, auch wenn sie nicht darauf abzielen, den Gefangenen zu demütigen oder zu erniedrigen. Sie verletzen Art 3 MRK, wenn sie erhebliches psychisches oder physisches Leid verursachen, die Menschenwürde beeinträchtigen oder Gefühle von Demütigung und Erniedrigung erwecken. Zu berücksichtigen sind dabei alle Umstände, so etwa Überbelegung, mangelhafte Heizung oder Lüftung, übergroße Hitze, sanitäre Verhältnisse, Schlafmöglichkeit, Ernährung, Erholung und Außenkontakte sowie gegebenenfalls ihr kumulativer Effekt (RIS-Justiz RS0123229 [T4]; EGMR 15. 7. 2002, 47095/99, *Kalashnikov/Russland*; *Meyer-Ladewig*, EMRK[3] Art 3 Rz 29).

Bei der Auslieferung in einen Konventionsstaat ist die Verantwortlichkeit des ausliefernden Staats eingeschränkt, wenn der Betroffene im Zielstaat ausreichenden und rechtzeitigen Rechtsschutz gegen Konventionsverletzungen erlangen kann (*Göth-Flemmich* in WK[2] ARHG § 19 Rz 10 mwN). Eine dahingehende Vermutung ist aber widerlegt (vgl § 4 Abs 3 AsylG 2005), wenn das Gegenteil vom Betroffenen (nach den zuvor genannten Kriterien) schlüssig nachgewiesen wurde oder dessen konkrete Gefährdung vom Gericht schon auf Basis objektiver Quellen wegen im Zielstaat ungeachtet dessen rechtlicher Verpflichtungen (insbesondere nach der MRK) bestehender systemischer Defizite im Grundrechtsschutz angenommen werden muss (EGMR Urteile vom 21. 1. 2011 [GK], 30696/09, *M.S.S./Belgien und Griechenland* [insbesondere Rz 326, 328, 330 f, 342 f, 352 ff und 362 ff] und vom 4. 1. 2014 [GK], 29217/12, *Tarakhel/Schweiz* [insbesondere Rz 101 ff]; *Grabenwarter/Pabel*, EMRK5 § 20 Rz 44).

Zwar fällt das Auslieferungsverfahren selbst nicht in den Anwendungsbereich des Art 6 MRK, doch können dessen Verfahrensgarantien für die Entscheidung über die Zulässigkeit der Auslieferung dann (ausnahmsweise) Relevanz erlangen, wenn die betroffene Person nachweist, dass ihr im ersuchenden Staat eine offenkundige Verweigerung eines fairen Verfahrens („a flagrant denial of justice") droht (vgl EGMR 7. 7. 1989, 14038/88, *Soering/Vereinigtes Königreich*, EuGRZ 1989, 314; RIS-Justiz RS0123200; *Meyer-Ladewig*, EMRK[3] Art 6 Rz 167; weitere Nachweise bei *Göth-Flemmich* in WK[2] ARHG § 19 Rz 14).

Vor diesem Hintergrund begegnet der ursprüngliche Ansatz des Beschwerdegerichts, unter dem Aspekt der Art 3 und 6 MRK auf einen Nachweis durch die betroffene Person abzustellen, keinen Bedenken.

Geht das Gericht nach seiner Prüfung vom Vorliegen aller rechtlichen Voraussetzungen für die Auslieferung und vom Fehlen von Auslieferungshindernissen aus, hat es die Auslieferung für zulässig zu erklären. Bestehen hingegen noch Zweifel am Vorliegen eines Auslieferungshindernisses, muss das Gericht versuchen, sie vor der Entscheidung über die Zulässigkeit der Auslieferung auszuräumen. Gelingt dies nicht, hat es die Auslieferung für unzulässig zu erklären (vgl *Göth-Flemmich* in WK² ARHG Vor §§ 10-25 Rz 7; *Murschetz*, Auslieferung und Europäischer Haftbefehl 189, 295 f).

Diesen Prüfkriterien entspricht der Beschluss des Oberlandesgerichts vom 20. Jänner 2015, AZ 22 Bs 296/14m, nicht.

Das Beschwerdegericht hat vorliegend „die Risken einer Verletzung des Art 3 MRK" als (nur) dadurch ausreichend herabgesetzt erachtet, dass es den ersuchenden Staat zur Einhaltung bestimmter (im Spruch ersichtlicher) Verfahrensgarantien als Bedingung „für den Fall der Auslieferung" verpflichtete (BS 1 f und 7).

Eine Erklärung der Zulässigkeit der Auslieferung setzt aber als Ergebnis der Prüfung das Nichtvorliegen von Auslieferungshindernissen voraus. Den Ausspruch über die Zulässigkeit der Auslieferung an die Bedingung zu knüpfen, dass sich die Russische Föderation in Bezug auf die betroffene Person in Zukunft konventionskonform verhält, widerspricht § 33 Abs 1 und 3 ARHG iVm Art 3 und 6 MRK.

Auf eine diplomatische Zusicherung darf übrigens nur dann vertraut werden, wenn sie geeignet ist, die Gefahr für die betroffene Person zu beseitigen, sie muss aus Sicht des Gerichts verbindlich und verlässlich sein (vgl *GöthFlemmich* in WK² ARHG Vor §§ 10-25 Rz 7).

Wenn objektive Quellen von der Anwendung oder Tolerierung von Praktiken berichten, die den Prinzipien der Konvention entgegenstehen, sind diplomatische Zusicherungen generell nicht ausreichend, um adäquaten Schutz vor Folter oder Misshandlung der ausgelieferten Person zu gewährleisten (EGMR 20. 5. 2010, 21055/09, *Khaydarov/Russland*; vgl auch *Göth-Flemmich* in WK² ARHG Vor §§ 10-25 Rz 8). In diesen Fällen schließt es die allgemeine Menschenrechtslage im Empfangsstaat bereits von vornherein aus, irgendeine Zusicherung zu akzeptieren (vgl EGMR 17. 1. 2012, 8139/09, *Othman [Abu Qatada]/Vereinigtes Königreich*).

Mit der Erwägung des Oberlandesgerichts, im Fall der Nichteinhaltung der Bedingungen wäre „pro futuro jedenfalls die Verlässlichkeit russischer Zusicherungen" in Auslieferungsverfahren derart in Frage gestellt, dass „künftige Überstellungen sogar als unzulässig eingestuft werden müssten", wird eine Timur I***** allenfalls betreffende Gefahr einer Art 3 MRK widersprechenden Behandlung im Empfangsstaat nicht ausgeräumt (vgl zum Ganzen AZ 13 Os 27/15t, 30/15f).

Da eine Benachteiligung der betroffenen Person durch die aufgezeigte Gesetzesverletzung nicht ausgeschlossen werden kann, sah sich der Oberste Gerichtshof veranlasst, ihre Feststellung auf die im Spruch ersichtliche Weise mit konkreter Wirkung zu verbinden (§ 292 letzter Satz StPO).

Zum Erneuerungsantrag:

Für den subsidiären Rechtsbehelf eines wie hier nicht auf ein Urteil des EGMR gestützten Erneuerungsantrags gelten alle gegenüber dem EGMR normierten

Zulässigkeitsvoraussetzungen der Art 34 und 35 MRK sinngemäß (RISJustiz RS0122737; 14 Os 103/14z; 14 Os 28/15z).

Da demnach Erneuerungsanträge gegen Entscheidungen, die der Erneuerungswerber mit Beschwerde anfechten kann, unzulässig sind (für viele: 13 Os 47/11b, 54/11g), war der Antrag, soweit er sich (inhaltlich) gegen den Beschluss des Landesgerichts für Strafsachen Wien vom 5. September 2014, GZ 353 HR 244/14w128, richtet, schon deshalb zurückzuweisen.

Mit seinem den Beschluss des Oberlandesgerichts Wien betreffenden Vorbringen zu einem Verstoß gegen Art 3 MRK kann der Erneuerungswerber mit Blick auf den Erfolg der von der Generalprokuratur erhobenen Nichtigkeitsbeschwerde zur Wahrung des Gesetzes auf deren Erledigung verwiesen werden, weil sich die Nichtigkeitsbeschwerde in Ansehung dieser reklamierten Grundrechtsverletzung mit dem Erneuerungsantrag deckt und deren Feststellung verbunden mit der nach § 292 letzter Satz StPO verfügten konkreten Wirkung einen angemessenen Ausgleich hiefür darstellt (RIS-Justiz RS0126458).

Soweit der Antrag ebenfalls bezogen auf die Entscheidung des Beschwerdegerichts darüber hinaus eine Verletzung von Art 6 sowie „Art 8 bzw Art 9" MRK behauptet, erweist er sich als teils als (im Sinn des Vorgesagten) unzulässig gemäß Art 35 MRK, teils als unbegründet:

Ausgehend von der Feststellung, dass das in der Russischen Föderation gegen den Betroffenen durchgeführte Abwesenheitsverfahrens nicht den Anforderungen des Art 6 MRK entsprach, hat sich das Oberlandesgericht mit der ergänzten und erweiterten Zusicherung der Behörden des Zielstaats (wonach zusammengefasst gemäß der russischen Strafprozessordnung Abwesenheitsurteile [jedenfalls] „aus prozessualen Gründen" aufzuheben und die Verfahrensakten zur Neudurchführung des Verfahrens an das Gericht zu übermitteln sind, welches sodann eine ordentliche Gerichtsverhandlung durchzuführen hat, in der die Rechte der Verteidigung gewahrt werden, wenn die hievon betroffene Person erklärt, mit dem Urteil nicht einverstanden zu sein und anlässlich ihrer Festnahme oder ihres Erscheinens vor den Rechtsschutzorganen selbst oder durch ihren Verteidiger einen entsprechenden Antrag stellt, wobei eine solche Vorgangsweise im Fall diesbezüglicher Erklärungen und Anträge des Timur I***** auch vorliegend garantiert werde; ON 50, ON 93 und ON 101) ausführlich auseinandergesetzt und diese teilweise durch (zulässigen; vgl RIS-Justiz RS0124017 [insbesondere T2, T3 und T4]) Verweis auf die Entscheidung des Beschwerdegerichts vom 21. Mai 2014, AZ 22 Bs 140/14w (ON 111) mit ausführlicher Begründung zutreffend als ausreichend im Sinn des Art 3 Abs 1 zweiter Satz des Zweiten Zusatzprotokolls zum Europäischen Auslieferungsübereinkommen sowie des § 19a Abs 2 ARHG beurteilt (BS 5 f; vgl dazu *Murschetz*, Auslieferung und Europäischer Haftbefehl, 205; vgl auch [den vorliegend allerdings nicht anwendbaren] § 11 Abs 1 Z 4 EUJZG sowie die in diesem Verfahren ergangene Entscheidung des Obersten Gerichtshofs vom 28. Jänner 2014, AZ 14 Os 149/13p, 179/13z, 180/13x).

Indem der Erneuerungswerber auf Basis eigener Interpretation der in Rede stehenden Erklärungen und deren Inhalt großteils ignorierender Spekulationen zu „allenfalls" bereits abgelaufenen Fristen und zur (mangelnden) Qualität der zugesicherten Verfahrenserneuerung die gegenteilige Ansicht vertritt und daraus eine Verletzung von Art 6 MRK abzuleiten trachtet, setzt er sich nicht substantiiert mit den relevanten Erwägungen in der als grundrechtswidrig bezeichneten Entscheidung auseinander (RISJustiz RS0124359) und vermag solcherart keine Fehlbeurteilung des Oberlandesgerichts darzulegen. Dass nur eine Garantieerklärung genügen würde, in der zugesichert wird, dass „das Abwesenheitsurteil ... keinerlei Wirkungen entfaltet", wird in diesem Zusammenhang ohne methodengerechte Ableitung aus dem Gesetz bloß behauptet (RISJustiz RS0128393).

Soweit auf Basis der (unbegründeten) These, die „Privatsphäre" und „Religionsausübung" des Erneuerungswerbers sei aufgrund seiner „Religions- und Volksgruppenzugehörigkeit (Moslem/Tadschike)" im Falle seiner Inhaftierung „jedenfalls ... in unzulässiger Weise eingeschränkt" eine Verletzung von „Art 8 bzw Art 9" MRK, reklamiert wird, scheitert der Antrag an der fehlenden Rechtswegausschöpfung, weil Derartiges in der Beschwerde gegen den Beschluss des Landesgerichts für Strafsachen Wien vom 5. September 2014, GZ 353 HR 244/14w128, nicht geltend gemacht wurde (vgl RIS-Justiz RS0122737 [T13]).

Im Übrigen wird mit diesem Vorbringen eine bloß nominell angesprochene Grundrechtsverletzung nicht deutlich und bestimmt aufgezeigt (erneut RISJustiz RS0122737 [T17], RS0128393).

Insoweit war dem Erneuerungsantrag daher gemäß § 363c Abs 2 StPO (teilweise analog; vgl dazu 17 Os 11/12i, EvBl 2013/41, 273) nicht Folge zu geben.

4. Asylum/Asyl

FF.VII.4.

Constitutional Court, Decision U528/2013 of 7 October 2015

Verfassungsgerichtshof, Erkenntnis U528/2013 vom 7. Oktober 2015

Keywords

Violation of the prohibition of discrimination among aliens as regards the rejection of an asylum application – omission of conducting the necessary investigations regarding the persecution of an Iraqi member of the armed forces/interpreter – political opinion

Verletzung im Recht auf Gleichbehandlung von Fremden untereinander durch Abweisung des Asylantrags – Unterlassung erforderlicher Ermittlungen hinsichtlich der Verfolgung eines irakischen Generals/Dolmetscher – politische Meinung

Facts and procedural history (summary)

The complainant illegally entered the federal territory on 24 August 2007 and filed an application for international protection. In his application, he stated that he had been a fighter pilot for the Iraqi armed forces. His colleagues had been persecuted, tortured and murdered by the 'Mahdi army'. After he also had been persecuted, he decided to bring himself and his family to safety.

His application for international protection was rejected by the Federal Asylum Authority on 8 April 2008. He was granted subsidiary protection, and received a temporary residence permit until 8 August 2009.

The complainant appealed against this decision regarding the non-granting of asylum, which was dismissed by the Asylum Court. In this regard, the Asylum Court pointed out that it could not find as proven that the complainant would be threatened by a well-founded fear of persecution in Iraq. Although it noted that 'police men, soldiers, journalists, intellectuals and all members of the governments as well as so-called "colloberators" were particularly threatened, it found that this did not qualify as one of the exhaustively listed asylum grounds listed in the Geneva Refugee Convention, which required to belong to a certain social group.

The complainant appealed against this decision, in reliance on constitutionally guaranteed rights, particularly Art. I(1) of the Federal Constitutional Act on Elimination of Racial Discrimination, Article 14 of the European Convention on Human Rights, and Article 47(2) of the Charter of Fundamental Rights of the European Union (fair and public hearing).

The Constitutional Court held (excerpts)

The Constitutional Court has considered [...]:

1. According to the constant jurisprudence of the Constitutional Court – going back to Constitutional Court Collection No 13.836/1994 ([...]), Article I(1) of the Federal Constitutional Act on Elimination of Racial Discrimination, Federal Law Gazette No 390/1973, contains the general prohibition, directed at the legislative and executive authorities, to refrain from any discrimination among aliens which is not based on objective distinctions. This constitutional provision includes the dictate to treat aliens in a like manner, in application of the requirement of objectivity; their distinct treatment is therefore only acceptable if and to the extent that there are reasonable grounds discernible therefor and the unlike treatment is not disproportionate.

1.1. This subjective right of an alien which is guaranteed by Article I(1) *leg.cit.* is breached if a decision is based on a law in violation of this provision ([...]), if the Asylum Court falsely interpreted the law to come to a conclusion that [...] would be in contradiction with the Constitutional Act on Elimination of Racial Discrimination (Federal Law Gazette No 390/1973 ([...]), or if it [the Asylum Court] acted arbitrary when making its decision ([...]).

1.2. The authorities behave in an arbitrary manner which reaches into the constitutional sphere, if the state of law is repeatedly misapplied, or if the authority omits to conduct any research on a decisive point or in total, particularly in connection with party submissions or carelessy deviating from the contents of the file and leaving out specific factual content ([...]). Arbitrary conduct is particulary given if the authorities base their decision on arguments which do not possess any rationale ([...]). Finally, if the authorities severely misjudge the legal status, this also amounts to arbitrariness ([...]).

2. The Asylum Court has made such a mistake in the present case:

2.1. In its reasoning [as introduced above], the Asylum Court has failed to assess the submissions made by the complainant as regards his persecution on the grounds of his political opinion. 'Political' can entail everything that is of relevance for the state as well as for the shaping and safeguarding of the community and orderly coexistence of human individuals in society ([...]). Hence, circumstances such as a high ranking position in the former Iraqi armed forces of Saddam Hussein's regime are relevant, but also the subsequent position as an interpreter for the American occupying forces. For arriving at the conclusion that there exists a well-founded fear of persecution due to political opinion, it suffices that the persecutors act in belief thereof, whether or not the applicant actually possesses this opinion (Article 10(1) lit. e, in connection with (2) Qualification Directive; [...]).

2.2. The Asylum Court determined that the complainant had been a pilot and officer in the ranks of a general with the Iraqi air force. Later he worked as an interpreter for the US armed forces (hence, as a 'collaborator'). He thus qualified in a two-fold manner as a member of one of the groups fearing persecution in the country report that the decision was based on. Moreover, according to these determinations, the state authorities are not able to ensure the safety of these persons, even if the persecution is conducted by oppositional groups and paramilitary entities. [Even if some of the facts alleged by the complainant] are not deemed sufficient to constitute a well-founded fear of persecution on their own, they constitute indications that serve to prove the fear of the complainant, he is being persecuted for his political opinion, without him being able to count on state authorities for his protection.

2.3. As the Asylum Court did not examine the complainant's submission also for the well-founded fear of persecution for the concept of political opinion, and omitted to conduct any investigations in this regard, it grossly misconstrued the legal situation ([...]).

German Original

Entscheidungsgründe:

I. Sachverhalt, Beschwerde und Vorverfahren

1. Der Beschwerdeführer reiste am 24. August 2007 illegal in das Bundesgebiet ein, stellte einen Antrag auf internationalen Schutz und brachte vor, dass er bis 2003 *Kampfpilot* in der irakischen Armee gewesen sei. Kollegen von ihm seien von der „Mahdi Armee" verfolgt, gefoltert und ermordet worden. Als er – etwa zwei Monate vor seiner Ausreise – selbst von der „Mahdi Armee" verfolgt worden sei, habe er seine Familie in Sicherheit gebracht. Am 17. August 2007 seien bewaffnete Männer mit vier Toyota Landcruisern vor seinem Haus aufgetaucht und hätten ihn verschleppen wollen. Ihm sei jedoch die Flucht gelungen. Zudem sei er von 2006 bis 2007 für die amerikanische Armee als *Dolmetscher* tätig gewesen. Eines Tages habe er einen Drohbrief erhalten, wonach er diese Tätigkeit beenden solle, sonst würde ihm oder seiner Familie etwas zustoßen.

2. Der Antrag des Beschwerdeführers auf internationalen Schutz wurde mit Bescheid des Bundesasylamtes vom 8. April 2008 gemäß §3 Abs1 iVm §2 Abs1 Z13 des Bundesgesetzes über die Gewährung von Asyl (Asylgesetz 2005 – AsylG 2005), BGBl I 100/2005 idF BGBl I 50/2012, bezüglich der Zuerkennung des Status des Asylberechtigten abgewiesen. Gemäß §8 Abs1 AsylG wurde dem Beschwerdeführer der Status des subsidiär Schutzberechtigten zuerkannt und gemäß §8 Abs4 AsylG eine befristete Aufenthaltsberechtigung bis zum 8. August 2009 erteilt.

3. Gegen diesen Bescheid erhob der Beschwerdeführer hinsichtlich der Nichtzuerkennung von Asyl Berufung an den Unabhängigen Bundesasylsenat, die der Asylgerichtshof nach dem Übergang der Rechtssache als Beschwerde behandelte und mit dem in Beschwerde gezogenen Erkenntnis als unbegründet abwies.

3.1. Der Asylgerichtshof stellt – insoweit das Vorbringen des Beschwerdeführers als erwiesen annehmend – ua. fest:

„Der Beschwerdeführer ist Staatsangehöriger des Irak und sunnitischer Religionszugehörigkeit. Er lebte bis zu seiner Ausreise aus dem Irak im August 2007 gemeinsam mit seiner Ehegattin, seinen vier Söhnen und zwei Töchtern in Bagdad. Seine Familie ist erst zu einem späteren Zeitpunkt aus dem Irak ausgereist und hält sich mittlerweile auch in Österreich auf.

In seiner Heimat war der Beschwerdeführer während des Regimes von Saddam Hussein Pilot bzw. zuletzt Offizier im Range eines Generals bei der irakischen Luftwaffe und anschließend als Dolmetscher für die Amerikaner tätig.

Es kann nicht festgestellt werden, dass dem Beschwerdeführer im Irak eine asylrelevante – oder sonstige – Verfolgung oder Strafe maßgeblicher Intensität oder die Todesstrafe droht."

3.2. Im Rahmen der Länderberichte stellt der Asylgerichtshof zu den besonders gefährdeten gesellschaftlichen Gruppen und zur Menschenrechtslage Folgendes fest:

„Polizisten, Soldaten, Journalisten, Intellektuelle, alle Mitglieder der Regierung bzw. sog. ‚Kollaborateure' sind besonders gefährdet. Auch Mitarbeiter der Ministerien sowie Mitglieder von Provinzregierungen werden regelmäßig Opfer von gezielten Anschlägen, mit zunehmender Tendenz seit Anfang 2011.

Ministerien der Zentralregierung, Hotels in Bagdad, die auch von irakischen Abgeordneten, hohen Beamten sowie internationalen Gästen regelmäßig genutzt werden, sowie ausländische Vertretungen zählen weiterhin zu den Orten mit erhöhtem Anschlagsrisiko. […]

Die Menschenrechtslage ist weiterhin katastrophal. Nichtstaatliche Akteure, insbesondere Aufständische, sind für viele Menschenrechtsverletzungen (gezielte Morde, ethnische Säuberungen, Anschläge, Entführungen) im Irak verantwortlich. Angehörige staatlicher Organe (Polizei, Streitkräfte) begehen ebenfalls Menschenrechtsverletzungen. Die irakischen Sicherheitskräfte sind bislang nicht in der Lage, gefährdete oder verfolgte Bevölkerungsgruppen effektiv zu schützen."

3.3. Der Asylgerichtshof verneinte das Vorliegen eines Asylgrundes. Dem vom Beschwerdeführer geschilderten Vorfall könne keine „Verfolgungsrelevanz" beigemessen werden. Dem Vorbringen des Beschwerdeführers, am 17. August 2007 habe er gesehen, wie vier Autos vor seinem Haus angehalten hätten und bewaffnete Männer zu seinem Haus gekommen seien, wobei er zwar hätte flüchten können, aber diese Männer jedoch das Haus durchsucht hätten, könne nicht gefolgt werden, da die Vornahme von Hausdurchsuchungen für sich allein noch keine relevante Verfolgungshandlung darstelle. Detailliertere Angaben zur behaupteten Hausdurchsuchung seien vom Beschwerdeführer nicht gemacht worden. Dem behaupteten Erhalt von Drohbriefen erkannte der Asylgerichtshof keine Glaubwürdigkeit zu.

3.4. Eine Verfolgung auf Grund einer gewissen beruflichen Tätigkeit könne den in der Genfer Flüchtlingskonvention taxativ aufgezählten Gründen nicht entnommen werden, weshalb im konkreten Fall ein asylrelevanter Anknüpfungspunkt an die Genfer Flüchtlingskonvention lediglich auf eine Zugehörigkeit zu einer bestimmten sozialen Gruppe gestützt werden könne. Sofern nun im Bericht des deutschen Auswärtigen Amtes zu besonders gefährdeten gesellschaftlichen

Gruppen im Irak u.a. festgehalten werde, dass „Polizisten, Soldaten, Journalisten, Intellektuelle, alle Mitglieder der Regierung bzw. sog. ‚Kollaborateure' [...] besonders gefährdet" seien, so sei dazu grundsätzlich auszuführen, dass dieser Bericht lediglich aussage, welche Personenkreise aus welchen Gründen auch immer als besonders gefährdete Gruppe im Irak anzusehen seien und es werde aber demgegenüber keine Bewertung bzw. Beurteilung der Asylrelevanz der Zugehörigkeit zu diesen Personengruppen vorgenommen. Die individuelle Beurteilung, ob ein Asylwerber, der den in diesem Bericht genannten Personengruppen angehört, die Voraussetzung für die Erteilung des Status eines Asylberechtigten erfülle oder der jeweils vorgebrachte Sachverhalt unter die Bestimmungen der Genfer Flüchtlingskonvention zu subsumieren sei, obliege ausschließlich der Asylbehörde oder dem Asylgerichtshof.

4. Gegen diese Entscheidung richtet sich die vorliegende, auf Art144a BVG in der bis zum Ablauf des 31. Dezember 2013 geltenden Fassung gestützte Beschwerde, in der die Verletzung in verfassungsgesetzlich gewährleisteten Rechten, insbesondere auf Gleichbehandlung von Fremden untereinander (ArtI Abs1 des BVG BGBl 390/1913 und Art14 EMRK) und auf Durchführung einer mündlichen Verhandlung (Art47 Abs2 GRC) geltend gemacht werden und die kostenpflichtige Aufhebung der angefochtenen Entscheidung beantragt wird.

5. Der Asylgerichtshof legte die Verwaltungs- und Gerichtsakten vor, sah von der Erstattung einer Gegenschrift ab und beantragte die Abweisung der Beschwerde.

II. Rechtslage

1. Die maßgeblichen Bestimmungen des Abkommens über die Rechtsstellung der Flüchtlinge vom 28. Juli 1951 (im Folgenden: Genfer Flüchtlingskonvention) lauten:

„Artikel 1

Definition des Begriffs ‚Flüchtling'

A.

Im Sinne dieses Abkommens findet der Ausdruck ‚Flüchtling' auf jede Person Anwendung:

1. Die in Anwendung der Vereinbarungen vom 12. Mai 1926 und 30. Juni 1928 oder in Anwendung der Abkommen vom 28. Oktober 1933 und 10. Februar 1938 und des Protokolls vom 14. September 1939 oder in Anwendung der Verfassung der Internationalen Flüchtlingsorganisation als Flüchtling gilt.

Die von der internationalen Flüchtlingsorganisation während der Dauer ihrer Tätigkeit getroffenen Entscheidungen darüber, dass jemand nicht als Flüchtling im Sinne ihres Statuts anzusehen ist, stehen dem Umstand nicht entgegen, dass die Flüchtlingseigenschaft Personen zuerkannt wird, die die Voraussetzungen der Ziffer 2 dieses Artikels erfüllen;

2. die infolge von Ereignissen, die vor dem 1. Januar 1951 eingetreten sind, und aus der begründeten Furcht vor Verfolgung wegen ihrer Rasse, Religion, Nationalität, Zugehörigkeit zu einer bestimmten sozialen Gruppe oder wegen ihrer politischen Überzeugung sich außerhalb des Landes befindet, dessen Staatsangehörigkeit sie besitzt, und den Schutz dieses Landes nicht in Anspruch nehmen kann oder wegen dieser Befürchtungen nicht in Anspruch nehmen will; oder die sich als staatenlose infolge solcher Ereignisse außerhalb des Landes befindet, in welchem sie ihren gewöhnlichen Aufenthalt hatte, und nicht dorthin zurückkehren kann oder wegen der erwähnten Befürchtungen nicht dorthin zurückkehren will.

Für den Fall, dass eine Person mehr als eine Staatsangehörigkeit hat, bezieht sich der Ausdruck „das Land, dessen Staatsangehörigkeit sie besitzt," auf jedes der Länder, dessen Staatsangehörigkeit diese Person hat. Als des Schutzes des Landes, dessen Staatsangehörigkeit sie hat, beraubt, gilt nicht eine Person, die ohne einen stichhaltigen, auf eine begründete Befürchtung gestützten Grund den Schutz eines der Länder nicht in Anspruch genommen hat, deren Staatsangehörigkeit sie besitzt.

[...]

Artikel 33

Verbot der Ausweisung und Zurückweisung

1. Keiner der vertragschließenden Staaten wird einen Flüchtling auf irgendeine Weise über die Grenzen von Gebieten ausweisen oder zurückweisen, in denen sein Leben oder seine Freiheit wegen seiner Rasse, Religion, Staatsangehörigkeit, seiner Zugehörigkeit zu einer bestimmten sozialen Gruppe oder wegen seiner politischen Überzeugung bedroht sein würde.

2. Auf die Vergünstigung dieser Vorschrift kann sich jedoch ein Flüchtling nicht berufen, der aus schwer wiegenden Gründen als eine Gefahr für die Sicherheit des Landes anzusehen ist, in dem er sich befindet, oder der eine Gefahr für die Allgemeinheit dieses Staates bedeutet, weil er wegen eines Verbrechens oder eines besonders schweren Vergehens rechtskräftig verurteilt wurde."

Die Einschränkung des Flüchtlingsbegriffs auf fluchtauslösende Ereignisse, die sich vor dem 1. Jänner 1951 zutrugen, wurde durch das Protokoll über die Rechtsstellung der Flüchtlinge vom 31. Jänner 1967 (im Folgenden: New Yorker Protokoll) beseitigt. Die Genfer Flüchtlingskonvention sowie das New Yorker Protokoll wurden mit BGBl 55/1955 und BGBl 78/1974 in innerstaatliches Recht – auf einfachgesetzlicher Ebene – transformiert.

2. Die Richtlinie 2004/83/EG des Rates vom 29. April 2004 über Mindestnormen für die Anerkennung und den Status von Drittstaatsangehörigen oder Staatenlosen als Flüchtlinge oder als Personen, die anderweitig internationalen Schutz benötigen, und über den Inhalt des zu gewährenden Schutzes (im Folgenden: Statusrichtlinie) enthält folgende relevante Bestimmungen:

„Artikel 2

Begriffsbestimmungen

Im Sinne dieser Richtlinie bezeichnet der Ausdruck

a) [...]

b) „Genfer Flüchtlingskonvention" das Genfer Abkommen über die Rechtsstellung der Flüchtlinge vom 28. Juli 1951 in der durch das New Yorker Protokoll vom 31. Januar 1967 geänderten Fassung;

c) „Flüchtling" einen Drittstaatsangehörigen, der aus der begründeten Furcht vor Verfolgung wegen seiner Rasse, Religion, Staatsangehörigkeit, politischen Überzeugung oder Zugehörigkeit zu einer bestimmten sozialen Gruppe sich außerhalb des Landes befindet, dessen Staatsangehörigkeit er besitzt, und den Schutz dieses Landes nicht in Anspruch nehmen kann oder wegen dieser Furcht nicht in Anspruch nehmen will, oder einen Staatenlosen, der sich aus denselben vorgenannten Gründen außerhalb des Landes seines vorherigen gewöhnlichen Aufenthalts befindet und nicht dorthin zurückkehren kann oder wegen dieser Furcht nicht dorthin zurückkehren will und auf den Artikel 12 keine Anwendung findet;

d) – k) [...]

[...]

Artikel 6

Akteure, von denen die Verfolgung oder ein ernsthafter

Schaden ausgehen kann

Die Verfolgung bzw. der ernsthafte Schaden kann ausgehen von

a) dem Staat;

b) Parteien oder Organisationen, die den Staat oder einen wesentlichen Teil des Staatsgebiets beherrschen;

c) nichtstaatlichen Akteuren, sofern die unter den Buchstaben a) und b) genannten Akteure einschließlich internationaler Organisationen erwiesenermaßen nicht in der Lage oder nicht willens sind, Schutz vor Verfolgung bzw. ernsthaftem Schaden im Sinne des Artikels 7 zu bieten.

[...]

Artikel 10

Verfolgungsgründe

(1) Bei der Prüfung der Verfolgungsgründe berücksichtigen die Mitgliedstaaten Folgendes:

a) Der Begriff der Rasse umfasst insbesondere die Aspekte Hautfarbe, Herkunft und Zugehörigkeit zu einer bestimmten ethnischen Gruppe.

b) Der Begriff der Religion umfasst insbesondere theistische, nichttheistische und atheistische Glaubensüberzeugungen, die Teilnahme bzw. Nichtteilnahme an religiösen Riten im privaten oder öffentlichen Bereich, allein oder in Gemeinschaft mit anderen, sonstige religiöse Betätigungen oder Meinungsäußerungen und Verhaltensweisen Einzelner oder der Gemeinschaft, die sich auf eine religiöse Überzeugung stützen oder nach dieser vorgeschrieben sind.

c) Der Begriff der Nationalität beschränkt sich nicht auf die Staatsangehörigkeit oder das Fehlen einer solchen, sondern bezeichnet insbesondere auch die Zugehörigkeit zu einer Gruppe, die durch ihre kulturelle, ethnische oder sprachliche Identität, gemeinsame geografische oder politische Ursprünge oder ihre Verwandtschaft mit der Bevölkerung eines anderen Staates bestimmt wird.

d) Eine Gruppe gilt insbesondere als eine bestimmte soziale Gruppe, wenn

— die Mitglieder dieser Gruppe angeborene Merkmale oder einen Hintergrund, der nicht verändert werden kann, gemein haben, oder Merkmale oder eine Glaubensüberzeugung teilen, die so bedeutsam für die Identität oder das Gewissen sind, dass der Betreffende nicht gezwungen werden sollte, auf sie zu verzichten, und

— die Gruppe in dem betreffenden Land eine deutlich abgegrenzte Identität hat, da sie von der sie umgebenden Gesellschaft als andersartig betrachtet wird.

Je nach den Gegebenheiten im Herkunftsland kann als eine soziale Gruppe auch eine Gruppe gelten, die sich auf das gemeinsame Merkmal der sexuellen Ausrichtung gründet. Als sexuelle Ausrichtung dürfen keine Handlungen verstanden werden, die nach dem nationalen Recht der Mitgliedstaaten als strafbar gelten; geschlechterbezogene Aspekte können berücksichtigt werden, rechtfertigen aber für sich allein genommen noch nicht die Annahme, dass dieser Artikel anwendbar ist.

e) Unter dem Begriff der politischen Überzeugung ist insbesondere zu verstehen, dass der Antragsteller in einer Angelegenheit, die die in Artikel 6 genannten potenziellen Verfolger sowie deren Politiken oder Verfahren betrifft, eine Meinung, Grundhaltung oder Überzeugung vertritt, wobei es unerheblich ist, ob der Antragsteller aufgrund dieser Meinung, Grundhaltung oder Überzeugung tätig geworden ist.

(2) Bei der Bewertung der Frage, ob die Furcht eines Antragstellers vor Verfolgung begründet ist, ist es unerheblich, ob der Antragsteller tatsächlich die Merkmale der Rasse oder die religiösen, nationalen, sozialen oder politischen Merkmale aufweist, die zur Verfolgung führen, sofern ihm diese Merkmale von seinem Verfolger zugeschrieben werden.

[...]

Artikel 13

Zuerkennung der Flüchtlingseigenschaft

Die Mitgliedstaaten erkennen einem Drittstaatsangehörigen oder einem Staatenlosen, der die Voraussetzungen der Kapitel II und III erfüllt, die Flüchtlingseigenschaft zu."

3. §2 Abs1 Z15 und §3 AsylG 2005, BGBl I 100/2005 idF BGBl I 135/2009, lauten:

„Begriffsbestimmungen

§2. (1) Im Sinne dieses Bundesgesetzes ist

1. – 14. [...]

15. der Status des Asylberechtigten: das dauernde Einreise- und Aufenthaltsrecht, das Österreich Fremden nach den Bestimmungen dieses Bundesgesetzes gewährt;

16. – 25. [...]

(2) – (3) [...]

Status des Asylberechtigten

§3. (1) Einem Fremden, der in Österreich einen Antrag auf internationalen Schutz gestellt hat, ist, soweit dieser Antrag nicht wegen Drittstaatsicherheit oder Zuständigkeit eines anderen Staates zurückzuweisen ist, der Status des Asylberechtigten zuzuerkennen, wenn glaubhaft ist, dass ihm im Herkunftsstaat Verfolgung im Sinne des Art1 Abschnitt A Z2 Genfer Flüchtlingskonvention droht.

(2) Die Verfolgung kann auch auf Ereignissen beruhen, die eingetreten sind, nachdem der Fremde seinen Herkunftsstaat verlassen hat (objektive Nachfluchtgründe) oder auf Aktivitäten des Fremden beruhen, die dieser seit Verlassen des Herkunftsstaates gesetzt hat, die insbesondere Ausdruck und Fortsetzung einer bereits im Herkunftsstaat bestehenden Überzeugung sind (subjektive Nachfluchtgründe). Einem Fremden, der einen Folgeantrag (§2 Z23) stellt, wird in der Regel nicht der Status des Asylberechtigten zuerkannt, wenn die Verfolgungsgefahr auf Umständen beruht, die der Fremde nach Verlassen seines Herkunftsstaates selbst geschaffen hat, es sei denn, es handelt sich um in Österreich erlaubte Aktivitäten, die nachweislich Ausdruck und Fortsetzung einer bereits im Herkunftsstaat bestehenden Überzeugung sind.

(3) Der Antrag auf internationalen Schutz ist bezüglich der Zuerkennung des Status des Asylberechtigten abzuweisen, wenn

1. dem Fremden eine innerstaatliche Fluchtalternative (§11) offen steht oder

2. der Fremde einen Asylausschlussgrund (§6) gesetzt hat.

(4) Einem Fremden ist von Amts wegen und ohne weiteres Verfahren der Status des Asylberechtigten zuzuerkennen, wenn sich die Republik Österreich völkerrechtlich dazu verpflichtet hat.

(5) Die Entscheidung, mit der einem Fremden von Amts wegen oder auf Grund eines Antrags auf internationalen Schutz der Status des Asylberechtigten zuerkannt wird, ist mit der Feststellung zu verbinden, dass diesem Fremden damit kraft Gesetzes die Flüchtlingseigenschaft zukommt."

III. Erwägungen

Der Verfassungsgerichtshof hat über die – zulässige – Beschwerde erwogen:

1. Nach der mit VfSlg 13.836/1994 beginnenden, nunmehr ständigen Rechtsprechung des Verfassungsgerichtshofes (s. etwa VfSlg 14.650/1996 und die dort angeführte Vorjudikatur; weiters VfSlg 16.080/2001 und 17.026/2003) enthält ArtI Abs 1 des Bundesverfassungsgesetzes zur Durchführung des Internationalen Übereinkommens über die Beseitigung aller Formen rassischer Diskriminierung, BGBl 390/1973, das allgemeine, sowohl an die Gesetzgebung als auch an die Vollziehung gerichtete Verbot, sachlich nicht begründbare Unterscheidungen zwischen Fremden vorzunehmen. Diese Verfassungsbestimmung enthält ein – auch das Sachlichkeitsgebot einschließendes – Gebot der Gleichbehandlung von Fremden untereinander; deren Ungleichbehandlung ist also nur dann und insoweit zulässig, als hiefür ein vernünftiger Grund erkennbar und die Ungleichbehandlung nicht unverhältnismäßig ist.

1.1. Diesem einem Fremden durch ArtI Abs 1 leg.cit. gewährleisteten subjektiven Recht widerstreitet eine Entscheidung, wenn sie auf einem gegen diese Bestimmung verstoßenden Gesetz beruht (vgl. zB VfSlg 16.214/2001), wenn der Asylgerichtshof dem angewendeten einfachen Gesetz fälschlicherweise einen Inhalt unterstellt hat, der – hätte ihn das Gesetz – dieses als in Widerspruch zum Bundesverfassungsgesetz zur Durchführung des Internationalen Übereinkommens über die Beseitigung aller Formen rassischer Diskriminierung, BGBl 390/1973, stehend erscheinen ließe (s. etwa VfSlg 14.393/1995, 16.314/2001) oder wenn er bei Fällung der Entscheidung Willkür geübt hat (zB VfSlg 15.451/1999, 16.297/2001, 16.354/2001 sowie 18.614/2008).

1.2. Ein willkürliches Verhalten der Behörde, das in die Verfassungssphäre eingreift, liegt unter anderem in einer gehäuften Verkennung der Rechtslage, aber auch im Unterlassen jeglicher Ermittlungstätigkeit in einem entscheidenden Punkt oder dem Unterlassen eines ordnungsgemäßen Ermittlungsverfahrens überhaupt, insbesondere in Verbindung mit einem Ignorieren des Parteivorbringens und einem leichtfertigen Abgehen vom Inhalt der Akten oder dem Außerachtlassen des konkreten Sachverhaltes (zB VfSlg 15.451/1999, 15.743/2000, 16.354/2001, 16.383/2001). Ein willkürliches Vorgehen liegt insbesondere dann vor, wenn die Behörde die Entscheidung mit Ausführungen begründet, denen jeglicher Begründungswert fehlt (s. etwa VfSlg 13.302/1992 mit weiteren Judikaturhinweisen, 14.421/1996, 15.743/2000). Schließlich ist von einem willkürlichen Verhalten auch auszugehen, wenn die Behörde die Rechtslage gröblich bzw. in besonderem Maße verkennt (zB VfSlg 18.091/2007, 19.283/2010 mwN, 19.475/2011).

2. Ein solcher Fehler ist dem Asylgerichtshof hier unterlaufen:

2.1. Mit seiner oben wiedergegebenen Begründung verabsäumt es der Asylgerichtshof, das Fluchtvorbringen des Beschwerdeführers nach dem viel näherliegenderen Tatbestand der Verfolgung wegen seiner politischen Überzeugung zu beurteilen. Als politisch kann alles qualifiziert werden, was für den Staat sowie für die Gestaltung bzw. Erhaltung der Ordnung des Gemeinwesens und des geordneten Zusammenlebens der menschlichen Individuen in der Gemeinschaft von Bedeutung ist (VwGH 12.9.2002, 2001/20/0310 mwN), weshalb davon Umstände wie die Bekleidung eines hohen Ranges in der ehemaligen irakischen Armee des Regimes Saddam Husseins, aber auch die nachfolgende Tätigkeit als Dolmetscher für die amerikanische Besatzungsmacht mit eingeschlossen sind. Für die Annahme einer asylrechtlich relevanten Verfolgung aus Gründen der politischen Gesinnung reicht es dabei aus, dass diese von den Verfolgern bloß unterstellt wird (Art10 Abs1 lite iVm Abs2 Statusrichtlinie; s. auch VwGH 12.9.2002, 2001/20/0310 sowie VfSlg 19.838/2013).

2.2. Nach den Feststellungen des Asylgerichtshofes war der Beschwerdeführer als Pilot bzw. zuletzt Offizier im Range eines Generals bei der irakischen Luftwaffe und anschließend als Dolmetscher für die US-Streitkräfte (insoweit also auch als „Kollaborateur") tätig, er gehörte daher in zweifacher Hinsicht auch zufolge der der Entscheidung zugrunde liegenden Länderberichte besonders verfolgungsgefährdeten Gruppen an, wobei auch dann, wenn die Verfolgung von oppositionellen Gruppen und paramilitärischen Verbänden ausgeht, die Staatsmacht nach diesen Feststellungen nicht in der Lage ist, die Sicherheit der verfolgten Personen zu gewährleisten. Mag auch der – vom Beschwerdeführer behauptete und vom Asylgerichtshof nicht in Zweifel gezogene – Vorfall des auf die beschriebene Weise erfolgten Eindringens von vier Männern in sein Haus isoliert betrachtet nicht zwingend „verfolgungsrelevant" sein, so ist er aber doch geeignet, die Befürchtung des Beschwerdeführers, er werde aus politischen Gründen verfolgt, ohne auf die Hilfe der Staatsmacht zählen zu können, im Sinne eines realen Risikos als begründet erscheinen zu lassen.

2.3. Soweit der Asylgerichtshof also das Vorbringen des Beschwerdeführers nicht auch unter dem Aspekt der Verfolgung aus politischen Gründen beurteilte und demgemäß die in diesem Zusammenhang erforderlichen Ermittlungen unterlassen hat, ist ihm eine grobe Verkennung der Rechtslage vorzuwerfen (vgl. VfSlg 19.838/2013).

IV. Ergebnis und damit zusammenhängende Ausführungen

1. Der Beschwerdeführer ist somit durch die angefochtene Entscheidung im verfassungsgesetzlich gewährleisteten Recht auf Gleichbehandlung von Fremden untereinander verletzt worden.

2. Die angefochtene Entscheidung ist daher aufzuheben.

3. Die vorliegende Entscheidung konnte gemäß §19 Abs4 VfGG ohne mündliche Verhandlung in nichtöffentlicher Sitzung getroffen werden.

4. Die Kostenentscheidung beruht auf §88 VfGG. In den zugesprochenen Kosten ist Umsatzsteuer in Höhe von € 400,– enthalten.

VIII. Human rights and fundamental freedoms/
Menschenrechte und Grundfreiheiten

See also FF.VII.2.-1, FF.VII.2.-2, FF.VII.4.

FF.VIII.

Supreme Administrative Court, Judgment Ro 2014/09/0053 of 20 May 2015

Verwaltungsgerichtshof, Urteil Ro 2014/09/0053 vom 20. Mai 2015

Keywords

Freedom of expression – European Convention on Human Rights – Art 10 ECHR – Art 17 ECHR – Art 9 Austrian State Treaty – prohibition of National Socialism – doubt expressed by a university professor regarding the Holocaust – Art 6 ECHR – applicability of fair trial rights to disciplinary proceedings – impartiality of judges

Freie Meinungsäußerung – Europäische Menschenrechtskonvention – Art 10 EMRK – Art 17 EMRK – Art 9 Staatsvertrag von Wien – Verbot des Nationalsozialismus – Anzweifeln des Holocaust durch einen Universitätsprofessor – Art 6 EMRK – Anwendbarkeit des Rechts auf ein faires Verfahren auf Disziplinarverfahren – Unparteilichkeit von Richtern

Facts and procedural history (summary)

The appellant was a university professor employed under public law at an Austrian university. Following statements made by him towards several students and a journalist that qualified the occurrence of the Holocaust, he was initially suspended and then convicted to a monetary fine in the amount of one monthly salary by a disciplinary commission. It considered that the penalty was justified under Art 10 (2) ECHR. The appellant appealed the decision of the disciplinary commission and argued that it violated his right to freedom of expression under Art 10 ECHR as well as the academic freedom under Art 17 Basic Law on the General Rights of Nationals (*StGG*). The authority of second instance in essence upheld the decision of the disciplinary commission. The appellant appeal against that decision.

The Supreme Administrative Court held

The appellant, born in 1960, is in employment under public law at the federal state as a university professor and is working at the institute for R at the S-university in N (anonymization by the Supreme Administrative Court).

With the decision of the disciplinary commission at Federal Ministry of Science and Research from 13 February 2013, following oral proceedings, the appellant was found guilty as follows:

'1. b.) *The appellant* is guilty of having made, toward the students MN, SR and SG, statements to the effect of: "The question of genocide during the period of National Socialism is not definitely resolved, as there has not yet been a discussion on that question that was objective and free of ideology. Some historical books contain one opinion, others the opposite. I cannot assess the events during the period of National Socialism, as I have not been present. I do however by no means want to whitewash the events."

Thereby he has intentionally violated Sec 43(2) Civil Service Employment Act (*BDG*) and thereby committed a breach of official duty within the meaning of Sec 91 Civil Service Employment Act (*BDG*).

1. b.) *The appellant* is guilty of having made, toward the students MN, SR and SG, statements to the effect of: "There is an abuse of the term of antisemitism: non-religious Jews, which were criticized for their exploitative business activities, defend themselves with the argument of antisemitism. This abuse is in part the reason for the mass murder of religious Jews in the past. The actually religious Jews opposed profiteering with compound interest."

Thereby he has in the context of his other statements subject to these proceeding intentionally violated Sec 43(2) Civil Service Employment Act (*BDG*) and thereby committed a breach of official duty within the meaning of Sec 91 Civil Service Employment Act (*BDG*).

1. c.) *The appellant* is guilty of having made, toward the students MN, SR and SG, statements to the effect of: "If a genocide committed by the national socialists is discussed, the currently ongoing genocide by the US should be discussed as well. I cannot answer the question whether gas chambers existed during the period of National Socialism. These events are too long ago; I have not been present. I have no opinion on gas chambers. In light of the more pressing, more current problems it is more important to concern oneself with the future rather than the past." With regard to the shortcomings present in the knowledge society he referred to the example of a technician, who wanted to demonstrate that gas chambers could not have worked for technical reasons. This had caused a stir. "In such situations the matter should be evaluated objectively and not disregarded by

reason that a law is violated. It should be possible that such a matter is debated openly and, as the case may be, also refuted."

Thereby he has intentionally violated Sec 43(2) Civil Service Employment Act (*BDG*) and thereby committed a breach of official duty within the meaning of Sec 91 Civil Service Employment Act (*BDG*).

2.) *The appellant* is guilty of having made, in a telephone conversation with Mag TM, which should serve to prepare an article in S (a daily newspaper), the statements "It does not make sense to talk about this from today's perspective" and "How do you define objectivity? Everything we have are building remains, photographs and descriptions." – both with reference to the holocaust.

Thereby he has intentionally violated Sec 43(2) Civil Service Employment Act (*BDG*) and thereby committed a breach of official duty within the meaning of Sec 91 Civil Service Employment Act (*BDG*).

3.) *The appellant* is guilty of having again recited his theses on knowledge by way of reference to mass extermination camps in a letter to the S (a daily newspaper) on 26 January 2012, by explaining: "As an expert for knowledge management and the philosophy of science who teaches and researches in the field and has several international publication to show, I advocate for an originary notion of knowledge. Accordingly, there are two types of knowledge: 1) expert knowledge, which originates from the postulation, verification and refutation of theories by scientists trained therefore, as well as 2) experience knowledge, which originates from personal participation in events and their interpretation against the background of subjective life experience. In this regard, the reading of books and listening to reports and lectures by laypersons does not lead to the development of knowledge but belief. Against the backdrop of this notion of knowledge I have to reject the statement "I know that mass extermination camps were operated under the criminal regime of the Third Reich" based on mere logical reasons, as I am neither a historian (expert knowledge) nor a contemporary witness (experience knowledge). I do however agree with the statement "We know that mass extermination camps were operated under the criminal regime of the Third Reich", as this "we", referring to the society as a whole, also includes experts in the subject matter (historians) and contemporary witnesses. I also agree with the statement "I believe that mass extermination camps were operated under the criminal regime of the Third Reich", as I trust both the statements of experts in the subject matter (historians) as well as of relevant contemporary witnesses.'

Thereby he has intentionally violated Sec 43(2) Civil Service Employment Act (*BDG*) and thereby committed a breach of official duty within the meaning of Sec 91 Civil Service Employment Act (*BDG*).

...

Due to the convictions handed down in counts 1.b., 1.c., 1.d., 2. and 3., the defendant is sentenced to a monetary penalty in the amount of one monthly salary excluding child benefits pursuant to Sec 92(1)(3) Civil Service Employment Act (*BDG*) in conjunction with Sec 126(2) Civil Service Employment Act (*BDG*).'

In sum, the authority of first instance justified its decision by having based its determinations on the oral testimony of the appellant and the witnesses SG, MN and SR as well as on transcripts of the statements of the appellant prepared by these three witnesses. Although the appellant has stated that he made the statements he is accused of not as his own opinion, but merely used them as metalinguistic statements, the witnesses in contrast consistently and convincingly testified that they have had the impression that the statements referred to in the judgment were the opinion of the appellant. The appellant also had not disputed his statements, as sent to him per email by the witnesses subsequently to the interview. Similar considerations applied with regard to the appellant's statements toward a journalist of S, who was also questioned during the oral proceedings.

The authority of the first instance explained that the appellant has committed a breach of official duty in accordance with Sec 43(2) Civil Service Employment Act (*BDG*) through the statements he is accused of in Points 1.b.), 1.c.), 1.d.), 2.) and 3.) of the decision. The National Socialism Prohibition Act (*VerbotsG*), which has the status of a constitutional law, belonged to the essential elements of the Austrian legal system. It were part of the professional duties of a civil servant, at least in an official capacity, to avoid making public statements that question the underlying basis of justification (*Wertungsgrundlage*) of the National Socialism Prohibition Act (*VerbotsG*), that is denying the holocaust and the existence of gas chambers as an historical fact. This duty particularly applies to civil servants that work in education, such as university lecturers, as these are entrusted with the education of students. Especially of those at least restraint is demanded with regard to statements that cast doubt on the factual basis mentioned and thereby on the remembrance of victims of the holocaust. This duty also existed in the context of statements on the possibility of knowledge and insight and reference to the past. The interference in the appellant's right to freedom of expression effected by disciplining the appellant was justified pursuant to Art 10(2) ECHR (the authority of first instance extensively cited jurisprudence of the European Court for Human Rights, for instance the judgment of 23 September 1998 in the Case *Lehideux und Isorni versus France*, Zl. 55/1997/839/1045).

Against this disciplinary decision the appellant lodged an appeal, in which he in essence argued that the prosecution of him under disciplinary law based on the statements he is accused of was impermissible under Art 17 Basic Law on the General Rights of Nationals (*StGG*) and Art 10 ECHR. Moreover the appellant argued a procedural defect, as those three members of the senate handing down the decision of the authority of first instance were biased in this respect, as they already had taken part in the decision on his suspension for the same allegations. Moreover the appellant disputed that he had made the statements he is accused of as statements of his own and requested the questioning of further witnesses as evidence therefore.

With the decision appealed against of the authority of second instance the first appeal was denied and the disciplinary decision appealed against confirmed with regard to both guilt and punishment.

The decision appealed against [of the authority of second instance] had in essence been justified by the circumstance that the appellant had not contested his participation in the pertinent interview with the students listed by name in the decision and that he also had not substantially opposed the individual statements reproduced of which he is accused. In the appeal, he had brought no substantial new arguments that are of pertinent legal relevance. For purposes of authorization, the appellant had been made aware of the statements he is accused of as his own statements in an email on 11 January 2012, it would have been on him to react in any form, to oppose the records presented of the contents of the conversation and correct his statements reproduced therein or demand their correction or clarify possible apparent errors that from his standpoint had arisen. However, the appellant had refrained from doing so. Further, he had also refrained from reacting to the journalist of the newspaper S and his email of 25 January 2012 and sending him a response. The witnesses requested by the appellant had also according to his own submissions not directly witnessed the interview conducted by the three students on 21 December 2011 and also not personally listened to the telephone conversation with journalist Mag TM. Therefore questioning these witnesses had been unnecessary. The appellant also had not argued for producing the audiotape transcripts of the interview of 21 December 2011. Therefore, the disciplinary commission had assumed that the appellant had made the statements he is accused of in the decision in that form.

Admittedly the public prosecutor's office had discontinued criminal proceedings under the National Socialism Prohibition Act (*VerbotsG*) pending against the appellant, as in case of (potentially also only pretended) personal uncertainty with regard to the existence of gas chambers, according to the jurisprudence of the Supreme Court, neither a direct nor indirect denial or negation is present, as required for the existence of the offense by denial (14 Os 24/96). However, this would by no means exclude that the appellant may be culpable of violations of his official duties with regard to the same set of facts, thus the discontinuation of criminal proceedings by the public prosecutor's office had no binding effect within the meaning of Sec 95 (2) Civil Service Employment Act (*BDG*). Especially the statement the appellant is accused of in Point 1.c.) of the decision, which solely reflects evaluations and whereby a part of the population (in particular those of mosaic faith) is being or should be debased or shown in a bad light, reminded to a shocking degree of the language of the National Socialist propaganda machinery. The appellant had had to be well aware of that already as a citizen and even more so as a professor at an Austrian university. The repeated oral as well as written statements in public or semi-public by the appellant, a university professor researching and teaching at an Austrian university, had been suitable, within the meaning of Sec 43 (2) Civil Service Employment Act (*BDG*), to seriously impair and permanently call into question the confidence not only of the remaining faculty, the non-tenured academic staff and the students, but also of the public outside of the university into his impartiality, his objective conducting of official duties as well as overall the appropriateness of the discharge of his office. According to the deciding authority, this could not seriously be doubted. The statements of the appellant were particularly suited to damage the reputation of the university, at which he carries out research and teaches, both domestically and abroad.

The connection of the conduct in question to the service as required by jurisprudence in case of violations of the pertinent duties of civil servants (Sec 43 (2) Civil Service Employment Act (*BDG*)) were unquestionably given in this case, as the appellant, by virtue of his office as university professor, were entrusted with the teaching of lectures and conducting exams as well as supervising of students, in particular of degree and doctoral candidates and junior researchers (Sec 165 Civil Service Employment Act (*BDG*)). In doing so, he is necessarily in continuing, repeated, also close professional contact with predominately young or younger people and had, as a teacher as well as figure vested with academic authority, already for these reasons to display special responsibility and sensibility with regard to statements made in front of an audience or intended for a broader readership – especially in connection with the historical subject matter in question here.

Insofar as the appellant argues in his appeal that he had not expressed his own personal opinion on the reign of terror of the national socialists and the Third Reich in his oral and written statements and that the statements made by him were coherent with his teaching activity in the area 'knowledge management', it had to be replied that the statements of the appellant and the choice of words in his theoretical remarks according to their meaning, both taken in isolation as well as in context, are well suited to veer the ordinary understanding of (newspaper) readers towards a questioning, doubting or conveying of personal uncertainties in relation to completely confirmed knowledge of the society regarding the pertinent historical facts. A 'neutral' position towards the Third Reich and the crimes committed therein would in no case be possible. The appellant must have had been aware of that. Thus the appellant could not successfully argue a lack of fault, also with regard to his defense that he had only made 'meta-linguistic statements'.

The authority of second instance cited jurisprudence of the Constitutional Court on the permissibility of restrictions of the constitutionally guaranteed rights contained in Art 17 Basic Law on the General Rights of Nationals (*StGG*) (academic freedom: *e.g.* VfSlg. 11.737/1988) and Art 10 ECHR (freedom of expression: *e.g.* VfSlg. 15.827/2000)

The authority of second instance affirmed the assessment of the severity of the disciplinary violation the appellant is accused of as being overall extremely significant and considered as an aggravating factor that the appellant had made repeated public or semi-public pertinent remarks and that, due to his position and function as university professor, he had a special responsibility and role model effect in particular towards the students. His lack of prior criminal, administrative or disciplinary convictions was deemed a mitigating factor by the authority of second instance, as was the duration of the proceedings of almost one year. The appellant had made statements, which objectively express a doubting, distanced or uncritical attitude towards National Socialism and the endless suffering of a nameless number of people caused by the authorities of that regime. He had gravely violated his duty deriving from the statutory provisions not to damage the reputation of the university to which he belongs. The appellant must be aware that he would provoke a critical and negative media response due to his position and that thus his university would be negatively mentioned in the public.

[...]

On the appeal, which was initially lodged with the Constitutional Court, rejected by it by decision of 6 June 2014, B 1343/2013-7 and transferred to the Supreme Administrative Court, the Supreme Administrative Court has deliberated:

[...]

The appellant considers the decision appealed against as unlawful, as he had only expressed his professional opinion by reference to political examples, he thoroughly rejected National Socialism and had repeatedly affirmed and explained that towards the students as well as the journalist. His statements had to be understood against the background of the fact that he had amongst other things engaged in theory of knowledge and knowledge management respectively.

Thereby the appellant does not demonstrate that the authority of second instance had unfoundedly or erroneously established or assessed the statements the appellant is accused of or that the findings of the authority of second instance came into existence through a defective procedure. The authority of second instance rather justified its findings comprehensibly and coherently. It is not unlawful, when it ascribed the statements of the appellant the objective of denying crimes of National Socialism and when it did not follow the argument of the appellant, that they merely were neutral statements in the context of an academic discourse on the topic of knowledge management. Such statements by a civil servant definitely constitute a considerable threat to the interests of the service within the meaning of Sec 43 (1) and (2) Civil Service Employment Act (*BDG*) (see the decision of this court of 3 July 2000, Zl. 2000/09/0006, of 5 September 2013, Zl. 2013/09/0114, of 3 October 2013, Zl. 2013/09/0077).

Both the authority of first instance as well as the authority of second instance have extensively and accurately demonstrated that there is no violation of the appellant's rights to respect of the freedom of science and its teaching pursuant to Art 17 Basic Law on the General Rights of Nationals (*StGG*) as well as to freedom of expression pursuant to Art 10 ECHR. Thus, from the point of view of these freedoms there was also no erroneous application of the disciplinary provisions with regard to the appellant. In this regard it may be referred to the decision of this court of 3 July 2000, Zl. 2000/09/0006, of 5 September 2013, Zl. 2013/09/0114, and of 3 October 2013, Zl. 2013/09/0077, to the jurisprudence of the Constitutional Court cited, especially its judgment VfSlg 18.405/2008, as well as the jurisprudence of the European Court of Human Rights for instance its judgment of 23 September 1998 in the case of *Lehideux and Isorni v France*, 55/1997/839/1045, paras 47 ff; and its decision of 24 June 2003 in the case of *Garaudy v France*, No 65831/01. Even if, in the present case, one does not assume a forfeiture of the rights under Art 10 ECHR by virtue of Art 17 ECHR, the interference caused by the decision appealed against may be considered as justified for the protection of public order pursuant to Art 10 (2) ECHR (see the judgment of the ECtHR of 10 July 2008, in the case of *Soulas et autres v France*, No 15.948/03, MN 48).

The constitutional provision of Article 9 State Treaty of Vienna, Federal Law Gazette No 152/1955 as amended by Federal Law Gazette No 164/1959 reads:

'Article 9

Dissolution of Nazi Organizations

1. Austria shall complete the measures, already begun by the enactment of appropriate legislation approved by the Allied Commission for Austria, to destroy the National Socialist Party and its affiliated and supervised organizations, including political, military and para-military organizations, on Austrian territory. Austria shall also continue the efforts to eliminate from Austrian political, economic and cultural life all traces of Nazism, to ensure that the above-mentioned organizations are not revived in any form, and to prevent all Nazi and militarist activity and propaganda in Austria.

2. Austria undertakes to dissolve all Fascist-type organizations existing on its territory, political, military and para-military, and likewise any other organizations carrying on activities hostile to any United Nation or which intend to deprive the people of their democratic rights.

3. Austria undertakes not to permit, under threat of penal punishment which shall be immediately determined in accordance with procedures established by Austrian

Law, the existence and the activity on Austrian territory of the above-mentioned organizations.'

The National Socialism Prohibition Act 1947, State Gazette 13/1945, as amended by Federal Law Gazette No 143/1992 which has the status of a federal constitutional law reads in excerpts:

'Sec 3g. Whoever performs an activity inspired by the National Socialist ideology that does not fall within the scope of § 3a to 3f will be punished with a prison sentence of between one and ten years or, if the perpetrator or the activity should pose a particularly grave danger, with a prison sentence of up to twenty years, unless the offence is subject to a more severe sanction under a different provision.

Sec 3h. In accordance with § 3g, anybody who denies, grossly minimises, approves or seeks to justify the National Socialist genocide or any other National Socialist crimes against humanity in a publication, a broadcasting medium or any other medium publicly and in any other manner accessible to a large number of people will also be punished.'

Art III(4) Introductory Act to the Administrative Procedure Acts 2008 – EGVG, Federal Law Gazette No 87 reads

'Article III(1) Persons who
...
4. disseminate national socialist-ideology as defined by the National Socialist Ideology Prohibition Act, National Law Gazette No. 13/1945, as amended by the Federal Constitution Act, Federal Law Gazette No. 25/1947, commit, with regard to the offence under sub-paras 3 or 4 only in cases not subject to a more stringent penalty according to other provisions on administrative offences, an administrative offence punishable by the district administration authority – in cases of sub-para 2 and 4 for areas of a municipality in which the Land police directorate simultaneously is security authority of first instance: by the Land police directorate – in cases of sub-para 1 and 2 by a fine of up-to 218 Euros, in cases of sub-para 3 a fine of up-to 1090 Euros, and in cases of sub-para 4 a fine of up-to 2180 Euros. In cases of sub-para 4, an attempt to commit the offence is punishable and objects used in committing the offence may be declared forfeited.'

The rejection and prohibition of National Socialism and of the dissemination of national socialist ideology are of fundamental importance for the re-establishment of the Republic of Austria after 1945 and the Austrian legal system. This objective clearly and unambiguously follows from the legal provisions described. Even though the appellant was not convicted under these provisions, the Supreme Administrative Court has no doubt that he put into question and violated the values enshrined in these provisions through his relativizing and trivializing statements.

The appellant's penalty under disciplinary law was also necessary to uphold these values, and thus for the protection of public order within the meaning of Art 10(2) ECHR, for the reasons accurately pointed out by the authorities of the first and second instance and, as a monetary penalty in amount of a monthly salary, was proportionate.

The appellant also considers the decision appealed against as unlawful, as the witnesses requested by him to prove that the reputation of the S-University had not been damaged through his statements have not been questioned. However, thereby the appellant does not demonstrate an unlawfulness of the decision appealed against, as the question whether the appellant's statements are suitable to damage the reputation of the S-University is a question of law.

By his submissions regarding the findings of the authority of second instance, the appellant does not demonstrate a lack of coherency in the assessment of evidence or a need for supplementation of the facts of the case.

The appellant considers the decision appealed against to be unlawful, because the senate of the authority of first instance (the disciplinary commission) decided on the decision of first instance in the same composition in which it had already decided on the motions of the appellant on lifting the interim suspension as well as on the discontinuation of the disciplinary proceedings.

Thereby the appellant does not point out an unlawfulness of the decision appealed against in the present case and no reason for recusal under Sec 7(1) General Administrative Procedure Act (*AVG*) with regard to the authority of first instance.

The reason for recusal in Sec 7(1) No 4 General Administrative Procedure Act (*AVG*),[1] according to which administrative officers shall abstain from exercising their office, if 'there are any other important reasons resulting in doubts as to them being fully unbiased', is to be interpreted and applied in light of Art 6(1) ECHR in this case (on the application of Art 6(1) ECHR on disciplinary proceedings regarding decisions on guilt and punishment see, *e.g.*, the decisions of this Court of 14 October 2011, Zl. 2008/09/0125).

For the assessment whether there is bias in this sense it is determinative whether a party to the proceedings has, in reasonable appreciation of all specific circumstances, reason to doubt the impartiality and objective attitude of the official (see the decision of this Court of 27 March 2012, 2009/10/0167). Under constitutional law, within the scope of application of Art 6 ECHR, the bias of a member of a tribunal is already then to be presumed, if the official lacks the appearance of impartiality (*Hengstschläger/Leeb*, AVG, Vol 1 2004 MN 14 on Sec 7 General Administrative Procedure Act (*AVG*), see the decision of this Court of 24 April 2014, Zl. 2013/09/0049), the impartiality may be examined from a subjective and an objective viewpoint (see *e.g.* the judgment of the ECtHR from 15 December 2005, *Kyprianou*, Zl. 73797/01, paras 118 ff).

---

[1] The Supreme Administrative Court apparently intended to refer to Sec 7(1) No 3 General Administrative Procedure Act (AVG).

The mere circumstance that a judge of first or second instance has issued decisions may by itself not substantiate a suspicion of bias. However, if a judge had already, for instance in decisions on pretrial detention or in an earlier stage of the proceedings, dealt with the guilt of the accused with a high degree of clarity and expressed an opinion thereon, that may in light of Art 6 (1) ECHR give rise to suspicion of bias in the decision on the merits themselves (see the judgments of the ECHR from 24 May 1989 in the Case *Hauschildt versus Denmark*, Series A No, 154, paras 49ff und from 22 July 2008 in the Case *Gomez de Liaño y Botella versus Spain*, No 21369/04, paras 67 ff).

According to the records, the disciplinary commission in the present case decided on the motion of the appellant on lifting his suspension on 13 February 2013, thus on the same day as on the decision in first instance and apparently subsequent to that decision. On 5 March 2012 the disciplinary commission has ordered the suspension of the appellant, while two members were part of the disciplinary commission who also took part in ruling on the disciplinary decision of first instance. In its decision on the suspension, the disciplinary commission also had to determine whether retaining the appellant in service 'would compromise the reputation of the position or substantial interests of the service due to the nature of the violation of official duties he or she is accused of' (Sec 112 (1) No 3 Civil Service Employment Act (*BDG*) as amended by Federal Law Gazette I No 120/2012). With their decision of 13 February 2013 it lifted the suspension of the appellant. No declarations on guilt and punishment are contained in these decisions, rather on the existence of a suspicion and the threat to interests of the service. Lifting the suspension was justified in the decision of 13 February 2013, as a further suspension was no longer justified as the suspicions are presently examined.

With decision of 3 December 2012, the disciplinary commission rejected a motion of the appellant to discontinue the disciplinary proceedings, reasoning that the suspicions mentioned in the opening decision remain valid also after the discontinuance of the criminal proceedings against the appellant. Also that decision contains no declaration on guilt and punishment.

Therefore the reasons to assume bias of members of the disciplinary commission when issuing the disciplinary decision of first instance, as invoked by the appellant, are not evident.

The appellant thus was not violated in his subjective public rights by the decision appealed against. The complaint was thus to be denied as unfounded in accordance with Sec 42(1) Administrative Court Act 1985 (*VwGG*).

[…]

German Original

Spruch

Die Beschwerde wird als unbegründet abgewiesen.

Der Beschwerdeführer hat dem Bund Aufwendungen in der Höhe von EUR 748,90 binnen zwei Wochen bei sonstiger Exekution zu ersetzen.

Begründung

Der im Jahr 1960 geborene Beschwerdeführer steht als a. o. Universitätsprofessor in einem öffentlich-rechtlichen Dienstverhältnis zum Bund und ist am Institut für R-Wesen an der S-Universität in N (Anonymisierungen durch den Verwaltungsgerichtshof) tätig.

Mit Bescheid der Disziplinarkommission beim Bundesministerium für Wissenschaft und Forschung vom 13. Februar 2013 wurde der Beschwerdeführer nach Durchführung einer mündlichen Verhandlung wie folgt für schuldig erkannt:

„1. b.) *Der Beschwerdeführer* ist schuldig, gegenüber den Studierenden MN, SR und SG sinngemäß folgende Aussagen getätigt zu haben: ,Die Frage des Genozids zur Zeit des Nationalsozialismus ist nicht endgültig geklärt, weil es noch keine objektive und ideologiefreie Diskussion über diese Frage gegeben hat. In einigen historischen Büchern steht eine Meinung, in anderen eine gegenteilige. Ich kann die Geschehnisse zur Zeit des Nationalsozialismus nicht beurteilen, weil ich nicht dabei gewesen bin. Ich möchte aber die Ereignisse keinesfalls schönreden.'

Er hat dadurch vorsätzlich gegen § 43 Abs 2 BDG verstoßen und dadurch eine Dienstpflichtverletzung im Sinn des § 91 BDG begangen.

1. c.) *Der Beschwerdeführer* ist schuldig, gegenüber den Studierenden MN, SR und SG sinngemäß folgende Aussagen getätigt zu haben: ,Es kommt zu einem Missbrauch des Antisemitismusbegriffs: nicht-religiöse Juden, die aufgrund ihrer ausbeuterischen Geschäftstätigkeit kritisiert werden, verteidigen sich mit dem Antisemitismus-Argument. Dieser Missbrauch ist teilweise auch der Grund für den massenweisen Mord an gläubigen Juden in der Vergangenheit. Die wirklich gläubigen Juden setzen sich der Geschäftemacherei mit dem Zinseszins entgegen.'

Er hat dadurch im Kontext seiner übrigen verfahrensgegenständlichen Äußerungen vorsätzlich gegen § 43 Abs 2 BDG verstoßen und dadurch eine Dienstpflichtverletzung im Sinn des § 91 BDG begangen.

1. d.) *Der Beschwerdeführer* ist schuldig, gegenüber den Studierenden MN, SR und SG sinngemäß folgende Aussagen getätigt zu haben: ,Wenn ein von Nationalsozialisten ausgeübter Genozid diskutiert wird, sollte der gegenwärtig stattfindende Genozid der USA ebenso diskutiert werden. Ich kann die Frage,

ob es während der Zeit des Nationalsozialismus Gaskammern gegeben hat, nicht beantworten. Die Geschehnisse sind schon zu lange vergangen; ich bin nicht dabei gewesen. Ich habe keine Meinung zu Gaskammern. Es ist angesichts der viel dringender aktuelleren Probleme wichtiger, sich mit der Zukunft anstatt mit der Vergangenheit zu befassen.' Bezüglich der vorherrschenden Mängel der Wissensgesellschaft hat er auf das Beispiel eines Technikers verwiesen, der aufzeigen wollte, dass Gaskammern technisch nicht funktioniert haben können. Dies habe sehr viel Aufsehen erregt. ‚In einer solchen Situation sollte die Sache objektiv geprüft werden und nicht mit der Begründung abgetan werden können, dass gegen ein Gesetz verstoßen wird. So etwas solle offen diskutiert und gegebenenfalls auch widerlegt werden können.'

Er hat dadurch vorsätzlich gegen § 43 Abs 2 BDG verstoßen und dadurch eine Dienstpflichtverletzung im Sinn des § 91 BDG begangen.

2.) *Der Beschwerdeführer* ist schuldig, in einem Telefongespräch mit Mag. TM, das einen Artikel im S. (eine Tageszeitung) vorbereiten sollte, die Aussagen ‚Es macht keinen Sinn, aus heutiger Perspektive darüber zu reden' und ‚Wie definieren Sie Objektivität? Alles, was wir haben, sind Gebäudereste, Fotos und Beschreibungen.' - beides bezogen auf den Holocaust - getätigt zu haben.

Er hat dadurch vorsätzlich gegen § 43 Abs 2 BDG verstoßen und dadurch eine Dienstpflichtverletzung im Sinn des § 91 BDG begangen.

3.) *Der Beschwerdeführer* ist schuldig, in der Aussendung an den S. (eine Tageszeitung) am 26.1.2012 seine Thesen zum Wissen erneut anhand der Massenvernichtungslager vorgetragen zu haben, indem er ausgeführt hat: ‚Als Experte für Wissensmanagement und Wissenschaftstheorie, der in diesem Bereich lehrt und forscht und mehrere internationale Publikationen vorweisen kann, vertrete ich einen originären Wissensbegriff.

Danach existieren zwei Arten von Wissen: 1) Fachwissen, welches durch Aufstellung, Überprüfung und Widerlegung von Theorien durch dazu ausgebildete Wissenschaftler entsteht sowie

2) Erlebniswissen, welches durch persönliche Teilnahme an Ereignissen und ihre Interpretation vor dem Hintergrund der subjektiven Lebenserfahrung entsteht. Durch das Lesen von Büchern und Hören von Berichten und Vorträgen durch fachliche Laien entsteht in diesem Sinne kein Wissen sondern Glaube. Vor dem Hintergrund dieser Wissensdefinition muss ich die Aussage ‚Ich weiß, dass unter dem verbrecherischen Regime des 3. Reichs Massenvernichtungslager betrieben wurden' aus rein logischen Gründen ablehnen, da ich weder Historiker bin (Fachwissen) noch Zeitzeuge (Erlebniswissen). Der Aussage ‚Wir wissen, dass unter dem verbrecherischen Regime des 3. Reichs Massenvernichtungslager betrieben wurden' stimme ich hingegen zu, da dieses ‚wir', auf die gesamte Gesellschaft bezogen, auch die Fachexperten (Historiker) sowie Zeitzeugen

umfasst. Auch der Aussage ‚Ich glaube, dass unter dem verbrecherischen Regime des 3. Reichs Massenvernichtungslager betrieben wurden' stimme ich zu, da ich sowohl den Aussagen der Fachexperten (Historiker) als auch der diesbezüglichen Zeitzeugen vertraue.'

Er hat dadurch vorsätzlich gegen § 43 Abs 2 BDG verstoßen und dadurch eine Dienstpflichtverletzung im Sinn des § 91 BDG begangen.
...

Aufgrund der in den Punkten 1.b., 1.c., 1.d., 2. und 3. erfolgten Schuldsprüche wird über den Beschuldigten gemäß § 92 Abs 1 Z 3 BDG in Verbindung mit § 126 Abs 2 BDG eine Geldstrafe in der Höhe von einem Monatsbezug unter Ausschluss des Kinderzuschusses verhängt."

Die Behörde erster Instanz begründete ihren Bescheid zusammengefasst damit, dass sie ihre Feststellungen auf die in der mündlichen Verhandlung gemachten Aussagen des Beschwerdeführers und der Zeugen SG, MN und SR sowie auf ein von diesen drei Zeugen erstelltes Protokoll der Aussagen des Beschwerdeführers gestützt habe. Zwar habe der Beschwerdeführer ausgeführt, die ihm vorgeworfenen Aussagen nicht als eigene Meinung geäußert zu haben, sondern sie nur als metasprachliche Aussagen verwendet zu haben, demgegenüber hätten die Zeugen jedoch übereinstimmend überzeugend ausgesagt, dass sie den Eindruck gehabt hätten, die im Spruch genannten Aussagen seien die Meinung des Beschwerdeführers. Der Beschwerdeführer habe seine ihm von den Zeugen per E-Mail nach dem Interview übermittelten Aussagen auch nicht bestritten. Ähnliches gelte hinsichtlich der Aussagen des Beschwerdeführers gegenüber einem Journalisten des S, der ebenfalls in der mündlichen Verhandlung einvernommen worden sei.

Die Behörde erster Instanz führte aus, dass der Beschwerdeführer durch seine in den Spruchpunkten 1. b.), 1. c.),

1. d.), 2.) und 3.) vorgeworfenen Aussagen eine Dienstpflichtverletzung gemäß § 43 Abs. 2 BDG 1979 begangen habe. Das im Verfassungsrang stehende Verbotsgesetz gehöre zu den wesentlichen Bestandteilen der österreichischen Rechtsordnung. Es gehöre zu den Dienstpflichten des Beamten, jedenfalls im Zusammenhang mit dem Dienst öffentliche Stellungnahmen zu vermeiden, welche die Wertungsgrundlagen des Verbotsgesetzes in Frage stellen, also den Holocaust und die Existenz von Gaskammern als historisches Faktum zu leugnen. Diese Pflicht gelte im besonderen Maße für Beamte, welche in Erziehung und Ausbildung tätig sind, wie Universitätslehrer, weil diesen die Ausbildung von Studierenden anvertraut sei. Von diesen sei daher in erhöhtem Maße zumindest Zurückhaltung bei Äußerungen gefordert, welche die genannte Faktengrundlage und damit die Erinnerung an die Opfer des Holocaust in Zweifel zögen. Diese Pflicht bestehe auch im Zusammenhang mit Aussagen zur Möglichkeit von Wissen und Erkenntnis und Bezug auf die Vergangenheit. Der durch die Diszi-

plinierung des Beschwerdeführers bewirkte Eingriff in die Meinungsfreiheit des Beschwerdeführers sei gemäß Art. 10 Abs. 2 EMRK gerechtfertigt (die Behörde erster Instanz zitierte ausführlich Rechtsprechung des Europäischen Gerichtshofs für Menschenrechte, etwa das Urteil vom 23. September 1998 im Fall Lehideux und Isorni gegen Frankreich, Zl. 55/1997/839/1045).

Der Beschwerdeführer erhob gegen dieses Disziplinarerkenntnis Berufung, in welcher er im Wesentlichen ausführte, dass seine disziplinarrechtliche Verfolgung auf Grund der ihm vorgeworfenen Aussagen gemäß Art. 17 StGG und Art. 10 EMRK unzulässig sei. Der Beschwerdeführer machte weiters als Verfahrensmangel geltend, dass jene drei Mitglieder des erkennenden Senates der Behörde erster Instanz im Hinblick darauf befangen gewesen seien, als sie bereits an einer Entscheidung über seine Suspendierung wegen derselben Vorwürfe mitgewirkt hätten. Weiters bestritt der Beschwerdeführer die ihm vorgeworfenen Aussagen als eigene Aussagen getan zu haben und beantragte zum Beweis dafür die Befragung von weiteren Zeugen.

Mit dem angefochtenen Bescheid der belangten Behörde wurde der Berufung keine Folge gegeben und das angefochtene Disziplinarerkenntnis sowohl hinsichtlich Schuld als auch hinsichtlich Strafe bestätigt.

Der angefochtene Bescheid wurde im Wesentlichen damit begründet, dass der Beschwerdeführer nicht bestritten habe, das in Rede stehende Interview mit den im Schuldspruch namentlich angeführten Studierenden geführt zu haben und dass er den wiedergegebenen, ihm spruchgemäß zur Last gelegten einzelnen Aussagen auch nicht substanziell entgegen trete. In der Berufung bringe er keine wesentlichen neuen Argumente von entsprechender rechtlicher Relevanz vor. Dem Beschwerdeführer seien die vorgeworfenen Aussagen als seine Aussagen in einem Mail am 11. Jänner 2012 zur Autorisierung zur Kenntnis gebracht worden, es wäre an ihm gelegen, in irgendeiner Form zu reagieren, der vorgelegten Dokumentation des Gesprächsinhaltes entgegenzutreten und seine darin wiedergegebenen Aussagen richtig zu stellen oder deren Richtigstellung zu verlangen bzw. aus seiner Sicht allfällig entstandene offensichtliche Irrtümer aufzuklären. Der Beschwerdeführer habe dies aber unterlassen. Er habe es auch unterlassen, dem Journalisten der Tageszeitung S gegenüber auf dessen E-Mail vom 25. Jänner 2012 zu reagieren und diesem eine Rückmeldung zukommen zu lassen. Auch in diesem Falle habe der Beschwerdeführer eine Korrektur der ihm zur Kenntnis gebrachten Mitschrift des Inhaltes des Telefongespräches nicht vorgenommen. Die vom Beschwerdeführer beantragten Zeugen hätten auch nach seinem eigenen Vorbringen das vom Beschwerdeführer mit den drei Studierenden am 21. Dezember 2011 geführte Interview nicht aus eigener unmittelbarer Wahrnehmung miterlebt und auch das Telefongespräch mit dem Journalisten Mag. TM nicht persönlich angehört. Daher sei die Einvernahme dieser Zeugen entbehrlich gewesen. Der Beschwerdeführer habe sich auch nicht für die Vorlage des Tonbandprotokolls des Interviews vom 21. Dezember 2011 ausgesprochen. Daher gehe die Disziplinaroberkommission davon aus, dass die dem Beschwerdeführer spruchgemäß angelasteten Aussagen von diesem in dieser Form tatsächlich getätigt worden seien.

Zwar habe die Staatsanwaltschaft ein nach dem Verbotsgesetz gegen den Beschwerdeführer anhängiges Strafverfahren eingestellt, weil nach der Rechtsprechung des OGH bei (allenfalls auch nur vorgetäuschter) persönlicher Unsicherheit hinsichtlich der Existenz von Gaskammern weder ein direktes noch ein indirektes Abstreiten bzw. Verneinen, wie es für die Verwirklichung des in Rede stehenden Tatbestandes durch Leugnen erforderlich ist, vorliege (14 Os 24/96). Damit sei jedoch noch keineswegs ausgeschlossen, dass dem Beschwerdeführer hinsichtlich des sachgleichen Sachverhalts schuldhaftes Verhalten gegen die ihm auferlegten Dienstpflichten zur Last liege, eine Bindungswirkung im Sinne des § 95 Abs. 2 BDG 1979 komme der Einstellung des Strafverfahrens durch die Staatsanwaltschaft nicht zu. Insbesondere die im Spruchpunkt 1. c.) inkriminierte ausschließlich Wertungen wiedergebende Äußerung des Beschwerdeführers, mit der ein Teil der Bevölkerung (im Speziellen jener mosaischen Bekenntnisses) herabgewürdigt und in ein schlechtes Licht gerückt werde oder werden solle, erinnere in erschreckender Weise an die hetzerische Diktion der nationalsozialistischen Propaganda-Maschinerie. Dies hätte dem Beschwerdeführer bereits als Staatsbürger und noch vielmehr als a. o. Professor an einer österreichischen Universität sehr wohl bewusst sein müssen. Die wiederholt getätigten sowohl mündlichen als auch schriftlichen Äußerungen in der Öffentlichkeit bzw. Halb-Öffentlichkeit durch den Beschwerdeführer, einen an einer österreichischen Universität forschenden und lehrenden außerordentlichen Universitätsprofessor, sei im Sinne der Bestimmung des § 43 Abs. 2 BDG 1979 die Eignung immanent, das Vertrauen nicht nur des übrigen akademischen Lehrkörpers, des universitären Mittelbaus und der Studierenden, sondern auch der außeruniversitären Öffentlichkeit in die Unparteilichkeit, die sachliche Wahrnehmung der dienstlichen Aufgaben durch ihn und insgesamt in die Ordnungsgemäßheit seiner Amtsführung ganz empfindlich zu beeinträchtigen, ja nachhaltig in Frage zu stellen. Dies könne nach Ansicht der erkennenden Behörde nicht ernsthaft in Zweifel gezogen werden. Die Ausführungen des Beschwerdeführers seien in ganz besonderer Weise geeignet, das Ansehen der Universität, an der er forsche und lehre, sowohl im Inland als auch im Ausland zu beschädigen.

Der bei Verstößen gegen die einschlägigen Beamtenpflichten (§ 43 Abs. 2 BDG 1979) von der Rechtsprechung geforderte Dienstbezug des inkriminierten Verhaltens liege hier fraglos schon deshalb vor, weil der Beschwerdeführer als Universitätsprofessor kraft seines Amtes mit der Durchführung von Lehrveranstaltungen und dem Abhalten von Prüfungen sowie mit der Betreuung von Studierenden, insbesondere Diplomanden und Dissertanten und des wissenschaftlichen Nachwuchses betraut sei (§ 165 BDG 1979). Dabei stehe er notwendigerweise in laufendem, wiederholtem, auch engerem fachlichen Kontakt mit zum weitaus überwiegenden Teil jungen bzw. jüngeren Menschen und habe er als Lehrer sowie als mit wissenschaftlicher Autorität ausgestattete Persönlichkeit bei von ihm vor Publikum getätigten Äußerungen bzw. für eine breitere Leserschaft bestimmten Aussagen - gerade im Zusammenhang mit der hier in Rede stehenden historischen Thematik - schon deshalb besondere Verantwortung und Sensibilität an den Tag zu legen.

Wenn der Beschwerdeführer in seiner Berufung vorbringe, er habe mit seinen mündlichen und schriftlichen Ausführungen nicht seine eigene persönliche Meinung zur Schreckensherrschaft der Nationalsozialisten und des Dritten Reiches zum Ausdruck gebracht und es stünden die von ihm getätigten Aussagen mit seiner Lehrtätigkeit im Bereich „Wissensmanagement" im Einklang, so müsse dem entgegnet werden, dass die Gesprächseinlassung durch den Beschwerdeführer nach der Bedeutung der von ihm bei seinen theoretischen Ausführungen gebrauchten Wortwahl sowohl isoliert als auch im Sinnzusammenhang durchaus geeignet sei, das durchschnittliche Verständnis von (Zeitungs) Lesern in Richtung eines Infragestellens, Bezweifelns bzw. Vermittelns von persönlichen Unsicherheiten in Bezug auf vollkommen gesichertes Wissen der Gesellschaft hinsichtlich der einschlägigen historischen Faktenlage auszulösen. Eine „neutrale" Haltung dem Dritten Reich und den darin verübten Verbrechen gegenüber könne es keinesfalls geben. Dies hätte dem Beschwerdeführer bewusst sein müssen. Der Beschwerdeführer könne daher mangelndes Verschulden auch mit seiner Verteidigung, er habe bloß „metasprachliche Aussagen" getätigt, nicht mit Erfolg geltend machen.

Die belangte Behörde zitierte aus der Rechtsprechung des Verfassungsgerichtshofes zur Frage der Zulässigkeit der Einschränkung der in Art. 17 StGG (Wissenschaftsfreiheit: zB VfSlg. 11.737/1988) und Art. 10 EMRK (Freiheit der Meinungsäußerung: zB VfSlg. 15.827/2000) verfassungsgesetzlich gewährleisteten Rechte.

Die belangte Behörde schloss sich der Beurteilung der Schwere der dem Beschwerdeführer vorgeworfenen Dienstpflichtverletzung als insgesamt überaus bedeutend an und wertete als erschwerend, dass sich der Beschwerdeführer öffentlich bzw. halb-öffentlich zu wiederholten Malen einschlägig geäußert habe und dass ihm kraft seiner dienstlichen Stellung und Funktion als außerordentlicher Universitätsprofessor besondere Verantwortung und Vorbildwirkung insbesondere gegenüber den Studierenden zukomme. Seine Unbescholtenheit in straf-, verwaltungs- und disziplinarrechtlicher Hinsicht wertete die belangte Behörde als strafmildernd, ebenso wie die Verfahrensdauer von nahezu einem Jahr. Der Beschwerdeführer habe Äußerungen getätigt, aus denen objektiv eine anzweifelnde, distanzierte oder unkritische Haltung gegenüber dem Nationalsozialismus unter dem von den Machthabern dieses Regimes verschuldeten unendlichen Leid einer namenlosen Zahl von Menschen zum Ausdruck komme. Er habe seine aus den gesetzlichen Bestimmungen folgende Pflicht, dem Ansehen der Universität, der er angehöre, nicht zu schaden, in gravierender Weise verletzt. Dem Beschwerdeführer müsse klar sein, dass er auf Grund seiner Stellung ein mediales Echo der Kritik und Ablehnung hervorrufen werde und dass auf diese Weise eine unnötige negative Erwähnung seiner Universität in der Öffentlichkeit bewirkt werden würde.

Was die spezialpräventive Funktion der Disziplinarstrafe betreffe, müsse festgestellt werden, dass auch noch aus der Berufung des Beschwerdeführers dessen Mangel an Einsicht in das disziplinäre Unrecht seines verfahrensgegenständlich wiederholten Fehlverhaltens hervorleuchte.

Von der beantragten Durchführung einer mündlichen Verhandlung durch die belangte Behörde habe gemäß § 125a Abs. 3 Z. 5 BDG 1979 Abstand genommen werden können, weil der Sachverhalt in den entscheidungswesentlichen Punkten klar sei bzw. unzweifelhaft feststehe und es der Beschwerdeführer vor der Erstinstanz unterlassen habe, auf präzise formulierte Fragen entsprechend konkrete, eindeutige Antworten zu geben.

Der Verwaltungsgerichtshof hat über die zunächst an den Verfassungsgerichtshof erhobene und von diesem mit Beschluss vom 6. Juni 2014, B 1343/2013-7, abgelehnte und dem Verwaltungsgerichtshof abgetretene Beschwerde erwogen:

Die nach dem 31. Dezember 2013 dem Verwaltungsgerichtshof abgetretene Beschwerde gilt analog § 4 VwGbk-ÜG (vgl. dazu die hg. Erkenntnisse und Beschlüsse vom 25. April 2014, Ro 2014/10/0029, vom 9. Mai 2014, Ro 2014/17/0052, vom 23. Mai 2014, Ro 2014/02/0082, und vom 17. Juni 2014, Ro 2014/04/0046, jeweils mit näherer Begründung) als Revision (Anmerkung: die Bezeichnung im Text erfolgt weiterhin als Beschwerde bzw. als Beschwerdeführer).

Der Beschwerdeführer hält den angefochtenen Bescheid deswegen für rechtswidrig, weil er lediglich seine fachliche Meinung anhand von politischen Beispielen geäußert habe, er lehne den Nationalsozialismus kompromisslos ab und habe dies gegenüber den Studenten und auch gegenüber den Journalisten mehrmals bekräftigt und dargelegt. Seine Äußerungen seien vor dem Hintergrund der Tatsache zu verstehen, dass er sich unter anderem mit der Wissenstheorie respektive dem Wissenschaftsmanagement befasst habe.

Damit zeigt der Beschwerdeführer nicht auf, dass die belangte Behörde die dem Beschwerdeführer vorgeworfenen Aussagen, auf unzutreffende oder fehlerhafte Weise festgestellt oder gewertet hätte oder dass die Feststellungen der belangten Behörde in einem mangelhaften Verfahren zustande gekommen wären. Die belangte Behörde hat ihre Feststellungen vielmehr auf nachvollziehbare und schlüssige Weise begründet. Es ist nicht rechtswidrig, wenn sie den Aussagen des Beschwerdeführers die Zielrichtung der Leugnung von Verbrechen des Nationalsozialismus beimaß und der Verantwortung des Beschwerdeführers nicht folgte, es habe sich dabei bloß um wertfreie Aussagen im Rahmen eines wissenschaftlichen Diskurses zum Thema Wissensmanagement gehandelt. Solche Aussagen durch einen Beamten stellen durchaus eine erhebliche Gefährdung von dienstlichen Interessen im Sinne der § 43 Abs. 1 und 2 BDG 1979 dar (vgl. die hg. Erkenntnisse vom 3. Juli 2000, Zl. 2000/09/0006, vom 5. September 2013, Zl. 2013/09/0114, vom 3. Oktober 2013, Zl. 2013/09/0077).

Sowohl die Behörde erster Instanz als auch die belangte Behörde haben auch ausführlich und zutreffend dargelegt, dass eine Verletzung des Beschwerdeführers in seinen Rechten auf Achtung der Freiheit der Wissenschaft und ihrer Lehre gemäß Art. 17 StGG sowie der Freiheit der Meinungsäußerung gemäß Art. 10 EMRK und zu verneinen ist. Unter dem Gesichtspunkt dieser Freiheiten erfolgte daher auch keine fehlerhafte Anwendung der dienstrechtlichen Vorschriften gegenüber dem Beschwerdeführer. Diesbezüglich kann auf die hg. Erkenntnisse vom 3. Juli 2000, Zl. 2000/09/0006, vom 5. September 2013, Zl. 2013/09/0114, vom 3. Oktober 2013, Zl. 2013/09/0077, auf die vom Verfassungsgerichtshof zitierte Rechtsprechung, insbesondere auf dessen Erkenntnis VfSlg. 18.405/2008 sowie auf die Rechtsprechung des Europäischen Gerichtshofes für Menschenrechte etwa im Urteil vom 23. September 1998 im Fall Lehideux and Isorni gegen Frankreich, 55/1997/839/1045, par 47 ff; und dessen Entscheidung vom 24. Juni 2003 im Fall Garaudy gegen Frankreich, Nr. 65831/01, hingewiesen werden. Auch wenn man im vorliegenden Fall nicht von einer Verwirkung des Rechts nach Art. 10 EMRK im Sinne des Art. 17 EMRK ausgeht, durfte der durch den angefochtenen Bescheid bewirkte Eingriff gemäß Art. 10 Abs. 2 EMRK zur Aufrechterhaltung der Ordnung als gerechtfertigt angesehen werden (vgl. das Urteil des EGMR vom 10. Juli 2008, im Fall Soulas et autres gegen Frankreich, Nr. 15.948/03, RdNr. 48).

Die Verfassungsbestimmung der Artikel 9 des Staatsvertrages von Wien, BGBl. Nr. 152/1955, idF BGBl. Nr. 164/1959, lautet:

„Artikel 9.

Auflösung nazistischer Organisationen

1. Österreich wird die bereits durch die Erlassung entsprechender und von der Alliierten Kommission für Österreich genehmigter Gesetze begonnenen Maßnahmen zur Auflösung der nationalsozialistischen Partei und der ihr angegliederten und von ihr kontrollierten Organisationen einschließlich der politischen, militärischen und paramilitärischen auf österreichischem Gebiet vollenden. Österreich wird auch die Bemühungen fortsetzen, aus dem österreichischen politischen, wirtschaftlichen und kulturellen Leben alle Spuren des Nazismus zu entfernen, um zu gewährleisten, daß die obgenannten Organisationen nicht in irgendeiner Form wieder ins Leben gerufen

werden, und um alle nazistische oder militaristische Tätigkeit und Propaganda in Österreich zu verhindern.

2. Österreich verpflichtet sich, alle Organisationen faschistischen Charakters aufzulösen, die auf seinem Gebiete bestehen, und zwar sowohl politische, militärische und paramilitärische, als auch alle anderen Organisationen, welche eine irgendeiner der Vereinten Nationen feindliche Tätigkeit entfalten oder welche die Bevölkerung ihrer demokratischen Rechte zu berauben bestrebt sind.

3. Österreich verpflichtet sich, unter der Androhung von Strafsanktionen, die umgehend in Übereinstimmung mit den österreichischen Rechtsvorschriften festzulegen sind, das Bestehen und die Tätigkeit der obgenannten Organisationen auf österreichischem Gebiete zu untersagen."

Das im Rang eines Bundesverfassungsgesetzes stehende Verbotsgesetz, StGBl. 13/1945, idF BGBl. Nr. 148/1992, lautet auszugsweise:

„§ 3g. Wer sich auf andere als die in den §§ 3a bis 3f bezeichnete Weise im nationalsozialistischen Sinn betätigt, wird, sofern die Tat nicht nach einer anderen Bestimmung strenger strafbar ist, mit Freiheitsstrafe von einem bis zu zehn Jahren, bei besonderer Gefährlichkeit des Täters oder der Betätigung bis zu 20 Jahren bestraft.

§ 3h. Nach § 3g wird auch bestraft, wer in einem Druckwerk, im Rundfunk oder in einem anderen Medium oder wer sonst öffentlich auf eine Weise, daß es vielen Menschen zugänglich wird, den nationalsozialistischen Völkermord oder andere nationalsozialistische Verbrechen gegen die Menschlichkeit leugnet, gröblich verharmlost, gutheißt oder zu rechtfertigen sucht."

Art. III Z 4 Einführungsgesetz zu den Verwaltungsverfahrensgesetzen 2008, EGVG, BGBl. Nr. 87, lautet:

„Artikel III (1) Wer

...

4. nationalsozialistisches Gedankengut im Sinne des Verbotsgesetzes, StGBl. Nr. 13/1945, in der Fassung des Bundesverfassungsgesetzes BGBl. Nr. 25/1947, verbreitet, begeht, in den Fällen der Z 3 oder 4 dann, wenn die Tat nicht nach anderen Verwaltungsstrafbestimmungen mit strengerer Strafe bedroht ist, eine Verwaltungsübertretung und ist von der Bezirksverwaltungsbehörde, in den Fällen der Z 2 und 4 für das Gebiet einer Gemeinde, für das die Landespolizeidirektion zugleich Sicherheitsbehörde erster Instanz ist, von der Landespolizeidirektion, in den Fällen der Z 1 und 2 mit einer Geldstrafe von bis zu 218 Euro, im Fall der Z 3 mit einer Geldstrafe von bis zu 1 090 Euro und im Fall der Z 4 mit einer Geldstrafe von bis zu 2 180 Euro zu bestrafen. Im Fall der Z 4 ist der Versuch strafbar und können Gegenstände, mit denen die strafbare Handlung begangen wurde, für verfallen erklärt werden."

Die Ablehnung und das Verbot des Nationalsozialismus und der Verbreitung von nationalsozialistischem Gedankengut sind für das Wiedererstehen der Republik Österreich ab 1945 und die österreichische Rechtsordnung von wesentlicher Bedeutung. Diese Zielsetzung geht aus den dargestellten Rechtsvorschriften klar und eindeutig hervor. Auch wenn der Beschwerdeführer nicht nach den angeführten Bestimmungen bestraft worden ist, so besteht für den Verwaltungsgerichtshof kein Zweifel, dass er durch seine relativierenden und verharmlosenden Äußerungen gerade die in diesen Vorschriften zum Ausdruck kommenden Werte in Frage gestellt und verletzt hat.

Die disziplinarrechtliche Bestrafung des Beschwerdeführers war auch zur Aufrechterhaltung dieser Werte und damit zum Schutz der Ordnung im Sinne des Art. 10 Abs. 2 EMRK aus den von den Behörden erster und zweiter Instanz zutreffend angeführten Gründen erforderlich und in Form der Verhängung der Geldstrafe in der Höhe eines Monatsbezuges angemessen.

Der Beschwerdeführer hält den angefochtenen Bescheid auch deswegen für rechtswidrig, weil von ihm zum Beweis dafür beantragte Zeugen, dass durch seine Aussagen das Ansehen der S-Universität nicht geschädigt worden sei, nicht befragt worden seien. Damit zeigt der Beschwerdeführer eine Rechtswidrigkeit des angefochtenen Bescheides jedoch nicht auf, weil die Frage der Eignung der Äußerungen des Beschwerdeführers zur Schädigung des Ansehens der S-Universität eine Rechtsfrage ist.

Mit seinem Vorbringen gegen die Feststellungen der belangten Behörde zeigt der Beschwerdeführer eine Unschlüssigkeit der Beweiswürdigung oder eine Ergänzungsbedürftigkeit des Sachverhaltes nicht auf.

Der Beschwerdeführer erblickt eine Rechtswidrigkeit des angefochtenen Bescheides darin, dass der Senat der Behörde erster Instanz (der Disziplinarkommission) in derselben Zusammensetzung über den erstinstanzlichen Bescheid befunden habe, in welcher er bereits über die Anträge des Beschwerdeführers auf Aufhebung der vorläufigen Suspendierung sowie auf Einstellung des Disziplinarverfahrens entschieden habe.

Damit zeigt der Beschwerdeführer im vorliegenden Fall keine Rechtswidrigkeit des angefochtenen Bescheides und keinen Befangenheitsgrund des § 7 Abs. 1 AVG hinsichtlich der erstinstanzlichen Behörde auf.

Der Befangenheitsgrund des § 7 Abs. 1 Z 4 AVG, wonach sich Verwaltungsorgane der Ausübung ihres Amtes zu enthalten haben, wenn „sonstige wichtige Gründe vorliegen, die geeignet sind, ihre volle Unbefangenheit in Zweifel zu ziehen", ist hier im Lichte des Art. 6 Abs. 1 EMRK auszulegen und anzuwenden (zur Anwendung des Art. 6 Abs. 1 EMRK auf Verfahren zu Entscheidungen über die disziplinarrechtliche Schuld und Strafe vgl. etwa die hg. Erkenntnisse vom 14. Oktober 2011, Zl. 2008/09/0125).

Für die Beurteilung, ob eine Befangenheit in diesem Sinne vorliegt, ist maßgebend, ob ein am Verfahren Beteiligter bei vernünftiger Würdigung aller konkreten Umstände Anlass hat, an der Unvoreingenommenheit und objektiven Einstellung des Organwalters zu zweifeln (vgl. das hg. Erkenntnis vom 27. März 2012, 2009/10/0167). Im Anwendungsbereich des Art. 6 EMRK ist die Befangenheit eines Mitglieds eines Tribunals in verfassungskonformer Weise dann anzunehmen, wenn einem Organwalter auch nur der äußere Anschein der Unparteilichkeit mangelt (Hengstschläger/Leeb, AVG, 1. Teilband 2004 RZ 14 zu § 7 AVG, vgl. das hg. Erkenntnis vom 24. April 2014, Zl. 2013/09/0049), die Unparteilichkeit kann in subjektiver und in objektiver Hinsicht betrachtet werden (vgl. zB das Urteil des EGMR vom 15. Dezember 2005, Kyprianou, Zl. 73797/01, par. 118 ff).

Der bloße Umstand, dass ein Richter erster oder zweiter Instanz Entscheidungen getroffen hat, kann zwar für sich allein die Annahme einer Befangenheit nicht begründen. Hat sich ein Richter jedoch etwa in Entscheidungen über die Untersuchungshaft oder in einem früheren Verfahrensstadium bereits mit hoher Klarheit mit der Schuld des Beschuldigten auseinander gesetzt und darüber eine Meinung geäußert, so kann dies am Maßstab des Art. 6 Abs. 1 EMRK als Grund für die Annahme seiner Befangenheit bei der Entscheidung in der Sache selbst gesehen werden (vgl. etwa die Urteile des EGMR vom 24. Mai 1989 im Fall Hauschildt gegen Dänemark, Serie A Nr. 154, par. 49ff und vom 22. Juli 2008, im Fall Gomez de Liaño y Botella gegen Spanien, Nr. 21369/04, par. 67 ff).

Im vorliegenden Fall hat die Disziplinarkommission nach der Aktenlage über den Antrag des Beschwerdeführers auf Aufhebung seiner Suspendierung am 13. Februar 2013, sohin am selben Tag wie über den Bescheid erster Instanz und offensichtlich nach dieser Entscheidung entschieden. Am 5. März 2012 hatte die Disziplinarkommission die Suspendierung des Beschwerdeführers verfügt, dabei hatten der Disziplinarkommission zwei Mitglieder angehört, die auch an der Entscheidung über das Disziplinarerkenntnis erster Instanz teilnahmen. Bei ihren Entscheidungen über die Suspendierung hatte die Disziplinarkommission darüber zu befinden, ob durch die Belassung des Beschwerdeführers im Dienst „wegen der Art der ihm oder ihr zur Last gelegten Dienstpflichtverletzungen das Ansehen des Amtes oder wesentliche Interessen des Dienstes gefährdet würden" (§ 112 Abs. 1 Z 3 BDG 1979 idF BGBl. I Nr. 120/2012). Mit ihrer Entscheidung am 13. Februar 2013 hat sie die Suspendierung des Beschwerdeführers aufgehoben. Aussagen über Schuld und Strafe sind in diesen Entscheidungen nicht enthalten, vielmehr über das Vorliegen eines Verdachtes und die Gefährdung dienstlicher Interessen. In der Entscheidung vom 13. Februar 2013 wird die Aufhebung der Suspendierung damit begründet, dass die weitere Suspendierung angesichts der nunmehrigen Klärung der Verdachtsmomente nicht mehr gerechtfertigt sei.

Mit Bescheid vom 3. Dezember 2012 hat die Disziplinarkommission einen Antrag des Beschwerdeführers auf Einstellung des Disziplinarverfahrens abgewiesen und dies damit begründet, dass die im Einleitungsbeschluss angeführten Verdachtsmomente auch nach der Einstellung des Strafverfahrens gegen den Beschwerdeführer noch aufrecht seien. Auch in dieser Entscheidung ist eine Aussage über die Schuld und Strafe nicht enthalten.

Die vom Beschwerdeführer gerügten Gründe für die Annahme einer Befangenheit von Mitgliedern der Disziplinarkommission bei Erlassung des Disziplinarerkenntnisses erster Instanz sind daher nicht zu ersehen.

Der Beschwerdeführer wurde durch den angefochtenen Bescheid sohin nicht in seinen subjektiv-öffentlichen Rechten verletzt. Die Beschwerde war daher gemäß § 42 Abs. 1 VwGG als unbegründet abzuweisen.

Die Kostenentscheidung beruht auf §§ 47 ff VwGG iVm der VwGH-Aufwandersatzverordnung 2014.

HH. Jurisdiction of the state/Jurisdiktion (Hoheitsgewalt)

II. Types of jurisdiction/Arten der Jurisdiktion

2. Jurisdiction to adjudicate/Urteilsjurisdiktion

HH.II.2.

Supreme Court, Decision 8Ob28/15y of 24 March 2015

Oberster Gerichtshof, Beschluss 8Ob28/15y, vom 24. März 2015

Keywords

Bilateral enforcement agreement between Austria and Turkey – (partial) recognition (by analogy) of foreign court decisions – *ordre public* – right to be heard – contestation of legitimacy – nullification of paternity – *res judicata* – jurisdiction to adjudicate

Bilaterales Vollstreckungsabkommen zwischen Österreich und der Türkei – (Teil-)Anerkennung gesonderter Spruchpunkte von Entscheidungen ausländischer Gerichte (per Analogie) – ordre public – rechtliches Gehör – Ehelichkeitsbestreitung – Aufhebung der Abstammung – Grundsatz der entschiedenen Rechtssache – internationale Zuständigkeit

Facts and procedural history (summary)

The petitioner was born out of wedlock on ***** in *****. She and her mother are Turkish citizens. In 1983, the mother of the petitioner married a Turkish national, who soon after ensured that he would be be listed as the father of the petitioner in her personal status.

R***** T*****, the legal predecessor of the opponent, passed away on *****. The estate of the deceased has since passed to his successor. The baptismal certificate issued by the parish office of *****, lists "R***** T*****" as the father of the petitioner, but such paternity was never acknowledged by him.

In the case at hand, on 18 September 2012, the petitioner filed for a declaratory judgment seeking determination on the parentage of R***** T*****. Later, on 12 July, 2013, she contested the paternity of her mother's husband before the Civil Court of Cesme [Turkey]. By (final and enforceable) judgment of 23 August, 2013, that court determined that the actual father of the petitioner was, in fact, R***** T***** and nullified the parentage of the Turkish husband of the petitioner's mother. Although both the mother and legal father of the petitioner (husband of the petitioner's mother), were parties to these Turkish proceedings, the opponent of the present proceedings was neither notified of nor included in them.

In the present case, the petitioner argued that she was the biological daughter of the opponent's legal predecessor, given that he had been listed as her father in her baptismal certificate and various other personal documents. She claimed that her mother's husband had only provided her with his name, to avoid her being excluded from Turkish society as a fatherless child. A medical expert opinion since issued, so she argued, had removed all doubt.

The opponent argued that there were several reasons to doubt the veracity of this claim, not least the lack of an acknowledgment of paternity by his legal predecessor. He also had never attained knowledge of the proceedings in Turkey.

The court of first instance rejected the original petition seeking acknowledgment of paternity. It reasoned that the judgment of the Turkish court had no effect in Austria, given that it had not been (formally) recognized and the opponent had not been included in the relevant proceedings. Additionally, any determination of paternity would necessarily be subject to Turkish law, which, so the court, would permit no such action, considering the appropriate statute of limitations.

The appellate court granted the petitioner's appeal and recognized the parentage of R***** T*****. It determined that the Turkish court had, in fact, enjoyed jurisdiction and its decision, whereby paternity had been nullified, was subject to *ipso jure* recognition in Austria. That ruling further caused no incompatibility with domestic or foreign determinations of personal status, or an infringement upon *ordre public*. The appellate court did, however, hold that the Turkish judgment was not legally binding insofar as it recognized paternity of R***** T*****, given that the opponent in the present proceedings had not been included in the Turkish ones. As a result, it was Austrian courts that enjoyed jurisdiction over determinations paternity. The law applicable to that issue turned on the nationality of the petitioner, meaning that an Austrian court was competent to rule on paternity pursuant to a Turkish statute. The applicable Turkish Civil Code stipulated a time limit of one year from birth for such decisions. Where a child had, however, previously legally had a father, that period would commence with nullification of parentage. As a result, in the case at hand that period had begun on 28 August 2013, the date the decision of the Turkish court had become final and binding. The relevant paternity petition had therefore been submitted on time and findings had shown that the legal predecessor of the opponent had indeed been the biological father of the petitioner. An appeal to the Supreme Court was therefore considered justified, given that the Court had never ruled on the relationship between recognition of a Turkish paternity decision and the Austrian procedural norm invoked by the opponent.

It is this decision that has been challenged by the opponent, who now seeks restoration of the dismissive ruling at first instance and reevaluation of costs. The petitioner and her mother request that such challenge be thrown out or rejected on the merits.

The Supreme Court held

Contrary to the finding of the appellate court, which is not binding upon the Supreme Court, the present appeal is, in fact, inadmissible, given the lack of a requisite hitherto unclarified point of law essential to the decision at hand and requiring Supreme Court determination as envisaged by Section 62 (1) Non-Contentious Matters Act [Außerstreitgesetz, AußStrG].

1. The opponent's reference to Section 84 AußStrG is inexpedient. That provision regulates the consolidation of multiple proceedings concerning the paternity of a particular child. Such consolidation would require, among other things, that one and the same court were competent both *ratione loci* and *materiae* pursuant to Section 108 Jurisdiction Act [Jurisdiktionsnorm, JN] (*DeixlerHübner* in *Rechberger*, AußStrG² § 84 MN 1). This includes international jurisdiction.

In the case at hand, the opponent himself acknowledges that the Turkish court did, in fact, enjoy international jurisdiction for the purpose of nullifying the paternity of the mother's husband.

2.1 The decision of the Turkish court determines both that the petitioner is not the daughter of her mother's husband (contestation of legitimacy) and that she is, in fact, the daughter of the legal predecessor of the opponent in the present proceedings.

Both case-law and academic literature recognize the admissibility of partial recognition, for instance, where a divorce decree issued by a foreign court includes further dicta (RISJustiz RS0121413; *Neumayr* in *Burgstaller/Neumayr/ Geroldinger/Schmaranzer*, Internationales Zivilverfahrensrecht § 97 AußStrG MN 16). Partial recognitions of decisions concerning parental contact are another case in point (*Schütz* in *Burgstaller/Neumayr/Geroldinger/Schmaranzer*, l.c., Art 30 ESÜ, MN 31).

The agreement applicable in the case at hand is the Treaty of 23 May 1989 Between the Republic of Austria and the Republic of Turkey on the Recognition and Enforcement of Judicial Decisions and Settlements in Civil and Commercial Matters (bilateral enforcement agreement). Pursuant to Article 7 of the Treaty, matrimonial and other concerns of family status are equated, which constitutes a logical consequence of the relatedness of such status matters. As a result, in the context of matters of parentage (as matters governing the status of children), partial recognition of a foreign judicial decisions is admissible, where separable claims are adjudged and thus declared upon in distinct dicta.

2.2 Here, these requirements are fulfilled. Distinct decisions on the nullification of paternity of the mother's husband and determination of the paternity of the biological father are admissible both under Austrian (Section 151 of the Austrian Civil Code [Allgemeines Bürgerliches Gesetzbuch, ABGB]) and Turkish law (Article 287 of the Turkish Civil Code).

3.1 The opponent argues that Austrian proceedings do not permit the implicit, in the sense of without a relevant and specific petition, recognition of the Turkish decision.

Under consideration of the case-law of the Supreme Court that assertion does not appear tenable.

3.2 Jurisprudence has shown that the principle of *res judicata* also applies in an international context and that violations of final and enforceable foreign decisions subject to recognition in Austria, are to be treated as having occurred in absence of domestic jurisdiction (6 Ob 96/11b with further references). As a result, decisions of foreign courts subject to recognition in Austria are legally binding and to be heeded *ex officio* (2 Ob 238/13h with further references).

3.3 The AußStrG, as amended, contains explicit rules on the recognition of foreign decisions in Sections 97 ff (decisions on the dissolution of marriage), Sections 112 ff (custody and contact rights) and Sections 91a ff (adoption). The Brussels IIA Regulation and other applicable treaties governing recognition and enforcement enjoy primacy.

As previously mentioned, the bilateral enforcement agreement concluded between Austria and Turkey applies. Pursuant to Article 11 (1) of the Treaty, recognition is governed by the law of the requested State, meaning Austrian law in the present case.

The admissibility of analogies derived from the AußStrG in the context of recognition of foreign decisions has long been recognized in Austrian law (1 Ob 190/03b on a Greek adoption; 6 Ob 170/04z on an Indian Adoption;

1 Ob 21/04a on a Chinese Adoption). The Supreme Court has already clarified that the provisions on recognition contained in Sections 91a ff AußStrG - which were introduced with the Family Law Amendment Act 2009 [Familienrechtsänderungsgesetz, FamRÄG 2009], Federal Law Gazette I 2009/75, effective from 1 January 2010, for the purpose of recognizing foreign adoption decisions and based on Sections 97 ff AußStrG (foreign matrimonial decisions) and Sections 112 ff AußStrG (foreign custody decisions) - constitute an appropriate basis for analogy with a view to recognition of foreign parentage decisions, given the relatedness of the subject matter considering that, similar to adoption, such matters [of parentage], govern the status of children (2 Ob 238/13h).

The procedural question (Article 11 (1) of the bilateral enforcement agreement), of whether or not an implicit evaluation of the recognizability of the parentage decision taken by the Turkish court were admissible, is thus governed by analogy to Sections 91a ff AußStrG.

3.4 Pursuant to the second sentence of Section 91a (1) AußStrG, recognition may autonomously be evaluated as a preliminary question without requiring distinct proceedings. With this provision, the principle of implicit recognition of final and enforceable foreign adoption decisions became enshrined in law (2 Ob 238/13h; see 6 Ob 96/11b on Section 97 (1) AußStrG). As a result of the appropriate analogy, this also applies to final and enforceable foreign decisions on the parentage of children.

4.1 In the case at hand, the recognizability of the decision taken by the Turkish court must be evaluated to determine whether or not that decision is legally binding. In absence of overriding norms of European Union law, such evaluation must be performed in application of relevant treaties, presently the bilateral enforcement agreement, and subsidiarily by analogy to Sections 91a ff AußStrG.

Pursuant to Article 3 of the bilateral enforcement agreement, decisions of the other contracting State must be recognized, insofar as they are both final and enforceable and taken by a competent court under Articles 6 to 9. According to Article 11 (1) of the bilateral enforcement agreement, competence in questions of matrimonial or family status is recognized, where the respondent (opponent) was a national, constant or habitual resident of that State at the time proceedings were initiated.

Under Article 4 (1) of the bilateral enforcement agreement, recognition may (among other reasons) be refused, where manifestly at odds with the *ordre public* of the requested State (Subparagraph a; see also Section 91a (2) AußStrG).

4.2 The opponent does not contest the existence of a foreign final and enforceable decision on parentage.

With respect to the decision of the Turkish court, its competence to nullify paternity of the mother's husband (contestation of legitimacy) is recognized pursuant to Article 7 (1) of the bilateral enforcement agreement.

4.3 An infringement upon *ordre public* requires that the application of foreign statutes result in a breach of fundamental values of the domestic legal order, which includes a sufficient domestic nexus (RISJustiz RS0110743; 3 Ob 186/11s). As an exception which is inconsistent with the legal order, an *ordre public*-clause merits especially sparing application (RISJustiz RS0077010). Mere inequity of a particular result or sheer contradiction of mandatory Austrian provisions will not suffice (6 Ob 138/13g). Rather, application of foreign norms must result in an unbearable infringement upon core fundamental values of the Austrian legal order (8 Ob 118/12d).

Procedural *ordre public* has the purpose of ensuring that parties enjoy the possibility of participating in proceedings (2 Ob 238/13h). Therefore, the right to be heard constitutes a particular manifestation of procedural *ordre public*. It has the purpose of protecting the respondent (opponent) from foreign decisions being passed without their participation. It must therefore be ensured that the respondent (opponent) has enjoyed the possibility of effectively participating in proceedings (6 Ob 96/11b on Section 97 (1) AußStrG).

4.4 With a view to the decision of the Turkish court on the contestation of legitimacy, no recognizable infringement upon *ordre public* has occured. In proceedings pertaining to nullification of paternity of a mother's husband (Section 151 ABGB), a possible biological father (and thus the opponent as legal successor) is, under Austria law too, not eligible to petition the court (*Hopf* in KBB4 §§ 151-153 ABGB, MN 3) and does not enjoy substantive party status (see *DeixlerHübner* in *Rechberger*, AußStrG² § 82 MN 9).

4.5 The recognizability of the Turkish decision on the contestation of the petitioner's legitimacy and thus the binding nature of that decision must therefore be affirmed as regards Austrian jurisdiction.

Any verification of the decision of the Turkish court now subject to recognition, in terms of whether or not it decided correctly, thus cannot occur in the context of Austrian (recognition) proceedings. In this regard, the opponent claims that the petitioner had submitted the relevant contestation of legitimacy after the pertinent statute of limitations had lapsed pursuant to Article 289 of the Turkish Civil Code. By relying on a statute of limitations, the opponent is precisely not invoking an infringement upon *ordre public* (see 6 Ob 559/95).

4.6 Insofar as the decision of the Turkish court contains a determination on the paternity of the legal predecessor of the opponent, recognition must, for one, be refused due to the fact that the Turkish court cannot be considered competent pursuant to Article 7 (1) of the bilateral enforcement agreement, considering that the opponent (the same would have applied to his legal predecessor) is neither a Turkish national nor a permanent or habitual resident of that State.

Additionally, an infringement upon procedural *ordre public* has occured, which merits refusing recognition of this decision taken by the Turkish court. The opponent was not included in the Turkish proceedings and thus did not participate in any stage of them. Pursuant to Section 82 (2) AußStrG, in the context of parentage proceedings, the relevant child, the person whose parentage can be constituted or nullified by such proceedings and the other parent of such child, insofar as that parent is alive and capable of sound judgment, are, in any event, parties to such proceedings (see also Section 148 (1) ABGB). Determination of paternity without heeding the right to be heard of the person affected or their legal successor as the case may be (see *DeixlerHübner* in *Rechberger*, AußStrG² § 82 MN 3), constitutes a breach of the right to be heard and thus the domestic *ordre public*. Naturally, it cannot be assumed that the opponent manifestly approves of the decision taken by the Turkish court, regarding the alleged paternity of their legal predecessor (see Subsection 2 of Section 91a (2) AußStrG).

4.7 Thus, recognition of the decision of the Turkish court, whereby the paternity of the legal predecessor of the opponent was determined, is excluded.

5. As a result, the appellate court was justified in assuming that a determination of parentage was at issue in the present proceedings.

In its submissions before the Supreme Court, the opponent did not contest the view taken by the appellate court, whereby Turkish law were applicable to the merits of this issue, the petitioner had (before an Austrian court) heeded the requisite term stipulated under Article 303 of the Turkish Civil Code and was, in fact, a descendant of the legal predecessor of the opponent.

6. The assertion advanced at this instance pertaining to pending legal action (Subparagraph b of Article 4 (1) of the bilateral enforcement agreement), could conceivably only refer to the question of determining paternity, given that contestation of legitimacy does not constitute an independent component of the proceedings conducted in Austria. Furthermore, considering the temporal sequence of the pertinent petitions, any assessment of whether or not legal action were pending, could only possibly refer to the Turkish proceedings. Recognition of the determination of paternity contained in the decision taken by the Turkish court, has, however, already been rejected on other grounds.

7. As a result, the decision of the appellate court does reflect the legal principles illustrated herein. Thus, no erroneous decision requiring correction was taken.

Given the lack of a requisite hitherto unclarified point of law essential to the decision at hand and requiring Supreme Court determination, the present appeal has been rejected.

The decision on costs reflects Sections 78, 83 (4) AußStrG in conjunction with Section 50 of the Austrian Code of Civil Procedure [Zivilprozessordnung, ZPO]. The decisions on costs taken by the previous instances cannot be contested in the context of proceedings before the Supreme Court.

German Original

Begründung:

Die Antragstellerin wurde am ***** in ***** außerhalb der Ehe geboren. Sie und ihre Mutter sind türkische Staatsangehörige. Am 17. 12. 1983 heiratete die Mutter der Antragstellerin einen türkischen Staatsangehörigen, der im Jahr 1984 dafür sorgte, dass er im Personenstand der Antragstellerin als deren Vater aufschien.

R***** T*****, der Rechtsvorgänger des Antragsgegners, ist am ***** gestorben. Der Nachlass wurde zwischenzeitlich dem Antragsgegner eingeantwortet. Im Taufschein des Pfarramts ***** scheint als Vater der Antragstellerin „R***** T*****" auf; dieser hat die Vaterschaft zur Antragstellerin bis zu seinem Tod nicht anerkannt.

Im vorliegenden Anlassverfahren stellte die Antragstellerin am 18. 9. 2012 den Antrag auf Feststellung ihrer Abstammung von R***** T*****. Nachher, nämlich am 12. 7. 2013, erhob sie vor dem Zivilgericht Cesme eine Ehelichkeitsbestreitungsklage nach Art 285 bis 294 des türkischen Zivilgesetzbuchs (tZGB). Mit (rechtskräftigem) Urteil vom 23. 8. 2013 stellte das türkische Gericht fest, dass der richtige Vater der (hier) Antragstellerin R***** T***** sei, und hob weiters das Abstammungsverhältnis zwischen dem türkischen Ehemann der Mutter und der (hier) Antragstellerin auf. An diesem türkischen Verfahren waren neben der Antragstellerin ihre Mutter sowie ihr rechtlicher Vater, nämlich der Ehemann der Mutter, beteiligt. Der Antragsgegner des vorliegenden Verfahrens wurde vom türkischen Verfahren weder verständigt noch diesem beigezogen.

In ihrem Antrag auf Feststellung der Vaterschaft brachte die Antragstellerin im Anlassverfahren vor, dass sie die leibliche Tochter des Rechtsvorgängers des Antragsgegners sei. Dieser scheine im Taufschein des Pfarramts ***** als ihr Vater auf. In diversen Personaldokumenten sei „R*****" als ihr Vater eingetragen. Der Ehemann der Mutter habe ihr lediglich seinen Namen gegeben, damit sie in der Türkei nicht als vaterloses Kind von der Gesellschaft ausgeschlossen werde. Aus dem zwischenzeitlich vorliegenden medizinischen Gutachten ergebe sich, dass der Rechtsvorgänger des Antragsgegners ohne Zweifel ihr Vater sei.

Der Antragsgegner erwiderte, dass eine Reihe von Gründen an der Vaterschaft seines Rechtsvorgängers zweifeln ließen. Insbesondere liege kein Vaterschaftsanerkenntnis vor. Von dem in der Türkei geführten Verfahren habe er keine Kenntnis erlangt.

Das Erstgericht wies den Antrag auf Feststellung der Abstammung ab. Das Urteil des türkischen Gerichts entfalte in Österreich keine Rechtswirksamkeit, weil diese Entscheidung in Österreich nicht (formell) anerkannt und der Antragsgegner des vorliegenden Verfahrens dem türkischen Verfahren nicht beigezogen worden sei. Auf die Feststellung der Abstammung sei materielles türkisches Recht anzuwenden. Davon ausgehend habe die Antragstellerin die Frist nach § 303 tZGB versäumt.

Das Rekursgericht gab dem Rekurs der Antragstellerin Folge und stellte fest, dass sie von R***** T***** abstammt. Die Entscheidung des türkischen Gerichts über die Aufhebung der Abstammung sei in Österreich (ipso iure) anzuerkennen. Die internationale Zuständigkeit des türkischen Gerichts zur Führung dieses Verfahrens sei zu bejahen. Eine Unvereinbarkeit mit einer inländischen oder früheren ausländischen Statusentscheidung liege nicht vor. Die Entscheidung verstoße auch nicht gegen den ordre public. Demgegenüber entfalte das türkische Urteil in Bezug auf die Feststellung von R***** T***** als Vater keine Bindungswirkung, weil der Antragsgegner des vorliegenden Verfahrens dem türkischen Verfahren nicht beigezogen worden sei. Damit sei über die Feststellung der Abstammung vom österreichischen Gericht zu entscheiden. Nach dem Personalstatut der Antragstellerin sei türkisches Recht anzuwenden. Nach Art 303 tZGB bestehe für die Feststellung der Vaterschaft eine Frist von einem Jahr nach der Geburt. Bestehe aber zwischen dem Kind und einem anderen Mann ein Abstammungsverhältnis, so beginne die einjährige Frist im Zeitpunkt der Beendigung dieses Verhältnisses. Im Anlassfall habe die Frist daher mit dem Eintritt der Rechtskraft der Entscheidung im türkischen Verfahren am 28. 8. 2013 zu laufen begonnen. Der Antrag auf Feststellung der Vaterschaft sei daher als rechtzeitig anzusehen. Ausgehend von den Feststellungen sei der Rechtsvorgänger des Antragsgegners der leibliche Vater der Antragstellerin. Der ordentliche Revisionsrekurs sei zulässig, weil „zur Frage der Anerkennung der vom türkischen Gericht gefällten Entscheidung und der Anwendung des § 84 AußStrG im Abstammungsverfahren" höchstgerichtliche Rechtsprechung fehle.

Gegen diese Entscheidung richtet sich der Revisionsrekurs des Antragsgegners, der auf eine Wiederherstellung der abweisenden Entscheidung des Erstgerichts abzielt. Außerdem bekämpft der Antragsgegner die Kostenentscheidung des Rekursgerichts.

Mit ihrer Revisionsrekursbeantwortung beantragt die Antragstellerin, das Rechtsmittel des Antragsgegners zurückzuweisen, in eventu diesem den Erfolg zu versagen. Die Mutter der Antragsgegnerin schließt sich deren Revisionsrekursbeantwortung an.

Rechtliche Beurteilung

Entgegen dem den Obersten Gerichtshof nicht bindenden Ausspruch des Rekursgerichts ist der Revisionsrekurs mangels Vorliegens einer entscheidungsrelevanten erheblichen Rechtsfrage im Sinn des § 62 Abs 1 AußStrG nicht zulässig.

1. Der Hinweis des Antragsgegners auf § 84 AußStrG ist nicht zielführend. Diese Bestimmung betrifft die Verbindung mehrerer Verfahren über die Abstammung des selben Kindes. Voraussetzung für die Verfahrensverbindung ist unter anderem, dass für alle Anträge dasselbe Gericht im Sinn des § 108 JN sachlich und örtlich zuständig ist (*DeixlerHübner* in *Rechberger*, AußStrG[2] § 84 Rz 1). Dies gilt auch für die internationale Zuständigkeit.

Im Anlassfall gesteht der Antragsgegner selbst zu, dass für das Verfahren über die Nichtabstammung vom Ehemann der Mutter das türkische Gericht international zuständig war.

2.1 Die Entscheidung des türkischen Gerichts bezieht sich einerseits auf die Feststellung, dass die Antragstellerin nicht vom Ehemann der Mutter abstamme (Ehelichkeitsbestreitung), und andererseits auf die weitere Feststellung, dass sie vom Rechtsvorgänger des Antragsgegners abstamme.

In Rechtsprechung und Literatur ist anerkannt, dass auch eine Teilanerkennung etwa eines Scheidungsausspruchs zulässig ist, wenn eine Entscheidung eines ausländischen Gerichts über die Ehescheidung auch andere Spruchpunkte enthält (RISJustiz RS0121413; *Neumayr* in *Burgstaller/Neumayr/Geroldinger/Schmaranzer*, Internationales Zivilverfahrensrecht § 97 AußStrG Rz 16). Auch eine Teilanerkennung einer Entscheidung über das Kontaktrecht kommt in Betracht (*Schütz* in *Burgstaller/Neumayr/Geroldinger/Schmaranzer*, aaO, Art 30 ESÜ, Rz 31).

Auf den Anlassfall gelangt das Abkommen vom 23. Mai 1989 zwischen der Republik Österreich und der Republik Türkei über die Anerkennung und die Vollstreckung von gerichtlichen Entscheidungen und Vergleichen in Zivil- und Handelssachen (bilateraler Vollstreckungsvertrag) zur Anwendung. Nach Art 7 leg cit werden Rechtssachen über den Ehe oder den Familienstand einander gleichgestellt, was als logische Konsequenz aus der Sachnähe der Statussachen resultiert. Daraus folgt, dass auch in Abstammungssachen (als kindschaftsrechtliche Statussachen) eine Teilanerkennung einer ausländischen Entscheidung zulässig ist, wenn sie über trennbare Ansprüche abspricht und insofern gesonderte Spruchpunkte enthält.

2.2 Diese Voraussetzungen sind hier gegeben. Die Feststellung der Nichtabstammung vom Ehemann der Mutter einerseits und die Feststellung der Abstammung vom biologischen Vater andererseits sind sowohl nach österreichischem Recht

(§ 151 ABGB) als auch nach türkischem Recht (Art 287 tZGB) jeweils selbständig möglich.

3.1 Der Antragsgegner steht auf dem Standpunkt, dass eine inzidente Anerkennung des türkischen Urteils, also ohne darauf gerichteten Antrag, im österreichischen Verfahren unzulässig sei.

Damit ist der Antragsgegner auf Basis der Rechtsprechung des Obersten Gerichtshofs nicht im Recht.

3.2 Es entspricht der Rechtsprechung, dass der Grundsatz der entschiedenen Rechtssache auch im internationalen Kontext gilt und der Verstoß gegen eine im Ausland rechtskräftig entschiedene und in Österreich anzuerkennende Rechtssache gleich wie der Mangel der inländischen Gerichtsbarkeit zu behandeln ist (6 Ob 96/11b mwN). Auch die Entscheidungen ausländischer Gerichte, die im Inland anzuerkennen sind, entfalten daher Bindungswirkung, die von Amts wegen wahrzunehmen ist (2 Ob 238/13h mwN).

3.3 Das neue AußStrG enthält in §§ 97 ff (eheauflösende Entscheidungen), §§ 112 ff (Obsorge und Kontaktrecht) und §§ 91a ff (Adoption) ausdrückliche Regelungen zur Anerkennung ausländischer Entscheidungen. Die Brüssel IIaVO oder sonst maßgebende völkerrechtliche Anerkennungs und Vollstreckungsverträge gelangen vorrangig zur Anwendung.

Wie schon erwähnt, gelangt auf den Anlassfall das bilaterale Vollstreckungsabkommen zwischen Österreich und der Türkei zur Anwendung. Nach Art 11 Abs 1 leg cit richtet sich das Anerkennungsverfahren nach dem Recht des ersuchten Staats, hier also nach österreichischem Recht.

Im österreichischen Recht ist die Analogiefähigkeit der im AußStrG enthaltenen Regelungen über die Anerkennung ausländischer Entscheidungen seit langem anerkannt (1 Ob 190/03b zu einer griechischen Adoption; 6 Ob 170/04z zu einer indischen Adoption; 1 Ob 21/04a zu einer chinesischen Adoption). Der Oberste Gerichtshof hat ebenfalls bereits geklärt, dass die Anerkennungsregeln nach §§ 91a ff AußStrG die mit dem FamRÄG 2009, BGBl I 2009/75, ab 1. 1. 2010 für die Anerkennung ausländischer Adoptionsentscheidungen eingefügt wurden und sich an den §§ 97 ff (ausländische Eheentscheidungen) und den §§ 112 ff AußStrG (ausländische Obsorgeentscheidungen) orientieren aufgrund der besonderen Sachnähe als geeignete Analogiegrundlage zur Anerkennung von ausländischen Entscheidungen in Abstammungsangelegenheiten heranzuziehen sind, zumal diese neben den Adoptionssachen ebenfalls zu den kindschaftsrechtlichen Statussachen zählen (2 Ob 238/13h).

Die verfahrensrechtliche Frage (Art 11 Abs 1 des bilateralen Vollstreckungsvertrags), ob eine inzidente Prüfung der Anerkennungsfähigkeit der Abstammungsentscheidung des türkischen Gerichts zulässig ist, richtet sich somit nach den §§ 91a ff AußStrG (analog).

3.4 Nach § 91a Abs 1 Satz 2 AußStrG kann die Anerkennung als Vorfrage selbständig beurteilt werden, ohne dass es eines besonderen Verfahrens bedarf. Damit wurde für rechtskräftige ausländische Adoptionsentscheidungen der Grundsatz der InzidentAnerkennung gesetzlich verankert (2 Ob 238/13h; siehe 6 Ob 96/11b zu § 97 Abs 1 AußStrG). Aufgrund des gebotenen Analogieschlusses gilt dies ebenso für rechtskräftige ausländische Entscheidungen über die Abstammung des Kindes.

4.1 Im Anlassverfahren ist somit die Anerkennungsfähigkeit der Entscheidung des türkischen Gerichts zu prüfen, um deren Bindungswirkung beurteilen zu können. Die Prüfung erfolgt in Ermangelung vorrangiger unionsrechtlicher Normen anhand einschlägiger völkerrechtlicher Verträge, hier auf Basis des bilateralen Vollstreckungsvertrags, subsidiär in analoger Anwendung der §§ 91a ff AußStrG.

Nach Art 3 des bilateralen Vollstreckungsvertrags sind die Entscheidungen des anderen Vertragsstaats anzuerkennen, wenn sie rechtskräftig sind und das Gericht nach den Art 6 bis 9 zuständig war. Nach Art 11 Abs 1 des bilateralen Vollstreckungsvertrags ist die Zuständigkeit in Rechtssachen über den Ehe oder Familienstand anzuerkennen, wenn der Beklagte (Antragsgegner) zur Zeit der Einleitung des Verfahrens Angehöriger dieses Staats war oder seinen Wohnsitz oder gewöhnlichen Aufenthalt im Gebiet dieses Staats hatte.

Nach Art 4 Abs 1 des bilateralen Vollstreckungsvertrags darf die Anerkennung (unter anderem) versagt werden, wenn sie mit der öffentlichen Ordnung des ersuchten Staats offensichtlich unvereinbar ist (lit a; siehe auch § 91a Abs 2 AußStrG).

4.2 Das Vorliegen einer ausländischen rechtskräftigen Entscheidung über die Abstammung wird vom Antragsgegner nicht bestritten.

Hinsichtlich der Entscheidung des türkischen Gerichts über die Feststellung der Nichtabstammung vom Ehemann der Mutter (Ehelichkeitsbestreitung) ist die Zuständigkeit des türkischen Gerichts nach Art 7 Abs 1 des bilateralen Vollstreckungsvertrags anzuerkennen.

4.3 Ein Verstoß gegen den ordre public setzt voraus, dass das Ergebnis der Anwendung fremden Rechts Grundwertungen der inländischen Rechtsordnung verletzt, wozu auch eine ausreichende Inlandsbeziehung gehört (RISJustiz RS0110743; 3 Ob 186/11s). Als systemwidrige Ausnahme erfordert die ordre publicKlausel einen besonders sparsamen Gebrauch (RISJustiz RS0077010). Eine schlichte Unbilligkeit des Ergebnisses genügt ebenso wenig wie der bloße Widerspruch zu zwingenden österreichischen Rechtsvorschriften (6 Ob 138/13g). Das fremde Recht muss im Ergebnis vielmehr zu einer unerträglichen Verletzung tragender Grundwertungen der österreichischen Rechtsordnung führen (8 Ob 118/12d).

Der verfahrensrechtliche ordre public soll sicherstellen, dass die Parteien die Möglichkeit hatten, sich am Verfahren zu beteiligen (2 Ob 238/13h). Die

Verletzung des rechtlichen Gehörs ist somit eine besondere Ausprägung des verfahrensrechtlichen ordre public. Sie soll den Beklagten (Antragsgegner) davor schützen, dass die ausländische Entscheidung ohne seine Beteiligung erlassen wurde. Es muss daher sichergestellt sein, dass für den Beklagten (Antragsgegner) die Möglichkeit bestanden hat, sich effektiv am Verfahren zu beteiligen (6 Ob 96/11b zu § 97 Abs 1 AußStrG).

4.4 Hinsichtlich der Entscheidung des türkischen Gerichts zur Ehelichkeitsbestreitung ist kein Verstoß gegen den ordre public erkennbar. Im Verfahren auf Feststellung der Nichtabstammung vom Ehemann der Mutter (§ 151 ABGB) kommt dem möglichen biologischen Vater (und damit ebenso dem Antragsgegner als Rechtsnachfolger) auch nach österreichischem Recht keine Antragslegitimation (*Hopf* in KBB4 §§ 151-153 ABGB, Rz 3) und auch keine materielle Parteistellung zu (vgl *DeixlerHübner* in *Rechberger*, AußStrG² § 82 Rz 9).

4.5 Die Anerkennungsfähigkeit der Entscheidung des türkischen Gerichts über die Bestreitung der Ehelichkeit der Antragstellerin und damit die Bindungswirkung dieser Entscheidung für den österreichischen Rechtsbereich ist demnach zu bejahen.

Eine Überprüfung der anzuerkennenden Entscheidung des türkischen Gerichts dahin, ob dieses inhaltlich richtig entschieden hat, kommt im österreichischen (Anerkennungs)Verfahren nicht in Betracht. Der Antragsgegner beruft sich in dieser Hinsicht darauf, dass die Antragstellerin die Ehelichkeitsbestreitungsklage gemäß Art 289 tZGB verspätet eingebracht habe. Indem sich der Antragsgegner auf eine zeitliche Beschränkung des Anfechtungsrechts beruft, macht er gerade keine ordre publicWidrigkeit geltend (vgl dazu 6 Ob 559/95).

4.6 Zur Feststellung der Vaterschaft des Rechtsvorgängers des Antragsgegners im Verfahren vor dem türkischen Gericht scheitert die Anerkennung dieser Entscheidung schon daran, dass nach Art 7 Abs 1 des bilateralen Vollstreckungsvertrags die Zuständigkeit des türkischen Gerichts nicht gegeben und daher nicht anzuerkennen ist, weil der Antragsgegner (dies hätte auch für seinen Rechtsvorgänger gegolten) weder türkischer Staatsangehöriger ist noch seinen Wohnsitz oder gewöhnlichen Aufenthalt im Gebiet der Türkei hat.

Außerdem liegt auch ein Verstoß gegen den verfahrensrechtlichen ordre public und damit ein Grund für die Versagung der Anerkennung dieser Entscheidung des türkischen Gerichts vor. Der Antragsgegner wurde dem türkischen Verfahren nicht beigezogen, er war an diesem gesamten Verfahren also nicht beteiligt. Gemäß § 82 Abs 2 AußStrG sind in einem Abstammungsverfahren jedenfalls das Kind, die Person, deren Elternschaft durch das Verfahren begründet oder beseitigt werden kann, und der andere Elternteil des Kindes, soweit er einsichts- und urteilsfähig sowie am Leben ist, Parteien (vgl auch § 148 Abs 1 ABGB). Die Feststellung der Vaterschaft ohne rechtliches Gehör des Betroffenen bzw seines Rechtsnachfolgers (vgl *Deixler/Hübner* in *Rechberger*, AußStrG² § 82 Rz 3) verstößt gegen den inländischen ordre public. Von einem offenkundigen Einverständnis des Antragsgegners mit der türkischen Entscheidung über die Vaterschaft seines Rechtsvorgängers (vgl § 91a Abs 2 Z 2 AußStrG) kann naturgemäß nicht ausgegangen werden.

4.7 Eine Anerkennung der Entscheidung des türkischen Gerichts über die Feststellung der Abstammung der Antragstellerin vom Rechtsvorgänger des Antragsgegners scheidet damit aus.

5. Das Rekursgericht ist demnach zu Recht davon ausgegangen, dass über die Feststellung der Vaterschaft im vorliegenden Verfahren zu entscheiden ist.

Der Beurteilung des Rekursgerichts, wonach auf diese Frage türkisches Sachrecht anzuwenden ist, die Antragstellerin für den Antrag auf Feststellung der Abstammung (vor dem österreichischen Gericht) die Frist des Art 303 tZGB eingehalten hat und diese vom Rechtsvorgänger des Antragsgegners abstammt, tritt der Antragsgegner im Revisionsrekurs nicht entgegen.

6. Die im Revisionsrekurs noch angesprochene Rechtshängigkeit (Art 4 Abs 1 lit b des bilateralen Vollstreckungsvertrags) kann sich hier nur auf die Feststellung der Vaterschaft beziehen, weil die Bestreitung der Ehelichkeit nicht selbständiger Gegenstand des österreichischen Verfahrens ist. Außerdem könnte die Prüfung der Rechtshängigkeit aufgrund der zeitlichen Abfolge der Rechtsschutzanträge nur das Verfahren vor dem türkischen Gericht betreffen. Die Entscheidung des türkischen Gerichts über die Feststellung der Vaterschaft ist aber schon aus anderen Gründen nicht anzuerkennen.

7. Das Rekursgericht ist im Ergebnis von den hier dargestellten Rechtsgrundsätzen ausgegangen. Eine korrekturbedürftige Fehlbeurteilung liegt nicht vor.

Mangels Aufzeigens einer erheblichen Rechtsfrage war der Revisionsrekurs zurückzuweisen.

Die Kostenentscheidung stützt sich auf §§ 78, 83 Abs 4 AußStrG iVm § 50 ZPO. Die Kostenentscheidung der Vorinstanzen kann im Verfahren vor dem Obersten Gerichtshof nicht bekämpft werden.

3. Jurisdiction to enforce/Durchsetzungsjurisdiktion

See HH.II.2.

SS. Legal aspects of international relations and cooperation in particular matters/Rechtliche Aspekte der internationalen Beziehungen und Zusammenarbeit in bestimmten Bereichen

I. General economic and financial matters/Wirtschaftliche und Finanzwirtschaftliche Angelegenheiten

3. Investments/Investitionen

See CC.II.3.

PART II
Austrian Diplomatic and Parliamentary Practice in International Law/ Österreichische Diplomatische und Parlamentarische Praxis zum Internationalen Recht[*]

Markus P. Beham[**] and *Gerhard Hafner*[***]

Index of Documents[****]

BB. Sources of international law/Völkerrechtsquellen

II.-1 – Work of the International Law Commission on Customary International Law 369

V. – *See BB.II.-1.*

VII. – *See CC.II.1.-1.*

IX. – *See BB.II.-1.*

---

[*] In the last years, the Office of the Legal Adviser of the Austrian Foreign Ministry published its own annual reports on 'Recent Austrian practice in the field of international law' in the Zeitschrift für Öffentliches Recht.. These reports have been available to the present authors prior to publication and have been drawn upon in the past digests of Austrian diplomatic and parliamentary practice in international law.

Considering the change in the nature of the 'Recent Austrian practice in the field of international law' from a digest of practice to, largely, a compilation of viewpoints of the Office of the Legal Adviser on various issues of international law, the authors have refrained from reproducing sections of the recent report and concentrated on compiling and translating original documents produced in 2015. The reader is called upon to also consult the 'Report for 2015' of the 'Recent Austrian practice in the field of international law' in the Zeitschrift für Öffentliches Recht for further views on issues of public international law of the Office of the Legal Adviser. See Konrad Bühler, Philip Bittner, Ulrike Köhler and Helmut Tichy, 'Recent Austrian Practice in the Field of International Law. Report for 2015' (2016) 71 Zeitschrift für Öffentliches Recht 103.

[**] Lecturer at the Section for International Law and International Relations of the University of Vienna and Associate at Freshfields Bruckhaus Deringer LLP.

[***] Professor ret. of International and European Law, Department for European, International and Comparative Law, Section for International Law and International Relations, University of Vienna.

[****] The digest covers the period from 1 January 2015 to 31 December 2015.

CC. The law of treaties/Recht der Verträge

I.2-1 – Objection to the reservation of El Salvador to the Second Optional Protocol to the International Covenant on Civil and Political Rights, Aiming at the Abolition of the Death Penalty 371

I.2.-2 – Withdrawal of Austria's Reservation to the Convention on the Elimination of All Forms of Discrimination against Women 372

I.2.-3 – Withdrawal of Austria's Reservations and Declarations to the Convention on the Rights of the Child 372

I.3.-1 – Work of the International Law Commission on Provisional Application of Treaties 373

II.1.-1 – Enquiry concerning binding nature of the financial agreement between Italy and South Tyrol 374

II.3.-1 – Work of the International Law Commission on the Most-Favoured-Nation Clause 385

III.-1 – Work of the International Law Commission on Subsequent Agreements and Subsequent Practice in Relation to the Interpretation of Treaties 386

VI. – *See CC.II.1.-1.*

DD. Relationship between international law and internal law/Völkerrecht und innerstaatliches Recht

II. – *See LL.II.2.-1.*

II.-1 – Inclusion of the Crime of Aggression in the Austrian Criminal Code 388

EE. Subjects of International law/Völkerrechtssubjekte

II.1.-1 – Amendment of the Federal Law on the Granting of Privileges to Non-Governmental International Organisations 390

II.1.b.bb.-1 – Withdrawal from the Common Fund for Commodities 394

II.2.d. – *See also EE.II.1.-1.*

II.2.d.-1 – Asian Infrastructure Investment Bank 394

III.6. – *See EE.II.1.-1.*

FF. The position of the individual (including the corporation) in international law/Die Stellung der Einzelperson (einschließlich der juristischen Person) im Völkerrecht

IV. – *See CC.II.1.-1.*

FF.VII.4.-1 – Five approaches to handling the refugee crisis 396

FF.VII.4.-2 – Enquiry concerning the distribution of refugees within Europe 399

VIII. – *See also CC.I.2-1, CC.I.2.-2,* and *CC.I.2.-3.*

VIII.-1 – Enquiry concerning the Qu'ran distribution events 404

X. – *See DD.II.-1.*

X.-1 – Joint declaration on the occasion of the centenary of the Armenian genocide 405

X.-2 – Work of the International Law Commission on Crimes Against Humanity 407

XI. – *See also DD.II.-1, FF.X.-2,* and *GG.-1.*

XI.-1 – Retroactive Application of Amended Rule 68 of the Rules of Procedure and Evidence of the International Criminal Court 409

GG. Organs of the State and their legal status/Die Staatsorgane und ihr rechtlicher Status

1 – Work of the International Law Commission on Immunity of State Officials from Criminal Jurisdiction 410

VIII. – *See also RR.IV.-1.*

VIII.-1 – Memorandum of Understanding between the United Nations and the Federal Government of Austria Contributing Resources to the United Nations Interim Force in Lebanon (UNIFIL) 412

LL. Air Space, outer space and Antarctica/Luftraum, Weltraum, Antarktis

II.2.-1 – Outer Space Regulation 418

QQ. The law of armed conflict and international humanitarian law/Recht des bewaffneten Konfliktes und internationales humanitäres Recht

　　I.2.b.-1 – Work of the International Law Commission on Protection of the Environment in Relation to Armed Conflicts 429

　　I.2.i.-1. – Joint Statement on the Humanitarian Consequences of Nuclear Weapons 431

RR. Neutrality, non-belligerency/Neutralität, Nicht-Kriegführung

　　IV.-1 – Enquiry concerning US soldiers in Schwechat 433

SS. Legal aspects of international relations and cooperation in particular matters/Rechtliche Aspekte der internationalen Beziehungen und Zusammenarbeit in bestimmten Bereichen

　　I.1. – *See CC.II.3.-1.*

　　I.1.-1 – Report of the United Nations Commission on International Trade Law 438

　　I.1.-2 – Enquiry concerning the renegotiation of the Comprehensive Economic and Trade Agreement (CETA) 439

　　I.1.-3 – Free Trade Agreement between the European Union and its Member States, of the one part, and the Republic of Korea, of the other part 445

　　I.3. – *See EE.II.2.d.-1.*

　　I.6. – *See EE.II.2.d.-1.*

　　III.-1 – Work of the International Law Commission on Protection of the Atmosphere 446

　　IV. – *See EE.II.1.b.bb.-1.*

　　VII.-1 – Convention on the Means of Prohibiting and Preventing the Illicit Import, Export and Transfer of Ownership of Cultural Property 1970 447

　　IX. – *See RR.IV.-1.*

BB. Sources of international law/Völkerrechtsquellen

II. Custom/Völkergewohnheitsrecht

BB.II.-1

Work of the International Law Commission on Customary International Law

Arbeit der Völkerrechtskommission betreffend Völkergewohnheitsrecht

On 4 November 2015, the Austrian representative to the 70th session of the General Assembly delivered the following statement to the Sixth Committee regarding the Report of the International Law Commission on the Work of its 67th Session concerning the topic 'Identification of Customary International Law':

> Austria supports the Commission's aim to clarify important aspects of this source of public international law by formulating 'conclusions' with commentaries. We commend Special Rapporteur Sir Michael Wood for the work undertaken in his third report focusing on the evidentiary aspects of the two constituent elements of custom, 'general practice' and 'accepted as law'.
>
> However, my delegation was surprised by the use of the term *lex ferenda* in paragraph 70 of the Commission's report, concerning the introduction by the Special Rapporteur of his third report. In this paragraph, the Special Rapporteur is quoted as having said that 'it was important to distinguish between those [rules] that were intended to reflect existing law – *lex lata* – and those that were put forward as emerging law – *lex ferenda*'. This wording seems to suggest that the expression *lex ferenda* would relate to law *in statu nascendi*, to emerging law. In Austria's understanding, *lex ferenda* is not law beginning to be formed, but simply the expression of the political wish that new legal rules be adopted.
>
> Austria notes that, as reflected in paragraph 88 of the Commission's report, several members of the Commission were of the opinion that the work of the ILC could not be equated to 'writings' or teachings of publicists. However, in paragraph 104 of the report we can see that the Special Rapporteur thought that a separate conclusion on the work of the ILC was not justified. Austria believes that the work of the ILC has special importance for the identification of customary rules of international law. The results of the Commission's work normally lead to General Assembly resolutions. The role of such resolutions is reflected in draft conclusion 12 adopted by the Drafting Committee regarding 'Resolutions of international organizations and intergovernmental conferences'. While this conclusion covers large parts of the work of the ILC, the remaining work would fall under draft conclusion 14 regarding 'Teachings'. For us, it is difficult to apply the expression 'Teachings of the most highly qualified publicists of the various nations' contained in this draft conclusion to the ILC and to other international expert bodies as well as to international scientific institutions. Austria believes that there should be a

specific reference to the role of the ILC and other expert bodies and institutions in the draft conclusions, or at least in the commentary.

As far as the other draft conclusions are concerned, we would like to point out that draft conclusion 4 paragraph 3 on the irrelevance of the conduct of other actors does not do justice to the important contribution of the International Committee of the Red Cross to international practice.

As far as draft conclusion 11 (1)(c) on the role of treaties is concerned, my delegation believes that it will be important to clarify in the commentary that the 'general practice' to which a treaty has given rise, referred to in this provision, must include also the practice of non-state parties to the treaty concerned and not only the practice of the states-parties.

Austria welcomes the fact that the draft conclusions address the difficult issue of the persistent objector in draft conclusion 15. We welcome the explicit restriction of the effect of persistent objections to the opposing state, which, therefore, is not in a position to prevent the creation of a rule of customary international law. Nevertheless, it would be necessary to further develop some issues relating to persistent objection, like the non-effect of persistent objections to rules of *ius cogens* and their relation to obligations *erga omnes*.

V. Opinions of writers/Lehrmeinungen

   See BB.II.-1.

VII. Unilateral acts, including acts and decisions of international organisations and conferences/Einseitige Akte, einschließlich der Akte und Beschlüsse von internationalen Organisationen und Konferenzen

   See CC.II.1.-1.

IX. Codification and progressive development/Kodifikation und progressive Weiterentwicklung

   See BB.II.-1.

CC. The law of treaties/Recht der Verträge

I. Conclusion and entry into force of treaties/Abschluß und Inkrafttreten völkerrechtlicher Verträge

2. Reservations and declarations/Vorbehalte und Erklärungen

CC.I.2-1

Objection to the reservation of El Salvador to the Second Optional Protocol to the International Covenant on Civil and Political Rights, Aiming at the Abolition of the Death Penalty

Protest gegen den Vorbehalt El Salvadors zum Zweiten Fakultativprotokoll zum Internationalen Pakt über bürgerliche und politische Rechte, das auf die Abschaffung der Todesstrafe abzielt

On 7 April 2015, Austria deposited an objection to the reservation of El Salvador to the Second Optional Protocol to the International Covenant on Civil and Political Rights, Aiming at the Abolition of the Death Penalty made upon accession on 8 April 2014:[1]

> The Government of Austria has examined the reservation made by the Republic of El Salvador upon accession to the Second Optional Protocol to the International Covenant on Civil and Political Rights, aiming at the abolition of the death penalty, adopted on 15 December 1989.
>
> The Government of Austria recalls that it is the object and purpose of the Second Optional Protocol to abolish the death penalty in all circumstances and that no reservations are permitted other than reservations made within the limits of Article 2 of the Protocol. In the light of the wording of Article 2 (1), a reservation to the Protocol is allowed to the extent that it concerns the application of the death penalty in times of war pursuant to a conviction for a most serious crime of a military nature committed during wartime. According to Article 2 (2), the State Party making such a reservation shall at the time of ratification or accession communicate to the Secretary-General of the United Nations the relevant provisions of its national legislation applicable during wartime.
>
> According to the information available, the applicable provisions of the national legislation of El Salvador specifying the application of the death penalty to the most serious crimes of a military nature in wartime were not communicated to the Secretary-General.
>
> The Government of Austria therefore objects to this reservation.
>
> This objection shall not preclude the entry into force of the Protocol between Austria and the Republic of El Salvador.[2]

---

[1] The text of the declaration reads as follows: 'The commitment of the State of Kuwait to the Convention is without prejudice to its Arab and Islamic obligations in respect of the definition of terrorism and the distinction between terrorism and legitimate national struggle against occupation.'

[2] C.N.243.2015.TREATIES-IV.12.

CC.I.2.-2

Withdrawal of Austria's Reservation to the Convention on the Elimination of All Forms of Discrimination against Women

Rücknahme von Österreichs Vorbehalt zur Konvention zur Beseitigung jeder Form von Diskriminierung der Frau

On 10 June 2015, Austria delivered the following declaration on the withdrawal of its reservation to the Secretary General of the United Nations:[3]

> The Republic of Austria ratified the Convention on the Elimination of All Forms of Discrimination against Women on 31 March 1982 subject to reservations to Article 7 (b) and Article 11. The reservation to Article 7 (b) was withdrawn in 2000 and the reservation to Article 11 was partly withdrawn in 2006.
>
> Following a review of the remaining reservation, the Republic of Austria has decided to withdraw its reservation to Article 11 in accordance with Article 28 (3) of the Convention.[4]

CC.I.2.-3

Withdrawal of Austria's Reservations and Declarations to the Convention on the Rights of the Child

Rücknahme von Österreichs Vorbehalten und Erklärungen zum Übereinkommen über die Rechte des Kindes

On 28 September 2015, Austria delivered the following declaration on its withdrawal of all reservations to the Secretary General of the United Nations:[5]

> The Republic of Austria has decided to withdraw its reservations to Articles 13, 15 and 17, as well as its declarations to Art 38(2) and (3) of the Convention on the Rights of the Child, in accordance with Article 51(3) of the Convention.[6]

---

[3] C.N.336.2015.TREATIES-IV.8; Federal Law Gazette III No 82/2015.

[4] Article 11 concerns the elimination of discrimination against women in the field of employment.

[5] C.N.504.2015.TREATIES-IV.11; Federal Law Gazette III No 138/2015. See on the reasoning for this step already Markus Beham and Gerhard Hafner, 'Austrian Diplomatic and Parliamentary Practice in International Law/Österreichische diplomatische und Parlamentarische Praxis zum Internationalen Recht' (2014) 19 ARIEL 305, at 318, CC.I.2.-3.

[6] The reservations to Articles 13, 15, and 17 had concerned the protective standard of the European Convention and Human Rights, whereas the declaration in accordance with Article 38 was considered obsolete. See already Konrad Bühler, Philip Bittner, Ulrike Köhler and Helmut Tichy, 'Recent Austrian Practice in the Field of International Law. Report for 2014' (2015) 70 Zeitschrift für Öffentliches Recht 123, at 126-128.

3. Provisional application and entry into force/Vorläufige Anwendung und Inkrafttreten

CC.I.3.-1

Work of the International Law Commission on Provisional Application of Treaties

Arbeit der Völkerrechtskommission betreffend die vorläufige Anwendung von Verträgen

On 9 November 2015, the Austrian representative to the 70th session of the General Assembly delivered the following statement to the Sixth Committee regarding the Report of the International Law Commission on the Work of its 67th Session concerning the topic 'Provisional Application of Treaties':

[...]

As to the form of the document to be elaborated we concur with the suggestion to produce draft guidelines which can be used by treaty-makers contemplating provisional application. The Austrian delegation takes note of the debate within the Commission with regard to the relevance of internal law. While we agree with the Special Rapporteur that it is not necessary to study in detail and on a broad comparative basis the different national constitutional provisions that address the possibility of provisionally applying treaties, we are of the firm view that the possibility of such provisional application always depends on the provisions of internal law.

With regard to draft guideline 1 as proposed by the Special Rapporteur, we would suggest that the Drafting Committee consider the following: The current formulation of this draft guideline appears like a presumption in favour of provisional applicability. In our view it should be reformulated in terms insisting that the possibility of provisional application depends on the provisions of internal law. This does not mean that a state could avoid its obligations once it has committed itself internationally to the provisional application of a treaty. However, whether or not such a commitment can be made is determined by its internal law.

The Austrian delegation supports the Special Rapporteur's approach in his draft guideline 5 to limit the instances of termination of the provisional application of treaties to those provided for in the Vienna Convention on the Law of Treaties and to abstain from introducing the vague additional grounds of a 'prolonged period' of provisional application and the 'uncertainty of the entry-into-force' of the treaty.

With respect to the three draft guidelines provisionally adopted by the Drafting Committee, which seem to contain only general introductory language, my delegation understands draft guideline 1 as encompassing also the provisional application of treaties by international organizations and expects that this will be clarified in the commentary.

As to draft guideline 2 it must be made clear that the reference to 'other rules of international law' does not detract from the purpose of these guidelines, which is to supplement the rules of the Vienna Convention and not to suggest changes to them.

As to draft guideline 3 my delegation thinks that some questions might arise with regard to the words 'or if in some other manner it has been so agreed'. This wording goes beyond Article 25 paragraph 1 subparagraph b of the Vienna Convention on the Law of Treaties, which only refers to the agreement of the negotiating states on provisional application. Thus, the provisional application by states which were not negotiating states is only possible if the treaty so provides or all the other negotiating states so agree. Similarly, if only some of the negotiating states agree on the provisional application, this provisional application must be qualified as an agreement that is separate from the original treaty.

II. Observance, application and interpretation of treaties/ Einhaltung, Anwendung und Auslegung von Verträgen

1. Observance of treaties/Einhaltung von Verträgen

CC.II.1.-1

Enquiry concerning binding nature of the financial agreement between Italy and South Tyrol

Anfrage betreffend betreffend völkerrechtliche Verbindlichkeit des Finanzabkommens zwischen Italien und Südtirol

On 19 February 2015, a number of representatives of the Austrian parliament raised a follow-up enquiry to their earlier enquiry regarding the *note verbale* of Austria to Italy of 23 February 2010,[7] to the Minister for Europe, Integration and Foreign Affairs:[8]

In response 2979/AB of 20 January 2015 to my enquiry 3140/J of 20 November 2014 you gave the following information regarding the content of the verbal note of 23 February 2010:

'In this verbal note, Austria gives notice to the Italian government that Austria was informed of the planned new financial regulation in the region Trentino-South Tyrol and the autonomous provinces of Trento and Bozen/Bolzano and the corresponding modifications of the Statute of Autonomy and that it acknowledged

---

[7] See Parliamentary Materials, 3140/J (XXV. GP).
[8] Parliamentary Materials, 3737/J (XXV. GP).

it favourably in light of the consensual approach between the competent organs of the Republic of Italy and the autonomous provinces of Trento and Bozen/Bolzano and the region Trentino-South Tyrol.'

With regard to the postulated legal certainty, you wrote that the exchange of notes respective letters as well as the verbal note of 23 February 2010 are suitable for this purpose.

These statements contradict each other in so far as the simple acknowledgment cannot create treaty-based legal certainty. Furthermore, the *verbatim* statement of the content of the verbal note was refused.

Furthermore, the following information has been transported across the media since December of last year.

In December of last year, Prime Minister Renzi informed Chancellor Faymann of the financial agreement. The newspaper Südtiroler Tageszeitung printed the content of the letter *verbatim*:

'Dear Werner,

I inform you that the Italian government has negotiated a new form of mutual financial relations with the two provincial governors Arno Kompatscher and Ugo Rossi. The agreement, a copy of which is enclosed, will be implemented with specific legal provisions. This initiative is based on the verbal note of 25 April 1992, which offered a list of measures for the implementation of the package, including the financial measures.

In the spirit, in which the Italian-Austrian relations were always held, the Italian government will continue to ensure approval in order to guarantee in the future the protection of ethnic minorities and the exercise of autonomous legislative and enforcement competences in the respective areas.'

Chairman of the South Tyrolean People's Party, Mr. Achammer, explained to the media that by signing this written 'note' to the Austrian Chancellor, Prime Minister Renzi paved the way for the first time for the international guarantee of a financial agreement between South Tyrol and the Italian state. The exchange of notes with Austria was at the level of a masterly achievement and would grant additional security. He also referred to the financial agreement as an important step forward with regard to the autonomy policy.

In your questionnaire, you state that the financial agreement is neither a bilateral agreement nor a treaty under international law. It was only done with an eye to an exchange of letters between Italy and Austria – no talk of legal safeguards whatsoever.

In an interview with the newspaper Südtiroler Tageszeitung, the provincial governor of South Tyrol, Dr. Arno Kompatscher, said that the response was made with regard to the Milan Agreement, which is simply wrong, as the enquiry expressly asked for the relevance of the currently concluded financial agreement, the so-called 'security pact', under international law. He emphasised that this exchange of notes regarding the security pact was now absolutely relevant under international law. It is generally confirmed by the South Tyrolean People's Party that, whereas it is not a treaty under international law, this is not necessary due to the Paris Treaty (Südtiroler Tageszeitung of 26 December 2014).

Recently, it could be read in media reports that Chancellor Faymann had signed a letter to Italian Prime Minister Matteo Renzi on 22. Jänner 2015, which supposedly constituted the final act making the exchange of letters an exchange of notes, thereby lifting the financial agreement 'to the level of international law'.

In this regard, the undersigned representatives address to the Minister for Europe, Integration and Foreign Affairs the following

Enquiry

1. Is there or was there ever any form of legal certainty regarding compliance with the

    a. Milan Agreement,

    b. Security Pact

    c. If so, how is it guaranteed?

2. On the basis of the correspondence between Prime Minister Renzi and Chancellor Faymann, in case of a violation of the current security pact with regard to the financial regulation between Rome and Bozen/Bolzano, before which international legal body can Austria bring a claim for Italy to honour the agreement?

3. Why was it not possible for you to publish a copy of the verbal note of 23 February 2010 or at least present it to the members of the Foreign Affairs Committee?

4. Is it possible now for you to repeat the exact content of the verbal note of 23 February 2010 *verbatim* or at least present it to the members of the Foreign Affairs Committee?

5. Is it true that Chancellor Faymann signed a letter on 22 January 2015, as mentioned above?

6. If so, what is the exact content *verbatim*?

7. Wherefrom does the exchange of letters between Prime Minister Renzi and Chancellor Faymann derive its relevance under international law and how is it defined?

8. From which section(s) of the text in this exchange of letters is the relevance under international law derived and how is it defined?

9. Through which Austrian steps does the relevance under international law arise in the case of a violation of the financial agreement by Rome?

10. What does it mean from the legal perspective and the perspective of international law that the financial agreement was now 'lifted to the level of international law' and what is the binding effect under international law for Italy?

11. What are the benefits/disadvantages for

   a. South Tyrol?

   b. Italy?

   c. Austria?

12. With regard to the present financial agreement, what separates this 'level of international law' from a 'treaty under international law'?

13. What is the difference legally and content-wise between the exchange of notes regarding the present financial agreement and the verbal note of 23 February 2010 regarding the Milan Agreement?

14. In how far does the present exchange of notes grant more legal certainty than the verbal note of 23 February 2010?

15. Is an exchange of letters between Prime Minister Renzi and Chancellor Faymann really sufficient to be able to derive a valid guarantee under international law?

16. Did an exchange of letters take place between you and Prime Minister Renzi?

17. If so, what content do(es)/did this/these letter(s) have *verbatim*?

18. Would not the Italian government need to give a binding assurance that it will comply with the agreement negotiated with South Tyrol, in writing and ratified by decision of the Italian parliament for an obligation under international law, on the basis of which Austria can base a claim?

19. Would not the Austrian parliament also decide to ratify in order to guarantee the binding character of such an agreement between states?

20. Can you confirm the claim made by the South Tyrolean People's Party that no additional treaty under international law is necessary to secure the presently discussed financial agreement because of the existence of the Paris Treaty of 1946 (Südtiroler Tageszeitung of 26 December 2014)?

   a. If so, why is such an effort made around the 'exchange of notes' that are supposed to lift the agreement to the level of international law?

   b. If so, on the basis of which provisions of the Paris Treaty?

21. What is the legal basis for the obligation of upholding the Paris Treaty?

22. When was the Paris Treaty ratified by the Austrian parliament?

23. How can the contradiction that the chairman of the South Tyrolean People's Party, Achammer, and Provincial Governor Kompatscher emphasised the protection of the financial agreement under international law from the start but you only speak of a corresponding 'exchange of letters' in your response?

The German original reads as follows:

In der Anfragebeantwortung 2979/AB vom 20. Jänner 2015 zu meiner Anfrage 3140/J vom 20. November 2014 teilen Sie bezüglich des Inhalts der Verbalnote vom 23. Februar 2010 Folgendes mit:

„In dieser Verbalnote teilt Österreich der italienischen Regierung mit, dass Österreich über die geplante neue Finanzordnung der Region Trentino-Südtirol und der autonomen Provinzen Trient und Bozen und der damit verbundenen Modifikation des Autonomiestatuts informiert wurde und diese in Hinblick auf die einvernehmliche Vorgangsweise zwischen den zuständigen Organen der Republik Italien und der autonomen Provinzen Trient und Bozens und der Region Trentino Südtirol zustimmend zur Kenntnis nimmt."

In Bezug auf die behauptete Rechtssicherheit, schreiben Sie, dass dafür sowohl der Noten- bzw. Briefwechsel, als auch die Verbalnote vom 23. Februar 2010 geeignet sei.

Diese Aussagen widersprechen einander insofern, als die bloße Kenntnisnahme keine vertraglich begründete Rechtssicherheit schaffen kann. Des Weiteren wurde wiederum die Angabe des Inhalts der Verbalnote im Wortlaut verweigert.

Des Weiteren konnte man den Medien seit Dezember des Vorjahres folgende Informationen entnehmen:

Im Dezember des Vorjahres informierte Ministerpräsident Renzi Bundeskanzler Faymann in einem Brief über das vereinbarte Finanzabkommen. Die Südtiroler Tageszeitung druckte den Inhalt des Briefes im Wortlaut:

„Lieber Werner,

ich informiere dich, dass die italienische Regierung mit den beiden Landeshauptleuten Arno Kompatscher und Ugo Rossi eine neue Form der gegenseitigen Finanzbeziehungen vereinbart hat. Das Abkommen, das ich in Kopie beilege, wird mit spezifischen Gesetzesbestimmungen umgesetzt werden. Diese Initiative beruht auf der Verbalnote vom 25. April 1992, mit dem eine Liste von Maßnahmen zur Durchführung des Pakets mitgeteilt wurde, darunter auch die Finanzregelung.

Im Geiste, von dem die italienisch-österreichischen Beziehungen immer geprägt waren, wird die italienische Regierung auch weiterhin das Einvernehmen garantieren, um auch in Zukunft den Schutz der ethnischen Minderheiten und die Ausübung der autonomen Gesetzgebungs- und Vollzugsgewalt für die betreffenden Gebiete zu gewährleisten."

SVP-Obmann Achammer erklärt dazu gegenüber Medien, dass Ministerpräsident Renzi mit der Unterzeichnung dieser schriftlichen „Note" an den österreichischen Bundeskanzler den Weg für eine erstmalige internationale Absicherung eines Finanzabkommens Südtirols mit dem italienischen Staat geebnet hätte. Der Notenwechsel mit Österreich komme einer Meisterleistung gleich und gewähre zusätzliche Sicherheit. Weiter bezeichnet er das Finanzabkommen als einen bedeutenden autonomiepolitischen Fortschritt.

In Ihrer Anfragebeantwortung halten Sie fest, dass es sich beim Finanzabkommen weder um ein bilaterales Abkommen, noch um einen völkerrechtlichen Vertrag handelt. Es sei dazu nur begleitend ein Briefwechsel zwischen Italien und Österreich in Aussicht genommen – keine Rede von rechtlicher Absicherung in irgendeiner Form.

Der Südtiroler Landeshauptmann Dr. Arno Kompatscher meint dazu in einem Interview mit der „Südtiroler Tageszeitung", dass sich die Beantwortung auf das Mailänder Abkommen beziehe, was schlicht falsch ist, da ausdrücklich nach der völkerrechtlichen Relevanz des aktuell geschlossenen Finanzabkommens, des sogenannten „Sicherungspakts" gefragt wurde. Er betont, dass dieser Notenwechsel zum Sicherungspakt nun absolut völkerrechtliche Relevanz habe. Von Seiten der SVP wird generell bestätigt, dass es sich zwar nicht um einen völkerrechtlichen Vertrag handelt, dieser sei aber aufgrund des geschlossenen Pariser Vertrages gar nicht notwendig (Südtiroler Tageszeitung vom 26. Dezember 2014).

Kürzlich war Medienberichten zu entnehmen, dass Bundeskanzler Faymann am 22. Jänner 2015 einen Brief an Italiens Premier Matteo Renzi unterschrieben hätte, mit dem der letzte Akt erfolgt sein soll, der den Briefwechsel zu einem Notenwechsel macht und damit das Finanzabkommen zwischen Südtirol und Rom „auf eine völkerrechtliche Ebene" hieven soll.

In diesem Zusammenhang stellen die unterfertigten Abgeordneten an den Bundesminister für Europa, Integration und Äußeres folgende

Anfrage

1. Besteht bzw. bestand jemals irgendeine Rechtssicherheit in Bezug auf die Einhaltung des

   a. Mailänder Abkommens,

   b. Sicherungspakts

   c. Wenn ja, wodurch ist eine solche gewährleistet?

2. Vor welcher internationalen rechtlichen Instanz kann Österreich aufgrund des diesbezüglichen Schriftwechsels zwischen Premier Renzi und Bundeskanzler Faymann bei Verletzung des derzeitigen Sicherungspakts in Bezug auf die Finanzregelung zwischen Rom und Bozen Klage auf Einhaltung der getroffenen Vereinbarungen erheben?

3. Warum war es Ihnen nicht möglich, eine Abschrift der Verbalnote vom 23. Februar 2010 zu veröffentlichen, oder sie zumindest den Mitgliedern des außenpolitischen Ausschusses vorzulegen?

4. Ist es Ihnen zum jetzigen Zeitpunkt möglich, den genauen Inhalt der Verbalnote vom 23. Februar 2010 im Wortlaut wiederzugeben, bzw. zumindest den Mitgliedern des außenpolitischen Ausschusses vorzulegen?

5. Entspricht es der Tatsache, dass Bundeskanzler Faymann einen Brief, wie oben erwähnt, am 22. Jänner 2015 unterzeichnet hat?

6. Wenn ja, wie lautet der exakte Inhalt im Wortlaut?

7. Woraus ergibt sich die völkerrechtliche Relevanz des Briefwechsels zwischen Premier Renzi und Bundeskanzler Faymann und wie wird diese definiert?

8. Durch welche Textpassage(n) in diesem Briefwechsel ist diese völkerrechtliche Relevanz begründet und wie wird diese definiert?

9. Wie kommt die völkerrechtliche Relevanz durch welche österreichischen Schritte im Falle einer Verletzung des Finanzabkommens durch Rom zum Tragen?

10. Was bedeutet es in rechtlicher und völkerrechtlicher Hinsicht, dass das Finanzabkommen nun „auf eine völkerrechtliche Ebene gehievt" wurde und welche völkerrechtliche Bindewirkung ergibt sich daraus für Italien?

11. Welche Vor- und/oder Nachteile ergeben sich daraus für

a. Südtirol?

b. Italien?

c. Österreich?

12. Was unterscheidet diese „völkerrechtliche Ebene" von einem „völkerrechtlichen Vertrag" in Bezug auf das vorliegende Finanzabkommen?

13. Worin besteht rechtlich und inhaltlich der Unterschied zwischen dem Notenwechsel bezüglich des aktuellen Finanzabkommens und der Verbalnote vom 23. Februar 2010 bezüglich des Mailänder Abkommens?

14. Inwiefern bietet der aktuelle Notenwechsel nun mehr Rechtssicherheit als die Verbalnote vom 23. Februar 2010?

15. Genügt tatsächlich ein Briefwechsel zwischen Premier Renzi und Bundeskanzler Faymann, um daraus eine völkerrechtlich wirksame Garantie abzuleiten?

16. Hat auch ein Briefverkehr zwischen Ihnen und Premier Renzi stattgefunden?

17. Wenn ja, welchen Inhalt hatte(n) der(die) Brief(e) im Wortlaut?

18. Müsste nicht die italienische Regierung eine gegenüber Österreich schriftliche bindende und durch Beschluss des italienischen Parlaments ratifizierte Zusage auf Einhaltung der mit Südtirol getroffenen Vereinbarung abgeben, damit sich daraus eine völkerrechtliche und durch Österreich einklagbare Verbindlichkeit begründen kann?

19. Müsste nicht das österreichische Parlament ebenso einen Ratifizierungs- Beschluss fassen, um die völkerrechtliche Verbindlichkeit einer derartigen zwischenstaatlichen Vereinbarung zu gewährleisten?

20. Können Sie die Behauptung seitens der SVP bestätigen, dass man keinen zusätzlichen völkerrechtlich relevanten Vertrag brauche, um das zur Debatte stehende Finanzabkommen rechtlich abzusichern, weil man dafür ja ohnedies bereits den Pariser Vertrag von 1946 habe (Südtiroler Tageszeitung vom 26. Dezember 2014)?

a. Wenn ja, warum stellt man dann diese Bemühungen um den „Notenwechsel" an, die das Abkommen auf eine völkerrechtliche Ebene hieven sollen?

b. Wenn ja, auf welche Bestimmung des Pariser Vertrages begründet sich dies?

21. Auf welcher rechtlichen Grundlage basiert die Verpflichtung zur Einhaltung des Pariser Vertrages?

22. Wann wurde der Pariser Vertrag im österreichischen Parlament ratifiziert?

23. Wie ist der Widerspruch zu erklären, dass SVP-Obmann Achammer und Landeshauptmann Kompatscher von Beginn an die völkerrechtliche Absicherung des Finanzabkommens hervorgehoben haben, Sie in der Anfragebeantwortung aber nur von einem „begleitenden Briefwechsel" sprechen?

On 17 April 2015, the Minister for Europe, Integration and Foreign Affairs gave the following response:[9]

On questions 1, 2, 15, 18 to 20:

The Italian Minister President Matteo Renzi informed his counterpart, Chancellor Werner Faymann, in writing that new provision for the regulation of the financial relations between Rome and Bozen/Bolzano (as well as Trento) had been agreed upon that, where necessary, would be implemented through separate legal provisions. This letter clearly puts the new financial regulations in the context of the existing internationally guaranteed rules on the autonomy of South Tyrol, which serves the international security of exactly the new financial regulations as part of the autonomy.

Austria assumes that the Italian government will honour its assurances. Domestically, these assurances and their implementation are subject to the control of the Italian Constitutional Court. Furthermore, both South Tyrol as well as Austria in exercising its protective function over South Tyrol consider the assurances of the Italian government as a development of the autonomy of South Tyrol that underlies the final control through the International Court of Justice since the settlement of the dispute in 1992.

On questions 3 and 4:

The content of the verbal note of 23 February 2010 was already made public in my response to the parliamentary enquiry 3140/J-NR/2014 of 20 January 2015. The text of the verbal note is as follows: 'The Austrian embassy would like to pay its regards and has the honour to inform that Austria was notified of the planned new financial regulation of the region Trentino-South Tyrol and the autonomous provinces of Trento and Bozen/Bolzano und the corresponding modifications of the Autonomy Statute and that it favourably acknowledges it in light of the consensual approach between the competent organs of the Republic of Italy and the autonomous provinces of Bozen/Trento and Bolzano and the region Trentino-South Tyrol.'

---

[9] Parliamentary Materials, 3589/AB (XXV. GP).

On questions 5 and 6:

The answer to this question does not fall within the competence of the Ministry for Europe, Integration and Foreign Affairs. Furthermore, I would like to point out that the content of the response of 22 January 2015 was printed *verbatim* in the South Tyrolean newspaper 'Dolomiten' on 12 February 2015.

On questions 7 and 8, 10 and 11:

An official exchange of letters between two heads of government is relevant under international law. Generally, such an exchange of letters expresses that the issues discussed are such as fall within the mutual state interest. In the present case, the letter of the Italian Prime Minister Matteo Renzi contains the assurance that the Italian government will continue to ensure a consensual bilateral approach in the spirit of past Italian-Austrian relations, in order to guarantee the protection of linguistic minorities in the autonomous province Bozen/Bolzano as well as the implementation of the autonomy in the legislative and administrative branches in the future. The reply by Chancellor Werner Faymann attributes particular importance to this assurance and the consensual bilateral approach emphasised by the Italian government.

On question 9:

In that case, Austria, in exercise of its protective function, would approach the Italian government and stand up for the interests of South Tyrol.

On question 12:

On the relevance of an official exchange of letters under international law, I refer to the above elaborations. A treaty under international law is a legal instrument negotiated between two subjects of international law, such as the Paris Convention of 1946, in which specific rights and obligations are laid down in binding form under international law. In this context, I would like to refer to my reply to the parliamentary enquiry 3140/J-NR/2014 of 20 January 2015, in which I explained that the financial agreement between South Tyrol and the Italian Government is not a treaty under international law.

On questions 13 and 14:

The exchange of letters of 2014/2015 is a notification of the financial agreement agreed at the intergovernmental level concerted between the two heads of government. The verbal note of 23 February 2010 was transmitted to the Italian Ministry of Foreign Affairs by the Austrian embassy in Rome.

On questions 16 and 17:

No.

On question 21:

On the basis of the customary international law principle of 'pacta sunt servanda' as codified in Article 26 of the Vienna Convention on the Law of Treaties (Federal Law Gazette No. 40/1980).

On question 22:

The fact that the Paris Treaty was not subject to any parliamentary approval on the Austrian side is to be understood from the circumstances at the time of its conclusion and does not alter the binding character of this agreement under international law. This legal understanding is also confirmed by the state practice of Austria and Italy. *E.g.*, Austria was notified of the implementation of the 137 package measures by Italy on 22 April 1992 with explicit reference to the Paris Treaty.

On question 23:

There is no contradiction here. The corresponding exchange of letters between Italy and Austria was undertaken to guarantee the financial agreement under international law.

The German original reads as follows:

Zu den Fragen 1, 2, 15, 18 bis 20:

Der italienische Ministerpräsident Matteo Renzi hat seinen österreichischen Amtskollegen, Bundeskanzler Werner Faymann, schriftlich darüber informiert, dass neue Bestimmungen zur Regelung der Finanzbeziehungen zwischen Rom und Bozen (sowie Trient) vereinbart wurden, die, wo dies erforderlich ist, durch eigene Rechtsvorschriften umgesetzt werden. In diesem Schreiben wird ein klarer Zusammenhang zwischen den bestehenden und international abgesicherten Regelungen der Autonomie Südtirols und den neuen Finanzregelungen hergestellt, was der internationalen Absicherung eben dieser neuen Finanzregelungen als Teil der Autonomie dient.

Österreich geht davon aus, dass die italienische Regierung ihre Zusagen einhält. Innerstaatlich unterliegen diese Zusagen und ihre Umsetzung der Kontrolle durch das italienische Verfassungsgericht. Darüber hinaus betrachten sowohl Südtirol als auch Österreich in Ausübung seiner Schutzfunktion für Südtirol die Zusagen der italienischen Regierung als eine Fortentwicklung der Autonomie Südtirols, die seit der Streitbeilegung 1992 letztlich der Kontrolle durch den Internationalen Gerichtshof unterliegt.

Zu den Fragen 3 und 4:

Der Inhalt der Verbalnote vom 23. Februar 2010 wurde bereits in meiner Beantwortung der parlamentarischen Anfrage 3140/J-NR/2014 vom 20. Jänner 2015 bekannt gegeben. Der Text der Verbalnote lautet wie folgt: „Die österreichische Botschaft entbietet dem Ministerium für auswärtige Angelegenheiten ihre Grüße und beehrt sich mitzuteilen, dass Österreich über die geplante neue Finanzordnung der Region Trentino-Südtirol und der autonomen Provinzen Trient und Bozen und der damit verbundenen Modifikation des Autonomiestatuts informiert wurde und diese in Hinblick auf die einvernehmliche Vorgangsweise zwischen den zuständigen Organen der Republik Italien und der autonomen Provinzen Trient und Bozens und der Region Trentino Südtirol zustimmend zur Kenntnis nimmt."

Zu den Fragen 5 und 6:
Die Beantwortung dieser Frage fällt nicht in die Vollziehung des Bundesministeriums für Europa, Integration und Äußeres (BMEIA). Im Übrigen weise ich darauf hin, dass der Wortlaut des Antwortschreibens vom 22. Jänner 2015 in den Südtiroler „Dolomiten" vom 12. Februar 2015 (S. 13) abgedruckt wurde.

Zu den Fragen 7 und 8, 10 und 11:
Ein offizieller Briefwechsel zwischen zwei Regierungschefs hat völkerrechtliche Relevanz. Ganz allgemein bringt ein solcher Briefwechsel zum Ausdruck, dass es sich bei den in ihm angesprochenen Fragen um solche zwischenstaatlichen Interesses handelt. Im konkreten Fall enthält der Brief des italienischen Ministerpräsidenten Matteo Renzi die Zusage, dass die italienische Regierung im Geiste der bisherigen italienisch-österreichischen Beziehungen auch weiterhin eine einvernehmliche bilaterale Vorgangsweise gewährleisten wird, um den Schutz der sprachlichen Minderheiten in der Autonomen Provinz Bozen sowie die Umsetzung der Autonomie in Gesetzgebung und Verwaltung auch in Zukunft zu garantieren. Im Antwortbrief von Bundeskanzler Werner Faymann wird dieser Zusage und der von der italienischen Regierung bekräftigten einvernehmlichen bilateralen Vorgangsweise besondere Bedeutung zugemessen.

Zu Frage 9:
Österreich würde in diesem Fall auf Ersuchen Südtirols in Ausübung seiner Schutzfunktion an die italienische Regierung herantreten und sich für die Interessen Südtirols einsetzen.

Zu Frage 12:
Zur völkerrechtlichen Relevanz eines offiziellen Briefwechsels verweise ich auf meine obigen Ausführungen. Ein völkerrechtlicher Vertrag ist ein zwischen zwei Völkerrechtssubjekten vereinbartes Rechtsinstrument, wie etwa das Pariser Abkommen von 1946, in dem in völkerrechtlich verbindlicher Weise konkrete Rechte und Pflichten festgelegt werden. Ich verweise in diesem Zusammenhang auf meine Beantwortung der parlamentarischen Anfrage Zl. 3140/J-NR/2014 vom 20. Jänner 2015, in der ich dargelegt habe, dass es sich daher beim Finanzabkommen zwischen Südtirol und der italienischen Regierung nicht um einen völkerrechtlichen Vertrag handelt.

Zu den Fragen 13 und 14:
Beim Briefwechsel von 2014/2015 handelt es sich um eine zwischen den beiden Regierungschefs abgesprochene Notifikation des Finanzabkommens auf zwischenstaatlicher Ebene. Die Verbalnote vom 23. Februar 2010 wurde von der österreichischen Botschaft in Rom dem italienischen Außenministerium übermittelt.

Zu den Fragen 16 und 17:
Nein.

Zu Frage 21:

Auf dem völkergewohnheitsrechtlichen Grundsatz „pacta sunt servanda", wie er in Art. 26 der Wiener Vertragsrechtskonvention (BGBl Nr. 40/1980) kodifiziert wurde.

Zu Frage 22:

Der Umstand, dass das Pariser Abkommen aus Gründen, die aus der Zeit seines Abschlusses zu verstehen sind, auf österreichischer Seite keiner parlamentarischen Genehmigung unterzogen wurde, ändert nichts an der völkerrechtlichen Geltung dieses Abkommens. Diese Rechtsauffassung wird auch durch die Staatenpraxis Österreichs und Italiens bestätigt. So wurde z.B. Österreich von Italien am 22. April 1992 die Durchführung der 137 Paketmaßnahmen unter ausdrücklicher Bezugnahme auf das Pariser Abkommen notifiziert.

Zu Frage 23:

Es besteht hier kein Widerspruch. Der begleitende Briefwechsel zwischen Italien und Österreich wurde zur völkerrechtlichen Absicherung des Finanzabkommens vorgenommen.

3. Interpretation of treaties/Auslegung von Verträgen

CC.II.3.-1

Work of the International Law Commission on the Most-Favoured-Nation Clause

Arbeit der Völkerrechtskommission der Vereinten Nationen betreffend Meistbegünstigungsklausel

On 2 November 2015, the Austrian representative to the 70th session of the General Assembly delivered the following statement to the Sixth Committee regarding the Report of the International Law Commission on the Work of its 67th Session concerning the topic 'Most-Favoured-Nation Clause':

Austria specifically welcomes the adoption of five summary conclusions reflecting the main outcome of the Study Group's work. It concurs with the Commission's view that the scope of MFN clauses is to be determined by the interpretation rules laid down in the Vienna Convention on the Law of Treaties. It further shares the Commission's view expressed in conclusion e) that the central, controversial question to what extent MFN clauses encompass dispute settlement provisions can be most appropriately solved by explicit language in the relevant treaties. However, there is a minor point concerning this conclusion which my delegation would like to raise: we are not fully convinced of the accuracy of the sentence stating that '[o]therwise the matter will be left to dispute settlement tribunals to interpret MFN clauses on a case-by-case basis.' The introductory word 'otherwise' suggests that only in the absence of explicit language in the relevant treaty dispute settlement tribunals have the power to interpret MFN clauses on a case-by-case basis. In fact, however, any application of a treaty requires the interpretation of this treaty, even if such interpretation appears obvious. Thus, a more nuanced formulation could have been adopted by the Study Group indicating that in the absence of explicit language dispute settlement tribunals enjoy a broader margin of interpretative freedom.

III. Amendment and modification of treaties/Änderung und Modifikation von Verträgen

CC.III.-1

Work of the International Law Commission on Subsequent Agreements and Subsequent Practice in Relation to the Interpretation of Treaties

Arbeit der Völkerrechtskommission der Vereinten Nationen betreffend die spätere Übereinkunft und Übung in Bezug auf die Interpretation von Verträgen

On 4 November 2015, the Austrian representative to the 70th session of the General Assembly delivered the following statement to the Sixth Committee regarding the Report of the International Law Commission on the Work of its 67th Session concerning the topic of subsequent agreement and practice in relation to the interpretation of treaties:

> We welcome the provisional adoption of draft conclusion 11 on constituent instruments of international organizations. This conclusion reflects the growing importance of the role of international organizations both as actors in their own right and as important fora for the collective action of their member states. The report rightly elaborates on the distinction between these two emanations of international organizations and their contribution to the interpretation of treaties.
>
> The practice of international organizations is of particular importance for the interpretation of their constituent instruments since it entails even the possibility of the application of the implied powers doctrine. Accordingly, the ICJ has already emphasized the particular nature of the constituent instruments of international organizations.
>
> Nevertheless, certain clarifications are still needed: First, the term 'international organizations' should be understood as referring only to intergovernmental organizations, as the expression was used by the ILC in texts for conventions such as *e.g.* the 1986 Vienna Convention on the Law of Treaties between States and International Organizations. Second, for the purposes of the draft conclusions, the term 'constituent instruments' only comprises instruments that are treaties. However, this does not exclude that organizations can be based on constituent instruments not having treaty character.
>
> As to paragraph 2 of draft conclusion 11 we would be interested to know how the term 'practice of an international organization in the application of its constituent

instrument' relates to the term 'established practice of the organization'. The latter expression has been used as part of the 'rules of the organization' defined in Article 2 paragraph 1 subparagraph (j) of the 1986 Vienna Convention. Generally speaking, it is difficult to determine the meaning of 'practice of international organizations', in particular whether it includes all acts that are attributable to the organization as mentioned in the commentary. The commentary, in paragraph 24, calls for a 'cautionary approach' in this regard but does not answer this question.

My delegation specifically appreciates the report's rich elaboration on the existing judicial and other dispute settlement practice which has been the basis for the elaboration of draft conclusion 11. With regard to the commentary on conclusion 11 paragraph 4 we appreciate the mentioning of the WTO but would have liked to have an express reference to Article IX paragraph 2 of the WTO Agreement on the authentic interpretation of the WTO Agreement as well as the multilateral trade agreements. While the case concerning United States measures affecting production and sales of clove cigarettes discussed in the commentary is reflective of some of the problems, the WTO Agreement demonstrates how difficult it often is to reconcile the institutionalized rules of an organization on interpretation with the role of member states as parties to the constituent instrument of an organization in interpreting this instrument.

Finally, the Austrian delegation is in favour of reflecting the practice of international organizations as such also in other draft conclusions, as suggested in footnote 354 of the Commission's report. In our view, draft conclusion 4 paragraph 3, which currently only refers to 'conduct by one or more parties' of a treaty, should be broadened and refer also to the conduct of an international organization established by such a treaty. This understanding would correspond to conclusion 1 paragraph 4, which refers to other subsequent practice without limiting it to state parties.

VI. Consensual arrangements, other than in treaty-form/ Willensübereinkünfte in anderer Form

See CC.II.1.-1.

DD. Relationship between international law and internal law/ Völkerrecht und innerstaatliches Recht

II. Application and implementation of international law in internal law/Innerstaatliche Anwendung und Durchführung des Völkerrechts

See LL.II.2.-1.

DD.II.-1

Inclusion of the Crime of Aggression in the Austrian Criminal Code

Aufnahme des Verbrechens der Aggression in das österreichische Strafgesetzbuch

As mentioned in the previous digests,[10] Austria recently implemented various provisions of international criminal law, including a newly adopted Chapter 25 of the Austrian Criminal Code, which came into force on 1 January 2015. Following Austria's ratification of the Kampala Amendment,[11] new §321k was introduced into the Austrian Criminal Code:[12]

Crime of Aggression

§321k.

(1) A person in a position effectively to exercise control over or to direct the political or military action of a State that initiates or executes an act of aggression which by its character, gravity, and scale constitutes a manifest violation of the Charter of the United Nations is punishable with imprisonment from ten to twenty years.

(2) Who plans or prepares such an act of aggression under the conditions named under paragraph 1, is punishable with imprisonment from five to ten years.

(3) For the purpose of paragraph 1, 'act of aggression' means the use of armed force by a State against the sovereignty, territorial integrity, or political independence of another State, or in any other manner inconsistent with the Charter of the United Nations.

The German original reads as follows:

Verbrechen der Aggression

§321k.

(1) Wer tatsächlich in der Lage ist, das politische oder militärische Handeln eines Staates zu kontrollieren oder zu lenken, und eine Angriffshandlung, die ihrer Art,

---

[10] See Markus Beham and Gerhard Hafner, 'Austrian Diplomatic and Parliamentary Practice in International Law/Österreichische diplomatische und Parlamentarische Praxis zum Internationalen Recht' (2012) 17 ARIEL 395, at 414, DD.II.-2; Markus Beham and Gerhard Hafner, 'Austrian Diplomatic and Parliamentary Practice in International Law/Österreichische diplomatische und Parlamentarische Praxis zum Internationalen Recht' (2014) 19 ARIEL 305, at 324, DD.II.-1.

[11] See Markus Beham and Gerhard Hafner, 'Austrian Diplomatic and Parliamentary Practice in International Law/Österreichische diplomatische und Parlamentarische Praxis zum Internationalen Recht' (2014) 19 ARIEL 305, at 371, FF.X. 1.

[12] Federal Law Gazette I No 112/2015.

ihrer Schwere und ihrem Umfang nach eine offenkundige Verletzung der Satzung der Vereinten Nationen darstellt, einleitet oder ausführt, ist mit Freiheitsstrafe von zehn bis zu zwanzig Jahren zu bestrafen.

(2) Wer unter den in Abs. 1 bezeichneten Voraussetzungen eine solche Angriffshandlung plant oder vorbereitet, ist mit Freiheitsstrafe von fünf bis zu zehn Jahren zu bestrafen.

(3) Im Sinne des Abs. 1 bedeutet „Angriffshandlung" eine gegen die Souveränität, die territoriale Unversehrtheit oder die politische Unabhängigkeit eines Staates gerichtete oder sonst mit der Satzung der Vereinten Nationen unvereinbare Anwendung von Waffengewalt durch einen anderen Staat.

The Explanatory Memorandum clarifies the scope of the provision:[13]

The criminal offence of §321k of the Austrian Criminal Code is largely oriented along the structure of Article 8bis of the Rome Statute. In accordance with the guiding principle of the Charter of the United Nations of maintaining international peace and security, §321k of the Austrian Criminal Code applies both to attacks against the Republic of Austria and those against other States. The acts include the following acts listed in UN General Assembly Resolution 3314 (XXIX) of 14 December 1974: [...]

The crime of aggression is a violation related special obligation offence. The offender must in fact be able to control or direct the political and military action of a state (Intraneus). However, he does not have to be the immediate perpetrator; it is sufficient if he is involved in the offense in any form in the sense of §12 Austrian Criminal Code. If there is no Intraneus involved in the act, the involved Extranei are not punishable.

The Austrian jurisdiction for crimes of aggression committed abroad is already adequately regulated by §64(1)(4c) of the Austrian Criminal Code, as amended, as a result of the reference to criminal offenses under Chapter 25.

The relevant parts of the German original read as follows:

Der Tatbestand des §321k StGB orientiert sich weitgehend an der Struktur des Art. 8bis RS. In Einklang mit dem leitenden Gedanke der Satzung der Vereinten Nationen, den Weltfrieden und die internationale Sicherheit aufrechtzuerhalten, bezieht sich §321k StGB gleichermaßen auf Angriffshandlungen gegen die Republik Österreich und solche gegen andere Staaten. Angriffshandlungen gemäß §321k StGB umfassen die folgenden, in der Resolution 3314 (XXIX) der Generalversammlung der Vereinten Nationen vom 14. Dezember 1974 aufgezählten Handlungen: [...]

Das Verbrechen der Aggression ist ein unrechtsbezogenes Sonderpflichtdelikt. Der Täter muss tatsächlich in der Lage sein, das politische und militärische Handeln eines Staates zu kontrollieren oder zu lenken (Intraneus). Er muss jedoch

---

[13] Explanatory Memorandum, Parliamentary Materials 689 (XXV. GP).

nicht unmittelbarer Täter sein; es genügt, wenn er in irgendeiner Täterschaftsform des §12 StGB an der Tat beteiligt ist. Wirkt kein Intraneus an der Tat mit, sind die beteiligten Extranei straflos.

Die österreichische Gerichtsbarkeit für im Ausland begangene Verbrechen de r Aggression ist durch §64 Abs. 1 Z 4c StGB idgF aufgrund des Verweises auf strafbare Handlungen nach dem 25. Abschnitt bereits angemessen geregelt.

EE. Subjects of International law/Völkerrechtssubjekte

II. International organisations/Internationale Organisationen

1. In general/Allgemeines

EE.II.1.-1

Amendment of the Federal Law on the Granting of Privileges to Non-Governmental International Organisations

Novelle des Bundesgesetzes über die Einräumung von Privilegien an nichtstaatliche internationale Organisationen

In order to accommodate legal entities that do not enjoy the full status of an international organisation and, thus, cannot conclude headquarters agreements, Austria amended the Federal Law on the Granting of Privileges to Non-Governmental International Organisations to include the category of 'quasi-international organisations'. The amendment entered into force on 1 January 2016:[14]

§7. (1) Quasi-international organisations within the meaning of para. 2 shall be granted privileges in accordance with paragraphs 3 and 4.

(2) A quasi-international organisation within the meaning of this federal law is an organisation

1. which has been recognised by decision as a non-profit organisation in accordance with §6,

2. if its activities are closely related to the activities of an international organisation within the meaning of Section 1(7) of the Federal Law on the Granting of Privileges and Immunities to International Organisations, Federal Law Gazette No. 677/1977, as amended.

3. that maintains a permanent and adequately staffed office in Austria,

4. a) the majority of members being states, international organisations or bodies fulfilling the functions of states or international organisations,

---

[14] Federal Law Gazette I No 160/2015.

b) which is at least 25% financed by states, international organisations or bodies fulfilling the functions of states or international organisations;

5. that has a similar structure is inter-governmental organisations,

6. that is active in two or more states.

(3) At the beginning of a calendar year, the Federal Government shall decide by decree which organisations respectively fulfil the requirements of para. 2. The decree shall be limited to one calendar year. Regarding the organisations listed in the decree, a separate decision within the meaning of §1 is not necessary. The provisions of §§4, 5, and 8 shall apply directly to the organisations listed in the decree.

(4) The quasi-international organisations (paragraph 2) listed in the decree in accordance with paragraph 3 enjoy the following privileges:

1. In respect of its official activities, the exemption of the organisation from:

a) the fee for any tenancy contracts pursuant to Section 33 TP 5 of the Fee Act 1957, Federal Law Gazette No. 267/1957, as amended;

b) the standard consumption tax for official vehicles of the organisation;

c) the motor-related insurance tax for official vehicles of the organisation;

d) the vehicle tax on for official vehicles of the organisation;

e) the municipal tax.

2. exemption from the property transfer tax for gratuitous acquisitions (§7(1)(1) Property Transfer Tax Act 1987) of a property in the sense of §2 of the Property Transfer Tax Act 1987, Federal Law Gazette No. 309/1987, as amended, by an organisation, in so far as the property serves the official activity.

3. exemption of the employees of the organisation from the income tax on the earnings (salaries and other forms of remuneration) which they receive from that organisation for their official activities. Such exemption shall not prejudice the right of the Republic of Austria to take into account these assets in determining the tax to be levied on income from other sources.

The relevant parts of the German original read as follows:

§7. (1) Quasi-Internationalen Organisationen im Sinne des Abs. 2 werden nach Maßgabe der Abs. 3 und 4 Privilegien eingeräumt.

(2) Eine Quasi-Internationale Organisation ist eine Organisation im Sinne dieses Bundesgesetzes,

1. die mit Bescheid gemäß §6 als gemeinnützig anerkannt worden ist,

2. deren Tätigkeit in einem engen Zusammenhang mit der Tätigkeit einer Internationalen Organisation im Sinne des §1 Abs. 7 des Bundesgesetzes über die Einräumung von Privilegien und Immunitäten an internationale Organisationen, BGBl. Nr. 677/1977, in der jeweils geltenden Fassung, steht,

3. die in Österreich ein ständiges und personell angemessen ausgestattetes Büro unterhält,

4. a) deren Mitglieder mehrheitlich Staaten, Internationale Organisationen oder Einrichtungen sind, die Aufgaben von Staaten oder Internationalen Organisationen erfüllen, oder

b) die zu mindestens 25% von Staaten, Internationalen Organisationen oder Einrichtungen, die Aufgaben von Staaten oder Internationalen Organisationen erfüllen, finanziert wird;

5. die über ähnliche Strukturen wie eine zwischenstaatliche Organisation verfügt und

6. die in zwei oder mehr Staaten tätig ist.

(3) Die Bundesregierung hat mit Verordnung festzustellen, welche Organisationen jeweils zum Beginn eines Kalenderjahres die Voraussetzungen des Abs. 2 erfüllen. Die Verordnung ist jeweils auf ein Kalenderjahr zu befristen. Hinsichtlich der in der Verordnung genannten Organisationen ist die gesonderte Erteilung eines Bescheides im Sinn des §1 nicht erforderlich. Die Bestimmungen der §§4, 5 und 8 finden auf die in der Verordnung genannten Organisationen unmittelbar Anwendung.

(4) Den in der Verordnung gemäß Abs. 3 angeführten Quasi-Internationalen Organisationen (Abs. 2) werden folgende Privilegien eingeräumt:

1. die Befreiung der Organisation in Bezug auf ihre amtliche Tätigkeit von folgenden Abgaben:

a) der Gebühr auf Bestandverträge gemäß §33 TP 5 des Gebührengesetzes 1957, BGBl. Nr. 267/1957, in der jeweils geltenden Fassung;

b) der Normverbrauchsabgabe für Dienstfahrzeuge der Organisation;

c) der motorbezogenen Versicherungssteuer für Dienstfahrzeuge der Organisation;

d) der Kraftfahrzeugsteuer für Dienstfahrzeuge der Organisation;

e) der Kommunalsteuer.

2. die Befreiung von der Grunderwerbsteuer für den unentgeltlichen Erwerb (§7 Abs. 1 Z 1 GrEStG 1987) eines Grundstückes im Sinne des §2 des Grunderwerbsteuergesetzes 1987 (GrEStG 1987), BGBl. Nr. 309/1987, in der jeweils geltenden Fassung, durch eine Organisation, sofern das Grundstück der amtlichen Tätigkeit dient.

3. die Befreiung der Arbeitnehmer der Organisation von der Einkommensteuer auf Aktivbezüge (Gehälter, Bezüge und sonstige Vergütungen), die sie für ihre Dienste von dieser Organisation in Bezug auf ihre amtliche Tätigkeit erhalten. Eine solche Befreiung berührt nicht das Recht der Republik Österreich, diese Aktivbezüge bei der Festsetzung der von Einkünften aus anderen Quellen zu erhebenden Steuer zu berücksichtigen.

The Explanatory Memorandum further clarifies:[15]
[...] §7 [...]:
[...] 3. Paragraph 3 concerns the employees of the organisation. Their earnings and benefits from an active employment in the organisation is exempt from income tax – and at the same time from 'pay-as-you-earn', whereas the exempt earnings may be considered with regard to the progression proviso. However, earnings and benefits from a previous employment in the organisation are not within the scope of the provision. The exemption only applies to employees that are employed 'with regard to the official activity of the organisation', not, *e.g.*, to cleaning personnel, kitchen staff, or IT service desk employees.

[...] §9(1) [...]:
The deletion of the reference to §7 in §9(1) clarifies that the privileges granted to the quasi-international organisations cannot be withdrawn within a calendar year. The binding granting of privileges for a calendar year is the prerequisite for the legal certainty of the persons concerned (*e.g.*, employees of the organization) and the administrability of the tax exemptions by intermediaries (*e.g.*, notaries, insurance companies). The consequence of any misconduct within the meaning of §9(1) is that the privileges are no longer granted in the following calendar year.

The relevant parts of the German original read as follows:

Zu Z 3 (Art. I §7):
[...] 3. Ziffer 3 betrifft die unselbständigen Beschäftigten der Organisation. Deren Bezüge und Vorteile aus einem bestehenden Dienstverhältnis zur Organisation sind von der Einkommensteuer – und gleichzeitig auch vom Lohnsteuerabzug befreit, wobei die befreiten Einkünfte gegebenenfalls zum Progressionsvorbehalt heran zu ziehen sind. Dagegen sind Bezüge und Vorteile aus einem früheren Dienstverhältnis zur Organisation nicht erfasst. Die Befreiung gilt nur für Dienstnehmer, die „in Bezug auf die amtliche Tätigkeit der Organisation" beschäftigt werden, nicht aber für z.B. Reinigungspersonal, Küchenpersonal oder IT-Servicedesk-Mitarbeiter.

Zu Z 4 (Art. I §9 Abs. 1):
Durch die Streichung des Verweises auf §7 in §9 Abs. 1 wird klargestellt, dass die den Quasi-Internationalen Organisationen gewährten Privilegien nicht innerhalb eines Kalenderjahres aberkannt werden können. Die verbindliche Zuerkennung der Privilegien jeweils für ein Kalenderjahr ist Voraussetzung für die Rechtssicherheit der Betroffenen (z. B. Arbeitnehmer der Organisation) und für die Administrierbarkeit der Steuerbefreiungen durch Intermediäre (z.B. Notare, Versicherungsunternehmen). Konsequenz eines allfälligen Fehlverhaltens im Sinne des §9 Abs. 1 ist, dass die Privilegien im folgenden Kalenderjahr nicht mehr gewährt werden.

---

[15] Explanatory Memorandum, Parliamentary Materials 889 (XXV. GP).

b. Participation of States in international organisations and in their activities/Mitgliedschaft in internationalen Organisationen, Teilnahme an ihren Aktivitäten

bb. Suspension, withdrawal, expulsion/Suspension der Mitgliedschaft, Austritt, Ausschluß

EE.II.1.b.bb.-1

Withdrawal from the Common Fund for Commodities

Rücktritt vom Übereinkommen zur Gründung des Gemeinsamen Rohstofffonds

On 9 January 2015, the Secretary-General was informed by the Common Fund for Commodities that Austria had notified the Fund of its decision to withdraw from the Fund.[16]

2. Particular types/Arten internationaler Organisationen

d. Other types of organisations/Andere Arten von Organisationen

See also *EE.II.1.-1.*

EE.II.2.d.-1

Asian Infrastructure Investment Bank

Asiatische Infrastruktur-Investitionsbank

On 23 March 2015, the Austrian Council of Ministers approved the signature of the Memorandum of Understanding on Establishing the Asian Infrastructure Investment Bank. The undersigned Memorandum was handed over by the Austrian Federal President to the President of the People's Republic of China during an official visit on 27 March 2015. Since that moment, Austria participated in the negotiation of the Articles of Agreement of the Asian Infrastructure Investment Bank. These were finalised 22 May 2015 and the text was accepted by the conference by way of acclamation. On 28 June 2015, Austria signed the

---

[16] C.N.716.2015.TREATIES-XIX.21. See also already Markus Beham and Gerhard Hafner, 'Austrian Diplomatic and Parliamentary Practice in International Law/ Österreichische diplomatische und Parlamentarische Praxis zum Internationalen Recht' (2014) 19 ARIEL 305, at 350, EE.II.1.b.bb.-1.

treaty and ratified it on 5 December of the same year. The Explanatory Memorandum points out:[17]

Through the participation of Western states such as Austria in the negotiations on the establishment of the AIIB, important cornerstones of the European position concerning governance and environmental and social standards could be asserted. Above all, this included securing the principle of sustainable development and an adequate conception of the rights of the Board of Directors. The principles of the oversight mechanisms such as transparency and independence were inserted into the treaty. The principle of 'best practices' with regard to operative policies and the consideration of debt sustainability in the recipient countries can be found in the explanatory notes of the Chief Negotiator's Report, which assist the authentic interpretation of the treaty. The envisaged environmental and social guidelines and the applicable standards are prepared by the chief negotiators and must be adopted by the future Board of Directors following the entry into force of the agreement and prior to the initiation of project financing. They are largely in accordance with the existing provisions of the Asian Development Bank and are based on the experience and practices of other international financial institutions active in the region such as the Asian Development Bank, the European Investment Bank, the World Bank Group or the European Bank for Reconstruction and Development (EBRD). The same holds true for the procurement rules which are based heavily on those of the EBRD.

The relevant parts of the German original read as follows:

Durch die Teilnahme westlicher Staaten wie Österreich an den Verhandlungen zur Gründung der AIIB, konnten wichtige Eckpunkte der europäischen Position betreffend Governance und Umwelt- und Sozialstandards durchgesetzt werden. Diese betreffen vor allem die Verankerung des Nachhaltigkeitsprinzips und eine adäquate Ausgestaltung der Rechte des Direktoriums. Die Prinzipien der Oversight Mechanismen wie Transparenz und Unabhängigkeit wurden ebenfalls in das Übereinkommen aufgenommen. Das Prinzip der „best practices" in Bezug auf die operativen Policies und die Berücksichtigung einer nachhaltigen Schuldentragfähigkeit in den Empfängerländern findet sich in den Erläuterungen aus dem Bericht der Chefunterhändler, die der authentischen Interpretation des Übereinkommens dienen, wieder. Die geplante Umwelt- und Sozialrichtlinie und die anzuwendenden Standards werden von den Chefunterhändlern vorbereitet und müssen vom zukünftigen Direktorium nach Inkrafttreten des Übereinkommens und vor Aufnahme der Projektfinanzierung angenommen werden. Sie sind weitestgehend in Übereinstimmung mit den geltenden Bestimmungen der Asiatischen Entwicklungsbank und bauen auf Erfahrungen und Praktiken anderer, in der Region tätigen internationalen Finanzinstitutionen wie der Asiatischen Entwicklungsbank, der Europäischen Investitionsbank, der Weltbank Gruppe oder der Europäischen

---

[17] Explanatory Memorandum, Parliamentary Materials 798 (XXV. GP).

Bank für Wiederaufbau und Entwicklung (EBRD) auf. Das Gleiche gilt für die Procurement Regeln, die stark an diejenigen der EBRD angelehnt sind.

III. Other subjects of international law and entities and groups/ Andere Völkerrechtssubjekte, Einheiten und Gruppen

6. Special regimes/Besondere Regime

See EE.II.1.-1.

FF. The position of the individual (including the corporation) in international law/Die Stellung der Einzelperson (einschließlich der juristischen Person) im Völkerrecht

IV. Members of minorities/Angehörige von Minderheiten

See CC.II.1.-1, CC.I.2.-2, and CC.I.2.-3.

VII. Immigration and emigration, extradition, expulsion, asylum/ Einwanderung und Auswanderung, Auslieferung, Ausweisung, Asyl

4. Asylum/Asyl

FF.VII.4.-1

Five approaches to handling the refugee crisis

Fünf Ansätze zur Behandlung der Flüchtlingskrise

On 22 August 2015, the Austrian Ministry for Europe, Integration and Foreign Affairs released its five approaches to handling the refugee crisis:[18]

[...]

1. Tackling Root Causes

- Conflict resolution: The Iran deal negotiated by the E3/EU+3 in Vienna has the potential for a new dynamic in the Near and Middle East. This should be instrumentalised for progress in the difficult and arduous diplomatic efforts for conflict resolution (in particular of the United Nations) in Syria and Libya.

---

[18] Parliamentary Materials, 6839/J (XXV. GP).

- International action against Islamist terror: The alliance against IS terrorism led by the United States is supported by Austria, as all other EU Member States. However, a UN Security Council mandate for operations against IS and for the protection of the civilian population would also be desirable to broaden the basis for the fight against IS. This will also be put on the agenda by the EU at the forthcoming UN General Assembly. Furthermore, it requires the willingness to support with certain non-military equipment, *e.g.* For Kurdish Peschmerga, who fight against the IS.

2. Safety on site

- Protected areas: To provide greater security, increased protected and buffer zones should be set up in the war zones and areas affected by crises. In the Syrian conflict, due to the understanding between the USA and Turkey, there is hope for a positive development that the EU should support, *e.g.* with the prospect of humanitarian aid. There is no such initiative in North Africa as of yet.
- Humanitarian aid: Once the protected and buffer zones have been established, there should be an extension of humanitarian aid.
- Reception centres in areas of origin/neighbouring countries: In countries of origin or neighbouring countries, reception centres with the possibility of applying for asylum outside the EU would be necessary. At the same time, however, there is also the need for information and support centres to raise awareness about the risks of illegal migration to the EU as well as the mobilisation of the EU-MS to participate in the common programme for the resettlement of refugees in order to deprive traffickers of their subsistence.

3. Protection of the external borders of the EU

- Control of the eastern Mediterranean Sea route: As in the central Mediterranean, a common approach with regard to monitoring the external borders of the EU is also necessary off the coasts of Greece and Bulgaria.
- Operations: Strengthening Frontex missions. In the mid-term, the EU needs a common, integrated EU external border protection
- Reception centres: EU funding for reception centres in Greece and Italy ('hotspots')

4. Cooperation and control of the Western Balkan transit route

- Cooperation: Reinforcement of police cooperation and support of local authorities in the Western Balkans. Active involvement of the Western Balkan states in internal considerations of the EU.
- Support: If need be, recourse to additional IPA resources.
- EU-internal coordination: Joint classification of 'safe countries of origin'. Support for migration conferences on the Western Balkan route, such as the Western Balkans Conference in Vienna on 27 August as well as in Budapest.

5. *Treatment of refugees within the EU*
- EU asylum rules: The quotas must continue to be enhanced.

The relevant parts of the German original read as follows:
[...]

1. Ursachenbekämpfung
- Konfliktlösung: Der von den E3/EU+3 ausgehandelte Iran-Deal in Wien hat Potential zu einer neuen Dynamik im Nahen und Mittleren Osten. Diese sollte für Fortschritte bei den bisher schwierigen und zähen diplomatischen Konfliktlösungsbemühungen (v.a. seitens VN (Vereinte Nationen)) in Syrien und Libyen genützt werden.

- Internationaler Einsatz gegen islamistischen Terror: Die von den Vereinigten Staaten geführte Allianz gegen den IS-Terrorismus unterstützt Österreich, wie auch alle anderen EU-Mitgliedsstaaten. Erstrebenswert wäre aber auch ein UNO-Sicherheitsratsmandat für Einsätze gegen IS und zum Schutz der Zivilbevölkerung, um die Basis für den Kampf gegen IS zu verbreiten. Dies wird auch seitens der EU anlässlich der kommenden UNO-Generalversammlung thematisiert. Weiters bedarf es der Bereitschaft zur Unterstützung mit bestimmten nicht-militärischen Ausrüstungsgegenständen z.B. für kurdische Peschmerga, die gegen die IS kämpfen.

2. Sicherheit vor Ort
- Schutzzonen: Um für mehr Sicherheit zu sorgen könnten verstärkt Schutz- und Pufferzonen in den Kriegs- und Krisengebieten eingerichtet werden. Im Syrien-Konflikt gibt es aufgrund der Verständigung zwischen USA und Türkei die Hoffnung auf eine positive Entwicklung die die EU z.B. mit der Perspektive auf humanitäre Hilfe unterstützen sollte. In Nordafrika gibt es dazu bis dato noch keine Initiative.

- Humanitäre Hilfe: Sobald die Schutz und Pufferzonen eingerichtet wurden, sollte es eine Ausweitung der humanitären Hilfsleistungen geben.

- Aufnahmezentren in Ursprungsgebieten/Nachbarländern: In Ursprungs- oder benachbarten Ländern wären Aufnahmezentren mit der Möglichkeit, Asylanträge außerhalb der EU stellen zu können, notwendig. Gleichzeitig braucht es aber auch Informations- und Beratungszentren zur Aufklärung über Risiken illegaler Migration in die EU genauso wie die Mobilisierung der EU-MS zur Beteiligung am gemeinsamen Programm zur Neuansiedlung („Resettlement") von Flüchtlingen, um den Schleppern die Existenzgrundlage zu entziehen.

3. Schutz der EU-Außengrenze
- Kontrolle Ostmittelmeerroute: Wie im zentralen Mittelmeer bräuchte es auch vor Griechenland und Bulgarien ein gemeinsames Vorgehen bei der Kontrolle der EU-Außengrenze.

- Missionen: Stärkung von Frontex Missionen. Mittelfristig braucht die EU einen gemeinsamen, integrierten EU-Außengrenzschutz
- Aufnahmezentren: EU-Finanzmittel für Aufnahmezentren in Griechenland und Italien („Hotspots")

4. Kooperation und Überwachung auf der Westbalkan-Transitroute
- Kooperation: Verstärkung der polizeilichen Kooperation und Unterstützung für lokale Behörden in den Westbalkanstaaten. Aktive Einbindung der Westbalkanstaaten in EU-interne Überlegungen.
- Unterstützung: Allenfalls Rückgriff auf zusätzliche IPA-Mittel.
- EU-interne Koordinierung: Gemeinsame Einstufung von „sicheren Herkunftsstaaten" mitausarbeiten. Unterstützung für Migrations-Konferenzen zur Westbalkanroute wie der Westbalkankonferenz in Wien am 27.8. sowie in Budapest.

5. Umgang mit Flüchtlingen innerhalb der EU
- EU-Asylregelung: Die Quotenregelung muss weiterhin forciert werden.

FF.VII.4.-2

Enquiry concerning the distribution of refugees within Europe

Anfrage betreffend die Verteilung von Flüchtlingen innerhalb von Europa

On 24 September 2015, a number of representatives of the Austrian parliament raised a parliamentary enquiry to the Minister of the Interior:[19]

According to media reports, the Ministers of the EU agreed *to distribute 120,000 refugees within Europe*. While this agreement counts as a success, there are currently far more than 120,000 refugees in Europe. Critics also warn that not every country will voluntarily honour the agreement. Penalties for countries that do not comply with this distribution are not planned. Since not all EU Member States are affected by the current refugee influx, it is not perceived as a 'European problem' everywhere.

In this connection, the undersigned representatives address to the Minister of the Interior the following

Enquiry

1. According to which allocation key will these 120,000 refugees be distributed in Europe?

2. How many refugees must Austria accommodate according to this key?

3. What will happen to refugees exceeding the 120,000?

4. Which countries voted against the proposal of the EU Commission?

---

[19] Parliamentary Materials, 6606/J (XXV. GP).

5. Which countries abstained?

6. Why did it take until now for a positive decision on the distribution of refugees across the EU?

7. How will it be ensured that the countries comply with the distribution?

8. Will it be possible to trust in the solidarity of the EU countries in this regard?

9. Which consequences must those countries that do not comply with the distribution expect?

10. How is the determination whether the refugee influx is a 'European problem' made?

The relevant parts of the German original read as follows:

Medienberichten zufolge haben sich die EU-Innenminister darauf geeinigt, dass *120.000 Flüchtlinge innerhalb Europas verteilt werden sollen.* Diese Einigung ist zwar als Erfolg zu verbuchen, doch befinden sich aktuell bei weitem mehr als 120.000 Flüchtlinge in Europa. Kritiker warnen außerdem davor, dass nicht jedes Land freiwillig der Vereinbarung nachkommen wird. Strafzahlungen für Länder, die dieser Verteilung nicht nachkommen soll es allerdings keine geben. Da nicht alle EU-Mitgliedsländer vom aktuellen Flüchtlingsstrom betroffen sind, wird dieser nicht allerorts als „europäisches Problem" wahrgenommen.

In diesem Zusammenhang richten die unterfertigten Abgeordneten an die Bundesministerin für Inneres folgende

Anfrage

1. Nach welchem Schema werden die erwähnten 120.000 Flüchtlinge in Europa verteilt?

2. Wie viele Flüchtlinge muss Österreich diesem Schema nach unterbringen?

3. Was geschieht mit den Flüchtlingen, die über die 120.000 hinausgehen?

4. Welche Länder haben gegen den Vorschlag der EU-Kommission gestimmt?

5. Welche Länder haben sich der Stimme enthalten?

6. Warum wurde über die EU-weite Verteilung der Flüchtlinge erst jetzt positiv abgestimmt?

7. Wie will man sichergehen, dass die Länder der Verteilung nachkommen?

8. Kann man diesbezüglich auf die Solidarität der EU-Länder vertrauen?

9. Welche Folgen müssen jene Länder erwarten, die der Verteilung nicht nachkommen?

10. Wie wird definiert ob sich die Flüchtlingsströme als ein „europäisches Problem" darstellen oder nicht?

On 18 November 2015, the Minister of the Interior gave the following response:[20]

On question 1:

The distribution takes place in accordance with the tables set out in the annex to Council Decision (EU) 2015/1601 of 22 September 2015 establishing provisional measures in the area of international protection for the benefit of Italy and Greece.

On question 2:

Council Decision (EU) 2015/1601 of 22 September 2015 establishing provisional measures in the area of international protection for the benefit of Italy and Greece envisions for Austria an allocation of 462 persons to be resettled from Italy and 1491 persons to be resettled from Greece. In total, 66,000 people shall be relocated from Italy and Greece. The resettlement of a further 54,000 persons shall be determined at a later date according to an analogous distribution key.

On question 3:

Multilateral European measures relating to the refugee policy will continue to be adopted on the basis of the applicable legal acts, in particular the Common European Asylum System.

On question 4:

Slovakia, Romania, the Czech Republic, and Hungary voted against the decision.

On question 5:

Finland abstained.

On question 6:

In recent years, a large number of legislative and non-legislative steps were taken to develop the European Asylum System. Austria has always been committed to the further development of the Common European Asylum System with a focus on improving the quality of national asylum systems and bringing into line the decision-making practice in the individual Member States.

Due to the massive increase in asylum applications in some Member States – caused by the armed conflicts in the Middle East –, the decision to establish a quota system with a fair, objective distribution key has recently been demanded. The relocation of 120,000 refugees decided by the Ministers of the Interior on 22 September 2015 is another important step towards a fair asylum system based on solidarity in Europe.

On questions 7 and 9:

In its meeting of 22 September 2015, the Council of Ministers of the Interior, in accordance with the principle of solidarity and equitable distribution of responsibilities among the Member States, which applies to the Union's policy on asylum and immigration, adopted by qualified majority the resettlement of 120,000

---

[20] Parliamentary Materials, 6353/AB (XXV. GP).

persons being undoubtedly in need of international protection. This decision is legally binding for all Member States. In case of non-compliance, the European Commission has the possibility to initiate an infringement proceeding against the respective Member State.

On question 8:

Opinions and appraisals are not subject to the parliamentary right of interpellation.

On question 10:

Given the persistent instability and conflicts in the Near and Middle East, the migratory pressure on the southern external land and sea borders has drastically increased. The migratory influx has, thus, shifted further from the central to the eastern Mediterranean and to the Western Balkan route and, consequently, to other Member States, which shows the European dimension of the migration flows. Articles 77 and the following of the TFEU establish a common EU policy on border control, asylum and immigration.

The relevant parts of the German original read as follows:

Zu Frage 1:

Die Verteilung erfolgt entsprechend den im Anhang des Beschlusses (EU) 2015/1601 des Rates vom 22. September 2015 zur Einführung von vorläufigen Maßnahmen im Bereich des internationalen Schutzes zugunsten von Italien und Griechenland enthaltenen Tabellen.

Zu Frage 2:

Im Beschluss (EU) 2015/1601 des Rates vom 22. September 2015 zur Einführung von vorläufigen Maßnahmen im Bereich des internationalen Schutzes zugunsten von Italien und Griechenland ist für Österreich eine Zuweisung von 462 umzusiedelnden Personen aus Italien, respektive von 1491 umzusiedelnden Personen aus Griechenland vorgesehen. Insgesamt sollen aus Italien und Griechenland 66.000 Personen umgesiedelt werden. Die Umsiedlung weiterer 54.000 Personen soll zu einem späteren Zeitpunkt nach einem analogen Verteilungsschlüssel festgelegt werden.

Zu Frage 3:

Gesamteuropäische Maßnahmen betreffend die Flüchtlingspolitik werden weiterhin auf Grundlage der geltenden Rechtsakte, insbesondere dem Gemeinsamen Europäischen Asylsystem, ergriffen.

Zu Frage 4:

Die Slowakei, Rumänien, Tschechien und Ungarn haben gegen den Beschluss gestimmt.

Zu Frage 5:

Finnland hat sich der Stimme enthalten.

Zu Frage 6:

In den letzten Jahren wurden zahlreiche legistische und nicht legistische Schritte gesetzt, um das Europäische Asylsystem weiterzuentwickeln. Österreich hat sich stets für die Weiterentwicklung des Gemeinsamen Europäischen Asylsystems eingesetzt, wobei der Fokus auf der Verbesserung der Qualität der nationalen Asylsysteme und der Angleichung der Entscheidungspraxis in den einzelnen Mitgliedsstaaten lag. Auf Grund des - durch die kriegerischen Auseinandersetzungen im Nahen Osten bedingten - massiven Anstiegs von Asylanträgen in einigen Mitgliedsstaaten wurde zuletzt verstärkt die Festlegung eines Quotensystems mit einem fairen, objektiven Verteilungsschlüssels gefordert. Die von den Innenministern am 22. September 2015 beschlossene Relokation von 120.000 Flüchtlingen ist ein weiterer, wichtiger Schritt in Richtung eines fairen, solidarischen Asylsystems in Europa.

Zu den Fragen 7 und 9:

Der Rat der Innenminister hat in seiner Tagung vom 22. September 2015 im Einklang mit dem Grundsatz der Solidarität und der gerechten Aufteilung der Verantwortlichkeiten unter den Mitgliedstaaten, der für die Politik der Union im Bereich Asyl und Einwanderung gilt, die Umsiedlung von 120.000 Personen, die unzweifelhaft internationalen Schutz benötigen, per qualifizierter Mehrheit beschlossen. Dieser Beschluss ist für alle Mitgliedstaaten rechtlich bindend. Im Falle der Nicht-Einhaltung hat die Europäische Kommission die Möglichkeit ein Vertragsverletzungsverfahren gegen den betreffenden Mitgliedstaat einzuleiten.

Zu Frage 8:

Meinungen und Einschätzungen sind nicht Gegenstand des parlamentarischen Interpellationsrechtes.

Zu Frage 10:

Angesichts der anhaltenden Instabilität und Konflikte im Nahen und Mittleren Osten hat sich der Migrationsdruck an den südlichen Land- und Seeaußengrenzen drastisch erhöht. Die Migrationsströme haben sich infolge weiter vom zentralen zum östlichen Mittelmeerraum und zur Westbalkanroute und in Folge in andere Mitgliedssaaten verlagert, was die europäische Dimension der Migrationsströme zeigt. Die Artikel 77 ff AEUV legen eine gemeinsame EU-Politik im Bereich Grenzkontrollen, Asyl und Einwanderung fest.

VIII. Human rights and fundamental freedoms/Menschenrechte und Grundfreiheiten

See also CC.I.2.-1., CC.I.2.-2, and *CC.I.2.-3.*

FF.VIII.-1

Enquiry concerning the Qu'ran distribution events

Anfrage betreffend Koran-Verteilung

On 12 November 2014, a number of representatives of the Austrian parliament raised a parliamentary enquiry to the Minister of the Interior:[21]

1. How many Qu'ran distribution events took place across Austria in 2014? (listed by province)
2. How many copies were distributed during these events?
3. How many of these distribution events were undertaken by the 'Lies!-Stiftung'?
4. Who undertook the rest of the Qu'ran distribution events?

The relevant parts of the German original read as follows:

1. Wie viele Koran Verteilaktionen gab es im Jahr 2014 österreichweit? (aufgeschlüsselt nach Bundesländer)
2. Wie viele Exemplare wurden im Zuge dieser Aktionen verteilt?
3. Wie viele dieser Verteilaktionen wurden von der „Lies!-Stiftung" durchgeführt?
4. Wer hat die übrigen Koran-Verteilaktionen durchgeführt?

[...]

On 23 December 2014, the Minister of the Interior gave the following response:[22]

The right to exercise one's religion without interference by the state is given high value in constitutional law from a fundamental rights point of view (Art 63 Austrian State Treaty of Saint-Germain, Art 9 ECHR). Generally, the existence of certain religious communities or communities with a particular world view does not create a competence of the security authorities. These only become active within the framework of the Security Police Act, the Code of Criminal Procedure, or other relevant substantive legislative grounds in the case of a corresponding suspicion of criminal activity. The distribution of the Qu'ran free of charge to an interested group of persons cannot be subsumed under a provision that would be relevant from a criminal law perspective.

Considering that there is no legal basis for the security authorities to become active, neither the number of events for the distribution of the Qu'ran, nor the persons responsible or the number of copies distributed are known.

[...]

---

[21] Parliamentary Materials, 3045/J (XXV. GP)

[22] Parliamentary Materials, 2873/AB (XXV. GP).

The relevant parts of the German original read as follows:

Der staatlich unbehelligten Religionsausübung wird vom Verfassungsrecht (Art. 63 Staatsvertrag von St. Germain, Art. 9 EMRK) ein hoher grundrechtlicher Stellenwert beigemessen. Allein durch das Bestehen von bestimmten glaubens- und weltanschauungsbezogenen Gemeinschaften wird grundsätzlich keine Zuständigkeit der Sicherheitsbehörden begründet. Nur bei entsprechender Verdachtslage wegen eines strafbaren Verhaltens werden die Sicherheitsbehörden im Rahmen des Sicherheitspolizeigesetzes, der Strafprozessordnung bzw. anderer einschlägiger Materiengesetze tätig. Die unentgeltliche Verteilung des Korans an einen interessierten Personenkreis ist in Österreich nicht unter einen strafrechtlich relevanten Tatbestand subsumierbar.

Da keine Rechtsgrundlage für ein Tätigwerden der Sicherheitsbehörden bestehen sind weder die Anzahl der Koran-Verteilaktionen noch die dafür Verantwortlichen oder die Anzahl der verteilten Exemplare bekannt.

[...]

X. Crimes under international law/Völkerrechtliche Verbrechen

See DD.II.-1.

FF.X.-1

Joint declaration on the occasion of the centenary of the Armenian genocide

Gemeinsame Erklärung anlässlich des 100. Jahrestages des Genozids an Armeniern

On 22 April 2015, the parliamentary group leaders of all parties represented in the Austrian parliament made the following joint declaration on the occasion of the centenary of the atrocities committed against the Armenian population of the Ottoman Empire during World War I:[23]

> On the 24 April the genocide, which was committed by the Ottoman Empire against 1.5 million Armenians, commits its 100th anniversary. Against this background, we commemorate the victims of violence, murder, and expulsion, including tens of thousands of members of other Christian communities in the Ottoman Empire, such as the Arameans, the Assyrians, the Chaldeans, and the Pontic Greeks.
>
> Because of the historical responsibility – the Austro-Hungarian monarchy was an ally with the Ottoman Empire during World War I – it is our duty to recognise and condemn the terrible events as genocide. It is also the duty of Turkey to honestly

---

[23] Parliamentary correspondence No 383 of 22 April 2015.

confront its treatment of dark and painful chapters of its past and recognize the crimes committed against the Armenians in the Ottoman Empire as genocide.

In times, in which international crises present an ever-greater threat to the world and its values, it is essential to take decisive action against atrocities and persecution of people all over the world. The crime against the Armenians one hundred years ago, which Pope Francis called 'the first genocide of the 20th century,' highlights the necessity of memory cultures. For the awareness of our inviolable values of freedom, peace, and human rights is inextricably linked to a dignified remembrance of the victims of violence, persecution, expulsion, and mass murder.

The parliamentary group leaders are committed to consistently pursuing the proven Austrian path of dialogue and reconciliation in the resolution of international conflicts. This also with regard to historical events that drive a wedge between ethnic groups and states, as in the case of Turkey and Armenia. On the part of Turkey, it is necessary to bring light into the darkness of the past in the spirit of a transparent reappraisal.

In order to promote reconciliation, the intention is to actively support confronting the historical events as well as their reappraisal by Turkey and Armenia as a first step towards reconciliation and the long overdue improvement of Turkish-Armenian relations, both bilaterally and at European level.

The Resolution of the European Parliament of 15 April 2015 (European Parliament resolution of 15 April 2015 on the centenary of the Armenian Genocide (2015/2590(RSP))) on the reconciliation of Turkey and Armenia is welcomed by the parliamentary group leaders of all parties represented in the Austrian parliament – irrespective of the formal assessment under international law.

The German original reads as follows:

Am 24. April jährt sich der Genozid, welcher durch das Osmanische Reich an 1,5 Millionen Armeniern verübt wurde, zum hundertsten Mal. Vor diesem Hintergrund gedenken wir der Opfer von Gewalt, Mord und Vertreibung, zu denen auch zehntausende Angehörige anderer christlicher Bevölkerungsgruppen im Osmanischen Reich, wie jene der Aramäer, der Assyrer, Chaldäer und der Pontos-Griechen gehören.

Aufgrund der historischen Verantwortung – die österreich-ungarische Monarchie war im Ersten Weltkrieg mit dem Osmanischen Reich verbündet – ist es unsere Pflicht, die schrecklichen Geschehnisse als Genozid anzuerkennen und zu verurteilen. Ebenso ist es die Pflicht der Türkei, sich der ehrlichen Aufarbeitung dunkler und schmerzhafter Kapitel ihrer Vergangenheit zu stellen und die im Osmanischen Reich begangenen Verbrechen an den Armeniern als Genozid anzuerkennen.

In Zeiten, in denen internationale Krisenherde eine immer größere Gefahr für die Welt und ihre Werte darstellen, gilt es, entschieden gegen Gräueltaten und Verfolgung von Menschen in aller Welt aufzutreten. Das Verbrechen an den Armeniern vor einhundert Jahren, das von Papst Franziskus als „erster Genozid des 20. Jahrhunderts" bezeichnet wurde, macht die Notwendigkeit von Gedächtniskulturen deutlich. Denn das Bewusstsein für unsere unantastbaren Werte der Freiheit, des Friedens und der Menschenrechte ist untrennbar verbunden mit einem würdigen Andenken an die Opfer von Gewalt, Verfolgung, Vertreibung und Massenmord.

Die Klubobleute bekennen sich dazu, den bewährten österreichischen Weg des Dialogs und der Versöhnung bei der Beilegung von internationalen Konflikten im Rahmen der Möglichkeiten konsequent fortzusetzen. Dies auch in Hinblick auf historische Geschehnisse, die einen Keil zwischen Ethnien und Staaten treiben, wie im Falle der Türkei und Armenien. Seitens der Türkei gilt es, im Sinne einer transparenten Aufarbeitung Licht in das Dunkel der Vergangenheit zu bringen.

Um die Aussöhnung zu fördern, wird die Absicht erklärt, eine Auseinandersetzung mit den historischen Ereignissen sowie deren Aufarbeitung durch die Türkei und Armenien als ersten Schritt zur Versöhnung und zur längst überfälligen Verbesserung der türkisch-armenischen Beziehungen sowohl bilateral als auch auf europäischer Ebene aktiv zu unterstützen.

Die am 15. April 2015 im Europäischen Parlament verabschiedete Resolution (European Parliament resolution of 15 April 2015 on the centenary of the Armenian Genocide (2015/2590(RSP)) zur Aussöhnung der Türkei und Armenien wird – unbeschadet der formalen völkerrechtlichen Beurteilung – von den Klubobleuten der im Nationalrat vertretenen Parteien begrüßt.

FF.X.-2

Work of the International Law Commission on Crimes Against Humanity

Arbeit der Völkerrechtskommission der Vereinten Nationen betreffend Verbrechen gegen die Menschlichkeit

On 4 November 2015, the Austrian representative delivered the following statement to the Sixth Committee during the 70th session of the General Assembly regarding the Report of the International Law Commission on the Work of its 67th Session:

According to the first draft article, on the scope, the future convention will apply to the prevention and punishment of crimes against humanity. My delegation is in favour of the proposed extension of the scope of the convention also to the prevention of such crimes. The commentary on this draft article spells out that the draft articles avoid any conflict with the obligations of states arising under the constituent instruments of international or hybrid criminal courts or tribunals, in particular the obligations resulting from the Rome Statute of the ICC. This is an important point for the Austrian delegation. However, the text of this draft article does not yet reflect this legal relationship, and we hope that it will be explicitly reflected in the final draft articles. Otherwise, the *lex posterior* regime of the Vienna Convention on the Law of Treaties could lead to different results.

Draft Article 2 relating to the general obligation to prevent and punish qualifies crimes against humanity as 'crimes under international law'. Although the 1996 Draft Code of crimes against peace and security of mankind has used this term, it has not yet received a clear understanding in international law and is unknown to the Rome Statute of the ICC. According to the commentary, this qualification should indicate that these crimes are punishable even when they are not incorporated in national criminal codes. This, however, applies only to international courts; in order to be punishable at the national level, the crimes need to be incorporated into national law. This should be clearly spelt out in the articles and the commentary.

Moreover, various legal instruments use the expression 'international crimes'. To us it is not clear what is the difference between the term 'international crimes' and the term 'crimes under international law'. We would be interested in a clarification if there is a distinction between the two expressions; if not, the term 'crimes under international law' should be avoided.

As to draft Article 3 containing the definition of crimes against humanity, my delegation supports the definition of these crimes which corresponds, as much as possible, to Article 7 of the Rome Statute, which is considered to reflect customary international law. Any other approach would create major obstacles, both to the further work on this topic and to the practice of states, since a number of states have used Article 7 of the Rome Statute as a model for their own legislation. This is also the case for Austria which has introduced, as of 1 January 2015, new provisions on international crimes into its criminal code, including a definition of crimes against humanity based on Article 7 of the Rome Statute.

Draft Article 4 on the obligation of prevention should be understood as extending not only to the prevention, but also to the punishment of such crimes, because of the preventive effect of legislative measures providing for punishment. This view has been confirmed by a judgment of the European Court of Human Rights, which explicitly refers to the connection between preventive effect and measures of punishment in the case of *Makaratzis v Greece*.

Paragraph 1 (a) of Article 4 obliges states to take legislative and other measures in any territory under their jurisdiction or control. My delegation supports this definition of the geographical scope which corresponds also to various judgments of the European Court of Human Rights, such as in the case of *Jaloud v The Netherlands*, where the Court discussed at length the question of control and jurisdiction.

XI. Criminal responsibility of the individual (see MM.)/ Strafrechtliche Verantwortlichkeit des Einzelmenschen (siehe MM.)

See also DD.II.-1, FF.X.-2, and GG.-1.

FF.XI.-1

Retroactive Application of Amended Rule 68 of the Rules of Procedure and Evidence of the International Criminal Court

Rückwirkende Anwendung von Regel 68 der Verfahrensordnung und der Beweisregeln des Internationalen Strafgerichtshofs

In reaction to Kenya's intervention that the use of previously recorded testimony as envisioned by amended Rule 68 of the Rules of Procedure and Evidence of the International Criminal Court not be applied retroactively, Austria, Liechtenstein, and Switzerland made the following statement at the 12th plenary meeting of the 14th session of the Assembly of State Parties on 26 November 2015:[24]

1. Mr. President, I have the honour of delivering the following statement on behalf of Austria, Liechtenstein and Switzerland.

2. We have not blocked consensus on the document just adopted in a spirit of compromise and utmost flexibility, but not without serious concerns on both substance and process. We would like to acknowledge though the hard work that went into the preparation of the report and thank all those involved.

3. Mr. President, the strength of the Rome Statute system lies in three factors:

(a) Voluntariness: States Parties signed up to the Rome Statute because they are convinced that it is in their long – term interest and that of the world. We are here, because we want to be here.

(b) Inclusiveness: It is a sovereign right of every State to join the Statute. The ambition is universal, no one is left behind.

(c) A common sense of purpose: We are united in the fight against impunity and the quest for justice for the victims of the worst crimes.

4. Mr. President, the Court, a court of law, is the centrepiece of the system. The Assembly's role is to provide strategic oversight and support to the Court, not to get involved in matters that pertain to the Prosecution or the Judiciary. Rather, the Assembly must preserve the integrity of the Statute and fully respect the Court and its independence.

5. Regarding paragraph 61 of the report, we would like to state for the record that this understanding only reflects the precise meaning of resolution ICC - ASP/12/Res.7, operative paragraph 2, which emphasized article 51, paragraph 4, of the Rome Statute.

6. So much on substance, now on process:

(a) The Assembly's own work has to be guided by respect for all voices, those of each and every State Party, observers, civil society representatives and, of course, of the Court.

---

[24] ICC-ASP/14/20, Annex V.

(b) The proceedings of the Assembly must be conducted in a spirit of inclusiveness and full transparency. Each and every delegation must be allowed to be heard and to take part in the decision making on an equal footing. Procedures, once established by this Assembly, need to be followed or be amended by this Assembly. We believe we should not follow the precedent to appoint representatives of geographical groups to discuss matters of substance.

7 . Mr. President, in moving forward, we all need to remind ourselves of the guiding principles and strengths of the Rome Statute system, and act accordingly.

8 . Mr. President, we would kindly ask that this statement be reflected in the records of this session of the Assembly.

GG. Organs of the State and their legal status/Die Staatsorgane und ihr rechtlicher Status

GG.-1

Work of the International Law Commission on Immunity of State Officials from Criminal Jurisdiction

Arbeit der Völkerrechtskommission betreffend die Immunität von Staatsorganen von strafrechtlicher Gerichtsbarkeit

On 9 November 2015, the Austrian representative to the 70th session of the General Assembly delivered the following statement to the Sixth Committee regarding the Report of the International Law Commission on the Work of its 67th Session concerning the topic of 'Immunity of State Officials from Criminal Jurisdiction':

> [...] My delegation is grateful to Special Rapporteur Concepcion Escobar Hernandez for her fourth report on this topic, which provides a lot of material for further discussion and clearly shows the complexity of defining 'acts performed in an official capacity'.
>
> The draft definition which the Special Rapporteur had presented to the. Commission in draft article 2 (f) defined an 'act performed in an official capacity' as an act which 'by its nature, constitutes a crime'. This was open to a misunderstanding, as it could have been read as implying that all such acts were necessarily crimes. The possibility of such a misunderstanding has been recognized by the Commission and taken care of by the Drafting Committee.
>
> Generally speaking, commenting on the considerations of the Special Rapporteur as reflected in the report and the discussion in the Commission, it must be emphasized that there are major differences between the rules governing immunity from civil jurisdiction and immunity from criminal jurisdiction. Immunity from

civil jurisdiction addresses the state as an entity, whereas immunity from criminal jurisdiction addresses individuals acting on behalf of the state. Criminal responsibility of juridical persons is only the exception, in certain states, for example in Austria, and only for certain crimes. Accordingly, references to state immunity from civil jurisdiction, as laid down in the UN Convention on Jurisdictional Immunities of States and their Property of 2004, are only of little help for the discussion of the present topic.

The issue of criminal jurisdiction for acts of the officials of a foreign state needs to be addressed irrespective of whether the acts concerned are acts *iure gestionis* or *iure imperii*. Therefore, the definition of an 'act performed in an official capacity' should comprise all acts that are attributable to the state, and not only those performed in the exercise of state authority, a limitation which the Drafting Committee has proposed in its draft Article 2 (f). Whether an act was performed in the exercise of state authority depends on the internal rules of the state concerned, which means that the borderline between acts performed in the exercise of state authority and other acts attributable to the state can differ from state to state. If an 'act performed in an official capacity' comprises all acts attributable to a state, there is no need to distinguish between acts performed as part of the sovereignty of the state or its governmental authority, as it is done, for instance, in paragraph 189 of the ILC report, and other acts. However, a broad approach to 'official acts' requires a thorough discussion of the exceptions from the immunity for such acts. This discussion will probably show that many, but not all acts *iure gestionis* are outside the immunity enjoyed by state officials from foreign criminal jurisdiction.

The Memorandum of the Secretariat on 'Immunity of State officials from foreign criminal jurisdiction', submitted in 2005, emphasized that state practice offers reasonable grounds for considering that *acta iure gestionis* performed by a state organ would still qualify as 'official'. It referred to a decision of the Austrian Supreme Court of 1964 which held that, contrary to state immunity, the immunity of heads of state also covered *acta iure gestionis*. This decision proves, irrespective of the fact that it concerned a head of state, that *acta iure gestionis* may be considered not as private, but as official acts *(Supreme Court, Prince of X Road Accident Case, 1964, International Law Reports, vol. 65, p. 13)*.

Accordingly, the Commission will have to put special emphasis on the criteria for the attribution of acts to a state. Although not all criteria employed in Articles 4 to 11 of the State Responsibility Articles can be used in the present context, they nevertheless serve as an appropriate starting point for the discussion. In particular, a discussion on acts performed by *de facto* officials will undoubtedly be needed.

For the time being, the scope of the draft articles under this topic seems to be limited by two conditions: the acts must have been performed by state officials – which excludes acts performed by persons who are not officials, but – for instance – act on instructions of a state, and they must be attributable to a state. The commentary on the definition of 'State officials' adopted last year by the Commission indicated a relatively broad meaning to be given to this definition. Such broad meaning of the term 'state officials' enlarges the number of acts performed in an official capacity. Therefore, it is even more important to develop clear criteria for the attribution of acts to a state.

Already last year we have pointed out that the issue whether persons acting in excess of authority (*ultra vires*) or in contravention of instructions should also enjoy immunity merits further consideration. We support the approach taken by some members of the Commission, see paragraph 199 of the report, that also this issue should be dealt with in the framework of the limitations or exceptions from immunity. The same is true for the issue of international crimes. This very important issue is to be dealt with once the exceptions to the immunity from criminal jurisdiction are under consideration.

VIII. Armed forces/Streitkräfte

See also RR.IV.-1.

GG.VIII.-1

Memorandum of Understanding between the United Nations and the Federal Government of Austria Contributing Resources to the United Nations Interim Force in Lebanon (UNIFIL)

Vereinbarung zwischen der Österreichischen Bundesregierung und den Vereinten Nationen über die Beistellung von Ressourcen für die „United Nations Interim Force in Lebanon" (UNIFIL)

On 2 February 2015, Austria signed a Memorandum of Understanding between the United Nations and the Federal Government of Austria Contributing Resources to the United Nations Interim Force in Lebanon (UNIFIL) which entered into force on 1 May 2015.[25]

[...]

Article 7 bis

United Nations standards of conduct

7.2 The Government shall ensure that all members of the Government's national contingent are required to comply with the United Nations standards of conduct set out in annex H to the present memorandum of understanding.

7.3 The Government shall ensure that all members of its national contingent are made familiar with and fully understand the United Nations standards of conduct. To this end, the Government shall, inter alia, ensure that all members of its national contingent receive adequate and effective pre-deployment training in those standards.

---

[25] Federal Law Gazette III No 46/2015.

7.4 The United Nations shall continue to provide to national contingents mission-specific training material on United Nations standards of conduct, mission-specific rules and regulations, and relevant local laws and regulations. Further, the United Nations shall conduct adequate and effective induction training and training during mission assignment to complement pre-deployment training.

Article 7 ter

Discipline

7.5 The Government acknowledges that the commander of its national contingent is responsible for the discipline and good order of all members of the contingent while assigned to the United Nations Interim Force in Lebanon (UNIFIL). The Government accordingly undertakes to ensure that the Commander of its national contingent is vested with the necessary authority and takes all reasonable measures to maintain discipline and good order among all members of the national contingent to ensure compliance with the United Nations standards of conduct, mission-specific rules and regulations and the obligations towards national and local laws and regulations in accordance with the status-of-forces agreement.

7.6 The Government undertakes to ensure, subject to any applicable national laws, that the Commander of its national contingent regularly informs the Force Commander of any serious matters involving the discipline and good order of members of its national contingent including any disciplinary action taken for violations of the United Nations standards of conduct or mission-specific rules and regulations or for failure to respect the local laws and regulations.

7.7 The Government shall ensure that the Commander of its national contingent receives adequate and effective pre-deployment training in the proper discharge of his or her responsibility for maintaining discipline and good order among all members of the contingent.

7.8 The United Nations shall assist the Government in fulfilling its requirements under paragraph 3 above by organizing training sessions for commanders upon their arrival in the mission on the United Nations standards of conduct, mission-specific rules and regulations and the local laws and regulations.

7.9 The Government shall use its welfare payments to provide adequate welfare and recreation facilities to its contingent members in the mission.

Article 7 quater

Investigations

7.10 It is understood that the Government has the primary responsibility for investigating any acts of misconduct or serious misconduct committed by a member of its national contingent.

7.11 In the event that the Government has prima facie grounds indicating that any member of its national contingent has committed an act of serious misconduct, it shall without delay inform the United Nations and forward the case to its appropriate national authorities for the purposes of investigation.

7.12 In the event that the United Nations has prima facie grounds indicating that any member of the Government's national contingent has committed an act of misconduct or serious misconduct, the United Nations shall without delay inform the Government. If necessary to preserve evidence and where the Government does not conduct fact-finding proceedings, the United Nations may, in cases of serious misconduct, as appropriate, where the United Nations has informed the Government of the allegation, initiate a preliminary fact-finding inquiry of the matter, until the Government starts its own investigation. It is understood in this connection that any such preliminary fact-finding inquiry will be conducted by the appropriate United Nations investigative office, including the Office of Internal Oversight Services, in accordance with the rules of the Organization. Any such preliminary fact-finding inquiry shall include as part of the investigation team a representative of the Government. The United Nations shall provide a complete report of its preliminary fact-finding inquiry to the Government at its request without delay.

7.13 In the event that the Government does not notify the United Nations as soon as possible, but no later than 10 working days from the time of notification by the United Nations, that it will start its own investigation of the alleged serious misconduct, the Government is considered to be unwilling or unable to conduct such an investigation and the United Nations may, as appropriate, initiate an administrative investigation of alleged serious misconduct without delay. The administrative investigation conducted by the United Nations in regard to any member of the national contingent shall respect those legal rights of due process that are provided to him or her by national and international law. Any such administrative investigation includes as part of the investigation team a representative of the Government if the Government provides one. In case the Government nevertheless decides to start its own investigation, the United Nations provides all available materials of the case to the Government without delay. In cases where a United Nations administrative investigation is completed, the United Nations shall provide the Government with the findings of, and the evidence gathered in the course of, the investigation.

7.14 In the case of a United Nations administrative investigation into possible serious misconduct by any member of the national contingent, the Government agrees to instruct the Commander of its national contingent to cooperate and to share documentation and information, subject to applicable national laws, including military laws. The Government also undertakes, through the Commander of its national contingent, to instruct the members of its national contingent to cooperate with such United Nations investigation, subject to applicable national laws, including military laws.

7.15 When the Government decides to start its own investigation and to identify or send one or more officials to investigate the matter, it shall immediately inform the United Nations of that decision, including the identities of the official or officials concerned (hereafter 'National Investigations Officers').

7.16 The United Nations agrees to cooperate fully and to share documentation and information with appropriate authorities of the Government, including any National Investigations Officers, who are investigating possible misconduct or serious misconduct by any member of the Government's national contingent.

7.17 Upon the request of the Government, the United Nations shall cooperate with the competent authorities of the Government, including any National Investigations Officers, that are investigating possible misconduct or serious misconduct by any members of its national contingent in liaising with other Governments contributing personnel in support of the United Nations Interim Force in Lebanon (UNIFIL), as well as with the competent authorities in the mission area, with a view to facilitating the conduct of those investigations. To this end, the United Nations shall take all possible measures to obtain consent from the host authorities. The competent authorities of the Government shall ensure that prior authorization for access to any victim or witness who is not a member of the national contingent, as well as for the collection or securing of evidence not under the ownership and control of the national contingent, is obtained from the host nation competent authorities.

7.18 In cases where National Investigations Officers are dispatched to the mission areas, they would lead the investigations. The role of the United Nations investigators in such cases will be to assist the National Investigations Officers, if necessary, in the conduct of their investigations in terms of, *e.g.* identification and interviewing of witnesses, recording witness statements, collection of documentary and forensic evidence and provision of administrative as well as logistical assistance.

7.19 Subject to its national laws and regulations, the Government shall provide the United Nations with the findings of investigations conducted by its competent authorities, including any National Investigations Officers, into possible misconduct or serious misconduct by any member of its national contingent.

7.20 When National Investigations Officers are deployed in the mission area, they will enjoy the same legal status as if they were members of their respective contingent while they are in the mission area, or host country.

7.21 Upon the request of the Government, the United Nations shall provide administrative and logistic support to the National Investigations Officers while they are in the mission area or host country. The Secretary-General will provide, in accordance with his authority, financial support as appropriate for the deployment of National Investigations Officers in situations where their presence is requested by the United Nations, normally the Department of Peacekeeping Operations, and where financial support is requested by the Government. The United Nations will request the Government to deploy National Investigations Officers in high-risk, complex matters and in cases of serious misconduct. This paragraph is without prejudice to the sovereign right of the Government to investigate any misconduct of its contingent members.

Article 7 quinquiens

Exercise of jurisdiction by the Government

7.22 Military members and any civilian members subject to national military law of the national contingent provided by the Government are subject to the Government's exclusive jurisdiction in respect of any crimes or offences that might be committed by them while they are assigned to the military component of the United Nations Interim Force in Lebanon (UNIFIL). The Government assures the United Nations that it shall exercise such jurisdiction with respect to such crimes or offences.

7.23 The Government further assures the United Nations that it shall exercise such disciplinary jurisdiction as might be necessary with respect to all other acts of misconduct committed by any members of the Government's national contingent while they are assigned to the military component of the United Nations Interim Force in Lebanon (UNIFIL) that do not amount to crimes or offences.

Article 7 sexiens

Accountability

7.24 If either a United Nations investigation or an investigation conducted by the competent authorities of the Government concludes that suspicions of misconduct by any member of the Government's national contingent are well founded, the Government shall ensure that the case is forwarded to its appropriate authorities for due action. The Government agrees that those authorities shall take their decision in the same manner as they would in respect of any other offence or disciplinary infraction of a similar nature under its laws or relevant disciplinary code. The Government agrees to notify the Secretary-General of progress on a regular basis, including the outcome of the case.

7.25 If a United Nations investigation, in accordance with appropriate procedures, or the Government's investigation concludes that suspicions of failure by the contingent Commander to

(a) Cooperate with a United Nations investigation in accordance with article 7 quater paragraph 7.14, it being understood that the Commander will not have failed to cooperate merely by complying with his or her national laws and regulations, or the Government's investigation; or

(b) Exercise effective command and control; or

(c) Immediately report to appropriate authorities or take action in respect of allegations of misconduct that are reported to him are well founded, the Government shall ensure that the case is forwarded to its appropriate authorities for due action. The fulfilment of these aspects shall be evaluated in the contingent Commander's performance appraisal.

7.26 The Government understands the importance of settling matters relating to paternity claims involving a member of its contingent. The Government will, to the extent of its national laws, seek to facilitate such claims provided to it by the

United Nations to be forwarded to the appropriate national authorities. In the case that the Government's national law does not recognize the legal capacity of the United Nations to provide such claims, these shall be provided to the Government by the appropriate authorities of the host country, in accordance with applicable procedures. The United Nations must ensure that such claims are accompanied by the necessary conclusive evidence, such as a DNA sample of the child when prescribed by the Government's national law.

7.27 Bearing in mind the contingent commander's obligation to maintain the discipline and good order of the contingent, the United Nations, through the Force Commander, shall ensure that the contingent is deployed in the mission in accordance with agreement between the United Nations and the Government. Any redeployment outside the agreement will be made with the consent of the Government or contingent commander, in accordance with applicable national procedures.

[...]

Article 9

Claims by third parties

9. The United Nations will be responsible for dealing with any claims by third parties where the loss of or damage to their property, or death or personal injury, was caused by the personnel or equipment provided by the Government in the performance of services or any other activity or operation under this MOU. However, if the loss, damage, death or injury arose from gross negligence or wilful misconduct of the personnel provided by the Government, the Government will be liable for such claims.

Article 10

Recovery

10. The Government will reimburse the United Nations for loss of or damage to United Nations-owned equipment and property caused by the personnel or equipment provided by the Government if such loss or damage (a) occurred outside the performance of services or any other activity or operation under this MOU, or (b) arose or resulted from gross negligence or wilful misconduct of the personnel provided by the Government.

[...]

Article 14

Entry into force

14.1 The present MOU shall enter into force on the first day of the second month following the day on which both Parties have informed each other of the fulfilment of the legal requirements for the entry into force.

14.2 The present MOU shall be applied provisionally by each Party which has informed the other Party of its intention to do so.

14.3 The present MOU shall become effective retroactively on 14 November 2011. The financial obligations of the United Nations with respect to reimbursement of personnel, major equipment and self-sustainment rates start from the date of arrival of personnel or serviceable equipment and self-sustainment rates start from the date of arrival of personnel or serviceable equipment in the mission area, and will remain in effect until the date personnel or serviceable equipment depart the mission area as per the agreed withdrawal plan or the date of effective departure where the delay is attributable to the United Nations.

LL. Air Space, outer space and Antarctica/Luftraum, Weltraum, Antarktis

II. Outer space/Weltraum

2. Uses/Nutzungen

LL.II.2.-1

Outer Space Regulation

Weltraumverordnung

On the basis of §12 of the Federal Law on the Authorisation of Space Activities and the Establishment of a National Registry (Outer Space Act),[26] the Federal Minister for Transport, Innovation and Technology passed the following regulation, implementing the legislation:[27]

Scope of Application

§1. By this regulation the implementations necessary according to §12 of the Outer Space Act are carried out.

Request for Authorisation

§2.(1) As evidence of the necessary reliability, capability and expertise to carry

---

[26] Federal Law Gazette I No 132/2011.

[27] Federal Law Gazette II No 36/2015. The translation has been provided by Irmgard Marboe, Associate Professor at the Section of International Law and International Relations of the University of Vienna, and Cordula Steinkogler, Research Assistant at the Section of International Law and International Relations of the University of Vienna, and was originally made available at the websites of the NPOC Space Law Austria, http://www.spacelaw.at/wp-content/uploads/2016/05/Austrian-Outer-Space-Regulation-2015.pdf, and UNOOSA, http://www.unoosa.org/documents/pdf/spacelaw/national/austria/Austrian_Outer_Space_Regulation_German_original_BGBLA_2015_II_36E-unofficial-translation.pdf.

out the space activity (§4, subparagraph 1, letter 1 of the Outer Space Act) the operator has to submit:

1. a certificate about a security review undertaken in accordance with the Federal Security Police Act, BGBl No 566/1991, as amended, or of a reliability review in accordance with the Federal Military Authority Act, BGBl I No 86/2000, as amended, of the operator, or, in case of a juridical person, of the representative responsible for the space activity,

2. evidences of qualification of the operator as well as of the persons cooperating in the space activity,

3. a list of activities previously carried out by the operator in the field of space technology or related fields,

4. evidence of the financial capacity of the operator as well as a costs projection and financing plan of the space activity,

5. all contracts in relation to the space activity, in particular the launch contract and supply contracts,

6. a concept demonstrating the planned task, purpose and objective of the space activity,

7. evidence that presents the technical details of the space activity, in particular the envisaged frequency spectrum and orbital position, the energy supply, the description of the intended payload, the communication strategy, the technical details of the ground station, technologies used at subsystem level and

8. documentation about the duration and termination of the space activity.

(2) As evidence that the space activity does not pose an immediate threat to public order, the safety of persons and property and to public health (§4, subparagraph 1, letter 2 of the Outer Space Act), the operator has to submit:

1. evidence of compliance with state of knowledge based on the relevant scientific knowledge of advanced techniques, facilities, construction and operation methods, whose functional operability has been tested and proven. If compliance is not an option in the case at hand or if evidence of it is not possible, it must be credibly demonstrated that the space activity nevertheless does not pose an immediate threat to public order, the safety of persons and property and to public health,

2. the results of the tests carried out to verify the safety and solidity of the space object according to the state of the art,

3. the emergency plans developed for the event of a failure of the communication or data connections, the loss of control over the space object, the failure of essential systems for power supply, attitude control or control of the trajectory and similar exceptional operating events and

4. information to what extent the space activity involves the observation of the Earth and what kind of data is thereby collected. In particular, the degree of

resolution of possible images of the surface of the Earth as well as the planned transfer of raw or processed data must be indicated. In case the space activity involves the processing of data within the meaning of the Data Protection Act 2000 (BGBl I No 165/1999, as amended), the necessary licenses for the processing and transfer of these data must be provided.

(3) As evidence that the space activity does not run counter to national security, Austria's obligations under international law or Austrian foreign policy interests (§4, subparagraph 1, letter 3 of the Outer Space Act), the documents provided in accordance with subparagraph 1 are reviewed, in addition the operator has to submit in particular:

1. documents providing information on the planned use and the recipients of the data collected in accordance with subparagraph 2, letter 4,

2. information on the payload of the space object.

(4) As evidence of appropriate provisions for the mitigation of space debris in accordance with §5 of the Outer Space Act (§4, subparagraph 1, letter 4 of the Outer Space Act), the operator has to submit:

1. a report [on the measures adopted] according to the state of the art and in consideration of the internationally accepted guidelines, in particular

a) for the avoidance of space debris and mission residue released during normal operations,

b) for the prevention of on-orbit break-ups of the space object,

c) for the removal of the space object from Earth orbit at the end of the space activity, either by controlled re-entry or by moving the space object to a sufficiently high Earth orbit ('graveyard orbit'), while for non-manoeuvrable space objects the Earth orbit is to be chosen such that they do not remain in Earth orbit for more than 25 years after the end of their operation,

2. a demonstration of measures adopted for the prevention of on - orbit collisions with other space objects.

(5) As evidence that the space object does not contain dangerous substances or substances harmful to health, which could cause harmful contamination of outer space or adverse changes in the environment (§4, subparagraph 1, letter 5 of the Outer Space Act), appropriate documents must be submitted by the operator.

(6) As evidence that the frequencies and orbital positions necessary for the radio operation of the space object may be used lawfully, the operator must submit the appropriate licenses or the documents required for the frequency coordination with the International Telecommunication Union (ITU) (§4, subparagraph 1, letter 6 of the Outer Space Act).

(7) As evidence of having taken out insurance according to §4, subparagraph 4 of the Outer Space Act, the operator must submit appropriate documents, unless he applies for exemption from the insurance requirement or a reduction of the

insurance sum according to §3 or the Federal State itself is the operator of the space activity.

Application for exemption from the insurance requirement or reduction of the insurance sum

§3. The operator may apply for exemption from the insurance requirement or a reduction of the insurance sum according to §4, subparagraph 4 of the Outer Space Act. For that purpose, he must provide documents demonstrating

1. to what extent the space activity serves science, research or education,

2. the risks connected to the activity and

3. the operator's financial capacity to cover liability for damages caused to persons or property.

Procedure

§4.(1) The provisions of the General Administrative Procedures Act 1991, BGBl No 51/1991, as amended, apply to the procedure, unless otherwise provided by the present Regulation or by the Outer Space Act.[28]

(2) The operator has to submit all the documents required for the request for authorisation according to this Regulation to the competent authority. These documents should, as far as possible, be provided in electronic form.

(3) The operator has to specifically identify documents, which, in his view, contain trade or business secrets. The protection of trade and business secrets is to be taken into account.

(4) If documents required under subparagraph 2 are missing in the request for authorisation or if the information provided in the request for authorisation is not complete, even when this turns out in the course of the procedure, the authority has to assign the operator to complete the request for authorisation.

(5) The request for authorisation is to be dismissed at any stage of the procedure, if in the course of the procedure it turns out in an undoubted manner that the project is in conflict to specific conditions for authorisation to an extent that the deficiency cannot be remedied by conditions or requirements.

(6) If the submission of documents according to §2, subparagraph 1, letter 5 and §2, subparagraph 2, letter 2 is not possible at the time of submitting the request for authorisation, the operator must inform about and justify this fact in the request. The launch service provider envisaged according to §2, subparagraph 1, letter 5 must be stated at the time of the decision regarding the request for authorisation at the latest. The submission of missing documents according to §2, subparagraph 1, letter 5 and §2, subparagraph 2, letter 2 is to be requested from the operator by means of conditions and requirements.

---

[28] Translation of this paragraph amended by the present authors.

Review of the conditions for authorisation

§5.(1) The review of the conditions for authorisation according to §2 and of the exemption from the insurance requirement or the reduction of the insurance sum according to §3 is incumbent on the Federal Minister for Transport, Innovation and Technology.

(2) If the nature, the extent or the complexity of the request so requires, the Federal Minister for Transport, Innovation and Technology may appoint additional certified experts. There is no entitlement to the appointment as certified expert.

(3) With regard to the review under subparagraph 1 the Federal Minister for Transport, Innovation and Technology may request an opinion from the Austrian Research Promotion Agency (FFG) and/or the European Space Agency (ESA).

(4) The continuing supervision and control of the space activity according to §7 and §13, subparagraph 1 of the Outer Space Act is to be exercised by the Federal Minister for Transport, Innovation and Technology.

Registration

§6.(1) The operator must provide the information according to §10 of the Outer Space Act as well as the information listed in subparagraphs 2 and 3 immediately after the launch, and at the latest within two weeks, in the German and in the English language.

(2) In addition to the information according to §10 of the Outer Space Act, the operator must provide the following information for the registration of the space object:

1. the Committee on Space Research (COSPAR) international designator, where appropriate,

2. the date and the Coordinated Universal Time (UTC) as the time of the launch,

3. the expected date and Coordinated Universal Time (UTC) of the re-entry of the space object,

4. the date and the Coordinated Universal Time (UTC) of moving the space object to a disposal orbit,

5. the web link to the official information on the space object,

6. the spacecraft which is or was used to launch the space object, and

7. the celestial body the space object is orbiting.

(3) In case of a change of operator the original operator must provide the following information:

1. the date and the Coordinated Universal Time (UTC) of the change of operator,

2. the identification of the new operator,

3. in case of a change of orbital position, the parameters of the original orbital position as well as the parameters of the new orbital position, and

4. any change of function of the space object.

(4) The operator shall be issued a certificate attesting the registration.

(5) Access to the register is open to any person, who can demonstrate a legitimate interest.

Costs of review

§7.(1) The costs for the review of the operator's reliability according to §2, subparagraph 1, letter 1 are borne by the operator. They are determined according to §5 of the Security Fees Regulation (BGBl No 389/1996, as amended).

(2) The costs for the review by qualified experts according to §5, subparagraph 2 are borne by the operator.

Fees

§8. The fees for the authorisation and registration procedures amount to 6 500 euros.

Competent authority

§9. The competent authority for the implementation of the authorisation procedure and the maintenance of the registry is the Federal Minister for Transport, Innovation and Technology, notwithstanding the agreements to be reached according to §17 of the Outer Space Act.

References to persons

§10. With respect to references to persons used in this Regulation, the form of reference selected shall apply to both genders.

The German original reads as follows:

Geltungsbereich

§1. Mit dieser Verordnung werden die im Sinne des §12 Weltraumgesetzes notwendigen Ausführungen getroffen.

Genehmigungsantrag

§2. (1) Zum Nachweis der nötigen Zuverlässigkeit, Leistungsfähigkeit und Fachkenntnis zur Durchführung der Weltraumaktivität (§4 Abs. 1 Z 1 des Weltraumgesetzes) sind vom Betreiber beizulegen:

1. ein Zertifikat über eine erfolgte Sicherheitsüberprüfung im Sinne des Sicherheitspolizeigesetzes, BGBl. Nr. 566/1991, in der geltenden Fassung, oder Verlässlichkeitsprüfung im Sinne des Militärbefugnisgesetzes, BGBl. I Nr. 86/2000, in der geltenden Fassung, des Betreibers oder, soweit es sich um eine juristische Person handelt, des für die Weltraumaktivität verantwortlichen Vertreters,

2. Qualifikationsnachweise des Betreibers sowie der an der Weltraumaktivität verantwortlich mitwirkenden Personen,

3. ein Verzeichnis der bisher vom Betreiber durchgeführten Aktivitäten im Bereich der Weltraumtechnologie oder verwandten Bereichen,

4. ein Nachweis der finanziellen Leistungsfähigkeit samt Kosten- und Finanzierungsplan der Weltraumaktivität,

5. sämtliche Verträge im Zusammenhang mit der Weltraumaktivität, insbesondere Startvertrag und Zulieferverträge,

6. ein Konzept zur Darstellung der geplanten Aufgabenstellung, Zweck und Ziel der Weltraumaktivität,

7. in Nachweis, welcher die technischen Details der Weltraumaktivität darstellt, insbesondere das angestrebte Frequenzspektrum und die Orbitalposition, die Energieversorgung, die Beschreibung der vorgesehenen Nutzlast, die Kommunikationsstrategie, die technischen Details der Bodenstation, verwendete Technologien auf Subsystemebene und

8. Unterlagen über die Dauer und Beendigung der Weltraumaktivität.

(2) Zum Nachweis, dass die Weltraumaktivität keine unmittelbare Gefahr für die öffentliche Ordnung, die Sicherheit von Personen und Sachen und für die Gesundheit darstellt (§4 Abs. 1 Z 2 des Weltraumgesetzes), sind vom Betreiber beizulegen:

1. ein Nachweis zur Einhaltung eines auf den einschlägigen wissenschaftlichen Erkenntnissen beruhenden Erkenntnisstandes fortschrittlicher Verfahren, Einrichtungen, Bau- oder Betriebsweisen, deren Funktionstüchtigkeit erprobt und erwiesen ist. Kommt die Einhaltung im konkreten Fall nicht in Betracht oder ist der Nachweis nicht möglich, so ist glaubhaft zu machen, dass die Weltraumaktivität dennoch keine unmittelbare Gefahr für die öffentliche Ordnung, die Sicherheit von Personen und Sachen und für die Gesundheit darstellt,

2. die Ergebnisse der Tests, mit denen nach dem Stand der Technik die Sicherheit und die Solidität des Weltraumobjekts geprüft wurde,

3. die, für den Fall des Ausfalls der Kommunikations- oder Datenverbindungen, den Verlust der Kontrolle über den Weltraumgegenstand, den Ausfall wesentlicher Systeme zur Stromversorgung, zur Lageregelung oder zur Flugbahnkontrolle und ähnlicher außergewöhnlicher Betriebsereignisse erarbeiteten Notfallpläne und

4. Angaben, inwiefern die Weltraumaktivität die Beobachtung der Erde miteinschließt und welche Daten dabei gewonnen werden. Insbesondere ist auf den Grad der Auflösung etwaiger Aufnahmen der Erdoberfläche wie auf die geplante Weitergabe von Daten, in rohem oder in verarbeitetem Zustand, hinzuweisen. Sollen im Zuge der Weltraumaktivität Daten im Sinne des Datenschutzgesetzes 2000, BGBl. I Nr. 165/1999, in der jeweils geltenden Fassung, verarbeitet werden, sind die für die Verarbeitung und Übermittlung dieser Daten erforderlichen Genehmigungen vorzulegen.

(3) Zum Nachweis, dass die Weltraumaktivität der nationalen Sicherheit, völkerrechtlichen Verpflichtungen oder außenpolitischen Interessen Österreichs nicht zuwiderläuft (§4 Abs. 1 Z 3 des Weltraumgesetzes), werden die unter Abs. 1 beigelegten Unterlagen der Beurteilung herangezogen sowie sind vom Betreiber insbesondere beizulegen:

1. Unterlagen, welche über die geplante Nutzung und den Empfängerkreis der gewonnenen Daten im Sinne des Abs. 2 Z 4 Auskunft geben,

2. Angaben zur Fracht des Weltraumgegenstandes.

(4) Zum Nachweis entsprechender Vorkehrungen für die Vermeidung von Weltraummüll im Sinne des §5 des Weltraumgesetzes (§4 Abs. 1 Z 4 des Weltraumgesetzes) sind vom Betreiber beizulegen:

1. ein Bericht über die entsprechend dem Stand der Technik und unter Berücksichtigung der international anerkannten Richtlinien, insbesondere

a) zur Vermeidung von Weltraummüll und Missionsrückständen während des gewöhnlichen Betriebs,

b) zur Vermeidung des Auseinanderbrechens des Weltraumgegenstandes in der Erdumlaufbahn,

c) zur Entfernung des Weltraumgegenstandes nach Ende der Weltraumaktivität, entweder durch kontrollierten Absturz oder durch das Verbringen in eine ausreichend hohe Erdumlaufbahn („graveyard orbit"), wobei bei nicht manövrierfähigen Weltraumobjekten die Erdumlaufbahn so zu wählen ist, dass diese nach Ende ihres Betriebs voraussichtlich nicht länger als 25 Jahre in der Erdumlaufbahn verbleiben,

2. eine Darstellung über die zur Vermeidung von Zusammenstößen mit anderen Weltraumgegenständen im Weltraum getroffenen Maßnahmen.

(5) Zum Nachweis, dass der Weltraumgegenstand keine gefährlichen oder gesundheitsschädlichen Substanzen enthält, die zu einer schädlichen Verunreinigung des Weltraums oder schädlichen Veränderung der Umwelt führen können (§4 Abs. 1 Z 5 des Weltraumgesetzes), sind vom Betreiber geeignete Unterlagen beizulegen.

(6) Zum Nachweis, dass die für den Funkbetrieb des Weltraumobjektes erforderlichen Frequenzen und Orbitalpositionen rechtmäßig genutzt werden dürfen, sind vom Betreiber geeignete Bewilligungen, oder die für eine Frequenzkoordination mit der Internationale Fernmeldeunion (ITU) erforderlichen Unterlagen (§4 Abs. 1 Z 6 des Weltraumgesetzes) beizulegen.

(7) Zum Nachweis über den Abschluss einer Haftpflichtversicherung im Sinne des §4 Abs. 4 des Weltraumgesetzes, sind vom Betreiber geeignete Unterlagen beizulegen, wenn er nicht nach §3 eine Befreiung von der Versicherungspflicht oder Herabsetzung der Versicherungssumme beantragt oder der Bund selbst Betreiber der Weltraumaktivität ist.

Antrag auf Befreiung von der Versicherungspflicht oder Herabsetzung der Versicherungssumme

§3. Der Betreiber kann die Befreiung von der Versicherungspflicht oder Herabsetzung der Versicherungssumme nach §4 Abs. 4 des Weltraumgesetzes beantragen. Dazu hat er Unterlagen beizulegen,

1. inwiefern die Weltraumaktivität der Wissenschaft, Forschung oder Ausbildung dient,

2. welches Risiko von der Weltraumaktivität ausgeht und

3. inwiefern er in der Lage ist, seiner Haftpflicht für Personen- oder Sachschaden finanziell nachzukommen.

Verfahren

§4.(1) Auf das Verfahren finden, soweit diese Verordnung oder das Weltraumgesetz nichts anderes bestimmen, die Vorschriften des Allgemeinen Verwaltungsverfahrensgesetz 1991, BGBl. Nr. 51/1991, in der jeweils geltenden Fassung, Anwendung.

(2) Der Betreiber hat die für den Genehmigungsantrag gemäß dieser Verordnung erforderlichen Unterlagen bei der zuständigen Behörde einzubringen. Diese Dokumente sind, soweit möglich in elektronischer Form einzubringen.

(3) Der Betreiber hat jene Unterlagen besonders zu kennzeichnen, welche, nach dessen Auffassung Geschäfts- oder Betriebsgeheimnisse enthalten. Auf die Wahrung von Betriebs- und Geschäftsgeheimnissen ist Bedacht zu nehmen.

(4) Fehlen im Genehmigungsantrag Unterlagen gemäß Abs. 2 oder sind die Angaben im Genehmigungsantrag unvollständig, so hat die Behörde, auch wenn sich dies erst im Zuge des Verfahrens ergibt, dem Betreiber die Ergänzung des Genehmigungsantrages aufzutragen.

(5) Der Genehmigungsantrag ist in jeder Lage des Verfahrens abzuweisen, wenn sich im Zuge des Verfahrens auf unzweifelhafte Weise ergibt, dass das Vorhaben bestimmten Genehmigungsvoraussetzungen in einem Maße zuwiderläuft, dass diese Mängel durch Auflagen oder Bedingungen nicht behoben werden können.

(6) Ist die Vorlage der Unterlagen nach §2 Abs. 1 Z 5 und §2 Abs. 2 Z 2 zum Zeitpunkt der Antragstellung über den Genehmigungsantrag nicht möglich, ist dieser Umstand vom Betreiber im Antrag anzuführen und zu begründen. Der nach §2 Abs. 1 Z 5 in Aussicht genommene Startanbieter ist spätestens zum Zeitpunkt der Entscheidung über den Genehmigungsantrag anzugeben. Die Nachreichung der Unterlagen nach §2 Abs. 1 Z 5 und §2 Abs. 2 Z 2 ist dem Betreiber mittels Auflagen oder Bedingungen aufzutragen.

Überprüfung der Genehmigungsvoraussetzungen

§5.(1) Die Überprüfung der Genehmigungsvoraussetzungen nach §2 und der Befreiung von der Versicherungspflicht oder Herabsetzung der Versicherungssumme nach §3 obliegt der Bundesministerin/dem Bundesminister für Verkehr, Innovation und Technologie.

(2) Erfordert es die Art, der Umfang oder die Komplexität des Antrages, kann die Bundesministerin/der Bundesminister für Verkehr, Innovation und Technologie zusätzlich geeignete sachverständige Personen bestellen. Auf eine Bestellung zum Sachverständigen besteht kein Rechtsanspruch.

(3) Im Hinblick auf die Überprüfung nach Abs. 1 kann die Bundesministerin/ der Bundesminister für Verkehr, Innovation und Technologie insbesondere die Österreichische Forschungsförderungsgesellschaft (FFG) und/oder die European Space Agency (ESA) um Stellungnahme ersuchen.

(4) Die weiterführende Kontrolle und Aufsicht der Weltraumaktivität nach §7 und §13 Abs. 1 des Weltraumgesetzes ist von der Bundesministerin/dem Bundesminister für Verkehr, Innovation und Technologie durchzuführen.

Registrierung

§6.(1) Der Betreiber hat die Informationen nach §10 des Weltraumgesetzes und die in Abs. 2 und 3 angeführten Informationen unverzüglich nach dem Start, spätestens aber nach zwei Wochen, sowohl in deutscher als auch in englischer Sprache zu übermitteln.

(2) Der Betreiber hat zusätzlich zu den Informationen nach §10 des Weltraumgesetzes folgende Informationen für die Registrierung beizubringen:

1. die Committee on space research (COSPAR) Bezeichnung, wenn anwendbar,

2. das Datum und die koordinierte universelle Zeit (UTC) als Zeitpunkt des Starts,

3. das erwartete Datum und die koordinierte universelle Zeit (UTC) des Wiedereintritts des Weltraumgegenstandes,

4. das Datum und die koordinierte universelle Zeit (UTC) der Verbringung des Weltraumgegenstandes in einen Entsorgungsorbit,

5. den Weblink zur offiziellen Information des Weltraumobjekts,

6. das Raumfahrzeug, mit dem der Weltraumgegenstand gestartet wird oder wurde und

7. den Himmelskörper, den der Weltraumgegenstand umkreist.

(3) Im Fall eines Betreiberwechsels hat der ursprüngliche Betreiber folgende Informationen zu übermitteln:

1. das Datum und die koordinierte universelle Zeit (UTC) des Betreiberwechsels,

2. die Identifizierung des neuen Betreibers,

3. bei einem Wechsel der Umlaufbahn, die Parameter der ursprünglichen Umlaufbahn sowie jene der neuen Umlaufbahn und

4. allfällige neue Funktion des Weltraumgegenstandes.

(4) Über die Eintragung ist dem Antragsteller eine Bescheinigung auszustellen.

(5) Die Einsichtnahme in das Register steht jedermann frei, soweit ein berechtigtes Interesse dargelegt wird.

Kosten der Überprüfung

§7.(1) Die Kosten für die Überprüfung der Zuverlässigkeit nach §2 Abs. 1 Z 1 trägt der Betreiber. Sie richten sich nach §5 der Sicherheitsgebühren-Verordnung, BGBl. Nr. 389/1996, in der jeweils geltenden Fassung.

(2) Die Kosten für die Überprüfung durch sachverständige Personen nach §5 Abs. 2 trägt der Betreiber.

Gebühren

§8. Die Gebühren für das Genehmigungs- und Registrierungsverfahren betragen 6 500 Euro.

Behördenzuständigkeit

§9. Die zuständige Behörde für die Durchführung des Genehmigungsverfahrens und die Führung des Registers ist die Bundesministerin/der Bundesminister für Verkehr, Innovation und Technologie unbeschadet der im §17 des Weltraumgesetzes vorgesehenen Einvernehmensherstellungen.

Personenbezogene Bezeichnungen

§10. Bei den in dieser Verordnung verwendeten personenbezogenen Bezeichnungen gilt die gewählte Form für beide Geschlechter.

QQ. The law of armed conflict and international humanitarian law/Recht des bewaffneten Konfliktes und internationales humanitäres Recht

I. International armed conflict/Der internationale bewaffnete Konflikt

2. The laws of international armed conflict/Das Recht des internationalen bewaffneten Konflikts

b. The commencement of international armed conflict and its effects (*e.g.* diplomatic and consular relations, treaties, private property, nationality, trading with the enemy, locus standi personae in judicio)/ Der Beginn des internationalen bewaffneten Konfliktes und seine Rechtsfolgen (z.B. diplomatische und konsularische Beziehungen, Verträge, Privateigentum, Staatsangehörigkeit, Feindhandel, locus standi personae in judicio)

QQ.I.2.b.-1

Work of the International Law Commission on Protection of the Environment in Relation to Armed Conflicts

Arbeit der Völkerrechtskommission betreffend den Schutz der Umwelt im Zusammenhang mit bewaffneten Konflikten

On 9 November 2015, the Austrian representative to the 70th session of the General Assembly delivered the following statement to the Sixth Committee regarding the Report of the International Law Commission on the Work of its 67th Session concerning the topic 'Protection of the Environment in Relation to Armed Conflicts':

> [...] The Special Rapporteur proposed a number of definitions, including a definition of armed conflict, that was left pending by the Drafting Committee for the time being. Concerning this definition, my delegation has already stated last year that it is in favour of applying the definition used in international humanitarian law; we are not convinced of the usefulness of a new definition of armed conflict for the purposes of these draft articles.
>
> Concerning the draft principles provisionally adopted by the Drafting Committee I would like to start with a few general remarks. We do not regard it as necessary in this context to address the relationship between human rights and humanitarian law, since this would exceed the scope of the present topic. What is needed, however, are explanations concerning the relationship between environmental law and humanitarian law.
>
> The introductory provision on the scope of the draft principles, *i.e.* that they apply to the protection of the environment before, during or after an armed conflict, is far too broad and seems to address environmental law in its entirety. We also question the phrase that the principles 'apply to the protection of the environment', as the protection of the environment is the objective of these principles and not its field of application.
>
> We would also like to draw attention to the issue referred to in paragraph 148 of the report of the Commission, relating to nuclear weapons and other weapons of mass destruction. Such weapons undoubtedly have a major detrimental effect on the environment, as was already recognized by International Court of Justice in its advisory opinion on the use of nuclear weapons. Last year, this issue was also discussed by the Vienna Conference on the Humanitarian Impact of Nuclear Weapons, organized by Austria in December 2014. We believe that the draft principles should also apply to nuclear weapons and other weapons of mass destruction.
>
> Draft principle I-(x) referring to the designation of protected zones in a general manner raises problems since state practice in the field of international humanitarian law shows the existence of a wide variety of protected zones with different legal consequences. Examples for such zones are nuclear weapons free zones,

demilitarized zones, hospital and safety zones, neutralized zones or open towns and non-defended localities. The term 'protected zone' does not yet exist in international humanitarian law. If this term were to be used, it would be necessary to define its relationship with already existing special zones. A particular issue that also needs discussion is to what extent the designation of protected zones, in particular those unilaterally declared, affects third states.

We agree that it was appropriate for the Drafting Committee to concentrate immediately on the phase during armed conflict, since this is the very core of the principles. However, the absence of a definition of the environment makes it difficult to assess the scope of the principles drafted so far, and it seems that the Commission has not yet reached a clear position whether it should address the natural or the human environment. Since the various existing instruments use different definitions of the environment, it is even more important to agree on a definition of the environment that would be the basis for these draft principles. Otherwise, the draft principles could hardly be interpreted clearly.

As to paragraph 2 of draft principle 11-1 on the general protection of the environment during armed conflict, my delegation would favour to use, also in this paragraph, the wording of Article 55 paragraph 1 of Additional Protocol I that directly addresses warfare and is therefore more focused on the conduct in armed conflicts than the general obligation now to be found in paragraph 2 of draft principle II-1. Paragraph 3 on the prohibition to attack parts of the environment also suffers from the absence of a definition of the environment.

For my delegation it is not clear why draft principle 11-2 on the application of the law of armed conflict to the environment specifically refers to the principles and rules of distinction, proportionality, military necessity and precautions in attack. In our understanding the law of armed conflict necessarily contains these principles and rules, which makes it superfluous to reiterate them in this context, unless it is for a specific reason. It would be sufficient to state in this principle that the law of armed conflict shall be applied to the environment, with a view to its protection. Such an understanding coincides with the objective of draft principle 11-3 on environmental considerations, which would suggest a merger of these two provisions.

As to draft principle 11-4 on the prohibition of reprisals, my delegation is in favour of this new general prohibition. We believe that it should apply to all forms of armed conflicts, including those of a non-international nature. This is also necessary in view of the growing difficulty to distinguish international from non-international armed conflicts and it is equally in line with the clear tendency to apply the same rules to all kinds of armed conflicts.

Draft principle II-5 on protected zones seems to presuppose an understanding that all protected zones are of the same legal nature. But in view of the differences between protected zones, to which we have already referred, a more differentiated approach seems advisable.

i. Conventional, nuclear, bacteriological and chemical weapons/ Konventionelle, nukleare, bakteriologische und chemische Waffen

QQ.I.2.i.-1.

Joint Statement on the Humanitarian Consequences of Nuclear Weapons

Gemeinsame Erklärung über die humanitären Auswirkungen von Atomwaffen

On 28 April 2015, at the Review Conference of the Parties to the Treaty on the Non-Proliferation of Nuclear Weapons, the Austrian Minister for Europe, Integration and Foreign Affairs gave the following Joint Statement on the 'Humanitarian Consequences of Nuclear Weapons':

> Our countries are deeply concerned about the catastrophic humanitarian consequences of nuclear weapons. Past experience from the use and testing of nuclear weapons has amply demonstrated the unacceptable humanitarian consequences caused by the immense, uncontrollable destructive capability and indiscriminate nature of these weapons. The fact-based discussion that took place at the Conferences on the Humanitarian Impact of Nuclear Weapons, convened respectively by Norway in March 2013, Mexico in February 2014 and Austria in December 2014, has allowed us to deepen our collective understanding of those consequences. A key message from experts and international organisations was that no State or international body could address the immediate humanitarian emergency caused by a nuclear weapon detonation or provide adequate assistance to victims.
>
> The broad participation at those Conferences, with attendance most recently in Vienna by 159 States, the ICRC, a number of UN humanitarian organisations and civil society, reflected the recognition that the catastrophic humanitarian consequences of nuclear weapons are a fundamental and global concern. We firmly believe that it is in the interests of all States to engage in discussions on the humanitarian consequences of nuclear weapons, which aim to further broaden and deepen understanding of this matter, and we welcome civil society's ongoing engagement.
>
> This work is essential, because the catastrophic consequences of nuclear weapons affect not only governments, but each and every citizen of our interconnected world. They have deep implications for human survival; for our environment; for socioeconomic development; for our economies; and for the health of future generations. For these reasons, we firmly believe that awareness of the catastrophic consequences of nuclear weapons must underpin all approaches and efforts towards nuclear disarmament, including in the work of the 2015 Review Conference of the Nuclear Non-Proliferation Treaty (NPT).
>
> This is not, of course, a new idea. The appalling humanitarian consequences of nuclear weapons became evident from the moment of their first use, and from that moment have motivated humanity's aspirations for a world free from this

threat, which have also inspired this statement. The humanitarian consequences of nuclear weapons have been reflected in numerous UN resolutions, including the first resolution passed by the General Assembly in 1946, and in multilateral instruments including the NPT. The world's most eminent nuclear physicists observed as early as 1955 that nuclear weapons threaten the continued existence of mankind and that a war with these weapons could quite possibly put an end to the human race. The First Special Session of the General Assembly devoted to Disarmament (SSOD-1) stressed in 1978 that 'nuclear weapons pose the greatest danger to mankind and to the survival of civilisation.' These expressions of profound concern remain as compelling as ever. In spite of this, the humanitarian consequences of nuclear weapons have not been at the core of nuclear disarmament and nuclear non-proliferation deliberations for many years.

We are therefore encouraged that the humanitarian focus is now well established on the global agenda. The 2010 Review Conference of the NPT expressed 'deep concern at the catastrophic humanitarian consequences of any use of nuclear weapons'. That deep concern informed the 26 November 2011 resolution of the Council of Delegates of the Red Cross and Red Crescent Movement, and the decision in 2012 of the General Assembly to establish an open-ended working group to develop proposals to take forward multilateral nuclear disarmament negotiations. It underlies the Special Declaration of the 3 Summit of the Community of Latin American and Caribbean States' in January 2015 on the urgent need for a nuclear weapons free world. In September 2013, at the High-Level Meeting on Nuclear Disarmament, numerous leaders from around the world again evoked that deep concern as they called for progress to be made on nuclear disarmament. More than three quarters of all countries supported the Joint Statement on the Humanitarian Consequences of Nuclear Weapons delivered at the 2014 First Committee of the UN General Assembly. Today's statement again demonstrates the growing political support for the humanitarian focus.

It is in the interest of the very survival of humanity that nuclear weapons are never used again, under any circumstances. The catastrophic effects of a nuclear weapon detonation, whether by accident, miscalculation or design, cannot be adequately addressed. All efforts must be exerted to eliminate the threat of these weapons of mass destruction.

The only way to guarantee that nuclear weapons will never be used again is through their total elimination. All States share the responsibility to prevent the use of nuclear weapons, to prevent their vertical and horizontal proliferation and to achieve nuclear disarmament, including through fulfilling the objectives of the NPT and achieving its universality.

We welcome the renewed resolve of the international community, together with the ICRC and international humanitarian organisations, to address the catastrophic humanitarian consequences of nuclear weapons. By raising awareness about this issue, civil society has a crucial role to play side-by-side with governments as we fulfil our responsibilities. We owe it to future generations to work together to do just that, and in doing so to rid our world of the threat posed by nuclear weapons.

RR. Neutrality, non-belligerency/Neutralität, Nicht-Kriegführung

IV. Policy of neutrality and non-alignment/Neutralitätspolitik, Bündnisfreiheit

RR.IV.-1

Enquiry concerning US soldiers in Schwechat

Anfrage betreffend US-Soldaten in Schwechat

On 17 September 2015, a number of representatives of the Austrian parliament raised a parliamentary enquiry to the Minister of the Interior:[29]

> Recently, a questionable incident occurred at Vienna airport: As reported by the newspaper Kurier, 9 members of the US forces together with war materials (M-16 rifles and pistols), attempted to travel via Vienna to Ukraine without the necessary permits in accordance with the Act on the Presence of Foreign Troops (Truppenaufenthaltsgesetz) contemplates. The 'attempt by the American Embassy to retrospectively obtain the authorisations' was 'rejected on legal grounds'.
>
> There is no public information on the assignments of the American soldiers in Ukraine, but it appears likely that their journey is related to the so-called 'military advisors' who were sent from the USA to Ukraine in order to train troops there.
>
> Theoretically, the transit could, therefore, even have been permitted under §2(1) (5) of the Act on the Presence of Foreign Troops, since 'participation in exercises and training' is mentioned as a possible reason.
>
> This option is also often applied: As the Minister of Defence elaborated in enquiry response 4617/AB, 2000 such permits for the presence of foreign troops were granted for the 'participation in exercises and training'.
>
> However, even if the close relation to a current military conflict is not always as obvious as in the case of the US soldiers in Schwechat, such exercises are increasingly an issue within a broader geopolitical context, which makes the transit permission as the standard outcome appear from a neutrality policy perspective.
>
> Russia, China, and NATO are trying to outdo each other with new large-scale exercises, the threat of which is superficially denied at best. It is precisely in the Eastern European NATO countries that manoeuvres aim to demonstrate presence and to present strength.

---

[29] Parliamentary Materials, 6494/J (XXV. GP)

This new arms race cannot be in the interests of the Austrian national security policy. The permission of transit for such operations is highly problematic with regard to Austria's neutrality.

Hence, the undersigned representatives make the following

ENQUIRY

1) What was the purpose of the travel of the nine US soldiers into Ukraine?

2) Which unit did the soldiers belong to?

3) How many of them belonged to the 173th Airborne Division?

4) How did the US justify the incident?

5) On what legal grounds was the attempt by the American Embassy to subsequently obtain the authorizations, described in the newspaper Kurier, based?

6) What was the reason for refusing this request?

7) Do you know that several hundred so-called 'military advisors' from the USA are actively involved in Ukraine in the training of troops for armed conflict in Eastern Ukraine?

8) Was this fact an element in the legal assessment of the subject matter and, if so, in how far?

9) Do you have any evidence that military advisors from the USA are also involved in fighting in the Ukraine?

10) According to the report of the newspaper Kurier of 29 July 2015, the spokesman of the BMLS (Federal Ministry of Defence and Sports), Colonel Michael Bauer, reacted to the incident: 'Since there were problems with their connecting flight after the stopover in Schwechat, they had to rebook and, to do so, leave the transit area.' In the process, during a security check, M-16 assault rifles and pistols were noticed in the luggage. Is it, thus, correct that the war material would have remained completely unnoticed had there not been 'problems with their connecting flight'?

11) Must weapons that are transported during air travel in the travel baggage be reported?

12) If so: Are the Austrian authorities informed if such reports concern a layover in Austria?

13) If so: Is the transport of war material controlled in the transit area?

14) If not: Why not?

15) Why were the weapons, which were undeclared and, thus, brought to Austria illegally, not confiscated from the US soldiers?

16) Do we allow everything going on in the transit area from NSA to armed soldiers?

The relevant parts of the German original read as follows:
Kürzlich kam es zu einem bedenklichen Vorfall am Flughafen Wien Schwechat: wie der Kurier berichtete versuchten 9 Angehörige der US-Streitkräfte mitsamt Kriegsmaterial (M-16 Sturmgewehre und Pistolen) im Gepäck über Wien in die Ukraine zu reisen, ohne dass entsprechende Genehmigungen nach dem Truppenaufenthaltsgesetz vorlagen. Der „Versuch der amerikanischen Botschaft, die Genehmigungen nachträglich zu erwirken", sei „aus rechtlichen Gründen abgelehnt" worden.

Über die Aufgaben der amerikanischen Soldaten in der Ukraine wurde öffentlich nichts bekannt, es liegt aber nahe, dass ihre Reise im Zusammenhang mit den sogenannten „Militärberatern" steht, die von der USA in die Ukraine entsandt wurden und dort Truppen ausbilden sollen.

Theoretisch hätte die Durchreise daher sogar nach §2 Abs 1 Z 5 Truppenaufenthaltsgesetz gestattet werden können, da dort die „Teilnahme an Übungen und Ausbildungsmaßnahmen" als ein möglicher Grund genannt wird.

Von dieser Möglichkeit wird auch rege Gebrauch gemacht: wie der Verteidigungsminister in der Anfragebeantwortung 4617/AB erläuterte, werden seit 2010 jährlich weit über 2000 Genehmigungen für Truppenaufenthalte zur „Teilnahme an Übungen und Ausbildungsmaßnahmen" erteilt.

Doch auch wenn der enge Bezug zu einer aktuellen militärischen Auseinandersetzung nicht immer so offensichtlich ist wie im Fall der US-Soldaten in Schwechat, stehen derartige Übungen zunehmend in einem großen geopolitischen Kontext, der die Transiterlaubnis als Standardfall neutralitätspolitisch heikel erscheinen lässt.

Russland, China und die NATO versuchen sich gegenseitig mit neuen Großübungen zu übertrumpfen, deren Drohpotential bestenfalls oberflächlich bestritten wird. Gerade in den osteuropäischen NATO-Staaten soll durch Manöver Präsenz gezeigt und Stärke präsentiert werden.

Dieses neue Wettrüsten kann nicht im Interesse österreichischer Sicherheitspolitik liegen. Die Gestattung von Durchreisen zu derartigen Operationen ist im Hinblick auf Österreichs Neutralität höchst problematisch.

Die unterfertigenden Abgeordneten stellen daher folgende

ANFRAGE

1) Zu welchem Zweck erfolgte die Reise der neun US-Soldaten in die Ukraine?

2) Welcher Einheit gehörten die Soldaten an?

3) Wie viele von ihnen gehörten der 173th Airborne Division an?

4) Wie begründeten die USA den Vorfall?

5) Auf welchen Rechtsgrund stützte sich der im Kurier beschriebene Versuch der amerikanischen Botschaft, die Genehmigungen nachträglich zu erwirken?

6) Aus welchem Rechtsgrund wurde dieser Antrag abgelehnt?

7) Ist Ihnen bekannt, dass mehrere hundert sogenannte „Militärberater" der USA in der Ukraine aktiv an der Ausbildung von Truppen für den Kriegseinsatz in der Ostukraine beteiligt sind?

8) Spielte dieser Umstand eine Rolle in der rechtlichen Bewertung der gegenständlichen Angelegenheit und falls ja welche?

9) Verfügen Sie über Hinweise, dass Militärberater der USA in der Ukraine auch an Kampfhandlungen teilnehmen?

10) Nach dem Bericht des Kurier vom 29.7.2015 erklärte der Sprecher des BMLS, Oberst Michael Bauer, zu dem Vorfall: „Da es nach der Zwischenlandung in Schwechat jedoch Probleme mit ihrem Anschlussflug gab, mussten sie umbuchen und dafür den Transitbereich verlassen." Dabei seien bei einer Sicherheitskontrolle M-16 Sturmgewehre und Pistolen im Gepäck bemerkt worden. Ist es daher zutreffend, dass der Transit samt Kriegsmaterial ohne „Probleme mit dem Anschlussflug" gänzlich unbemerkt geblieben wäre?

11) Müssen Waffen, die bei Flugreisen im Reisegepäck transportiert werden, gemeldet werden?

12) Falls ja: werden die österreichischen Behörden informiert, wenn derartige Meldungen einen Transitfall in Österreich betreffen?

13) Falls ja: wird der Transport von Kriegsmaterial im Transitbereich kontrolliert?

14) Falls nein: warum nicht?

15) Warum wurden den US-Soldaten die nicht deklarierten und damit illegal nach Österreich eingeführten Kriegswaffen nicht abgenommen?

16) Lassen wir uns von NSA bis bewaffnete Soldaten im Transitbereich alles bieten?

On 12 November 2015, the Minister of the Interior gave the following response:[30]

On question 1:

The purpose of travel is unknown.

On questions 2 and 3:

The soldiers belong to the United States Marine Corps. How many of them belong to the 173rd Airborne Division is unknown.

On question 4:

The commander of the soldiers stated in his interrogation that, according to his information, all official steps for the flight and transport of the soldiers and the baggage had been regulated by the superior authorities.

On questions 5 to 10 and 16:

Opinions and appraisals are not subject to the parliamentary right of interpellation.

---

[30] Parliamentary Materials, 6275/AB (XXV. GP).

On question 11:

Generally, transported firearms and ammunition must always be declared at the airport of departure. The respective airline is responsible for complying with these legal requirements (IATA regulations). In Austria, the police additionally carries out an inspection of the transported firearms on the basis of weapons law.

On questions 12 to 14:

Since neither a reporting requirement nor a control obligation ('one-stop security concept') exists due to aviation security regulations, a transport of war materials from a US airport arriving in the course of a stopover is not known by officials from the aviation security point of view.

On question 15:

The weapons of the US soldiers were safely deposited in a security gate, accessible only to police forces. Upon directive of the Public Prosecutor's Office Korneuburg, a temporary attachment of the weapons took place.

The relevant parts of the German original read as follows:

Zu Frage 1:

Der Zweck der Reise ist nicht bekannt.

Zu den Fragen 2 und 3:

Die Soldaten gehörten dem US-Marine-Corps an. Wie viele von ihnen der 173th Airborne Division angehörten ist nicht bekannt.

Zu Frage 4:

Der Kommandant der Soldaten gab in seiner Vernehmung an, dass nach seiner Information alle behördlichen Schritte zum Flug und Transport der Soldaten und des Gepäcks durch die vorgesetzten Dienststellen geregelt wurden.

Zu den Fragen 5 bis 10 und 16:

Meinungen und Einschätzungen sind nicht Gegenstand des parlamentarischen Interpellationsrechts.

Zu Frage 11:

Grundsätzlich müssen mitgeführte Schusswaffen und Munition immer am Abflughafen deklariert werden. Für die Einhaltung dieser rechtlichen Bestimmungen (IATA Vorschriften) ist die jeweilige Fluglinie verantwortlich. In Österreich erfolgt darüber hinaus eine waffenrechtliche Überprüfung der transportierten Schusswaffen durch die Polizei.

Zu den Fragen 12 bis 14:

Da aufgrund der luftfahrtsicherheitsrechtlichen Vorschriften weder eine Meldepflicht noch eine Kontrollverpflichtung („One-Stop-Security-Konzept") besteht, wird aus luftfahrtsicherheitsrechtlicher Sicht ein Transport von Kriegsmaterial von einem US-Flughafen ankommen im Zuge eines Transitaufenthaltes behördlich nicht bekannt.

Zu Frage 15:
Die Waffen der US-Soldaten wurden in einem Sicherheitsgate, zu welchem nur Polizeikräfte Zutritt haben, sicher verwahrt. Über Weisung der Staatsanwaltschaft Korneuburg erfolgte eine vorläufige Sicherstellung der Waffen.

SS. Legal aspects of international relations and cooperation in particular matters/Rechtliche Aspekte der internationalen Beziehungen und Zusammenarbeit in bestimmten Bereichen

I. General economic and financial matters/Wirtschaftliche und Finanzwirtschaftliche Angelegenheiten

1. Trade/Handel

See CC.II.3.-1.

SS.I.1.-1

Report of the United Nations Commission on International Trade Law

Arbeit der Kommission der Vereinten Nationen für internationales Handelsrecht

On 19 October 2015, the Austrian representative to the 70th session of the General Assembly delivered the following statement regarding the Report of the United Nations Commission on International Trade Law on the work of its 48th session:

> [...]
>
> Austria strongly supports the work of the Commission concerned with *technical cooperation and assistance* in the field of international trade law reform and development. In this regard, we recognize the need to strengthen support to Member States, upon their request, in the domestic implementation of their respective international obligations through enhanced technical assistance and capacity building. Austria welcomes the efforts of the Secretary-General to ensure greater coordination and coherence among United Nations entities and with donors and recipients and, welcomes in this regard the *guidance note* on strengthening United Nations support to States to implement sound commercial law reforms. It is our hope that the guidance note referenced in the draft resolution will meet with the approval of all member states.
>
> I would also like to recall that last year, the United Nations *Convention on Transparency in Treaty-based Investor-State Arbitration* was adopted, and already has

16 signatories. The Convention constitutes an efficient and flexible mechanism by which the Transparency Rules elaborated by the Commission in 2013 will apply to disputes arising under the existing 3,000 bilateral and multilateral investment treaties currently in force. Together with the Rules on Transparency, the Convention contributes to the enhancement of transparency in treaty-based investor-State arbitration, and to the dissemination of knowledge about peaceful dispute resolution proceedings and to the continuous strengthening of the rule of law. In this regard, we commend the efforts by the UNCITRAL Secretariat to operationalize the *repository of published information under the Rules on Transparency* in Treaty-based Investor-State Arbitration, consistent with the aim to enhance transparency in treaty-based investor-State arbitration.

[...]

SS.I.1.-2

Enquiry concerning the renegotiation of the Comprehensive Economic and Trade Agreement (CETA)

Anfrage betreffend die Neuverhandlung von CETA

On 22 October 2015, a number of representatives of the Austrian parliament raised a parliamentary enquiry to the Federal Chancellor based on the following grounds:[31]

CETA, the already fully negotiated EU trade agreement with Canada, is considered a blueprint for TTIP. It includes investment protection provisions that fall short of the ISDS reform proposals put forward by EU Trade Commissioner Malmström in September 2015. Despite these new proposals, the EU Trade Commissioner is unwilling to reopen the negotiations on CETA concluded in 2014. However, she announced that she would discuss with Canada how the ISDS clauses in CETA can be fine-tuned in accordance with her recent reform proposals. It is unclear how and in which legally binding form this undertaking will be approached.

At the same time, the retention of investment protection clauses in international agreements with states with developed legal systems (*e.g.* USA and Canada) stands in contradiction with the decision of the Austrian parliament of 24 September 2014. It held that the 'sense of the inclusion of ISDS clauses in agreements with (these) states (...) is not comprehensible from today's point of view'.

The relevant parts of the German original read as follows:

CETA, das bereits fertig ausverhandelte Handelsabkommen der EU mit Kanada, gilt als Blaupause für TTIP. Darin enthalten sind Investitionsschutzbestimmungen, die hinter die von EU-Handelskommissarin Malmström im September 2015 vorgelegten ISDS-Reformvorschläge zurückfallen. Trotz dieser neuen

---

[31] Parliamentary Materials, 6839/J (XXV. GP).

Vorschläge ist EU Handelskommissarin nicht gewillt, die 2014 abgeschlossenen Verhandlungen über CETA wieder aufzunehmen. Sie hat jedoch angekündigt, mit Kanada zu erörtern, wie die in CETA verankerten ISDS-Klauseln im Einklang mit ihren jüngsten Reformvorschlägen feinabgestimmt werden können. Offen ist, in welcher Weise und in Form welcher rechtsverbindlichen Verankerung dieses Vorhaben angegangen wird.

Gleichzeitig steht das Festhalten an Investitionsschutzklauseln in internationalen Abkommen mit Staaten mit entwickelten Rechtsystemen (z.B. USA und Kanada) im Widerspruch zum Beschluss des Nationalrates vom 24.9.2014. Danach ist die „Sinnhaftigkeit der Aufnahme von ISDS-Klauseln bei Abkommen mit (diesen) Staaten (…) aus heutiger Sicht nicht erkennbar".

On 22 December 2015, the Federal Chancellor gave the following response:[32]

On question 1:

- In which aspects are the ISDS rules in CETA different from the reform proposals on international investment protection put forward by EU Trade Commissioner Malmström in September 2015?

Briefly summarising, in CETA, the following changes have been envisioned in comparison to previous comparable agreements:

- Assurance of transparency regarding all documents and hearings within the course of the arbitration procedure,
- a ban on 'forum shopping',
- review of the interpretation of the agreement by governments,
- a strict code of conduct for arbitrators,
- a right of refusal for unfounded claims, and
- the introduction of the loser pays principle, in order to prevent frivolous and unfounded arbitration proceedings.

The proposals of the European Commission in the context of TTIP envision, in particular, the establishment of a permanent court system with an appeal body (as opposed to *ad hoc* arbitration), an established distribution of business for the allocation of cases, strict decision deadlines, a ban on judges to act as lawyers in investment proceedings as well as strict ethical rules for judges and an obligation for the parties to disclose who is financing the claim as further differences.

On question 2:

- How does the Federal Chancellery perceive these differences with regard to the requirements for public, independent judicial systems?

The present proposals show that it was and is important to be critical with regard to the subject of investment protection. Some progress can be seen, but the need

---

[32] Parliamentary Materials, 6588/AB (XXV. GP).

and the added value of arbitration in agreements between states with developed legal systems must continue to be questioned in general.

On questions 2 a., 3 d., 4 a., 5 c., and 6 c:

- In which way are you ensuring that the Federal Minister of Science, Research and Economy, whose department is heading the negotiations at the EU level to take this position at the European level?

The Federal Chancellery uses the possibilities of the coordination mechanisms at the national level, in order to introduce its position into the decision-making process. Austria has also expressed its position, in particular at the European Council in March 2015, in the form of a declaration which corresponds to the resolution of the Austrian Parliament of September 2014, and, thus, holds the view that the sense of including ISDS clauses in agreements with states with developed legal systems is not conceivable from today's point of view. A declaration to this extent was also made at the European Council in December 2015.

On question 3:

- Are you standing up to secure the new proposals on investment protection put forward by the Commission as legally binding within the framework CETA?

    a. If yes, what possibilities for a legally binding implementation do you see and which one are you promoting?

    b. If so, compared to the Commission's proposal for reform, for which points do you see the need for further fine-tuning – as Commissioner Malmström has called it?

    c. If not, why not?

COM Malmström has already stated several times that the European Commission does not intend to resume the CETA negotiations concluded in 2014. However, the on-going process of legal review of the CETA text still offers the possibility for changes in the investment protection chapter. Recourse to this possibility should be taken in any case. Austria took this position in the Foreign Affairs Council (Trade) on 27 November 2015. In addition, the President of the European Commission, Jean-Claude Juncker, was also contacted in this regard.

On question 4:

- Is and to what extent is a separate investment protection mechanism in CETA really necessary against the background of the 'right to regulate'?

Investment protection provisions may not restrict the scope of state regulation – the political freedom for action or decision-making in order to achieve legitimate political objectives in the interest of the common good must be preserved.

On question 5:

- If the Commission puts CETA before the Council in the current form without any amendments, additions, or fine-tuning with regard to the investment protection chapter, will you take the position during the inner-Austrian approval process that Austria should approve the treaty within the Council?

   a. If so, why?

   b. If not, why not?

The CETA treaty text is currently undergoing the legal review process. Once this has been completed and the individual language versions have been prepared, the final version will be subject to a thorough examination and evaluation.

On question 6:

- Should the Commission submit CETA to the Council for adoption in its present form for the purpose of a provisional application of CETA, will you utilise the inner-Austrian approval process in order for Austria to approve the provisional application within the Council?

   a. If so, why?

   b. If not, why not?

So far, it is unclear which parts of the agreement should be subject to provisional application. Hence, an evaluation is currently not possible.

On question 7:

- Since having seen the final CETA treaty in August 2014, have you upheld the view that CETA is a mixed agreement?

   a. If so, why?

   b. If not, why not?

In the understanding of Austria, CETA is a mixed agreement that requires ratification by the national parliaments.

On question 8:

- Which indications do you have from the European Commission that it will submit CETA to the Council as a mixed agreement respective not as a mixed agreement?

In this connection, we refer to the Commission's request for information to the European Court of Justice pursuant to Article 218(11) of the Treaty on the Functioning of the European Union, which seeks to clarify whether the already initialled free trade agreement with Singapore is to be considered as a mixed agreement.

The relevant parts of the German original read as follows:

Zu Frage 1:

- In welchen Punkten unterscheiden sich die ISDS-Regelungen in CETA von den von EU-Kommissarin Malmström im September 2015 vorgeschlagenen Reformvorschlägen zum internationalen Investitionsschutz?

In CETA sind, kurz zusammengefasst, die folgenden Änderungen im Vergleich zu bisherigen, vergleichbaren Abkommen vorgesehen:
- die Sicherstellung von Transparenz betreffend alle Dokumente sowie Anhörungen
- im Rahmen der Schiedsverfahrens,
- ein Verbot des „Forum Shoppings",
- Kontrolle der Interpretation des Abkommens durch die Regierungen,
- ein strenger Verhaltenskodex für Schiedsrichter,
- ein Ablehnungsrecht für unbegründete Ansprüche und
- die Einführung des Verliererzahlt-Prinzips, um unseriöse und unbegründete Schiedsklagen hintanzuhalten.

Die Vorschläge der Europäischen Kommission im Rahmen von TTIP sehen als weitere Unterschiede insbesondere die Einrichtung eines permanenten Gerichtssystems mit Berufungsinstanz (anstelle von ad hoc einberufenen Schiedsgerichten) vor, eine feste Geschäftsverteilung für die Zuweisung der Fälle, strenge Entscheidungsfristen, ein Verbot für Richter, als Anwälte in Investitionsstreitigkeiten tätig zu sein, sowie strenge ethische Regeln für Richter und eine Verpflichtung der Streitparteien offenzulegen, wer ihre Klage finanziert.

Zu Frage 2:
- Wie wertet das Bundeskanzleramt diese Unterschiede im Hinblick auf die Anforderungen an öffentliche, unabhängige Justizsysteme?

Die vorliegenden Vorschläge zeigen, dass es wichtig war und ist, beim Thema Investitionsschutz kritisch zu sein. Es zeigt sich ein gewisser Fortschritt, allerdings ist weiterhin grundsätzlich die Notwendigkeit und der Mehrwert von Schiedsgerichten in Abkommen zwischen Staaten mit entwickelten Rechtssystemen zu hinterfragen.

Zu den Fragen 2 a., 3 d., 4 a., 5 c. und 6 c:
- Auf welche Weise wirken Sie auf den Bundesminister für Wissenschaft, Forschung und Wirtschaft ein, dessen Ressort die Verhandlungen auf EU-Ebene führt, diese Position auf europäischer Ebene zu vertreten?

Das Bundeskanzleramt nutzt die Möglichkeiten der Koordinierungsmechanismen auf nationaler Ebene, um seinen Standpunkt in die Entscheidungsprozesse einzubringen. Österreich hat seine Position insbesondere auch beim Europäischen Rat vom März 2015 in Form einer Erklärung dargelegt, die der Entschließung des österreichischen Nationalrates vom September 2014 entspricht und somit die Ansicht vertritt, dass die Sinnhaftigkeit der Aufnahme von ISDS-Klauseln bei Abkommen mit Staaten mit entwickelten Rechtssystemen aus heutiger Sicht nicht erkennbar sei. Auch beim Europäischen Rat im Dezember 2015 wurde in diesem Sinne eine Erklärung abgegeben.

Zu Frage 3:

- Setzen Sie sich dafür ein, dass die von der Kommission vorgelegten neuen Vorschläge zum Investitionsschutz auch im Rahmen von CETA rechtsverbindlich verankert werden?

    a. Wenn ja, welche Möglichkeiten für eine rechtsverbindliche Verankerung sehen Sie und für welche setzen Sie sich ein?

    b. Wenn ja, in welchen Punkten erachten Sie im Vergleich zum Reformvorschlag der Kommission weitere Feinabstimmungen – wie EU-Kommissarin Malmström es genannt hat – mit Kanada für notwendig?

    c. Wenn nein, weshalb nicht?

KOM Malmström erklärte bereits mehrmals, dass die Europäische Kommission nicht beabsichtige, die 2014 abgeschlossenen Verhandlungen über CETA wieder aufzunehmen. Allerdings bietet der derzeit laufende Prozess der rechtlichen Überprüfung des CETA-Textes noch die Möglichkeit für Änderungen im Investitionsschutzkapitel. Diese Möglichkeit sollte auf jeden Fall genutzt werden. Österreich hat diese Position beim Rat Auswärtige Angelegenheiten (Handel) am 27.11.2015 vertreten. Außerdem wurde diesbezüglich auch Kontakt mit dem Präsidenten der Europäischen Kommission Jean-Claude Juncker aufgenommen.

Zu Frage 4:

- Ob und inwieweit ist ein eigener Investitionsschutzmechanismus in CETA vor dem Hintergrund des „right to regulate" tatsächlich erforderlich?

Investitionsschutzbestimmungen dürfen das staatliche Regulierungsrecht nicht einschränken – die politischen Handlungs- bzw. Entscheidungsspielräume zur Erreichung von legitimen politischen Zielen im Interesse des Allgemeinwohls müssen gewahrt werden.

Zu Frage 5:

- Wenn die Kommission dem Rat CETA in der derzeit vorliegenden Form, d.h. ohne Änderungen, Ergänzungen, Feinabstimmungen beim Investitionsschutzkapitel, zur Ratifikation vorlegt, werden Sie sich im innerösterreichischen Abstimmungsprozess dafür einsetzen, dass Österreich im Rat dem Vertrag zustimmt?

    a. Wenn ja, weshalb?

    b. Wenn nein, weshalb nicht?

Der CETA Vertragstext durchläuft derzeit den Prozess der juristischen Überprüfung. Wenn dieser abgeschlossen ist und die einzelnen Sprachfassungen erstellt worden sind, wird die zu diesem Zeitpunkt vorliegende, finale Fassung einer gründlichen Prüfung und Bewertung unterzogen werden.

Zu Frage 6:

- Wenn die Kommission dem Rat CETA in der derzeit vorliegenden Form zur Beschlussfassung vorlegt und dabei die vorläufige Anwendung von CETA

vorsieht, werden Sie sich im innerösterreichischen Abstimmungsprozess dafür einsetzen, dass Österreich im Rat der vorläufigen Anwendung zustimmt?
a. Wenn ja, weshalb?
b. Wenn nein, weshalb nicht?
Bislang ist nicht bekannt, welche Teile des Abkommens vorläufig angewendet werden sollen. Eine Beurteilung ist aktuell daher nicht möglich.

Zu Frage 7:
- Sind Sie nach Vorliegen des CETA-Vertrags seit August 2014 nach wie vor der Auffassung, dass es sich bei CETA um ein gemischtes Abkommen handelt?
a. Wenn ja, weshalb?
b. Wenn nein, weshalb nicht?

Nach Auffassung Österreichs handelt es sich bei CETA um ein gemischtes Abkommen, das der Ratifikation durch die nationalen Parlamente bedarf.

Zu Frage 8:
- Welche Hinweise aus der Europäischen Kommission haben Sie, dass diese CETA dem Rat als gemischtes Abkommen vorlegen bzw. nicht als gemischtes Abkommen vorlegen wird?

In diesem Zusammenhang wird auf das Auskunftsersuchen der Europäischen Kommission gemäß Artikel 218 Absatz 11 des Vertrags über die Arbeitsweise der Europäischen Union an den Europäischen Gerichtshof verwiesen, der klären soll, ob das bereits paraphierte Freihandelsabkommen mit Singapur als gemischtes Abkommen zu betrachten ist.

SS.I.1.-3.

Free Trade Agreement between the European Union and its Member States, of the one part, and the Republic of Korea, of the other part

Freihandelsabkommen zwischen der Europäischen Union und ihren Mitgliedstaaten einerseits und der Republik Korea andererseits

On 13 December 2015, the Free Trade Agreement between the European Union and its Member States, of the one part, and the Republic of Korea, of the other part, entered into force. The Austrian Explanatory Memorandum contains the following comments with regard to the character of the treaty as a mixed agreement:[33]

[...] Since the present agreement contains provisions that fall both under the competence of the European Union as well as the Member States, it constitutes a

---

[33] Explanatory Memorandum, Parliamentary Materials 1635 (XXIV. GP).

mixed agreement and requires the approval of all Member States on the side of the European Union. [...]

The relevant parts of the German original read as follows:

[...] Da das vorliegende Abkommen Bestimmungen enthält, die in die Kompetenz sowohl der Europäischen Union als auch der Mitgliedstaaten fallen, handelt es sich um ein gemischtes Abkommen und bedarf auf EU- Seite auch der Genehmigung durch alle Mitgliedstaaten.[...]

3. Investments/Investitionen

See EE.II.2.d.-1.

6. Development/Entwicklung

See EE.II.2.d.-1.

III. Environment/Umwelt

SS.III.-1

Work of the International Law Commission on Protection of the Atmosphere

Arbeit der Völkerrechtskommission betreffend den Schutz der Atmosphäre

On 2 November 2015, the Austrian representative to the 70th session of the General Assembly delivered the following statement to the Sixth Committee regarding the Report of the International Law Commission on the Work of its 67th Session concerning the topic 'Protection of the Atmosphere':

Concerning the topic of the 'Protection of the atmosphere', Austria is grateful to the Special Rapporteur Shuinya Murase for his very rich second report which contains five guidelines regarding definitions, scope, basic principles, the common concern of mankind and international cooperation. We also welcome the dialogue the Commission has had with scientists on the protection of the atmosphere, which certainly promoted a better understanding of the complex physical phenomena connected with this topic.

Permit me now to turn to the guidelines provisionally adopted by the Drafting Committee. We agree that there is a pressing need to address this topic, as it is stated in the preamble of the guidelines.

As to guideline 1 on the use of terms, it is to be asked why the definition of 'atmospheric pollution' limits the scope of the guidelines only to transboundary effects of atmospheric pollution. In the atmosphere, every pollution inevitably has transboundary effects. Thus, the qualification of 'transboundary' is certainly redundant. It also complicates the matter since using that qualification any assertion of pollution would first require proof of its transboundary effects. For this reason, my delegation favours a deletion of this redundant qualification.

We also question whether it was appropriate to delete, in the same definition contained in guideline 1, 'energy' from the factors causing pollution, in view of the fact that the United Nations Law of the Sea Convention, in its Article 1 (1)(4), explicitly refers to energy as a cause of pollution. We don't see the reason for the difference between these two definitions. Although we note that the commentary on this guideline refers to energy among the substances causing atmospheric pollution, for the sake of clarity it would be better to include energy also in the definition of 'atmospheric pollution' itself.

Paragraph 4 of guideline 2 on the scope of the guidelines refers to the status of airspace under international law. However, since airspace is under the complete and exclusive sovereignty of the relevant state, its status is governed not only by international, but also by national law. Therefore, it should also be clarified in the guidelines that they do not affect the national legal regulation of the airspace. Accordingly we propose to reformulate this phrase, so that instead of saying that it does not affect the 'status of airspace under international law' it would say that it does not affect 'the legal status of the airspace'. In connection with this paragraph 4 of guideline 2, I would also like to agree with the statement contained in the commentary that the question of the delimitation between airspace and outer space has been under discussion in the Legal Subcommittee of the Outer Space Committee for a long time, and that, therefore, there is no need to discuss it in the present context.

IV. Natural Resources/Natürliche Ressourcen

See EE.II.1.b.bb.-1.

VII. Cultural matters/Kulturelle Angelegenheiten

SS.VII.-1

Convention on the Means of Prohibiting and Preventing the Illicit Import, Export and Transfer of Ownership of Cultural Property 1970

Übereinkommen über Maßnahmen zum Verbot und zur Verhütung der unzulässigen Einfuhr, Ausfuhr und Übereignung von Kulturgut

On 15 July 2015, Austria deposited its ratification of the Convention on the Means of Prohibiting and Preventing the Illicit Import, Export and Transfer of Ownership of Cultural Property 1970 with the United Nations Educational, Scientific and Cultural Organization, which entered into force for Austria on 15

October 2015.[34] The Explanatory Memorandum highlights and clarifies that the obligations of restitution under Articles 7 and 13 of the Convention shall not be applied retroactively:[35]

> Articles 7 and 13 envision that states take 'necessary measures' to secure restitution of cultural property in exchange for adequate compensation by the state of origin. This obligation does not have retroactive effect but – as explicitly evident from Article 7(b) and in accordance with Article 25 of the Vienna Convention on the Law of Treaties – only applies to situations occurring after accession; hence, the Convention does not apply to earlier acquisitions, in particular not to historically accumulated collections.

The relevant parts of the German original read as follows:

> Die Art. 7 und 13 des Übereinkommens sehen vor, dass die Vertragsstaaten „geeignete Maßnahmen" setzten, um die Rückgaben von Kulturgut gegen die Zahlung einer angemessenen Entschädigung durch den Herkunftsstaat sicherzustellen. Diese Verpflichtung wirkt jedenfalls nicht rückwirkend, sondern – wie sich auch ausdrücklich aus Art. 7 lit. b und in Übereinstimmung mit Art. 25 des Wiener Übereinkommens über das Recht der Verträge, BGBl. Nr. 40/1980 i.d.g.F., ergibt – nur auf Sachverhalte, die nach dem Beitritt verwirklicht wurden; das Übereinkommen wirkt daher nicht auf frühere Erwerbungen, insbesondere nicht auf die historisch gewachsenen Sammlungsbestände zurück.

IX. Military and security matters/Militärische Angelegenheiten, Sicherheitsangelegenheiten

See RR.IV.-1.

---

[34] Federal Law Gazette III No. 139/2015.
[35] Explanatory Memorandum, Parliamentary Materials 456 (XXV. GP).

Book Reviews

Jens David Ohlin, *The Assault on International Law*. Oxford University Press, Oxford, 2015, ISBN 9780199987405, xi + 304 pp., EUR 26.99

Jens David Ohlin's book deals with the way the Bush administration approached international law in general and particularly sensitive topics like the prohibition of torture in particular. In so doing, above all those not trained in US law gain new perspectives into the specific international law-related aspects of the US constitution, the role of legal advisors, some of the relevant cases, and the US legal system in general.

While those adhering to the idea of a liberal world order, first and foremost – officially, at least – Bill Clinton or Barack Obama, emphasize the role of international law as a tool working for the benefit of the entire international community and thus *also* for the US, the Bush administration seemingly viewed it as, if at all, one of several factors shaping their policy. The US would thus only adhere to international law as long as it was not considered as being detrimental to the broad definition of their vital interests. International law was thus relegated to the status of 'law improperly so called', as John Austin famously put it.

Ohlin tells the story of how a rather less-renowned law professor like John Yoo raised to prominence by arguing in favour of a restrictive interpretation of the prohibition of torture. How big names like Jack Goldsmith managed to be considered as voices of reason while simultaneously engaging (together with Eric Posner, the co-author of *The Limits of International Law*[1]) in what Ohlin calls an assault on international law. He shows how these scholars became the architects of a strong executive by formulating the theoretical and philosophical background, *e.g.*, by (deliberately or not) misconstruing the leading cases on the role of international law in the US legal system.

In so doing, Ohlin *inter alia* refers to the writings of Carl Schmitt, characterized by some as the key legal thinker of the Third Reich (at least in its initial phase). On a side note, however, it shall be briefly noted that the passage referred to by Ohlin from Schmitt's *Die geistesgeschichtliche Lage des heutigen Parlamentarismus*[2] (The Crisis of Parliamentary Democracy) is less a piece of advocacy in favour of a strong executive than an observation on the worrisome state of the Weimar democracy during the troublesome 1920s. Schmitt primarily noted that it was

---
[1] Jack L Goldsmith and Eric A Posner, *The Limits of International Law* (2007).
[2] Carl Schmitt, *Die geistesgeschichtliche Lage des heutigen Parlamentarismus* (1923/1991) 62f.

inevitable to bypass the parliament by governing in closed circles and specialized committees without actually arguing in favour of a strong executive. On the contrary, he even lamented that it thereby lost its original foundation and purpose.

However, Schmitt and his views on (constitutional) law in times of crisis – or their reception at least – had a renaissance in the wake of 9/11. During these times, constitutionalism and the idea of a strong Congress was seen as an impediment to the need for effective and decisive actions. Ohlin however convincingly argues how a strong and active parliament not only can function better than a nefarious strong man in times of crisis but also that the thought of the need for a strong executive is misleading in the first place.

In sum, reading *The Assault on International Law* provides a dramatic insight into the legal, academic, and – ultimately – political battles over the place of international law in US domestic law and the US conceptualization of sovereignty. For those with a particular fondness for international law, it reads like a thriller – a pretty good one, for that matter.

Ralph Janik

Susan Pedersen, *The Guardians: The League of Nations and the Crisis of Empire*. Oxford University Press, Oxford, 2015, ISBN 9780199570485, xiv + 571 pp., EUR 31.99

Susan Pedersen successfully provides a detailed – at times, a bit too detailed (but this is obviously my personal opinion, others are definitely happy with, *e.g.*, her discussion of appointments to and debates in the Permanent Mandates Commission) – and definitely read worthy account of how the mandate powers administered the former Ottoman and German territories. One can almost feel the hours of research and writing put into the final text when turning the pages.

The topic chosen remains highly relevant until this very day. Already in the introduction and in Chapters 7 and 9, in particular, Pedersen describes the struggle between those advocating in favour of annexation and the middle path chosen by the Permanent Mandates Commission and the administering powers alike. How the right to self-determination, although it raised hopes outside of Europe, *e.g.*, among the Kurds, was initially not meant to be extended to these territories and the related struggle over the notion of civilization – one must not forget that international law maintained the divide between civilized, semi-civilized and non-civilized entities even after the horrors of the First World War.[3] After all, the Permanent Court of International Justice's statute still referred to *civilized*

---

[3] See, among countless examples, *e.g.*, Frederick S Dunn, *The Protection of Nationals* (1932) i.

nations – a connotation the drafters deemed as being applicable to *all* nations[4] – in turn seemingly excluding any 'semi-civilized' or even 'backward peoples' from its scope of application: Already in 1919 the Allied Supreme Council agreed on what would later become Article 22 of the Covenant which spoke of colonies and territories 'which are inhabited by peoples not yet able to stand by themselves under the strenuous conditions of the modern world.' (at p. 29) From the Arab perspective, this stream of thought, also visible in related documents such as the notorious Sykes-Picot Agreement:

> spoke of Arabs as children and of Europeans as grown-ups who would take care of them until they could do grown-up things like feed themselves—such was the language directed at a people who, if the Muslim narrative were still in play, would have been honored as the progenitors of civilization itself—and who still retained some such sense of themselves.[5]

A few words on her descriptions of Belgian rule in Rwanda are also due at this point. Pedersen generally seems to have tried to avoid linking past and contemporary events. Interestingly enough, she thus also refrains from mentioning the 1994 genocide or other preceding massacres when describing Belgian 'indirect rule' through Tutsi chiefs. A particularly noteworthy quote reveals how the Tutsi were described by the Belgian Minister of Colonies Louis Franck and Belgium's 1925 report to the Council of the League of Nations as 'long-established, intelligent and capable' while 'majority Hutu were "typical Bantus", "expansive, noisy, cheerful and without guile", but the Tutsi—"proud", "distant", "pitiless", and "polite", "using the lance against the weak and posing against the strong"—were "destined to rule".' (at p. 241).

One gets the impression that Belgium created the artificial and inherently tremendously conflicting division between Hutu and Tutsi. One should nevertheless not forget that the system of indirect rule and the quasi-appointment of the Tutsi were already introduced by the Germans. Belgium simply 'went further', *e.g.*, by introducing identity cards – which essentially froze belongingness to one of the groups forever –, introducing a Tutsi administrative apparatus, and favouring their education.[6]

That being said, Susan Pedersen's *The Guardians* is one of those history books that provide even the most avid reader with a new perspective and understanding

---

[4] *Cf.* Allain Pellet, 'Article 38' in Andreas Zimmermann, Karin Oellers-Frahm, Christian Tomuschat and Christian J Tams (eds) *The Statute of the International Court of Justice: A Commentary* (2012) 731, para 261.

[5] Tamim Ansari, *Destiny Disrupted: A History of the World Through Islamic Eyes* (2009) 311.

[6] Martin Meredith, *The State of Africa: A History of Fifty Years of Independence* (2005) 158f.

of contemporary events. From the perspective of international relations, the First World War and its aftermath arguably had a more last impact than the Second – after all, this period shaped the contours of some of the most troublesome regions until this very day. Be it the origins of the multi-ethnic composition of Iraq, Germany's attempts to regain its former status – even inadvertently supporting the independence of states such as Tanganyika by protesting against any British attempts towards annexation – and later the naïve (in hindsight) idea of conceding to Nazi Germany's claims as a means to preserve peace in Europe, the British and international approach towards the creation of a Jewish state, or the general relationship between the former colonial or mandate territories and their European rulers (along with South Africa and its mandate over South West Africa),– to name just a few examples – the crucial impact of this period cannot be overstated.

Ralph Janik

Michael Potacs, *Rechtstheorie*. facultas, Wien, 2015, ISBN 9783708944354, 210 pp., EUR 20.60

Concise introductions to legal theory and juridical methodology in the German language produced in Austrian faculties and, hence, representative of this particular tradition of Germanophone doctrine are, unfortunately, rare. Until this recent publication, the late Franz Bydlinski's *Grundzüge der juristischen Methodenlehre*[7] was one of the few such works in current circulation. Most other contributions are usually restricted to journal articles[8] – often only available in Austrian databases – or *Festschriften*.[9]

In light of the recent turn towards theory in international law,[10] Michael Potacs book is a welcome contribution to the promulgation of 'Austrian' thought on that matter. His claim is that the book equally serves as a handbook as well as a theory of positive law (p. 5). However, it quickly becomes clear throughout the first pages that the book is less of the former and more the development of the latter. His restrictive definition of legal theory leaves little room for much of what has been happening in international legal theory (although Potacs shows

---

[7] Franz Bydlinski, *Grundzüge der juristischen Methodenlehre* (2011).

[8] For example, the Journal für Rechtspolitik.

[9] Notable exceptions by Austrians outside textbook literature are the topical contributions by Jörg Kammerhofer and Alexander Somek.

[10] See, *e.g.*, Jeffrey L Dunoff and Mark A Pollack (eds), *Interdisciplinary Perspectives on International Law and International Relations* (2013) as well as the recent publications by Jean D'Aspremont, Jörg Kammerhofer and others.

a solid understanding of international law doctrine),[11] particularly none of the interdisciplinary contributions of the 'law and ...' character. At the centre of his understanding lies the question of the quality of positive law (p. 15), which makes it more a book about methods of interpretation than anything else.

Potacs develops the framework for his argument by progressing in seven steps which also make up the individual chapters of the book: definition ('Begriff'), theories ('Theorien'), subject matter ('Gegenstand'), knowledge ('Erkenntnis'), structure ('Struktur'), science ('Wissenschaft'), and methods ('Methoden'). In the introductory chapter, he distinguishes his understanding of legal theory from legal philosophy (pp. 18-19), legal policy (pp. 20-21), sociology of law (pp. 21-24), and legal dogmatics ('Rechtsdogmatik', pp. 24-26) – a start to a book on legal theory that might irritate the reader of its international exponents, used to an amalgamation of these concepts.

He continues with a presentation of individual 'theories', beginning with Hart (pp. 29-33) and leading from legal realism (pp. 34-37) over Kelsen (pp. 38-41) to MacCormick and Weinberger (pp. 42-44). At the end of his elaborations, he suggests an understanding of positive law as meaning derived from language, in which he uses the epistemic interest in insights for interpretation as an underlying benchmark (p. 45). Thereby, he arrives at 'positive law' as an order created by humans and understood as a 'legal system' in common parlance (p. 50). While it is a legitimate proposition, it appears that his understanding of legal theory is predetermined by his requirements for assessing the law through means of interpretation (as he himself contends, p. 15).

The chapter is followed by a discussion of the sources of law as manifestations of the subject matter of legal theory. It is followed by a problematisation of different epistemological approaches, including hermeneutics (pp. 75-79), discourse analysis, in particular Habermas and Alexy (pp. 80-82), as well as Kelsen's Grundnorm (pp. 83-87). In the end, Potacs resorts to what he calls 'objective legal studies' ('Objektive Rechtswissenschaft'), seeking the intent of the legislator, as a conception for his understanding of positive law (pp. 88-92). Based on his requirements, the reader must already have suspected that all other models are bound to fail.

The final chapters deal with structure and, as the core theme of the book, interpretation. First, Potacs discusses various problems of hierarchy and conflict. In his treatment of the relationship between domestic and international law (pp. 112-118), he offers a dualist position with the possibility for 'monistic densification' ('monistische Verdichtung', p. 118). He then presents a more or less descriptive account of the various forms of interpretation, taking into account

---

[11] Equally, older 'standard' contributions such as by Kennedy, Koskenniemi, Kratowchil, or Onuf.

both specificities of international law and US approaches, and preceded by their contextualisation and derivation within theory.

Overall, the individual chapters oscillate between descriptive accounts of legal theory – a resource for students acquainting themselves with the basics of the topic – and the development of Potacs' own argument. In order for the book to serve as a handbook, aside from the bibliography and index, the elaborations would have benefitted from concise assessments or conclusions at the end of each chapter as well as a conclusion towards the end. Even the reader following Potacs' development of a theory of positive law is left hanging in the air in the final chapter, retracing the individual steps to tie the threads together. The character as a reference work is further limited by the omission of some of the standard literature in German such as Canaris' and Larenz's *Methodenlehre der Rechtswissenschaft*.[12] This is joined by some formal, though negligible errors such as having forgotten Bydlinski (cited, *inter alia*, at p. 26, n. 60) and Canaris (cited at p. 143, n. 49) – these two of all authors – in the bibliography.

For an international audience, Potacs' restrictive definition of legal theory may make reception of the ideas as difficult and untranslatable as 'Rechtsdogmatik' (although he does garnish his thoughts with input from US legal doctrine and meditation on issues of international law throughout the book). However, this should rather serve as an impetus for international legal theory to grapple with and adapt these ideas of Germanophone doctrine. Hopefully, the publication will come to have provided the groundwork for a second, more comprehensive edition with a corresponding translation into English.

Markus P. Beham

---

[12] Karl Larenz and Claus-Wilhelm Canaris, *Methodenlehre der Rechtswissenschaft* (1995).

Book Notes

Matthias Niedobitek (ed.), *Europarecht – Grundlagen der Union*. De Gruyter, Berlin *et al*., 2014, ISBN 9783110271683, xl + 966 pp., EUR 69.95 and Matthias Niedobitek (ed.), *Europarecht – Politiken der Union*. De Gruyter, Berlin *et al*., 2014, ISBN 9783110271393, lvi + 1374 pp., EUR 69.95

The blurb of the first volume of this two edition textbook on EU law promises contributions by 'experienced and renown scholars of European law': Aside the editor, it contains contributions by Joachim Gruber, Ines Härtel, Dieter Kugelmann, Roman Lehner, Siegfried Magiera, Karl-Peter Sommermann, and Wolfgang Weiß, as well as three representatives of Austrian universities, Walter Obwexer and Werner Schroeder, both University of Innsbruck, and Stefan Storr, University of Graz. The second volume includes chapters by Hermann-Josef Blanke and Robert Böttner, Stephanie Jungheim and Wolfgang Weiß, Ludwig Gramlich, Matthias Rossi, José Martinez, Ulrike Davy, Astrid Epiney, Kerstin Odendahl, Eckhard Pache, Hans-Joachim Cremer, and another Austrian representative from the University of Innsbruck, Peter Hilpold. Still, it is quite visible in all issues relating to the relationship between EU and domestic law that it is written for a mostly German audience, with the *Grundgesetz* serving as the primary background for discussion.

The structure of the first volume follows and covers the treaty basis and institutions, membership in the Union, the common values of the Union and its member states, fundamental rights, the relationship between EU law and domestic law, the competences of the Union, the forms, in which the Union may act, and the overall legislative process, the implementation of EU law, the financial structure of the Union, the concept of enhanced cooperation, and, finally, the methodological specificities of EU law. The second volume touches upon a number of substantive subject matters of EU law. Each chapter has a detailed index, allowing for an easy orientation within each topic.

One particularly valuable chapter is that by Joachim Gruber on the methodological specificities of EU law which almost represents a sociological endeavour, reminding of such work as by Tobias Nowak and others on the attitudes of domestic judges towards EU law.[1] While Gruber could have been more comprehensive on one or two dogmatic issues such as *effet utile*, in particular informed the

---

[1] Fabian Amtenbrink, Marc LM Hertogh, Tobias Nowak and Mark H. Wissink, *National Judges as European Union Judges: Knowledge, Experiences and Attitudes of Lower Court Judges in Germany and the Netherlands* (2011).

reader as to its connection with the public international law concept of 'implied powers', the chapter goes beyond a mere textbook synthesis in portraying an institution in its everyday function.

Markus P. Beham

Printed in the United States
By Bookmasters